Starring Red Wing!

THE INCREDIBLE CAREER OF LILIAN M. ST. CYR, THE FIRST NATIVE AMERICAN FILM STAR

Linda M. Waggoner

UNIVERSITY OF NEBRASKA PRESS | LINCOLN

Library of Congress Cataloging-
in-Publication Data
Library of Congress
Control Number: 2019006781

Set in Adobe Text by Mikala R. Kolander.
Designed by N. Putens.

For my mother, Elaine Ursula Edwards

She exists in me now, just as I will and already do within my grandchildren. No one ever truly dies. The desires of our hearts make a path. We create legacy with our thoughts and dreams.

—Joy Harjo

CONTENTS

ILLUSTRATIONS

PREFACE

Red Wing came from a prominent Ho-Chunk (or Winnebago) family, but she was orphaned by the time she was four. She grew up in a racist world that did not recognize her complete humanity or her worth. With guts, grace, and determination she became America's first Native film star. She left a legacy that still inspires young Native women today. They in turn inspired me to tell Red Wing's story.

Red Wing left few of her own words, but nearly every word she did leave is quoted or summarized in this book. She was born in 1884, so no one remains to remember her youth or young womanhood. Moreover, Red Wing was born on the Winnebago reservation in Nebraska but spent over a decade of her childhood far from home in Indian boarding schools. Her early performing years also found her in distant places, and she lived the last fifty years of her life in New York City. If Red Wing's parents had raised her to adulthood, the course of her life would certainly have been different. Instead, she became a film star, an educator, a regalia maker, and a political leader of the intertribal New York Metropolitan Group of American Indians. Still she honored the cultural practices of the Ho-Chunk people all her life, despite her separation from their home.

There are no archives that hold a collection of Red Wing's papers. A few possess her extant silent films, but most of these archives are in Europe. I was not able to travel that far. However, I was overjoyed to discover that I could watch five of these rare films online. I also viewed two films at the Museum of Modern Art in New York, one that was Red Wing's and one that was erroneously attributed to her, and likewise two at the Green Library at Stanford University in Stanford, California, that were helpful to see but weren't hers. I also purchased three of her later motion pictures, including her claim to fame, Cecil B. DeMille's *The Squaw Man*, released in 1914. However, the book's film research is extensive. Although

Red Wing did the bulk of her motion pictures before the invention of credits, I searched through hundreds of digitized film production trade magazines and newspapers to determine what films were hers and what were possibilities (the results are in the appendix).

I found early on that if I could identify the other actors and crew Red Wing worked with, I would have more luck identifying her films and fleshing out the people she spent so much time with. Whenever I found film ads with photos or other images of her cast and crew, I ran them through the iPhoto facial identification process. I also used my own facial recognition abilities to try to confirm who was who. Once I identified the bulk of her costars and colleagues, it was much easier to give an account of their role in Red Wing's life and career and create her filmography.

I did most of the tribal research on Red Wing's family well before I started researching this book. Her father's family and my father's family are among two of fifty "mixed-blood" Ho-Chunk families who became naturalized citizens in Minnesota. I have been avidly researching this group and their many relatives for more than twenty-five years. I'm very familiar with Ho-Chunk names, but I used both the English translation and the phonetic rendering as shown in tribal or other records to avoid confusion and to reflect the times in which Red Wing lived.

There is not one term to describe the United States' indigenous population that fits all situations. There is also no good expression to represent people in Red Wing's orb who were racially mixed. In this book I employ a variety of terms, such as "Indian," "Native American," "American Indian," "Native," "squaw," "half-breed," "mixed-blood," "full-blood," and "mulatto." I used words as they were given in sources or to reflect specific historical contexts. Unfortunately, racism and ethnocentrism imbue all these signifiers.

This is not an academic text, but it is research laden. I tried to keep the story moving by relegating "more than you want to know" details in the notes. However, I do hope silent film buffs, students of Native American studies, and readers who are interested in one of the story's personalities will welcome the additional information.

Finally, there were many times when I simply did not know something, and I say that. To lend context to the many silent intervals I encountered,

I turned to experts in film, American history, indigenous studies, anthropology, psychology, and narrative theory. Obviously, a life cannot be adequately represented or summed up in a book. This biography is an interpretive composition based on inscriptions and images I discovered that Red Wing left behind. I hope its melody is in tune with her experiences.

ACKNOWLEDGMENTS

The completion of this book depended on many people and institutions, and I am truly grateful for their help and support. Any errors or misrepresentations in this book are mine alone.

I'd like to first thank my dear friend David Lee Smith, who joined his creator, Earthmaker, much too soon. Smith served as the tribal historian for the Winnebago Tribe of Nebraska. He shared his incomparable knowledge of the Winnebago (Ho-Chunk) people with me, and we shared a close friendship over the years that can't be replaced.

Matt Bokovoy, acquisitions editor for the University of Nebraska Press, deserves my extreme gratitude. He helped me bring my last book to fruition, and he continues to encourage and support my work. Matt, Philip Burnham, and Akim Reinhardt reviewed the verbose and gangly first draft of the manuscript. Their editorial critiques proved invaluable. Akim also checked for historical accuracy and political correctness, while Philip offered insightful suggestions that made me feel he was actually interested in the subject matter. His comments inspired me to add more "long shots" and to hone in on what an everyday reader might find of interest. I also thank Joeth Zucco and Mary M. Hill for their invaluable editorial contributions, as well as Heather Stauffer for helping whenever needed.

I depended on Anne Slatin, Josephine Tarrant, and Louis Mofsie to tell me about Red Wing's New York years. Anne shared stories from her late husband, Harvey Slatin, who was a close friend of Red Wing before she died. She also sent me a wonderful file that held some of Red Wing's personal documents and things others had written about her, as well as a very special historic family letter. If that wasn't enough inspiration, Anne also passed on to me Red Wing's leftover bead stash. Anne's generosity came at a time when I really needed a sign from the heavens, and I thank her profusely.

Josephine Tarrant and Louis Mofsie, both descended from Red Wing's niece Vina Lowry Mofsie, who moved with her aunt to New York in the early 1920s, shared their knowledge about Red Wing. Although they couldn't provide a lot of factual detail, they offered wonderful insights into her personality and her place as a role model in their still-performing and still-activist family. They knowingly and lovingly continue her legacy and deserve my warmest thanks.

James L. Hansen, retired genealogical consultant for the Wisconsin State Historical Society, is always there when I need him. The research he shared with me includes early records of the St. Cyr family in Wisconsin.

I also appreciate the scholars who invited me to present my research on Red Wing, including Elaine Nelson (Missouri Valley History Conference, 2014); Barbara Landis ("American Indians in Show Business: How the Carlisle Indian School Influenced the Entertainment World," Carlisle Journeys: American Indians in Show Business conference, 2014); Adrienne Greci Green, Clyde Ellis, and Rebecca Wingo (Native American and Indigenous Studies Association conferences, 2015, 2017, and 2018); Sherri Smith-Ferri ("Our People, Our Land, Our Images," Grace Hudson Museum, 2018); and Michael Ezra, chair of the Department of Native American Studies, Sonoma State University, Rohnert Park, California. Michael brought me back to the department in 2017 to teach Native American Cinema. Prepping for the course helped me to coalesce my research. I also thank my forty students for their patience and encouragement.

I'm an independent scholar and relish time spent with human beings who share my interests. I'd like to thank the following colleagues, friends, and acquaintances for their insights and support on this project: Sherri Smith-Ferri, Adrienne Greci-Green, Clyde Ellis, Katie Phillips, Barbara Landis, Philip Deloria, Grace Slaughter, Carma Foley, Stephen Bottomore, Kent Blansett, Angela Aleiss, Henry Payer, Bob Smith, and Rick Kerns.

This book would not have been possible without the incredible wealth of free online searchable digital archives. The early cinema publications from the Media History Digital Library enriched this book beyond measure. I particularly want to thank Eric Hoyt, founder of the Media History Digital Library, for contributing high-resolution scans for many of the images I discovered on the site. I also consulted the wonderful Carlisle

Indian School Digital Resource Center, the California Digital Newspaper Collection, the Edward E. Ayer Digital Collection at the Newberry Library, the Library of Congress collection of digitized films, and FamilySearch. These sites are well worth exploring.

The following archives and their archivists (named and unnamed) greatly contributed to my knowledge about Red Wing, her family, the Ho-Chunk people, and the history of silent westerns: John Cahoon, Seaver Center, Natural History Museum of Los Angeles, California; Faye Thompson, Academy of Motion Picture Arts and Sciences, Margaret Herrick Library, Beverly Hills, California; James D'Arc, L. Tom Perry Special Collections Library, Brigham Young University, Provo, Utah; Ashley Swinnerton, Film Study Center, Museum of Modern Art, New York, New York; Paul Bourcier, Division of Museums and Historic Sites, Wisconsin Historical Society, Madison; Bob Knecht, Kansas Historical Society, Topeka; Mary Frances Ronan, National Archives and Records Administration (NARA), Washington DC; NARA Central Plains Region, Kansas City, and NARA St. Louis, Missouri; Raynor Library, Special Collection and Archives, Marquette University, Milwaukee, Wisconsin; Family History Library, Salt Lake City, Utah; Los Angeles County Court Archives, Los Angeles, California; City of Orange Public Library, California; Autry Museum of the American West, Los Angeles, California; Green Library, Stanford University, Palo Alto, California; Hampton University Archives, Hampton, Virginia; Brooklyn Historical Society, New York; Nebraska State Historical Society, Lincoln; Blue Earth Historical Society, Mankato, Minnesota; Blue Earth County Courthouse, Mankato, Minnesota; Thurston County Courthouse, Pender, Nebraska; and Wisconsin State Historical Society, Madison.

Marc Wanamaker of Bison Company Production Archives deserves my thanks for allowing me free use of several images for this book. My appreciation also goes out to the following photo curators and institutions. Mary K. Huelsbeck, Wisconsin Center for Film and Theater Research, Madison; Marilyn Van Winkle, Institute for the Study of the American West, Autry National Center, Southwest Museum, Los Angeles, California; Daisy Njoku, Smithsonian National Anthropological Archives, Suitland, Maryland; Richard Tritt, Cumberland County Historical Society, Carlisle,

Pennsylvania; Ben Harry and Cindy Brightenburg, L. Tom Perry Special Collections Library, Brigham Young University, Provo, Utah; and Kristine Krueger, Academy of Motion Picture Arts and Sciences, Margaret Herrick Library, Beverly Hills, California.

Finally, I'd like to express my love to my children, Biba Bell, Brooke Vermillion, Hilary Carson, Gelsey Bell, and Neal Carson, and their significant others, for their encouragement. I also thank the heavens for the unwavering support of my husband, Roger V. Bell Jr. Roger had my back through the long and arduous process of birthing this book. He also formatted many of the images in this book. I would be lost forever in the wilderness without him.

INTRODUCTION

In the spring of 1958 *New York Times* journalist Meyer Berger paid a visit to an elderly American Indian woman living in a modest walk-up in Manhattan's West End neighborhood. They had been acquainted for some time, but Berger, master of the human-interest story, decided it was time to feature his Indian friend in his popular column About New York. Shortly after his visit, "Red Wing, Once a Film Star, Now Makes Indian Regalia on West End Ave." appeared in the *Times*. Two striking photographs of Red Wing accompany the piece. They show a still lovely and lively woman with thick gray upswept hair framing her round face. In both photos she wears a dress of her own making. In one she poses with a threaded needle, pretending to finish her handiwork, a Plains Indian bonnet made for a woman and made just for show. In the second photo Red Wing exudes an air of proud dignity, but something about her expression tells us she has seen it all.

"When Red Wing was a girl, about fifty-five years ago," Meyer's column begins, "her pretty face and her lovely eyes were known almost all over the world. She played in the earliest silent films—'Squaw Man,' 'Thundering Herd,' and 'The Mended Lute.' She starred in 'Pioneer Days,' an Indian whooper staged in the old Hippodrome, where the pale concrete parking garage stands now, opposite Stern's." "Now Red Wing is 74 years old," Meyer continues, and "works all day, sometimes through the night, in her dark two-room lodge. . . . She sews authentic Indian war bonnets, war shirts, beaded suits and leggings of buckskin, cowhide or elk." Some of her "handwork goes to her own tribe, the Winnebagos in Nebraska," Meyer explains, but "she sews for other clans, too." She also made Indian costumes for "the Order of Red Men, a national lodge of whites," he adds.

Meyer portrays Red Wing with a hearty dose of vanishing Indian nostalgia to resonate with his readers. He gives her Indian name,

Rupa-Hu-Sha-Win, to emphasize her exotic American origins. He doesn't mention that Red Wing had already lived in the metropolis for more than two decades or that the "traditional dress" she wore was actually a copy of the dress she made for *The Squaw Man*, one of her films from 1914. He also fails to mention that Red Wing's real name from birth was Lilian Margaret St. Cyr and that she had European American ancestry, as well as Winnebago or, more properly, Ho-Chunk. Meyer phonetically renders the Indian names of Red Wing's parents, Mitchell and Julia Decora St. Cyr, in the Ho-Chunk language: "Her father was the chieftain Waunk-Shik-Sto-he-Gah—He Who Gathers His People. Her mother was Nah-Gu-Pingah—Pretty-Hair Woman." However, few readers, including him, could recognize that his translation for "Red Wing" is not Ho-Chunk at all but Lakota.

Meyer takes his readers inside Red Wing's home, telling us he sees images of her parents and "pictures of Red Wing's five brothers and sisters" that "fade on the dark tenement wall." He also points out "the image of Young Deer, the Delaware she married in 1906," without realizing that it's the first time since her marriage that Red Wing gave her former husband this particular tribal affiliation. "Red Wing's eyes often lift from her work to look upon her vanished kin," Meyer states wistfully. "When she speaks, the syllables are soft and low. She tells of how Episcopal missionaries put her through private school in Philadelphia; how, at Carlisle School, she knew the great athlete Jim Thorpe and Chief Bender, pitcher for the Philadelphia Athletics." Red Wing may have known Jim Thorpe, but they were not classmates at Carlisle, because she graduated from the Indian school before Thorpe enrolled. No matter. Red Wing knew how to craft her image, and Meyer simply followed her lead.

Meyer focuses much of his column on Red Wing's costume and regalia making, which, one hopes, resulted in more business for her. The income she received from her handiwork allowed her to stay independent. She did not want to depend on family or friends to take care of her. Meyer tries to capture Red Wing's personality in the rest of the column. He offers a nostalgic nod to her glory days, when she was the first American Indian silent film star. He notes that though she is less socially inclined than she used to be, she never refuses an invitation to appear for "the Friends," who "have ever been good to my people," she said. If "the Friends, the Quakers, ask her to sing, dance, or lecture for them," Meyer explains, "she puts on her ancient buckskin dress and hurries to oblige."

Meyer concludes Red Wing's story by emphasizing her advancing age and nobility of character. Although his insights ring true, Meyer misses the bundle of energy those closest to Red Wing knew her to be. "Sometimes she cooks special Indian dinners for church groups," he writes. "Sometimes she entertains for the benefit of mentally retarded children. Then she goes back to her dark tenement lodge to sit with the faded wall pictures, far from the home of her people, but always with them in spirit."[1]

Yes, "with them in spirit" but fully spirited herself. Red Wing embodied pep and daring all her life up to her death at ninety years old. As her great-nephew Louis Mofsie remembered during a conversation I had with him in 2014, she was "a feisty woman" and "a go getter," and she always "liked to keep busy." The youngest of six siblings, she survived all of them by decades. She also lived long past the death of her actor-director (and allegedly "Delaware") husband, not to mention practically everyone else she had worked with during her film career, the bulk of which spanned 1908 to 1917.

The secret to Red Wing's energy and long life, given the great obstacles she indeed encountered, remains hers. The story of her remarkable career is ours to share. Red Wing was so much more than the first Native American film star. She made a substantial contribution to the silent film industry, specifically to westerns. She made at least seventy films, perhaps many more. Her claim to fame was her role as Naturitch in Cecil B. DeMille's first film, *The Squaw Man*. No wonder she made the film's dress her signature piece. She was an actress, yes, but also a writer, a prop maker, a costume designer, a cultural consultant, and her own incredible stunt woman well before Hollywood proper existed. When she arrived with the second motion picture company to locate in the Los Angeles area in 1909, Red Wing made history as a film pioneer.

Her career shaped the genre of silent westerns. Her film persona was so popular by 1912 that competing motion picture companies introduced their own "Red Wing" characters. However much she portrayed a stereotypical

Indian princess, on-screen Red Wing played women imbued with not only loyalty and love but also incredible strength and courage. A fitting persona for President Teddy Roosevelt's era, Red Wing was a bareback-riding, gun-toting, sprightly western gal who, yes, sometimes died tragically—like a proper Indian princess—at the end of her films. However, before the curtain closed Red Wing usually broke several taboos and always saved the day. Clearly, Red Wing's evolution as a stock film character owes its mass appeal to her namesake's effervescent and heroic spirit.

Red Wing's film career waned dramatically with World War I. Not one to feel sorry for herself, she became an educator-performer, first full-time and then part-time until she died. She met many famous people during her life. They admired her for her early career but loved her for her wonderful spirit. She participated with them in political activism to give recognition to American Indians. A National Indian Day was one of her causes. Her steady political activism starting in the 1920s culminated in the burgeoning Red Power movement. Red Wing died in 1974, the year after the American Indian Movement's (AIM) occupation of Wounded Knee.

Red Wing honed her skills in bead, leather, and feather work to help support herself later in life. These skills kept her connected to the traditions of her family, the Ho-Chunk people, as well as to a cosmopolitan network of American Indians who lived in and around New York City. If Red Wing was not performing, lecturing, cooking, or just helping out, her hands were busy with scissors and needle and thread. Her handiwork also kept her connected all her life to her legacy, Native performance.

Life held many hardships for Red Wing, but she overcame them because she did not wait for change, she created it. Extremely independent, she was not averse to taking the bull by the horns and wrangling a life and livelihood for herself. Certainly, she was not immune to pain and experienced much tragedy in her nine decades, but she just kept on, one step after the other. Moreover, through all her personal trauma, seemingly insurmountable challenges, and inevitable change, what protected and sustained her was her alter ego, Red Wing, the persona she created for herself early on and then whom she became after all.

STARRING RED WING!

CHAPTER 1

Lilian Margaret St. Cyr of the Winnebago Tribe of Nebraska

Lilian Margaret St. Cyr was born a member of the Winnebago Tribe of Nebraska.[1] The Winnebago call themselves the "Ho-Chunk" and are a Siouan people, like the Otoe, Iowa, and Missouri, who speak a language derivative of theirs. The name translates as "big voice" (*ho*, "voice," and *chunk*, "big") and is also interpreted as "people of the parent speech." Many ethnologists believe Ho-Chunk ancestors made the second of four Siouan migrations from the southeastern United States to the western shore of Lake Michigan. Ho-Chunk oral tradition maintains that the people originated at Red Banks, located at the shore of Green Bay, Wisconsin, where they first encountered the French in 1634.

The Ho-Chunk population suffered extreme decimation in the early eighteenth century during the French and Fox Wars. As a result, the people intermarried extensively with their primarily Algonquin neighbors, like the Menominee, who called them "Winnebago," a term that refers to the stagnant water at Red Banks. The Ho-Chunk also married Pottawatomie, Ojibwe, and Ottawa from the north, Sac and Fox from the south, and Dakota from the west, as well as French Canadian fur traders, who had arrived in Wisconsin by the early eighteenth century.

According to tribal records, Lilian was "three quarters Winnebago," which typically means that one of her grandparents was white. However, blood quantum is often an arbitrary assignment that fails to reflect the rich complexity of Native American ancestry. The essentialist notion of a "full-blood" tribal member is a nineteenth-century creation that grants authenticity through "blood" while undermining and obfuscating how Natives themselves reckoned family, clan, and tribal membership. Lilian was often described as "a full-blood" throughout her film career, lending her authenticity in relation to the many white actresses who played Indian maids. Obviously, blood cannot be measured, so "blood quantum" is an imaginary distinction to describe not only one's relative "Indianness" but also one's essential difference from whites. The begging question becomes, what exactly does "full-blood" call up in the American imagination that makes it to this day a problematic descriptor for Native people? The answer is a stereotype or trope. Whether it is applied to a stoic cigar-store Indian or an ethereal Indian princess sitting by a stream pining for her lover (while illustrating an advertisement for butter, fruit, or beer), the image comes from the collective national fantasy about Indians. Lilian manipulated and made her own the mythic Indian princess stereotype in the early years of her career in order to be viewed by the public as a "real Indian." However, her family of origin is anything but stereotypical.

Lilian, also called Lily, Lillia, and Ochsegahonegah (Fifth Daughter), was born to Julia Decora and Mitchell St. Cyr on February 13, 1884.[2] She was their last child, one of five girls and three boys. (See appendix A for Lilian's family.) Except for the eldest sibling, all the St. Cyr children were born on the Winnebago reservation, which is located at the northeastern corner of Nebraska in Thurston County. Both the St. Cyr and the Decora families belonged to the Winnebago Tribe of Nebraska and served as political and cultural intermediaries. Both families had French Canadian ancestors from whom their surnames derived. The Decora family line includes respected civil chiefs and peacemakers who sacrificed for their people in times of need. These leaders favored egalitarianism and strove to accommodate cultural difference while adhering to Ho-Chunk traditions. The diplomatic St. Cyrs were more patriarchal and family oriented, more French perhaps, yet still expressed an abiding loyalty to their Ho-Chunk people.

For forty years the Ho-Chunk Nation suffered unrelenting upheaval. This diaspora, known euphemistically as the "Indian removal period," involved more than one "trail of tears" for the Ho-Chunk. Today the Winnebago Tribe of Nebraska and the Wisconsin Ho-Chunk Nation exemplify the fissure created by this long-drawn-out uprootedness of one people who became two. From the 1830s through the 1870s, U.S. government policies supported encroachers, land speculators, agrarian settlers, and lead miners who forced the Ho-Chunk ever to the west. Lilian's family miraculously survived this traumatic period, which took them from Wisconsin to Iowa to Minnesota to South Dakota and finally to Nebraska.

Little is known about Lilian's mother, Julia Decora St. Cyr. She was born about 1846 near Fort Atkinson, Iowa, which was built allegedly "to protect the Winnebago." The eldest daughter of Younkaw (Queen Woman) and Baptiste "Tall" Decora, Julia's Indian name was Naw jin pin win kaw (Pretty Hair Woman).[3] Julia's father was the son of Ho-Chunk civil chief Conokaw Decorah, whose father was Chougeka (Wooden Spoon). Chougeka's parents were Wahopoeka (called by whites Glory of the Morning) and Joseph Sabrevois Decarrie, a French Canadian fur trader. "Decora" and its many spellings derive from this ancestor's name.[4]

The Ho-Chunk people recognize Wahopoeka's marriage as the first non-Native union. It occurred shortly after 1729, when Decarrie left Canada to enter the fur trade in the Pays d'en Haut, or "Upper Country," as the Great Lakes area was known. The marriage was an important alliance, likely arranged by Wahopoeka's brothers according to the Ho-Chunk custom. Decarrie brought useful European technologies and trade items to the Ho-Chunk, and they in turn provided him with pelts, comfort, and a wife.

Wahopoeka and Decarrie had two sons and a daughter: Chougeka (Wooden Spoon), the oldest; White Breast, the second son; and Oak Woman, their only daughter. Oral tradition recalls that Decarrie took Chougeka and Oak Woman back to Canada. Eventually, Oak Woman married a fur trader, but Chougeka became terribly homesick even though his father's family treated him very well. Decarrie felt pity on his son and allowed him to return to Wisconsin and his mother's family. Chougeka's Ho-Chunk uncles immediately taught him to fast so that he could be spiritually ready to lead his people.

Wahopoeka lived out her days on a small island on Lake Winnebago.

One explorer who encountered her in the late eighteenth century believed she was a queen. He particularly noticed her dignified demeanor and the respect her people afforded her. Was she a chief? It's unknown. But Waho-poeka served as a powerful role model for all of her female descendants, including Lilian. Her stature and the social status of her brothers, who were chiefs or sons of a chief, afforded her own sons membership into the Thunderbird clan, although clanship was customarily passed from father to child. The Ho-Chunk's sanction of these first *métis* (mixed) children initiated the acceptance and recognition of many others to come.

Lilian's great-great-grandfather Chougeka wed the daughter of Chief Carrimonie (Walking Turtle). Chougeka and his wife (or wives, since the Ho-Chunk practiced plural marriage) had six or seven sons and five daughters, including two who, like their aunt Oak Woman, married French Canadian or *métis* men involved in the fur trade. Chougeka's multicul-tural background proved a valuable asset when the Great Lakes fur trade thrived. During his lifetime he allied with the French and the British and negotiated with the Americans. All three of these colonial powers desired Ho-Chunk resources, first their furs and daughters and then their land.

Following the War of 1812, Americans flooded into the Ho-Chunk's Wisconsin and northern Illinois territory. "Choukeka, or Dekare, the Spoon," signed an "X" next to his name on the first "peace-making treaty" with the U.S. government in June 1816.[5] Chougeka died shortly after he signed the treaty, so Conokaw (First Son) resumed his father's role.[6] Conokaw had several names over the course of his life. "My father's name, among the French, was Zhuminaka, which I am told is from a French word having to do with wine," stated Conokaw's son Spoon. "His Winnebago name was Warrahwikoogah, or Bird Spirit. The Americans called him Grey-headed Decorah."[7] Conokaw's "X" mark appears on the second, fifth, and sixth Winnebago treaties with the United States under his other Ho-Chunk name, White War Eagle.[8]

Americans knew Conokaw Decorah "as a man of temperance." Conokaw spoke at least Ho-Chunk, French, English, and Chippewa, the lingua franca of the fur trade. He presented the exceptional qualities of a Ho-Chunk civil chief, having a "well-balanced temper, not easily provoked, and . . . good habits." After signing the treaty of 1829, which ceded 2.5 million acres, including the Ho-Chunk's ancestral lead mines in Illinois, the elderly chief headed a large village on the Wisconsin River near Portage, Wisconsin. The U.S. military made its presence known there by constructing Fort Winnebago at the eastern edge of the one-mile fur trade "portage" in 1828. Shortly after, the government hired local *métis* men to construct a house near the fort for the new Winnebago agent to administer treaty stipulations. The agent and his wife came to respect Conokaw for his nobility, courage, and modest demeanor. Still, when U.S. officials leaned on him to negotiate in times of conflict, he protested that he did not have the authority they vested in him because he was "half white and half red."[9]

In 1832 the Ho-Chunk's neighbor, Sac and Fox chief Black Hawk, banded together with several tribesmen and some disaffected Kickapoo to protest and resist land cessions from a previous treaty. The ensuing Black Hawk War cinched the fate of the Ho-Chunk. Conokaw counseled his warriors to stay neutral during the conflict, but many felt sympathy for Black Hawk's cause, and some, like the prominent Winneshiek family, who had Sac and Fox relatives, allied with their kinsmen. The United States defeated Black Hawk and removed his tribe to Iowa. However, the Winneshiek alliance bolstered the government's position to enact President Jackson's Indian Removal Act of 1830, which proposed to remove all Indians to west of the Mississippi.

The Ho-Chunk faced starvation in the winter of 1833 because of delayed annuities. When the agent's wife offered Conokaw enough food for his family, he refused it. If all his people "could not be relieved," he declared, his family would starve with them.[10] Meanwhile, smallpox and starvation ravaged Ho-Chunk communities, particularly around Portage and Prairie du Chien. Whether from disease, starvation, or old age, Conokaw became seriously ill. His *métis* brother-in-law baptized him informally (*endoyer*) into the Catholic faith as he lay dying.[11] The chief's conversion was not surprising. One of his sons later recalled that Conokaw retained warm memories of the "Black Robes" who visited his village during his childhood. When Conokaw died in 1836, all hopes for his people to retain their homeland died with him. His passing marked not only the waning of the Ho-Chunk and their *métis* kin's prominent role in the fur trade but also the end of the friendship between "white and red." Conokaw left his eldest son to lead in his stead, but he died within six months of his father. Next in line was Tall Decora's older brother, the more pacific Little Decora.

Little Decora's Thunderbird clan name was Mauhecooshanakzhe (One That Stands and Reaches the Skies), but he was nicknamed White French. A terrible calamity challenged this gentle leader. A fraudulent treaty coerced by government officials and signed in Washington DC in 1837 by those without authority ordered the Ho-Chunk's complete removal from their homelands. Little Decora pleaded for the relief of his people when military forces arrived in 1840 to force stragglers across the Mississippi River to Fort Atkinson, Iowa. Having been recently baptized Catholic like his father, he hoped an appeal to Christian brotherhood might soften the heart of a government official: "Father, you know our family was a large one. Since we left the Portage my mother and two brothers have died, and now I am left alone with a little brother and sister, both of whom are sick. This is not only my situation, but that of all the other chiefs. These few chiefs are all that were able to come to see you. All the rest are sick. Father, though I call myself a Winnebago, I live under the love of the Great Father above."[12]

Little Decora's entreaty changed nothing. Hundreds of Ho-Chunk perished from harsh conditions, disease, and dysentery during this first removal to Iowa.[13] Unfortunately, it would not be the last—many, many more deaths would follow. The 1837 treaty forced the Ho-Chunk to remove to the so-called Neutral Territory in northern Iowa, where they essentially served as a buffer between warring tribes.

Lilian's seemingly effortless "accommodation" to European American culture rested not only on her descent from the Decora "half red and white" family but also on the influence of their *métis* in-laws. Lilian's father, Michel St. Cyr Jr., more commonly known as Mitchell, also came to play a leadership role in the tribe. The St. Cyrs typified fur trade families inhabiting the old Northwest in the eighteenth and early nineteenth centuries. Like Lilian's mother's surname, St. Cyr appears on several Winnebago treaties, but not as a signatory. Lilian's grandfather Michel St. Cyr Sr. was one among several Ho-Chunk *métis* to receive a section of land "hereinbefore ceded" as "a descendant of said [Winnebago] Indians" as put forth by the treaty of 1829. The 1837 treaty also assigned $1,000 to his father, Hyacinth St. Cyr, "for supplies and services to the nation."[14]

Michel St. Cyr Sr. served as a government interpreter and go-between. He spoke Ho-Chunk, French, English, and probably Sac.[15] Some believed he was "a white man" because he favored his father. His multiethnic makeup lost its function and context by the mid-nineteenth century. The nation's fascination with fractions of race like "Negro quadroon" or "octaroon" bled over to those with Native American parents. Protoethnographer Henry Schoolcraft, who himself had an Ojibwa wife, demonstrated this fetish with racial mixing in his "description and comparison of the hair of the North American Indians":

> Michel St. Cyr, a di-mestisin—Winnebago and French—has curled hair and by his wife, a pure Winnebago, with straight black hair, has four children, one, fourteen years of age, has chestnut hair, brown complexion, and black eyes; another, aged twelve, has dark chestnut hair[,] brown complexion, and dark [eyes]; the third, a brunette, has blackish brown hair and black eyes; the fourth has blackish brown hair, brown complexion, and black eyes; while a sister of St. Cyr, married to a Pole, has one child that has blonde hair, and light eyes; and another who has light brown hair, copper complexion, and black eyes.[16]

While Schoolcraft found Michel's attributes a veritable variation of the species, Michel's community of origin perceived his looks as common. He was born about 1811 and baptized near the juncture of the Wisconsin and Mississippi Rivers at St. Gabriel's Catholic Church in Prairie du Chien, Wisconsin.[17] Prairie du Chien served as a well-traveled crossroads for the fur trade, and it was where various tribal groups and European ethnic groups intersected and married. Michel's father, Hyacinth St. Cyr, was one of Prairie du Chien's early traders. Hyacinth, a New France descendant, was born in St. Louis, Missouri. Michel's mother was called Josette. Henokaw (or Hinuga) was her birth-order name, because she was the first daughter of The Spaniard, an alleged Winnebago chief.[18]

Michel married Angelique Nausaresca in the Indian custom before 1837. St. Gabriel's Church records identify her as Sac not Ho-Chunk, unbeknownst to Schoolcraft. However, one of her parents may have been

Ho-Chunk, since she spoke the language fluently. Before her marriage to Michel, Angelique had a son in 1836. Church records identify his father as "Jos. Causic."[19] Michel adopted the boy who would become Lilian's father and had him baptized in 1839 at St. Gabriel's as "Michel St. Cyr, Jr."[20] Three days later, eighteen-month-old "Michel," son of Michel and Angelique, was also baptized at St. Gabriel's. As was the French custom, the name "Michel" was attached to each of the son's names, but as the eldest son, Lilian's father was always known by the name of his adoptive father, which was pronounced "Mitchell" by the Ho-Chunk, as his name is often spelled. The family called the eighteen-month-old Michel "Augustus," even though he was Michel's first biological son.

Michel and his growing family resided at his trading post on Lake Mendota, one of the "Four Lakes" near present-day Madison, Wisconsin. They raised "corn, oats, potatoes, and vegetables." The isolated twelve-by-twelve-foot log cabin that Michel purchased from another Indian trader offered a dirt floor and few comforts.[21] Even so, it sometimes served as an inn for weary travelers. Portage fur trade clerk John DeLaronde recalled fondly a visit he made to St. Cyr's post around July 4, 1837, to "trade some red deerskins." DeLaronde, married to a Decora daughter, brought along some of his in-laws. The St. Cyrs, DeLaronde's group, and several French Canadian and *métis* men "engaged in hunting and fishing" nearby and feasted together on venison and fish, made more festive with St. Cyr's stock of "flour, pork, tea, coffee, sugar and whisky." One of Conokaw Decora's grandsons played the fiddle. Wisconsin history declares this group the "first white men" to celebrate Independence Day in Madison, indicating the fluidity of racial identity.[22]

Strangers often mistook Michel for a non-Native French Canadian because in their estimation he acted more like an Indian trader than an Indian. For example, Alexander Pratt left Fort Atkinson, Iowa, to arrive at Michel's post in February 1838. Pratt beheld Michel's modest accommodations as a haven in the wilderness. The trading post "was the first building of the kind we had seen since leaving Fort Atkinson," he explained. Cold and hungry Pratt and his men "bolted in" after no one answered the door. They "found a squaw and some four or five papooses" and tried speaking "to her in the Pottawattamie language, but she made no reply."[23] After Pratt and his men had exhausted all of their nonverbal communication skills, Michel walked through the door. "He informed us that he was a Canadian, that the squaw was his wife, and that the children were also his. The squaw belonged to the Winnebago tribe, and spoke a different language from the other Indians in the vicinity," recalled Pratt. Michel informed his guest that he had been in the Indian trade "for years." Angelique made supper while the men talked. "It was a kind of pot-pie" made from muskrat, and Pratt and his crew "relished [it] very well." Pratt and his men spent the night after supper and left in the morning.[24]

The St. Cyrs departed for Prairie du Chien not long after Pratt's visit. Michel sold his valuable Lake Mendota property for a song to future governor of Wisconsin James Doty and his partner.[25] Michel and Angelique legally married on April 16, 1838, and settled with their children in the fur trade village where Michel was born. Late that summer Michel made a claim for 1837 treaty money set aside for "mixed-blood relations of the Winnebago tribe."[26]

In 1839 Angelique gave birth to Michel John, known as John, in Prairie du Chien.[27] The next year the St. Cyrs followed the Ho-Chunk to their new agency at the Turkey River near Fort Atkinson, Iowa. Michel obtained a trading license that would help support his family along with annuities they received.[28] Angelique gave birth to Alexander in the fall of 1841. A priest blessed Angelique and Michel's marriage at St. Gabriel's the next year. The blessing may have soothed Angelique's fears when her husband took Mink Woman (Chaejunsickaw) for his second wife.[29] Mink Woman delivered Moses to Michel in 1843. Angelique delivered Mary Elizabeth the same year. The St. Cyr household brimmed with children when violence erupted. The Sac and Fox murdered several Ho-Chunk, leading government officials to propose removal again.

The Ho-Chunk signed another treaty in the fall of 1846 in Washington DC. This one "sought to remove the Winnebagoes from the 'neutral ground' in Iowa, to a point more remote from the centres of civilization." Authorities also planned to remove tribal members who resisted the first removal to Iowa. Dakota chief Wabasha generously offered the Ho-Chunk a plot of land near Winona in Minnesota Territory. After all, the Dakota and Ho-Chunk were intermarried and traditional allies. The land bordered the Mississippi River, and La Crosse, the Ho-Chunk's easternmost village, was only thirty miles downstream. Wabasha's promise "threatened trouble," however. The Ho-Chunk "wished to remain at the Winona prairie," while U.S. government representatives obtained "Long Prairie" from the Ojibwe in the summer of 1848.[30]

Military troops corralled the Ho-Chunk to the new reservation in the fall of 1848, but the Ho-Chunk didn't like the new environment. It was remote. It sat fifty miles northeast of Minneapolis in Minnesota Territory and was over two hundred miles from La Crosse.[31] The Ho-Chunk also rightly feared there would be trouble with the Chippewa (Ojibwe), whose land abutted theirs. The woods were impenetrable and made it hard to hunt or to see if an enemy was approaching. Consequently, many individuals and families fled back to Wisconsin, joining a band led by Chief Dandy, who had resisted the first removal.

Most of the Ho-Chunk *métis* lived around the Winnebago Agency. The men worked for the agency as farmers, carpenters, assistant blacksmiths, and common laborers.[32] Their wives raised children, planted and tended gardens, and took care of their homes. Mink Woman gave birth to Mary Louise at Long Prairie in 1847, while Edward was born to Angelique the same year. Another St. Cyr daughter seems to have been born in 1849, but she died young, and her mother is unknown. Mink Woman parted with Michel soon after. She married Little Priest, who came to be one of the Ho-Chunk's most revered warriors.

Michel advocated for his children's education, a desire he passed on to his son Mitchell. Protestant missionaries received the government's sanction to run the agency school, as they had at Turkey River, but Michel and the other *métis* persuaded Ho-Chunk chiefs to support their efforts to establish a Catholic mission and school instead. The men organized a petition, whose cosigners included all the men DeLaronde encountered on that first July Fourth in Madison, as well as Chief Little Decora and his brother Tall Decora, Lilian's maternal grandfather.[33] They were successful, and a Catholic mission came to Long Prairie.

Angelique delivered three more children to Michel during the Long Prairie years: William in 1851, Hyacinthe in 1852, and Valentine in January 1855. Again, intertribal conflict with the Ojibwe necessitated the

Ho-Chunk's removal in 1855. The government established a new agency in the little village of St. Clair, just east of Mankato in Blue Earth County. The Ho-Chunk *métis* soon formed a Catholic congregation, and the parish priest baptized Michel and Angelique's last child, Julia, who was born in 1859.[34]

The Blue Earth County reservation held promise. The Ho-Chunk built wigwams and frame houses, tilled farms, sent their children to school, buried those who passed on, and began finally to put down roots. An 1859 treaty promised allotments to Ho-Chunk heads of families and adult individuals, but some traditional leaders felt justifiably suspicious about officials dividing up their reservation and selling off what didn't get allotted. Still, Ho-Chunk *métis*, now dubbed "the civilized band," campaigned to own the land they farmed. Michel was one of the first to be allotted, but it was over a decade before he received his deed.

The Dakota War of August 1862 dashed all hopes for a permanent home. As Minnesota's lieutenant governor put it to Minnesota's governor, the war began with an "accidental outrage."[35] The Dakota agent surmised that "the die was cast" for war on "Sunday, the 17th day of August, A.D. 1862, at the village of Acton," in Meeker County. "Four young men from Shakopee's band at the Lower Sioux Agency . . . part of a hunting party composed of fourteen, obtained whiskey, became intoxicated, and killed six persons, including a man named Jones, from whom it is alleged they obtained the whiskey." The agent insisted that these murders were "the spark which ignited the train leading to the magazine in which, for more than ten years, had been accumulating the combustibles of discontent, dissatisfaction, and premeditated devilment."[36] The "magazine" was the Dakota's loss of their land by government treaties, growing frustration with constant broken treaty promises, and anger over favors granted to nontraditional tribal members.

In the early hours of August 18, Dakota chief Little Crow, after hearing about the Acton murders, worried that all his people would be punished for the deeds of a few. Consequently, he reluctantly agreed to condone what he feared was a "hopeless war against the whites." According to historians, "The fighting lasted six weeks and took the lives of nearly five hundred whites, mostly civilians, and an unknown but substantial number of Indians."[37]

A five-man military tribunal convicted 323 men of war crimes between September 28 and November 5, 1862; 304 of those faced execution.[38] However, Ho-Chunk chiefs remained neutral during the conflict. Little Decora even warned the Winnebago agent after Dakota approached him to ally with them against the whites. The military tribunal also tried fourteen Ho-Chunk men for joining the Dakota, but only one, who had a Dakota relative, was convicted, and only on circumstantial evidence.

President Abraham Lincoln interceded against the wishes of Minnesota citizens and dramatically reduced the number of men to be executed. Still, thirty-eight Dakota were hanged to their death in Mankato on the day after Christmas in 1862. Some Ho-Chunk tribal members from nearby St. Clair attended the execution, which marked the largest mass hanging in America. Authorities also sent over two hundred prisoners to be held in Davenport, Iowa, including the one Ho-Chunk man convicted.

Minnesota citizens united to banish the Dakota and the Ho-Chunk from the state, in great measure because farmers coveted their fertile lands. In May 1863 government officials crammed nearly two thousand Ho-Chunk men, women, and children into steamer ships bound for Crow Creek, South Dakota. When the people disembarked, they found themselves in a barren land with scant food and few basic necessities. They also found themselves surrounded by a militia that threatened to shoot and kill anyone who attempted escape. The banished Dakota, mostly women, children, and the elderly, shared meager supplies with the Ho-Chunk.

Lilian's father, Mitchell, and his brothers Gus (Augustus), John, and Alex accompanied their kin to Crow Creek. Soon after, Angelique died, but whether in Minnesota, in Crow Creek, or on the Missouri River in between is unknown.[39] Most members of the civilized band returned to Blue Earth County, joining those who had not left. They lobbied the government to give them the allotments that had already been selected for them. Officials offered them a deal: if they became naturalized citizens and relinquished their tribal allegiance, then they would be paid the remainder of the annuities owed them and receive 40 acres of land per adult or 80 acres per family. Michel and fifty others agreed to the terms. He received his money and land in exchange for his tribal membership in 1871.[40] He married a young Ho-Chunk *métis* woman in 1865 and with her had seven more children. However, only one of these children lived to be over thirty, indicating that Michel's choice did not insure a viable future for his family.

As time passed and settlers came to Blue Earth County, Lilian's grandfather Michel became more of an Indian and less of a "white man." Locals remembered him as having a dark complexion with dark eyes and hair and perceived his Indianness as a curiosity rather than a threat because it was an interesting remnant of the town's past as an Indian agency. Michel died on his allotment on February 27, 1896, at nearly sixty years of age. His funeral at St. Clair's Catholic Church "was largely attended." "There seems to be no record of his birth to be found," stated a newspaper report, "but he must have been a very old man as he has lived here nearly half a century and was not considered a very young man when he first came here in the early days."[41]

Michel's widow and surviving daughter had moved away by 1900, and except for Mink Woman's daughter, who had a large family with a white farmer, the rest of Michel's children with Angelique and Mink Woman migrated to homes near or on the Nebraska reservation, where they lived out their days with their Ho-Chunk kin.

Lilian's eldest brother, David Reuben St. Cyr, was born at the Crow Creek internment camp on Christmas Day of 1864. Shortly after his birth, the St. Cyr and the Decora families escaped their imprisonment with the surviving Ho-Chunk. They carved dugout canoes and paddled south on the Missouri River, which flowed through Crow Creek, until they reached Sioux City, Iowa. There they crossed the border into northern Nebraska. They set up camp on the reservation of the Omaha people. The Omaha, closely related to the Ho-Chunk, took pity on them. The following year, the Omaha granted their cousins the northern section of their reservation.

The Dakota's plight was horrendous to be sure, but the Ho-Chunk's removal to Crow Creek cost hundreds, perhaps a thousand, lives. Some estimate that nearly one-third of the population had died of disease, starvation, and exposure by the time David was born. Lilian's birth was a full generation later, but the deaths of so many Ho-Chunk people during and shortly after their stay at Crow Creek reflect her inheritance, the tragedy and trauma of the removal years.

Lilian's father, Mitchell, acted as agency interpreter and spokesperson for the Nebraska Ho-Chunk. Although he was technically a citizen, his marriage to Julia Decora brought him back into the fold of the tribe. A photograph of the Ho-Chunk delegates who traveled to Washington DC in 1865 to obtain their reservation shows Mitchell standing just to the left of Chief Little Decora. Lilian's father has a mustache and dark wavy hair combed straight back from his brow. He is strikingly handsome.[42] Although no pictures of Lilian's mother have surfaced, Lilian clearly resembles her father down to the dimple on her chin.

The Winnebago Tribe of Nebraska numbered 1,335 individuals in 1868. At this time, tribal leaders, with Mitchell as their interpreter, called a council to adopt eighteen "Laws and Regulations" that would govern life on the reservation. The last of these regulations stipulated that the "Executive and Judicial power of the Tribe shall be lodged in fourteen Chiefs." The chiefs would "have jurisdiction of all cases arising under the Tribe"; "guard with vigilance the interests of the Tribe, irrespective of distinct bands and individuals"; and make sure "laws are rigidly enforced" and that "all offenders, without respect to person or rank, are brought to quick and prompt punishment." The council's declaration exemplifies the status of the tribe as a sovereign nation within the United States.[43]

President Ulysses S. Grant's Indian commissioner, E. S. Parker, a Seneca attorney who served with Grant as his assistant adjutant general during the Civil War, appointed Major Howard White as the Winnebago agent in 1869. White was a Quaker, and Quaker appointments for such positions were commensurate with Grant's Indian policy. Joseph A. Paxson, also a Quaker, served as reservation physician. Paxson kept a diary during his appointment that affords a rare glimpse of the conditions of the reservation in its early years. He visited the various bands that were spread across more than one hundred thousand acres to administer care and medicine. His diary entry for July 26, 1869, states that he visited Little Decora's camp, where presumably Lilian's grandparents lived. The conditions were not good. "Saw 15teen that are complaining," he wrote.

"Some with 'Sore eyes' [trachoma] some 'Rheumatism' 'Gout' 'Scrofula,' and one case of 'Coxalgia.'"[44] Paxson blamed unsanitary living conditions for most of the diseases he treated, but he did not attribute the unsanitary conditions themselves to the involuntary poverty and hardship caused by the removal years. His observations lack deep sympathy for the Ho-Chunk's situation. Instead, he exhibits typical cultural chauvinism.

Paxson's diary reveals that the government had not yet banned "pagan" ceremonies from the reservation. He writes about a dance he witnessed that was apparently connected to the traditional Medicine Lodge religion the Ho-Chunk practiced.

> After dinner we all went over to see the dance out. Their doings were most peculiar. There was about 200 Indians dressed in the gayest colors they could find, and trimmed with beads & ribbon & bells. Each member carries a "medicine bag." Some of their bags are most beautiful, being the skin of some animal, as the rat, beaver, otter, skunk, opossum, muskrat, of something of the kind. These "bags" were trimmed in the most gaudy style with beads, ribbon, & bells. While to see this dance was quite interesting I do not think it is best for the Indian to encourage such things.[45]

Paxson observed the Ho-Chunk asserting their own cultural beliefs. What he and other white officials wanted to see, however, was the Ho-Chunk's expression of Christian piety, individuality, and industry. Paxson helped with land surveys in November 1869 to achieve this end. Dividing tribal land into allotments discouraged communal ownership and thus tribal sovereignty.[46] A school was also constructed that year to teach children to be industrious and independent.

New York Quakers sent "the little children attending the Winnebago Indian School" new clothes not only for their comfort but also to transition them from "savage" to civilized. New Year's Day of 1870 was "set apart as the most appropriate of all to distribute the clothing," Paxson wrote. "A number of the smallest & most destitute of the children were selected by the teachers to come to the office this morning and be fitted out in a comfortable suit, as a New Year's gift." Children arrived early "accompanied by their mothers, older sisters, & brothers, and a few of the men." School staff brought them "into the office one at a time," removing their "old clothes, rags & blankets" and replacing them, according to Paxson, with a "good warm suit, from head to foot." Paxson pronounced the change "wonderful," observing that "from a dirty little Indian, wrapped in a blanket, came a neat well formed little Indian boy."[47] He didn't remark on the girls, because their dresses needed to be fitted, cut, and sewn. His demeaning remarks about the boys, however, reveal the dark side of "Indian education," best represented by Richard Henry Pratt's future prescription "Kill the Indian in him, and save the man." Lilian's brother David may have also stood in line for new clothes, though he probably wouldn't have been deemed as "destitute" as the other boys, since his father was employed at the agency. Still, the St. Cyr children, like their kinsfolk, endured government-sanctioned cultural genocide and the terrible sense of shame it elicited.

Just before the summer solstice of 1870 the reservation suffered a dramatic political shake-up. The fourteen chiefs noticed that "civilizing influences," apparently from the Quaker administration, had usurped their sovereignty. Having "lost all their authority to white man's justice," they were forced to resign.[48] Leaders called a council, and the fourteen chiefs selected their replacements. The new chiefs were younger and less traditional men, including Mitchell, Lilian's father. "During the council each of the old chiefs made a retiring speech," wrote Paxson. "Some nice some not much so." Little Priest's brother, Grey Wolf, "made a flaming speech—denouncing everything and everybody," according to Paxson.[49]

Another shake-up occurred in 1873 when the U.S. military rounded up the Ho-Chunk living in Wisconsin and shipped them to the Nebraska reservation. It was nice to have families reunited, but almost immediately illness and other hardships struck. Several of the newly transplanted left Nebraska and made their way back to their "old haunts" by 1875. Other Nebraska folk, fed up with conditions, also departed. The elderly Little Decora eagerly returned to the land where his family and ancestors were buried. The continued resistance of the Wisconsin contingent finally wore down the government's resolve. Heads of families were encouraged to apply for homesteads in counties surrounding Black River Falls in the next decade. These lands became the de facto reservation and home of the Wisconsin Ho-Chunk Nation.

Meanwhile, Mitchell St. Cyr's family grew. His first daughter, Julia J., was born in 1867. Shortly after, he took a second wife, Ocseeahoononickaw, the "Sixth Daughter" of White Elk and Good Red Bird Woman.[50] Sixth Daughter gave birth to Abner St. Cyr in 1869. The same year Julia Decora gave birth to Annie. Minnie was born to Julia in 1870, while Sixth Daughter gave birth to Levi the next year. Sixth Daughter died shortly after, so Abner and Levi lived with their grandmother Red Bird Woman.[51] Julia had another son, Louis Laurence, in 1876. Two years later she delivered Pauline, but she died in infancy. Julia gave birth to Eugene in 1881, and he also died quite young.

Conditions in Nebraska were dire in 1881. Mitchell had already contracted trachoma, a painful eye disease, when he accompanied several Ho-Chunk and Omaha chiefs to Washington DC, where he spoke as a delegate. A reporter described the Ho-Chunk as "well-dressed men" who "spoke English fluently." He noted that only two of the Omaha had been educated, "but all wore the garb of civilization, blue flannel or black cloth suits." "Chief St. Cyr, an intelligent fellow, was the first to speak," he wrote. Mitchell requested $40,000 in Winnebago annuity money to buy horse teams and lumber and to "set their saw-mill in operation again." The secretary of the interior balked at Mitchell's request, retorting, "The Indians should show a disposition to help themselves." Speaking for "the industrious class," Mitchell replied that "those Indians who did not work" did not expect assistance. Other delegates supported his request, explaining that the Winnebago "had a bad year, their crops have failed," and, consequently, they need "an advance on our cash annuity." Addressing Mitchell, the secretary replied, "I understand that a number of your tribe are well off, and own large and profitable farms. Now would you be willing for us to advance money to the needy class only, or do you desire an equal division?" "Why we will want our share, of course," responded Mitchell. "We are entitled to it."[52]

Mitchell was no stranger to the government's political manipulation. In the end, it only fueled his desire to represent the interests of the tribe and his family as tribal members. Given the government's domination over their lives, Mitchell believed it was paramount that his children be educated "in the white man's way" so they could maneuver a system that was almost always tipped against them. After enrolling David and Julia J. in the reservation school, he gave his permission in 1880 for the siblings to attend the brand new Indian Department at Hampton Institute in faraway Hampton, Virginia.

Hampton Institute, a large freedman's school, had added the smaller Indian Department in 1878. Famed alumnus turned teacher Booker T. Washington remembered Julia well. She enrolled at age twelve but had already been the organist for the reservation school in Nebraska, he remembered. He was struck by how well she spoke English. "No Indian girl has ever been able to enter the Preparatory class" at Hampton, Washington wrote, "but Julia, I think, can enter the Junior class."[53] Julia was certainly brighter than most, but her attendance at the boarding school initiated a lifelong love-hate relationship with Hampton. She found toeing the assimilationist line challenging, and as a result staff locked her in a small cell in the basement of the school, where she was served bread and water. Not surprisingly, she wrote home concerning her situation.

Her letter upset her parents, so Mitchell wrote to the head of Hampton's Indian Department on February 17, 1882.[54] His letter clearly states his desire that Julia complete her education while at the same time asking for more indulgence and some grace on the part of Hampton staff.

> Yesterday I received a letter from Julia St. Cyr (my daughter) saying that she had been in some trouble, had been locked up some time, & asking me to write & ask you not to punish her in that way. Now I wish to request that you & the other lady (Matron I suppose) will be indulgent & as she promises "never to do anything wrong again" that you will forgive her.
>
> The mother has been greatly distressed & cried a great deal about it, & we fear our daughter may hurt or kill herself, in trying to escape. So that if she can not get along without being punished anymore in that way, we would want her sent home. But we want our daughter to be dutiful & if you can get along with her, without too much trouble, we want her to stay out her time & finish her education.[55]

Julia remained at Hampton for two more years. She learned many useful skills, including an uncommon racial tolerance toward African Americans that she assuredly passed on to Lilian. Still, Julia's ambivalence about the Hampton Institute never resolved itself.

Lilian was born to Julia Decora and Mitchell St. Cyr on February 23, 1884. People remembered that winter as simply terrible. Ten percent of the Plains Indian population succumbed to malnutrition and various diseases. The worst case occurred in Montana, where six hundred Piegan (Blackfeet) Indians starved to death. The mass extermination of the buffalo made the Indigenous population especially dependent on the federal government, which was slow in responding, if it did at all.[56] Although the Ho-Chunk weren't dependent on buffalo for sustenance, they were all too familiar with the indifference of their Great Father.

Indian reformer and protoethnographer Alice Fletcher visited the Nebraska Winnebago briefly during the year of Lilian's birth. She was busy allotting land to the Omaha and collecting ethnographic data, but she wanted to record a Winnebago syllabary.[57] She met Mitchell on the reservation and perhaps held his new baby. She had already met Julia J., apparently through staff at Hampton Institute. Consequently, Julia J. turned to Fletcher in the summer of 1885: "Dear Miss Fletcher my dear darling mother died last week Tuesday morning at four o'clock. It was the time I was just coming back in the boat from Hampton. I didn't tell you while I was in Washington that I wished you would help David my brother that he can come home. Oh! it is so lonely here. If I had gotten here in time it will not be so hard, but I came three days after Tuesday after my darling mother died."[58]

Julia J. arrived home from boarding school to find a grieving father suffering the late stages of trachoma. He'd apparently taken another wife, but she left him and went to Wisconsin. Mitchell was hard-pressed to take care of all his children, especially Lilian, who was only sixteen months old. "I am willing to do anything to help my poor father now," Julia wrote Fletcher. "My father has sore eyes very badly and our mother's loss is so great to him, and he wishes that David would come home soon and help us. I really do miss my mother very much. . . . Father sends his regards to you. I am trying my best all the time. I feel so sorry but I trust in God, for he knew best to take our most beloved mother away."[59]

Julia also conveyed Tall Decorah's grief and, like Little Decora, emphasized her family's piety to win Fletcher's support. "He is my mother's father poor man! he is just mourning now but he says she is safe in heaven and tries to comfort us all. My mother was a good Christian, Mrs. Fletcher, so I feel so much better. When you have the time write to me and advise me. I feel so sick and lonesome. I will close now and say good bye to you."[60]

Julia returned from school to a motherless home, a blind father, and a baby sister who needed care. No one was there to celebrate her historic accomplishment as a member of Hampton's first Indian Department graduating class. Soon Julia would find, as she later wrote, "what a hard place West was for educated Indians." Meanwhile, David returned from the East to manage the farm for his father.[61] Minnie was away in Genoa, Nebraska, attending Indian boarding school. Annie and perhaps her grandmother Younkaw likely took care of Lilian and Louis. Life was hard.

Despite her ambivalent feelings about Hampton, Julia served as a recruiting agent for the school. Her participation in finding new students from the reservation allowed her to attend Hampton normal school classes in 1887 and to train as an assistant teacher.[62] Unfortunately, Hampton staff or teachers failed to meet Julia's expectations. She confided her problems to a local townswoman. Her confidante immediately wrote President Grover Cleveland, complaining about the treatment of Hampton students. The letter initiated a congressional investigation of the school that fall.[63]

Meanwhile, Lilian's sister Annie gained an appointment as assistant teacher for the reservation school from December 1886 to June 1887 and then again the following year.[64] The first real glimpse of Lilian as a small child appears during this time. Apparently, the sisters boarded together in town, as shown by a letter to "Anni and Lillia" from their father dated September 1887 or 1888. The letter, written on old-school ruled notepaper, now shows signs of wear and tear and repair, but its message of love is undimmed. A proud father missed his daughters and hoped they were well.

My Dear Lovly Daughters

Anni and Lillia
I am trying to write you a few lines let you know I am well and
I hope my few line will fine you the same health. Papa thinking

About you all the times Kiss My Little girl [Lilian] tell her Papa send her his kiss Take good care of your Little Sister Me and David still living alone yet Minnie has not come home yet I hope you are contented I hope you will not get lonesome I am keeping house my eyes are the same The times are dull at this Agency Now my dear child take good care of yourself be honest a true girl so you can have a good name and can be trusted any where I no you are good girl I am proud of it all the time

You must excuse me to not have written to you more offen I can't see good enough but I gesss by all my written this all I hope my few line will fine you and your sister in good health tell Lillia the Little Pony is big now

> From your father
> Michel St. Cyr[65]

In July 1888 Julia started work as an assistant teacher at the Sac and Fox Agency in Tama, Iowa.[66] Mitchell died sometime before the end of September that year, leaving four-year-old Lilian and her siblings orphaned and grieving. Lilian learned powerful lessons in her first years of life. She would take nothing for granted. She would try to get along wherever she went. She would not make a fuss. She would try to bring a smile to someone's face. "Papa's kisses" faded into memory, but the tiny missive he sent "Anni and Lillia" still survives. Lilian kept the cherished heirloom of parental love till the day she died in 1974. It served as a reminder to find comfort in her past and to hold tight to the heritage that was hers to claim.

CHAPTER 2

Ochsegahonegah at the Lincoln Institute

It was a clear and unseasonably warm evening in Philadelphia on March 2, 1889, as the assembly room of the Lincoln Institute on South Eleventh Street filled to capacity with "some of the most fashionable people of the city." The crowd took their seats to watch a production of Gilbert and Sullivan's *H.M.S. Pinafore*, but the philanthropically inclined among them came mostly for charity's sake. Nearly everyone in the audience anticipated a novel experience, since the Lincoln Institute was not a theater. It was an Episcopal boarding school that had opened wide its Christian doors in 1882 to educate American Indian children. The evening's true reformers believed in "the possibility of thoroughly civilizing the Indian." Other attendees were not so sure. They agreed that instructing the nation's Indian wards in industrial skills was a noble endeavor, but teaching them the fine arts was unrealistic. A *Philadelphia Times* reviewer challenged their lack of faith, pronouncing that American Indians had a gift for the stage. It was not just his opinion. Audience members also "expressed their surprise as well as their satisfaction at the excellent manner" in which the Indian pupils performed. Despite makeshift stage sets and an insufficient solo piano accompaniment, the reviewer deemed the performance equal to any given by "the whites of our city schools." His ambiguous compliment disguised the diversity of the students, some of whom had white fathers or grandfathers who loved Indian women only briefly or for life.[1]

The Lincoln Institute provided the female cast, while the affiliated

Educational Home for Boys in West Philadelphia lent the production its cast of Indigenous males. Students hailed from across the country, including New York, California, and Alaska. These "dusky lads and maidens" won the reviewer's highest acclaim in pursuing a "a new line of usefulness and accomplishments."[2] Their accomplishments were not just limited to the stage. Joshua Givens (Kiowa), a twenty-seven-year-old Educational Home student, was about to be ordained as a Presbyterian minister. Chosen to be the speaker for the event, Givens reiterated the hopes of the day's Indian reform movement by confronting the infamous conviction attributed to Indian fighter General Philip Sheridan: "The theory, that there is no good Indian but a dead Indian is disproved by this presentation here to-night, in which Indian boys and girls have delighted and won the applause of a large, fashionable, intelligent and critical audience. They must be good to have done so well, and their achievement shows you, our white friends, that if you educate our people we will help you solve the Indian problem."[3]

The *Times* review provided the male cast members' phonetically rendered Indian names that so fascinated the eastern elite. The male leads were Karoutowanen (Iroquois) as Captain Corcoran, Thonwenjorem (Iroquois) as Sir Joseph Porter; Sha-go-wash (Chippewa) as Ralph Rackstraw, and Shaoanes (Iroquois) as Dick Deadeye. The report also gave the English names of the female leads, including Louisa Chubb or Chull (Mohawk) as Josephine, Nettie Hansell or Wanske (Modoc) as Buttercup, and Lucy Gordon or Wiciyaci (Sioux) as Cousin Hebe. The reviewer pointed out that Chubb, "a prepossessing girl of 16" who was gifted "with a more than fair soprano voice," noticeably suffered stage fright. Despite her emotional state, Chubb's enunciation was clear and "without a trace of alien accent." "In fact," the reviewer remarked, "the ear gave no intimation" that she or any of the other singers "were not of the Aryan race."[4]

Nettie Hansell, the darling of the Lincoln Institute, was the star of the performance. Her remarkable mezzo-soprano vocals captured everyone's praise. An adorable child who was dressed in crimson silk and mistaken for Sioux (though her birth-order name marked her as Ho-Chunk) equally stole the show. "Ochsegahonegah, or Lillie St. Cyr, a pretty and phenomenally bright little Sioux girl of five years," the reviewer wrote, "evoked hearty applause and many charming compliments." It's difficult to know if Lilian remembered the moment when fate put her on the pathway to a performance career. She did not leave an account of the evening or mention if the boarding school influenced her choice to become an actress.[5] No one could have guessed that night—still five years before Indians were first captured on film—that the little girl in crimson silk would one day become the first "real Indian" motion picture star.

Scant documentation exists to account for Lilian's years in Philadelphia, but her peers and teachers, the school's administration and history, and the school's prominent visitors during her stay provide a framework for understanding its influence. One of Lilian's siblings enrolled her in the school when she was only four. She remained in Philadelphia until she was nine years old. Lilian must have learned during these crucial developmental years not only to obey authority figures outside her family but also to win their love.

Contemporaneous reformers viewed off-reservation Indian boarding schools like Hampton Institute in Virginia and the famous Carlisle Indian Industrial School in the town of Carlisle, outside Harrisburg, Pennsylvania, as the most effective means for assimilating Indian children into white society.[6] Tragically, they also suppressed the reality that American Indian children suffered immeasurably when the government attempted to obliterate their familial and cultural ties in order to inculcate in them Anglo-Saxon or "Aryan" values. Some children and their parents actively resisted this attempt, while others, like Lilian and her family, viewed such policy as the only means to escape impoverished reservation life and to achieve success in the white world. Most, however, like Lilian, would question and confront this policy in their later years when the effects of historical trauma on America's Indian population became chillingly apparent. By the 1910s government officials were unconvinced that adhering to a stringent policy of assimilation was making much of a difference. The so-called Indian problem, which reformers like those who attended *Pinafore* were determined to solve, resisted resolution.[7]

Mary McHenry Bellangee Cox, the widow who established and ran both the Lincoln Institute and the Educational Home, was a powerhouse reformist. She was also fiercely dedicated to her female students, perhaps insuring that Lilian's early experience of Indian boarding school was at least survivable. Lincoln Institute also offered Lilian exemplary role models like Nettie Hansell, the school's best singer, and star pupils like Jane Eyre and Lucy Gordon, whom Cox nurtured to become teachers. Several Ho-Chunk girls, including the Frenchmans, whom Lilian's brothers would marry, and the Tyndalls, family friends from the Omaha reservation, also attended the school. Lilian's sisters Annie and Minnie were also role models, but, more importantly, they watched over her.

David St. Cyr was the oldest sibling left to care for Lilian when their father died because Julia was working in Iowa. David was unmarried and in charge of the family farm, so he had little time or female support to care for his younger siblings. A recruiter from the Lincoln Institute and the Educational Home, together known as "the Homes," arrived at the Winnebago reservation in the fall of 1888, solving the dilemma. With David's permission, the recruiter took the orphaned St. Cyrs, Annie (eighteen), Minnie (about seventeen), Louis (about eleven), and Lilian (four), and a few other reservation children on the long train ride from Sioux City, Iowa, to Philadelphia.

Lilian was technically too young to be admitted to the Homes (six was the minimum age requirement), but she was in desperate need of care, as the *Philadelphia Times* reported: "There are now fifteen more Indians under instruction [at the Homes] than the government pays for, owing to the pressure brought upon the managers by the destitution of some little Indian children from the Winnebago Reservation."[8] Lilian, as one of the destitute, later gave two brief reports of her time in Philadelphia. First, she stated that she "was placed in a family at Philadelphia where she entered the kindergarten," and later, she said, "Episcopal missionaries put her through private school in Philadelphia."[9] Apparently, she boarded with a local family until she was old enough to enroll in the school.

The original Lincoln Institute arose from the philanthropic impulse of Mary Cox. Sister of railroad tycoon James McHenry and wife of Philadelphia attorney John Bellangee Cox, Cox began her educational career in 1856 when she opened a school in her own home. Ten years later she established the Lincoln Institute for the education and training of Civil War orphan boys age twelve to twenty-one. She opened the Educational

Home in 1871 at Sixty-Fifth Street and Greenway Avenue for boys under twelve. Most of the orphans were adults by 1881, so Cox put the Lincoln Institute building up for sale and transferred her remaining charges to the Educational Home.[10]

Cox's mission changed dramatically when the indomitable Richard Henry Pratt came to Philadelphia the next year from Carlisle, Pennsylvania. Pratt was the zealous superintendent of the prototypical Indian boarding school, Carlisle Indian Industrial School, which he founded in 1879. He decided to promote Indian education and the value of his school in particular by exhibiting "his most successful students" in Philadelphia's bicentennial parade. The crowd cheered as floats with Pratt's students portraying the three stages of civilization, primitive to barbaric to civilized, passed down the parade route. Pratt had already employed a similar strategy to promote his school using before and after photographs of his students. These cabinet cards portrayed single or groups of students as they arrived at Carlisle from their respective reservations as "uncivilized" paired with an image of the same individual or group with their hair cut and dressed in a school uniform as "civilized." Pratt was pleased to see that these opposing photographs translated well into a living diorama.

Pratt, referred to as the "Red Man's Moses," was dedicated to the pursuit of civilizing as many American Indians as humanly possible.[11] Cox was well aware of Pratt's stature and graciously hosted his students, housing them in the vacant Lincoln Institute building. Pratt's students enjoyed their time in Philadelphia, even if they didn't relish the public display. One of Pratt's female students gave an account of her stay, which was published in an Indian education journal: "The people were all very kind to us all, and gave us good beds to sleep on, and very good food, indeed, to eat. We were all treated well by the kind white people. Mr. Johnson and Mrs. Cox went all around Philadelphia trying to get beds enough for us all to sleep upon when we got there, and I think it was very kind in them to do that."[12]

The Carlisle students were not the first to whom Cox opened her doors. She boarded Clarence Three Stars and Luther Standing Bear earlier that year while they worked for John Wanamaker's famous department store in Philadelphia. The Lakota boys enrolled in Carlisle the year Pratt established the school. Three Stars came from the Pine Ridge Agency in South Dakota, while Standing Bear, son of Chief George Standing Bear (Brulé Lakota), arrived from the Rosebud Agency. Standing Bear became Pratt's model student but later recalled both painful and happy memories of the school. As soon as he arrived at the school he was forced to have his long hair cut and relinquish his Lakota name, Ota Kte (Plenty Kill). On the other hand, he felt honored when Pratt chose him to play the bugle call each morning.

Many criticized Carlisle's military emphasis, but Standing Bear learned to take pride in the daily drills boys were forced to perform. His stay at Cox's Educational Home left him shocked by the behavior of the white boys who were the children of soldiers. "A big wagon left the school every morning, carrying several of the boys who worked out," he wrote. "We were invited to ride with them. After the first few mornings however, I preferred to ride in the street cars, rather than listen to the rough, pro-fane language which these boys used on their way to work. And these boys were supposed to be civilized, having had good teachers and good education." Three Stars decided to return to Pine Ridge partly due to the white boys' offensive behavior but mostly because of the mundane work at Wanamaker's. Standing Bear found himself alone in Philadelphia, determined to prove that Indians were not "good-for-nothing."[13]

Standing Bear's behavior so impressed Cox that she was more than will-ing to accommodate Carlisle students. Besides, she needed new charges. Cox and her board of managers sent a letter in the fall to Attorney Gen-eral Benjamin Harris Brewster in Washington DC, "offering to change [Lincoln] institution into a training school for Indian girls."[14] She and the board sought funding for fifty to one hundred girls to mark the institution as a legitimate Indian industrial training school. Cox was experienced in seeking funding for her Civil War orphans, but Pratt surely prepped her on how to establish a government-contract school. Pratt was informed by his own experience haggling with Congress since he founded Carlisle. He probably also advised her to downplay her missionary zeal. Cox was well aware of his feelings on the subject. "The missionary does not citizenize," he often complained.[15] Pratt wanted American Indian *citizens* to be the outcome of Indian education, not religious converts.

The secretary of the interior informed Cox and her board of managers that their request depended on a congressional appropriation. Massachusetts senator Henry L. Dawes and Pennsylvania senator Simon Cameron, both avid Pratt supporters, were in their corner. Dawes sat on the Indian Affairs Committee and was already preparing the ground for his lasting legacy, the Dawes Severalty Act of 1887. The kingpin of U.S. assimilationist policy, the Dawes Act attempted to destroy tribal sovereignty by dividing tribal land into individual allotments for single adults and heads of family. It also gave to the government's discretion land that was leftover from the allotments, further fueling pan-Indian resistance movements such as the Ghost Dance.

Cameron's ties to Indian issues reached back fifty years when he served as a special disbursing agent for the 1837 treaty stipulation that gave $100,000 to mixed-blood Ho-Chunk people, including the St. Cyr family. He and his co-agent were charged with fraud during the disbursement; nonetheless, he managed to rise above public scandal and build a formidable political career.[16] He served as President Lincoln's secretary of war until he resigned under new corruption charges. His checkered past was apparently disregarded under the era's patronage system, which Pratt certainly exploited. Cameron immediately requested an appropriation for the Lincoln Institution, "which was referred to the Committee on Appropriations."[17]

Cox and the board received approval by the next summer. "The corporators of the Lincoln Institute met to-day," reported the *New York Times*, "and made the necessary amendments to the charter for converting [the Homes] into a training school for Indian children."[18] Civil War orphans under fifteen still at the Educational Home would be transferred to the Northern Home for Friendless Children. Two "missionary ladies" who served in Dakota Territory recruited eleven girls from the Rosebud, Pine Ridge, and Cheyenne reservations later that summer. This was not an easy task. Policy dictated that the girls would be enrolled for five years, returning home at the government's expense. Children and their parents faced a long, painful separation, since very few parents could afford to travel east to visit their children. "Some of the parents were very reluctant to allow their children to leave them," the Lebanon, Pennsylvania, newspaper reported in September, "and one mother followed the party one hundred miles on foot, and recovered her child."[19] However, this outcome was rare. Most children, like the St. Cyrs, had no one who could reclaim them.

The ten remaining Lakota girls ranged in age from ten to seventeen and were enrolled in the Lincoln Institute on September 8. One of the girls, Iron Owl, was the great-niece of Hunkpapa leader Sitting Bull and so a great coup for Cox.[20] Seven more girls arrived from the West in December, while five Ojibwe girls came from the White Earth Agency in Minnesota, where an Episcopal mission aided the recruitment process considerably. The minimum requirement for the new school was fifty pupils, but the crafty Pratt transferred twenty-seven of his girls from Carlisle on January 3, 1884.[21]

The report of the Board of Commissioners of Public Charities explained the Homes' transformation into an Indian contract school. It noted the visit from Pratt's students, which led to Cox and the board's "deeper interest in the Indian cause" and "desire to do what they could to assist in their civilization." It also revealed that reformers, however benevolent and holy in their intentions, believed their mission was decreed by their racial superiority. "It seems to be settled that the wisest and surest way to settle the Indian question is not only to educate but to bring the Indians in contact with the whites in daily intercourse, so that with their natural perceptions and imitative tendencies they may imitate the ways and manners of the Anglo-Saxon race."[22]

This patronizing, chauvinistic, and racist attitude toward Native people permeated every nook and cranny of the country in various ways. For example, Pratt was not essentially racist, but he rejected the value of Native culture. He wanted Indians to become American citizens and to act like white people. For him, it was not a matter of nature but of nurture, an Enlightenment era view.[23] Racism based on pseudoscience was steadily replacing Pratt's old-school universalism, however, and many came to believe that environment could not change an Indian's essential "savage" nature. Franz Boas's concept of cultural relativism was about to be introduced to the scientific community, but it would take decades for it to reach mainstream society.

It is unclear if Cox shared Pratt's total rejection of American Indian culture. Her close relationship with the missionaries of the White Earth reservation in Minnesota indicates that her beliefs aligned with those of Bishop Henry B. Whipple, who had established the Ojibwa mission at White Earth. Whipple was not as fanatic as Carlisle's founder about wiping out all vestiges of what Pratt called "Indianisms." Many Minnesota Indians loved Whipple because he exposed government corruption in Indian affairs. He also successfully pleaded with President Lincoln to grant clemency to the more than three hundred Dakota men sentenced to be hanged in Mankato following the 1862 conflict. His efforts helped bring the executions down to thirty-eight. Nevertheless, he was as paternalistic as Pratt, working unceasingly to replace Native religion with his own. Cox aspired to do the same.

Lilian also experienced the attitude fostered by scientific evolutionism, which was probably closer to Cox's approach to education. Indians, despite their individual characters, were not strictly racially determined *if and only if* they worked very hard to achieve "progress." Hampton Institute wholeheartedly embraced this approach, which is telling, given that Julia St. Cyr and other Hampton students felt their teachers' and mentors' disappointment keenly and often solicited their approval even years after they left school.[24] Lilian grew to adulthood during the height of these conflicting ideologies, all unified by the notion that American Indians were socially and morally bereft.

Lilian also came from an ethnically mixed family in a time when the terms "half-breed" and "squaw man" were commonly used expressions that scarcely disguised white people's disgust for miscegenation. Finally, she was a Catholic, not a Protestant, the preferred religion of Anglo-Saxon Americans. How was a young orphaned girl supposed to fend off feelings of shame and navigate the whirlwind of beliefs animating "Indian reform"? With no parents to guide her, no home culture to ground her, and no role models to show her an alternative path, Lilian, perhaps as early as kindergarten, began to craft a public persona to secure her survival.

Lincoln Institute had enrolled "Eighty-Four Indian maids" by May 1884. The first order of business was to modify or change the girls' Indian names because staff and teachers could not easily write or pronounce their original names. The change also implicitly disassociated the children from their tribal identities. Some students already had English names, like Henrietta, or Nettie, Hansell, whose English name had been given to her by her father, John Hansell, a Modoc mixed-blood man. Most students, like Chtahkah, a Pawnee girl dubbed "Jane Eyre," were given new names. "After the ordeal of giving the names has been passed then comes the real work," one newspaper reported. "Some of them are so wedded to their wild customs that it takes quite a while to make them accept contentedly the civilized ways. Many upon first entering would prefer to lie down upon the floor or a hard bench to pass the night and it is only by the strictest vigilance that this is prevented."[25]

Later that year Congress passed an appropriation of $33,400 for both the Lincoln Institute and the Educational Home, stipulating: "For care, support, and education of two hundred Indian children at Lincoln Institution (or the Homes), Philadelphia, Pennsylvania, at a rate not to exceed one hundred and sixty-seven dollars per annum for each child." Senator Cameron had requested $175. The government also allotted $1,000 for "the education, support, and transportation" for thirty-four additional students.[26] However, the Homes could not be maintained with a government contract alone. Cox also depended on local philanthropists. Two of her most prominent benefactors were George W. Childs and Anthony Joseph Drexel. Childs was the editor of the *Philadelphia Ledger*. Drexel, a Catholic and uncle to Saint Katharine Drexel, was an art patron and banker who later teamed up with J. P. Morgan to amass a fortune. In 1891 he also founded Philadelphia's Drexel Institute of Art, Science, and Industry, a school that provided "practical training for students of modest means," including those from ethnically diverse backgrounds. Several students from the Homes, Carlisle, and the Hampton Institute attended his school.[27]

Cox managed the Homes with the help of women volunteers and paid male employees, although the pay was not generous. When Lilian and her siblings arrived in Philadelphia in 1888, the Homes' student body consisted of "Sioux, Chippewa, Ojibway, Santee, Osage, Omaha, Pawnee, Navajo, Cheyenne, Miami, Modoc, Wichita, Mohawk, Oneida, Iroquois, Winnebago, Crow, and Kiowa," as the *Philadelphia Times* reported.[28] The girls were housed in seven dorms headed by an older student who served as dorm captain. She made sure the children said their prayers every night and went straight to bed and not on the floor, if they were so inclined. Annie St. Cyr at eighteen may have served as a teacher's assistant, but she may have come to the school simply to watch over Lilian. Hampton Institute had set a precedent to allow parents to stay with their little ones if that was the only option to ensure the children's enrollment. For example, Eva Johnson, a Ho-Chunk girl who enrolled at Lincoln Institute sometime after the St. Cyrs, wrote: "Three of us children and my mother went to Lincoln Institution Philadelphia, Penn. for school my mother stayed there a year with us and then went home because my grandfather was sick."[29]

Cox understood her mission as "nothing less than to educate and train in the arts of civilized life the sons and daughters of the warriors and chiefs from the various Indian tribes in the United States." One may infer that her mission was politically expedient. After all, the children of warriors and chiefs, such as Sitting Bull, might prevent disputes and encourage assimilation when they returned home. Cox also hoped to dispel the stereotype that her students were savage. She introduced a common view of many female educators. Indian children were docile if treated with care, they took readily to religious instruction, and, like Lilian, they loved music. "All those who have lived among these 'native Americans,'" she stated, "bear their testimony that they are as I have found them—faithful, affectionate and grateful." She confronted a neighbor's misconception regarding Educational Home boys. "We do not see, nor do our pupils have such things as war dances, war paint, scalping; not even in their play hours do they desire to indulge in such things." Cox assured her fellow Philadelphians that all of her students indulged in civilized entertainments. These included "base ball, cotillions, round dances, singing comic songs, and other amusements of like kind." She also boasted that the Homes' "church choir is as good as any in our city churches. The Indians are naturally religious, and delight in singing sacred chants, and never desire to miss a church service, as so many of our own race do. The more I see of these people," she explained, "the more my respect and affection for them increases." She hoped to influence the public "to a just appreciation of their character and capabilities."[30]

Nonetheless, the Homes served another purpose that undermined Cox's belief that Indian children were equally worthy of respect. Indian tribes were viewed as a vanishing race, underscored by the notion that God had gifted the Anglo-Saxons a "Manifest Destiny" to conquer the continent ever westward. Scientific enquiry also took up this racial myth not as a hypothetical idea but as a reality. Scientists placed Native people's culture and physiognomy on an artificial spectrum between "Caucasians" and "Negroids" in order to prove white superiority. Meanwhile, a massive ethnographic salvage effort filled museums with Indigenous-made objects, as well as human remains. Photographers made their living creating stereoscopic images of both "wild" and "civilized" Indians. Even Lilian's father and brother David were photographed front and side view with ethnographic identifiers like "Michel St. Cyr, Winnebago Half-caste" when they visited Washington DC during treaty negotiations.[31]

One publication noted "praiseworthy" government efforts to "secure and preserve . . . ethnographical features of the fast-disappearing Indian tribes—their dresses, adornments, occupations, sports, and pastimes." It further declared that the Lincoln Institute's student body was a tribally diverse "collection" of the "children of the 'noble savage'" and might be "regarded as one of the most interesting and useful museums for the study of feature and character."[32] Lilian loved to perform for the public and was encouraged to do so by those in charge of the Lincoln Institute, but how strange it must have been for her to slowly realize that the audience was not just judging her by her talent and charisma but also viewing her as an object of study.

The curriculum of the Homes reflected Carlisle's, which was founded to promote assimilation, offer a "common school education," and provide industrial training to boys and girls. School was year-round. The girls usually spent the second half of their day sewing and knitting, but the first half included reading, writing, and arithmetic, as well as lessons in housekeeping and typewriting. They also received music lessons. Boys' instruction included farm work, harness making, blacksmithing, wheelwrighting, carpentry, and industrial baking.[33] Students also participated in field trips, according to Anna Bender, an Ojibwe girl from White Earth who attended school with the St. Cyr girls. She recalled that her teachers took them "to places of historical interest such as Carpenters and Independence Halls." They also visited "the mint to see how money was coined and to the Academy of Natural Sciences and Zoological Gardens."[34]

The Homes were also represented as nonsectarian. Cox often averred that students could attend whatever church they chose. However, she answered to a higher authority. The schools were in fact Episcopal-run missions with the directive to expose children to Protestantism and to prepare them to "go back to their tribes and either teach or engage in mission work." With this goal, akin to Hampton Institute's but contrary to Carlisle's, pupils had to retain some knowledge of their Native culture and language in order to communicate with the people back home when they returned. Although Cox hoped to guide her students into mainstream European American society and away from their reservations á la Pratt, reports indicate that a student such as Jane Eyre, who graduated from a Philadelphia high school and was subsequently hired as a teacher on her reservation, was deemed a Lincoln Institute success story.[35]

Government contracts required that Indian schools be nonsectarian. Catholic authorities in particular carefully monitored the Homes for coerced Episcopal conversions. Philadelphia Episcopal Church records demonstrate the validity of the Catholics' concerns. Various Episcopal churches in Philadelphia baptized and confirmed large groups of Indian students, including those from Catholic families. The Reverend Henry J. Rowland presided over the Educational Home's onsite chapel and baptized two dozen boys in the fall of 1889, including Louis St. Cyr and several other Ho-Chunk Catholics.[36] Bishop Ozi W. Whitaker had confirmed Annie St. Cyr earlier that spring.[37] The Episcopal Church may have also baptized or confirmed Lilian and Minnie St. Cyr, but their records have not yet been located. Church records clearly show that several Homes students returned to their reservation as Episcopalian, regardless of their original religion. Lilian remained a practicing Catholic until she died, even though Louis and Annie apparently retained their devotion to a Protestant supreme being.[38]

Lilian's experience in Philadelphia had long-lasting effects. The Lincoln Institute's music program encouraged her innate abilities, but its emphasis on domestic training at the expense of higher education left her with few options later in life. The training girls received in all Indian schools of the time meant that "the light of the home" more often became a domestic servant in a white woman's household. A deep prejudice underlay this training, which was based on the fear that Indian women's households were not only health hazards but also uncouth domiciles. Educators ignored the reality of unrelenting poverty and rejected the precepts of the natural world Indian mothers inhabited. They taught girls impractical skills such as the aesthetic presentation of meals. "The tables in the dining room are all most tastefully decorated with flowers and fruit," a visitor wrote of the Lincoln Institute.[39] "The girls serve by turns in each of the departments, so that they become thoroughly conversant and learned in all matters essential to the comfort and convenience of home." The visitor further praised the school for producing "capital domestics" for weary homemakers who "would give a hearty welcome to these Indian maidens." Yes, privileged white women across the land certainly gave Indian maids "a hearty welcome" to clean their homes and take care of their children. Lilian experienced their appreciation firsthand when she could not find employment in her early thirties.

It took focused dedication to keep the doors of a government contract school open, and Cox learned skillful political maneuvering to assure funding, whether from Congress or from philanthropists. To encourage benefactors, she emphasized the academic aspects of the Lincoln Institute's curriculum and her pride in her students' performance in a "competitive examination." "In writing and arithmetic the girls showed great readiness and proficiency," she stated, as well as "on some cardinal points of chronology and history, even of our own country." She further confessed that her "well-taught Sioux and Modoc girls" assured that the Lincoln Institute students won the competition.[40] The school's music program also encouraged benefactors by partaking in an allegory familiar to the public. Music tamed the savage and led him or her to civilization. The music program visibly and audibly impressed potential benefactors with the reward of Indian education done right. The production of *H.M.S. Pinafore,* with its skillful vocalist Nettie Hansell and endearing cast member little Lillie St. Cyr demonstrated money well spent.

The Lincoln Institute shone next to its brother school, the Educational Home. The Homes' board of managers apparently had worked out some of the kinks by the time Louis St. Cyr was enrolled there, but some serious issues still loomed large. A huge problem that never seemed to resolve itself was the employment of competent management. One of the early superintendents actually feared some of his students. Unfortunately, the Homes took any student that recruiters could get their hands on, including grown men. Some of these men from Pine Ridge reservation rebelled and acted out by bringing liquor into the school. The superintendent summarily sent them to a local prison, from which most were released the next day.

The worst cases involved beatings, which were afterward investigated by the Society for the Prevention of Cruelty to Children. An unidentified representative for the boys' school penned a letter to Indian rights activist Herbert Welsh after scathing public criticism of an Educational Home superintendent. The official had been charged with spanking boys "without intervention of clothing." Although Cox condemned the superintendent's actions, the unnamed writer, who was perhaps the perpetrator, expressed his belief that such bare-bottom beatings, so familiar to his upbringing, were of "great service to the beneficiaries."[41]

The boys' school had serious problems beyond its sadistic superintendent. It provided little industrial training. Although public relation material advertised that boys were trained in vocations such as baking and shoemaking, the reality was that many of the boys were left idle. This ensured that managing them would be a challenge, but worse, it indicated that the school was a sham. How did Lilian's brother Louis fare at the Educational Home? Certainly not as well as his sisters did at the Lincoln Institute. He was trained in cooking or baking, according to a later record, but the fatherless boy desperately needed a worthy male role model, which the Educational Home was clearly lacking.

Louis, a fine athlete, probably had fun playing baseball with Anna Bender's brother Charles "Chief" Bender, whom Lilian later claimed as a friend.[42] Bender is better known for having been a star athlete at Carlisle Indian School and for tying a 1911 World Series record for pitching three consecutive games.[43] Bender's presence was not enough to prevent the

Educational Home from failing, however, not only in the school's aim to educate boys but also as a humane institution. After Louis left Philadelphia in 1893, he bounced from school to school, never having achieved the sterling reputations his sisters Annie, Minnie, and Lilian acquired.[44]

Cox's hands-on management of the Lincoln Institute made all the difference. She placed a few students, including Minnie St. Cyr, as nurse trainees in Philadelphia's Lying-In Hospital for expectant mothers.[45] Teaching and nursing were viewed as advanced careers for Native women at the time, so this was no common feat. In 1891 Nebraska's Genoa Indian Industrial School paper boasted about Minnie's progress in Philadelphia: "We hear that Minnie St. Cyr, who was one of Genoa's pupils from Winnebago agency, has been appointed nurse . . . and was found to be so efficient in every way that they couldn't give her up. We are glad to hear such excellent reports from one of our girls, and to know that she is making herself useful in a good work, and doing credit to herself and those that have been her instructors."[46]

Clearly, Lilian and her sisters were exceptionally intelligent high achievers and in another time and place could have succeeded at Harvard, Yale, Johns Hopkins, or Juilliard. Cox realized that Native children suffered the biting prejudice of a racist public, but did she understand how much they suffered from the unjust and ineffective policies of the U.S. government? Could she see that the St. Cyr girls and their peers were much more than docile, musically inclined, service-oriented females? Perhaps she could, or she would have in another time and place. If she couldn't, then her dedication to the Indian reform movement blinded her to the full humanity and great potential of her wards.

CHAPTER 3

Role Models and Visitors

Little Lilian found herself far from home before she had scarcely begun to understand what home meant. Annie, Minnie, and Louis surely helped her to deal with so many strangers and to adapt to urban living. The St. Cyrs also spent their time away from Nebraska beyond the city limits of Philadelphia, because many pupils at the Homes went on "outings" during the summertime. Carlisle and Hampton Indian schools began the outing program, in which students usually stayed with and worked for farm families in the countryside for a small wage. Summer outings with a farm family provided students with hands-on experience in European American culture and society. Some students loved their outing program experiences, but some also ran away. Older runaways sometimes even made it back to their home reservations. Hampton Institute staff sent Julia and David St. Cyr on outings to the Berkshires in Massachusetts, a popular rural area for Indian student placement. The St. Cyrs left no record of praise or complaints.

An outing served other purposes as well. It offered country living and fresh air, providing relief from the hot and humid eastern summers, which most children from the Great Plains were not used to. Many students died in Indian boarding schools, particularly from pulmonary tuberculosis, or "consumption."[1] Consumption ravaged reservation people and often went undetected in school enrollees until it was too late. Students also contracted the disease in the confines of the boarding school. Rural environments provided open air that helped prevent the spread of the disease and also eased its symptoms.

Outings also kept students away from so-called bad influences at home. Ethnocentric educators absolutely dreaded that students would "go to the bad" and "return to the blanket." This meant donning tribal clothing again or just practicing traditional culture. Female representatives from Hampton visited the Winnebago reservation every summer to keep track of the "progress" or lack thereof of returned Indian students. They were upset to find that many returned girls practiced the Ho-Chunk custom of marriage, which was not legally binding. The school's representatives deemed it pagan and the girls immoral. They also hated to learn that returned students practiced the Peyote Religion, common on the Nebraska reservation, even though it had distinctive Christian elements and discouraged the use of alcohol.

Cox established a summer retreat for her students with all of these factors in mind. Homes benefactor George W. Childs provided the old vacated Spread Eagle Inn, which he had recently acquired. The Wayne train depot, northeast of Philadelphia, was only two miles away. Cox's summer home was also conveniently located nearby. Cox had the old tavern renovated and brought the first group of Indian students there in the summer of 1884. A chaplain provided "moral direction" to the children at a community hall in Wayne every Sunday. The lessons of the school year continued, but the atmosphere at the summer home was more relaxed.

Performances for the locals became a mainstay of the summer school agenda. That September, before they returned to the city, students enacted twenty-two tableaux from Longfellow's popular *Hiawatha*.[2] A large audience enjoyed the production, especially the "Wedding Feast." "In this scene the stage was filled with the girls and boys of the Institute, all in striking costumes brilliant in color and beads, feathers, tassels, fringes and other trinkets," according to a review. "A wedding song was sung, then came the dance, after which a chorus of over thirty Indians sang a hymn in the Dakota language."[3]

Lilian's fellow student Anna Bender spent seven years at the Lincoln Institute and could not even remember her father when she finally returned to White Earth. Nevertheless, she remembered her summer outings fondly.

My brothers went to the Education at Home [*sic*] on forty-ninth street leaving me at the girls' school on eleventh street. Here I spent the happy days of my childhood with other children, brought as I had been, from their western homes. October to May we went to school in the city, but the summer months we spent in the country eighteen miles out from Philadelphia and five miles from Valley Forge at a place called Wayne. These days are the pleasantest of all in my memory for they recall long walks through the country with our teachers gathering flowers, picking berries and cherries, and in the fall hunting nuts.[4]

Students preferred the summer school, but not more than home, as one prominent visitor discovered. When Buffalo Bill's Wild West show passed through Philadelphia that summer, some of the Indian performers made a brief stopover on the train to visit student relatives. Chief Sitting Bull and his wife, "resplendent in scarlet blankets and leggings," were among the party, and they wanted to check in on pretty Iron Owl, their great-niece. Cox intended to show Sitting Bull and the other visitors the benefits of her program so they would "favor sending other children to the Indian schools." However, Sitting Bull grew concerned when he found Iron Owl terribly homesick and "frequently [giving] way to tears." After a grand tour of the country grounds and the nicely renovated tavern, Sitting Bull kept Iron Owl "constantly by his side." He enjoyed watching the Indian girls write in English, but his pleasure had slowly ebbed by evening. He tried to lighten the mood during the dinner the students prepared especially for him. He addressed the Lakota girls in their native tongue, joking that he would rather have brandy than the milk he was served. The girls sang hymns after the meal and finally brought a smile to Sitting Bull's face when they performed calisthenics.[5]

Sitting Bull's relatively positive impression of the summer school did not outweigh his great-niece's tears. As his party awaited the train to Philadelphia that evening, he asked if he could take Iron Owl "back home with him." His "request was, of course, refused," presumably by Cox. Iron Owl was granted permission to ride with her great-uncle as far as Philadelphia, but Cox instructed her to go directly to the Lincoln Institute. When the chief and his great-niece arrived at the depot on

Broad Street, Sitting Bull bid Iron Owl a sad farewell, after which she walked down the street, "crying bitterly."[6]

By the next summer Iron Owl seemed transformed. "I don't no more like a blanket. It is bad dress," she told a reporter. "Not nice and pretty, like this." The reporter noted the "coquettish complacency" with which "she smoothed out the folds of her checked calico apron." Presumably, Iron Owl had succumbed to Indian school indoctrination, and Cox probably encouraged the interview. "When I go back to my people I say to all," she continued, "Indian way not good. Live like white people."[7] At least Iron Owl was relatively healthy. Between 1884 and 1893, the year Lilian returned home, more than fourteen children died at the Homes, and homesickness aggravated their illnesses. An 1885 report shows that at least five girls were sent home ill within the year, while three died in Philadelphia of consumption.[8]

The summer school was moved from the old tavern to some buildings on an adjoining property in 1886. Sun House was its first name, but soon after the country home was christened Ponemah after *Hiawatha*'s "land of the hereafter." Cox invited future Omaha physician Susan La Flesche to visit Ponemah that summer, offering her a respite from her medical training at Philadelphia's Women's Medical College. La Flesche accepted the invitation, as she was eager to see her friend from home, Mary Tyndall. La Flesche experienced outings while she and Julia St. Cyr attended Hampton together, but Ponemah really impressed her with its bucolic splendor. "The place was beautiful, right in the woods and hills, the stumps still standing where the clearing had been made," she wrote to her sister. "It was a long frame building—3 stories high. It was a lovely building with long piazzas. There were a lot of Indian girls around and . . . a beautiful brook."[9]

Even though many visitors found the summer home an idyllic spot for the "children of nature," seven homesick girls begged to be sent back to their reservations that summer. Visiting physician Dr. C. McClelland offered his diagnosis that "no medicine can cure the homesickness of the Indians," who "mope and mope and pine away," losing "their appetite and their health." He justified suspending the children's mandatory five-year term with "the only effective prescription," sending them home "to their people and their native hunting-grounds."[10]

Ellen Hansell, not as musically inclined as her older sister, Nettie, was one of the children returned home that summer for health reasons. Clara Richardson, apparently Iron Owl's sister, suffered from consumption and was also sent home.[11] Cox finally released Iron Owl as well. Having "moped and pined" for at least two years, Iron Owl and her pretty calico frock eagerly boarded the train back to her home on the plains. Even La Flesche alluded to the problem of homesickness as she relayed to her sister Mary Tyndall's reaction to her visit: "Oh, Susan it seems just like a dream to me. Are you really here?"[12]

By the time the St. Cyrs arrived in Philadelphia some of the first students were reaching adulthood. Ponemah made romance between students more common because both sexes were housed on the same property. The music program was also co-ed, so Lilian may have noticed the budding romance between Lakota musician Philip Roubideaux and Nettie Hansell. If not, Lilian still enjoyed singing in the summers every day with boys and girls all together.

Lincoln Institute and Ponemah offered Lilian lessons beyond domestic training, religious instruction, and music. Homesick children bonded with other children despite tribal affiliations. Some formed lifelong relationships though they lived far apart.[13] Indian boarding school friendships in fact engendered a network for civil rights support that eventually spawned the Society of American Indians in 1911, America's first formal intertribal, or pan-Indian, organization. Apart from the SAI, intertribal friendships had simpler implications. It is likely the St. Cyrs' relationships with the Omaha Tyndalls led Lilian to team up professionally with one of their nephews years later. Marriages also resulted from Indian school friendships. The St. Cyr brothers married Frenchman sisters, while Philip Roubideaux married Nettie Hansell.

The Homes provided intertribal role models as well. Lilian surely paid attention to Nettie Hansell, who became the star singer of the Ponemah Musical Society, born of the summer's music program. The society was a popular feature of the Homes' musical productions and eventually performed at the World's Columbian Exposition in Chicago in 1893. Cox let

Nettie board at the school for ten years, undoubtedly because she wanted Nettie to develop her musical talent. Nettie was at Lincoln during Lilian's entire stay, so Lilian had several years to emulate her.

Nettie, unfortunately, had darker lessons to teach the Lincoln Institute girls. A policeman sexually assaulted her and Ettie Tyndall on the way to and from church in the winter of 1892. Nettie, encouraged by Cox, lodged a complaint with the police department that resulted in the policeman's immediate discharge from the force. A few days later the policeman shot himself in the head.[14] His suicide was widely publicized, but how it touched his victims and their school friends can only be imagined. Nettie died tragically soon after. She married Roubideaux in 1893, the year Lilian returned to Nebraska. Nettie gave birth to their son in May the next year, but she died a few months later from a heart condition. The baby boy remained at Lincoln Institute until he died of bronchitis before he turned two. His Lakota father returned to South Dakota.[15] Nettie's death proved that life and happiness were fleeting even for the gifted.

Representatives of living history visited the Homes and exposed Lilian and her siblings to the state of Indian affairs in the country. One of the most interesting groups came to Philadelphia in early February 1891 just before Lilian's seventh birthday and shortly after the horrific Wounded Knee massacre at Pine Ridge reservation in South Dakota. A Lakota delegation stopped at Lincoln Institute both before heading to Washington DC to speak to the president and right after the meeting. The *Philadelphia Times* headlined the first visit "Great Chiefs in Town."[16] Lilian, though too young to truly comprehend, likely witnessed one or two of the historic meetings in Philadelphia between Lakota leaders who sought justice and prominent white men who had differing opinions about what that justice should be.

With typical bias both *Times* reports on the visits minimized the tragedy of Wounded Knee. The reports also neglected to mention Sitting Bull's recent assassination, even though he proved to be Philadelphia's and the world's favorite Indian chief. Moreover, Sitting Bull's death directly connected to the massacre, and both were the results of white men's paranoia of the Ghost Dance.[17]

On December 15, 1890, Standing Rock reservation agent James McLaughlin sent Indian police to arrest Sitting Bull. McLaughlin feared the chief would go to the Pine Ridge Agency to incite the scores of Ghost Dancers camped at Wounded Knee Creek. The chief wasn't a true believer, but he'd let Ghost Dancers camp on his land. Chaos ensued as police took Sitting Bull into custody, and one of the Indian policemen shot Sitting Bull.[18] Two weeks later, on December 29, U.S. soldiers fired into the Wounded Knee camp, allegedly because a Lakota had fired a shot first.

Several of the Lakota visitors had relations at the Homes and surely alerted the children about Sitting Bull and Wounded Knee. The *Times'* report of the first visit suppressed the United States' trigger-happy role in the massacre. Instead, the newspaper reporter employed the trope that a visit by Indians equals "invasion," a joke cliché that newspapers continued to employ into the late twentieth century: "A band of Sioux Indians invaded the city of William Penn yesterday. They were friendly Indians, although they are fresh from the disorder and carnage at the Pine Ridge Agency, and they come . . . as the guests of the Universal Peace Society."[19] "Carnage" represents the terrible truth when U.S. soldiers murdered two hundred mostly unarmed Lakota, but the word "disorder" camouflages the military's role in the slaughter of so many women and children.

The *Times* reporter described the respected visitors as "fine specimens . . . dressed in ordinary citizens' clothes." Clearly, government officials considered these "specimens" as "friendlies," the common term for Indians thought to be sympathetic to the U.S. policy of assimilation. They included Chief John Grass, "the life-long enemy of Sitting Bull"; Young Man Afraid of His Horses, "a veteran friendly and a Christian"; Hollow Horn Bear, a young chief; Clarence Three Stars, former Educational Home and Carlisle student; interpreter Lewis Shaugran, a former Indian scout and Chief Red Cloud's "half breed" nephew, "who has a daughter, a son and a niece in the Lincoln Institution"; Lakota clergyman Rev. Charles S. Cook, "who has a church in the Pine Ridge Agency, which is now used as a hospital"; and the chief of Pine Ridge's police, Major George Sword, dressed in his uniform.[20]

The delegation visited with "friends and relatives at the Lincoln Institution," after which they attended the Homes' board of managers meeting.

Cox brought out her "singing girls" to ease the tension and then showed the men around the school. Next, the visitors were given a tour of the city, including Wanamaker's department store, where Three Stars had been employed; "the lamp emporium of R. J. Allen, Son, & Co."; and "Strawbridge & Clothier's." The delegation was in no mood to be awed by the white man's civilization, apparently. In fact, the excursion made some men "very sick."[21] After a "much needed rest," the men were escorted to the Christ Reformed Church, where a serious meeting hosted by the Universal Peace Union convened.

When they arrived at the church, the pews were nearly full. One hundred fifty students from the Homes sat in the middle front rows, including, presumably, the St. Cyrs. The Indian visitors were seated across from the children facing the audience. A church quartet played music, a prayer was offered, and the pastor welcomed all. Next, Alfred H. Love set the tone. Love, a Philadelphia woolens merchant and a noted Quaker pacifist, headed the Universal Peace Union, which he founded shortly after the Civil War. Love exemplified the true Quaker to whom Lilian felt loyalty in her later years. He protested the Indian wars, government corruption, and the misconduct of Indian agents, and he advocated for the civil rights of American Indians, including their citizenship. "Our brethren from the far West are with us tonight," he began, "and they had only a few days ago arrived from Pine Ridge, from a scene of disorder and bloodshed to a city of peace and civilization."[22]

Love then introduced Thomas J. Morgan, the U.S. commissioner of Indian Affairs. Morgan shared a utopian vision of assimilation with Richard H. Pratt, with whom he often conversed. Two years earlier Morgan had ordered that "tribal relations should be broken up, socialism destroyed, and the family and autonomy of the individual substituted. The allotment of lands in severalty, the establishment of local courts and police, the development of a personal sense of independence, and the universal adoption of the English language are a means to this end."[23] Morgan's dictates clearly convey the inviolate tenets of capitalism to which the United States still adheres.

"There were 250,000 Indians all over the country, some lower than the lowest animal and some to a certain degree civilized," Morgan declared blatantly to the Christ Church audience. He went on to point out the government's colonialist control over its Indian wards, stating that the United States "held in trust $23,270,569 belonging to the principal tribes." Morgan, a shrewd politician, admitted there was "difficulty" at Wounded Knee, but he concluded it was not the Indian agent's fault. He proposed that the Bureau of Indian Affairs be separated from the Civil Service to avoid further problems. Morgan's speech was mostly "a long statement of statistics," after which the children in waiting sang a hymn. They "were much applauded."[24]

Herbert Welsh of the National Indian Rights Association followed the children's song with a "ringing speech" that challenged Morgan's speech and attacked political cronyism. "In Dakota the blood of 500 people had been shed to enlighten the minds of the savages," he exclaimed with sarcasm. "The difficulties all come about through the officials—the positions are political spoils." Welsh declared Pine Ridge agent Daniel F. Royer (whom some Lakota nicknamed "Young Man Afraid of Indians") "a coward." "At Pine Ridge," Welsh continued, Royer "withdrew his police and called out the military, and the advent of the soldiers precipitated the bad feeling and drove the Indians into the Bad Lands." "I say to you all, write to your President and ask him to carry out the fundamental principle of true government," he implored. "Choose fit and honest men, and do not dismiss them. That is the crisis of the hour. Will we meet it?"[25]

The Indian leaders responded. Reverend Cook spoke in his native tongue, while an interpreter addressed the audience: "In looking into your faces and touching your hearts we feel we are friends." How different in tone, especially from Morgan's patronizing, objectifying, and insulting words. John Grass of the Standing Rock reservation also addressed the audience in his native tongue. He hoped for justice, and again his words conveyed respectful diplomacy. "This evening I seem to have seen all the good men and all the good women in this great country," his interpreter translated. "My friends and myself have come to see the President, but we have seen you first and I am glad to see you. . . . At last God had taken pity on us and put it into the hearts of good men to help our people." Grass further explained that though he and his delegation represented "civilized Indians," the "effort to become so" brought them much trouble.

"With hearts full of sorrow we come on an errand of peace," he affirmed. "That is all I have to say, and I shake hands with you in my heart."[26]

Two of the Indian delegates tactfully expressed their gratitude for the evening, after which female students sang a farewell hymn. If Lilian had not experienced it before, then she learned that evening how Native leaders conducted themselves with strangers. Did she notice how the honorific manners of the visitors contrasted with the paternalistic and defensive attitude of some of their hosts? If nothing else, she learned they were different.

The next week an unusual advertisement appeared in the *Times*: "Sioux delegation from the Battle-field of Pine Ridge, friendlies and hostiles forty in number, at Horticultural Hall, Broad Street, above Spruce, on Friday, February 13, at 7:45 P.M. Two hundred Indian Children will conduct the music, vocal and instrumental. Reserved seats, 50c.; admission, 25c."[27] When Friday arrived a *Times* reporter with a different tone counted "forty-three warriors and interpreters" whom he depicted as a "motley crowd of redskins and half-breeds" or "very big injuns."[28] The mayor of Philadelphia "offered them the freedom of the Quaker City," after which they were photographed and then taken to visit the Supreme Court judges, police headquarters, and George Childs, who "showed them how to print a newspaper." Finally, they were "regaled with a Quaker collation" at the home of Joseph Elkinson, who early on established the Tunesassa Friends Indian School at Quaker Bridge, New York.[29]

The Lincoln Institute and Alfred Love of the Universal Peace Union hosted the delegation once again. Seating was arranged as before, with the Indian guests and the students, some from Carlisle this time, seated in front. "When the applause had died away," reported the *Times*, "Mr. Love alluded to the great occasion, unprecedented in the annals of history, when such a large band of hostiles and friendlies had been brought together after a peaceable and successful conference with the 'Great Father.'"[30] The student program began with everyone singing "My Country, 'Tis of Thee." Nettie Hansell and Lucy Gordon also performed, the latter singing "Saved from the Storm," an eerie tribute to the survivors of Wounded Knee. The youngest girls, including presumably Lilian, performed a "dolls' drill." A few Homes students also gave readings and speeches.

The Reverends Cook and Walker addressed the audience for John Grass and American Horse, while Love conveyed the remarks of Lakota Brulé leader Two Strikes. The newspaper report labeled the first two men "friendlies," while it marked Two Strikes a "hostile." Both friendly and hostile suffered exhaustion upon returning to Philadelphia from Washington DC. "Two Strikes only said a few words and John Grass was suffering with fatigue," reported the *Times*. American Horse rose to the occasion, however. Reverend Walker read American Horse's typewritten speech, in which he described "how the soldiers had shot down defenseless women and children without provocation, and how the tribes had been put back fifteen years in their progress toward civilization."[31] Although his speech was masked in assimilationist rhetoric, American Horse finally broke the silence regarding Wounded Knee. It was not a battle; it was a massacre.

After American Horse's impassioned speech, a "prominent figure," Lilian's sister Minnie, took the stage. Her entry seemed so antithetical to the horror story conveyed by American Horse, and yet she seemed to present herself as the healing hope for the Indians' future. "Once a Winnebago squaw, but now a nurse at the Lying-in Charity and Nurse School, at Eleventh and Cherry," wrote the *Times* reporter, Minnie "looked really pretty in her neat dress and clean white apron and cap." Pretty, indeed, but Lilian's sister embodied an admonishing angel of mercy. If "the tribes had been put back fifteen years in their progress toward civilization," then their only hope was Indian education.[32]

As fate would have it, the ghosts of the Ghost Dance and Wounded Knee arose to haunt America in 1973, the year before Lilian's death. Although she may not have remembered the important delegates who visited her school, the people who loved her would commemorate her life by honoring their sacrifices at her death.

CHAPTER 4

Home and Away Again

The St. Cyr siblings departed Philadelphia for Nebraska in the summer of 1893, having completed their five-year commitment. They traveled by train to Chicago, perhaps stopping over to see the Ponemah Musical Society perform in the "White City" at the World's Fair. Their journey ended after a twenty-mile wagon ride that brought them home to Winnebago from the train station in Sioux City. If the family farm was a welcome sight, it also elicited feelings of grief, for both their parents were gone. Lilian probably did not remember her mother, but her father's absence was palpable. He was no longer there to show little "Leillia" how much her pony had grown. He also would not see how much she had grown. If the future was any indication, then Lilian emanated grace and poise beyond her nine years. Would her father have noticed that her polished demeanor derived not just from maturity? Would he perceive she bore the vestiges of an Indian boarding school education, where she had to learn to be other than Ho-Chunk? He may have, but if he didn't, others living on the reservation noticed that she emanated a peculiar strangeness like all the children who returned home from government institutions of assimilation. Evidently, Lilian learned a lesson in boarding school. To protect her cherished Ho-Chunk origins and disguise her "mixed-blood" heritage, she would have to create an alternative Indian identity.

In addition to her two older siblings, new family members welcomed Lilian home. Cora Frenchman, whose sisters attended Lincoln Institute, had married her brother David. The couple already had two children, David

Jr., nearly three, and Martha, one and a half. Julia had a two-year-old, Leo Cecil White. George Whitewing Sr. was Leo's father but not Julia's husband. Notably, George Whitewing Jr., Leo's much older half brother, would become an Indian performer like Lilian. He'd also appear as the blanketed Indian subject of California artist Maynard Dixon's striking painting *Iesaka Waken*.[1]

While David managed the family farm, Julia worked as a domestic helper for the large multiracial Nash family, whose mother was Ho-Chunk. Julia lived with the Nashes eight miles from the Winnebago Agency. Earlier that spring Julia wrote to Samuel Armstrong, Hampton Institute's director and founder, in preparation for her siblings' return. She hoped to acquire a job as an assistant teacher at the Winnebago reservation school and solicited his recommendation. "General, you know I am an orphan and our home is broken up," she implored, "so I wish to have a good home again for my sisters, and brother."[2]

Julia found herself in the midst of a crisis brought on by her "Indian education," however, shortly before or after she penned the letter to Armstrong. The crisis reveals the depth of the era's institutional racism and its total disregard for the civil rights of American Indians, not to mention their right to privacy. U.S. commissioner of Indian Affairs Thomas J. Morgan provoked the conflict when he ordered a report on Hampton Institute's returned students. Hampton staff agreed to compile the report, after which the federal government published a hardback copy of the report and disseminated its findings nationwide in 1892, a few months before Julia's letter reached Armstrong.[3] The publication, which essentially rated all Hampton students from "bad" to "excellent," ruined the chances for many returned students to find employment, particularly with the "Indian Service," as the Bureau of Indian Affairs was called.[4] The report used the following criteria to measure the return students' progress toward "civilization" and Americanization: whether they were married legally (good) or by Indian custom (bad); whether in character they were "honest and industrious"; whether they practiced temperance with regard to alcohol and peyote; and whether they lived "a life which we can point to as an example for others to follow and improve upon." The report further gave intimate biographical details of students and deemed Julia, given her *potential* "for good," "one of the worst." Obviously, school faculty and staff looked unfavorably upon the congressional investigation brought on by Julia's white confidante in 1887. Nor were they pleased when they learned that the "bright but headstrong" Julia seemed to have "returned to the blanket" because she sometimes dressed as a traditional Ho-Chunk. They really bristled when they discovered she bore a son without a husband, even though one staff member noted that Julia "lavishes an intelligent mother's care and devotion" upon him.[5]

Julia's letter does not reveal whether she knew about the returned students report when she wrote to Armstrong, but he certainly did. Unfortunately, Julia often found herself at the mercy of white authority figures, but how on earth would she and David feed so many more mouths? The St. Cyrs may have lacked physical resources, but they did not lack acuity. The family reshuffled itself that fall. Minnie wed Benjamin Lowry in November. He was a Ho-Chunk Carlisle school graduate. Annie married St. Pierre Owen, the son of a white man and the grandson of Ho-Chunk chief Baptiste Lasallieur on his mother's side. A recruiter whisked Louis away to Hampton Institute in October 1893, suggesting that Julia still had some influence at the school. Meanwhile, the Winnebago agent appointed David agency interpreter, which along with farming helped him to support his growing family.[6]

By the following spring of 1894 David and Cora had added another daughter to their family. Annie gave birth to a son that summer, though Minnie remained childless for some time. Lilian probably helped out her siblings with child care and housekeeping, living with whichever sibling needed her. Julia finally received an entry-level, low-paying appointment to look after the boys in the reservation boarding school. Lilian attended the school briefly.

Many parents and guardians on the Winnebago reservation and across the country were against sending their children to boarding school, but some had no choice. Some recruiters even abducted children without parental permission. The Office of Indian Affairs prohibited kidnapping and required a guardian's signature, but few Native people knew how to fight for their rights, especially when the particular reservation agent aided and abetted the kidnappings. For example, a recruiter abducted

Lilian's cousin Angel De Cora after De Cora's father left the family and her mother remarried. Promised a train ride, De Cora found herself enrolled in Hampton Institute in Virginia in the fall of 1883. Julia St. Cyr later took credit for De Cora's "recruitment," but De Cora speculated that the Winnebago agent might have "signed the papers, etc.," which she said was sometimes the case in "the pioneer days of Indian education." De Cora also wondered if her maternal uncle "had a voice in the matter."[7] If he had, he never informed her mother. She cried and grieved for months until she found out what happened to her daughter.

Such extreme measures were not always necessary. Poor guardians of Native children, especially those with European American ancestry and/or with absent fathers, voluntarily signed permission slips to send their children far from home to off-reservation boarding schools. Why was this so? Commissioner of Indian Affairs Morgan asserted that "half breeds . . . are more willing to go to school," but the immediate reason was often dire and more racially encompassing.[8] Indian boarding schools, whether near or far, secular or nonsecular, fed and clothed Indian children. Mitchell St. Cyr may have believed that eastern boarding schools afforded his children the opportunity to survive in a "white man's world," but sometimes families simply could not care for all of their children on meager government annuities and unreliable farming.[9] The reservation offered few opportunities, but extreme poverty threatened more than the lack of a prosperous future. Poverty threatened lives. The St. Cyr siblings were one among many families in Winnebago who faced this terrible dilemma.

Lilian arrived by train at Carlisle Indian Industrial School in late October 1894 with her family's blessing. Most likely, Julia had a hand in enrolling Lilian at the boarding school where Pratt's program stood as a nationwide model for the government's assimilation policy. Lilian's time in Philadelphia made her an attractive enrollee, since Lincoln Institute was a principal feeder school for Carlisle. At ten years old Lilian had already spent half her life at boarding school, so unlike many of her peers, at least she had some inkling of what was expected of her. Her enrollment form marks her as "half Indian," indicating not only that she spoke English well and dressed in "civilized" clothing but also that whoever enrolled her believed her father was white. The record also shows she was just fifty-three inches tall and weighed eighty-five pounds. She enrolled the same day with three Omaha children who likely traveled with her from Nebraska.[10]

When Lilian disembarked from the train that bordered the school grounds, she immediately noticed that the campus was much larger than Lincoln Institute, though it was located in a much smaller city. Carlisle Indian Industrial School, which now houses the U.S. Army War College, included young and older girls' and boys' quarters, teachers' quarters, staff housing, a chapel, an auditorium, a hospital, an athletic building and field, trade shops and stables, a covered bandstand, a cemetery for deceased children, and an old guard house, which was sometimes used to incarcerate students.[11]

Carlisle's townspeople welcomed or tolerated the Indian schoolchildren when they were about. Aside from the townsfolk, Lilian noticed that the quaint town with its brick architecture was much older than Winnebago. Carlisle was also not far from the Gettysburg battlefield and steeped in Civil War history. However, Pratt's experience serving in the Plains Indian Wars set the military tone for Lilian's tenure at the school. After his Civil War service, Pratt reenlisted in 1867, serving as an army officer for an African American, or "Buffalo Soldier," regiment that served on the Great Plains. As Carlisle archivist Barbara Landis explains, "In April, 1875, seventy-two warriors from the Cheyenne, Kiowa, Comanche and Caddo Nations, were rounded up for exile to St. Augustine, Florida. There they would be held hostage in exchange for the ransom of the good behavior of their kinfolk with Richard Henry Pratt as their jailer. These men were shackled and transported by rail to Ft. Marion Prison far from their homelands to a hot, humid climate unfamiliar to them."[12]

Pratt immediately decided to single-handedly "civilize" the hostages in military fashion. He replaced their clothes with army uniforms, cut their long hair, and set them practicing daily drills. He assigned them menial jobs, some of which paid, and then began the task of teaching them English. Later, with the help of some "excellent ladies," he taught the men basic academic skills. He also exposed them to Christian precepts in the expectation they would give up their traditional spiritual practices, which he deemed barbaric. Moreover, he welcomed visitors to the prison to witness the transformation in order to, as he stated, "correct the unwarranted prejudice promoted among our people against the Indians through race hatred and the false history which tells our side and not theirs."[13]

The government released the Fort Marion prisoners back to their reservations in 1877, but Pratt wanted the younger men to be further educated and serve as "a civilizing influence." He persuaded Samuel Armstrong "to partake in an experiment and allow Indian students to attend Hampton," established as a freedman's school following the Civil War.[14] Armstrong admitted seventeen of the former prisoners into Hampton's newly established Indian Department in the spring of 1878. He soon realized the potential of the new department and welcomed forty-nine mostly teenaged children from western reservations Pratt recruited. Pratt discovered that his vision of Indian education was not quite in line with Armstrong's, however. While Armstrong had a strong missionary bent and hoped to train African American and American Indian children alike to return home to exert a "civilizing" influence on their people, Pratt wanted to sever the ties that bound Indian students to their traditional families, lives, and homes, as well as to the U.S. government. Soon after, Pratt acquired the use of the army barracks in Carlisle, Pennsylvania, and founded Carlisle Indian Industrial School in 1879 to accomplish his mission.

"Can the Indian be civilized?" was the question of the day, better known as the "Indian problem." Pratt's answer to the question and response to the problem was nothing less than cultural genocide: "Kill the Indian in him, and save the man," or, as he stated it in other words, "To civilize the Indian, get him into civilization. To keep him civilized, let him stay."[15] Pratt was determined to eliminate anything that smacked of "Indianism," including the Office of Indian Affairs, tribal sovereignty, and American Indian cultural practices. Unlike Armstrong, Pratt dissuaded his students from returning home. He concluded that segregation for Indians began on the frontier and ended at the reservation, where he believed lack of industry and initiative was commonplace. He further asserted that civilization was a learned habit, not a "biological consequence." He planned to coerce Indian children to revere Anglo-Saxon culture and Protestant values and live among America's white population, even intermarrying if possible. He dismissed every solution to the "Indian problem" that did not embrace citizenship, equating the situation of Native Americans with American immigrants. "An Indian can do no better thing for himself than to spend years among the best whites," he said, "gaining their language, intelligence, industry and skill in the fullest and quickest way."[16] He did not want his students learning from African Americans, as they naturally did at Hampton. African Americans, from Pratt's experience in the military, had their own problems and hardships to overcome, with slavery leading to segregation the most worrisome.

How could Lilian and so many other Native children fall in line with Pratt's pedagogical mission, which attempted to strip them of their tribal identities? The answer is complicated and as varied as the children themselves. Lilian's father held similar views. However, while Pratt expressed an unrelenting zeal to eradicate Native cultures, Mitchell St. Cyr was simply pragmatic. He believed "learning the ways of whites" provided the only opportunity for his children to succeed in the world into which they were born, but he did not want them to reject their Indian kin, cultural practices, and homes to do so.[17]

It's interesting to consider how the public perceived Carlisle Indian School with Pratt's directive in mind. By the turn of the century, many viewed Carlisle as the Ivy League of Indian schools. Carlisle's popular football team played the Ivy League, so the school was often mistaken for a college. Adult men willingly attended Carlisle to play sports because doing so offered them prestige, though the men received only a tenth-grade education at most. Many Carlisle teachers and alums came to inhabit the upper echelon of pan-Indian society, and their descendants are among the most famous Native people today. Native teachers included artist Angel De Cora; musician, author, and activist Gertrude Simmons Bonnin (Zitkála-Šá); and physician and author Charles Eastman. Sport figures Chief Bender, Gus Welch, and Olympic gold medal winner Jim Thorpe are famous alums. Future film actors such as Chauncey Yellow Robe, Luther Standing Bear, and, of course, Lilian also graduated from Carlisle. Native people in the limelight often boasted they'd gone to the school, whether they had or not. Lilian touted her graduation from Carlisle for the rest of her life.

Certainly, Lilian cared little about prestige as a ten-year-old. Here she was again far from home, but this time without her sisters to watch over her. Fortunately, her half brother Levi St. Cyr worked at the school. He was a fine athlete and singer and had played in Carlisle's famous band. Levi graduated in 1891, but the school hired him to work in its print shop because he was so well regarded. Still, it's hard to imagine Lilian's state of mind when the train stopped at the south end of campus. Was she excited? Was she anxious? Was she sad? Was she angry? While her older siblings surely felt relief that their youngest sister had a place to live and grow for the next five years, Lilian apparently buried her deepest feelings and learned to keep busy to ward off despair. Her experience at Carlisle solidified lessons begun in Philadelphia, but how she adapted to the stricter demands of Pratt's school is unknown. Her name appears only once in copies of the school newspaper before 1900. Notably, the publication reported that she participated in a musical performance.

Like Lincoln Institute, Carlisle exposed students to music and performance studies, and its school band was nearly as famous as its football team. It also offered art classes, as well as literary and debating clubs, but Lilian's studies focused on domestic and industrial training first and foremost. Pratt's view that Native children should be self-sufficient and not depend on government annuities drove the curriculum. Pratt was also a great believer in the outing experience, which he hoped would further inculcate European American values.

Lilian's outing record suggests where her love of the Quakers blossomed. "The Friends," as she told journalist Meyer Berger, "have ever been good to my people. I would never refuse them." Her first outing began on May 30, 1895, with Frank and Annie Gaskell of Rancocas, New Jersey, a town located about 5 miles west of Mount Holly, on the east side of the Delaware River, and about 160 miles due east of Carlisle.[18] Rancocas has great significance to the New Jersey Quakers. The Friends held their first meeting there in 1661 and had established a school by 1720. John Woolman, the avid Quaker abolitionist, was born in Rancocas, where he discovered his calling.[19] The Gaskells were also an early Quaker family of the area. Frank was a steward and then a cook who served on the New Jersey state board of health. He and his wife were in their twenties and had at least three small children, whom Lilian helped tend. Lilian may also have helped on the Gaskells' farm that summer.[20]

Her next outing began the first week of May 1896. This time she stayed with Quakers Mary and William Whitaker at Roslyn, a community of Abington, Pennsylvania, not far from Rancocas.[21] The Quakers established a meetinghouse in Abington in 1702. The Whitakers were in their fifties, with older children, and Lilian probably helped Mary around the house. She probably also attended Quaker church services, where she was exposed to meditative principles antithetical to Catholicism. "The meeting house is not a consecrated edifice," William Wistar Comfort instructed, "and if there is anything holy about it, it must be the lives of the people who meet there. The Friends feel that there must be a vital and sustained connection between worship and daily life. When their ideal is attained, their meeting is merely the community search for that guidance which they covet for every important act of their lives."[22]

Lilian went on her third outing to a Quaker home in September 1897. She stayed with Dr. Joseph and Marion Currie, who had adult children.[23] The Curries previously lived next door to the Gaskells but had moved to Beverly, New Jersey, not far from Rancocas, when Lilian stayed with them. Joseph was a homeopathic doctor and as an alternative medical practitioner was probably liberal minded. Joseph's wife, Marion, was the daughter of William Woolman Haines. As her father's name suggests, Marion's Quaker roots ran deep—not only to the Woolman family but also to Robert Haines, who married "educated Indian" Mary Carlisle, the daughter of a local Lenape chief, in 1720. Carlisle was a legendary Quaker heroine who received her education at the first Friends school in Rancocas.[24] Lilian undoubtedly heard the family story that included this revered "Indian princess." She may also have attended the Quaker school in Beverly, since she began her outing with the Curries in September.

Lilian spent her last outing with the Richard Hall family. The Halls had a home in Smithville, New Jersey, just north of Atlantic City and in Easthampton, New Jersey, which, again, was not far from Rancocas. Hall, a farmer who later became a policeman, and his wife, Mary, had two small children. Lilian probably stayed with them at Smithville beginning in early May 1898. She returned to Carlisle for school in the fall. Apparently,

Lilian's time with these Quaker families impressed her with the idea that the Friends were "true friends of the Indian."[25]

In the meantime, Julia St. Cyr became concerned for her little brother's welfare at Hampton Institute. After all, Louis, who was now about twenty-one and who was learning shoe making and wheelbarrow construction at Julia's alma mater, had not been adequately cared for at the Educational Home. Julia feared he was vulnerable, having lost his parents at so young an age. Samuel Armstrong had died, so Julia wrote to Hampton's new superintendent, asking him to keep an eye on her little brother: "I wish you would talk to my brother St. Cyr at your school. He is doing well. I see from his letters, and I want him to get into the Normal School and graduate. He was always a good boy, and I hope you will give him your kind advise [*sic*]—often."[26] School officials discharged Louis for "unsatisfactory" behavior in June 1895 despite Julia's request.

How was the rest of Lilian's family faring? Most of them found employment with the Indian Service. David St. Cyr worked as a clerk for the Winnebago agency. The Hampton Institute school newsletter publicized his "progress": "'I have built a nice little house about a mile from the agency. It cost me over four hundred so I have got a home for my little ones. I hope you will come again and see my new Home.' D. St. Cyr."[27] Minnie and Benjamin Lowry separated briefly. She had lost three children and was supporting herself and her only daughter, Alvina, who was born in 1897. Meanwhile, Julia received a brief appointment as a cook for the Indian school in Morris, Minnesota, but was let go soon after for "lack of ability." She received her next appointment as a seamstress at the Clondorf Indian School in St. Paul, Minnesota. Annie and her husband, St. Pierre Owen, began work at the Red Moon Agency boarding school in Hammon, Oklahoma, in early 1898. Annie was appointed assistant matron, and St. Pierre was hired as an industrial teacher.

Indian Service appointments were usually temporary, and employment didn't last long, whether or not employees were qualified for their positions.[28] The school Julia worked for closed, and the Owens served their appointments and returned home. However, the St. Cyr family was skilled at adapting to change and pooling their resources. St. Pierre headed a large household by the summer of 1900, including a son, Devillo (their other child died), and Annie's family members Minnie and Alvina Lowry, Julia, Leo, and their paternal uncle Hyacinth St. Cyr.

By the summer of 1898 Julia or another family member miraculously managed to get Louis transferred to Carlisle. At sixteen he was reunited with his little sister Lilian, now fourteen. Lilian was learning office skills by assisting school clerk Anna Luchenbach for half days.[29] Luchenbach often trained boys, but only the most advanced girls received her instruction. Office skills afforded the girls better-paying jobs, particularly in the Indian Service.

A photo taken at Carlisle about this time shows what a beauty Lilian had become and why she eased so effortlessly into performing rather than office or domestic work. Posed with her brothers Louis and Levi, she exudes charm and an endearing vulnerability. After the picture was taken, Levi (nicknamed "Doc") returned home to marry Annie Frenchman, David's sister-in-law.[30] Carlisle's school paper, the *Indian Helper*, reported on the marriage and on Levi's popularity: "'Doc' St. Cyr, the staunch bachelor when here, has finally come to the conclusion that 'man is not complete till he has got a wife' so he is going to be 'completed' Jan. 31st. No one has more friends at Carlisle than Mr. St. Cyr, who will pour out congratulations by the 'bushel' when the good news is learned."[31]

Less than two months later, in March 1900, Louis left school allegedly to enlist in the navy.[32] However, by June he was working as a night watchman for a hotel just north of Boston.[33] Lilian wasn't left completely on her own. Several children and teens from the Nebraska reservation attended school with her at this time.[34] She had also bonded with Ella Romero, an older Cheyenne / Mexican American student. Ella was allegedly orphaned at a young age like Lilian, though actually her father outlived her. The girls came from very different backgrounds, but both loved to sing and perform. Ella played the mandolin as well.

The girls also shared the experience of having had extensive stays in Indian boarding schools. Mennonite missionary Elizabeth Welty Hirschler became Ella's guardian when Ella was quite young. Elizabeth's family was another in the long line of missionaries hoping to save the souls of Indian children. Elizabeth's brother-in-law established the first Mennonite mission in 1880 at the Arapaho Agency, which also served the Cheyenne, in Darlington, Oklahoma.[35] In 1882 the Indian agent hired Elizabeth to be assistant matron, while D. B. Hirschler, her future husband, served as school superintendent.[36] Elizabeth and her family transferred to Canton, Oklahoma, soon after, where she presumably became Ella's guardian. Oklahoma missionaries aimed to place "Indian youths" like Ella in Mennonite homes like Elizabeth's "where they were well cared for and attended school." In 1885 Elizabeth enrolled Ella in the newly established Mennonite Indian Industrial School in Halstead, Kansas.[37] Elizabeth died two years later, however, so her newly married brother, Joel Welty, became Ella's guardian. Welty was a prominent Indiana businessman who published Mennonite literature.[38] Ella moved with the Weltys to Fort Wayne, Indiana, where she attended public school for a time. She lived with the Mennonite Weltys for several years and enrolled in Carlisle in 1896 when she was fourteen.[39]

How much Lilian discovered about her friend's origins is unknown, but the history of Ella's family is filled with pathos, not unlike the story lines Lilian later developed for her films. Ella's father, Rafael Romero, served as one of Pratt's interpreters at Fort Marion in Florida. Romero was born about 1843 in Texas to Mexican parents, though some believed his mother was Arapaho.[40] The story goes that he was sold to the Kiowas after having been kidnapped by Comanches as a boy. He later settled with the Cheyenne and then accompanied the prisoners to Fort Marion in 1875.[41]

Romero was notorious for the role he played in General George Armstrong Custer's love life. The setting for Custer's "romance" was the Washita River Valley, where the Seventh U.S. Cavalry led "a surprise dawn attack against the Southern Cheyenne village of Peace Chief Black Kettle on November 27, 1868."[42] That winter Custer hired Romero to be one of his scouts. He sent Romero and two of his other scouts to locate Black Kettle's village and assess how many dwellings were there. "Romero entered the village and counted all fifty-one lodges," according to one source. Allegedly, Custer put him in charge of the fifty-three Cheyenne women and children the army captured, after which Romero became "Romeo." Early accounts of the battle, including Custer's autobiography, claim Romero's nickname derived from his way with women. Some soldiers found this incredible, given what they viewed as his unattractive "Ethiopian features." Others gave accounts about his name that seem more likely—that it derived from Romero's role as a "go-between" and interpreter.[43]

The story of Ella's father is part of the Cheyenne's oral history.[44] Evidently, "Romeo" struck a devil's bargain with the Cheyenne women prisoners. If the women would "service" the military, their lives and the lives of their children would be spared. One soldier recalled, "Romero would send squaws around to the officers' tents every night." Custer "took first choice" of Maotsi (or Monaseta), "a fine looking one" whom he raped "in his tent every night." Some said Maotsi gave birth to a boy two months after Custer chose her. They also allege that she later gave birth to a second son, who was Custer's.[45]

Romero chose Woman Stands in the Sand Hill for himself. They had a child, Rosa Romero, about a year or two later. After Rosa's mother left Romero, he "picked out" a fifteen-year-old Cheyenne girl named Woman Coming in Sight to be his next wife. She gave birth to George Romero in 1878 and Ella in about 1881. What happened to George and Ella's mother is unknown.[46] However, Ella's father appears on the 1900 federal census as Romeo with a wife named Loving, with whom he had at least two more children.[47]

If Lilian was unaware of Ella's family story, she had certainly heard similar accounts passed down from her grandmother's generation. Historical documents confirm that army privates and officers took Ho-Chunk women as sex slaves at Fort Winnebago, Wisconsin, in the late 1820s and early 1830s. Ho-Chunk and Dakota women also prostituted themselves to feed their children at Crow Creek in the 1860s.[48] Children born of these relationships appear later in government records seeking heirship rights from these absent fathers. No wonder the captured Indian woman appears so often in Lilian's early films.

Carlisle students had many opportunities to share intimate stories with their peers, since they also shared sleeping quarters. But speaking one's native language was strictly prohibited and could elicit punishment. On the other hand, students forced to speak English acquired a lingua franca that enabled intertribal relationships to blossom. As much as the children enjoyed talking to each other, they did not relish public speaking. Teachers who encouraged European American individuality often prodded Native children to speak up, if not with confidence, then at least in volume. Some children experienced extreme culture shock when they spoke in public. At home, children were seen, not heard, and public speaking was left to a few orators in their tribe.

Student-run literary clubs were popular at Carlisle and competed in debates. Boys could join the Standard Literary Society or the Invincible Debating Society, while girls could choose between the Mercer Literary Society and "the Susans," named for Susan Longstreth, an early Quaker benefactress of the school. Lilian opted for the Susans, and in February 1900 she defended the pro side of "a lively challenge-debate" whose subject was "poverty causes more crime than wealth." Several visitors attended, including a former student named Hugh Lieder, whom the Carlisle *Indian Helper* described as "one of our Indian soldier boys." The Spanish-American War intimately touched many Carlisle students who learned their brothers and cousins sailed on ships across the ocean to engage in battle, some never to return. Following the debate, Lieder, whose mother was Crow, spoke passionately to the Susans: "My sisters, I will be . . . among the troops soon to sail from New York for the Philippines. I am an Indian; I am an American citizen. I go to fight under the flag I love and I am willing to give my life to the country which has done so much for me."[49] The president of the Susans thanked him, and Lilian and the girls broke out in the songs "America" and "God Be with You till We Meet Again." Lieder, or Shield Necklace, hailed from Montana and served in the Fourth Infantry, where his commanders lauded his dedication. The girls' patriotic songs had been good medicine. He returned to Montana from the war in 1902.[50]

The Susans were not just a debate team; they also put on musical performances similar to those given at Lincoln Institute. Piano solos, vocals, and recitations made up the Susans' repertoire. Students also designed and made the sets and costumes, a skill that Lilian would put to good use in the future. The Susans entertained Carlislers in March 1900, and the school paper reported: "Lilly St. Cyr, Juliet Smith, Amelia Metoxen and Louisa Rogers appeared in appropriate costumes as 'The Seasons' and showed careful study of their quotations."[51]

Early the next year Lilian appeared as Morning for the Susans' tableau of female literary figures, including Minnehaha and Pocahontas, the latter played by Ella Romero.[52] "The entire performance was so gracefully and admirably done," reported the school paper, "that the audience, to show its appreciation, voted a request to have the entertainment repeated, which the young ladies agreed to do." No special mention was given to Lilian's performance, but it's certain she played her part "admirably" and "gracefully" as well.[53]

Lilian did not return to the reservation for the summer of 1901. Instead, she did clerical work for Anne S. Ely. Ely, also a Quaker, worked as a faculty member at Carlisle for twenty-eight years.[54] She never married, but her life partner was Miss Marion Burgess, the pen behind the "Man on the Bandstand" featured in Carlisle's school paper.[55] Burgess described Ely as "wise, discreet, magnanimous, [and] true." She also found her "lighthearted yet deeply in earnest, social without society pretense." Whether Lilian shared this regard for Ely, under her tutelage Lilian learned "office tactics and courtesies," as well as "business efficiency and dispatch office skills."[56] Clearly, Lilian got along well with authority figures. She continued her studies at Carlisle into the fall. In December her sewing teacher treated her to a trip to visit friends in Mechanicsburg, ten miles east of Carlisle.[57] Two months later, Lilian graduated from Carlisle Indian Industrial School. She probably believed she could now find office work so her family would not have to support her.

Lilian returned home after commencement. A photo of her taken in Sioux City at this juncture shows that she had grown into a lovely young woman. The photo is rare, because it is the only one known in which she wears traditional Ho-Chunk dress.[58] The photo also signifies that Lilian faced a crossroads: either take the traditional path (stay on the reservation, marry, and have children) or venture out into the wide world.

Lilian intended to continue her schooling, but whether it was her idea or sister Julia's, she sought a future different from the one the reservation could at that time provide her. The reservation at the turn of the century was not a healthy place to live. Decades of historical trauma had taken their toll. Illnesses such as trachoma, tuberculosis, and venereal disease were rampant among the reservation population. Multiple marriages and pairings were frequent, leading government authorities to press for legal unions not only to set European American moral standards but also to simplify heirship concerns regarding allotted land. Poverty loomed large, and death visited nearly every household.

Lilian wrote to Carlisle Indian School staff from Nebraska that August after receiving a standard questionnaire on how she was doing as a returned student. She said she planned to start school in September and "intend[ed] to clinch the lessons driven in at Carlisle." She expected to take "a post-graduate course somewhere." Carlisle educators expected a return on their investment, responding, "We hope and expect always to hear of her that she is living a life of earnest endeavor in the right direction."[59]

Her brother Louis relinquished his hopes (or Julia's) of furthering his own education. He returned home from the East and married Rosa Frenchman in November 1903.[60] Now all four St. Cyr brothers were married to all four Frenchman sisters, since Abner St. Cyr, Levi's full brother, had married Lizzie Frenchman in about 1894.[61] The families were well matched. The pretty Frenchman girls, daughters of Charles and Catherine Tebo Frenchman, were Ho-Chunk and French, like the St. Cyrs. The St. Cyr boys had all attended Indian boarding schools in the East, and all the Frenchman children except David's wife had attended the Lincoln Institute. Meanwhile, Julia had married George Travis, a Citizen Band Pottawatomie employed at the Pottawatomie and Great Nemaha Agency in Nadeau, Kansas. They apparently met there when they both worked for the agency boarding school.

After Lilian returned home to the reservation, she started attending St. Augustine's Catholic Church regularly. She also became ill, but the cause is unknown. She hoped to further her education and spent her free time reading, taking music lessons, and, perhaps, learning beadwork skills from her female relatives. At the close of the year, despite her own health issues, Lilian traveled to Newton, Kansas, located twelve miles east of Halstead, to visit Ella Romero.[62]

Why Ella was no longer living with the Weltys is unknown. She had intended to graduate in June 1902 but was sent home in February that year with the debilitating symptoms of tuberculosis. Lilian watched in agony as terrible coughing fits wracked Ella's frail body. All she could do was comfort her dear friend and watch as she wasted away. Ella died with Lilian by her side on January 31, 1903. Upon her poor friend's death Lilian returned to Winnebago.[63]

Grief for a peer is very different from the grief one feels for the loss of a parent. The latter reminds us of our past and origins, while the former forces us to reckon with the future. Ella's dreams would go unfulfilled, while Lilian's future still held promise. In fact, Lilian's life path took a dramatic turn soon after her friend passed away. The family of Kansas senator Chester Long invited her to spend the summer with them at their home in Medicine Lodge, Kansas.[64]

Chester Isaiah Long had just been elected to the Senate when Lilian arrived. He would serve three terms. While staying in Medicine Lodge, Lilian helped Long's wife, Anna, with the housework and the children. Later, Lilian claimed she was the Longs' protégée. Some accounts state that Lilian met Long's family while she lived in Philadelphia, but how this occurred is unclear. Long's wife was a native Kansan, and although Long was born in Greenwich, Pennsylvania, his family had moved to Kansas by 1879. He was already practicing law in Medicine Lodge when Lilian and her siblings arrived in Philadelphia.

Lilian and Anna Long were both orphaned at a young age, so Anna may have felt empathy for her young helper. Anna met her husband in grade school. Later, Anna taught music and Chester taught elocution in the same school. They married in 1895 and had two daughters, Agnes and Margaret, two years apart. Acquaintances and friends characterized Anna as "soft-spoken and refined." She traveled extensively in the United States and twice visited "abroad." She studied music in the East and in Kansas City. She was not one to follow fashion trends. She usually dressed in blue and wore her hair the same way for years. She was an avid reader and hoped to pass on this habit to her children. "While Mrs. Long will confess to no fads, she owns to a few hobbies," reported the *Kansas City Star*. "One of these she emphatically announces is the determination that her girls shall be useful as well as ornamental."[65]

Lilian's host family seems to have been a good match for her, at least at first. Expert equestrian Chester Long may have taught Lilian horseback-riding skills beyond those she learned on the reservation. Anna probably gave Lilian music lessons as well that enhanced Lilian's future endeavors. If Anna tried to instill in Lilian useful rather than ornamental qualities, then she was successful. Lilian never feared hard work and was not content to be an idle appendage on a man's arm. Anna struggled with illness throughout her marriage, however, which intensified her conservative and serious nature. Lilian claimed she "learned the whites' customs and graces, but never forsook the ways of her own people" while living with the Longs.[66] The statement begs the question, though, did the Longs attempt to suppress her Ho-Chunk ways?

After the summer with the Longs in Kansas, Lilian returned to Nebraska to live with Minnie. Her sister was now a single parent with three young daughters: Alvina, who was four and a half; Lillian Margaret, aged two; and Annie, born in January. Benjamin had remarried in March.[67] Lilian was surely a welcome addition to the household, but without a job prospect she was also a financial burden. Julia, ever the mother hen, wrote yet another letter in mid-September to the superintendent of Hampton Institute, again imploring him to help her family: "My sister Lillian St. Cyr who graduated from Carlisle a year ago last Feb. wishes to attend your school. . . . My sister is eighteen years of age and is a good girl. I know you will like her. She desires to go right away, so please send her transportation before the school has taken up."[68] Julia hoped Lilian could attain a normal school teaching certificate, but her request was denied, perhaps because a recruiter from the school had already come to the reservation to pick up new enrollees in August.[69]

Someone may have reached out to the Longs when Julia's plan fell through. In the fall of 1905 the couple invited Lilian to accompany them to Washington DC. From there it was a relatively short train ride to Carlisle, so Lilian visited friends and teachers at her alma mater in October.[70] Afterward she rejoined the Longs. Their beautiful home at 1455 Massachusetts Avenue was described as "one of the handsomest residences on that longest of avenues . . . midway between the German and Russian embassies, and in the very heart of the fashionable section."[71]

Those who knew Republican senator Long characterized him as "the man who does things." A gifted speaker, Long was a politician who could also "keep pat" on controversial issues. He supported President Theodore Roosevelt's push for stricter regulations on railroad freight charges, which Kansans liked, and he pressed for Oklahoma's admission to the Union. To deliberate on the latter issue, he joined a committee that traveled west, holding town meetings "to gather information relative to coal lands, asphalt leases, removal of restrictions on Indian lands, and other things vital to Indian Territory."[72] Long also served as U.S. commissioner to the Philippines, aligning with his proimperialist president at a time when it still appeared the United States could restrict and resist expansion. A picture of Napoleon hung on the wall in Long's Medicine Lodge office for years. Long claimed the portrait inspired his own ambitions, but it also suggests Long approved of the imperialistic ambitions of his own nation.

Lilian worked for the Long family all winter, surrounded by political forces beyond her complete comprehension. The capital city offered a cosmopolitan whirlwind of social engagements, but Lilian was more likely a servant than a guest at these functions. She observed the behavior of elite society and learned that its members were as human as she was. When Anna Long held a reunion for the wives of Kansas congressmen in January 1905, Lilian found herself surrounded by prominent women, among them Mrs. Charles Curtis of Topeka, whose husband would become the vice president in 1929; Mrs. Victor Murdock of Wichita, whose husband was the editor of the *Wichita Eagle* and succeeded Long as state legislator; and Mrs. J. D. Bowersock, wife of Justin Dewitt Bowersock, banker, manufacturer, and developer.[73] Only one of the wives at the reunion would rise to occupy a prominent government position herself. Mrs. J. M. Miller of Council Grove, wife of the county attorney, J. M. Miller, became the first woman appointed to a state office as the chairman of the Kansas Board of Control.

Lilian also observed the behavior of guests such as Anna's neighbors Baroness Emma von Leistner, the local royal, and Isabella Heth, who resided part-time at her family plantation in Radford, Virginia. It's unknown if she held racist views, but Isabella was the wife of Captain Stockton Heth, a staunch southern Democrat who served as military aide to his older brother, General Henry Heth of the Confederacy, best known for jumping the gun at the battle at Gettysburg.[74] Heth's DAR debutante daughters also attended the soirée. How they treated Lilian surely impressed her either favorably or not. Lilian's name does not appear on the list of guests reported by the newspaper, indicating she served as housemaid, cook, nanny, pianist, or just a curiosity. It was no matter; she would become the center of attention by and by.

CHAPTER 5

James Young Johnson
and Family Secrets

Lilian took the train to Carlisle to attend commencement exercises in mid-March 1905. Teddy Roosevelt's newly appointed commissioner of Indian Affairs, Francis Leupp, was among the passengers also bound for Carlisle. As commissioner Leupp began ushering in a new age of Indian education that was antithetical to Pratt's rejection of "Indianism." Leupp was an avid collector of Native arts and crafts and believed Indian schools should encourage their manufacture, even to the point of selling items to the public to raise money for schools.[1] Leupp had also secured a reduced fare to Carlisle for Lilian, but by whose request is unknown.[2]

Lilian arrived at Carlisle to joyous pandemonium. Graduation ceremonies and related events lasted for three days. Boys and girls put on a gymnastics exhibit and played team basketball. Students for the first time at graduation demonstrated their skills in "blacksmithing, printing, harnessmaking, carpentry, farming, and domestic sciences such as cooking, dressmaking and laundrying." Staff and teachers wanted to give the public "insight into the possibilities open to the Indian as a trade worker."[3] Carlisle's famous sixty-piece band also performed, which Lilian surely enjoyed.

Leupp handed out the diplomas to graduates, two of whom were Lilian's Ho-Chunk friends Emma Logan from Nebraska and Adeline Kingsley from Wisconsin. The girls' brothers had already graduated from Indian schools and smoothed the way for their sisters' achievement. Howard Logan graduated with Levi St. Cyr and was one of Carlisle's star

69

pupils. Ebenezer Kingsley, who had attended the Homes in Philadelphia, graduated from Hampton Institute with Julia St. Cyr. A model student, Kingsley took a teaching position with Annie and St. Pierre Owen at the Red Moon Agency Indian school. Thousands of Native children attended off-reservation boarding schools, but the Indian Service preferred to employ those who completed graduation.

The visit to Carlisle seems to have helped Lilian make up her mind concerning an important life advent. Shortly after she returned to Washington DC, she married James Young Johnson. "Lillian St. Cyr, a graduate of Carlisle, from Nebraska, who has been living in Washington with Mr. Long's family, senator from Kansas," Carlisle's school paper, the *Arrow*, reported, "was married on the 9th of April to J. Younger Johnston [*sic*], a young man [of] Indian and Spanish descent."[4] How Lilian met James is a complete mystery. He was a thirty-year-old native of Washington DC, so it is likely they met in the city. Very soon they would embark on an exciting career opportunity. However, the security of their future depended on both spouses transforming their identities. Lilian would change hers superficially, but society norms required that James change his identity completely.

James was not Spanish, but he may have been descended from a Native American woman who lived at least four generations before him. However, records identify his parents and grandparents as "mulatto" or "black." (See appendix B for Johnson's family.) Lilian never publicly admitted her husband had African American ancestry, but she surely knew. In fact, "B" is marked for the race of both husband and wife on their marriage certificate.[5] James hid his African American roots after his marriage to Lilian, but his mixed-race family was well known in Washington DC. No matter. James took his bride elsewhere and chose to pass as "Indian." In doing so, James denounced the incredible legacy his family left to him. One hundred years later James received recognition as the first Native American director. It may be time to reconsider that honor and tell his family story.

Courageous character came from both sides of James's family. His parents were George Durham Johnson and Emma Young Johnson, who had married in 1868 in Washington DC. George Johnson was born in Philadelphia in 1842 to "Major" Clarke and Lydia LeCount Johnson.

The Major owned a restaurant-tavern in the city, as did Lydia's brother. George's parents had ties to the so-called Moors of Delaware, a racially mixed community of Africans and European Americans, some of whom intermarried with the remains of a small Indigenous population that had managed to survive the ravages of colonialism on the eastern seaboard.[6] When George was born, the Johnson-Durham-LeCount family belonged to an elite group of mulatto property owners in Philadelphia who advocated education for their children and supported civil rights for "colored" Americans.

George volunteered for the army's Colored Troops division as a seaman in March 1865. He had moved to Washington DC by 1867, having obtained a job as clerk for the Freedman Bureau's educational department.[7] He became a staunch member of the Colored Soldiers and Sailors League, a Reconstruction era civil rights organization focused on veterans who felt they had not "received from the Government a due recognition for their services rendered in the hours of need." The group also proposed that "in sustaining the Union with the musket," African American men "have now their right to the ballot."[8]

George was a natural leader and fought strenuously for civil rights. He attended Howard University in Washington DC, graduating in January 1871. The spring before he graduated, he, his first cousin (James LeCount Jr.), and other classmates who hailed from Philadelphia "adopted a series of congratulatory resolutions in honor of the ratification of the fifteenth amendment." They sent the resolutions back to "fellow citizens in Philadelphia . . . uniting with them in thanks to Almighty God."[9] LeCount taught school for "colored" children in Washington DC and was closely connected to George's uplifting work at the Freedmen's Bureau.[10] LeCount, a cabinetmaker and undertaker, participated in Philadelphia's Underground Railroad by hiding escaped slaves in his coffins.[11]

Tragically, George's noteworthy accomplishments left less of an impression on his son James than his mother's heritage. Emma Young Johnson's family embodied the living legacy of the tangled and terrible history of slavery in the nation's capital, where James grew up. Emma's connection to the institution of slavery was much more conspicuous than the Johnsons'. Records designate her mother and siblings as "mulatto," like the Johnsons. They were also property owners, and at least Emma and one of her brothers attended school. However, the similarities between the families end there.

Ann Young, Emma's mother, was born into slavery in Maryland about 1812. It's likely her father or grandfather was a slave owner, since she was marked "mulatto." Ann grew to womanhood on the outskirts of the District of Columbia. Morduit Young bought or inherited Ann before she'd turned four years old.[12] The slaveholding Youngs were planters who owned vast landholdings in Maryland. Morduit's father, William Young Jr., inherited from his father the southern half of the Nock, a five-hundred-acre parcel. This property included forty squares of land that encompassed what would become eastern Capital Hill.[13] By 1780 the Young property "extend[ed] from what is today East Capitol Street down to the banks of the Anacostia." The Young home sat on a bluff above the river. Today the Congressional Cemetery encompasses Young's estate and holds William Young Jr.'s elaborate grave marker.[14]

No structures remain, but Young's "typical antebellum farm" boasted a frame house, a large outdoor kitchen, and four log buildings. The buildings almost certainly housed Young's slaves, which numbered ten in 1790.[15] When his estate was probated two years later, eleven slaves, age two to forty-four, were among his assets.[16] After Young died, his widow remained on the property, described as the "core of a plantation." At the turn of the nineteenth century, she held only two slaves and lived with Morduit and his two sisters.[17]

Morduit Young married Elizabeth Beall in 1813 and set up housekeeping on a farm she had inherited from her father. The Beall property was located in the historic Eastern Branch Tract about two and a half miles outside Washington DC.[18] The three-hundred-acre farm included quality timberland, springs, and superior soil, at least fifteen acres of which Morduit cultivated.[19] Five years after his advantageous marriage, Morduit could not pay taxes on the Capital Hill property he had inherited from his father. The next year he sold to his mother-in-law, Ann Beall, "four horses, a wagon and gear, six cows, three beds and bedsteads and furniture, one sideboard and twelve chairs," as well as four slaves. The $1,200 he received from her may have helped to pay his property taxes, and following a sale or sales of some of his inheritance, he seems to have paid her back, because she did not keep his four slaves. These individuals were described as "a Negro man named Gusty, a Negro boy named Charles, a Negro boy named Oscar, [and] a Negro girl named Ann," six years old, who grew up to become Emma Young Johnson's mother.[20]

Morduit's wife died in late 1819 or early 1820, probably due to complications of childbirth. She left him with three daughters under six, including an infant. The girls moved in with Grandmother Beall. Morduit lived next door with an elderly white woman and four slaves, who likely were Gusty, Charles, Oscar, and Ann.[21] Morduit's financial problems continued to plague him. A county official seized his property, a rowboat and ferry, in the summer of 1895 to satisfy his debts.[22] Five years later, still a widow, Morduit resided on his farm with a white teenage male and six slaves, including Gusty, Charles, and Ann. The other three slaves were Ann's children, though Ann was only seventeen.

Mother-in-law Beall held twenty-six slaves. When she died the next year in 1831, she willed the slaves to her surviving daughters and to Morduit's daughters.[23] Unable to pay his property taxes again, Morduit ended up in debtor's prison for eleven days in 1836.[24] Three years later, his health declining and feeling his mortality, Morduit made out a will.[25] He died near his home on July 19, 1844, having been "plagued by a long and painful illness."[26]

The Compensated Emancipation Act ended slavery in the District of Columbia in 1862 by offering financial recompense to slave owners. Nearly two decades earlier, however, Morduit realized that his slaves would be in jeopardy upon his death. Although Washington DC's slave owners "seemed relatively benign" compared to rural southern plantation owners, Morduit's slaves faced being separated from each other and "sold further south."[27] Morduit sought to remedy this situation through his will. His last request in the document directed that "my slave man Charles be set at liberty and be free and be paid twenty dollars out of my estate after my death," but most of his will focused on "my servant woman Anne [Ann] and the children." First he gave them their freedom upon his death. He also bequeathed Ann "control and direction" over her children to counteract the injustice that slave parents had no rights over their children. He asked Ann "to bound" her boys "to such trade or trades as she may select." Moreover, he willed Ann and each of her children, whom he named Minty, James Rodney, and William Pickney, several lots of his land in The Nock. Finally, he willed to Ann "two good milch cows, one good work horse and cart, thirty dollars at the discretion of my executor, two beds and furniture, six chairs, one table and all my kitchen furniture all of which property I wish to be equally divided among the children she has or may have before my death, share and share alike."[28]

Several years later, Washington DC city directories show Ann as the widow of Morduit Young. These entries, the provisions of Morduit's will, and the fact that Ann started having children after Morduit's wife died indicate that most or all of her children were Morduit's. The acts of emancipation directed in Morduit's will were not revolutionary by any means, especially his directive to Charles. Many of the district's citizens manumitted their slaves upon death or stipulated they were not to be sold to slave traders. What was radical about Morduit's will was the amount of property he willed to Ann and her children, particularly in contrast to what he willed to the daughters of his white wife. One sentence encompassed their inheritance: "I give devise and bequeath to my daughter Susannah G. Sheriff a mourning suit to cost twenty dollars *and no more* [my emphasis] and to my other two daughters Ann T. Magruder and Amelia T. B. Hollidy all the rest and residue of my estate real personal or mixed."[29] This terse passage implies that Morduit felt less obligated to his white daughters than to Ann and her children. He also chose a friend to be his executor, although his daughters' husbands were perfectly competent. Immediately following his death, his white daughters put up their inheritances for public auction.[30]

Morduit's will also stipulated the fate of Lilian's mother-in-law, Emma, who was born into slavery about the year Morduit died. She would "share and share alike" with the other children as the child Ann "has or may have before my death." While Morduit designated Ann and her children his legal heirs, they were also listed with his property and assigned a monetary worth when his estate was assessed for probate. Their worth was a significant portion of the personal property of his estate, a portion that his white daughters would not inherit. Ann, age thirty-three, was valued at $400; her oldest son, James Rodney, age twenty, $200; and her son William Pinkney, age fifteen, also $400. Ann's daughter Minty, nineteen, was valued the most, at $450, probably because she could bear children.[31]

Morduit's three white daughters owned a total of eighty-one slaves by 1850. Meanwhile, Ann Young and her children, the white daughters' half siblings, lived on their inherited property in a predominantly white neighborhood just southwest of the Capitol.[32] Ann worked as a laundress, and Minty earned a living as a seamstress. James R. was employed as a bartender, while William P., after a stint as a sailor, rose to the position of lithographer or plate printer. Emma Young attended school. She would learn to read and write, unlike her mother and sister Minty.

Just a year following the Compensated Emancipation Act, "Ann Young" "col'd [colored]," is listed as Morduit's widow in the city directory.[33] It's important to remember that Ann was barely a teenager when her first child, James Rodney, was born on Morduit's farm. As a slave, Ann could not reject the sexual advances of her owner—who was about thirty years her senior—or refuse to have his children. The only limitation on the relationship was that Morduit could not make it public. Having sex with slave girls was common enough, and children were conceived as a result, but the law forbade a man to claim those children as his own, even in his will. However, Morduit's will indicates, as one historian writes that "filial relationship was a clear probability in some cases of manumission with bequests of property."[34]

It's unknown if Lilian's husband knew about his white grandfather. If he had, how did it shape who he became? George Johnson moved in with Ann's family at 179 F Street South after he married Emma in 1868. Minty (whose real name was Maria Ann), James R., and William P. also lived in the household. Minty died of breast cancer soon after.[35] The 1870 census shows James R. as the head of Ann's household. The family's assets were given as $4,500 (approximately $79,004 today) in real estate and $500 ($8,778 today) in personal property. Emma and George lived at the same address but were enumerated as a separate household. George was listed as a clerk for the Freedmen's Bureau and Emma as "keeping house." Their household also included a two-year-old daughter, Marie, and a seventeen-year-old domestic, who was black.[36]

Little Marie died the next year when Emma was pregnant with George Jr. He was born in July 1871.[37] Two Julys later, Emma gave birth to Minnie.[38] Yet another death followed her birth, however, in October, when James R. Young died of pneumonia. At this point in time the Young-Johnson clan resided at 474 F Street Southwest, very near their former residence. Meanwhile, George found work as a court bailiff because the Freedmen's Bureau had been discontinued.[39]

Lilian's husband, James Young Johnson, was born on April 2, 1876, into a relatively elite urban mixed-race family. His mother's and grandmother's enslavement, however, was scarcely behind them. In fact, James's home was part of his great-grandfather's plantation, where his grandfather Morduit played as a boy. But here his grandmother Ann demanded her due. Whether lawful or not, she publicly declared herself Morduit's wife and refused to keep their relationship secret. Ironically, James was descended from a mulatto grandmother who fought for respect and a white master who loved his slave.

Harry W. was born to George and Emma in February 1878. The joy of their child's birth was short-lived again. Ann died that summer, suffering a "long and painful illness" like Morduit.[40] The only grandmother James ever knew was lost to memory, since he was only two years old at the time of her passing. His father died that December.[41] It's unknown how George Sr. died, but he was only thirty-four years old. James may have held a fleeting memory of his father, but he lost the role model that would allow him to embrace who he really was.

Although James later claimed he was Indian, he probably knew little about that part of his heritage. Despite his father's apparent link to a mixed-race group of Nanticoke, or Delaware, as Lilian later claimed, George Sr.'s family was deeply entangled in issues related to Reconstruction. Before George moved to Washington DC, he rallied for the Convention of Colored Soldiers and Sailors (CCSS) at the National Hall in Philadelphia in 1867. Caroline LeCount, George's first cousin, demanded to ride a whites-only Philadelphia streetcar the same year.[42] Her nonviolent protest preceded Rosa Park's bus ride by nearly one hundred years.

Caroline became engaged to the legendary Octavius R. Catto following her protest. Catto was a mulatto schoolteacher from the Institute for

Colored Youth, the alma mater of Caroline and her brother James. Catto supported "black veteranhood" with George at ccss meetings.[43] He also traveled to Washington DC in 1871 to "aid in the administration of the freedman schools," working with George and James LeCount. Catto returned to Philadelphia to his teaching job that fall. On the morning of October 10, when angry whites filled Philadelphia streets to protest the black vote, Catto determined he would cast his ballot. A fight erupted between black and white voters, mob violence ensued, and Catto was murdered.[44]

Catto's death set back Philadelphia's civil rights movement for decades. His "body was moved to a nearby police station, where in a heart rending scene Caroline LeCount identified her fiancé," reported the *Philadelphia Inquirer*.[45] Caroline devoted her life to the civil rights movement. She never married, and her fiancé became a martyr to the cause. She served as principal for a school named after Catto and advocated for the hiring of African American teachers. "Colored children should be taught by one of their own color," she declared. For decades Caroline served as a role model for African American women and educators. Lilian's husband, James, never spoke publicly about his notable cousin, but she lived until 1923.

James's mother, Emma, died at home on Saturday morning, August 9, 1890. She was counted among the city's African American community, some of whom descended from freed blacks and others from slaves. Her funeral was held on Monday afternoon at the historic Fifteenth Street Presbyterian Church, founded in 1841 as the "First Colored Presbyterian Church." Following the funeral, she was buried next to her husband and other family members in the Harmony Cemetery, established in 1829 for free blacks.[46] James's brother George Jr. was nineteen when his mother died, but Minnie, James, and Harry were underage. The court appointed Emma's executor, Elizabeth C. Savoy, a mulatto woman, as their guardian.[47] Savoy was middle-aged, unmarried, and a seamstress. She also taught in the "colored school" system.[48]

William P. Young, probably the family's main breadwinner, died in 1894.[49] James's sister Minnie married William Henry Fossett, a clerk, the same year. Fossett lived with Johnson's family until 1900, when he and Minnie moved to Cincinnati, Ohio, to be near his family. Fossett, employed as a mailman, was descended from one of the five slaves emancipated by

President Thomas Jefferson.[50] Despite struggling with slavery's devastation, the Cincinnati Fossett family was intact and accomplished. Family members rose to become important political and religious leaders in their community, just like the Johnsons and LeCounts.

James's older brother George Jr. married Lydia Annice Dickerson in 1897. Her parents were also categorized as mulatto, and her father was a "cart man." George and Lydia had only one child, Annice, born in 1898.[51] At first they lived at the Young residence, but then George headed another household in Washington DC that included Lydia's six siblings. George was employed as a hotel clerk, while his in-laws worked as a schoolteacher, piano repairer, express man, and dressmaker—good jobs for African Americans of the time.[52] George and Lydia's daughter Annice, who never married, graduated from Wellesley College in 1921 and became a high school teacher in Morristown, New Jersey. She apparently passed as white.[53]

Meanwhile, Elizabeth Savoy had already moved into the Young-Johnson home, which Emma had deeded to her. Harry was a student at this time, and Lilian's future husband apparently had no occupation.[54] Savoy's nieces and nephews lovingly called her "Aunt Banny," but whether she treated the Johnson boys with affection is unknown. What is known is that she was an avid proponent of African American education.

Oliver C. Black, whose mulatto wife was a schoolteacher, was also close to James's family. Black was an outspoken civil rights advocate when he was appointed trustee for the Johnson children's property. Black joined the navy as a messenger in 1882 but soon after charged his naval commander with ordering him to serve as his family's domestic servant. He publicly charged President McKinley's administration with giving seven times more positions to mulattos than blacks.[55]

James Young Johnson could not have grown up without a keen awareness of the early civil rights struggle with such incredible and accomplished role models. Unfortunately, what may have become most clear to him as a young man—as it certainly was for his niece Annice Johnson—was that the extraordinary and intelligent people who surrounded him could never attain the same success or position as whites of their same caliber or even whites well below it. Consequently, James grew up learning that being black, colored, or mulatto was a hopeless disadvantage. However open-minded Lilian may have been about her husband's racial makeup, she was certainly not stupid. It would be better for their future if her husband appeared "Indian and Spanish" rather than black.

While Lilian attended Carlisle, James Young Johnson arrived at the New York Naval Yard in Brooklyn on October 8, 1898. He walked to where the old and decrepit USS *Vermont* was permanently docked. He met with recruiting officer Captain Merrill Miller and soon after joined the U.S. Navy, which was combating the "insurrection" led by freedom fighter Emilio Aguinaldo in the Philippines. Following its victory in the Spanish-American War, the United States viewed the Filipino people as racially inferior spoils of war. Nevertheless, Johnson agreed to serve his country for three years. He may have viewed his enlistment as a rite of passage, given his father's devotion to the Colored Soldiers and Sailors League.[56]

Racial tensions in America had not improved in the three decades since James's father had joined the CCSS movement. James's naval service record does not reflect the ideals his father embraced. James shared his generation with W. E. B. Du Bois, who the year before James enlisted introduced the radical idea that African Americans suffered from an anxious double-consciousness: "It is a peculiar sensation, this double-consciousness, this sense of always looking at one's self through the eyes of others, of measuring one's soul by the tape of a world that looks on in amused contempt and pity," he wrote. "One ever feels his two-ness, an American, a Negro; two souls, two thoughts, two unreconciled strivings; two warring ideals in one dark body, whose dogged strength alone keeps it from being torn asunder."[57]

James certainly suffered from a fractured sense of self. On the one hand, he was partly white; on the other, he was always deemed black; and on another, perhaps he had an American Indian ancestor who left an indelible stamp on his father that his memory could not retrieve. The lofty ideals his father and Du Bois espoused did not ring true for him. After his naval service, he created an identity that was much more self-serving.

James's eyes, hair, and complexion were each categorized as "mulatto" on his enlistment form, making it clear to anyone concerned that miscegenation tainted his family history.[58] In addition, at twenty-one he was only five feet, three and a quarter inches tall and bow-legged. In an era that embraced rugged individualism and hypermasculinity, his stature and gait were distinct disadvantages. Captain Miller waived the navy's height requirement, however, and assigned his new recruit to the lowly position of mess attendant at sixteen dollars per month. After the ship's medical officer gave James an "excellent" bill of health, officials assigned him to the USS *Celtic*, docked at the New York Navy Yard since the end of the Spanish-American War.

James received his first evaluation two months after serving meals to the crew. His commanding officer, Nathaniel J. K. Patch, marked him down for an unknown "minor offense," while he received three out of five points for both sobriety and obedience. However, he raised his marks for the next three quarters of 1899, receiving top rating for professional conduct, sobriety, and obedience. James seemed to be adapting well to the daily routine despite his disadvantages, at least on paper.

James finally got a taste of sea life. The *Celtic*, supplied with meat, vegetables, and other goods for U.S. forces, deployed to the Philippines on October 12, 1899. The refrigerated stores ship "steamed down the United States east coast through Caribbean waters" and then "down the east side of South America bound to round Cape Horn on the long route to the Asiatic Station."[59] Patch again gave James high marks, but something changed dramatically soon after the crew arrived in the Philippine Islands.

The ship docked at the southern shore of Manilla Bay at the Asiatic Station in Cavite on March 30, 1900. Patch wrote up James's evaluation the following day. It showed he had been punished for another minor offense and given six hours' extra duty. From there his evaluations declined. By the next quarter James was put in solitary confinement with only bread and water for three days for "having liquor in possession." At the end of September Commanding Officer Forse found James "drunk from liberty." He was taken off mess duty, "put on deck," and made a landsman third class, the lowest rank of the navy.

Johnson served four hours' extra duty as a punishment in December. At the same time, he lost marks on his evaluations and served another four hours' extra duty as punishment.[60] By the end of December, James was put on restriction for one month for disobeying the master of arms and for "washing clothes out of hour." The infraction appears to have been trivial. He left the ship without permission two weeks later. James claimed the navy was a racist institution, as Charles Black had done before him. Was the master of arms targeting him because of his race? And what about his drinking? Did he have a drinking problem, or was he simply blowing off steam like the rest of the crew? If he was being targeted, he responded by acting out. "James Y. Johnson, landsman, tried by summary court-martial on board the 'Celtic' at sea, March 21, 1901, for an absence without leave," stated his next evaluation. James was again sentenced to solitary confinement with "bread and water for 30 days" and "full rations every 5th day." He was also sentenced "to lose 2 months pay, amounting to $32.00."[61]

Forse gave James one last evaluation after his release from solitary. Marks were all 1's for naval training exercises and obedience and a 5 for sobriety. Under "Offences, or, Causes for Disrating," Forse wrote "Retention undesirable," signifying a dishonorable discharge was at hand. However, his senior squadron commander received notification on April 30 that James had epilepsy. Three top medical officers signed the notification.[62]

Did Johnson have an epileptic fit while in solitary confinement? Apparently so, that is, if he did in fact suffer from epilepsy. There is no indication that he had the disease after he left the navy, however. Was he just acting? It's possible. James was transferred to the USS *Petrel* on May 4. The *Petrel*'s commanding officer noted again that "retention was not desirable." James was transferred to the hospital ship USS *Solace* on May 30. His health was rated "bad," indicating he had presented with epileptic seizures. The commanding officer of the *Solace* noted that Johnson was "slow in obeying orders" and "reduced to conduct second class." However, he was punished with five days in solitary confinement with only bread and water again, charged with being "insolent and defiant to an executive officer."[63]

James remained on the *Solace* until July 22, when he was transferred to the USS *Culgoa*. He continued to be evaluated as a landsman, receiving low marks on his naval training exercises, except for sobriety and obedience. He served out his term of three years and was honorably discharged on October 7 in Boston. Epilepsy assured his honorable discharge. The pay docked as a result of his court-martial was returned to him. The question remains: Did James feign seizures? Epilepsy was a surefire way to get discharged from the navy because it was still equated with mental illness, alcoholism, and bad character in general. Many with epilepsy went to asylums. If James was truly an epileptic, he kept it hidden for the rest of his days.

Eleven days after Lilian graduated from Carlisle, James was back in Washington DC. The *Colored American* reported on his "globe trotting" naval adventure on February 22, 1902.

> Mr. James Y Johnson of this city has inst. returned from a three years cruise in the South Atlantic and Pacific waters. He left the city in October 1898 and after passing Bahia, Brazil and other South American points, sailing around the Cape of Good Hope and by the Hawaiian Islands and to the Philippines. The Petrel followed the Oregon and Iowa with meat and other provisions for the Dewey fleet, whose work at Cavite is now an historical reminiscence. His enlistment expired not long ago and because of the great prejudice in the navy, he will not re-enlist.[64]

Epilepsy squelched James's dishonorable discharge. Although there was "great prejudice in the navy," he could not reenlist if he wanted to. Thrown in the ocean with common Americans, James experienced a more virulent racism than he had known at home. It's no wonder he put aside his past and his family and took on a new identity. Given his era's fascination with all things Plains Indian, his timing couldn't have been better.

Fig. 1. David St. Cyr (seated front far left) and Mitchell St. Cyr (seated front center) with the Winnebago delegation to Washington DC, 1886. Courtesy Edward E. Ayer Digital Collection, Newberry Library, Chicago.

Fig. 2. Julia St. Cyr (standing far right) and the Winnebago group at the Omaha Exposition, 1898. National Anthropological Archives, Smithsonian Institution, OPPS NEG 3796.

Fig. 3. Louis, Lilian, and Levi St. Cyr at Carlisle Indian Industrial School, John N. Choate, photographer, ca. 1900. Cumberland County Historical Society, Carlisle, Pennsylvania.

Fig. 4. Lilian St. Cyr in Ho-Chunk dress, ca. 1902. From the author's collection. Courtesy of David Lee Smith, Winnebago, Nebraska.

Fig. 5. Princess Red Wing. Obermüller & Son Cabinet Card, 1907.

Fig. 6. Red Wing, Young Deer, and Bison Co. actors with teepee, 1909–10. Courtesy Marc Wanamaker, Bison Productions/Archives, Los Angeles.

Fig. 7. Red Wing, Young Deer, and Bison Co. actors in the woods, 1909–10.
Courtesy Marc Wanamaker, Bison Productions/Archives, Los Angeles.

Fig. 8. Red Wing selling beads in *The Cowboy and the Schoolmarm*, 1910. Film 13404 from the EYE Collection, Amsterdam.

Fig. 9. The Bison stock company in Mexican costume, 1910. Women in front row (*left to right*): Evelyn Graham, Jewell Darrell, Red Wing, and Marguerite Favar. Young Deer, back row, second from right. Academy of Motion Picture Arts and Sciences, Margaret Herrick Library, Beverly Hills.

BISON FILMS

TRADE MARK

FOUR REELS A WEEK—Tuesday, a "Bison"—Wednesday, Ambrosio—Friday, a "Bison"—Saturday, Itala

B. B. B.
BISON BRINGS BUSINESS.

Exhibitors be on the jump and demand the "BISON" releases for the coming week. "Rivalry in the Oil Fields." Tuesday's release, is a sensational dramatic subject. This picture was taken in the California oil regions, much time and money having been spent in order to make it a subject of merit. Friday's "BISON" release, "Red Wing's Constancy," is the second subject of the "Red Wing" series about to be released by this company. We believe we have demonstrated our ability as producers of Western subjects and do not deem it necessary to go into detail concerning this picture, other than to say that the story is an exceedingly interesting one and the photography excellent.

"BISON"—Release, Tuesday, April 12th

"BISON"—Release, Friday, April 15th

"RIVALRY IN THE OIL FIELDS."

"AMBROSIO"—Release, Wednesday, April 13th

"RED WING'S CONSTANCY"

"ITALA"—Release, Saturday, April 16th

"LEGEND OF THE CROSS."
{ "FRICOT IN COLLEGE."

"THE THREE BROTHERS."
"A MISTAKE."

LITHOGRAPHS AND POSTERS FREE

We furnish all exchanges handling these productions with one sheet four colored lithograph posters with each reel. Demand same from your exchange as they will positively increase your box office receipts.
Brief description of all subjects will be found on another page.

NEW YORK MOTION PICTURE CO.
Manufacturers of "Bison" Life Motion Pictures
429 SIXTH AVENUE, Cor. 26th Street   -   NEW YORK CITY
Phone 6690-1-2 Madison Square   Cable Address : Nosib

Fig. 10. Bison Co. film ad for *Red Wing's Constancy. Moving Picture World,* April 16, 1910. Courtesy Media History Digital Library.

Fig. 11. Bison Co. group photo, 1910. Front row (*left to right*): Fred Balshofer, Buster Emmons, Bebe Daniels, Charles O. Bauman. Standing on sides in front of second row: Red Wing and Young Deer. Second row: Marin Sais, Madeline West, Phyllis Daniels, Margaret Favar, Evelyn Graham, and Edna Maison. Third row: Maxwell Smith (Bruzzel), unknown, Jess McGaugh, George Gebhardt, Jack Conway, Howard Davies, E. J. Allen. Fourth row: Art Acord, Milt Brown, Dick Stanley, Pat Hartigan, J. Barney Sherry, Frank Montgomery, and Roswell Emmons. Names and spellings are according to my research. Seaver Center for Western History Research, Los Angeles County Museum of Natural History.

Fig. 12. Red Wing at home in Edendale, 1910. Autry Museum, Los Angeles, 94.36.1.181.

CHAPTER 6

Princess Red Wing and Young Deer

James dreamed of escaping "the great prejudice" that oppressed him, while his future bride planned a way to return to the East. These two intentions sealed their fate. The home James grew up in was gone and sold by 1904.[1] Harry had moved to Manhattan by 1905 and found employment as a waiter. Harry married Gertrude Alexander, an African American woman, the same year James wed Lilian.[2] The brothers would lead very different lives, and it seems their choice of wives made all the difference.

Lilian and presumably her groom traveled to Saratoga Springs, New York, the summer following her marriage. Mohawk, Wabenaki, and Oneida people gathered annually at the popular vacation destination to earn money from the tourist trade. These communities had camped at the mineral springs for decades, selling their "ash splint baskets, beaded bags, and leather moccasins decorated with traditional symbols." "The Indian craze" sweeping the country by 1906 called for "more ornate baskets, wall pockets, fans and beadwork."[3] Lilian likely began to sell her souvenir beadwork as well, perhaps embellished with the words "Saratoga Springs," as was usual. She may have also learned non-Ho-Chunk techniques and beadwork designs from other women in the camp.

James sought his discharge papers from the Bureau of Navigation. Apparently, he needed them to apply for a job. He wrote to the bureau, stating, "My Discharge was in a bundle of papers and somehow they were destroyed by fire." Lilian had scurried for money since their marriage, as evidenced by a letter she wrote to Commissioner Leupp that August from

Indian Camp 1 in Saratoga Springs. She reminded Leupp of their train ride to Carlisle together and suggested she had made a favorable impression on him. Her request was the standard one. She hoped to speed up the slow machinery of bureaucracy in order to have dispersed the heirship proceeds from her maternal grandparents' allotments. Tall Decora died sometime between 1885 and 1888, and Younkaw, who probably taught Lilian beadwork, died in 1901. "We are anxious to receive our money," she wrote, "for one of my sisters would like to build (she has been farming her own allottment) and I am also anxious to make improvements on my land or else buy a lot here in Saratoga, they range from $150.00 up so I hope you will help us by hastening the approval and return of the deeds." She gave Leupp three references, including Senator Long and two Winnebago agents, "regarding my capability." "I am sorry to trouble you for I know you are a very busy man," she concluded, "but I am very anxious about this matter and hope you will give us your aid." "Hoping to receive a favorable reply," she signed her name "Lilian St. Cyr (Johnson)" and added Senator Long's Kansas address for good measure.[4]

Lilian's stress on her "capability" addressed a concurrent federal policy that Indians were regarded as government wards until they achieved a level of competency that equipped them for citizenship. If the Longs used Lilian as a glorified housekeeper, she was savvy enough to use them as exemplary character references. Moreover, her letter not only demonstrates Lilian's confidence and skill as a young woman in addressing a white authority figure but also indicates that she must have had close friends at the camp, if she was serious about settling in the area. Her plan to do so did not come to pass.

That fall the Johnsons traveled to New York City, where Lilian and probably James joined a large cast of Lakota Indians for the spectacular *Pioneer Days*. The musical extravaganza opened on November 24, 1906, in the newly built Hippodrome Theater. The fifty-two-hundred-seat venue, located on bustling Sixth Avenue between 44th and 43rd Streets, was billed as "the largest, safest, handsomest, costliest playhouse in the world."[5] Lilian did not "star" in the production, as Berger Meyer stated, but *Pioneer Days* offered her her first break into show business.

The show's cast members were not the only Indians on Manhattan

Island. One observer noted that the Hippodrome performers joined an existing population of "Iroquois or Six Nations from both Canada and New York State" and "Indians of Maine and Nova Scotia of Algonquin stock such as the Mic Macs and Abenaquis." Some Native families lived in the boroughs of the Bronx, Queens, and Richmond, while many resided in Brooklyn's Little Caughnawaga neighborhood. However, most at this time preferred "the Indian Village," a neighborhood based in Greenwich Village "bounded by Broadway, Canal street, the North River and Four-teenth street." "The Indians when not in shows or summer camps wear conventional white men's clothing," the observer stated. Men wore their hair long but usually kept it under "a broad brimmed soft hat." Many of the New York Indians kept a supply of Navajo blankets and "Indian goods" in their homes to sell. They also tended to have "a valuable store of Indian war bonnets and buckskin costumes," which they donned in winter when they got together to sing, dance, and resume "the way of an Indian."[6] Lilian would eventually find her rightful place in this unique community and continue its traditions.

Lilian was probably not thinking of her future but of the past when she played a Sioux Indian maid for *Pioneer Days*. The show certainly challenged her childhood memories of the educated Wounded Knee delegation that visited Lincoln Institute because the story cast Native actors as white folks wanted to see them—untutored and uncivilized. Some of the Native actors among the cast touted as "Sioux Chiefs" included Black Horn, Iron Bird, and Sitting Bull's son William, whose picture also appears in the playbill for the show. Others cast as "Medicine Men and Braves" included Spotted Eagle and Willie Red Shirt, as well as their wives (called "Squaws") and children ("Papooses"), including William's infant daughter Rose Gabriel Sitting Bull.[7] The cast of characters also featured outlaws, "half breeds," a "Keeper of the Store," a "fiddler," a "Chinese Laundry Man," three U.S. Army officers, and the beloved white heroine, "Miss Virginia Harrington."

Scene 1 of *Pioneer Days* opened in a South Dakota pioneer town "in the days when the white man was pushing his way toward the Pacific." The Indians in "war council" entered the Black Hills near the Pine Ridge reservation in scene 2 and then performed the government-forbidden

Ghost Dance in a fabulous costumed spectacle that thrilled the 288 large audiences that came to see the show. The Hippodrome program boasted that the last scene was "the greatest scene ever attempted on the stage of any playhouse."[8] It featured a stagecoach attack by Indians with army troops coming to the rescue of Miss Harrington.

Carlisle graduate Henry Standing Bear, who played the role of interpreter, had charge of the Lakota cast, which included his brother Luther Standing Bear. Like Lilian's, Luther's name does not appear on the playbill. However, his memoir confirms his participation in the show. It also sheds light on the life Lilian led at this time: "We stayed at one of the big hotels in New York, and had two acts a day in which to appear. We had a six months' contract, so when that ran out, all the Indians went home except myself. I concluded to stay to see if I could make my living among the white people. I appeared in theaters and side-shows. I lectured and did any sort of work I could find."[9]

Lilian and James partnered with Standing Bear, and the trio continued to perform together after the show closed. Lilian later stated that Standing Bear adopted her as his niece and gave her an Indian name.[10] Her naming ceremony, if there was one, occurred sometime between November 1906, when *Pioneer Days* debuted, and early January 1908, when the name "Red Wing" first appeared in print. "As you know most Indians have an English name in addition to their Indian name," Lilian wrote, "and my two names are Lilian St Cyr & Red Wing."[11] Lilian's statement implies that, like "most Indians," she received a clan name from a Ho-Chunk tribal member. However, until Standing Bear came along, Lilian only had a Ho-Chunk name to reflect her birth order in the family. Over the years, Lilian validated Standing Bear's influence by giving the press the Lakota rather than the Ho-Chunk rendering of Red Wing as Rupa-Hu-Sha-Win.[12] A Buffalo Bill Wild West show veteran, Standing Bear well knew that an Indian performer needed an Indian name to be considered authentic.

Pioneer Days closed in May 1907, and Red Wing and "Young Deer," the stage name Johnson adopted at this time, found their calling with names that expressed their new personas.[13] Buffalo Bill's Wild West shows had already made Indians playing Indian a standard form of entertainment for whites. The incredible popularity of the shows, which took performers all the way to Europe, provided Native people, as one historian notes, "class and geographic mobility, financial security, independence from the restriction of white reservation agents, opportunities for political and social activism, and access to a limited range of institutional power."[14] Lilian's new career choice offered the same to her.

Lilian's educated siblings sought "class mobility" and "financial security" as well, but through the Indian Service. "White reservation agents" certainly circumscribed the mobility of her brothers David and Abner St. Cyr, who both had large families. Lilian's older sister Julia was another matter, both more and less restricted. Julia had only one child to worry about, so she was free to travel away from the reservation to Indian Service jobs. Still, she was beholden to authorities in charge of the Indian schools she worked for, and they were not always pleased with her job performance. By 1901 Julia had carved out a new career path for herself as an "Indian lawyer" to make extra money. Her bright intelligence guided her to serve the interests of individuals on the reservation, although she never studied law formally. Many tribal members required assistance with their heirship claims, and Julia's mastery of English, as well as her ability to deal with white authority figures, made her an apt candidate for the job. Unfortunately, authorities indicted Julia for extorting money from one of her clients, Wehunkaw, in 1906. The jury acquitted her in the end, but she blamed her arrest on the agent of the Nebraska reservation:

> I went to great expense and great trouble, not at any one time, but during those ten years. From time to time I advanced money to We-Hun-Ka and when she got her money she thought it was no more than right that I should be paid back what I had loaned. If she had got no money I of course would have had nothing, but she is my aunt, and I did the best I could for her. . . . The truth is that if it hadn't been for a meddling Indian agent . . . all this trouble would have been avoided. Information given by him resulted in my arrest. I don't know whether he didn't understand the situation or whether he didn't want to understand. Anyhow, I'm exonerated.[15]

"The Only Indian Woman Lawyer" became a national headline. Some newspaper reports stated that a few Ho-Chunk men were so incensed when Julia shed tears during her testimony that they walked out of the courtroom. The reports portrayed Julia as an accomplished Indian woman, on the one hand, but found her untrustworthy as such, on the other hand. How the many sexist and racist portrayals of her sister influenced Lilian is unknown, but they certainly steered her to a less risky career path off reservation. If playing Indian had its pitfalls, at least Lilian could live her life creatively, actively, and, at least for a time, incognito as Red Wing.

It's unclear where Lilian and James ended up immediately after *Pioneer Days* closed. "Ever since childhood," James later claimed, "his life" ran "in amusement channels. For many years he trouped all over the country with the circuses of the period, among them being Barnum & Bailey, and 101 Ranch."[16] Although no evidence of his circus days has been discovered, he and Lilian and Luther Standing Bear may have briefly joined the famous 101 Ranch, known more properly as the Miller Brothers' 101 Ranch Wild West Show. The troupe was based in Oklahoma, but the show traveled to Virginia to wow the Jamestown Exposition that summer. At least Henry Standing Bear was at Jamestown, because he acted as interpreter for the fair's permanent Indian exhibit.[17] If one or both Standing Bear brothers made it to Jamestown, one or both undoubtedly appeared in the show. As one historian writes, "Tens of thousands of visitors made it a point to attend at least one performance of the Miller Brothers' 101 Ranch Wild West Show. The program, featuring sixteen distinct western acts, lasted a full ninety minutes. Many of the people came back to see the show several times before the long run ended, in mid-October."[18]

Lilian and James didn't have to go as far as Virginia. Brothers Joe and Zack Miller, "encouraged by the staggering response to their show in Virginia," returned to their Oklahoma ranch and "quickly assembled a second road show, and shipped it to Brighton Beach, New York," that summer.[19] Brighton Beach resort sat at the southern tip of Brooklyn. Like Coney Island, the resort was a destination spot for New Yorkers hoping to beat the summer heat. For six weeks that summer thousands of city slickers thrilled to the "fancy trick riding" and sharp shooting of the Miller

Brothers' cowboys and cowgirls. The show also featured "wild Indian" riders, a herd of real buffalo, and a young Will Rogers Jr. demonstrating "feats with the lariat."[20] Joe Miller may have also employed Lilian and James, who apparently could ride a horse fairly well.[21]

By the year's end the Johnsons had joined "Chief Charging Hawk" and his small crew of "Sioux Indians" for an act at Brighton Beach. One film scholar naturally assumed that Chief Charging Hawk and Sherman Charging Hawk, a Lakota performer born in 1874, were one and the same. However, Brighton Beach's Chief Charging Hawk was none other than Luther Standing Bear.[22] Standing Bear did not make up his character; it was based on Sherman's father. Charging Hawk Sr. joined Lakota and Cheyenne warriors led by Crazy Horse against the Seventh Cavalry in a last-ditch effort to thwart the invasion of their homeland. During the two-day battle at Little Big Horn, 263 U.S. soldiers were killed, including Lieutenant Colonel George Armstrong Custer. Standing Bear's persona exploited the public's fascination with this historic battle. Of course, it probably also gave him pleasure to reenact an event in which his people were the victors.

Standing Bear had debuted as Charging Hawk at Huber's Palace Museum. The entertainment center, also known as Huber's Fourteen Street Museum, was located in Greenwich Village. A typical "dime museum" that catered to the city's masses, Huber's was divided "with one stage for freak acts and another for variety shows." Entertainers performed several times a day, and the schedule was grueling. Performing monkeys, Unthan "the armless wonder," and an early Harry Houdini headlined. "Huber's was known in New York City for its variety of acts," according to one source, "but it was not a leading vaudeville house and did not feature top-name entertainers."[23] Along with Charging Hawk's act, the lineup included the French Hercules, Pierre Gasnier, as well as "the World's Renowned Esquimaux," Chief Debro, and his wife. Frank "Shorty" and Sarah Kendalville played the Debros, but they were achondroplastic dwarfs who hailed from Indiana. They posed in the tradition of the "Little Esquimaux Lady," Olaf Krarer, who initiated the public's fascination with exotic ethnic dwarves in the late nineteenth century.[24]

By December Standing Bear's act included "an interesting lecture of the American Indian of to-day."[25] The "Indian of today" was a common subject for Carlisle Indian School, going back at least as far as Pratt's parade in Philadelphia. Pratt transformed the stereotypes "good" and "bad" Indians to "before" and "after" Indians, depending on whether one was educated at Carlisle.[26] It is likely that Lilian, "an Indian of today," and James joined Standing Bear's act about this time.

The threesome took their show on the road in January 1908. They appeared at the Curio Hall of the Ninth and Arch Museum in Philadelphia. Another dime museum, the venue's first floor "had distorting mirrors, a penny arcade, and penny-in-the-slot peep shows; the second floor housed a menagerie; and the third floor contained a Curio Hall, a room in which people designated as 'freaks' stood along the walls in niches."[27] Red Wing posed as a sixteen-year-old Sioux along with Young Deer, Chief Charging Hawk, and whatever Sioux Indians came along. The show also featured Gasnier and another strong man, as well as the "greatest living authority" on the life of bees. "In the Sioux tongue the chief tells of Custer's last charge" at Little Big Horn, wrote a reviewer. "He was a boy at the time and his story as interpreted by Young Deer is very graphic. Red Wing, the girl, sings a song in her native tongue, later singing it again in English. They are from the Pine Ridge Agency in Dakota."[28]

Performing as Wild West show Indians engaged the two Carlisle alums in exactly the activity that Pratt abhorred. Hiding behind "Red Wing" helped Lilian maintain the moral high ground of a Carlisle graduate, even though, ironically, she was an "after" Indian playing a "before" Indian. Playing Charging Hawk allowed Standing Bear to separate himself from the obligations of Carlisle's model student. However, when Standing Bear wrote Carlisle staff two years later about his "progress," he defended his role as an Indian performer:

> The Schools may not be in favor of the shows, but that is where I have seen and learned [a] good deal from too. As the saying goes experience is a good teacher, during my travels I have been amongst good and bad. But I never forgot what I was taught at Carlisle, not to drink and to smoke, not chew tobacco or tell lies. I tell you I have been where temptation was strong especially in the Show life, but believe me I

have lived up to what I was taught. . . . It is easy to be good in school, but its hard when you get out into the world.[29]

Standing Bear taught Lilian the ropes of Indian performance. His lessons weren't always translatable across genders, however, nor were they always particularly well thought out. After the trio returned from Philadelphia in February 1908, the *New York Times* reported on their visit to the Bronx Zoo with the dubious headline, "Spanked a Paleface Boy": "Chief Charging Hawk, his 17-year-old daughter, Red Wing, and her brother, Running [Young] Deer, all three Sioux Indians on their way to Asbury Park, went out to the Bronx Zoo yesterday to see the animals. They met six boys, and by the time they had made a short visit to the Zoo at least 1,000 young Americans were following them around." The trio must have been performing somewhere nearby or were attempting to drum up business for their act, but when "Lucky Ned, the Boy Scout of the Bronx Plains, jerked a feather out of the Chief's headgear," Standing Bear chased the boy across the park and spanked him.[30] The spanking episode is telling. Standing Bear felt relatively comfortable asserting his authority over white children with impunity.

After the spanking episode Manhattan socialite Mrs. Albert Brooks invited the threesome to perform for the Gotham Club at the luxurious Waldorf-Astoria Hotel, where she and her husband resided. Brooks had recently organized the elite club, whose members met to muse on the arts and philanthropy and to discuss subjects like patriotism and hygiene. She set up an evening "of songs, recitations, violin solos, selections on the phonograph, speeches, and Indian war dances" in mid-March. Standing Bear and the Johnsons, dressed in their Sioux finery, including face paint, "danced to the rhythm of the tomtom" while Lilian sang "My Navajo" and "Arrowana."[31]

The trio's performance greatly pleased the audience, so Brooks hired them again to perform at the Prince George Hotel on April Fool's Day. She advertised the affair as an "evening of the occult," and she dressed accordingly. She wore a mink-fur-trimmed "cream silk gown" with black polka dots, topped with an embroidered "Jap kimono." She had artificial poppies in her hair and wore two dog collars around her neck, one a beaded Navajo and the other "a dull diamond" of "Oriental design." Clearly, Brooks was a devotee of the Aesthetic movement, which embraced the ethnically exotic, including Indian curios. Sculptor Solon Borglum also belonged to the club. He specialized in western themes and Indians. He was also brother to Gutzon Borglum and nephew to Lincoln Borglum, famed carvers of Mount Rushmore. Unfortunately, he could not attend the evening's festivities despite the enticing line-up "of fortune telling, ghost dances, crystal gazing, telepathic experiments, dream analyses, palm and tea leaf readings, Indian dances, amateur and professional 'incantations,' and table rappings."[32]

A *Sun* reporter found the whole evening amusing. "This much being established," he wrote, "it might also be stated emphatically that the printed slip handed out at the door explained that among others expected were Chief Charging Hawk, Princess Red Wing, Young Deer and Vesta La Viesta, who is a professional cosmologist and planetary explorer and who got back from Mars or Saturn just in time to tell about the astral folks."[33]

A *New York Times* report lacked the *Sun*'s sarcasm. "The April Fool's Day guests were Princess Red Wing, a young aboriginal who sings . . . with great fidelity to pitch; 'Young Deer,' *a Carlisle graduate* [my emphasis]; 'Chief Charging Hawk,' and 'Ramaswami,' a Brahmin priest, thus bringing together the East Indian and North American Indian."[34] Not only did the Orient meet the Occident that evening, but Brooks also paired a ghost costume contest with a "real Indian" Ghost Dance, presumably performed by Lilian and her partners. If the audience missed the irony, surely the Sioux performers found the pairing incongruous. Significantly, James's Indianness received an authoritative nod from the newspaper report. Since he wasn't born and raised on the plains like his bride, at least he could masquerade his urban childhood with a pretend "real Indian" education. And he would, from then on.

Although Lilian did not publicly disclose the odd bent of her early performances, she most certainly grappled with how the public perceived her. Still, she decided to get a publicity photo that met the expectations of her East Coast audience. She engaged photographer August Obermüller and entered his studio in the lower East Side sometime in 1907 or 1908. Obermüller, a German-born American, was in his late sixties, five feet, two inches tall and two hundred pounds wide. Slim and petite Lilian came decked out in buckskin with a long necklace and silver bracelets. A beaded headband with a single feather graced her long dark braids, which draped the bodice of her fringed dress.

Obermüller looked her over, and one of them decided that she should pose with one leg kneeling. Without a hint of supplication or coyness, however, Lilian peered directly into his camera—and poof! She was immortalized as "Princess Red Wing." It's hard not to assume that the eyes in the photo reflect her bizarre surroundings. Obermüller shot theatrical photographs, certainly, but, more specifically, photographs for sideshow "freaks," some of which may have been displayed on the walls of his studio.[35] Obermüller had taken at least one picture of an Indian Wild West performer, but the portraits of his usual subjects included dwarves, albinos, "midgets," giants, frizzy-haired "Circassian beauties" (primitive women of the northwestern Caucasus region), tattooed men, a female lion tamer, a snake woman, Siamese twins, and a boy with a parasitic twin emerging from his midsection.

Perhaps Lilian was nonplussed after having worked with the Debros and Pierre Gasnier. Other photographers specializing in "freaks of nature" had also captured their likenesses on cabinet cards. Still, it's hard to fathom how she felt as the small, rotund, older German man peered at her through the lens of his camera. Obermüller's image of Princess Red Wing, if removed from this context, appears to be simply a romantic vision of a vanishing Indian maid. However, when viewed as part of Obermüller's body of work, her photo taps into the dark racist and sexist fantasies of modernity.[36]

Lilian's new career path might have precipitated a rude awakening and a quick exit from show biz for someone less daring. Instead, she began to fashion a persona that met public expectations while still expressing her effervescent spirit. The public's fascination with the Indian princess ever pining "by the silv'ry light of the moon" seemed to limit her possibilities. Nevertheless, Lilian shaped the stereotype to meet her expectations. She sang and danced to the tom-tom and the piano, both of which she could play. She did voice performances in "her native tongue" and spoke eloquently like "the new Indian" she in fact was. Soon the public would realize that Lilian was much more than a genuflecting Indian princess.

By the early spring of 1908 a talent scout had taken notice, and Lilian attained a bit part for Kalem Company's production of *The White Squaw*. The one-reeler—twelve hundred feet of film—was shot in Fort Lee, New Jersey, just across the Hudson from Manhattan. When Kalem released the film that spring at least one reviewer exclaimed that it "proved a sensation." "The story is very exciting and holds its audience in deep interest," he raved, "rivaling the wild tale of Francis Slocum, the White Squaw of the Miami Indians."[37] The film has been lost, but Lilian's part was probably minimal. Still, the small role granted her entry into a new career that would lead her to a brief period of fortune and fame.

Standing Bear and the Johnsons continued their act through the summer of 1908, when Brighton Beach booked its third successive Wild West show, the Kemp Sisters' Hippodrome and Indian Congress.[38] Obermüller's headshot of "Princess Red Wing," along with photos of a performing nun, a pipe-smoking elephant, and a beautiful dancing Salomé, illustrated the *Brooklyn Daily Eagle*'s headline, "Big Shows at the Beaches and Elsewhere for Fourth of July Week."[39] The Johnsons and "an Indian encampment presided over by Chief Charging Hawk and several young braves" teamed up with "Uncle Dan Boyington and his trained mules, buffalo and yak."[40] "The Destruction of Jerusalem," a spectacular fireworks display, finished off the evening.

Since the Miller Brothers had employed Boyington as an animal trainer and performer the year before (and would again employ him in 1909), the Johnsons may have met him when and if they had in fact worked earlier for the 101 Ranch Show.[41] Teaming up with Uncle Dan was probably not a bad gig. Boyington expressed a gentle soul and was an interesting entertainer for his times. The public knew him for his humane treatment of animals. He believed that reward, not punishment, worked best to train the beast. "Mules are like women," he would say. "They have never been understood." He stressed that animals were intelligent and that "if you watch those you are working with, many a time they teach you."[42]

Sometime while working with Uncle Dan, Lilian, James, and Standing Bear ran into a stranded group of Lakota show Indians brought to New York by a stock raiser from near Pine Ridge, Elisha C. Swigert. Swigert recruited the group to perform in a Wild West show at the newly opened

Coney Island Hippodrome. Unfortunately, Coney Island's venue went out of business almost as soon as it opened, and a disagreement arose between Swigert and the Lakota over what they'd do instead. The disagreement, of course, had two sides. Standing Bear sent a letter to the Indian Rights Association, penned by Lilian, to plead for the Lakota:

> I write to appeal for aid for my people. If you can send a man or come right away yourself we can explain matters to you. There are 26 Sioux Indians here stranded and want the government to send them home. They were brought east by an Indian trader from Gordon, Neb. Please notify us or tell us what to do, of course we are doing our best for them but we cannot send them home as we have not the means. . . . Trusting you will investigate this matter right away as these Indians are very restless and some tried to walk home. We are trying to keep them together until we can get them home.[43]

"Chief Charging Hawk" signed the letter with a return address of the "101-Ranch" at Brighton Beach, suggesting that the Miller Brothers employed the trio, as well as Boyington. The letter precipitated an immediate investigation. Superintendent E. F. Merwin arrived to assess the Coney Island situation. He discovered that some of the twenty-four Indians were happily employed as performers. The majority still felt uncertain about the legality of a new contract with Swigert, however, given that there was no reservation agent to witness it. Merwin talked to "other Wild West managers," including a white performer called "Eagle Eye," whom Merwin mysteriously identified as Red Wing's uncle. Merwin concluded that Standing Bear and the Johnsons were not just innocent bystanders in the conflict. His assessment reveals their influence in the matter, as well as how Native performers in general navigated a for-profit system run predominantly by whites.

Merwin reported that the president of the "Springfield Bank" sent a railroad ticket to "Walk Under Ground," and the elderly Indian went home. Several others from Pine Ridge also returned home, and one elderly man planned to leave that week. Six of the performers contentedly worked at an amusement park in New Jersey. Merwin further stated that he "saw five of the Indians working at Uncle Dan's Wild West for which they were receiving satisfactory pay." The remainder worked for other shows, but he added, "both Luther Standing Bear or Charging Hawk as he now calls himself, and Young Deer are reticent and I could not learn where they had located these others." Since the Pine Ridge group was "well equipped with war bonnets, blankets and other paraphernalia," Merwin presumed they'd have no difficulty finding employment in the area, but since he also believed they were "all improvident," he worried they'd have "trouble in getting back home when they wish to go."

He also didn't believe that "the statements made by Young Deer and Luther Charging Hawk should obtain full credence." He learned "through different sources that the two men along with Young Deer's wife attempted to exploit a show in Dreamland [at Coney Island] themselves." Merwin's sources informed him that the trio "endeavored to get other Indians," but when they couldn't, they also went to the New Jersey amusement park "and engaged for the season." They were fired, however, because "they were not obedient." In response, at least one of the three told the management they would use their influence so no other Indians would take their place. However, Swigert stepped in and sent six of his Pine Ridge crew to the management. Merwin continued his complaint against Standing Bear and Young Deer.

Luther had tried to get Indians from Swigert and failed. . . . [This] furnished the motive which caused him to foment the troubles which followed Swigert and have acted so disastrously on him and reacted on the Indians. Luther has accomplished his purpose and now has five with him at Uncle Dan's and has placed some of the others, but where, he would not tell me. Indians on the ground fully equipped as these are a working capital and no doubt but Luther and Young Deer will reap a good harvest from what they have plainly stolen from Swigert as he had paid their expenses from Gordon, had furnished them with their war bonnets, blankets and other paraphernalia expecting a profit from the business done both for himself and the Indians. I do not suppose that Senator Curtis or the Indian Rights Association can prevent such low life trickery and rascality but they can withhold their moral support and should discountenance such proceeding. I have not seen Swigert since writing my letter of July 2; at that time he seemed thoroughly cast down and at his wits end.[44]

Low-life trickery and rascality aside, Standing Bear and the Johnsons continued to draw crowds at Brighton Beach because the five Indians from Pine Ridge boosted the authenticity of their act significantly. Merwin's account shows that Standing Bear and at least Young Deer, if not his wife, knew how to scramble and take advantage of the opportunity that presented itself. However, it also suggests that the men could be vengeful when they did not get their way or that, as Indians, whites found them untrustworthy.

Later in July the *Brooklyn Daily Eagle*'s column "Varied Amusements by the Sea" featured a headshot of "Chief Charging Hawk" in the requisite feathered headdress. The column also described Brighton Beach's other rousing attractions that exemplified the era's fascination with the thrilling, the exotic, and the ethnographic: "At another section of the 'pike' is an interesting Oriental tea garden, where Japanese Geisha girls serve tea, and exhibitions of jiujitsu and Japanese sports and drama are presented. Uncle Dan Boyington has added to his already clever show a large number of Indians, prominent among them being Princess Red Wing, Young Deer, both of Carlisle University Pa. Of the stationary devises Brighton Beach Park possesses the longest scenic railroad in the world, a handsome carousel, a fine roller skating rink, the sensational 'thriller' called the 'Ragged Edge,' [a roller coaster] and the shooting gallery."[45]

Brighton Beach also featured "A Night on a Houseboat" that summer. "On the gorgeous scenic setting of an elaborate double-decked houseboat, gayly decorated with garlands, flags and lanterns, a party of young people and their chaperon are summering," its description read.[46] Jesse L. Lasky directed the escape-from-the-summer-heat vaudeville show. Little did Red Wing know, if she saw the show, that Lasky would become a famed movie producer and she the star of his first silent film.

Near the end of the summer of 1908, the Johnsons, along with an apparently non-Native fellow calling himself "Falling Star," attended a luncheon in their honor given by three Brooklynites who said they met the couple through their association with the Miller Brothers. The *Brooklyn*

Daily Eagle covered the event and featured a photo of the group, showing "the three real Indians from the plains" in their standard Indian regalia. "Princess Red Wing is quite a fluent linguist and made the luncheon quite enjoyable," the reporter remarked. Why this was a newsworthy event is unknown, but at least it was publicity.[47]

The trio broke up either soon after or just before the luncheon. Standing Bear continued for a time performing as Charging Hawk in "Indian vaudeville," a term coined about 1894 for performers who were "real Indians," as well as those posing as such.[48] Standing Bear performed in H. A. Brunswick's Wild West Indian Vaudeville show in June 1909. An ad for the show reflects the developing aspects of specifically *Indian* vaudeville: "See the hair raising war dance" and "the greatest and most exciting Wild West Indian Picture. Bring the Children, it is Educational." Another ad for the show itemized its features: "See Chief Ocallala Fire, 86 years old, Leader in Custer's last fight. Also Chief Charging Hawk. See the War Dance. A complete lecture on the Western pictures (which change each night)."[49] Besides war dances, Native songs accompanied by the tom-tom, "real" chiefs in feathered war bonnets, princesses in traditional garb, not to mention educational lectures on Indian culture, Indian vaudeville was often performed at theaters in tandem with a silent western or two. Eventually, Lilian would conduct her own Indian vaudeville tour, but for now, she was destined for something greater.

It's unknown where the Johnsons went next. Did they stay in Manhattan? Did they return to Saratoga Springs to make and sell Indian curios? Did they visit the reservation or go to Washington DC? The erasure of James's racial makeup makes it easy to forget that his siblings lived nearby. His older brother George still resided in Washington DC with his wife and daughter.[50] His youngest sibling, Harry, and his wife, Gertrude, moved to Manhattan sometime before that summer when their only child, Thelma Johnson, was born. If Johnson kept in touch with Harry, perhaps Harry visited his show at Brighton Beach. Minnie and her husband, William Fossett, also joined Harry in Manhattan, where they all shared an apartment. Minnie's husband worked as a watchman, and Harry worked as a janitor, probably in the same building. Obviously, they led lives more mundane than their brother's.

Lilian and James ended up back in Philadelphia by 1909, or at least they worked for a film company based there. It's unknown if James made contact with his father's family. He and Lilian garnered roles in a Lubin Manufacturing Company film entitled *Falling Arrow*.[51] The film, released in April 1909, partially filled one reel and ran for about eleven minutes. This amount was typical of early silent films. The *Nickelodeon* summed up the story as "a romance in which Young Deer, an Indian chief, rescues the Mexican planter's daughter and is rewarded with her hand."[52] The *Film Index* advertisement shows James and the Mexican's daughter, played by Lilian. The *New York Dramatic Mirror* deemed the acting "on par with the story," which wasn't a compliment. "The Magic Arrow would have been a more appropriate title," wrote the reviewer, "for it travels in this picture further than any arrow ever traveled before without wings." Lilian's character, who was captured by a "bad outlaw," shoots the arrow, which "lands in an Indian camp ever so many miles away." Attached to it is a note to her "Indian lover." Said lover "mounts his horse and rides furiously through several scenes till he reaches the girl and rescues her." One critic seemed most distressed by the film's outdoor scenery and "Eastern atmosphere," which belied its western theme. However, one authentic detail greatly impressed another critic. He thought James's riding skills appeared "unusually good": "The Indian's horse had no saddle. The Indian merely jumped upon his back and rode swiftly away."[53] This desire for authentic detail—or at least what the public deemed as such—opened wide a door of opportunity for the Johnsons.

On June 26, 1909, a film crew from Manhattan's Biograph Company arrived at the small train depot in Cuddebackville, New York, near the Orange Mountains. The city folk, happy to escape the heat of the metropolis, took a five-hour trip by train via the Manhattan ferry departure at 125th Street. Two men destined to become filmmaking legends headed the group, the recent actor turned director David Wark "D. W." Griffith and Wilhelm "Billy" Bitzer, his skilled cameraman.[54]

The film crew's destination featured pristine landscape perfect for an Indian camp, rugged trails suitable for death-defying chases on horseback, and the winding, picturesque, and sometimes rapid Neversink

River. Tiny Cuddebackville also hosted a general store and lodging that were virtually empty for the summer. "Joy, but didn't they become delirious, the actors slated for a Cuddebackville . . . week in the mountains," exclaimed Griffith's wife, Linda Arvidson, "with no hotel bill, and pay checks every day! Few there were so ultra modern that they would take no joy in the bleating of lambs but would prefer their city third floor back." Still, the journey to the small hamlet took "much preparation": "We had to see that our best blouse was back from the laundry and our dotted swiss in order for evening, our costumes right, and grease-paint complete, for any of us might be asked to double up for Indians before the week was over."[55] Although Arvidson was unable to make the first trip to the Orange Mountains, she and others, like Mary Pickford, Mack Sennett, Florence Lawrence, and Lillian Gish, made several films there under Griffith's direction from 1909 until 1915.[56]

Alvin Predmore and his wife ran the Caudebec Inn. Predmore met Griffith's first crew at the railroad stop in his "Red Devil," a spiffy red driving machine trimmed with brass. At full capacity his converted farmhouse held close to eighty people—that is, if four men shared a room and extras slept on cots in the hallways or hammocks on the porch. As film idol Wallace Reid recalled, the inn "was a large three-story building encircled by a big porch and meant to hold a dozen guests. It defined 'rustic': spotlessly clean thanks to Mrs. Predmore, but only one bathroom, a tiny parlor, and a large dining room overlooking an apple orchard."[57] They weren't staying long, even though Griffith planned to shoot two westerns calling for "wild mountainous country," *The Mended Lute* and *The Indian Runner's Romance*.[58]

Griffith, Bitzer and his wife, and "the principals" ("movie star" was a future concept) got to ride in Predmore's automobile from the station, while an express wagon served to transport "big wads of canvas for the teepees, cameras, and costume baskets."[59] The rest of the cast and crew, including the newly recruited "Mr. and Mrs. Youngdeer," walked behind for a half mile or so to the inn. "Glad to see you come," said Mrs. Predmore as she welcomed the motley crew on the veranda. Frank Powell, an actor who also served as production manager (he played the old prospector in *The Indian Runner's Romance* and Chief Great Elk Horn in *The*

Mended Lute), signed about thirty people into the guest register. Along with "Griffith" and "Bitzer" these guests included several actors who would become Griffith favorites: Florence Lawrence (who played *The Mended Lute*'s Rising Moon); Owen Moore (who played Little Bear in *The Mended Lute* and Blue Cloud in *The Indian Runner's Romance*); Moore's soon-to-be wife and not yet America's sweetheart, Mary Pickford (who played Blue Cloud's wife and a bit part as an Indian maid in *The Mended Lute*); James Kirkwood (who played Standing Rock in *The Mended Lute* and a cowboy in *The Indian Runner's Romance*); and Lottie Smith, Mary Pickford's younger sister (who had a bit part in one or both films). Powell also signed in for "Young Deer" and "Red Wing," who were lodged in the farmhouse.[60] With so many people crammed into one place, it's a good thing the Tammany Hall Tavern was just across the dirt road to provide an evening haven for card playing and craps.[61]

Although Lilian later stated that she'd played a small part in *The Mended Lute*, she may have appeared briefly in both films, though it's difficult to be certain due to the films' condition today. *The Mended Lute*'s story line even then epitomized the western genre. The film's setting was Spirit Lake, Iowa, and the Indians were Plains Sioux. As one reviewer put it, "It is the familiar love story where the lover accepted by the Indian girl is objectionable to her father, and despite her protests she is given to someone else." Mary Pickford was not the leading lady for *The Mended Lute*, but she said Griffith liked to cast her as an Indian because her hazel eyes filmed dark. She also recalled that "a Mrs. Young Deer taught authentic Indian dances to the company after supper. Mr. Young Deer was in charge of costumes, bows and arrows and other props."[62] Griffith hired the Johnsons to enhance the believability of white actors playing Indian.

The plot of *The Mended Lute* was standard, except that the villains were white and the Indians triumphant in the final chase.[63] Although the Indians appeared "triumphant" in *The Mended Lute* and "the victors" in *The Indian Runner's Romance*, today their caricatured redface portrayal by white actors diminishes the effect no less than the white actors playing blackface villains in Griffith's notoriously racist *Birth of a Nation* (1915). Yet surprisingly, viewers of the time found *The Mended Lute* cutting edge. One review noted that the details appeared "true in every particular to

Indian life as it was known among the Sioux at that time" and that the film exhibits "an entirely new feature of that life." The critic acknowledged that the common stereotype was that the "Sioux is without sentiment of any kind," so he was amazed "to see here blended so much poetry and romance . . . based upon what appear to be actual facts." He pronounced the film a new "view of Indian character."[64]

Lilian's influence assuredly softened the "view of Indian character" portrayed in both films. Some scholars have noted that Griffith's racism is apparent in these early films, but it's equally evident that Young Deer and Red Wing played on Griffith's romantic portrayals of heroic Indians as their film careers progressed. Although Griffith did not realize the potential for "real Indians" *acting* as lead Indian characters, he nevertheless respected the Johnsons as *consultants* on all things Indian.[65] The Johnsons contributed materially to props and set design and consulted on customs and costumes. However, their influence had political consequences. During the Progressive Era, the authentic markers of exotic cultures became counterculture fetishes that served to anchor Anglo-Saxon superiority.

A scene in *The Indian Runner's Romance* supports Pickford's memories of Red Wing's dance lessons. The extant film, "a thrilling episode set in the Black Hills," features a brief dance during a wedding scene.[66] James, in Indian dress, leads the dance with the beat of his tom-tom. Lilian's choreography is comic by today's standards and for some even offensive. However, *The Indian Runner's Romance*'s viewing public found the dance convincingly authentic. Lilian received no credit for her contribution to the film, but *Moving Picture World* touted the contribution of *The Mended Lute*'s "Indian consultant." "Moving picture stories based on the life and customs of the American aboriginals have ever been attractive," the critic wrote, "and we conscientiously doubt if there has ever been a more intensely interesting subject presented than this Biograph production which, indeed, is a masterpiece." Then as now, authenticity *and* thrilling action made a winning combination, and *The Mended Lute*'s "exciting and skillfully handled" canoe chase conclusion left viewers breathless.[67] "Much thought and time were given the many details," the review continued, "and we may claim that as to costumes, manners, and modes of living, it is more than reasonably accurate, these details having been supervised by an expert in the matter."[68] James was undoubtedly this "expert," despite the fact that only Lilian could claim such expertise. But it was a man's world even if James was an Indian. Gender bias and her husband's desire for recognition and fame overshadowed Lilian's contribution to her films.

The Johnsons also began working that summer for director-cameraman Fred J. Balshofer. Balshofer looked more like a leading man than most actors of the time. He was tall and extremely handsome, with wide-set eyes and a luscious crop of light curly hair. He was also a big fan of cameraman Billy Bitzer, so a friendly repartee may have already existed between Biograph and Balshofer's enterprise, the New York Motion Picture Company (NYMPC). Balshofer was one of three partners for the newly incorporated company, which was headquartered at the corner of Sixth Avenue and 26th Street in Manhattan. Charles O. Bauman and Adam Kessell headed the plucky independent film production company, trademarked as Bison Life Motion Pictures but better known as Bison Co. Both men had formerly owned film exchanges, and both men were rogues. Balshofer acted as the company's secretary-treasurer, but, more importantly, he was put "in charge of picture making."[69]

The company's lead actors, Evelyn Graham and Charles Krause, whose stage name was Charles K. French, came from the "legitimate stage." Graham was a statuesque, unconventional beauty with thick dark hair and wide, dark, down-turned eyes that she accentuated with dark eye shadow. Graham could portray a gypsy, an Indian, or a pioneer woman as easily as a cowgirl. French, tall and husky with kindly blue eyes, had graying hair at his temples, making him appear dignified whether he was in a dress suit or a cowboy outfit. French and Graham played leads in Bison Co.'s first venture, *Davy Crockett in Hearts United*. "Davy Crockett was the type of picture we had decided we would make when we formed the Bison Company, and the sale of prints proved how right our judgment was," Balshofer explained.[70] *A Squaw's Revenge* followed, released in June 1909, and the sales convinced the partners "to make only westerns." Consequently, on June 25, Bison released *The Cowboy's Narrow Escape*, featuring an Indian character and his sister. This time, "for realism and color," Balshofer "added two authentic Indians," Young Deer and Red Wing, to play the siblings.[71]

A Cowboy's Narrow Escape met the expectations of the viewing public. James played an Indian boy meeting up with cowboys in a saloon who "treat him to whiskey." When the boy comes back for more drink (because as an Indian he can't help himself), he witnesses Bad Bill murdering the saloon proprietor. Like a good sister, Lilian's character keeps the whiskey away from her brother, and she rescues him when Bad Bill throws him over a cliff for having seen the crime. Tom, the cowboy in the white hat, is wrongfully accused of Bad Bill's crime and is persecuted by the mob. In the end, the Indian boy who was saved by his sister (who shows everyone that the proprietor was never killed in the first place) saves Tom for another day.

A photo of Lilian in Indian costume guiding her poor, injured brother through a rocky terrain appears in Bison Co.'s advertisement for the film.[72] The ad also includes a photo inset of several cowboys, including Art Acord, an up-and-coming western actor and real live broncobuster who joined the company that year.[73] The ad boasts a "thrilling western story" featuring "a genuine Indian man and woman as leading characters" and "a leading Cowboy who held the roping champion of Oklohoma [*sic*] for five years." *Moving Picture World* gave the film a great review: "The producers of this interesting picture have gone about the work of making it in such a common sense fashion that hypercriticism is disarmed, and we should think that the picture is one that would successfully appeal on its merits to the very large class of lovers of Indian subjects." The reviewer also raved about "some very powerful and convincing bits of acting," giving a nod to the Johnsons and Acord. The "simple, probable story" also received honorable mention. "This is carrying out our last week's suggestion and going straight to nature," the reviewer explained. The reviewer applauded Bison Co., concluding that "they are evidently engaging the right kind of talent, and we think that they have all the capacity for making a great success of their pictures."[74]

Balshofer hired one of Biograph's leading men, Charles C. Inslee, to act and direct, as well as Eddie Dillon, an actor and former jockey, for his next project, *A True Indian's Heart*. Inslee, a balding actor "with nearly transparent eyes," played a believable gypsy in Biograph's first film, *The Adventures of Dolly* (1908), as well as the Indian character George

Redfeather in Biograph's *Call of the Wild* (1908).[75] Inslee donned "a black wig parted in the center with two braids that reached below his shoulders" for *A True Indian's Heart*. His only other costuming was a loincloth, "giving him an excellent opportunity to display his fine physique," according to Balshofer. Evelyn Graham played Inslee's leading lady. There were no stars in this era, so everyone pitched in with whatever skills they had to make a moving picture, including constructing sets. Lilian recalled that French was the primary director, which was probably due to Inslee's ineptitude at directing.[76] Balshofer hired the Johnsons to be the ethnographic consultants, but they also contributed "scenarios," which were prototypes for film scripts. Lilian made costumes and props as well.

Balshofer shot *A Cowboy's Narrow Escape* and *A True Indian's Heart* in a neighborhood located in Fort Lee, New Jersey.[77] The area was named after a local merchant, R. Coyte. At that time no one dreamed the quaint little village would become the center for filmmaking. "Coytesville is one of the oldest neighborhoods in Fort Lee," one historian notes. "The streets are still very narrow and hilly as the one-time village sits atop the Palisades, much like an eagle's nest. The borders very loosely are the Palisades Interstate Parkway overpass bridge . . . , east to the end of the Palisades, north to the Englewood Cliffs border and west to Englewood."[78]

After the Bison Co. crew disembarked from the Manhattan ferry, they traipsed up First Street, a tree-lined dirt road with "wooded hills and forests" beyond, to Rambo's Saloon. The saloon offered western atmosphere, and its second story provided dressing rooms for the cast. Arthur C. Miller, who was Balshofer's teenage film developer and assistant cameraman at the time, remembered: "At the back of the saloon was a cistern with a pump where the 'Indians' washed the Bole Armenia or reddish water paint from their bodies after a hard day's work." He also explained that the company rented horses and cowboy equipment from Captain Anderson's livery stable, located just behind the saloon. A photo of the time shows both Johnsons in Indian costumes with leading cowgirl Evelyn Graham and her horse standing in front of a large teepee that Lilian constructed "according to Indian tradition."[79] It didn't matter that the traditional lodges of the Ho-Chunk were bark and woven mat wigwams. What mattered was that Indians in westerns needed teepees, and a real Indian maid constructed a semblance of one.

The crew met at the saloon in the early morning to begin filming. "Fred Balshofer, always conscious of the final effect," stated Miller, "was anxious to select pleasing compositions, so he insisted that western pictures to be successful, must consist of a series of beautiful pictures combined with fast-moving action to tell a story, with as few subtitles as possible." Balshofer demarcated scenes "by stretching sash cord from wooden pegs that were driven to the ground."[80] The director made sure the actors stayed within these boundaries so the camera wouldn't have to be moved.

After a morning or afternoon of filming, the company convened near the saloon under a long grape arbor. A huge planked table sat there, where more than one film crew at a time could enjoy the saloon's standard fare, "ham and eggs, bread and butter, coffee, and homemade apple pie." Lilian, who may have met Griffith at such a gathering, surely learned her craft during those amiable mealtimes. As Miller recalled, "The experience of sitting under the grape arbor with actors, directors, and cameramen and hearing them swap stories, gossip and ideas was delightful."[81]

A True Indian's Heart should have taken only two days to film, but the last scene almost shut down the whole operation. The crew erected a "slab log cabin deep in the woods" that was to be set on fire. No special effects—just kerosene and matches. As Miller told it, "Red Wing was to run in and rescue Miss Graham, who was supposed to be overcome with smoke." "When everything was in readiness," he said, "it somehow seemed a better idea not to put Miss Graham inside the cabin before starting the fire." The director's decision to "wait outside until the right amount of fire was burning, then run in and close the door" saved Graham's life, as well as Lilian's. "Fred was to start turning the camera," Miller explained, and then "Red Wing was to dash into the burning cabin, open the door, and help Miss Graham to safety." As the young women waited next to the cabin for their cue, Inslee signaled to the prop man who had prepared the cabin for the scene. The prop man lighted a piece of paper and tossed it toward the structure. "As soon as the burning paper reached the cabin," Miller recalled, "there was a tremendous explosion as the whole cabin burst into flames. The heat was unbearable. Both Fred and

Inslee ran to the aid of the girls under the impression that both must have been injured. Luckily, both Red Wing and Miss Graham had had enough presence of mind to cover their faces and back off from the fire." Miller and Balshofer were also concerned about the camera's safety, but one of the crew managed to save it. "Nobody was aware that the prop man had literally soaked the slabs of the cabin with kerosene," said Miller. "Needless to say, that was the end of the day as well as of that prop man." Fortunately, a nearby car rushed the women back to Rambo's, "where first aid was administered at once." Yet the show had to go on. "Fred had the front of the cabin rebuilt," continued Miller, "and shot the fire scene again with much more precaution."[82]

A True Indian's Heart was released on July 2. Like *Mended Lute*, it boasted a thrilling canoe chase, probably shot along Fort Lee's palisades. It was also billed as having "the best actors in America, and the scenes the most beautiful nature has produced."[83] Nevertheless, Inslee, "the Lone Indian," received more acclaim and fan mail than anyone else for his loinclothed virility. As Balshofer remarked, "Inslee made a striking appearance on the screen and the ladies simply went gaga over him."[84] Inslee's sex appeal aside, making movies was not a frivolous affair. A career as an actor in westerns in those days was fraught with danger. There were no stunt men or women and no special effects, yet the public expected a thrill ride for their few coins. Unfortunately, Lilian's near-death experience in *A True Indian's Heart* would not be her last.

In between the release of Lilian's Biograph films in August, Bison Co. released *Half Breed's Treachery* on August 20. Again, *Moving Picture World* applauded the company for "securing for the principal characters of this story a genuine Indian and his wife." As the film's title and many more like it reveal, mixed-race Natives suffered as much negative stereotyping as their "full-blood" kin. It's hard to fathom how Lilian dealt with this issue, given her father's ancestry and his role in the tribe. Still, having steady work and some small influence over how films portrayed Native people improved her life, as well as the lives of other Indian performers. On the reservation she might have been winning small cash prizes, like her relatives had, for best dancer and best costume at the reservation powwow. Or, like her sister, Lilian might have donned traditional Ho-Chunk dress for spectators at local, state, and world's fairs, such as Julia did for the 1898 Omaha Exposition.[85] Either way, the money and prestige her relatives received couldn't compare with what Lilian earned for appearing on the big screen.

The Johnsons' roles in *Half Breed's Treachery*, again shot in Coytesville, functioned pretty much the same as they had in *A Cowboy's Narrow Escape*. Still, the location was a problem, despite its picturesque scenery and proximity to Manhattan. Al "Slim" McCoy, a detective hired to protect Thomas Edison's camera patent, proved a great annoyance for Balshofer and his crew. The New York Picture Company refused to join the "Edison trust," which was established as the Motion Picture Patents Company (MPPC) in December 1908. Lilian had not worked for an independent company before, so the subterfuge was new to her. Kalem, Lubin, and Biograph were MPPC members, along with Edison's Manufacturing Company, George Kleine, Georges Méliès Company, Pathé Frères of France, Selig Polyscope, and the Vitagraph Company.[86]

McCoy hounded Bison Co. at Fort Lee so much that Balshofer gathered his crew, slipped out of the city, and set up a temporary studio at Neversink, New York, located in the Catskill Mountains at the northern end of the Neversink River Valley. "Our company consisted of Charlie French, Evelyn Graham, Young Deer and his wife Red Wing, J. Barney Sherry, Eddie Dillon, Charlie Inslee, Bill Edwards our property man, Arthur Miller and me," Balshofer recalled. A "broken-down boarding house" provided their lodging, while a barn housed interior shots. Locals served as extra cowboys and Indians, while the scenic beauty and the "clear mountain air" made for "sharp, brilliant photography."[87]

Lilian soon found her niche in the "Indian helper film," the genre exemplified by *A True Indian's Heart*. Throughout her career, she played various versions of the Indian princess helper, portraying the Indian maid who "stands alone as a romantic noble savage figure . . . willing to give her life for the western European culture that attracts her." Like the stock character, Lilian's portrayals emanated "youth, innocence, and gratefulness" and "incredible, child like sincerity." More importantly, her Indian princess appeared in stark contrast to the "uncivilized" and ignoble "savages" who peopled the pictures in which she appeared.[88] But there was another side to the story. Indian helper narratives "heightened the expected aura of tragedy by visually highlighting the helper's dangerous situation."[89] The fire at Fort Lee was the first among many treacherous scenarios Lilian would experience. The basis of her Indian princess character was more than just a helper. Her character made difficult rescues and performed spine-tingling feats, which her audience adored. Consequently, Lilian as "Red Wing" became first and foremost a modern heroine poised and ready to leap into action and save the day.

Bison Co. released *The Paymaster* on September 10. It was the story of "how Silver Bird, an Indian girl, saves Lieutenant Barns, the paymaster, from a band of outlaws."[90] Lilian may not have played Silver Bird, since she is not the Indian woman (who may be Graham) photographed in Bison's ad. Was this because Silver Bird loved a white man, and portraying such interracial love was still taboo, or was it because Graham was Bison Co.'s leading lady, regardless of the part? *The Paymaster* was either the last movie Bison Co. shot in New Jersey or the first filmed at Neversink. Bison Co.'s next films, *A Squaw's Sacrifice* (sequel to *A Squaw's Revenge* and released on September 24), *Dove Eye's Gratitude* (released on October 8), *Iona, the White Squaw* (released on October 22), and *Mexican's Crime* (released October 29), were most likely made near Neversink.[91] Although delicately featured, dark-haired Jewell Darrell played Iona, Lilian probably played the self-sacrificing Indian maid in *A Squaw's Sacrifice*. As *Moving Picture World* concluded, "The little squaw, feeling that his [Bob's] true happiness lies with Mabel, ends her life with a knife taken from Bob's belt. She places Mabel's hand in Bob's and dies in his arms." This over sentimentalized early western narrative ploy, lifted straight from Edwin Milton Royle's popular stage play, *The Squaw Man*, supported the Indian princess's function as a self-sacrificing helper to the superior white race. It also skirted the touchy issue of miscegenation—or at least the possibility of a mixed-race child raised by Indians—as it reasserted the proper Darwinian hierarchy. The *Moving Picture World* critic loved the film and the sentiment. "This picture teems with human feeling," he declared. "It is a story very well told and charmingly portrayed. The scenery and acting demand particular commendation."[92] Lilian also appeared presumably as

Dove Eye in *Dove Eye's Gratitude*, supporting Jewell Darrell's character. This Indian helper film was "beautifully colored" and portrayed "Indian life in all its phases."[93]

Meanwhile, Slim McCoy grew more determined to nail Bison Co. for patent infringement, but he couldn't figure out where Balshofer was making movies. The company managed to avoid the detective until snow season, when everyone returned to New York City. That fall *Variety* announced that Bison "swiped" ideas and "borrowed" actors from MPPC.[94] After all, Inslee had left Biograph for Bison Co., but he wasn't the only swap. Vitagraph, an MPPC company, hired the Johnsons in the late summer or early fall. Vitagraph kept a studio in the Midwood neighborhood of Brooklyn, but a company representative may have caught up with the Johnsons in the Catskills or under the arbor at Rambo's. Only four days after Bison Co. released *Dove Eye's Gratitude*, Vitagraph released the similarly titled *Red Wing's Gratitude*. The title suggests that Vitagraph representatives attempted to woo Lilian away from Bison Co. by giving her top billing. *Red Wing's Gratitude* also firmly established *gratitude* as a prominent characteristic of the Indian princess helper films "not simply for specific white favors, but for the gift of contact with civilization."[95] The form and function of the "scenario" of *Red Wing's Gratitude* exemplify the story line and stereotypes exploited over and over in early westerns. As *Moving Picture World*'s lengthy synopsis shows, these include the "savage" Indian father and the noble Indian daughter who begins as a "drudge" but meets her transformative fate as the self-sacrificing Indian heroine.

> Red Wing is a little Indian maiden, who is the drudge of her tepee. Her brutal father shares the Indian contempt for women and regards her as little better than a beast of burden, though she is developing into an attractive maiden who some day will bring him many ponies and blankets from some amorous brave. Finding her sitting beside the fire at the camp, he drives her forth to gather wild berries, and when her weary feet will carry her no further and she sinks exhausted to the ground, her father happens to cross her trail, and with blows and hard words drives her to her task. His brutality excites the anger of some emigrants who are hurrying to make camp, and the leader of the little

band of pioneers drives the cruel chief from the prostrate form upon which he is raining blows. Naiuchi is armed only with a knife against revolvers in the hands of several determined men and he slinks away. That night the emigrant camp is visited and the little daughter of the leader is carried off to be tortured. Red Wing recognizes in her the little daughter of her benefactor and in the early morning she rouses the child before the warriors are awake and leads her down to the river, where she places the wondering child in a canoe and swiftly paddles down the stream, where a second canoe is manned and some of the red fiends furiously paddle away while the rest of the band turn to rush across the country, hoping to reach a point below the fugitives by working in a straight line instead of following the many windings of the stream. Red Wing is overtaken and wounded by a bullet, but before the pursuers can come up to her, the emigrants, who have been searching for the little one, are attracted by the sound of the shot and they reach a bend in the river just in time to fight off the redskins. This is the point for which the land party has been heading, and though they come up in support of those in the canoe, they are beaten off and the sorrowing emigrants make easy the last moments of the grateful girl.[96]

The praise for the film was exemplary. The reviews complimented the "picturesque surroundings," the well-told graphic story, and, again, the novelty of "the leading roles being sustained by real Indians." "This is a notable Indian picture in many important particulars," one review stated. Without naming Lilian's certain contribution, the critic complimented the "rich bead work" and "handsome headdresses," the "native manufacture" of the Indian dress (worn authentically), and the "Indian customs . . . observed throughout under the direction of the real Indians, who take leading roles." The Indian camp settings were pronounced "splendid," and the "flight by water" was exciting. "One interesting point of minor importance," added the critic, "is the fact that the canoes are paddled Indian fashion, from one side of the boat only, where there is a single paddler, and not on alternate sides."[97]

The success of *Red Wing's Gratitude* depended on the story's ability to reach white audiences and allow them to *become* Indians—that is, to "play Indian"—as they identified with the film's main characters and experienced their pathos. Colonialist nostalgia for nature and "primitivism" afforded audience members a temporary escape from the harsh reality of an industrialized world. Most white women could also identify with Red Wing's noble, self-sacrificing, and unappreciated experience as a drudge. The faulty belief that Indian men were worse than white men in degrading and devaluing the "weaker sex" made white women's lives tolerable.

James also appeared in *Red Wing's Gratitude*. He wasn't as physically imposing as Inslee, so his smaller stature made him a perfect Indian helper. If Vitagraph hoped to tempt the couple away from Bison Co. with *Red Wing's Gratitude*, Balshofer responded in kind and more strategically to the head of the family rather than to Lilian. James starred in *Young Deer's Bravery* (released on November 5), which provided the perfect vehicle for him and also initiated his very own namesake character. "Just at the right minute when things look pretty dark for Young Deer, the cowboys come to his aid, the Indians are repulsed and everyone made happy through Young Deer's bravery. This picture is most entertaining, exciting and splendidly acted," concluded *Moving Picture World*.[98] It's unknown if Red Wing made an appearance in the film, as the heroine was a white actress.

Next, Balshofer cast James as "Little Bear" and perhaps Lilian as Little Bear's sister in a film that was a bit daring for the times, *An Indian's Bride* (released on November 19). The story centered on a young western girl's love for an Indian. Its "great care as to details" and "magnificent photography" seem to have assuaged the fear of on-screen miscegenation—though the titillation remained. Lilian and James next appeared in Bison Co.'s *The Message of an Arrow* (released on December 3), a story tweaked from the plot of *The Falling Arrow*. Described in the pejorative language of the day, its theme was "the jealousy of a young Indian buck," Gray Wolf, when a "squaw," White Swan, "openly declares she loves a white man," Slim. Only an average film, according *to Moving Picture World*'s review, it showcased only "reasonable" acting and "apparently correct" costuming. Both Johnsons appear prominently in Bison Co.'s ad for the film. As White Swan, Lilian poses in supplication on Slim's (portrayed by Inslee) right, while Gray Wolf (James) is in hand-to-hand combat on his left.[99]

Just before Thanksgiving Bison Co. shot its last film on the East Coast. *The Love of a Savage* (released on December 17) followed an interesting and logical narrative progression concerned again with Indian-white love. This time two Indians, White Elk, presumably played by James, and Spotted Tail, probably played by a white actor, competed for the Indian maid, Arrow Head, apparently played by Lilian. The denouement featured White Elk tied "to stakes in the water" and left to drown with the rising tide. Arrow Head "comes to his rescue and with him in a canoe paddles away."[100] Again, the Indian princess rises to the occasion to perform a dangerous rescue. These films, as short and unsophisticated as they seem now, firmly established petite Red Wing as the first Native American actress of the silent screen. Her story had just begun.

CHAPTER 7

Edendale, California

"After a long weary ride of four nights and five days," later wrote Fred Balshofer, "our small company, consisting of Evelyn Graham, Charles French and his wife, Charles Inslee, J. Barney Sherry, Young Deer and his wife Red Wing, Bill Edwards (the prop man), Maxwell Smith, who came in Arthur Miller's place, and I, arrived in Los Angeles the day after Thanksgiving, November 1909."[1] According to Balshofer, there were two reasons the Bison Co. cast and crew headed west. One was to elude Slim McCoy, and the other was to shoot westerns *in the West*, where the landscape lent authenticity. In addition, the weather generally supported filming year-round. Bison Co. wasn't the first to move its operation to California, but it was the second to permanently do so. Selig Polyscope of the MPPC came first to Los Angeles, setting up a temporary studio in an old Chinese laundry on Olive Street and then a permanent studio at 1845 Alessandro Street (now Glendale Boulevard), located in Edendale, three miles west of Los Angeles. Bison Co. joined Selig the next year, and Edendale became the epicenter for California filmmaking several years before Hollywood gained the title.[2]

Initially, Balshofer and French, now director and assistant manager of Bison Co.'s California stock company, intended to return to New York in the springtime.[3] They rented a "hilly" lot on Alessandro Street, a block from Selig's, for forty dollars a month. The fenced-in property included a barn, some shacks, and a four-room bungalow, where Balshofer set up a processing lab and office. The property also featured an old grocery and feed store, which the crew turned into a studio.[4] Red Wing and the rest of the stock company changed costumes in the old building and performed interior shots on an eighteen-by-eighteen-foot outdoor stage constructed by the crew.[5]

The day before Christmas, Bison Co. released its first California endeavor, *An Italian Love Story*, with Graham, Darrell, and Charles Avery, a short actor who often played a childlike imp.[6] Local orange groves provided plenty of scenery for Balshofer's new junior cameraman, Maxwell Smith Bruzzel, better known as Maxwell Smith.[7] The company followed with *The Red Cross Heroine*, released on New Year's Eve. When 1910 dawned in the Golden State, Balshofer decided to produce more westerns, as well as military films. Both were wildly popular, and both were good investments, costing as little as $112 to make.[8] Wages for stock actors like Red Wing amounted to about thirty-five dollars per week. Bison Co., according to Balshofer, often "turned out a one-reel picture in two days and sometimes finished a picture between sunup and sun-down." From November 1909 to July 1910 Balshofer completed a whopping 185 pictures, that is, two films every three days.[9] In an era that did not list film credits, employ stunt people, or acknowledge the status of "movie star," Red Wing's work was tough, thankless, and anonymous. Still, it was often exciting, it kept her busy, and it paid the bills.

Most of Bison Co.'s ads, which appeared in *Moving Picture World*, featured a photo inset of one or more cast members. Today these faded stills help identify some of the films that featured Red Wing. For example, she and French appear in an ad for *The Red Girl's Romance*, which was released on January 7, 1910. (See appendix C for Red Wing's filmography.) As the synopsis of the film concludes, "The red girl and Petro . . . go to a . . . beautiful spot where they plight their troth."[10] Red Wing as "the Red Girl," her Spanish hero, played by French, and his trusty steed pose in an idyllic mountain setting, gazing into a hopeful future.

California served as a virtual Eden. Filmmakers found sprawling landscapes that offered new possibilities for scenarios and for actors. In utopian California, Lilian Margaret St. Cyr Johnson faded into the past. Her birth name and her husband's surname no longer represented her. She was now and would be until she died Red Wing. In addition, her husband dropped Johnson like a hot potato and morphed permanently into Young

Deer. As Red Wing and Young Deer, they were *the* Indian actors to meet or beat in California, both hailing from Carlisle and the Winnebago tribe in Nebraska, if anybody asked. Notably, their stage names designated their authenticity as Indians. It's no wonder. The new moving pictures reflected the country's imperialistic, nationalistic, patriarchal, and white supremacist ideologies, deeming all Native actors—who were few and far between—über-Indians, usually of the Plains, regardless of origin. The complexity that was American Indian identity in the early twentieth century was lost on the general public. And no matter how many times film critics yearned for authenticity with regard to a film's ethnographic details, what counted as authentic *narrative* was a mythical, ahistorical view of Indians as enemies or helpers, as "good" Indians or "bad."

The motion picture industry contributed to the utopian promise of Southern California that Helen Hunt Jackson's 1884 novel, *Ramona,* propagated.[11] *Ramona* portrayed a Southern California love affair threatened by racism during the Spanish missionary period between beautiful Ramona, a Scotch Indian mixed-blood woman, and dashing Alessandro, a mission Indian. Jackson, who included a heartbreaking chapter on the Winnebago being ousted from Minnesota in her first nonfiction book, *A Century of Dishonor*, created her fictional account of Ramona's life to tug at the heartstrings of America in the same vein as *Uncle Tom's Cabin.* More specifically, she hoped that Ramona's story would gain sympathy for the plight of Indians as *Uncle Tom's Cabin* ostensibly did for America's enslaved population. But like Harriet Beecher Stowe's best seller, *Ramona*'s greatest influence was to romanticize a racist institution, in this case, the Spanish missionary system.[12] Subsequently, a distinct California aesthetic emerged that covertly celebrated colonialism. Spread through tourism and world's fairs, the "missionary style" also became California's regional expression of the nationalist Arts and Crafts movement.

The film industry was poised to popularize this California ideal. Red Wing's former employer, the Biograph Company, arrived in sunny Los Angeles that January of 1910 to contribute its influence. Under Griffith as director, the company stayed for three months "for the express purpose of making 'Ramona' in authentic locations."[13] Griffith returned later to set up a permanent studio for Biograph, but during his brief visit in 1910 he made several films with a Spanish colonial mission theme that virtually erased real Native resistance from memory. Griffith made three films at the San Gabriel Mission in Los Angeles County, the historic site of the 1775 Tongva (Gabrielino) Indian rebellion.[14] He also directed *In Old California*, replete with a Spanish señorita. Finally, he made *Ramona* in Ventura County at Camulos, "one of the five homes accredited to the real Ramona that Mrs. Jackson picked for her fictional one."[15] Not surprisingly, Griffith chose the adorable, photogenic, and skillful pantomimer Mary Pickford, with her high cheekbones and eyes that photographed dark, to play Ramona.

The story was so popular that four other Ramona ingénues followed Pickford's lead (Adda Gleason in 1916, Dolores del Rio in 1928, Loretta Young in 1936, and Esther Fernandez in 1946), not to mention those who played her annually at San Gabriel's Mission Play and the Ramona Pageant, performed in Hemet, California. Red Wing never played Ramona, but she played characters like her, such as the Indian maiden in *The Red Girl's Romance*.

Just as the Mission style promoted a mythic and timeless California, the state's landscape appeared in films as conveniently mutable. Shortly after Bison Co. moved to Edendale, the NYMPC leased a large ranch from the Santa Monica Water and Power Company. Covering at least a thousand acres, the property, according to Balshofer, was just north of Santa Monica "and included Santa Ynez canyon in the Santa Monica Mountains."[16] "There are orange and banana groves, grape vineyards, and in fact almost any kind of tropical scene can be found upon the ranch," *Moving Picture World* explained. Mount Lowe's snow-capped peaks, which anchored the site, afforded "winter scenes" year-round. The Pacific Ocean also bordered the ranch, offering the company "a fine beach front, a mile in length" to film "tales of the deep blue sea." The site also included "three hundred acres of prairie land" for films about "life on the plains." A colonial mansion was among the several buildings on the estate that, according to *Moving Picture World*, housed the members of the Bison Co. stock company, who enjoyed "the vast pleasures of this modern 'Garden of Eden.'"[17]

The Bison stock company, as Balshofer often called his company of actors and extras, did not really reside on the property, however. According to Balshofer, only a few cowboys who cared for Bison's horses lived in the shacks that dotted the property. Still, the "Garden of Eden" represented Old Mexico for some films and Wyoming or South Dakota for others, while the Pacific coast transformed easily into the Atlantic seaboard. The ranch represented "life on the plains" as easily as California's gold country. This variability of place allowed Red Wing a multitude of roles as well. Although she played mostly Indian maidens, she also portrayed a Mexican señorita, an Anglo pioneer girl, and a Gypsy vagabond. Still, her forte was a sufficiently picturesque and appropriately grateful "red girl." In this role she played the love interest of many dime-novel characters: an Indian chief's son, a Cheyenne warrior, a treacherous half-breed, a heroic cowboy, a gritty miner, or the ever-loving squaw man.

Other Bison Co. films for January release included *A Red Man's Devotion* (probably with Young Deer) and *A Cowboy's Reward*.[18] On February 11 the company also released another Young Deer vehicle entitled *Young Deer's Gratitude*. Although scant dialogue in the form of intertitles survive from these films, *Moving Picture World* recorded one of the lines for the film that conveys Young Deer's stock character: "White squaw no bad heart—me bring papoose to-night—when high moon—Angel Gulch."[19] One critic declared, "This is a fairly good Indian picture, but practically the same story has been told by Young Deer at least twice before, once for this same company and once for Vitagraph."[20] Apparently, the public did not find Young Deer as a film hero as compelling as the heroine, Red Wing.

When Bison's *Government Rations* (released February 15) appeared in theaters, it was clear that critics and moviegoers wanted to see an Indian's gratitude as a ward of the United States. The film was loosely based on the Dakota War of 1862, when the Indians "went on the warpath," according to *Moving Picture World*'s story synopsis. The plot point that radically differed from history involved a military officer who believed someone in the tribe stole rations. Taking it a step further and making it more California, the storyline scapegoated three Mexican men for the theft. As one critic wrote, "When the mistake is discovered by the finding of the Mexicans devouring the rations, the colonel calls a truce, apologizes to the Indians in a very gentlemanly manner indeed, they all smoke and peace reigns once more over the scene." The critic found "certain attractive features" in the film's resolution to elicit "a glow of satisfaction" from the audience.[21] The "glow" was self-serving. Indian women and children endured starvation as a result of the military's false accusation. However, when the tribe received its "gentlemanly" apology from military officials, tribal members felt more than happy to reside peacefully within the limits of their reservation. The moral of the tale was simple. As long as the Great Father acted civilly, the Indians would adjust to their lot in life. Red Wing played one of the starving Indian women and appears among several other Indian characters in Bison's ad. She may also have contributed to the story line, at least in terms of explaining why the Minnesota Indian "uprising" might have been justified in the first place.

A few days after the release of *Government Rations*, the *Los Angeles Times* featured a lengthy article describing the new film center in Edendale, headlined as "Quite a Colony." It explained that the Bison Co. followed Selig to the area and that more than fifty people from Biograph had just arrived. It also stated that there were "upwards to 200" actors residing in the Los Angeles area along with "about two-score trained horses with the outfits and almost a trainload of properties and costumes."[22] Eddie Dillon probably rejoined Biograph at this time. Bison's remaining stock company included French and his wife, Helen French, Inslee, Graham, Darrell, Sherry, Avery, and, of course, Red Wing and Young Deer, who received special praise in the article: "Indian pictures have occupied the attention of the New York Motion Picture Company to a large extent during the past month, and they have two genuine Indians to take part in the scenes. They are Young Deer and Miss Redwing, members of the Winnebago tribe, both of whom have posed for some of the best-known artists in the country, and are perfect types of their race."[23]

Major A. J. McGuire, an older, mustached, gray-haired actor, and several professional cowboys and broncobusters, such as Tex Cooper, William "Billy" Gibbons, Milt Brown, and Jess McGaugh, who also handled Bison's horses, joined Bison Co. about this time. Frank Montgomery signed on to play leads, and Jack Conway joined the stock company along with Eugene "Gene" Allen and Howard Davies.

Marguerite Favar, Edna Maison, and Marin Sais came on as ingénues. The camera absolutely loved the Australian-born Favar, with her radiant smile. She was slender, with dark hair and flirty dark eyes. Favar, born Adelaide Farwarth, emigrated from Australia to the United States with her mother, Alice, and first gained recognition as a dancer in the Lewis and Clark Exposition in Portland, Oregon, in 1905. Maison was an earth mother type who loved animals. She began her career as an opera singer. Born in San Francisco to a French father and a California-born mother, she had a distinctive square jawline and beautiful piercing dark eyes.[24] Sais was a beautiful, wide-eyed equestrian who didn't stay in the stock company as long as the other women.

In addition, the company hired two child actors, Buster Emmons and Virginia "Bebe" Daniels.[25] Emmons, born Marion Paul Emmons, was a native Californian born in 1905. Daniels came from Selig Polyscope, where she apparently played Dorothy in the first *Wizard of Oz*. Two of the children's parents also joined the company. Buster's father, Roswell Gay "Bob" Emmons, who hailed from Kentucky and had been a deputy sheriff in Nebraska, came on as an actor with deep-sea-diving skills. Bebe's divorced mother, Phyllis Griffin Daniels, acted in several Bison pictures, at least once as the Indian female lead, though Balshofer later described her as his secretary.[26] Finally, Red Wing's most prominent leading man, Swiss-born George Gebhardt (also "Gebhart") and his wife, Madeline West, who played Inslee's Gypsy wife for Griffith in 1908, joined the company. Gebhardt, born in 1879, was tall, dark, handsome, and brooding. Indian roles became his greatest contribution, at least in Young Deer's opinion. Maxwell Smith continued as assistant cameraman, and the multitalented Thomas K. Peters, who had previously worked as a cameraman and a magician, specialized in designing and building film sets.[27]

The Cowboy and the Schoolmarm (released March 1) is one of the few extant films Bison produced at this time that features Red Wing.[28] Preserved by the EYE in Amsterdam, it is tinted and displays Dutch titles.[29] The film is in remarkable condition, however, and is lively, endearing, and quite entertaining. Although the EYE has not identified the actors, it is not difficult to make them out. Jewell Darrell plays the sweet schoolmarm. Bebe Daniels and Buster Emmons play two of her students. Evelyn

Graham appears in a cameo as Bebe's mother. J. Barney Sherry stars as the classic villain, whose desire for the hand of the schoolmarm leads to a rousing horse chase. Frank Montgomery plays Jim, the schoolmarm's true love interest and foil for the villain.

Red Wing and Young Deer first appear in the film as the Indian helper couple in a western saloon scene. The saloon scene, introduced in *The Squaw Man*, became a typical entry scene for Red Wing's characters. She would walk into the saloon usually to sell beadwork, and one or more white men would harass her. This time she walks into the saloon with Young Deer, and Sherry's character plays the harasser. Sherry shoves Red Wing to the floor as she tries to show him her wares. Young Deer tries to stand up for her, but he is no match for Sherry, who towers over him. Nor are any of the other cowboys in the saloon, played by McGaugh, Avery, and George E. Stanley. In the nick of time, Frank Montgomery's character intervenes and points a gun at Sherry. The Indians leave peaceably, but not before Young Deer gives Sherry a once-over that surely would have included an "ugh" if it was not a silent film. Next, Sherry's character and two of his henchmen, played by William Gibbons and Major McGuire, abduct the schoolmarm. The Indian couple watch in the shadows as the foursome rides quickly by. Young Deer instructs Red Wing to follow the group on foot and lay down her beads like Gretel to mark their trail.

Up until this point in the film, Red Wing's acting is nonchalant and without the artifice of Indian stoicism that Young Deer displays. But given the impossibility of following the riders on foot, Red Wing's mannerisms become overly dramatic to the point of being comical. She falls several times, gets up, and places her hand on her chest to feign exhaustion. After this scene, Young Deer pairs up with Montgomery in pursuit of the villains, who have kidnapped Darrell's character. Red Wing catches up just in time to see Montgomery and his Indian sidekick save the day. They shoot the henchmen and capture the villain, who has been unhorsed—although Sherry's character could easily have shot both men before they reached him. The film ends happily with Jim and the schoolmarm's passionate kiss as they sit on their horses. A "kiss" between their horses concludes the film.

Just before the film was released, Red Wing took a bad fall from her horse, probably during one of the daredevil bareback-riding stunts for which she became known. It may have been while making *The Indian and the Cowgirl* (released March 8), since her character didn't ride a horse in *The Cowboy and the Schoolmarm. The Indian and the Cowgirl* had no Indian female characters, but Bebe Daniels played a child fastened to her horse by bad cattle rustlers, who "sent the beast careering over the plains." The film featured "some wild riding, ending by the discovery of the horse bearing the child and his capture by the dexterous use of the lasso."[30] Since Red Wing was small in stature, and since she admitted to doing stunts for others, she likely played Bebe's stunt double. In fact, she performed a similar stunt with a few tweaks that made it even more dangerous in a film the following year.

After the accident, Red Wing quickly returned to work, as the March 5 issue of *Moving Picture World* reported: "The many friends of Red Wing, the only full-blooded Indian actress posing for motion pictures, will no doubt be pleased to hear that she has fully recovered from the accident with which she met a few weeks ago." The general entertainment publication *Billboard,* as well as the more prestigious *New York Dramatic Mirror,* also mentioned her recovery.[31] Coverage of the accident firmly established her reputation as a serious western actor. Balshofer correctly decided the time was right to highlight his brave Indian heroine.

Following the release of a military film and two odd western love stories involving rattlesnakes (in one of them Red Wing played a minor role as a white woman), Bison released two films for its first series starring its perfect female "Indian type."[32] *Red Wing's Loyalty* (April 8) and *Red Wing's Constancy* (April 15) made Red Wing a household name. Bison's ad for the former exclaimed, "We predict for this release long lived memory, because of its superiority, having all previous films manufactured by this company beaten to a stand still."[33] An ad for the latter film boasted that "the story is an exceedingly interesting one and the photography excellent."[34]

A Bison ad declared the film series "a tremendous success." It preceded the first renowned silent movie serial, *The Perils of Pauline,* by four years, but the films no longer exist, as far as anyone knows. However, their themes again came directly from Edwin Milton Royle's *The Squaw Man*: "An Indian romance in which an Indian girl is represented as succoring the man who helped her in her hour of need." An ad, as well as a surviving photo still for *Red Wing's Loyalty*, shows Young Deer playing the "unscrupulous half breed" who frames a military officer, played by Frank Montgomery, for murder. This induces Red Wing to repay a debt of gratitude to the officer, who earlier aided her because she saved him from being burned at the stake by the Indians, who, of course, have been misled by the half-breed.[35]

Red Wing's Constancy departed from the standard Indian helper narrative, however. In fact, one reviewer was taken aback by the story line: "A picture in which death is rampant, though possibly it is somewhat softened in its effect by the fact that it comes in each instance in a fair combat. Red Wing could have shown her constancy to her cowboy husband quite as well in some other way than in pursuing and killing his murderer, even though that has some justification."[36] The ad for the film shows Red Wing kneeling on a grassy slope with her arm outstretched to the sky, perhaps holding a knife. A dead man lies in front of her, while several cowboys, including one played by Charles French, stand or sit on horses behind her, all witnesses to her act of vengeance.[37] This time the half-breed, probably again played by Young Deer, attempts to woo Red Wing away from her white husband. In response, Red Wing's spouse pursues the half-breed, overtakes him, and honorably decides on hand-to-hand combat, yet he is dishonorably stabbed and killed by his rival. Red Wing finds the body and seeks the sheriff, played by French. The sheriff and his cowboys (played by Avery, McGaugh, Gibbons, Blanchard, and McGuire) pursue the half-breed but can't find him. Red Wing "determines to capture the half breed herself," tracking him "to a woodland." Her tracking skills and her desire for retribution lead her right to him. She then slyly tricks him by coaxing him to a grave that has already been dug. The scene culminates in a short knife duel in which she stabs the half-breed to death. Apparently, Red Wing's *constancy* was a more potent form of Indian loyalty than the public—or at least one motion picture critic—could stomach. After leading the sheriff and the cowboys to the dead body in the grave, tough little Red Wing "spurns the reward offered for his death, feeling repaid by being her husband's avenger."[38]

Another Bison player suffered a serious accident, demonstrating how many dangers pioneer silent film actors faced. Twenty-five-year-old Marguerite

Favar, the ingénue with the fetching eyes and brilliant smile, fell out of a buggy and was struck unconscious during the filming of a scene on Los Feliz Road near Elysian Park, a popular location for filmmaking. As she stood up in the buggy to throw a kiss to her on-screen beloved, the horse bolted, and she was pitched from the carriage. An ambulance arrived to rush her to the Sister's Hospital, but not until a cameraman recorded the accident. The *Los Angeles Herald* reported on the event, taking special notice of "a new point in legal procedure": "This is the first instance on record in which an accident, threatening such serious consequences, has been caught in its entirety by a motion picture camera. . . . Should the young woman die it is likely that the pictures would be introduced in . . . evidence before the court."[39] Favar only suffered a concussion and did not choose to sue her employer, despite the "new point in legal procedure." Early Californian film companies gave little attention to safeguarding their actors because actors had not yet unionized to demand their safety. Bison Co.'s fast pace kept the stock players on their toes. They had little time to think about anything but the next film.

Maxwell Smith may have been the cameraman who recorded Favar's accident. He also placed the photos he took at this time in a scrapbook. One of the photos shows Red Wing in her home.[40] She is sitting on an oak Mission-style side table. To keep her legs from dangling in midair, one foot rests on the table's lower shelf, and the other is balanced on the head of an open-mouthed bearskin rug laid out in front of the table. Her hair is put up, she wears dangling earrings and a medallion necklace, and a beaded head-band beautifully frames her dark hair. White crocheted collar and cuffs ornament her dark dress. Peeking out from under the hem of her simple frock are dark silk stockings and little black Mary Jane shoes with small white ornaments. A sculpted Victorian vase sits next to her on the table. Magazines and newspapers have been arranged neatly on the shelf next to her tiny shoe. The shelf also holds some of the intricate beadwork items that appear in her films, including a beaded sash with a Great Lakes motif. Several beaded framed photographs surround her. One shows a woman in traditional Native dress, but it's not clear who she is. Red Wing appears in the other three photographs wearing a man's Plains Indian headdress.

Many publicity photos show Red Wing in Indian costume, but Smith's portrait of Red Wing is rare. Not only is she dressed in modern fashion like the "Indian of today," she is shown in her own home. This rare glimpse of her domicile in 1910 represents exactly what Meyer Berger witnessed in 1958: Native handiwork, pictures of family, and pictures of Red Wing all crowded neatly into a small, cozy space. Endearingly charming, Red Wing with her dimpled chin faces the camera while her sparkling dark eyes look coyly to the side. Despite the childlike quality Red Wing shared with Mary Pickford, she appears fierce enough to give the threatening bear rug a boot.

The photo offers an idealized vision of Red Wing's domestic life that probably didn't match her reality. Making silent films as a western actor proved mentally, emotionally, and physically demanding, but working with her husband day in and day out seems to have become increasingly difficult. The couple shows a remarkable on-screen chemistry for certain. But the basis of their intimacy might have been how much they enjoyed performing together in a make-believe world.

Red Wing and Young Deer differed greatly in how they expressed their desire for fame. Red Wing enjoyed posing and entertaining for their own sake. Moreover, the film industry allowed her to express strength without fear of reproach, despite her gender. Progressive Era values encouraged women to participate in physical activities as long as they did not compete with men or were violent, a line her character crossed in *Red Wing's Constancy*. Red Wing used her athletic abilities to advantage, making the character "Red Wing" synonymous not only with "Indian gratitude" but also with female prowess. On the one hand, Red Wing's contributions made "real Indians" visible to the public and demonstrated how they outshone white actors acting in redface. On the other hand, Red Wing displayed courage equal to any man's. The Indian kitsch images of her wearing a man's headdress in Smith's photo advertise her power. Furthermore, the little lady holding the bear down with her tiny shoe was no damsel in distress. The next four years proved Red Wing an undefeatable, amazing heroine—with Young Deer's support and without.

The odds of reservation folks seeing any of Red Wing's Bison films was slim to none. The closest theaters were probably in Sioux City, Iowa, and

Omaha and Lincoln, Nebraska. Julia St. Cyr first spotted her little sister in a "moving picture show" sometime between 1910 and 1913. Seated in the dark theater, Julia gasped to see Lilian appear on the screen "seated on a pony in Indian trappings." She was so taken aback that she in turned surprised everyone in the movie theater when she burst out, "That's my sister—that's my sister."[41] The film may have been one of Bison's, but if it was produced after May 1910, it was not. Red Wing's employment with the New York Motion Picture Company was coming to a close. She played another Indian helper girl in *The Adventurers of a Cowpuncher* (April 22) and appears prominently in its ad, pointing the way to Major McGuire's character. Meanwhile, Young Deer played a comic role in blackface—of all things—in *Rattlesnakes* (April 26). One or both of them may have acted in *The Rescue of the Pioneer's Daughter* (April 29). Finally, Red Wing played an Indian girl in *Love and Money*. Her last film with Bison Co., released on May 6, was "full of action and very realistic," with every scene "well acted."[42]

CHAPTER 8

New Careers with Pathé Frères

In the late spring of 1910 Red Wing and Young Deer left Bison Co. for a better opportunity. Before they departed, they made several films to tide over Balshofer until he could replace them—or at least replace Red Wing. *The Mexican's Jealousy*, *Perils of the Plains*, and *The Tie That Binds* were released on May 20, 27, and 31, respectively. The ad for the former picture shows Young Deer in Mexican costume with two other bandito characters. Red Wing in Indian dress appears prominently with J. Barney Sherry in the ad for *Perils of the Plains,* though there is no Indian helper described in the film's synopsis. Red Wing and Young Deer are also pictured in a still from Maxwell Smith's scrapbook for *The Tie That Binds*, a domestic drama featuring Sherry, Maison, Favar, and Montgomery. The ad for the film seems more comic than dramatic, with Red Wing and Young Deer dressed in non-Indian clothing peeking out from a crowd of other actors.

Sometime shortly before the Johnsons left Edendale they posed in all their Indian finery with the stock company in front of the stage backdrop for *Love and Money*. Balshofer, NYMPC manager Charles O. Bauman, cameraman Maxwell Smith, and actor Pat Hartigan wore regular men's suits for the photo, while twenty others dressed as cowboys and cowgirls. A few people pictured in the photo have been lost to memory, but many more went on to make names for themselves in silent films and even in the talkies, though their early Bison films are largely unknown. Two important Bison actors are missing from the group, Charles Inslee and Jewell Darrell.

Red Wing and Young Deer appear in their best Indian costumes. They frame each side of the photo, leaning elbows on two large ceramic pedestals. Young Deer stands out, draped with articles of beautiful Native beadwork. He wears the requisite Plains Indian headdress and beaded vest, as well as gorgeous beaded moccasins. He also displays pieces that look to be Red Wing's handiwork, a sash and matching bandolier bag. Beaded choker, cuffs, and leggings adorn his outfit, while his cheek is ornamented with a painted Navajo symbol in the shape of a backward swastika.

Red Wing looks stunning in her floor-length Red Wing series fringed deerskin gown. She wears a headband and feather, which was not something Native women actually wore but which identified Red Wing as an Indian maid for her public. A Ho-Chunk-style beaded sash worn over one of her shoulders covers several long necklaces that fall Ho-Chunk style below her waist. The long tail of a silver concho belt descends to the hem of her dress, where beaded moccasins peak out. She radiates beauty.

Not long after the photo was taken, another film company "lured" Red Wing and Young Deer from Bison. "About 1910 the Pathe Co. came to America & signed me to a contract to make Western & Indian Films," Red Wing recalled. "We had our own Studios at Edendale & Hoot Gibson, Jack Hoxie, Milt Brown, Bebe Daniels & Lewis Stone were some of the actors who worked for us."[1] Pathé Frères, a large film company based in Paris, decided to make moving pictures in the United States, particularly westerns, which Europeans loved. Company heads chose New Jersey as home base and opened operations about fifty miles from Fort Lee in Bound Brook in April 1910. The well-known French photographer and director Louis Gasnier arrived to manage and direct for the company's American branch.[2]

Young Deer's varied experience, his Indian persona, and of course the acting talents of his "real Indian" wife made the couple a desirable commodity for the French company, whose westerns received criticism for lacking authenticity. Notably, Young Deer's little Indian wife, as shown by her recollection, did not see herself solely as a photoplayer, however, but as part of the western division's management team.

The initial trade magazine press for American Pathé asserted that its parent company was by and large well respected. "When Pathé Frères first proposed to make pictures in this country," stated the *Film Index*, "exchangemen and exhibitors awaited their first American release with interest, for they knew that, if Pathé Frères could produce good American subjects with the same photography and finish that they placed in their French films, they would have some great features for their audiences."[3] The American division released its first film, *The Girl from Arizona*, on May 16. Shot at Fort Lee, the film features Pearl White in her film debut. White began her career as a stage actress but became famous for her role as Pauline in the widely popular series *Perils of Pauline*, which debuted in 1914.

After *The Girl from Arizona*, White played in Young Deer's directorial debut for Pathé, *White Fawn's Devotion: A Play Acted by Red Indians in America*.[4] The restored film was added to the National Film Registry in 2008, but White has not been credited with the role of White Fawn, which some mistakenly attribute to Red Wing. White, wearing Red Wing's concho belt and perhaps her dress, played an Indian mother opposite Paul Panzer, who acted as her "squaw man" husband. *Moving Picture World* characterized the "dramatic story, with native life and customs as accurately depicted as possible," as "an improvement in this respect over some of Pathé's previous attempts at illustrating Indian life."[5] This was a coup for Pathé and its Indian director, although the *Nickelodeon* exaggerated Young Deer's Indian authenticity (as does the National Film Registry): "Pathé Frères announce that from now on they will release regularly each Saturday an American made film which will be a feature. For June 18 they announce an Indian picture, 'White Fawn's Devotion,' *which has been produced under the personal direction of a native Indian chief.*"[6]

Technical World Magazine also featured the "native Indian chief" and his "young wife" in its June issue. Henry M. Hyde, special correspondent for the *Chicago Tribune*, edited the progressive journal, which covered early to recent technologies. The June issue included a long article on cliff dwellings, as well as the story of Young Deer's five-pound vest, made up of "150,000 beads." This vest, which he wore in the Bison stock company photograph, shows up more times and on more characters than one can count in Red Wing and Young Deer films. An unnamed Lakota woman from Pine Ridge made the vest and apparently also constructed Young Deer's holster, cartridge belt, cuffs and sleeve band, as well as a bridle and saddle blanket, pictured in the article. She decorated the vest with "two Sioux warriors . . . carrying a feather-bedecked lance," "mounted on galloping ponies," and "attired in the war bonnets of the tribe." "The back of the vest is no less beautiful," stated the writer, "and likewise represents two mounted braves and two stags as well."[7] Young Deer in "his wonderful jacket of beads" is pictured front and back with an outfitted pony. Red Wing appears at the top of the page posed on a hill representing an iconic Indian maid praying to her god, Earth Maker. She wears her Red Wing series dress and concho belt. Interestingly, the article makes no mention of the couple's connection to the film industry.

The article made the standard claim that Young Deer graduated from Carlisle. It also claimed he was born on the Winnebago reservation but added something new—that he was "the son of Green Rainbow." Charles Green Rainbow was the only Green Rainbow living at this time on the reservation, but he had no surviving children.[8] He was an Indian policeman who followed the traditional Medicine Lodge religion and was known for his handmade snakeskin belts. Perhaps he "adopted" Red Wing's spouse during their visit to the reservation—maybe even that year. However, the adoption, if it occurred, was informal and not recognized by the tribe.

The alleged son of Green Rainbow continued directing for Pathé in New Jersey. He took on *Under Both Flags*, a lavish Civil War drama (released August 3), *The Red Girl and the Child* (released August 13), and *A Cheyenne Brave* (released August 17). Mrs. Young Deer's talents and appeal found fitting vehicles in the latter two films.[9] The *Film Index*, "a house organ" for Pathé and Vitagraph companies that later merged into the *Moving Picture World*, publicized Red Wing's first two Pathé films with several photo stills.[10]

The trade magazine advertised *The Red Girl and the Child* as "a Western Drama of the right kind with plenty of exciting situations and full of ginger and snap." The "right kind" meant it looked like an American western should look, while Red Wing's charming performance and the story's pacing provided the film's "ginger and snap." Today New York City's Museum of Modern Art holds a copy of the film, which offers a broad range of the acting talents and athletic prowess of Pathé's new Indian princess. The film opens with cowboy Dick Sutton saying good-bye to his wife and toddler before he rides to town. After entering the general store / saloon, Sutton stops cattle rustler Bill from bullying "the Red Girl," played by Red Wing, who is (again) selling her beadwork in the barroom. The lovely actress wears her own hair in two braids and her Red Wing series dress. Her performance displays poignant vulnerability and femininity as Sutton comes to her aid. Soon after, Sutton's wife arrives, crying out that the vengeful Bill has kidnapped their child. The ever-grateful Red Girl then effortlessly mounts her horse and rides off like the wind with Sutton to rescue the child.

George Larkin, who appeared in Young Deer's *Under Both Flags*, plays Sutton. Larkin began performing with his acrobat family at age six. Nicknamed "Daredevil Larkin," his agility equally matched that of his Indian heroine. Larkin was five years younger than Red Wing and cut a dashing figure with his thick dark wavy hair and piercing dark eyes.[11] As Sutton he dresses in white chaps and Young Deer's beaded vest. Larkin's sexy swagger complements Red Wing's feisty yet measured Red Girl.

When the two discover the child's skirt on the trail with "follow and I will kill the kid" etched in blood on it, the Red Girl decides to disguise herself as "a lad." Attired just like her leading man in little white chaps and a cowboy hat, the cross-dressed and fetching Red Girl creeps into the sleeping camp to rescue the child, who is played by Violet "Baby" Radcliffe. When the Red Girl finds the toddler, she "ties it on her back in her native way and starts back." Pursued by Bill and his henchmen, Red Wing scales a slate-covered hillside with the real child actor holding on for dear life. When the bad guys reach her, "the Indian woman hauls herself, with the child still on her back, hand over hand over a rope stretched across a wide and deep gully."[12] Only the depth of the gully appears contrived.

No stunt double stands in for Red Wing as she performs a feat most women couldn't do without a burden, let alone with a child strapped on. When the Red Girl reaches the other side of the ravine, she cuts the rope, and Bill and his gang fall into the chasm. The last scene of the film shows the Red Girl returning the child to the grateful and happy Suttons. The scene is joyful, made more so because Red Wing does not appear to be acting. She simply lights up when Baby Violette hugs and kisses her affectionately to say good-bye. As the *Film Index* critic rightly judges, "The action from the beginning is rapid and natural, and the bit of heart interest that centers about the child is sure to arouse a sympathetic interest."[13] The *Dramatic Daily Mirror* also responded with "liberal applause." However, the critic had some complaints: "Great pains were taken to select peculiarly romantic and striking scenes to go with the really novel and strongly interesting incidents that make up the story, but the basis of the plot is neither new nor plausible." The critic also noted a lack of care to detail, which the average filmgoer probably didn't notice.[14]

In contrast, critics viewed *A Cheyenne Brave* as "a straight Indian" picture, following the mode of Red Wing's earlier work with a thrilling fifteen-canoe-chase finale. Like *The Red Girl and the Child*, it displayed "spirited action from start to finish," but it lacked the emotional appeal of Red Wing's endearing performance in *The Red Girl and the Child*. "Some interest attaches to a love story of this character because it is a type of the heart stories of all men," *Moving Picture World* noted, "but the principal attraction of this story is the beautiful outdoor scenery, so well photographed and reproduced. The story may be needed to afford a reason for the long canoe journey, but there is little in it which appeals strongly to critics of love stories."[15]

The *Film Index* touted *A Cheyenne Brave* as "an Indian film with not a white man, woman or child in it," while *Moving Picture World* more accurately noted: "All the actors taking part in this picture are real Indians or sufficiently well made up to pass as such."[16] At least in terms of the three stills that remain, the film can be likened to Griffith's *Mended Lute*, because no other American Indian actors besides Red Wing appear in stills from the motion picture. This time, Larkin plays Red Wing's love interest. His acting as Red Shield, the Cheyenne brave—at least as shown in the photographs—reveals the telltale signs of a white actor playing Indian. Two fake braids frame his face as he folds his arms across his puffed-out bare chest. He juts his jaw forward and protrudes his lower lip to portray stoic defiance. Again, only the sound of "ugh" is missing to make him stereotypically Indian. "An Indian love story with a long chase through picturesque scenery is one feature and a duel between two Indians for another," summarized *Moving Picture World*. "But the girl's lover wins and, entering their canoe again, they depart for the land of the brave's people." A still from the last scene shows "the daughter of a Sioux chief" embraced by her lover, Red Shield, as they ride downstream in their honeymoon canoe, draped with a large quantity of leafy boughs.[17]

Meanwhile, Bison Co. released *Red Fern and the Kid* on July 15. It's possible Bison made the film with white actors after Red Wing and Young Deer left the company, but it had their stamp all over it.[18] Balshofer suffered the loss of his two "real Indian" actors, while Pathé American began reaping the rewards. Having proven their worth to Pathé, Red Wing and Young Deer returned to Los Angeles, shiny and new, near the end of July. They didn't go directly to Edendale but, according to the *Los Angeles Herald*, "registered at the Nadeau," a chic Los Angeles hotel in the heart of the city. "Mr. and Mrs. James Young Deer" were notably "full-blooded Winnebago Indians from New York city" and graduates of "Carlisle university," stated the *Herald*. Young Deer, a "representative of a French motion picture house," would "remain here for some time making outdoor western pictures in which Indians figure." Mrs. Young Deer would "assist her husband" and play "the leading roles in nearly all his picture plays."[19] Interestingly, both the *Los Angeles Times* and the *Herald* announced the sophisticated Indian couple's "arrival" as if they had never been in the area before.

While American Pathé began constructing its primary studio in Jersey City, Red Wing and Young Deer returned to Edendale to set up Pathé's West Coast Studio at 1807 Alessandro Street.[20] Selig Polyscope's large production studio, which boasted a new Mission-style facade, abutted the property at 1845 Alessandro.[21] Meanwhile, poor Balshofer, working for Bison at 1712 Alessandro, had more than his share of problems. On the plus side, Gebhardt and Inslee remained to play Indian leads. The company also acquired a handsome white stunt horse Balshofer lovingly named Snowball.[22] However, on the down side, Slim McCoy came to town, so Balshofer's problems with Edison's patent began anew. To make matters worse, Balshofer's "camera boy," Maxwell Smith, turned traitor. Balshofer and Gebhardt, armed with a .45 pistol, caught Smith in the act of nabbing the camera that McCoy suspected infringed on Edison's patent and that Balshofer kept locked up in his office. According to Balshofer,

Smith "blabbered out a confession that he had made sketches and used the office lights and our 5x7 still camera in an effort to make photographs for McCoy of the inside movement of my Pathé movie camera. . . . Smith nearly succeeded in his plan but almost lost his life for a few measly dollars."[23] Balshofer fired Smith and was out another member of his company.

Curiously, the Nestor and Champion film companies each released a film with a heroine named Red Wing that July.[24] Perhaps they didn't anticipate Red Wing's return from New Jersey. Red Wing, as her namesake or not, was hard to replace. Balshofer was left to cast white actresses for female Indian leads after Red Wing's departure. Marguerite Favar looks to be the Indian female lead in *A True Indian Brave* (released September 9) and *A Cowboy's Daring Rescue* (released October 11). Her obvious redface greasepaint made her look more like a female minstrel than an Indian princess. This lack of recognizable authenticity did not bode well for Bison Co. westerns.

Red Wing, Young Deer, and Smith weren't the only losses Balshofer suffered. Jewell Darrell got married and left the company. Unfortunately, she died sometime before Christmas of a heart condition at thirty-five years old. One trade paper listed her accomplishments on the stage and commemorated her wonderful comedic talent.[25] Bison Co. members and perhaps Red Wing and Young Deer paid tribute to their former colleague by filling a large wagon with flower arrangements they had designed themselves.

Charles K. French left Bison and came on board at West Coast Pathé in the fall. He served as assistant manager, director, and actor. Nearly six feet tall, French had brown hair and clear blue eyes. He was extremely athletic and much older than Red Wing, so playing her leading man was sometimes awkward. Born in Cleveland, Ohio, in 1860, French started his stage career at eighteen. He was best known for his blackface character Uncle Ned in the original stage production of *In Old Kentucky*.[26] The *New York Dramatic Mirror* reported that French was also "a great lover of horses" and had owned several prize-winning Thoroughbreds, making him a valuable asset to western films.[27] Why he jumped ship from Bison is unknown, but the new West Coast Studio offered opportunity with its established reputation, stable membership in the MPPC, and, perhaps, its more generous pay scale.

The Motion Picture Patents Company subpoenaed Balshofer for a deposition hearing in Los Angeles right after Smith's firing. "Kessel and Bauman came out to California post haste," said Balshofer, but "on the advice of all of our lawyers, they went back to New York, leaving me to face the situation alone." Balshofer fled to Big Bear Valley in the San Bernardino Mountains with the company just before the trial. At that time, the summer resort was "remote and practically unknown."[28] Apparently, no one had filmed there before—and with good reason. The terrain was so steep that Bison Co. cast and crew rode horses and hauled equipment on buckboards over the dirt road for the last twenty-five miles of the trek from the city limits of San Bernardino. Still, the mountain scenery and crystal-clear light filmed beautifully.

While Red Wing and Young Deer set up their new studio, hired actors, and scouted locations, Pathé American released the couple's New Jersey ventures to broad acclaim. That fall Bison Co. also released the last of the Red Wing and Young Deer series: *For the Love of Red Wing*, *Young Deer's Return*, *Red Wing and the White Girl*, and *The Flight of Red Wing* (September 20, October 4, November 4, and November 15, respectively). *Moving Picture World* panned *Red Wing and the White Girl*, asserting that the "acting and scenery are good" but that "there is the handicap that Western pictures which tell nothing in particular are no longer desirable."[29] The magazine had nothing to print about *The Flight of Red Wing*, since Balshofer was at Big Bear and too indisposed to send in publicity.[30] However, Jack Spears, film critic for *Film in Review*, lauded it as one of Red Wing's best for Bison Co.[31] Held by the British Film Institute today, it's the only extant film of the four. In this film Red Wing's father imprisons her after she refuses the man he wants her to marry, the disgusting Eagle Eye. Hal, a more pleasing cowboy, catches her eye. In the end Hal and his cowboys rescue her.

Smith's scrapbook includes a beautiful photo of Red Wing and Young Deer labeled "Young Deer's Return," though it is difficult to see its connection to the film's synopsis.[32] "Scorned by the father of the [white] girl he loved, whom he had saved from death in the burning desert," an ad for *Moving Picture World* summarized, "Young Deer goes back to savage life, discards civilized garments and weds a girl of his race." The film featured "splendid scenes of stirring interest, the fight with the bandits, the rescue from savage Indians, the winning of a sensational baseball game by Young Deer at Carlisle, etc., etc."[33] Smith's photograph, however, shows Young Deer and Red Wing in a saloon standing next to a seated cowboy, played by Pat Hartigan. Several cowboys, including George Gebhardt's character, drink and play cards in the background. Young Deer wears white man clothes except for his signature beaded vest and moccasins. On his arm in her long deerskin gown, Red Wing expresses disdain as Young Deer looks noticeably smug, holding a shot of whiskey while he talks to Harrington's character. If this photo represents the film, the scene must have been one of the film's last.

For the Love of Red Wing centered on the "terrible vengeance of an Indian for the death of his sweetheart result[ing] in the extermination of a band of settlers after a spectacular battle." Red Wing commits suicide so that a bad band of settlers can't recapture her after she escaped them. Young Deer plays her vengeful Indian sweetheart. "The finding of her body by her lover is intensely dramatic and pathetic," noted *Moving Picture World*'s reviewer, "and the weird funeral rites most interesting. The redskins are exhorted to a frenzied pitch, the settlers wiped out and their cabins burned."[34] Why the critic tolerated Indians wiping out settlers is unknown. They must have been extremely cruel to Red Wing.

Smith's scrapbook contains photos from this film, though they are mislabeled "Flight of Red Wing."[35] Young Deer, bare chested and loinclothed, wearing a Plains-style feathered bonnet, talks with J. Barney Sherry's character. Sherry looks to be playing an Indian chief in similar bonnet, vest, long pants, and beaded loincloth. The two men are outdoors, and Sherry points to the distance. Gebhardt, paying rapt attention to Sherry, plays a third Indian, scantily dressed with long braids. Sexy bare-chested and loinclothed younger males wait for direction. All the men express somber emotions, with their arms folded in front of their chests in the stereotypical Indian pose. Another of Smith's photos is set in an Indian camp. The same men and a few redface white women actresses express sadness; Red Wing's body lies dead in the foreground of the picture. The young men from the first photo carry her away from the Indian camp on a wooden stretcher.[36] *For the Love of Red Wing* literally and figuratively depicts Red Wing's final exit from Bison Life Motion Pictures.

Balshofer's troubles continued through the end of October. On his way to film at Cheney's Camp in the Santa Ynez Canyon, Balshofer, Gebhardt, Montgomery, and a friend found themselves stranded when their automobile broke down. The men separated to make their way back to civilization, but Balshofer and his friend lost their way in the dense brush. After three days and four nights without food, they were rescued.[37]

But conditions had already improved for Balshofer. "After an extended trip through Arizona," stated *Variety*, he "signed Mona Darkfeather to play the principal female Indian roles in all future Bison western pictures." Since Darkfeather's early films were set in snowy mountain scenery, she may have joined the company when they trekked to Big Bear. Balshofer promoted his new Indian princess by wildly exaggerating her qualifications, however, including her discovery and her uniqueness. "Real Indians have been prominent in photoplay for some time," *Variety* continued, "but none have attempted the leading characters."[38] Of course, the claim was blatantly false. What about Red Wing's large body of work?

Balshofer touted Darkfeather as a "full-blooded Indian girl" and promoted her as "Princess Mona Darkfeather." In reality his new leading Indian lady was a dark-eyed and dark-haired native Californian with Spanish ancestry who was born Josephine Workman. Darkfeather debuted in "the snappiest red skin picture of the season," *A Cheyenne's Love for a Sioux* (released November 25). She next appeared in *A Child of the West* (released on December 2).[39] Certainly, Balshofer felt compelled to stretch the truth about his new stock player to compete with West Coast Studio down the street. Even today some confuse Darkfeather and Red Wing. This may be because initially Balshofer mixed them up in his own memoir, published in the 1960s. His book includes a photo of Red Wing motioning to a canoe, but the illustration is mislabeled with the title of one of Darkfeather's films, *Little Dove's Romance* (released in 1911).[40] Another of his photos is identified as Darkfeather's "Little Dove's Gratitude," a title Bison never released. However, it's actually the photo still from Red Wing's *Dove Eye's Gratitude*. Balshofer understandably mixed up the films in his memory, but his clever promotion of Darkfeather during the 1910s significantly raised the appeal of Bison Co. westerns and probably allowed him at least a small taste of revenge against his former Indian leads.

Soon after New Year's Eve, Red Wing and Young Deer received great news. Pathé Frères released "the first picture received from our Coast Company," *The Yaqui Girl*. "A great Western picture with fine Mexican scenery," noted *Moving Picture World*, the film was probably shot in rural Los Angeles. Red Wing played Silver Leaf, the Yaqui Girl, but it is unknown who played Pedro, the Mexican troubadour who was her love interest. Although Silver Leaf became "fascinated" with Pedro, he was already in love with Marguerite, a Spanish maiden. Silver Leaf in a jealous rage threatens to go to authorities and inform them that Pedro is a bandito. Consequently, Pedro and Marguerite bind Silver Leaf flat on her back to a horse "without bridle or saddle" and "send the animal with its burden towards the boundless prairie." An Indian rescues Silver Leaf, and the story ends when Silver Leaf kills Pedro. As much as audiences found Silver Leaf's plight thrilling, *Moving Picture World* concluded that it was "not above the ordinary in any degree."[41] In addition, *Variety*'s critic deemed it inconsistent, stating flatly, "The arranger has taken liberty with Indian cunning, Mexican treachery and a form of punishment which lacks proper conception. Not badly photographed, but weak in construction."[42]

Young Deer, of course, was "the arranger" and used the same old ploy, tying Red Wing to a horse, that he had employed before and would use again. The stunt was extremely dangerous for his wife, no matter how unoriginal. *The Yaqui Girl* was also another story in which Red Wing's character crossed the line of racial and feminine propriety. Two of the three stills for the film, published by the *Film Index*, show her in an uncharacteristically negative light. In one she wields a knife or some other weapon, preparing to strike a kneeling Marguerite, while Pedro aims a gun at her from behind. In another she appears sullen and without remorse, standing among a group that includes a sheriff character, while Pedro lies on the ground dead, attended by Marguerite. Suffice it to say, the critics found Silver Leaf much too vengeful for their taste.

Red Wing and Young Deer lived in a house a couple of blocks from the studio at 1854 Alessandro Street. At the time Alessandro Street was a dirt road serviced from the city of Los Angeles by cable car. Most everyone in the cast and crew lived in the neighborhood, making it easy to gather them all up in the morning for a day of filming.[43] Just before winter they were also rounded up for company photographs, one of which appeared in *Moving Picture World*, entitled, "Pathé Stock Company—Operating at Los Angeles, California." The photo of nineteen individuals shows that a large portion of the company consisted of "vaqueros," the California moniker for cowboys. Another was taken outside the studio in and around Young Deer's spiffy Thomas-Detroit raceabout, which he was about to sell.[44] Edgar Willis, Carl E. House, Jesse E. Snow, Hart "Jack" Hoxie, Frank "Curly" Weinmann, Charles Davis, and "Pockets" Howland are the seven vaqueros.[45] Other company members pictured are former Bison Co. crew member Thomas K. Peters, set designer and builder; character actors Joseph De Grasse and Irvin Hay; actors Frank V. Biggy, William F. Ridgway, and Keith Breed (also the bookkeeper); assistant manager, director, and actor Charles K. French; and Young Deer, the prominent company head. Red Wing, the "Indian lead"; Virginia Chester, ingénue; Bessie Eyton, leading lady; and Miss Austin, whose first name is unknown, made up the stock company's ladies.

Several of those pictured went on to become well-known film actors. Tall, black-haired, and gray-eyed vaquero Hart Hoxie, who started as a circuit rodeo rider in Idaho at age fourteen, became one of the best-known cowboys on the early screen. Raised in modest circumstances, Hoxie never learned to read or write. He married five times. Marin Sais from the early Bison Co. was his third wife; they married in 1920. Hoxie changed the story of his origins to support the clean and shiny image of a western film star. His real name was John F. Stone or perhaps John Hartman Stone. Hoxie's family was extremely dysfunctional, so he doctored his family story for the press. His mother was identified as half Cherokee or half Nez Perce in publicity pieces, but neither was true. Calvin Scott Stone, whom the public only knew as Doc "Bart" Hoxie, was his father, a worse bad guy than any from Hoxie's westerns.[46]

Two other Bison actors, Joseph De Grasse and Bessie Eyton, also went on to carve out lasting names for themselves. De Grasse had aquiline features and light hair. He was French Canadian and brother to respected actor Sam De Grasse, who appeared in D. W. Griffith's *Birth of a Nation*. Joseph often played Indian chief fathers to Red Wing's characters in Pathé westerns. He acted in scores of films over the course of his career. He also wrote, produced, and directed. Joseph later teamed up professionally and in marriage with Ida May Park, a female director, rare for the times. The couple were directing and codirecting for Universal Pictures by 1917. They also nurtured the budding acting talents of Lon Cheney, with whom they became lifelong friends.

Auburn-haired, blue-eyed Eyton, born Bessie Harrison in Santa Barbara, California, was a talented actress not long at West Coast Studio. She had left the company by May 1911 to play leads for Selig Polyscope, where her husband, Charles F. Eyton, served as a producer.[47] Selig billed her as "one of the best swimmers on the West Coast," and she acted in "a number of aquatic pictures at Catalina Island."[48] Also an accomplished equestrian, Eyton became known for her western roles and later appeared with Red Wing in a Selig blockbuster. She was most known, however, for her 1916 portrayal of a Scarlett O'Hara–type southern belle in *The Crisis*, a Civil War picture. She remained with Selig Polyscope until the company went out of business in 1918.

Ingénue and soubrette Virginia Chester hailed from San Francisco and became one of West Coast Studio's more eccentric personalities.[49] She was only fifteen or sixteen when Young Deer hired her to play Marguerite in *The Yaqui Girl*. Chester suffered from mysterious illnesses while with West Coast Studio but acted in several roles in between recoveries. Chester later worked for Bison Co.'s second incarnation, Bison 101 Pictures. She also worked for Biograph, after which she married. "Admitting that her art means more to her than does married life," she left her husband in Utah in 1917, returning to Los Angeles to join the Mena Film Company. She and Marin Sais teamed up socially to put on "Bohemian gatherings" at Killarney Kottage, Chester's Hollywood bungalow. At this time, they also appeared together in Universal's *The Vanity Pool* with the equally bohemian Mary MacLaren, famed for her beauty and athleticism and later for her screenplay about a woman who unknowingly marries a homosexual. Although Chester eschewed traditional marriage, her leading lady status with the Mena Film Company represented a distinct move toward Christian values, as the company intended "to produce motion pictures that would illustrate, elucidate and popularize the various features of the Divine Plan of the Ages."[50]

Two other important cast members, Grave Digger and Black Demon, are pictured outside the studio, and they were known as the "two most famous death-dealing, cowpuncher-defying bronchos ever saddled." Hart Hoxie may have helped acquire at least Grave Digger after the horse fell and then crushed and killed Hoxie's former employer, famed broncobuster and Wild West showman Dick Stanley.[51] Broncobusting was terribly dangerous, but it was part and parcel of western films.

Pathé's vaqueros also performed steer riding, which was featured in the company's next film, *The Cowboy's Innocence* (released January 4, 1911). The story centered on Gertie and cowboy Bob, who meet at her uncle's ranch, where the cowboys put on a show for her, including riding "a savage steer." Bob is then framed when a Mexican character plants cards in the top of his boots, an old Bison Co. ploy. The Indian helper, played by Red Wing, witnesses the act and in the end saves Bob so that he can marry Gertie, but not until after the Mexican tracks her down and "attempts to make love to her."[52] The *New York Dramatic Mirror* deemed it a "great Western drama" that was "different from the ordinary."[53]

Just before moving into a brand new studio in Jersey City Heights in January 1911, American Pathé produced *The Battle at Redwood*, a story based on the Dakota War of 1862. Film critics deemed it "wild enough to suit almost anyone."[54] Obviously, no film sought to convey the extreme trauma Native people endured, including Red Wing's Minnesota relatives. Nonetheless, the success of the American Pathé films contrasted with the next West Coast Studio releases. Virginia Chester took the lead in Young Deer's next two films, *Trailed by an Indian* (released January 18, 1911) and *A Cowboy's Devotedness* (released February 4). The critics felt unmoved by the first story, although the *Nickelodeon* raved about the cinematography: "Pictures of such gem-like brilliancy are not often seen upon the screen. Whether this is due to the California atmosphere, or to clever manipulation of the photographic process is hard to say."[55] *Moving Picture World* expressed the same sentiment but more tersely: "The picture has scenic merit, but little else to commend it."[56]

Moving Picture World's critic found *A Cowboy's Devotedness* even less worthy: "Most of these Western pictures have a sameness to them that becomes monotonous with much repetition. They are interesting in a way, but unless some striking novelty is introduced they do not rise above the mass which has come from the studios in the past few months. The Pathes are masters of some subjects," the critic continued, "and would consult their own interests and conserve their reputation by devoting their efforts to the reproduction of some other variety of subject. Let the Western pictures go, and bring out those individual films which so often in the past have ranked among the masterpieces."[57]

This criticism struck at the core of Young Deer's professional reputation. It's unknown how the larger Pathé Frères organization responded to such negative reviews, but management must have been worried, given the investment it made in West Coast Studio. Nevertheless, Young Deer focused his attention on building "one of the largest and best-equipped plants on the Coast."[58] *Moving Picture World* reported that Pathé's "Edendale Studio holdings" covered an entire block, "which under the personal direction of Mr. James Young Deer, is being substantially improved as fast as a corps of artisans can perform the work."[59] A Mission-style facade replete with church bells would front the studio, nicely complementing Selig Polyscope's studio next door. *Moving Picture World* featured a photo of the street side of the new studio, pictured with an array of vaqueros, as well as a wonderfully descriptive write-up:

> The interior of the Pathe studio is beginning to resemble a "wild and wooly" frontier town of the early '70s. Here may be found a reproduction of the old frontier towns. Main street containing the "Sheriff's Office;" "Dance Halls;" several varieties of "Saloons;" "Hotel;" "Stage and Express Office;" "Gambling Halls," etc., too numerous to mention. Fill this street with cowboys and different characters in costume, and you are once again transported to the West of long ago—yet outside the wall modern electric trains whiz by at intervals, the tourist and commuter occupants staring in amazement at the cowboys, Indians, and posses in costume, galloping back to the studio after a hard day's work on exteriors.[60]

When the rains came nonstop in January 1911 the studio's continued construction was not the only challenge Young Deer and Red Wing faced.

Young Deer crashed into a lamppost in downtown Los Angeles when his Thomas-Detroit raceabout skidded on wet pavement. He and several friends were thrown out of the car onto "the muddy street," but fortunately no one sustained injuries.[61] It's unknown if Red Wing experienced the accident, but something had changed between her and her husband. She was no longer content with their marriage and perhaps with their business partnership as well. Meanwhile, the high rainfall severely impacted her filming schedule. Three other film companies kept studios in Southern California at this time, Selig, Bison Co., and Biograph. While Selig and Bison Co. had "a reserve supply of finished pictures," newer arrivals Biograph and West Coast Studio had to film whenever they could.[62]

Red Wing performed as the Indian lead in two motion pictures made about this time, *Silver Leaf's Heart* and *Lieutenant Scott's Narrow Escape*. She appears for the first time in a new dress with a Plains-style beaded yoke, a dress she later claimed she made herself.[63] The *Film Index* featured a wonderful photo of Red Wing in *Silver Leaf's Heart* wearing the new dress with her concho belt while she gestures to costar Charles K. French, who protects an unknown child. The film's narrative took off from *The Red Girl and the Child*, only this time an Indian abuses Red Wing's character, and his fellow tribal members kidnap the child. French's character intercedes, earning Silver Leaf's gratitude and, thus, the return of his daughter.

The *Film Index* critic also noted a scene that probably involved the infamous Grave Digger and Hart Hoxie: "Riding at breakneck speed one of the men is thrown from his horse, which stumbles and falls over him." This caused the horse behind him to fall, pinning the rider to the ground. It was a "nasty mix-up," reported the reviewer, that "might have resulted seriously but for the expertness of the riders."[64] As Balshofer had with Favar's accident, Young Deer filmed the accident and included it in the end product. Young Deer's innovative move was legally risky, as before, but Young Deer was becoming quite a risk taker.

Regardless of the film's exciting realism, *Moving Picture World*'s critic again found that the film's theme had run its course, and who could blame him for thinking so? "Another Indian subject, in which the gratitude of an Indian girl is made the basis for a lively and somewhat interesting conflict between the Indians and the white settler. There is a thrilling running fight, with one horse carrying three, and while the reproduction is as good as might be, the difficulty lies in the selection of the subject." The critic didn't mind a thought-provoking historical reference, but he complained that the "time has passed when these things occur in America."[65]

Despite criticism waged against West Coast Studio's worn-out scenarios, it must have been an exciting time to be involved in such a cutting-edge field. Young Deer received credit for another innovation, "discover[ing] a new photographic process for taking moonlight and firelight effects." "By his method," wrote *Moving Picture World*, "the negatives show a clearness of outline and background that could not be obtained by the old method." Young Deer utilized this "startling effect" in a new western that he claimed was "the best all around picture that he has so far taken."[66] Unfortunately, it's unknown which of his films featured this new special effect and if the film is extant. The process seems to have been particularly favorable for capturing western evenings, whether on the prairie or in an Indian camp.

Like Young Deer, Red Wing was no less a western motion picture innovator. Most of her films have been lost, but her contribution in those early years laid the groundwork for the rare "real Indian" actress—and many not so real—who followed her. It's likely she had a hand in other innovations as well, but gender bias toward Young Deer's achievements kept her influence, except as an actress, hidden from public recognition.

The first real Indian film actress appeared on the early February cover of the *Film Index* in a photo from *Lieutenant's Scott's Narrow Escape* (released on February 18). An unknown white actor playing Lieutenant Scott is pictured with Red Wing. His white horse and some Indian characters appear in the background in a romantic wooded landscape. Red Wing wears her new dress and holds a large southwestern water jar, to advertise the film's attention to ethnographic detail. But the water jar is also symbolic of the Indian maid's innate fertile and self-sacrificing nature, as Red Wing gazes with devotion toward the actor playing Scott, who is, in the end, the white man she rescues.

Motion Picture World's review of the motion picture fell a bit short of the promise of the *Film Index* cover. The critic found the "thrilling riding and other acts" as well as the "interpretation of plains life, representing cowboys and Indians . . . quite satisfactory." But again, the scenario was "nothing really new."[67] *Nickelodeon*'s critic found the film "fairly well done" but complained that it lacked "mental, moral," and "spiritual elements," as well as a love story: "As the action is neither very novel nor very thrilling it stirs only a mild degree of interest." Taking into account that the film was ultimately a Pathé Frères production that would be shown in Europe, the critic thought it might "serve to stir thrills where the Indian subject is not so well known as in America."[68]

It's no wonder the films' quality suffered. Young Deer and Red Wing pumped out new films one after the other in rapid succession. *Red Deer's Devotion*, *The Sheriff's Daughter*, *The Cattle Rustlers*, and *The Kid from Arizona* came out on March 8, 18, 22, and 25, respectively.[69] Young Deer acted as both Red Deer and "the kid." Red Wing and Bessie Eyton played Indian girls in *The Kid from Arizona*. Interestingly, Red Wing also played "the paleface lily" May, who attracted Red Deer's devotion.[70] The film's reception is incredibly ironic, given that Red Wing played a white woman. Although critics praised the cinematography as "commendably clear and steady," they were put off by Red Deer and May's cross-racial romance. "Melodrama pushed to the limit," wrote *Nickelodeon*'s critic. "The marriage between the Indian and the white heroine is not calculated to make the film popular; it hits one of America's most adamantine prejudices."[71] *Moving Picture World*'s review was even more scathing: "Another feature of this film will not please a good many. It represents a white girl and an Indian falling in love with each other. While such a thing is possible, and undoubtedly has been done many times, still there is a feeling of disgust which cannot be overcome when this sort of thing is depicted as plainly as it is here, even to the point where the girl decides to run away and join her Indian lover." Although May's father shows up with a gun to defuse "the tense situation" and send Red Deer running, apparently the scene occurred too late in the story to ease the anxiety of "a good many."[72]

On the other hand, contemporary scholars applaud Young Deer's daring for pushing the limits of racial prejudice and confronting the racist myth of miscegenation, which between a nonwhite male and a white female was much more taboo than its reverse. Although Mr. and Mrs.

Young Deer pulled a fast one in *Red Deer's Devotion*, apparently somewhere along the line Young Deer had tested Red Wing's devotion to its limit. Four days before the film's release, "Lillian St. Cyr Johnston [*sic*]" filed for a decree of divorce "against James Johnston, otherwise known as James Young Deer," and left him without an Indian female lead.[73]

It may simply be coincidence, but sometimes Young Deer's film scenarios coincided with events in his own life. Was he expressing feelings for a white woman, or was Red Wing upset that he asked her to play one? On the very day both the *Los Angeles Times* and *Herald* reported that Red Wing filed for divorce, *Moving Picture World* ran a lengthy public relations piece on Young Deer's ingénue, Virginia Chester. It touted the "very young" Chester, whose photograph accompanied the piece, as "one of the few actresses appearing in moving-picture work that has a special talent for Ingenue parts, and under the careful training and direction of Mr. Young Deer, the director, her future work in the pictures will help to maintain the high-class productions of the Pathe Frere's Studios."[74] The article means nothing on its own, but in time Young Deer gained a reputation for propositioning young actresses or would-be actresses. When Red Wing filed for divorce, California was not a no-fault divorce state and required a plaintiff to provide cause. Los Angeles County has lost her file, so there is no way to confirm what provoked her decision to file a decree. Whatever the cause, Red Wing held leverage to force change in her marriage. After all, she was not just Young Deer's Indian wife; she was West Coast Studio's most valuable asset.

CHAPTER 9

Leaving Young Deer

Moving Picture World reported that Red Wing was in New York City visiting friends a week after she filed for divorce. Young Deer apparently felt it necessary to divert attention from the real reason she left Edendale. Red Wing left no record of her stay in New York or if she actually did go there at all. Of course, she may have had friends there, but did she pursue another job opportunity? After all, she was a rare commodity that could lend authenticity to any western motion picture. She later stated that she received other job offers while working with her husband, and no doubt American Pathé in New Jersey would have snapped her up without hesitation.[1]

That Sunday during her absence the *Los Angeles Times* published a lengthy article on the local film industry. The piece featured a large photo inset of the "personnel of the Bison Company" with Red Wing and Young Deer in Indian costume and another photo of the company shooting a scene. "Few of us realize what a great and prominent industry this has become," the reporter declared, "or the enormous amount of money expended by the various companies in the fitting up of their studios, their rehearsal theaters, and in the general plants involved." The reporter explained in detail how the new trade was not only "good for the actors" and "a Godsend to the theatrical profession" but also a "tremendous boost for the city." "Edendale will be much appreciated," he concluded.[2]

West Coast Studio received top billing in the article, indicating that the reporter had conducted an informative interview with Young Deer: "The famous firm of Pathe Frères of Paris, Berlin, New York and London, has established a branch of studio at Edendale, where the 'western' pictures it is now exploiting are brought into being." He noted that "the branch studio" was "the smallest as yet operating on the Pacific Coast," yet "the company of players is second to none." He also stated that the quality of West Coast Studio's "natural scenes" equaled that of the scenes filmed by its parent company. If Young Deer deserved blame for his worn-out scenarios, he also deserved credit for the high cinematographic standard of his films.[3]

The report boosted the reputation of local film producers, who had not previously received such high acclaim. "The members of these companies are giving a vast amount of employment, are spending money freely, are advertising Los Angeles to the uttermost parts of the earth, are well ordered and comfortable citizens and are acquiring a permanent foothold," wrote the reporter. "Others are on their way, and they will be welcome."[4]

The report also reveals that Young Deer focused on drumming up publicity despite his emotional state. Although he'd lost his leading lady, he wasn't the type to mope around. When the skies finally cleared, the weather turned perfect for filming. He gathered up about twenty cast and crew and headed out to the Santa Monica Canyon and the Malibu Mountains "to take several Indian pictures" just after Balshofer and Bison Co. left the area. *Moving Picture World* described the "beautiful stretch of broken foothill and mountain land" that "partly faced the magnificent Pacific Ocean" as "isolated." The area was "devoid of modern buildings, cable cars, paved roads," which kept automobile traffic down to a minimum. Consequently, the location "offered scores of unspoiled vistas for the camera."[5] Unfortunately, the rains returned and nearly washed Young Deer's company down the canyon. Still, he managed to make one to three films in the week he was away from Edendale.[6]

Young Deer's wife abandoned him, but his friends seemed to be true blue. To commemorate his thirty-fifth birthday in the first week of April, they presented him with a lovely gold watch etched with his monogram and inscribed, "Presented to J. Young Deer by the Pathe Stock Company." They also gave him "a new summer suit of the latest approved weave of light colored cloth." Young Deer hosted his birthday party to music and comedy at the Olympic Theater on Broadway Street. After the show he treated his guests, including the Olympic stock company and its chorus girls, to "an enjoyable supper" at the Bristol Café in the heart of downtown Los Angeles. "Following the café supper," as *Moving Picture World* reported, "Young Deer rounded up a bunch of automobiles and the whole party were soon en route for the Log Cabin, a resort in the Santa Monica Canyon. It was in the 'wee' hours when the party finally returned to Los Angeles, just what hour the Pathe director declined to state."[7] Interestingly, a *Los Angeles Times* reporter caught one group in a bit of debauchery at the Log Cabin Resort that same weekend.[8] Their escapades resulted in the revocation of the establishment's liquor license. One newspaper report described the establishment as a "plague spot," a "lewd resort, and "a mecca for motorists . . . where everything goes from unlimited booze to silk underwear." "Two chorus girls from a Main-street theater," which is where the Olympic Theater was located, "with two young men, held the center of the stage at the Log Cabin a few nights ago," the report continued. "They arrived in a fine new automobile . . . half intoxicated . . . and soon accomplished the other half of their spree."[9] Whether or not the *Times* report involved Young Deer's party, the Log Cabin usually hosted Los Angeles joyriders seeking a naughty escapade.

If Red Wing kept up with the movie trades, she discovered that her husband's life—especially his nightlife—went on without her. Young Deer certainly had something to prove, since his personal and professional activities seemed to be of more public interest than usual. *Moving Picture World* reported that he took a camera downtown to "the retail shopping district" and convinced a policeman to halt traffic so he could capture the heart of Los Angeles on film.[10] What use he had for the footage is unknown. Perhaps he hoped to sell it to Pathé Frères for one of its newsreel features, which aired weekly in theaters across the globe. Next he spent several days photographing the grand Hollywood mansion of Paul de Longpre. Longpre was a French artist from Lyons famous for his floral paintings.[11] His estate with its acres of magnificent gardens afforded Young Deer subjects galore. Again, he may have been thinking of Pathé's newsreel, but *Moving Picture World* reported nothing else on the matter.

Meanwhile, Bessie Eyton and Virginia Chester became ill. This caused more than a health problem, because both actresses played Indian leads and substituted for Red Wing. Chester became seriously ill for two months, so Young Deer hired dark-eyed Margaret Ward Manners, "well known by her work in Western legitimate stock companies," to play leads. Manners didn't stay long. Apparently, she was also an accomplished thief. The following summer authorities arrested Manners and her husband for stealing tens of thousands of dollars worth of "securities" and jewelry.[12]

Young Deer also hired bank cashier Fred W. Gollum to act occasionally but primarily to manage the business, indicating that Red Wing with her clerical skills ordinarily had helped him in this area. Young Deer felt anxious to get the company in good working order because a Pathé Frères representative was due in April to inspect his studio. Representative K. W. Linn remained in Los Angeles for a week and accompanied Young Deer and the stock company to view West Coast Studio's latest western, *The White Squaw,* at the Optic Theater in downtown Los Angeles. What did Linn think about Young Deer's missing wife? It's possible her absence was the reason he came to check up on the West Coast division, but the trades mentioned nothing about her. *Moving Picture World* journalist Richard V. Spencer reported that "Mr. Young Deer" hosted Linn, Fred Gollum, and Charles K. French and his wife "at a local musical comedy theater." "Later in the week," said Spencer, "Mr. Linn will be shown places of local interest and will watch the Pathe Company at work."[13]

How the studio fared upon inspection is unknown. How Young Deer fared is another matter. Shortly after Linn's departure, Young Deer seemed to be feeling the effects of his new bachelor status for the worse. A *Los Angeles Herald* headline for April 29, 1911, stated, "Sioux Motion Picture Actor Goes on War Path." This was not exactly the kind of publicity he sought. *Times* readers could easily conjure up the image of a Plains Indian on the warpath, so the stereotype was denigrating enough. But the headline also demoted Young Deer from a manager-director to simply an actor, stripping him of all authority and power to refute the charges against him. Young Deer attempted to thwart the insult to his social status, however, as indicated between the lines of the *Herald*'s report:

James Youngdeer, a Sioux Indian, in every day life the heroic redman of many motion picture plays, went on the warpath last night at the Olympic theater in Main street while viewing one of the "wild west" scenes in which he appeared. Youngdeer's "pale face" brother, A. M. King, a special officer at the theater, was the object of the Indian's wrath when the latter attempted to quiet the obstreperous actor during his visit to the place.

Despite the fact that King is nearly twice the size of the Indian, the policeman was rolled on the sidewalk and handled roughly by the Indian actor. Patrolman Forthman heard the shouting occasioned by the struggle and hurried to King's aid. Youngdeer was arrested on a charge of disturbing the peace and was booked at central police station. When he arrived at the station the young Sioux could hardly be quieted. When he was asked if he could produce $25 bail, the tribesman brought out a roll of bills that widened the eyes of Desk Sergeant Smith. The actor was released on bail, and left the station vowing vengeance upon the haughty "pale face" who had caused his arrest. He will appear in police court today.[14]

Young Deer did nothing to dispel the myth of his Indianness, but what could he say? I'm not a Sioux tribesman. I'm a mixed-race man with proud ties to the African American community. In 1911 and for the decades that followed, it was better for someone with his complex ethnic background to be lampooned as a Plains Indian warrior than to be found out to be black, whatever the percentage.

A review for Young Deer's next picture, *Indian Justice* (May 3), helped to soothe his wounds. The film featured Leaping Elk, a Pawnee, whom Young Deer may have played, and his love interest, Swift Arrow, perhaps played by Manners. Young Deer set the story in prehistoric times, "before the white man sought to civilize the Indians with bad whiskey and a Carlisle education," according to the *Film Index*. The scenario was standard, but the film itself was tinted or "toned" to "striking effect." The new special effect gave Young Deer's production "artistic merit," raved the *Film Index*, and to his credit, "the fine scenic settings scarcely seem to need this aid."[15]

Four days later Young Deer received more acclaim when *Moving Picture World* published a biographical sketch illustrated with his sepia-toned photo.[16] Wearing a suit and broad-brimmed hat, he looks very much the part of a serious western film director. If Pathé management didn't initiate the public relations piece, then it suggests Young Deer's attempt to change the narrative from the negative publicity he'd received. It also reveals his desire to distance himself from his wife for abandoning him. Red Wing, except as her namesake character in a film title, is conspicuously missing from the lengthy article about his career.

The sketch identified "James Young Deer" as the "director and general manager" for West Coast Studio. Born again in the wrong place (Dakota City, Nebraska), Young Deer as a youth found employment in circuses and Wild West shows. The piece failed to mention his military service and stated incorrectly that he'd started in the film industry working with the Kalem and Lubin Companies in the 1890s. Obviously, Young Deer wanted to divert attention away from his years as a young man in Washington DC. "Although he little realized it at the time," the article asserted, "the moving picture field was destined to provide the medium for the outlet of his dramatic instincts. . . . Beside assisting in the production of the films, he wrote many of the scenarios on which they were based, and ofttimes played the leading roles or important character parts." The sketch further noted his work for *The Mended Lute* and that he "helped to produce the Vitagraph film 'Red Wing's Gratitude.'" Next it covered his early films with New Jersey Pathé and claimed that the westerns he made since his return to Edendale "have been very successful and are much in demand." "Young Deer has gathered about him a competent organization of professional men and women," the writer pronounced, "and is sparing neither effort nor expense to make the Pathe Frères productions topnotchers in the film market." The piece listed five of these "topnotchers," four of which starred Red Wing. Again, it made no mention of her at all. The story intimates that Young Deer believed their marriage was over and signals that he hoped to deny Red Wing her due.[17]

Despite the positive spin on Young Deer's career, critics, if not mainstream American theatergoers, grew tired of Young Deer scenarios. *Moving Picture World* journalist C. H. Claudy queried, "If Kalem and Pathe and Essanay et al[.] must live out West and hire troupes of cowboys and Indians and produce dramas, why can't they produce logical, interesting, livable dramas, instead of impossible slush." "It hurts the public's feelings," he implored, "it hurts the business, it hurts the producers. I know strong plots are hard to come by, but if so simple minded an individual as the present scribe can find in so beautiful a piece of photography only food for criticism and distaste and not even a suspicion of a thrill," he continued, "it seems to me a producer ought to be able to see the weakness of the story before they spend time and money on it."[18] Since Claudy singled out beautiful photography, was his critique aimed more at Young Deer than at Kalem and Essanay producers? Perhaps.

While Claudy's criticism may have given Young Deer pause, his immediate concern was finding a viable female who could play Indian leads. Virginia Chester ended up back in the hospital with appendicitis after a month's recovery from her mysterious "serious illness." Even worse, the talented Bessie Eyton quit the company completely to work for Selig Polyscope. Young Deer regrouped and planned to take the company, including lead actor De Grasse and female lead Manners, to Tijuana, Mexico, on May 5. He hoped "to make several films," including one with a real bullfight. Unfortunately, he couldn't get permission to cross into Tijuana because it was smack dab in the middle of a Mexican Revolution war zone.[19]

After losing Eyton, Young Deer recruited Vida Ramon from "a San Francisco moving picture company" to play leads. Nothing more is known about her. He also hired actor Dave Morris, a Choctaw Indian, to play character roles. Morris went by the name Joe Moonlight, and he had a short fuse, according to the *Los Angeles Herald*. Again, a reporter claimed that the Indian "went on the warpath," this time after a waiter refused him a cigarette. Moonlight fractured the waiter's jaw and landed in jail, allegedly responding: "No more city adventures for me."[20]

If the future is any indication, Young Deer's recruitment decisions were impulsive either because he was so intent on getting someone cheap or because he was just drawn to strange characters. On the one hand, the film industry attracted strange characters. While chaos reigned during Red Wing's absence, West Coast Studio released only a few films: *The White*

Squaw (April 8), *A Cowboy's Adventure* (April 12), *Indian Justice* (May 3), and, perhaps, *The Passing of Dappled Fawn*.[21] It seems a correlation existed between Red Wing's presence and Young Deer's production output.

Young Deer's fortune changed when Red Wing returned home on May 21.[22] The couple's mysterious separation and following reunion resulted in plans for a new film and apparently no final divorce decree. "Red Wing . . . since her return from New York recently, has been engaged in creating a new leading Indian role in a big Indian production that the Pathe director is putting on this week," reported *Moving Picture World*. "Mr. Young Deer is playing opposite to her in the other lead."[23] The item is telling. Part of wooing back his wife, at least in Young Deer's estimation, included his devotion to their performance partnership.

Moving Picture World reported that Virginia Chester left the company at the same time Red Wing returned home. But three weeks later the trade magazine revised its statement and said she was near "the point of death" in the Clara Barton Hospital: "Miss Virginia Chester, who formerly played ingénue leads with the Pathé West Coast Studio stock company, and who had just recovered from a dangerous operation, was again stricken with serious illness, forcing her to again return to the hospital for another operation."[24] Chester left several films that Young Deer hoped she'd complete "pending her recovery."

By the beginning of July Chester had recovered enough to "return to the camera," but another serious incident with a new actor, Joseph A. Oliver, occurred in late May or early June. Young Deer had just hired Oliver, a forty-seven-year-old veteran vaudeville actor. Something spooked Oliver's horse while the company filmed a scene in Griffith Park, and it took off, with the actor holding on for dear life. "A score of cowboys started in pursuit, yelling instructions to Mr. Oliver, who is quite elderly," reported *Moving Picture World*. "Hart Hoxie soon overtook the runaway and brought it to a sudden halt. The abrupt halt threw Mr. Oliver from the horse, and in falling he was seriously injured."[25] The crew hurried Oliver to the hospital with three broken ribs. The doctor prescribed bed rest for at least a month. Apparently, Oliver suffered a serious concussion, because besides enduring lasting hallucinations, he woke up in a strange boardinghouse near San Francisco in late March 1913 "to realize that he had suffered a complete loss of memory for almost two years."[26] It's doubtful anyone realized the extent of Oliver's injuries, and since he was a new hire, they probably lost touch with him.

After Oliver's accident, Young Deer and Red Wing took the company to Catalina Island, off the coast of Long Beach, to film Red Wing's first project since she returned home.[27] Entitled *Blue Wing and the Violinist* (released August 3), the film featured Red Wing as Blue Wing, "the belle of the tribe." Blue Wing falls in love with a violin-playing fur trapper captured by her tribe. Since "music charms the savage beast"—in this case, Indians—the trapper is freed and takes Blue Wing "back to civilization" with him. She eventually returns home, however, after the violinist leaves her with "a broken heart and a little baby to remind her of her life in the big city." *Moving Picture World*'s reviewer predictably characterized the film as "an emphasized example of the dangers of such alliances."[28] The review seems heavy-handed.

A critic for North Carolina's *Wilmington Dispatch* did not agree with *Moving Picture World*'s moral assessment. Since the film no longer exists, it's difficult to say who got it right, but the *Dispatch*'s review states: "The trapper wins the love of a beautiful Indian maiden and carries her home as his wife, but the call of her people is too strong and she goes back." The *Dispatch* critic characterized the story, "filled with the tenderest of emotion," as "a sweet tale that will pull at the heartstrings." Moreover, the critic declared that "the strong human-nature story . . . teaches an intensely interesting and powerfully helpful moral that every husband and wife should know."[29] This reviewer claimed that the film exemplified a universal love story, starkly contrasted with *Moving Picture World*'s denouncement of miscegenation.

Red Wing counted the film as one of her best, and she likely came up with the scenario, given her family history. Later she claimed she often wrote scenarios for her films, even though Young Deer took the credit at the time of their release. But to be fair, since his productions were internationally distributed, he received widely read criticism when they fell short. That summer, Britain's prestigious political and critical journal, the *Spectator*, printed the following critique of Young Deer's alleged talent as a scenario writer: "Recurring to the subject of directors who invent their own photoplays, a Los Angeles publication states that 'James Youngdeer is distinguished as one of the few directors who writes all his own scenarios,' and he is reported as saying that 'the only two that he has used other than his own were failures.' Goodness, gracious, mercy on us! Did all his own scenarios turn out to be stupendous successes? What?"[30] Perhaps Young Deer and Red Wing actually collaborated on scenarios, but he was certainly loath to give her any credit.

Pathé American summoned Young Deer to New York and New Jersey in July, and whether or not the company also summoned Red Wing, she accompanied him on the trip east. The break afforded the rest of the stock company a well-deserved two-week vacation in preparation for the "busy season" ahead.[31] If not a vacation for the Young Deers, the long train ride and time away from California allowed them to begin to repair their marriage. When they arrived at Penn Station, the bustling city welcomed them back to their beginnings. They met with manager-director Louis Gasnier to reaffirm their positions in the company and probably to receive instructions on how to proceed next.

Red Wing was Young Deer's best asset, and Linn likely tipped off Gasnier to her absence from Edendale. Gasnier probably also took note that Nestor Company released another film with a Red Wing character in July. Even when Red Wing was Blue Wing, she was an authentic Indian lead who easily upstaged any white actresses playing her namesake. The fact that white actresses played "Red Wing" at all was a tribute to her talent and marketability that was surely not lost on Pathé American's management.

The meeting with Gasnier resulted in an upsurge of roles for Red Wing. But before the couple returned to Edendale, they made a visit to the Nebraska reservation. Much had changed since Red Wing's childhood, including an expanding lively brood of nieces and nephews. Red Wing loved children, so what a treat to reunite with her family! Her half brother Abner had lost his oldest son that year, but Annie Frenchman St. Cyr was pregnant with their fifth child, whom they would name Lillian.[32] Levi's brother Abner and his wife, Elizabeth Frenchman St. Cyr, had just had their tenth child, Lucinda, in April. Red Wing's brother David had divorced Cora Frenchman, but they had five children. Their oldest,

David Jr., had just had his first child, whom he named after his grandfather Mitchell. Red Wing's nephew Jason Owen, son of Annie, was already a teenager, and his sister Pauline had just begun school. Despite the fact that their father left the household, Minnie St. Cyr Lowry's three daughters, Alvina, Annie, and Red Wing's other namesake, Lillian Margaret, thrived under the careful watch of their mother. Julia St. Cyr Travis's son Leo White was almost twenty. His mother doted on him, partly because he was an only child and partly because his father had little to do with him. Red Wing's brother Louis and his wife, Rosa Frenchman, lived in Emerson, Nebraska, near Minnie. They had no children, however, and would separate by the next year.[33]

Along with a dose of family love and childhood memories, Red Wing acquired lots of Indian clothing and accessories, most of which sister Julia probably acquired for her. When Young Deer and Red Wing returned to Edendale on July 22, *Moving Picture World* acknowledged Young Deer's visit to the reservation, but with no mention of Red Wing: "James Young Deer, producer of the Pathe Company, has returned to Los Angeles from a business trip to New York and vicinity. He has brought back two trunks of Indian costumes which he obtained from the Indian reservation in Nebraska, where he went to visit his people."[34] Apparently, again, Young Deer's Indian authenticity required Red Wing's support.

For the rest of the year Red Wing and Young Deer focused their energies on making films. It's difficult to determine all of the Pathé American westerns that were their productions and not New Jersey's. Productions definitely from West Coast Studio included *The Cheyenne's Bride* (released August 24), *Starlight's Necklace* (September 21), *Driven from the Tribe* (September 27), *The Romance of the Desert* (October 12), *A Western Postmistress* (November 16), *Cowboy Life* (November 23), *A Bear Hunt Romance* (December 2), *The Flower Girl of Las Palmas* (December 13), and *His Daughter's Bracelet* (December 28).[35]

The Cheyenne's Bride is probably the couple's reunion film. It's a love story between the son of a Cheyenne chief, played by Young Deer, and the daughter of a Sioux chief, played by Red Wing. With a classic Romeo and Juliet narrative, the film opens with Red Wing's and Young Deer's characters dressed in all their finery and mooning over each other beside a stream. "There is enmity between the Sioux and the Cheyenne tribes," *Moving Picture World*'s story synopsis explains. "And when a Cheyenne woos a Sioux maiden he is promptly taken prisoner and condemned to death, but the girl saves him. Her incensed father binds the girl on a horse and provides a horse to a Sioux brave and the Cheyenne but the Cheyenne wins." Red Wing performed her signature stunt in the extant film, which, *Moving Picture World* claimed, "brought the audience . . . out of their seats almost before it ended."[36] The stunt's formidability shows in the film. Red Wing has a difficult time getting her balance once Young Deer's character unbinds her from the horse. After the Sioux character loses to Young Deer's character, the Cheyenne, he takes a feather out of his hair and places it in the Cheyenne's hair to signify his bravery. Red Wing should have earned that honor. Her stunt performance is truly death defying, and she displays more grit and courage than any other actor in the film.

After three surgeries Chester returned to play lesser female soubrette roles, which were often comedic but not as physically taxing.[37] Several other actors joined the company as well, including Hazel Buckham, who became West Coast Studio's next accident victim. As the company filmed a canoe scene at Griffith Park or Echo Lake, the canoe tipped over, and Buckham and her costar Charles French fell headlong into the water. Neither could swim. Buckham lost consciousness and had to be revived with "stimulants."[38] She soon moved on to safer working conditions, became a successful film actress, and chose not to mention her early affiliation with West Coast Studio.

Still, Red Wing and company headed back to Catalina Island with several canoes in tow for a week's shooting. They planned to film exterior shots for at least *Starlight's Necklace*, another extant film.[39] The narrative exhibits suspicious undertones about Young Deer and Red Wing's marriage. Red Wing plays her namesake, and Joseph De Grasse plays her husband, Eagle Eye. Their love story revolves around Red Wing's jealousy of Starlight, a beautiful Indian maid. Starlight gave Eagle Eye a necklace during "a most unexpected and attractive encounter."[40] Afterward, the two females get into an argument, and Starlight attempts to stab Red Wing. When Eagle Eye intervenes to save his wife, Red Wing stops him from stabbing Starlight but allows him to chase her away. The couple's marriage is restored with Starlight's exit. *Moving Picture World* gave the "Indian story of love and jealousy" a mixed review, asserting that "the illusion of Indian life and character is not badly done." The critic liked seeing "some real Indians . . . in the cast," although he noted that he overheard audience members remarking that De Grasse looked more like a longshoreman than an Indian. "Some of the scenes are fairly artistic and have some beauty," praised the critic, but he thought the Indian village scenes resembled lesser versions of Bison Co. westerns.[41]

Red Wing and De Grasse also appeared on a fall cover of *Moving Picture World* posing in a scene from their film *The Romance of the Desert*. Red Wing in braids wears an Indian dress and stands in a rocky terrain; with praying hands, she gazes up at De Grasse, who's dressed in a kind of Apache costume. A large rock to their right is in shadow but bears a cross with the word "Jesus" etched below. In the film De Grasse plays a construction foreman who is "sun struck" into delirium and loses his memory. When he wanders from his camp, a group of Indians find him, and he lives with them in the mythic Southwest. Transforming spiritually into an Indian, he falls in love with Red Wing's character, and they marry. Their marriage becomes threatened when a white woman crosses their path and identifies De Grasse's character as her lost husband by the crucifix he wears. The *Moving Picture World* reviewer loved "the thread of religious sentiment" in the film and especially loved the story line, which ends when the hero returns to his white wife. "The religion that he had taught to the squaw prevents a tragedy," the reviewer declared. "The whole situation is very well handled. It's a good and acceptable picture."[42]

By the time the review appeared in print De Grasse had already left Edendale for New York and a mysterious job opportunity—perhaps with American Pathé. Along with his departure Young Deer probably suffered a bruised ego from *Moving Picture World*'s jab that his *Starlight's Necklace* scenes resembled lesser versions of Bison Co.'s. Balshofer had his own troubles, though. He'd just lost his popular "Indian" heroine, Darkfeather, as well as Frank Montgomery, Bison Co.'s longtime lead and part-time director. Selig Polyscope stole the couple away shortly after their marriage with a better offer, as it had done with Bessie Eyton. Now both West

Coast Studio and Bison Co. were on the lookout for new talent. Bison Co. immediately replaced Darkfeather with a white actress, Anna Little. Little didn't have Darkfeather's charisma or sex appeal, but her sensitive performances lent some dignity to Indian maid characters. Young Deer temporarily hired members of the Out West Club, a large group of "seasoned riders," to fill out his westerns. Club members may have appeared in *Driven from the Tribe* with De Grasse before he left for New York.[43]

Red Wing experienced the dawning of the photoplayer fan in 1911. Pathé Frères acknowledged the phenomenon in the fall when it published Red Wing's, De Grasse's, and Charles French's images with nine other New Jersey actors: Pearl White, Paul Panzer, Max Linder, Gwendolin Pates, Martha Spier, Octavia Handworth, Charles Arling, Billy Quirk, and William Cavanaugh. Their photographic portraits appear in four rows of three each for a full-page ad titled "Pathe's Popular Players." Among other publications, the ad appeared suitably in the new fan publication *Motion Picture Story Magazine* and states: "Everyone knows and admires the Pathé Players. We have prepared an elaborate set of 12 Photos, 10-inch by 12-inch done in sepia tone, of the Pathe stock."[44] Red Wing's fans could purchase the entire set for two dollars, allowing them all the time in the world to study their favorites. Red Wing's inclusion in the set points not only to her international popularity but also to her value to Pathé.

Red Wing's photo is a simple headshot on a dark background. The full-page close-up, with her dimpled chin and one braid facing the camera, shows her eyes glancing slightly sideways, her upper lip slightly pouted, and her dark arched eyebrows framing her kohl-lined dark eyes. She wears a light-colored headband with one pristine white feather. Beautiful beadwork jewelry adorns her neck. Indeed, she looks every bit the iconic Indian heroine, and the image surely secured her fan base.

The image also signifies Red Wing's return to Young Deer, at least as his company's beloved Indian heroine. If the couple's separation didn't quite strengthen their marriage, it certainly shored up Red Wing's position in Young Deer's stock company for the next two years.

Fig. 13. Red Wing and George Larkin in *The Red Girl and the Child*. *Film Index*, August 13, 1910. Courtesy Media History Digital Library.

Fig. 14. Red Wing in chaps in *The Red Girl and the Child*. From the Collection of the Celeste Bartos International Film Study Center, Museum of Modern Art, New York.

Fig. 15. Pathé Frères West Coast Studio stock company, *Moving Picture World*, March 11, 1911. Front row (*left to right*): Charles K. French and Young Deer. Second row: Red Wing, Virginia Chester, Bessie Eyton, and Miss Austin. Third row: Thomas K. Peters, Joseph De Grasse, Irvin Hay, Frank V. Biggy, William F. Ridgway, and Keith Breed. Fourth row: Edgar Willis, Carl E. House, Jesse E. Snow, Hart "Jack" Hoxie, Frank "Curly" Weinmann, Charles Davis, and "Pockets" Howland. Courtesy Media History Digital Library.

Fig. 16. Pathé Frères West Coast Studio stock company outside the studio, 1911. Courtesy Marc Wanamaker, Bison Productions/Archives, Los Angeles.

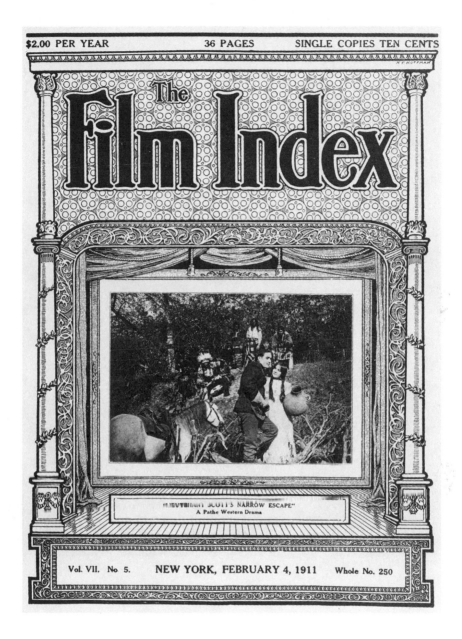

$2.00 PER YEAR   36 PAGES   SINGLE COPIES TEN CENTS

The Film Index

"LIEUTENANT SCOTT'S NARROW ESCAPE"
A Pathe Western Drama

Vol. VII. No 5.   NEW YORK, FEBRUARY 4, 1911   Whole No. 250

Fig. 17. *Lieutenant Scott's Narrow Escape. Film Index*, February 4, 1911 (cover).
Courtesy Media History Digital Library.

Fig. 18. *Silver Leaf's Heart. Film Index*, February 11, 1911. Courtesy Media History Digital Library.

Fig. 19. *Cheyenne's Bride*, 1911. Film 1498 from the EYE Collection, Amsterdam.

Fig. 20. Red Wing of Pathé Frères. *Motion Picture Story Magazine*, October 1911. Courtesy Media History Digital Library.

RED WING

MACE

EDNA MAISON

MIRIAM NESBITT

MONA DARKFEATHER

CRANE WILBUR

Fig. 21. Caricature sketch with Red Wing, Edna Maison, and Mona Darkfeather. *Motion Picture Story*, April 1914. Courtesy Media History Digital Library.

Fig. 22. Red Wing and George Gebhardt in a canoe at Silver Lake, Los Angeles, 1911–13. Courtesy Marc Wanamaker, Bison Productions/Archives, Los Angeles.

Fig. 23. Red Wing and DeMille in the snow near Keen Camp, 1914. Cecil B. DeMille Papers, L. Tom Perry Special Collections Library, Brigham Young University, Provo, Utah.

Fig. 24. Naturitch's death scene in *The Squaw Man*. Early 1914 photo still for *Life*, 1959.

CHAPTER 10

Keeping Up with the Competition

In the early fall of 1911, Red Wing and Young Deer added two more actors to their group of stock players. Their old compatriot Charles Inslee left Bison Co. to join them, as did newcomer Louise Glaum, formerly with Selig. Young Deer felt especially pleased with Glaum's acquisition, calling her "a valuable addition to his forces."[1] He was right to be enthused. Glaum became one of the most famous actresses in silent film and earned a star on the Hollywood Walk of Fame for the vamp roles she played that rivaled Theda Bara's.

Young Deer assembled some members of the company in October, including presumably Glaum, Inslee, and Red Wing, for a location shoot at the historic S & M Ranch in the Santiago Canyon near Santa Ana.[2] French had discovered the Orange County location the prior year when the ranch's foreman asked to borrow some of French's cowboys to help with the spring cattle roundup. French gleaned *The Dollar Mark* from the event, a picture featuring "a big husky cowpuncher" and a young girl. Critics praised the short film for its "rich settings" and "clear clean-cut photography."[3]

A Santa Ana reporter spotted Young Deer's "moving picture concern" as it traveled through the area. He noted that French took charge of the "outfit" of "ten cowboys and five women, and a complete lay-out for the taking of pictures." Young Deer again okayed French to lend cowboys for a roundup, and French planned to "take a lot of pictures." "The cowboys are to camp at the old ranch-house," explained the local reporter, "while the women and manager will stay in Santa Ana and go back and forth by automobile." "A number of Indian scenes are to be taken," he added, "in which cowboy actors would play Indians."[4] The new location couldn't have been better. The crew set scenarios on a real working ranch equipped with a corral and barn, grazing cattle, pristine running streams, and picturesque scenery.

The time was paramount for West Coast Studio to make more authentic westerns. Shortly after Anna Little replaced Darkfeather, Bison Life Motion Pictures became Bison 101 Pictures. The transformation began when Charles O. Bauman and Adam Kessell of the NYMPC hired Thomas Harper Ince to manage their western division. The now legendary silent film director showed up for the job interview in early October with a five o'clock shadow and a borrowed diamond ring to make him appear older. The men offered him $125 a week, and he accepted. Once Ince came on board Balshofer acted as general manager. Years later, Red Wing claimed she'd worked for Ince rather than Balshofer because Ince's name became synonymous with Bison 101 westerns, which were well known.[5]

Along with Ince and his wife, stage actress Elinor Kershaw, the NYMPC added new hires fresh from Carl Laemmle's Independent Motion Pictures (IMP): cameraman Ray Smallwood, leading lady Ethel Grandon, English actress Alice Inward, and director's assistant Charlie Weston. "When they arrived at the end of October," said Balshofer, they "immediately began making films at the Edendale Studio."[6] Actor Francis Ford, elder brother of director John Ford, also came on to direct the smaller cast's "Western comedies and dramas."[7]

NYMPC scored a remarkable coup, however, when Bauman made a bold and innovative business move to acquire the actors and livestock from the Miller Brothers' 101 Ranch Wild West Show, which wintered in Venice, California, after giving several performances in Southern California. "Our arrangement gave us the use of about seventy-five cowboys, twenty-five cowgirls, and about thirty-five Indians," Balshofer explained. "We hired Jim Brooks, manager of the show, who was a powerful ex-cowpuncher well about to rustle everybody up at sunrise and parade them up the coast to our sanctuary in the Santa Ynez Canyon."[8]

Kessell told a *Motography* journalist that the overhauled company was now the "largest in the world, comprising more than four hundred people, employed daily." "It includes the reorganized regular stock company of sixty people, and the Miller Bros. 101 Ranch Wild West Company of 350 people," he said. "We have been extremely fortunate in securing this famous aggregation and with the world's most daring riders—men and women who think but little of their lives when some hazardous feat is performed." The days of the "cut and dried western picture" were over, he predicted.[9]

The new Bison 101 company pitched camp on the acreage the original Bison Co. had leased from the Santa Monica Water and Power Company. How Miller Brothers performers felt about relocating to the isolated "sanctuary" from their quaint beach cottages in Venice can only be imagined. "It wasn't an easy task to arrange housing and a mess hall for the people and shelter and corrals for the livestock in such haste," Balshofer recalled. "Brooks helped ease the situation by having the Indians set up their own tepee village almost at the crest of the south ridge of the canyon, and there they lived all by themselves."[10]

The pressure for Young Deer and Red Wing to compete increased exponentially as the impressive "Inceville" arose where Sunset Boulevard meets the Pacific Coast Highway.[11] Ince "built an elaborate outdoor studio, with several open air stages, a Western town set, a ranch set, and other buildings," all fueled with an onsite electric power plant and connected to the outside world with a telephone system. The company also raised cattle and maintained a vegetable garden "to feed the growing workforce of people."[12]

Red Wing's honorary uncle Luther Standing Bear joined Inceville's workforce soon after. He'd been performing with the Miller Brothers in Oklahoma but couldn't tolerate the summer heat. "I had heard a great deal about the wonderful climate of Southern California, and concluded to go there," he recalled. "I wrote to Thomas Ince, then one of the big moving picture magnates. He had some Sioux Indians with him, and I thought I would like to be with them. He wrote a nice reply and sent me transportation to Los Angeles."[13] Standing Bear probably didn't live at Inceville proper, since he also worked for an archery concession at the Venice Beach boardwalk. Did he reconnect with Red Wing? It's unknown. There's no public record of their reunion until 1915.

West Coast Studio digs paled in comparison to Inceville, with its inexhaustible cast of authentic cowboys, Indians, and all the accouterments of the 101 Ranch. Clearly, Young Deer and Red Wing needed to step up their game. It was now vitally important for them to shoot westerns in wild and woolly locations with authentic-looking cowboys and Indians. Down in Orange County, Young Deer began to visualize the S & M Ranch as his version of Inceville, with Red Wing as his Indian princess in residence.

Everyone put their all into *A Western Postmistress* (released November 16), the first film shot in the new location, apart from *The Dollar Mark*. Red Wing appears as her namesake character in the film, and Louise Glaum likely played the postmistress. "There is a dash and spirit in this Western melodrama, which, despite the oft repeated plot of the story, makes it interesting," wrote the critic for the *New York Dramatic Mirror*. "The girl postmistress at Lonely Gulch has a sweetheart, for whom she sends when she gets a telegram from the express company to come and get a bag of money. But he doesn't get the message because the 'greaser' has overheard and intercepts Red Wing, the Indian girl messenger, binds her and tosses her over a cliff." Meanwhile, the "greaser's" gang pursues the postmistress through the Santiago Canyon. Of course, the Indian princess helper frees herself in time to save the white heroine.[14] *Moving Picture World* found the story line "stirring and sufficiently unusual."[15]

Next, *Cowboy Life* (released on November 23) "show[ed] real life on the ranch" and undoubtedly included footage of the roundup.[16] After Young Deer produced a few more films at the new locale, including *His Daughter's Bracelet* (released December 28), which probably featured Red Wing, the company returned to Edendale the first week of December.[17] It's difficult to determine the rest of Red Wing's films for this time because both East and West Coast Pathé Studios made several more films only identified generally as Pathé Frères films. *The Horse Thief* (released January 11), *The Strike on the Ranch* (released January 10), *The Squaw Man's Revenge* (released January 17), and *Swiftwind's Heroism* (January 27) seem to have been filmed at the S & M Ranch.[18] The latter film, a comedy-drama, centers on a white woman, probably played by Glaum, who is raised by Indians. Red Wing, however, held star attraction as the film's "full blood Indian actress."[19]

The Rebuked Indian (released January 4) and *The Sioux's Cave of Death* (released January 24) seem to have both been New Jersey productions, though the latter's origin is questionable. These films featured another prominent Native American actor, Chief Dark Cloud, who had begun acting for West Coast Studio by 1912.[20] The press touted Dark Cloud, born Elijah Tahamont in 1861, as a chief of the Abenaki of Quebec Province.[21] His Abenaki wife, Margaret Camp, aka Dove Eye, acted in films with him and also wrote film scenarios based on old legends.[22]

Red Wing probably knew the Dark Clouds when she lived on the East Coast. D. W. Griffith directed the couple in their first known film, *The Broken Doll*, released in 1910. The Tahamonts also served as Griffith's cultural consultants, so he may have hired the couple to replace Red Wing and Young Deer. Their beautiful daughters, Beulah and Bessie Dark Cloud, were educated in eastern public schools for white children and sometimes acted in their parents' films.[23] Although the public knew Red Wing and Young Deer as the first Indian silent film couple, the distinction of the first Native American family to act in silent films belongs to the Tahamonts.

Publicity stated that Dark Cloud was a Carlisle alum and "one of the most intelligent and educated of his race," though his enrollment at the Indian school can't be confirmed.[24] Dark Cloud also posed for western artist Frederick Remington over the course of nearly twenty years, as well as artists De Cost Smith, Edward Deming, and Maynard Dixon. He found it "most interesting work" that was technically distinct from motion picture "posing." Unfortunately, nothing is known about Red Wing posing for artists, as one article stated she had, but Tahamont's description of acting in film sheds light on Red Wing's work in the field. "For pictures, one poses in a still attitude," he stated. "For films, one poses in action. . . . The actor knows he must keep his pose—or rather the spirit of his pose, and yet uphold the action of the drama. He must show anger, delight, love, fear, just as he depicts these emotions, or feeling for the painter. But he must keep these emotions in action. It is not always so easy."[25]

Red Wing continued working through the holiday season. She traveled without Young Deer to the Southwest and arrived in El Paso, Texas, on Christmas Day with about twenty cast and crew. *Motography* magazine explained the reason for the excursion: "The Pathe company has stationed a company in El Paso, Texas, which will work throughout Texas and Mexico utilizing the scenery of this section in developing Indian and Mexican subjects. The work is in charge of Director George Connor [*sic*] and with the party are Redwing, the Indian girl, and Miss Lurline Lyons, leading lady."[26] Red Wing found herself in interesting company. George Washington Conner—better known as Buck Connors—was a newbie to film but eventually became a well-known sidekick in talkie westerns. Lyons, a California-born ingénue, was the favorite niece of one of the period's iconic writers, Jack London.[27]

Connors had amassed a broad range of skills applicable to the production of silent westerns in the years prior to working for West Coast Studio. His military service in the Spanish-American War garnered him a Bronze Medal for his unfaltering courage. He joined the Buffalo Bill Wild West show as a roughrider after he returned home.[28] When Colonel W. F. "Buffalo Bill" Cody and Major Gordon Lillie, aka Pawnee Bill, joined forces in 1907 to form Buffalo Bill's Wild West and Pawnee Bill's Great Far East shows, the "Two Bills" asked Connors to take on more responsibility. Connors wore several hats for the production, including recruiting reservation Indians and "rid[ing] the typewriter" as Lillie's personal secretary.[29] He may have met Red Wing and Young Deer about this time.

In the fall of 1909 Connors managed the show's winter headquarters in Trenton, New Jersey. One reporter observed him "teaching a cow pony to fall down and play dead when he told it to."[30] Spring rehearsals culminated in an extravagant Madison Square Garden show in the summer of 1910. Rehearsals began again the following spring in Trenton. "Everybody has responded to the call," reported *Variety*, "including Col. W. F. Cody (Buffalo Bill), who has come from his mines in Arizona to resume his farewell tour." In the meantime, Connors traveled to the Pine Ridge reservation to recruit "Chief Iron Tail and 100 Ogalalla Sioux Indians," as well as Red Wing's old Hippodrome alumnus William Sitting Bull to perform in the Two Bills' final show.[31]

It's unknown who asked Connors "to superintend the production of a Western borderland story in moving pictures," but he was surely more equipped to deal with roaming Zapatistas than Young Deer.[32] Moreover, Red Wing knew how to portray a Mexican señorita, while Lurline

Lyons, with her Latina beauty passed down from a South American grandmother, could portray Mexican ingénues.[33] The warmer borderland winters made for longer periods of filming, but scenarios set in the midst of the thrilling Mexican Revolution gave these West Coast Studio films a competitive edge over Bison 101's cowboy and Indian westerns, no matter how unpredictable.

The titles of Red Wing's El Paso films can't be confirmed, but *His Mexican Sweetheart* and *A Mexican Elopement* were released not long after she returned to Edendale (March 2 and March 28, 1912, respectively). Both films featured a Mexican heroine perfect for her or for Lyons. Whether or not Red Wing acted in either film, Connors's inexperience in filmmaking left her plenty of roles to play to help him succeed in his new endeavor.

Charles French may have also lent his expertise to Connors in El Paso. He and former Bison Co. cameraman Maxwell Smith tended to their copper mines in nearby Arizona while West Coast Studio folks filmed at the border.[34] French had firsthand experience with revolutionaries as well. He discovered "considerable anti-American feeling" when he earlier took a mining expedition through Central America. He barely escaped with his life after rebels captured and planned to execute him.[35] Although Red Wing knew about French's narrow escape, it did not stop her from leaving the safety of home. Again, her courage matched that of any of the men she knew.

West Coast Studio released *Indian Blood* (February 3) and *The Squaw's Debt of Gratitude* (February 28), both likely filmed at the ranch.[36] Red Wing probably played Gebhardt's Indian female lead in *Indian Blood*, which tells the story about a brave and his wife and son who are "banished from the tribe" after the "brave attacks a chief's son."[37] *The Squaw's Debt of Gratitude* followed as an action-packed Indian helper story typical of Red Wing's oeuvre: "An Indian girl, accidentally wounded, is nursed by a pale-face maiden, and when she regains her health, is sent back to her tribe," according to *Moving Picture World*. Glaum probably played the white female, who was captured and "destined to the tortures for which the Indians were famous." The grateful "little Indian squaw" comes to her rescue after "many thrilling adventures."[38]

Red Wing also played the Indian female lead in *A Victim of Firewater* (released March 27), but it's unknown if the following Pathé Frères March releases, *Cholera on the Plains, The Arrow of Defiance,* and *The Price of Gratitude,* were East or West Coast productions.[39] Young Deer may have played the "victim of firewater," a degenerate Carlisle graduate. The only interesting aspect of the film is its narrative contrast to earlier ones in which Young Deer played the heroic Carlisle alum. This new character "received small education and a great thirst" for whiskey, eventually becoming a thief and "a fugitive from justice."[40] What had changed to make the educated Indian such a cynical figure? Was it Young Deer or Red Wing or America?

Red Wing didn't have the lead and probably didn't even appear in any of the West Coast Studio productions released in April. Perhaps the films were shot before she returned from El Paso. *Brave Heart's Hidden Love* (released April 4) starred Louise Glaum, Charles Inslee, and Earl C. Simmons.[41] The rest of the films featured new hires for West Coast Studio because Bison Co.'s restructuring led some actors to leave. Red Wing's and Young Deer's former costar Edna Maison played the lead in their film *The Girl Sheriff* (released April 11).[42] George Gebhardt left Bison for West Coast Studio as well, while his wife, Madeline West, went to Kalem Pictures. He first appeared as an Indian hero in *For the Papoose* (released April 25).[43] The film's pathos derives from the misdeeds of White Buffalo, an unscrupulous "squaw man." White Buffalo dumps his Indian wife, takes away their child, and convinces his in-laws to slaughter white settlers so he can elope with one of their women. The "happy" ending comes after Gebhardt's Indian character kills White Buffalo and returns "the papoose" to its mother, who is also his sister. It's unknown who played White Buffalo, but his unsavory character certainly ran counter to Edwin Milton Royle's original play.

Jackie Saunders played the white love interest of the philandering squaw man. Saunders, born Anna Jackal, flaunted curly hair and big blue eyes. A Kewpie doll type, Saunders looked much younger than her twenty years. Curiously, as the extant though damaged film shows, Red Wing appears to be playing the wronged Indian wife in the first scene, but a white actress plays her character later in the film.[44] Interestingly, she had a troubled relationship with Saunders, which may have been the reason for her disappearance in the rest of the film.

It's unclear if Red Wing played Blue Fawn in *The Red Man's Honor* (released May 1), but *Moving Picture World*'s critic said it was "a first-class picture" and "among the very best wholly Indian pictures that we have ever seen." It's a big picture, dignified," the critic went on, and its "action is so straight forward and logical that it seems not manipulated but naturally dramatic." The reviewer also thought that the actors "impress one as being red," indicating Gebhardt may have been in the film.[45] *The Cowboy Girls* (May 2) and *Orphans of the Plains* (released May 15) included parts for Red Wing, Baby Violet Radcliffe, and Buster Emmons, who also came from Bison Co.[46] *The Justice of the Manitou* (May 16) and *The Prospector's Sweetheart* (May 26) followed, but Red Wing's presence in the latter films is unconfirmed. A review of the first compares with many of Young Deer's films. The critic deemed the cinematography "commendable" but found no justice in the story about "an insulted squaw."[47] The second film featured a young Mexican heroine, so it might have been made near El Paso.[48]

The same day *The Red Man's Honor* appeared in theaters, the *New York Dramatic Mirror* published an ad illustrated with George Gebhardt's painting. It shows a lone Indian standing under a tree, gazing up at a larger-than-life Indian maiden who floats in the upper corner of the page. A dreamy moon rises over a mountain lake in the background. The painting seems amateurish and hokey, and the figures are sloppily labeled "Geo. Gebhart" (misspelled) and "Princess Red Wing." The ad copy, obviously crafted by Young Deer, states: "George Gebhart [*sic*], as Young Buffalo, and Princess Red Wing who will appear, in the near future, in a series of Indian Dramas, written exclusively for them by Jas. Young Deer, manager and director of Pathe Frères Western Stock Company." The ad wasn't exactly up to *New York Dramatic Mirror*'s professional caliber, but it heralded a change in Red Wing's standing as a western film star: "Mr. Gebhart, in Mgr. Young Deer's opinion, as well as many others, is the truest portrayer of Indian nature of any man in or out of the profession, and, as Princess Red Wing is the only full-blooded Indian girl playing Indian leads, Mgr. Young Deer expects to give the public the best results to be obtained in motion pictures."[49]

Young Deer's assertion that the Swiss American Gebhardt surpassed all others in his portrayal of "Indian nature" followed shortly after the question man for a fan magazine told one of his inquirers, "No, the Bison leading man is not of Indian blood, but is a painted sham."[50] Obviously, Gebhardt as Red Wing's leading man required some serious branding. Young Deer couldn't lie about Gebhardt's racial authenticity, but he could highlight the leading man's acting-Indian skills. Moreover, Gebhardt filmed beautifully. He was exotic and sexy, and, like Charles Inslee before him, the girls went ga-ga over him.[51] More importantly, the ad implied that Kalem's "Princess Darkfeather" and Bison 101's Anna Little could not compete with Red Wing. The ad, despite its failings, sent a direct message about Red Wing's stature to the competition.[52] If they thought she was simply a stoic Indian princess helper, they had another think coming.

When Red Wing and Young Deer weren't making motion pictures, they promoted the company. One Friday night in May they participated in the Shriners Parade in Los Angeles, where thousands "pressed against the wire stretched along the streets and gazed in amazed wonder at more than a mile of glittering pageantry."[53] Young Deer entered a nearly fifty pony "Pinto Brigade" with riders decked out in "Western costumes." George Champion, who rented out horses to movie studios and appeared in at least one West Coast Studio film, won the best prize for his "cowpuncher's outfit." Judges awarded Mrs. Charles French second place for her western outfit. The parade ended with a spectacular electric pageant. It's unknown if Red Wing paraded, but it's difficult to imagine that she stood on the sidelines.[54]

The parade also included a California Mission Pageant that inspired Young Deer to make one or more Mexican-themed films. Selig Polyscope owned exclusive filming rights to the nearby San Gabriel Mission, so Young Deer came up with an idea. He bought a photo collection of a California mission and gave it to set designer Harry Radcliff.[55] After a week and more money than Young Deer intended, Radcliff reproduced a beautiful life-size version of the structure, which stood "in a big open space back of the studio." Young Deer hoped to recoup his losses by writing a few film scenarios featuring his new set.

In early June, *Moving Picture World*'s column Doings at Los Angeles ran an item about Gebhardt and Red Wing pairing up in Young Deer's films. A new and now iconic headshot of "Princess Redwing" accompanied the column.[56] The professional photo capturing Red Wing's beauty, dignity, and that characteristic dimple on her chin served to neutralize Gebhardt's contrived representation of her the month before. Perhaps Pathé Frères management realized it was time to invest in a professional photo of their Indian motion picture star, because the film business had changed. Fans wanted to get to know their favorite film personalities. The revival of her royal title is another notable aspect of the photo. Faux Indian princess Mona Darkfeather's popularity was getting under everyone's skin. Young Deer took the bait, and Red Wing bowed to the stereotype for the time being.

Meanwhile, Joseph De Grasse returned from New Jersey Pathé to West Coast Studio and made *A Redskin's Appeal* (released on June 13) with Red Wing and Gebhardt.[57] Red Wing played Lola and received special praise for her acting. *Moving Picture World* deemed the picture "more than ordinarily desirable" and "a very well-acted picture, especially the leading lady." Young Deer allegedly based the scenario on fact. Lola, the adopted daughter of General Branson, played by De Grasse, is betrothed to his son Jack. Just before their marriage Lola meets Strongheart, "an educated Indian," played by Gebhardt. He tells her who she really is and that the general played a part in the death of her Indian father. Consequently, Lola marries Strongheart rather than Jack and averts the touchy issue of miscegenation.[58]

The film had artistic merit that may have derived from the talented Harry Radcliff, who was also an electrical engineer. It displayed scenes as "moving illustrations in a book," a "conceit" that was not wholly new but was skillfully executed. "It would seem that historical pictures and all delicate, poetic romances . . . would be better shown as illustrations," *Moving Picture World*'s critic pronounced, leaving "realistic pictures of modern life" to be portrayed more naturally.[59] Critics loved the film, perhaps a sign that Pathé management urged Young Deer to highlight their star Indian lead with better productions.

Gebhardt starred in *The Gambler's Reformation* (released June 19) and opposite Red Wing in both *The Deerslayer's Retribution* (released June 27) and *An Indian Idyl* [*sic*] (released June 22). *Moving Picture World* gave *The Deerslayer's Retribution* little fanfare, summarizing its story as "an Indian failing to win the love of the daughter of the chief, commits a crime and swears that his rival committed the deed, but eventually the matter is all satisfactorily cleared up."[60] However, *An Indian Idyl* made a "beautiful picture of Indian life . . . woven about a love affair that springs up between the daughter of the Sioux Chief and a brave from the Crow tribe."[61]

While *A Redskin's Appeal* opened in Los Angeles in mid-June at Clune's Theater, the largest venue of its time, Young Deer, Red Wing, and their company returned to the S & M.[62] On the way they stopped at Sonora-town, an old Mexican quarter of Los Angeles. The Doings at Los Angeles columnist gave the film company credit for being the first to discover the colorful ethnic and now historic neighborhood. "With its low adobe buildings, its narrow streets and its quaint people, it resembles more a section of the city of Mexico than a part of a modern American city," he explained.[63] After Young Deer and Red Wing checked out the area as a potential location, they continued south to the Santiago Canyon. Accompanied by dogs, horses, camping equipment, and reels of blank film, the company arrived at the ranch ready to roll. The next day the local paper ran a tongue-in-cheek piece with the headline "Indians Will Run Wild in Canyon." "But hold before you call out the militia. It should be said that [massacres] will occur, pictorially speaking . . . so that the minimum of real blood will be spilled."[64]

The following Friday, June 21, the Electric Theater in the city of Orange, located about seven miles north of the company's camp, treated locals to "a special program" in honor of the visiting motion picture company. It was the largest attendance the theater had ever housed—and no wonder! "On the regular program were two especially interesting films, produced by the Pathe company on the Irvine ranch," the newspaper reported the next day, adding, "Many of the leading characters in the scenes were personally introduced on the stage, as the entire company were present at the performance."[65]

To kick off the event the Orange City band regaled the crowd as they lined up to buy tickets. After the audience was seated, an Indian tableau opened the program, followed by the appearance of Colonel William

A. Lavelle, a new stock player. Lavelle was a seasoned Wild West show performer known for his likeness to Buffalo Bill Cody, and he probably appeared in at least one of the two films shown that night, *Strike on the Ranch* and *Indian Blood*. Lavelle had a bit of a drinking problem but appeared to all intents and purposes sober in his Buffalo Bill attire, complete with goatee.[66]

Next, Young Deer introduced the other stock players, giving star billing to "Princess Red Wing, the only full-blood Indian acting female parts anywhere," and "George Gebhardt, the greatest portrayer of Indian parts by a white man." French, De Grasse, and Bison Co. alumnus Bob Emmons were also star attractions of the evening. However, little three-year-old Violet Radcliffe and her child costar, Buster Emmons, who was said to "ride like a cowboy or a Cossack," outshone them all. The young duo performed Red Wing's version of "the Grizzly Bear dance," which proved to be "the hit of the evening." Mazie Martell, a Vaudeville female impersonator, ended the evening with his performance.[67]

The audience loved Pathé night, so Young Deer and Red Wing brought the company back for an encore performance the following Friday evening in tandem with a showing of *A Redskin's Appeal*, which some of the company members had not yet seen. "This is a very beautiful and original story written by Mr. James Young Deer," a local reporter announced, "and in it his wife, Red Wing, is featured, along with Gebhardt and De Grasse." The night promised "Indians and Squaws a Plenty" and assured theatergoers that they would "get their money's worth"—which was ten or fifteen cents, depending on their seat.[68]

Gebhardt appeared in "complete makeup" in an Indian costume touted as "the most elaborate of any ever seen anywhere."[69] Certainly, Red Wing pulled out all the stops and came in her best Indian costume as well. The audience was also treated to *A Western Postmistress* and Chief Dark Cloud's *The Sioux's Cave of Death*.[70] Mazie Martell returned to delight the crowd with a "gladtime ragtime" finale. "Mr. Young Deer lost no time in securing Mr. Martell's services for some comedy scenarios," reported the local paper, in "which Mr. Martell plays the leading lady."[71] Whether he as a she or he as a he eventually acted in a West Coast Studio production is unknown.

Meanwhile, back at the ranch the company filmed *The Squaw Man's Sweetheart* (released June 29), starring again Red Wing, Gebhardt, and De Grasse.[72] Red Wing's brother Louis also shows up in the film as an Indian. He'd left his wife, Rosa Frenchman, moved to California, and gained employment at West Coast Studio at least long enough to appear in the one film.[73] Critics weren't particularly enthralled by the story, which was a takeoff of *For the Papoose*.[74] While the squaw man character was kinder, Red Wing portrayed his rejected and vengeful Indian wife. The French title of the extant film says it all: *Jalousie de Squaw* (Jealousy of the squaw).[75] Although a *Moving Picture World* critic thought *The Squaw Man's Sweetheart* had "some pretty scenes" and good cinematography, it had too "many small shortcomings" and "fail[ed] to appeal to the spectator's sense of justice."[76]

Jackie Saunders likely played the squaw man's white "sweetheart." Red Wing's character swallows her jealousy to rescue her character in the film, but in real life Saunders claimed that Red Wing actually victimized her. Consequently, Saunders filed suit against Young Deer in the Los Angeles County Court at the end of July. "A legal poultice of $5000 is the balm which Jackie Saunders asks the court to give her because Redwing Young Deer bit her on the arm," reported the *Los Angeles Herald*. "Redwing's teeth, the complaint charges, closed on Jackie Saunders's arm in the expensive bite during an altercation between the two women at the S. and M. ranch near Orange where the biter's [*sic*] husband, James Young Deed [*sic*] is employed."[77]

There's no evidence the case went to trial, so either Young Deer paid off Saunders or she simply dropped the suit. But the altercation indicates that Red Wing perceived Saunders as a threat to her person, her professional status, or, more likely, her marriage. Given the events of the following year, Young Deer's romantic attentions toward Saunders dwelled at the root of the women's conflict. Red Wing's ire didn't harm Saunders at all, however. Following her brief stint with the company, Saunders went to Balboa Films and became the "Mary Pickford of the West." She never mentioned her employment with West Coast Studio again.

Despite the tension at the ranch, Red Wing and Young Deer produced several more pictures, released in July. They included *The Greed of Gold*

(July 4),[78] *The Wooing of White Fawn* (July 6), *His Wife's Old Sweetheart* (July 11),[79] *The Unwilling Bride* (July 12), *A Brave Little Indian* (July 18),[80] *The Halfbreed's Foster Sister* (July 20),[81] *His Second Love* (July 24),[82] *The Redman's Friendship* (July 25),[83] and *For the Sake of the Papoose* (July 27), the latter film not to be confused with *For the Papoose*.[84] Of these, Red Wing took the lead in at least *The Wooing of White Fawn* and *The Unwilling Bride*.[85]

The Wooing of White Fawn told the tale of two Indian brothers in love with the same Indian maid. Red Wing played White Fawn, and Gebhardt played one of the brothers.[86] The brothers' loyalty to each other kept each from fulfilling his desire, but, of course, a twist of fate—and a bizarre twist at that—occurred to seal the deal, as related by *Moving Picture World*: "One day, in a desperate encounter, the younger brother is badly mutilated by the foes who attack the two brothers and loses the sight of one eye. Little White Fawn, with whom they are both in love, prefers the other brother after this event, until he finally dies from a snake bite and she finally marries the blind one."[87]

Critics found Red Wing's unwilling bride "delightful" and "a pleasure to watch."[88] *Moving Picture World*'s critic raved because the film featured "no burnings, no scalpings; no portrayal of the red man as always bad, the white man as always good." *Moving Picture World*'s critic also acknowledged the authority of the filmmakers regarding Indian character, noting that "Princess Redwing's" performance "materially enhanced the naturalness of the story." Young Deer's directing received special mention, "insofar that it is not the white man's way, and that it is the red man's way." Gebhardt likewise received acclaim for his "wonderful agility in movement."[89] *The Unwilling Bride* did not survive over time, but the film marks the apex of Red Wing's and Young Deer's careers. Still, Young Deer's passing as an "authentic Indian" visionary in the contemporaneous world of western films should be duly noted. How much his authentic Indian wife influenced his work escaped the notice of the film's reviewer as usual.

On the eve of the film's release, Orange's Electric Theater put on another Pathé Night, showing Red Wing's *The Squaw's Debt of Gratitude* and an unnamed film featuring the ever-popular West Coast Studio children, Emmons and Radcliffe.[90] Although Mazie Martell again performed, it doesn't appear that anyone from West Coast Studio provided live entertainment.

In August West Coast Studio released another Emmons/Radcliffe vehicle, *In God's Care*.[91] Other films out that month without an apparent Indian female lead but featuring Gebhardt include *The Famous Scout to the Rescue* (August 8),[92] *The Cactus County Lawyer* (August 17),[93] *Jealousy on the Ranch* (August 21),[94] and *The Hand of Destiny* (August 22).[95] De Grasse also appeared with Louise Glaum in *The $2,500 Bride* (August 24). Like *Jealousy on the Ranch*, the film featured a roundup.[96] Glaum may have appeared in other films released in August, but Young Deer's sultry dark-eyed actress was long gone. She left the company to work for Nestor Film Company and then by the end of the year for Universal.[97] Eventually, she joined Ince at Bison 101.

As the Saunders episode suggests, Red Wing had begun to feel the effects of the intense filming schedule and working with her impulsive husband day in and day out. She appeared prominently in only one August release, *Silver Wing's Two Suitors* (August 14). Like *The Cheyenne's Bride*, the characters were all Indian, and Young Deer and Gebhardt played her character's competing Indian suitors. The film featured whirling river rapids, this time on the fictional "Tecumseh River," where either Young Deer's or Gebhardt's character met his death.[98] The film's cinematography passed muster, but *Moving Picture World*'s critic found it "neither exciting" nor "convincing."[99]

Red Wing acted with Gebhardt in *The Penalty Paid* (released September 5). The film featured another "thrilling pursuit in canoes through the smooth waters of a shaded creek and a hand-to-hand combat in the water." The scenic Santiago Creek, a thirty-four-mile-long tributary of the Santa Ana River, served the scene well. *Moving Picture World*'s reviewer deemed the film a "fine picture," with Red Wing's and Gebhardt's performances meeting their "regular high standard." Further, he claimed, "There is splendid photography and rare scenery, especially panoramic views of mountains."[100]

Red Wing may have also played Silver Moon in *Silver Moon's Rescue* (released September 21). The story was a bit different for Red Wing, however. Instead of cowboys simply harassing her character for selling beadwork in a saloon, they try to force her to drink whiskey. An Indian brave (probably Gebhardt) intercedes and during a struggle accidentally kills one of the cowboys. Silver Wing is then captured, and "after a rattling good fight," her tribe rescues her.[101]

It's unclear how Red Wing felt about working at the isolated ranch, but Young Deer relished his time there. Given his urban upbringing as the son of a woman born into slavery, the ranch provided not only a respite from city life but also a place where he ruled the roost. He often invited his friends to come for a visit, including in August the "theatrical light" Lewis Stone, who acted in at least one of Young Deer's films.[102] And when he tired of ranch life—at least as a film subject—he could easily pack up his already nomadic cast and crew. For example, after the summer's films were in the can, Young Deer took everyone to the Mexican border, where they made "some war pictures" that likely included *The Bandit's Spur* (released September 18), which featured all Mexican characters.[103]

Afterward the company headed back to Edendale to film interior shots at the studio.[104] *A Redman's Loyalty* (released October 5), with Gebhardt as Indian "Bull Moose," and *The Horse Thieves* (released October 10), in which Red Wing played her usual Indian helper role, made up the remaining October releases definitely shot at the ranch.[105]

Plans were in the works to go to Catalina Island, where Red Wing and Gebhardt were set to play the leads in "an idyllic drama."[106] If that was enough to keep Red Wing busy, it wasn't enough for her husband, whose ambitions grew daily by leaps and bounds. Apparently, he was still dreaming of his own Inceville when he purchased thirty-five acres of land on Donegan's Hill, a rise in the landscape that once overlooked Edendale but has since been bulldozed to make room for urban development. Young Deer planned to build "a big modern motion picture plant" on the hill and to abandon West Coast Studio shortly thereafter because it was too small.[107] According to *Moving Picture World*, he intended to create "a small town of his own on the hill, with an inclined railroad connecting with the street car system, and a great amount of landscape and architectural embellishment." His empire never came to fruition, likely because Pathé Frères declined to expand its western division.

Besides living and breathing film production, Young Deer was an avid boxing fan. In fact, he'd played a water boy in Bison Co.'s *Dooley Referees the Big Fight* (1910), which featured Charles Avery as Dooley and an unknown African American man who was probably a boxer in real life.[108] By the summer of 1912 Young Deer's name had begun appearing in sports columns attached to Mexican lightweight boxer Joe Rivers, who later had a film-acting career.[109] "Young Deer, the moving picture man, is a good loser," the *Los Angeles Times* declared. "He has bet and won on Rivers a lot of times, and was a heavy loser Monday, but comes back with an offer to back Rivers for $5000 to beat Mandot in another match and is willing to deposit $1000 at any time as a forfeit."[110] In early September the *Los Angeles Times* sports column reported that Young Deer managed featherweight boxer Johnny Schiff, who would also later appear in one of Young Deer's films: "He intends to send Johnny out to Edendale and have him train for his coming match. Young Deer says he will feed Johnny up well and give him a fair chance to show what there is in him."[111] If Red Wing shared her husband's enthusiasm for boxing, it was never reported. She certainly may have been concerned about the amount of the bets he wagered. Still, she enjoyed diamond rings and fancy clothes, as befit a film star. Perhaps their match was even on that score.

After the boxing event, Young Deer took fifteen members of the company, including Red Wing, to Yuma, Arizona, where the town welcomed cast and crew with open arms. He intended "to make a drama dealing with the Yuma [Quechan] . . . an industrious tribe who have long lived in a state closely approximating civilization," reported *Moving Picture World*. Young Deer, "who is himself an Indian, though of another tribe and having besides the advantages of a college education," *Moving Picture World* further misstated, was said to have been "studying Yuma lore and is now to make use of it."[112]

Suddenly, Arizona attracted western film companies because it was not yet suburbanized and it was home to several Indian tribes. It also offered mining opportunities, which many in the western film industry enjoyed doing on their down time, as well as films focused on the subject. Charles French and Maxwell Smith had paired up to invest in some mining ventures near Tucson and had just named three of their mines, which had yielded several pounds of rich gold ore, after themselves: the French, the Camera Man Number One, and the Olive Number 1.[113] The latter mine was named for Olive Hunt, Smith's new bride and the daughter of the men's third partner, Oliver Hunt of California.

While West Coast Studio shot film in Arizona, Oliver Hunt accidentally shot Maxwell Smith, who had married Hunt's daughter just nine days before. The newlyweds slept in a wagon at the mining camp while Hunt rested nearby on the ground. When Smith got out of the wagon in the night, Hunt mistook him for "a wildcat or some other animal." Smith died in the hospital the next morning.[114] It's unknown if Red Wing or Young Deer attended his funeral or whether French was in the area to bid farewell to his young partner. Nonetheless, Camera Man Number One was about to strike it rich when Smith's father-in-law's bullet struck him down. Perhaps not coincidentally, French appeared soon after in Bison 101's *The Vengeance of Fate*, a tale of jealousy, mining, and murder.

By the end of September, Red Wing and Young Deer had "secured several pictures" in Arizona with "weird and peculiar backgrounds." *Jim's Partner* (released October 31) and *Broken Hearts* (released November 6) fit the description, and both films are mining dramas.[115] The company also filmed *Buster to the Rescue* (released in November 9), a story set in Arizona that undoubtedly starred Emmons and Radcliffe.[116] The two young actors were also featured in *The Branded Arm* along with Gebhardt and Maison, who played Indians.[117] Curiously, Red Wing acted, at least as an Indian female, in few of the Arizona films. Gebhardt starred in the mining story *Red Eagle, the Lawyer* (released November 23), which centered on the predicament of a Yuma Indian and the "unscrupulous spectators" who attempt to swindle him out of his "rich lands." It's unknown who played Red Eagle's love interest, White Feather.[118] Maison played the mother in *Fate's Decree* (released December 11) and Señorita Garcia, the lead in *Her Faithful Yuma Servant* (released January 15).[119] Gebhardt played the Yuma servant. Shortly after the film was shot, Maison left the company to play leads for the Nestor Company. She reconsidered returning to Pathé later that year but decided to stay with Nestor.[120]

Red Wing definitely played the Indian lead in *The Winning of White Dove* (released November 30), shot in Arizona.[121] Gebhardt played her love interest, Moose Head, "a Yuma brave." It's appropriate to wonder if Red Wing at twenty-eight felt content to play the one-dimensional Indian princess over and over again. Still, it was the only decent role for a Native American woman in early twentieth-century America. The "Indian drudge," a soulless beast of burden, was the other option. If Red Wing perpetuated the Indian princess stereotype—and she certainly did—at least she made it her own.

The same day West Coast Studio released *Red Eagle, the Lawyer*, Kalem Company released *Red Wing and the Paleface*. The film, which was highly publicized, ends with "Red Wing" taking her own life to join her dead lover in "the happy hunting ground."[122] Character actress Jane Wolfe portrayed Red Wing. Wolfe had Pennsylvania Dutch ancestry but was often cast in ethnic roles.[123] Wolfe was also slated to play Red Wing in *Buckskin Coat* (released February 15, 1913). If Red Wing felt put out by Wolfe's performances of her namesake, at least the fan magazine *Motion Picture Story Magazine* assured its readers, "Red Wing is a real Indian."[124]

The cast and crew had returned home by November in time for Tom Ince's surprise birthday party. After NYMPC reneged on a merger with several independent companies that would become Universal Company, it lost the use of its brand name "Bison." As a result, Ince's Bison 101 Ranch Pictures transformed into Broncho Pictures. Kessell and Bauman had also just hired Mack Sennett to head NYMPC's new Keystone Pictures division, famous today for the Keystone Cops and Charlie Chaplin films. Sennett had acted with Red Wing and Young Deer in Griffith's Cuddebackville pictures, but he eventually took the title of "the King of Comedy." Sennett moved his arm of the company into the old Bison studio on Alessandro Street, and soon thereafter Keystone Pictures became part of Kay-Bee Pictures (for Kessell and Bauman).[125]

"All the members of the Kay-Bee and the Broncho companies" attended Ince's party, according to *Moving Picture World*, "and a number of specially invited guests from other motion picture companies in the vicinity, among the latter being Mack Sennett and Mabel Normand of the Keystone, and Mr. and Mrs. James Young Deer of the Pathe Western Company." Although Red Wing and Young Deer's company competed directly with Ince's company, they were probably glad to be invited to his extravaganza. Young Deer may have felt a pang of jealousy, however, when Ince's friends presented him with a large topaz ring surrounded by diamonds. Ince later "made a speech forgiving everybody for their share in the conspiracy." The lavish party of three hundred or so attendees lasted into the wee hours of the night and featured "a banquet, an impromptu entertainment and a dance."[126]

Immediately after the party Red Wing and Young Deer traveled to New York on business. Gebhardt supervised the studio while they were gone, although one trade magazine said French took on the responsibility, though apparently he was still employed by Broncho Pictures.[127] While Red Wing and Young Deer conducted business meetings with East Coast Pathé, George F. Blaisdell, *Moving Picture World*'s At the Sign of the Flaming Arcs columnist, noted Young Deer's appearance in New York City. He reported Young Deer had just applied for a lifetime membership in the Screen Club.[128] Blaisdell himself belonged to the club, which at the time was located at West 45th Street. The club had been newly established by actor King Bagott in a Broadway café, and its members included "managers, directors, actors, authors, cameramen, and photoplay newspapermen."[129] Although the new organization stressed "unity, advancement and preservation of the motion picture art," it quickly degraded into a social club where favors were traded and the rights of the lower-paying echelon ignored. Whether Young Deer actually retained a membership is unknown.

Red Wing and Young Deer returned to Edendale for Christmas, a day of rest and feasting for most Californians. However, they had work to do and perhaps felt compelled to keep things moving forward after their meeting with Pathé management. They set up a Wild West scene near the studio, but before anyone took their spots, two of their Indian actors, Hilario Pino and William Eagle Eye, "had some words while standing on the sidewalk." Suddenly a large crowd formed when Eagle Eye pulled a knife on Pino, and the two began fighting viciously. Police Detective Rico arrived with a paddy wagon, but he flagged down an automobile, whose driver took Pino to the hospital with minor injuries.

After the police returned to the Central Station, a witness ran to West

Coast Studio and informed someone: "Their Indians had gone on a rampage, and half a dozen cowboys were instructed to round them up." The street-fight crowd laughed and taunted the studio's stock players when they discovered "the cowboys had come to capture the Indians." After angry cowboys steered their horses into the crowd, four detectives arrived on the scene. "When the cowboys saw the police . . . approaching," according to the *Los Angeles Times*, "they stuck their spurs into the flanks of their ponies and rode away in a cloud of dust."[130]

Meanwhile, Detective Rico hauled Eagle Eye to the city jail, and a judge found him guilty of an "intoxication charge." "Fast friends save when in liquor," Eagle Eye and Pino paid fifteen-dollar fines each for battery and walked out of the courtroom together. When a reporter interviewed Young Deer about the raucous event, he blamed nearby citizens for supplying liquor to his "moving picture Indians."[131] Pino was a Pueblo Indian born at White Rock, New Mexico, but did Young Deer know that Eagle Eye was in fact Mexican Chinese and not subject to the current laws prohibiting selling liquor to Indians?[132]

The year 1912 closed with the release of *The Bear Trap* (December 28). The film was likely shot at the ranch, with Gebhardt as Deer Foot, Red Wing as his wife, and De Grasse as a trapper. After the trapper's wife falls into a bear trap, Deer Foot risks his life to save her. The critics complimented the technical elements of the film, which may have included the work of French-born cameraman George Rizard, who became a well-known cinematographer in the 1920s.[133] Beyond that the story was oh-so-predictable and included another "bad Indian squaw" role for Red Wing.[134] *The Bear Hunter* followed (released February 6). The extant film features Red Wing as her namesake; William Eagle Eye as Eagle Feather; Gebhardt as Iron Spider, an Indian trapper; Maison as Miss Mason; and a live bear.[135] The acting bear earned his supper and became another West Coast Studio stock company novelty, taking its place with the beloved child duo and Peggy the horse.

By now, two years had passed since Red Wing had filed for divorce. If she doubted her decision to return to Young Deer as his wife, she nonetheless continued to work with him as his star Indian actress and business partner.

Perhaps real life was secondary in importance to them because they shared so much together on-screen. Red Wing was a natural actress who enjoyed the limelight, and her day-to-day life revolved around playacting and making scenarios come to life. Was fantasy life what kept the couple together? Certainly, early western filmmaking entailed more than fantasy. It meant hard work, long hours, dedication, and lots of derring-do to face inevitable danger. Red Wing's great-nephew Louis Mofsie elucidated the link between Red Wing and her rough-and-tumble life with Young Deer. Her motto was "go and do it," he said, and she wasn't one to hesitate or ponder matters. What more could one ask from a silent film actress? Red Wing obviously actively sought an action-packed life, and if they shared nothing else, Young Deer shared that with her. Was this courage or a way to avoid real-life problems? Undoubtedly, it was both. Young Deer's gutsy bravado and ambition equally matched Red Wing's highly spirited can-do—must-do—nature. As a team they were a force to be reckoned with, but like all cosmic energy, that force would one day burn itself out.

CHAPTER 11

The Calm before the Storm

The dawning of 1913 found Woodrow Wilson on the precipice of his presidential inauguration. The Mexican Revolution entered its third year. The first World War was not yet tangible, but it would take the United States from a policy of pacifism to a declaration of war. Like her country, Red Wing could no longer sustain a passive role in her marriage. The conflict, precipitated by Young Deer's indictment for a federal offense, destroyed their on-screen partnership for good.

In retrospect, the New Year presented the calm before the storm. Red Wing and Young Deer lived conveniently at 1854 Alessandro Street, just kitty-corner from the studio.[1] Their home has since been demolished, but when *Los Angeles Times* journalist Gertrude M. Price came to call for an interview with Red Wing, she found it "a delightful mixture of 'Americanism' and 'Indianism.'" Red Wing's home "has a gas stove and a bathroom and regular dining room furniture, etc., just as there might be in a regular American home," Price informed her untutored readers. "But her walls are dotted with all sorts of Indian trophies. Her portieres are wonderful Indian beadwork. Her rugs are Indian and scores of her ornaments on the table and walls are Indian too."[2] Price's human-interest story hit national newspapers in April and confirmed the image afforded by Maxwell Smith's 1910 photo. Red Wing was a modern Indian lady and not exactly the primitive one her fans so adored.

Like many of the so-called Red Progressives of her day, Red Wing approached the U.S. policy of assimilation as a hope for her people rather than as a hindrance. Yet like many of them she also believed Native American art forms and traditions should be treasured. As Smith's and Price's impressions concur, Red Wing proudly displayed Native-made items—hers included—throughout her home and on her person. The binary opposition between Richard Pratt's before-and-after Carlisle photos failed to define Red Wing. She wasn't an early or a late version of his Indian. She was a paradox and a survivor of cultural genocide. Time, natural talent, and life experience had shaped her into much more than a testimony to the success of Indian education. She fashioned herself into a unique cultural phenomenon, a thoroughly modern Indian woman who nonetheless portrayed a primitive Indian maiden in theaters across the world.

Young Deer exploited the trope of Pratt's before-and-after Indian, however, when he entered the annual Tournament of Roses Parade, held on New Year's Day in nearby Pasadena. On the one hand, his unoriginal idea was a no-brainer; it was soothing nationalistic fodder for a public eager to believe the myth. As Pratt had proved years ago when he marched his students in various stages of "civilization" through the streets of downtown Philadelphia, the two sides of Indianness provided a picturesque spectacle easily adapted to a parade and easy on the eyes and soul of America. On the other hand, the before-and-after idea may have been Red Wing's, a dusty remnant from her Carlisle days, dear to her heart like a fairy tale heard over and over.

The *Los Angeles Times* ran a lengthy piece on the parade, as did *Moving Picture World*, which declared, "The activity of the motion picture people of Southern California was by far the most noticeable feature" of the parade and "occupied nearly three-quarters of a mile of the five-mile floral parade." The Tournament of Roses parade entertained between 75,000 and 150,000 spectators.[3] This year, the usual floral floats played second fiddle to the photoplayers who acted out scenes here and there along the route before their company's cameraman. Mack Sennett and Fred Mace from Keystone Pictures acted as British "Famous Detectives" as they "surveyed the crowds with ludicrous solemnity." They were chauffeured through the parade route in a spiffy new automobile draped with flower garlands and garnished on top with pretty Mabel Normand, Keystone's up-and-coming leading lady.[4] The parade also featured a race between an elephant and two camels (the elephant won) from Selig Company's Wild Animal Farm near Eastlake Park.

Pathé Frères proper sent a cameraman to cover the event for its weekly newsreel, *Pathé Weekly*. West Coast Studio's elaborate float, Indian Life—Past and Present, caught everyone's attention and may have appeared in the newsreel. "One end . . . showed a smartly dressed college graduated Indian." The other exhibited "a teepee with an aged squaw sitting before it." An actor dressed as an Indian hunter faced the unknown actress, having just given her his hunt, the carcass of a deer. A live wolf stood at his side, while a "cavalcade of Indians and cowboys in costume" paraded behind the float.[5] The *Los Angeles Times* concluded that Young Deer's entry, "set forth in the midst of elaborate floral embellishments," included a "procession of Indians" that "add[ed] to the picturesqueness of the parade."[6]

The new Universal Company paraded cowboy and Indian stock players, but its entry lacked the artistry and excitement of Young Deer's. Again, Bison 101 Pictures, now part of Kay-Bee, provided West Coast Studio's only real competition. "100 Sioux Indians, men women and children" from Inceville, entertained the enthusiastic crowd with "demonstrations of Indian life." The actors made and broke camp, did a mock war march, and performed "a number of tribal dances and various games." Miller Brothers "rough riders, lariat tossers and broncho busters" showed off their skills, to the crowd's delight.[7]

After the Rose Bowl parade, Young Deer and Red Wing closed the studio for "overhauling," while Pathé Frères released several of their films shot in Arizona and at the ranch in January. These included *The Frame-Up* (January 2), *Peggy and the Old Scout* (January 8), *Her/The Faithful Yuma Servant* (January 15), *The Unfulfilled Oath* (January 22), *The Half Breed* (January 23), and *Saved by His Horse* (January 30). French played the old scout with Peggy the trained horse, who also appeared in *Saved by His Horse*. Gebhardt played an Indian chief in the latter film.[8] Gebhardt also starred in the rest of the January releases. Maison played Gebhardt's leading lady in *Her Faithful Yuma Servant* and perhaps also in *The Half Breed*. Red Wing played his Indian wife in *The Frame-Up*.[9] *Moving Picture World*'s critic noted that young boys in the audience "took especial delight in 'Princess Red Wing's' bare back riding."[10]

Red Wing also played Mexican heroine Julia Calero in *The Unfulfilled Oath*. After drunken Rurales killed Calero's father during the revolution, she gives her "oath of allegiance" to revolutionists, and she determines to avenge her father's death.[11] However, when rebels capture Gebhardt's character, General Maderez, Calero wavers on her oath. Again, gratitude drives Red Wing's character. "A story, not a picture of life," reported *Moving Picture World*. "It is clearly and smoothly told and entertains, but there is little power in such to stir emotions and little chance for sincere acting."[12] Red Wing's performance as a grateful female Mexican revolutionary couldn't compete with her bareback-riding Indian princess.

By 1913 the rage for social clubs that swept America had reached the West Coast. The Los Angeles Photoplayers Club, also known as the Reel Club, debuted shortly after New York's Screen Club. Officers included Keystone's president, Fred Mace, who organized the all-male organization; West Coast Studio's De Grasse; and Red Wing's old costars from Bison Co., J. Barney Sherry, Frank Montgomery, and Pat Hartigan.[13] Young Deer joined the club in January but a little too late to win the bid from Montgomery for the first ticket of the club's grand fund-raiser, the Valentine Day's Ball.[14] Even though Red Wing's gambling husband lost, he made sure she had a prominent seat at the festive ball. The club planned the lavish affair for the Shrine Auditorium on the Saturday night of Valentine's Day.

A night parade with the participation of all forty-five local motion picture companies kicked off the evening. "Wild animals, automobiles, Indians, cowboys and prize horses" paraded for spectators, along with Selig's Big Otto, the elephant that marshaled his company's procession in the Rose Parade.[15] The fund-raiser netted more than $13,000, most of it marked to construct a clubhouse. Club members sold ten thousand tickets, and more than five thousand attended, among them two thousand or so motion picture people, including Balshofer and NYMPC's Bauman. The headline for the event, "They Really Have Voices," was timely. Thomas Edison had just paid $50,000 for the patent of a machine that added sound to pictures.[16] But "talkies" were a promise, not a reality, and the public's desire to finally listen to their silent film idols boosted ticket sales.

"Friends of years standing heard one another speak for the first time last night at the photoplayers' inaugural ball in Shrine Auditorium," wrote Al G. Waddell in the *Times*. "Actors in the motion pictures met and mingled with their audience and greatly enjoyed the experience. The audience long had wondered what the voices of their favorites sounded like, and how these men and women of a make-believe world really looked in the flesh. Curiosity in this direction was pleasantly gratified at this remarkably successful affair." The actors wore formal attire to show fans how they "really looked in the flesh." Many of the women, like Red Wing, were only "familiar . . . in the guise of western heroines . . . attired in rough-and-ready garments." When Red Wing's fans picked her out from "the merry throng," they were delighted to see her in a "gorgeous gown," looking as beautiful, elegant, and adorable as her former co-actress, "little Mary Pickford," who also attended the gala.[17]

Mabel Normand and other lead actors performed a grand number to open the gala. The ball that followed featured twenty-four dances with motion picture–themed titles, including the "studio stumble," the "dramatic drug," the "silent slide," the "camera cavort," the "screen scoot," the "reel rave," the "actors' rumble," and the "directors' dirge."[18] Red Wing and Young Deer surely danced at least one selection but probably spent most of the night talking with friends and soaking in the adoration of their fans. The fund-raiser went well past midnight and was a smashing success. The historic event perhaps initiated the flood of Hollywood celebrity galas that followed.

Young Deer sought out a new stock player to fill the role of leading white lady. First he tried Oliver Skinner, French's former cast mate from *In Old Kentucky*. A *Moving Picture World* columnist made much of Young Deer's and Skinner's satisfaction with their new partnership, including that she felt eager to quit the stage for the silver screen. However, when one of Young Deer's scenarios required her to "fall unconscious across a railroad track" while a real train approached, he again pushed the limits of safety. "How close can you run without danger?" he asked the engineer of the rented train. "I can come within six feet of her," he responded to the director's satisfaction. Apparently, the engineer feigned confidence.

He put on the brake so late that the train brushed Skinner's clothing.[19] Skinner departed Edendale soon after.

Next, Young Deer tried out Lillian Wiggins, a beautiful blonde and statuesque showgirl. Wiggins (later known as Lillian Worth) was born in Brooklyn, and though she was gorgeous, she was no vapid Kewpie doll. She eventually won the vote for New York City's most popular actress. When Young Deer spotted her in Los Angeles in mid-November, she was playing the "nouveau riche" Mrs. Malaprop in the touring Broadway musical comedy *The Kiss Waltz*.[20] After the show he invited the performers to come see how a motion picture was made. Most of them lost interest in the process, but Wiggins, fascinated, stayed on, asking Young Deer question after question. A journalist who interviewed her later explained, "When the light began to fade and the day's work for the motion picture players was over she thanked the director and remarked that she would like to try acting of that sort herself. She . . . believed the day of the showgirl was drawing to a close and . . . didn't get one anywhere after all." Young Deer asked her to come back in the morning so he could "give her a trial."[21]

Wiggins showed up at 7:00 a.m. ready to audition for a western. Young Deer gave her what then amounted to a screen test, asking her to perform various scenes. She recalled that he was flabbergasted when he learned that she was "an expert horsewoman" and had been riding since she was a child. He staged some interior scenes so she could prove her acting ability.

Wiggins's recollection provides insight into Young Deer's directing style. "It is one thing to see the film as it is projected on the screen in a theater, and quite another to see the living persons 'acting it out' before the camera," she explained. "The latter is as unromantic as cooking a dinner. The actors rehearse each scene perhaps five minutes. The stage director speaks pointedly regarding their shortcomings. Then there is a sharp command and they start to go over it again. This time the camera whizzes monotonously; the stage director's remarks are as swift and sharp as arrows. The thing must be done right, for spoiling films means a loss of money and time."[22]

Wiggins impressed Young Deer with her beauty, talent, and athleticism. He immediately asked her to join the company and offered her a salary. She said, "Yes."[23] Wiggins played opposite Gebhardt and De Grasse in her first film, *The Clutch of Conscience* (released February 13, 1913).[24]

Two weeks later, West Coast Studio released *The Pioneer's Recompense* (February 27), starring Gebhardt and Red Wing. *Moving Picture World* gave it a solid review, calling it an "imaginative, up-to-date picture." *Moving Picture World* also praised Gebhardt and particularly "Princess Red Wing" for their accurate portrayals of the "primitive psychology" of "redmen."[25] Gebhardt gained further attention as "the perfect Indian type" when a California artist carved a bust of Gebhardt, intending to market copies through a distributing company. Whether the artist's plan came to fruition, his interest demonstrates that Gebhardt captured what the public viewed as attractive and essential male "Indianness."[26] However, Gebhardt moved on when Universal Pictures offered him the chance to both direct and act in Universal comedies. *The Love That Turned* (March 13) and *The Sheriff's Reward* (March 27) were Gebhardt's last March releases.[27] Red Wing probably played opposite him in the first film, another story that took place during the Mexican Revolution. Wiggins played De Grasse's wife in the second, while Gebhardt had the role of her "second lover."[28]

The studio shut down for two or three weeks at the beginning of April, at which time the company took a well-needed rest. When they returned to work, *Variety* lauded Lillian Wiggins as "the leading woman of this company of clever people," while *Moving Picture World* reported that George Larkin, Red Wing's first costar with Pathé American, planned to replace Gebhardt.[29] But Larkin left no evidence of his acting days with West Coast Studio. If anything, it was a short stint between acting for Éclair Films in February and Kalem in July. Gebhardt's name, on the other hand, continued to be associated with West Coast Studio films released in late April, which may have been held for release to tide over the studio upon his departure.[30] Meanwhile, Madeline West, Gebhardt's wife, played "heavies" for West Coast Studio, De Grasse took over Charles French's role as assistant manager of the company, and Red Wing waited in the wings for her next "big Indian picture."[31]

While she waited, Selig Polyscope released *The Tie of the Blood* (April 17). Lo and behold, the film's leading characters were Carlisle graduates "Red Wing" and "Deer Foot." What was going on? Was Selig honoring his next-door neighbors or spoofing them? "For actors in Indian roles the Selig players do as well as could be expected," stated one critic, "conforming closely to the popular conception of what an Indian looks like and how he moves. Harold Lockwood, cast as Deer Foot, the son of Sitting Bull, does capable work, while . . . Amy Trusk as Red Wing, the daughter of Big Eagle, is pleasing."[32] If imitation is the sincerest form of flattery, then Red Wing might have been pleased too, though her reaction is unknown.

Gertrude Price's human-interest story began appearing in newspapers across the country that April. Price's piece, one of several written about moving picture heroines, solidified Red Wing's reputation and fan base and also validated her as the real Red Wing. The article was titled "Picturesque Indian Maid Is Fearless, Ambitious, Clever," and Red Wing's professional head shot accompanied the piece with the caption, "Red Wing Keeps House and Acts, Too." The piece begins as Price relays Young Deer's introduction to Red Wing. "Up on the side of a hill not far from the Pathe studio, Young Deer led me one sunny afternoon last January to see his wife," Price wrote. "'Maybe the house won't be in just exactly American order,' Youngdeer [sic] told her. 'But you won't notice when you see Red Wing.'" "I found Red Wing sitting cross-kneed on his bed, half wrapped in a wonderful Indian blanket," Price explained, "her raven hair falling in two thick braids, one on either shoulder. 'The most picturesque little maid I ever saw,' I thought as she put out a very soft little hand for me to shake, and lifted her eyes from a delicate bit of fancy work."[33]

The publicity was a boon for the actress and, like the Valentine Ball, ostensibly showed her fans what she was like in real life. Price also published interviews with Bessie Eyton, Mona Darkfeather, and Red Wing's new stock player, Lillian Wiggins, whose star was fast ascending.[34] It's hard not to wonder if Red Wing felt some resentment toward West Coast Studio's new leading lady. In a metaphorical sense, she occupied the position of white queen, while Red Wing still held the status of red princess. It's easy to assume Red Wing displayed jealousy of her husband's attention to other women actors, who were invariably white women. On the other hand, Young Deer didn't seem to mind Red Wing's on-screen relationships with at least Gebhardt or De Grasse, but her trust in his fidelity to their marriage vows was about to undergo a serious inquest.

It all started with a stunt and ended with a scandal that rocked Los Angeles. To begin with, on April 23, as the *New York Dramatic Mirror* reported, "Manager James Young Deer, of the West Coast Studio . . . was fined heavily when his men tied a horse's feet and rolled the animal down a hill for a picture effect. The Humane Society pressed the case."[35] *Moving Picture World* alleged that the "inhumane realism" occurred when Young Deer, determined to "outdo all other motion picture producers in realism," filmed Red Wing's next big "Indian picture," titled *General Scott's Protégé* (released May 3).[36]

Red Wing plays her namesake, who lives with the family of General Scott. She leaves his family when her tribal chief's son commits a crime and her lover is sacrificed to pay the penalty. When Scott dies, the Indians try to get Red Wing to come back to the tribe, but she refuses. A battle with soldiers ensues, but "little Red Wing" ends the story as its heroine. It's not clear how the film involved a cowboy riding too close to the edge of a cliff and then saved himself by jumping off his horse to cling to the edge of a precipice, after which his trusty steed falls to his death, "dashed to pieces on the rocks below."[37] But this film was later identified as the culprit.

Whether Young Deer planned the stunt from the start or whether it occurred to him when he spotted the location for the scene, he decided that one of his "half dead" stock horses that contracted blood poisoning after an eye injury would do nicely as the cowboy's horse. After he placed his camera to get the best view of "the sheer drop" and yelled "action," one of his riders mounted the poor animal. The horse was sick, but he was not dumb. When the rider tried to edge him close to the cliff, he refused to budge. Young Deer realized his plan was not working, so he decided his horse handlers, including broncobuster Milt Brown, should hogtie the animal and push it over the brink. "The horse was led to the edge of the cliff, but while its legs were being tied it began to scream like a human being and to struggle," reported *Moving Picture World*. "The horse succeeded by its struggles in prolonging its miserable existence, for, instead of going over the place selected, it rolled and fell down a steep slope at one side and was merely injured, instead of being killed outright."[38]

The shrieking agony of the poor terrified animal brought local women running to the scene. When they saw the men push the horse over the cliff, they alerted the police, who arrested the three horse handlers and fined them fifty dollars apiece. Young Deer certainly wasn't the first movie man to be accused of cruelty to animals, but the event foreshadowed what was to come.[39] "The incident has done immense undeserved harm to the motion picture industry in this city," wrote *Moving Picture World*, "for the newspaper reports excited public sentiment, which, unfortunately, is not discriminating and is directed against all the producing companies." Newspaper readers filled editorial columns "with general condemnation of the motion picture producers."[40]

Word got out beyond Los Angeles, and it got out fast. *Moving Picture World* columnist George Blaisdell devoted his entire mid-April column to the debacle, quoting a letter he received from an unknown writer:

> Have you seen the Patheplay . . . called "General Scott's Ward [Protégé]"? The treatment that a dumb creature gets in that picture is enough to make boil the blood of any human being. I have been around horses pretty much all my life and have been with men who often had to depend upon their horses, and maybe I have more affection for these animals than others. But believe me, if there'd been any real men around when the bunch who took that picture chucked that horse into the coulee there would have been some real shooting.[41]

Blaisdell thought the film's release was "incomprehensible," since Young Deer included the pathetic scene in the film. Blaisdell noted that Milt Brown, George Champion, and Jim Kid paid fines as the horse's handlers, while the "fault unquestionably lay at the door of the director."[42]

If Red Wing's film exploited her husband's inhumane realism, it seems the incident or one like it was used a second time for *The Fugitive* (released May 28). The film's scenario includes a "thrilling scene" in which an innocent man has "a terrible fall" with his horse while making his escape. However, a *Moving Picture World* critic stated, "Only a bit of this is shown so that the mind is kept from seeing its brutality."[43]

Expediently following the exposure of his directing craft, Young Deer packed up everyone—lock, stock, and barrel—and headed for the ranch in Santiago Canyon. They brought some large dogs and "a great bear" and set up tents and a makeshift studio around the old S & M Ranch house. As before, the company filmed a roundup that featured three hundred range horses to add "realism to the next batch of westerns."[44] Although the hubbub about the horse cruelty subsided, the problems for Mr. and Mrs. Young Deer had just begun.

CHAPTER 12

Young Deer and the White Slavery Ring

The ranch provided a welcome respite for Red Wing's company that spring in particular. Camping under the scented oak trees, spotting deer, rabbits, foxes, and bobcat, and gazing at the shimmering stars in the immense night sky provided a tonic that kept the company focused on the present film schedule. However, on Thursday, May 1, law enforcement officials interrupted the company's peaceful intermission.[1] Orange County under-sheriff George C. Law and Los Angeles Police detective Louis Rico (the same official from the Pino and Eagle Feather altercation) showed up at the camp. First, they questioned one of the company's horse handlers. While the three chatted, a young white woman dressed in Indian costume began saddling her horse. Rico didn't pay much attention to her, but Law suspected that she planned to warn Young Deer of their arrival. He alerted Rico, and they followed the woman in their automobile. She halted her horse near an old coalmine where the cast and crew had just finished filming. When Rico spotted Young Deer, he served him a subpoena to testify in court regarding what the newspapers proclaimed was "a white slavery ring."

The case centered on Long Beach hotel owner and multimillionaire George H. Bixby but expanded to include other alleged perpetrators. Interestingly, Bixby came from an Orange County pioneer family who had owned the S & M Ranch.[2] Bixby was indicted for "contributing to the delinquency of minors," and Mrs. Josie Rosenberg and Mrs. Elizabeth Espy, who ran separate "rooming houses" in Los Angeles, were indicted for introducing "minor girls to men of wealth for immoral purposes." On May 3 the Los Angeles Superior Court charged Bixby with "specific acts of degeneracy in connection with the delinquency of two minor girls."[3] The alleged victims, Irene Brown Levy, a waitress, and Cleo Helen Parker, a nurse, were or near eighteen years old, but California law specified under twenty-one as minors.

Twenty-year-old Katie Phillips, said to be "a scenario writer" and "motion-picture actress," pressed the first charge against Bixby. Phillips started her career as a chorus girl and ended it as a burlesque performer. After beginning a relationship with Bixby, whose alias was "the Black Pearl," she claimed she ended it with a slap to his face when she discovered he was married. Aware of his illicit relations with minors, she then filed charges against him. Afterward she claimed Bixby threatened her and then indirectly paid her $100 to leave town. She also claimed he sent someone after her to San Francisco to "rough her up." Bixby hired a private detective to find evidence of blackmail, and law enforcement arrested Phillips in San Francisco for vagrancy. Phillips was taken back to Los Angeles to testify before the grand jury about the time Rico and Law served the subpoena on Young Deer.[4]

Young Deer was certainly aware of the situation when Law and Rico arrived at the ranch, since the *Los Angeles Times* first reported on the case in mid-April. On April 23 the *Times* further reported that nineteen-year-old Evelyn Nesbeith "led astray" "vivacious" seventeen-year-old Christine Neal, who came from Seattle, when she introduced Neal "to the night life of a great city." Allegedly, Neal "tasted the hidden joys, the late suppers at all-night cafes," and "the midnight dash in an auto to beach and Vernon."[5] The latter destination, just south of downtown Los Angeles, often hosted boxing matches attended by Young Deer and his many friends.

Neal and a few other women testified that they went to Vernon disguised as boys to attend a prizefight. Other witnesses spied the crossdressed girls ringside. They also saw them sharing "a lively night" with "several well-known men" at the Vernon Country Club following the fight.[6] Old Bison Co.'s Pat Hartigan was Neal's date. The police sent Neal to Juvenile Hall, but she refused to testify against her thirty-year-old paramour because "she loved him." The judge sentenced her to the Whittier

Reformatory in Orange County, where she was to remain until she reached twenty-one. Her girlfriend, Nesbeith, "proved more tractable." Nesbeith testified that they went on "joy rides," attended a prizefight, and visited "Hartigan's room" more than once.[7]

Young Deer, an avid boxing fan and trainer, was subpoenaed for a different case involving a minor, Evelyn Quick, and two automobile salesmen, William La Casse and Richard Hollingsworth. Both men were "charged with a statutory crime." Quick, born Florence Lavina Quick, was a fifteen-year-old Keystone actress. Although she wasn't involved with Bixby or Hartigan, she gave investigators "the names of other men with whom she associated," as well as "the names of a number of girls . . . treading the primrose path."[8]

Quick informed investigators that a "married film couple" who noticed "her beautiful blue eyes and luscious complexion" had discovered her in a drugstore. She was then fourteen. They offered her twenty-five dollars a week to act in their films, and she accepted. The coverage of her testimony gave no names, but Young Deer and Red Wing employed her about this time.[9] Quick was not just passing through an acting career like Katie Phillips. Shortly after the trial, she was savvy enough to change her name to Jewell Carmen. By 1915 she had played Douglas Fairbanks's leading lady; she then married screen director Roland West in 1918. After West had an affair with the beautiful actress Thelma Todd, Jewell Carmen became a suspect in Todd's headline-making murder. She was not convicted.

William La Casse declared he wanted a public hearing to prove his innocence, and public it was. When Young Deer showed up to court on May 5 for La Casse's preliminary examination, he received another subpoena, this time from the grand jury. When Quick showed up to court from the juvenile detention center that day, some "officials connected with the grand jury probe" declared her "the most beautiful young woman drawn into the case." "Handsomely gowned in a peculiar shade of blue that matched her eyes," Quick, according to the *Los Angeles Herald*, "told her story simply and directly." "I am 15 years old," she stated. "My next birthday will be July 13." She testified that she met La Casse through Richard Hollingsworth in January at the Vernon Country Club. "On January 26 I was asked by La Casse to go to Pasadena with him and a Miss Wilde and another man to have some pictures taken to advertise automobiles." "Mr. La Casse paid a great deal of attention to me," she said. "On one occasion I went to the Raphael Apartments with him. On another occasion I went with him to a bungalow he owned on Washington street [where] he put a $lo gold piece in my stocking."[10]

"I was at James Youngdeer's studio at San Juan Capistrano [near the S & M Ranch] when Mr. Hollingsworth appeared. Mr. Youngdeer introduced me and Mr. Hollingsworth apparently took a fancy to my eyes too, because he talked about them," she continued. "Well, unfortunately, I listened. I wish my eyes had not been so blue or so whatever it was."[11] A few days after her testimony, Nestor Film Company wooed Quick from Keystone Pictures to become its leading lady. As *Moving Picture News* reported, "Her beauty and talents have already won her high esteem."[12] Of course, no mention appeared in the trades about the charges.

Quick wasn't La Casse's only object of desire.[13] He also began an affair with Helen L. Daveys Engstrum, the "wife of a wealthy capitalist." One newspaper reported that if the court acquitted La Casse "of the charges brought by Miss Quick . . . he will marry Mrs. Engstrum soon as she is free from her present husband."[14] Paul Engstrum was granted a divorce in July based on his claim that his wife frequented the Vernon Country Club with La Casse and that subsequently he found her "scantily clad" in La Casse's apartment.[15]

The case was sordid, to say the least. Richard Hollingsworth's wife committed suicide at the end of April after the scandal hit the newspapers. He was also formally charged with contributing to the delinquency of Christine Neal. Young Deer apparently appeared for the prosecution, but his testimony at La Casse's preliminary hearing wasn't reported. Young Deer was described by a *Los Angeles Times* sports columnist as a man who "has many friends in Los Angeles" because "he does things on the square," and he undoubtedly frequented the Vernon Country Club with La Casse and Hollingsworth.[16]

On May 14 warrants were issued for the arrest of fourteen more men and one woman. All the alleged victims named in the warrants were girls "between the ages of 11 and 14." One of the arrests may have been of William Aldridge, a prizefight promoter, who was accused of contributing to Evelyn Nesbeith's delinquency.[17] The *Los Angeles Herald* reported that the probation officer's investigation led him to the conclusion that "all of the men wanted in connection with these cases were acting together in a systematic effort to corrupt the young girls and furnish recruits for the underworld," although this assertion is far-fetched.[18] The exaggeration made serious what was a common criminal offense: older men soliciting minor girls for status, companionship, and sex.

After the preliminary hearing Young Deer began training boxer Bert Fagan at the ranch.[19] Somehow in the chaos Red Wing continued making films. Following *General Scott's Protégé*, she starred with Gebhardt in *A Redskin's Mercy* (released May 14), which featured either Lillian Wiggins or Virginia Chester.[20] The rest of West Coast Studio's 1913 productions were all or nearly all filmed at the ranch. Notably, some of the film titles reflect the pathos that began in the spring of 1913 and ended in December: *The Fugitive* (released May 28), *The Squaw Man's Awakening* (May 31), *The Outlaw's Love* (June 19), *The Trapper's Mistake* (June 28), *The Friendless Indian* (July 1), *A False Accusation* (July 23), *The Erring Brother* (August 13), *The House Divided* (August 14), *The Mexican Gambler* (August 19), *$1000 Reward* (August 30), *The Price of Jealousy* (September 6), *An Accidental Shot* (September 11), *Her Brave Rescuer* (September 20), *The Blind Gypsy* (September 23), *The Secret Treasure* (September 24), *Lillian's Nightmare* (September 30), *A Yankee in Mexico* (October 14), *The Bullet's Mark* (October 17), *The Poisoned Stream* (October 21), *The Faithless Friend* (November 27), *A Break for Freedom* (December 3), *A Bear Escape* (December 5), and, finally, *An Indian Don Juan* (December 23).[21]

The May through August releases that featured Red Wing are unknown. Suffice it to say, however, that *The Fugitive* was a prophetic title. She may have appeared as De Grasse's Indian wife in *The Squaw Man's Awakening*, and if so, she played another "bad squaw."[22] Apart from that, Red Wing probably played in the Mexican-themed films, *The House Divided* and *The Mexican Gambler*.[23] By July De Grasse had left West Coast Studio for a position to direct for the Lubin Manufacturing Company. Virginia Chester, ever besieged with health problems, nursed a broken ankle. The company bear also suffered a mouth disease. When Young Deer decided to check on his animal star, the bear expressed its displeasure. Young Deer approached the animal after handlers roped it. In severe pain, the bear "folded" Young Deer "in loving embrace" and sank its fangs into Young Deer's face.[24] Since Selig Polyscope had established its own zoo, animal pictures were all the rage. Young Deer bandaged his wounds, determined to keep up with the competition, and the bear remained on the ranch.

La Casse's attorney presented his case in Los Angeles before the juvenile court jury on July 25. Young Deer's name isn't mentioned in the testimony given by the newspapers, but he may have driven into the city from the ranch to be a witness. A sign of the sexist times, the press demonized Quick: "As he [her attorney] talked the young girl sat before the Jurors as if to emphasize her girlishness. She was dressed in black and occasionally she would let a shy glance fall upon some of the grayhaired men in whose hands rests La Casse's fate."[25] Hollingsworth stated that he witnessed nothing improper between his friend and Quick. The defense tried to impeach Quick by introducing a family Bible into evidence that seemed to indicate that her birth year had been fudged to make her appear younger than she was. However, other official records clearly show her birthdate was July 13, 1897, as she stated.

For the time being, Red Wing remained under the radar. If she stayed at the ranch, she may have had little to do, as no films released in August seem to have been hers.[26] Fortunately, Gebhardt returned to the company that month, so plans were under way for more films for his Indian princess.[27] By mid-August, however, a tempest had gathered forces on the ranch. A witness complained to the local marshal that someone recklessly drove Young Deer's automobile, identified by its monogram, J.Y.D. One of the female passengers got out of the car, which was filled with "boisterous movie actors," and refused to go any further. "She asked the driver of the machine that had followed them for a ride to the Pathe camp," the local paper reported, "and was taken in." When her new ride approached Young Deer's automobile, one of the male passengers stood before the car and "covered" its driver "with a revolver." The driver stopped his car, and the armed man "ordered the girl to step out and get back into the Pathe car," according to the report. She did as she was told, and her rescuer drove away.[28] No charges were brought against the gunman, because by the time the marshal made it to the ranch all appeared peaceful. But later that month when a small truck left the ranch speeding for the city of Orange, the unknown driver skidded off the road head-on into a barbed-wire fence and landed in a ditch. The local paper ran a humorous item about the accident: "The driver climbed out and viewed the remains. 'What a realistic scene it would have made,' mused he as he footed it to Orange."[29]

About this time Red Wing also found herself the victim of a "realistic scene." The *Strand* magazine, a British publication featuring human-interest stories and fiction, ran an item about her under the title "Heroines of the Film." Young Deer probably submitted the story, which was illustrated with her Pathé publicity photo.

> The unauthorized acquisition of a settler's horse by an Indian is punished in the peculiarly drastic and effective method of the West— hanging upon the nearest tree. This was the fate which "Red-Wing," the talented full red-blooded actress of the Pathe Company, nearly experienced. The manager of the production had completed arrangements with a settler for such stealthy action, but, unfortunately, Red-Wing took the horse of the wrong man, who knew nothing about the matter. When he saw his horse being ridden off by an Indian the man gave chase with one or two pards, caught the runaway, and, without more ado, proceeded to put the unwritten law into execution. They whipped a lariat over her neck, and were just about to lift her up when the producer arrived upon the scene to explain. His argument was scarcely convincing; the rough boys thought he was in collusion; but when the man whose horse should have been stolen appeared during the harangue the apparent grievance was settled amicably amid a salvo of guffaws.[30]

This may have been simply a publicity piece, but whether exaggerated or completely untrue, it demonstrates that Red Wing, no matter how successful, endured overt racism. Clearly, it was not a laughing matter to find herself with a noose around her neck, even if it only happened in print.

Back in Los Angeles, another sensational "white slavery ring" story about fifteen-year-old Carol Mason hit the news. She acted for two film companies, including apparently West Coast Studio. Like Quick, Mason easily gained the attention of the press not so much because of her beauty but because she was younger. One reporter deemed her story "serious." Her large publicity photo appeared with the long report. The writer said she looked old for her age, but the image of her appears younger than ones published of Quick. Mason had gone missing for ten days from her mother's home and was then located at a boardinghouse. "After the girl, who had dyed her a hair a rich auburn, had been found by detectives, she related a tale which resulted in the speedy arrests of Henry W. Haskamp, a realty operator of Los Angeles who was said to be a son of Herman Haskamp, a millionaire lumberman of Prince Rupert, B.C., and Robert W. Burton, an automobile dealer of Los Angeles," stated the front page of a Bay Area, California, newspaper. "It was charged they had contributed to the girl's delinquency."[31] The crimes involved more than just "contributing," according to the coverage in an Illinois newspaper. "Using a battering ram to break in the door of his apartment, which he had barricaded with desks, chairs and tables, the police overpowered Haskamp after a tussle and placed him in jail." Police also arrested Robert Burton, who ran a tire company, "and both men were charged with rape." The court further issued a warrant for Dr. Royal Crist for "performing a criminal operation upon the Mason girl."[32]

Some of the pressure let up when Mason testified that she had left her mother's home willingly. All the accused were set free within three weeks. Notably, Burton decided to marry Mason, with her mother's permission. "Marriage Solves It," the *Los Angeles Times* headline read. "From a honeymoon in the mountains Mrs. Carol Mason Burton came today to Justice Summerfield's courtroom to clear her husband of charges which she, herself, instituted."[33] Since a wife did not have to testify against her husband, the court dropped the charge against Robert Burton. A week later, Mason testified against Haskamp, but Haskamp claimed he hadn't seen her for four months before his arrest. Since Mason "was uncertain as to dates and other material matters," Haskamp's attorney moved to dismiss the case and let his client return to Canada. The judge concurred. The doctor, who had presumably performed an abortion, was set free as well because, his attorney argued, "as a matter of fact the doctor saved the young girl's life when she was suffering from gross carelessness on her own part."[34] The new Mrs. Burton's case seemed to have been amicably resolved for all concerned, but it was not the end of her charges.

Young Deer's troubles started again with animal cruelty. In mid-September the *Santa Ana Register* reported, "Five moving picture cowboys who have been at work with the Pathe company in the Santiago canyon practiced roping a cow yesterday, and when they had finished with their fun the cow was so badly injured that she was unable to get off the ground." A local constable and deputy witnessed the act, but they assumed the cowboys were in the process of capturing the animal or butchering her. They visited the camp the next day, however, and found the cow's legs covered with rope burns and its hip badly injured. The lawmen determined the cowboys had "amused themselves by dragging the cow." The judge fined the cowboys ten dollars each for "cruelty to an animal." He also ordered them "to either kill the cow or take proper care of her."[35]

The ranch had become a no-holds-barred Wild West show. How was Red Wing coping? Perhaps she lodged in Santa Ana and missed the bulk of the chaos. A few days later, Young Deer drove into Los Angeles and was hit by another motorist. The other driver was arrested, and the newspaper report claimed that Young Deer suffered serious injury. He seems to have recovered quickly, however.[36]

Christine Neal escaped from the Whittier Reformatory, "aided by Evelyn Nesbeith," on July 21. The Whittier superintendent put out a ten-dollar reward for her arrest, but she was never located. The cases against Hartigan, Hollingsworth, and a third perpetrator, J. F. Manney, were dropped on October 3.[37] Consequently, Hartigan returned home to Edendale from San Francisco, where he'd sought sanctuary, and continued working in the film industry.

By the end of the month, the Los Angeles Superior Court had also dropped Nesbeith's case against William Aldridge. She declared to the press that she planned to "forsake the stage and become a nun." The "girl whom the stage and the night lights brought to the Juvenile court as a delinquent, has decided that after all the gay life does not pay," reported the *Oakland Tribune*.[38] She allegedly committed herself to the Home of the Good Shepherd to begin her repentance.

Red Wing and the company returned to Edendale at the end of

October, but not before a policeman again arrested an unidentified driver of their automobile for speeding.[39] Young Deer had managed up until this point to avoid serious legal charges, but his time had come. "Youngdeer, Accused by Girl, Denies Her Acquaintance," ran a headline for the *Los Angeles Times*. Now Red Wing was forced to reckon with her marriage. Was she suspicious of her husband from the start, or was she surprised by this sudden turn of events? Did the bite she inflicted on the young ingénue at the ranch the year before point to her husband's infidelity or simply her unfounded jealousy? Media coverage scarcely reveals how she negotiated the charges against her spouse. But Young Deer's sly handling of the scandal reaffirms his incredible ability to weasel his way out of trouble.

Deputy Sheriff Bradfield arrested Young Deer in Edendale or Los Angles on Saturday night, November 22, 1913, for the "startling accusations" of pretty Marie Wilkerson.[40] Wilkerson, who had only attended high school for one year, had just turned eighteen when Young Deer allegedly assaulted her.[41] The judge set Young Deer's bail at $1,500, and apparently Red Wing bailed him out the same day.[42] The court also charged businessman Frank Troxler for contributing to Wilkerson's delinquency. Both men were arraigned on November 25, but they both countercharged Wilkerson and her sister, Lulu Barkley, with extortion. Perhaps the extortion charges weren't entirely fallacious. After all, a witness claimed that Wilkerson demanded money from Troxler's brother so she could leave town. The one-hundred-dollar bill she received from him was marked, however, and she was sent to the juvenile detention center. As for Young Deer's case, his stenographer, Stella Stray, stated that she was "hidden behind the door" when Wilkerson's sister demanded $200 from him "to get her sister out of the city."[43] But the court wanted proof, so upon his release from jail, Young Deer set up a scheme right out of a Keystone comedy to catch Barkley in the act of extortion.

> An appointment was made for another hotel last night at 8 o'clock. In the meantime Youngdeer and his attorney went to Central Station and notified the detective department. Deputy District-Attorney McCartney was communicated with and advised that the appointment be kept and that Mrs. Barkley be arrested, providing she accepted

the money. Youngdeer and detectives went to the hotel, but in the meantime Mrs. Barkley had apparently heard of her sister's arrest and failed to put in an appearance. While Youngdeer, with the detectives, was keeping the appointment, his wife, fully cognizant of all that was happening, waited for her husband in a downtown café.[44]

At this juncture Red Wing stuck by her man. However, as she sat waiting in the café, she must have asked herself if the pittance of money Barkley demanded proved her husband had not committed a crime—against the girl, against the law, and against their marriage vows. Wilkerson stated she had been "engaged as an actress by Youngdeer" since June. She further elaborated that when she "appeared to get a position," he "lured her to a private office" and "made love to her." When Barkley discovered "the love affair," she brought charges against Young Deer. It's not difficult to imagine that Red Wing's heart sank when she read Wilkerson's statement in the newspaper, but how did she feel about her husband's response to the accusation? Did she believe him, or did she simply feel she needed to cover for him at all costs? The *Orange Daily News* report offers no clue:

> Youngdeer yesterday heatedly denied the charges. He said he had not employed the young woman and that he was not acquainted with her. He further stated that he believed a man who was formerly employed by him was using his name and posing as Youngdeer. He also said that he had secured evidence that two young women had gone to his camp on a Sunday, when he was not there, and had been offered positions by a young man posing as the manager. To both young women this man made insulting remarks according to Youngdeer.[45]

The alibi that someone posed as him would not be sustainable when the prosecution put the real Young Deer in front of Wilkerson and asked, "Is this the man?" Moreover, Young Deer's entrapment scheme with Wilkerson's sister didn't pan out. He asked the judge for a continuance, because forty actors awaited him "to direct a new motion picture." The judge gave him one day.

In the meantime, Barkley told the press that her sister had been living in Los Angeles for the last year and a half but that she wanted to take her back home to Oklahoma City. "What would you do, if you were me?" she asked the reporter. "Would you send my sister to Whittier, or would you take her back into your home, where you know she will not remain, or send her back to her parents with the same result, or would you cast her out altogether? I am going to try to reform the girl," she explained, "but I don't know just how. Somehow, in a case of this kind, the girl gets the worst of it nearly every time."[46] Given how many teenage girls skipped town, faced imprisonment, turned to the church, married, or changed their names, she was right. The court acquitted all of the well-to-do men who partook in the pleasure of the minor girls, including multimillionaire George Bixby.

The next day Pathé Frères released *Faithless Friend* (November 29), one of Red Wing and Gebhardt's better films. *Moving Picture World* published their photo in character along with a review of the film, which hadn't happened for quite some time. Inside Red Wing's teepee, Gebhardt (as a white man) lies with his head in her lap, exhausted and ailing, while she offers him water from the emblematic pottery jar. The review said it's "a very good and well acted story," but it was the same old story that pleased racist critics and so would not end happily for the Indian maid. The story's designated hero would return to a white woman, his first wife.[47]

The same day the film debuted, Young Deer and Red Wing arrived at the Los Angeles Superior Courthouse. "James Youngdeer, motion picture producer, was held for court today on a charge of contributing to the delinquency of Miss Marie Wilkerson, 18," the *Los Angeles Herald* reported. "Youngdeer was given a secret hearing. His wife, who is known as 'Red Wing,' waited outside. Miss Wilkerson testified that Youngdeer had taken her to his private office several times and made improper advances. Youngdeer attempted to prove an alibi. Mrs. Youngdeer did not testify."[48] The *Los Angeles Times* report offered more sordid detail: "Miss Wilkerson lays her downfall to James Youngdeer, a motion-picture man, in whose employ she was. She alleges he invited her to his private office and there mistreated her. After she had been discarded, the encounter with Troxler is alleged to have occurred."[49]

If Young Deer did not exactly introduce beautiful blue-eyed Quick to the "primrose path," Wilkerson claimed he had done so to her—and she was not the last one to make the claim. The next day the *Times* revealed the purpose of the secret hearing. Another minor, this time only fifteen, offered testimony "bearing on Young Deer's conduct." "Deputy District-Attorney McCartney says the charge of the young girl, whose name he declines to make public, is more serious," reported the *Times*. "He is rounding up other girls as witnesses as corroborative evidence. Mrs. Youngdeer was at the examination."[50]

The reports are contradictory concerning whether Red Wing "waited outside" or was privy to the hearing. She probably dressed fashionably and sat behind her husband and his counsel with her face perfectly composed. What was her state of mind, however, when Mrs. Carol Burton took the stand? Did she listen carefully as the plaintiff revealed the same crime with which Wilkerson had charged her husband, that he had "lured" her to his office "under promise to make her a moving-picture actress?"[51] Did Red Wing believe the teenager, or did she stand by the defendant?

Two days later West Coast Studio released *A Break for Freedom* (December 3) followed by *A Bear Escape* (December 5). The titles may have been coincidental or something Young Deer subconsciously created after his first subpoena. On December 8, after another arrest warrant was issued to Young Deer for "a statutory offense" against Carol Mason Burton, he skipped bail, applied for an emergency passport, and boarded a steamship headed for the British Isles.[52]

Constable George Lyons arrived at Red Wing and Young Deer's bungalow in Edendale shortly after. He found Red Wing at home alone. The constable "learned that Youngdeer had sold all his Edendale property, even to his household goods," shortly after he left the courtroom the week before.[53] What "household goods" did he leave behind for his wife? Was Red Wing forthcoming about her husband's whereabouts? It doesn't appear so. Lyons continued to search for Young Deer all week. He went to Pasadena and other "resorts" the fugitive frequented, which probably included Vernon. At last he found Young Deer's expensive automobile "stripped and 'tuned' as if for a fast drive" in a garage on Flower Street. This led him to believe that "Young Deer had planned to get away in it, but was forced to abandon that plan" when he discovered Lyons watching the garage.[54]

Young Deer's attorney, Samuel Pechner, claimed his client still owed him $200 for legal fees, so the court ordered an issuance of an attachment, leaving Red Wing unable to sell her husband's vehicle. Whether or not

Red Wing had any inkling where her husband had gone, Lyons reasonably assumed he must have headed south to Tijuana, Mexico.[55] Within the week the *Times* reported that presiding judge Taft had received a letter from the "Indian fugitive" and "motion-picture man." Young Deer reminded him that "the red man" received no justice "since the first day the white man set foot in this country." Therefore, Young Deer had to go "home" to raise a large sum of money to prove his innocence. Apparently, Young Deer hoped the judge would equate his home with an Indian reservation—any reservation would do. "I know from a reliable source," he told the judge, "that I am to be made the black sheep of the whole (white slave) happenings—Bixby, La Casse, Hollingsworth and the two men that were up for the Mason girl's trial." He compared his situation to Troxler's, "a white man who had no established business" and was nevertheless "released on his own personal bond." "I had an established business," he continued. "I was an Indian" and was "held for $1500." Underlying his claim to an Indian identity was his actual and problematic African American origins. If those had been discovered, Young Deer knew he'd be deemed more than "the black sheep." Troxler "may be set free," wrote Young Deer, "but I, God only knows what I will get. It is not one man that will try me; there will be twelve, most possibly all white." If he was to receive the "white man's justice," he told the judge, "I must prepare." He promised to return when he had sufficient funds to defend himself.[56]

Judge Taft, believing the stereotype that an Indian's pledge is trustworthy, took Young Deer at his word, and the case was struck from the calendar. "He is an Indian," Taft commented to the press. "I will wait and see."[57] Clearly, Young Deer's claim to be an Indian served more than one purpose. It framed the judge's perception of him; it diverted attention from his controversial ethnicity during the horrendous era of African American lynchings; and for the time being it kept Red Wing from learning whether Wilkerson or Mason Burton told the truth.

One week later *An Indian Don Juan* hit the theaters. It featured Gebhardt, Douglas Gerrard (an Irish actor who later turned to directing), and Fanchon Lewis, as well as a character called "Red Wing," presumably played by Red Wing. If Red Wing cared to see it that month, the irony of the film title could not have escaped her notice.[58]

Young Deer fled the country leaving several unreleased films. *Against Heavy Odds,* a two-reel western featuring Gebhardt, Gerrard, and Lillian Wiggins, was his last film with West Coast Studio (released March 14, 1914).[59] Red Wing appeared in *By the Two Oak Trees* (released December 31) and *Down Lone Gap Way* (released January 13, 1914).[60] The first was another Mexican drama "about treachery and thievery" that concluded with "a woman who nearly drowns by a slowly rising tide."[61] It featured Gerrard, Gebhardt, Madeline West, and George Champion. The scenario centered on a miner who marries Red Wing's character, an Indian girl. When gold eludes the miner, he asks his parents for money, but they tell him "he has made his bed and now he must lie in it."[62] Red Wing's character obviously represented the bed. As a result, the miner chooses a life of crime to support his Indian wife. The film did not go over well with the critic and apparently included the same sick horse footage already trashed by others. "Marred by the picture of a horse which is made to tumble head first down a steep incline and by the pitching of a man over the lip of a rock," wrote *Moving Picture World*'s critic, "this picture of a hold-up and its consequences lacks convincing humanity in places where it isn't trite." Not only did he find the film "one of the weakest Patheplays by the Western company in some weeks," it was also censored in Canada.[63]

Soon after, as Red Wing later wrote, "my company broke up." West Coast Studio transformed into a film distribution company called Pathé Exchange.[64] Pat Hartigan ran the enterprise, which made its historic mark in March 1914 with the first installment of *The Perils of Pauline,* starring Young Deer's former actress, Pearl White.

Like the drowning woman "by the two oak trees," Red Wing refused to be pulled under by her husband's turmoil. After all, as she had confided to Gertrude Price that January, "several companies" had tried to take her from West Coast Studio. "There's more money right down the road at the next moving picture place. But I'd have to leave my husband and he doesn't like that," she demurely explained.[65] In the end, her husband left her. Before the New Year, fate offered Red Wing an opportunity that delivered more than money. It gave her the role of her lifetime.

CHAPTER 13

Cecil B. DeMille and *The Squaw Man*

When New Yorkers Cecil B. DeMille and Jesse L. Lasky arrived in Los Angeles that December they held high hopes that their first film would be successful, but they never dreamed it would be celebrated for decades, even a century. Both men came from the theater business. DeMille worked as an actor, playwright, and stage director. Lasky produced vaudeville and was known for his popular burlesque show, *Folies Bergère*. He also put on *A Night on a Houseboat* at Brighton Beach when Red Wing performed there. The two men had just formed the Jesse L. Lasky Feature Play Company in New York along with Frank A. Tichenor and Lasky's brother-in-law, Samuel Goldfish (later Samuel Goldwyn), another historic figure in movies.[1] The company had theater productions in mind but quickly turned to planning moving pictures, specifically adaptations of "famous novels and plays." They also wanted to film the scenarios in locations where the literary works were set.[2] They wisely decided to begin with *The Squaw Man,* Edwin Milton Royle's highly successful four-act play.

They chose Dustin Farnum to play the lead, since he'd starred in the play's 1911 revival. Farnum was a popular stage actor, and according to columnist George Blaisdell, he was a natural fit for the screen. Farnum was of "commanding height, of generous mold, with a complexion that fills the requirements of the inexorable camera—black hair and dark eyes," and his "magnetism" appealed equally to women and men. Blaisdell also liked his "frankness, democracy," and "entire absence of affectation."[3] DeMille had no experience in filmmaking, and Farnum had made only a brief appearance in a short the year before, but both men were keen to enter the business.

The new film company cast Winifred Kingston as the hero's British love interest. She and Farnum had costarred in another theatrical production, and they would also marry after Farnum divorced his first wife in 1924. DeMille took the position of general stage manager and director, while Pathé American director Oscar Apfel was hired to codirect. American Pathé cameraman Alfredo Gandolfini also joined the company.

The western scenes in the play are set in Montana, but DeMille intended to make the film in Flagstaff, Arizona, because it was an easier destination by train. He soon discovered that in "Arizona, beautiful, healthful sunny Arizona," the sun didn't always shine, nor did Flagstaff resemble the high plains of Montana. With Farnum's encouragement the men boarded another train and headed west for California, where the "climate was good" and "there was a great variety of scenery." The West Coast put the new independent film company farther from the Edison trusts, which the men hoped would not take "a personal interest in their project."[4]

Some knew that the rain in Arizona sent the company to California to make the picture, but DeMille assured the media that the crew filmed in Montana, Wyoming, and Utah. As *Moving Picture World* reported, "The Lasky Company, numbering over one hundred persons, travelled from lower California nearly two thousand miles to Green River, Montana, covering seven states and crossing three mountain ranges in the making of 'The Squaw Man.'"[5] The company heads originally planned to hire as many actors as possible from the original stage production but instead decided to mine the local talent around Los Angeles.

On December 13 DeMille and Farnum arrived in the City of Angels and registered at the Alexandria Hotel.[6] The next day Farnum told a journalist he'd been "stung by the movie bug" when he'd visited a California "movie camp" the previous year. Working outdoors really appealed to the longtime stage actor. "Los Angeles is the greatest place on earth for picture making," he declared. "It is the ideal spot—God's own paradise! I love it here and if I don't stay here the remainder of my life it will not be because I do not want to."[7]

DeMille hired Young Deer's former stenographer and spy, Stella Stray, to keep records. She recalled that "operations" began on December 16.[8] The company leased the Burns and Revier Studio, "one of the best-equipped rental lots in Los Angeles." "The main building on the property was a barn that Burns and Revier adapted to serve as offices, dressing rooms, and film laboratory," according to DeMille's biographer, Robert S. Birchard. When everyone was assembled, they "settled down to a preproduction schedule that lasted all of seven days."[9]

The barn-studio sat near the corner of Selma Avenue and Vine Street in Hollywood, a location that was certainly less bustling then than it is now.[10] Today the location bears a historic landmark plaque that establishes *The Squaw Man* as the first Hollywood feature-length film. Red Wing had spent six prolific years in the motion picture business, and this six-reel film became her real claim to fame. "I remember going to the Van Nuys hotel to meet Mr. de Mille," she recalled. "He said I was too short. But just then Dustin Farnum, who played the lead, came in, looked at me, and said, 'Don't go any farther, she'll do.' That's how I got the part."[11] DeMille cast her as Naturitch, an Indian maid whose love and devotion transform Farnum's character from a wrongfully accused British nobleman into a bona fide American and heroic "squaw man."

Hollywood legend has it that DeMille wanted Mona Darkfeather to play Naturitch, but she was not available, although this can't be confirmed. DeMille claimed instead that he cast Red Wing "in preference to an experienced actress because I wanted a real Indian to play her part."[12] DeMille's explanation ultimately served to give the public impression his "little Indian girl," as he called her, was an ingénue and *his* discovery.

DeMille kept a record of the people he interviewed for his production in a small red notebook.[13] It lists forty names, some with notations and some only with addresses and phone numbers. Red Wing is the second actress listed. Unfortunately, DeMille's notations next to her name simply give her salary, address, and phone number. Virginia Chester and Madeline West also interviewed for unknown roles they did not get. DeMille noted that Chester "rides well, leads Pathe." DeMille also interviewed Jane Darwell, known today for her Academy Award–winning role as Ma Joad in the 1940 classic *The Grapes of Wrath*. Although Darwell did not get a part in the film, DeMille hired her for his next production, *Brewster's*

Millions, as well as several future films. If she had made the cut, he had planned to pay her sixty dollars per day, as he penned in his notebook. Her salary reflected that she "had already progressed in pictures," according to Birchard. This seems to be an accurate assessment, given the five dollars per day the not yet famous Hal Roach received, but in fact Darwell had just begun her film career that year when she appeared in a Bison 101 western directed by Francis Ford.[14] Again, in contrast, DeMille notated seventy-five dollars per day for his "inexperienced" Indian girl.

Farnum played opposite both Red Wing and Kingston as Sir James Wynnegate, an upper-crust British veteran apparently of the Boer War. Wynnegate changes his name to Jim Carston when he arrives in the United States. Joseph Singleton took the part of Naturitch's father, Tabywana, a Ute chief. Other cast members include Monroe Salisbury as Wynne-gate's cousin, Sir Henry, Earl of Kerhill; Dick La Reno as Wynnegate's true-blue friend and ranch foreman, Big Bill; and Dick Le Strange as Grouchy the ranch hand. "Baby" Carmen DeRue, a little girl actress, played Hal, Carston and Naturitch's son. Bison Co.'s Art Accord and Milt Brown received minor roles as cowboys. DeMille's notebook indicates that Accord tried out for Cash Hawkins, the film's villain, but Brown only made the part of one of Hawkins's "group." William Elmer Johns, aka Billy Elmer, who started out as a boxer to become one of DeMille's regular stock players, got the part instead. DeMille played a bit part as a western card dealer, beginning his life-long custom of appearing in cameos in his own films.

Certainly, Farnum carried the film as its hero, but the discrepancy between his salary and Red Wing's was enormous. Red Wing caught the drift and stood up for herself: "One day Mr. de Mille, apparently seeking to impress me, told me I ought to be proud because I was working with Mr. Farnum, a $1,000-a-week star. I said, 'What about him? He's working with a hundred per cent American,' which I am. 'My ancestry is recorded in the bureau of Indian affairs.'"[15] One film scholar states that Red Wing was the only Native American to act in the film, but that doesn't appear to be entirely accurate. Although Singleton, who played her Ute father, was Australian, several Native Americans portray Ute tribal members. Some even received a credit in trade publications. Jack Big Deer, who played the medicine man, and Old Elk, who played Baco White, probably belonged to tribes living near one of the film's locations.[16]

It's difficult to tally how many wives of "squaw men" Red Wing portrayed in her career, but Royle's play was the classic story. It's important to acknowledge how contemporaneous critics perceived DeMille's vision of the narrative. The following summary of the story from *Motography* provides a substantial description of the film's plot, but its plot point omissions reveal notable silence regarding Naturitch's controversial role in the love story:

> [It] starts off with an army officers' dinner at which James Wynnegate is made guardian of a trust fund provided for the widows and orphans of soldiers. Wynngate [*sic*] secretly loves the wife of his cousin, the Earl of Kerhill. The earl embezzles a large sum of the trust money and, to save the earl's wife from disgrace, Wynngate allows the blame for the stolen money to rest upon him.
>
> He departs for America, aboard a trading schooner. In mid-ocean the schooner is set afire and Wynngate is picked up by a vessel which brings him into New York. There, in a café, he meets a western man whom he saves from society pickpockets and the westerner invites him to visit the West where "people keep their hands in their own pockets." Wynngate goes and assumes the name Carston. He buys a ranch, incurs the enmity of "Cash" Hawkins, and the latter's attempt on Carston's life is frustrated by Nat-U-Ritch, an Indian girl, who kills Hawkins. Her guilt is known to none but Carston, and the death of Hawkins remains a mystery. Going out over snowy plains, one day Carston is afflicted with snow-blindness. He is found and saved from death from poisonous fumes, by the Indian girl, who cares for him at his home. When he is recovered Carston attempts to send the girl back to her people but she refuses to go. Carston marries her and is known thereafter as "the squaw-man." He has a son who becomes the pride of the ranchers.
>
> The Earl of Kerhill with his wife and party, are traveling in the Swiss mountains. The Earl falls over one of the precipices and before he dies, confesses to the theft of the trust money. His widow, her cousin and

the family barrister search for Wynngate in the West, find him and beg him to return home and assume his title. He refuses, but consents to send his son back that he may be educated to fill his rank. Nat-U-Ritch, sad over the taking-away of her child, commits suicide, leaving "the squaw-man" free to return to his own country and eventually, so the story suggests, his first love.[17]

Red Wing's Naturitch, or, more accurately, DeMille and Royle's (who was on-set for much of the filming), set the stereotype for the Indian princess helper for decades to come. On the surface she is a tragic heroine, but on a deeper level her character falls victim to love, racism, and Manifest Destiny. Although Naturitch's self-sacrificing character contrasts to that of her drunken and abusive father, Tabywana's stereotypical ignoble Indian, she also represents the stereotypical "shiftless Indian." The camera often captures her spying, sneaking, and scheming. More importantly, a fade-out transition suggests she seduced Carston. This is a significant plot point censored from the *Motography* review.

Following the fade-out, Naturitch demurely reveals a pair of baby moccasins of her own make to Carston, letting him know, as a white woman would, that she is pregnant with their child. When he realizes their predicament, he implores Big Bill to summon the justice of the peace to his ranch. Big Bill shakes Carston's hand in response to show the audience that Carston is truly an honorable man. He will sacrifice his social position to wed the pregnant "squaw," never mind that her child is his. The justice of the peace arrives to the ranch but refuses to marry the couple because Naturitch is an Indian. When Carston shows him the little moccasins, he begrudgingly administers the civil ceremony.

Naturitch suffers serious consequences for loving a white man. Near the end of the film the sheriff and his posse are on to her about Hawkins's murder, but before they can retrieve the murder weapon, which is hidden in her bureau, she takes the gun and shoots herself. Ostensibly, Carston's decision to send their son to England without her consent impels Naturitch to commit suicide. The audience understood not only that as an Indian she had no rights over her mixed-blood child but also that the ultimate paternal (male) authority belonged to her husband. Deeper cultural and historical implications belie Naturitch's suicide. First, as the title suggests, she is a "squaw" and, as a consequence, is unable to inculcate the values of European American civilization in her son. This duty is left implicitly to Wynnegate's first love, British-born Lady Diana, who waits in the wings.

Naturitch as an Indian mother passes on to Hal her primitive nature, an essence revered during the Progressive Era but only if it is nurtured by civilizing influences. Her name itself, Naturitch, refers to this dichotomy. Hal will grow up strong with his mother out of the picture, because Anglo-Saxon superiority infused with Indianness produces an authentic *American* identity. In addition, Naturitch kills herself with the same weapon she used on Hawkins, since she has transgressed the racial line. She killed a white man in order to protect the story's hero. The film's denouement resolves these issues by killing her off and erasing her very existence.[18] She is punished for her race, punished for her gender, punished for loving a white man, punished for killing a white man, and punished for miscegenation, the moral and national transgression for which only she is to blame.

The story ends with Lady Diana sheltering Hal while his dead mother lies in his father's arms. The Indian mother who saved the life of the white hero twice is narratively sacrificed for Hal's future and the moral health of the nation-state. The film's grand message is that the audience can mourn the vanishing Indians, but their demise is necessary and inevitable. Whether Indians appear as innocent, like Adam and Eve in the Garden of Eden, whether they relieve thirst, hunger, and loneliness, or whether they provide protection and a respite from civilization, Indians can never transcend their essential savage nature. American exceptionalism depends on it.

The filming began in late December at the Hollywood studio. Red Wing made a beaded floor-length doeskin gown for her role. At the end of January the *Los Angeles Herald* reported, "Pretty Red Wing, the Indian motion picture actress, daughter of the famous Cherokee chieftain, Winnebago," shot herself through the wrist during her suicide scene. "The revolver was thought to be loaded with blanks, but when she fired, a real bullet shattered her wrist."[19] One of DeMille's scrapbook photos looks to be related to Naturitch's suicide. It captures Red Wing's character in a romantic light standing pensively atop a grassy hill as the sun sets on the horizon. Some believe DeMille staged some scenes near the Hollywood sign, and as the report of the accident shows, codirector Apfel filmed the suicide scene in "the hills." Some also believe the accident never happened at all, since today DeMille is infamous for creating publicity stunts to promote his films. *Billboard*'s report suggests DeMille doctored the story: "Red Wing may have met the fate of the Indian girl of action," and the "ball went through her wrist instead of her hand. She was rushed to the doctor's office unconscious, but will recover without serious or permanent injury."[20] *Moving Picture World* gave an account that was less dire and probably accurate: "The bullet inflicted a slight flesh wound in the Indian girl's left arm, but she went through the scene without any demonstration of pain or injury. When the scene was completed . . . Red Wing showed a badly swollen and bloody arm."[21] This fits Red Wing's personality to a tee.

Birchard's biography gives several locations for the film. Sir Henry's mountain accident and confession were shot in the Santa Monica Mountains.[22] DeMille used stock footage for British references but filmed Wynnegate's British manor in "a mansion in the fashionable West Adams District of Los Angeles." The remaining scenes, Birchard noted, were filmed in California. The harbor scenes were set in San Pedro. The crew built Carston's cabin on the "Universal Ranch" (today's Universal City). The western saloon was constructed "beside railroad tracks in the vast desert that was once [the] San Fernando Valley." "The company did go as far afield as Keen Camp in Idyllwild and Hemet, California, to shoot footage of cattle on the open range." He also stated that the film's snow scenes were shot on Mount Palomar.[23]

Birchard's list requires some clarification and correction. DeMille's hazy memory and lengthy filmography are certainly to blame. Contemporaneous reports show that the 1914 version of the fire onboard the ship was actually staged in San Diego. There is also no evidence the 1914 company filmed at Mount Palomar.[24] Fifteen members of the film company, Red Wing, Farnum, La Reno, Singleton, DeMille, Apfel, and Gandolfini arrived in Hemet, California, on February 2, 1914. Salisbury might have come along as well, since he owned a ranch in Hemet. "The scenery around Hemet is the best we have found for producing motion pictures," a local reporter boasted, and he was not exaggerating.[25] The quaint town shared the beautiful San Jacinto Valley with its eastern neighbor, the city of San Jacinto. The magnificent San Jacinto granite mountain range, which encompasses Mount San Jacinto and Tahquitz Peak, borders the picturesque valley, which is located in Riverside County.

Compared to Mount Palomar at 6,000 feet, Tahquitz Peak reaches 8,846 feet, and Mount San Jacinto looms larger, at nearly 11,000 feet in elevation. (Mount Palomar is seventy miles southwest of Hemet and even farther from Hollywood.) When naturalist John Muir hiked to the summit of Mount San Jacinto in 1896, he exclaimed, "The view from San Jacinto is the most sublime spectacle to be found anywhere on this earth!"[26] Cameramen filmed several movies, including a few starring Gene Autry, as well as Frank Capra's 1937 classic, *The Lost Horizon*, in this scenic locale. The area is also the home of the Soboba Band of Luiseño Indians. Government officials established their reservation, which borders San Jacinto, only six months before the Lasky group arrived. In addition, the Cahuilla Band of Mission Indians lived just south of the mountains. Both these groups of desert-mountain dwellers survived the terrible reign of the California missions, as well as the destructive earthquake of 1890.

The cast and crew, followed by "two truck loads of baggage," left Hemet to ascend the narrow and winding mountain road for Keen Camp, based five miles south of the hamlet of Idyllwild. A Hemet reporter noted that the company "would be assisted by many local people," including some from "the Soboba and Cahuilla reservations." "Seventeen horses will be used in the production of the pictures to be made at Keen Camp, besides nearly 100 people."[27] The company planned to stay a week or so in the area to take advantage of "the deep snow that covers San Jacinto and Tahquitz peaks."[28]

It took two hours to get to Keen Camp by an "auto-stage" that ran from Hemet every day but Sunday. At five thousand feet the Lasky crew finally reached Keen Camp, a snow-covered resort run by a widow named Anita Walker.[29] Walker's oak-and-pine-tree-studded property sat on the eight-thousand-acre HJ Ranch. Keen Camp boasted a view of Tahquitz Peak and "good fishing, hunting and trapping," and it featured a "large dancing pavilion, tennis courts, billiards, and saddle livery." Guests could take day trips to Idyllwild, the peaks of Mount San Jacinto and Tahquitz, North Fork Falls, Lake Hemet, and the Garner Stock Ranch.[30] The hotel and cottages rented for fourteen dollars per week, with tent houses renting for two dollars less. Meals cost fifty cents and included fresh milk, fresh cream, and fresh eggs. Guests had access to the Keen Camp Store, which also served as a post office. The camp was a resort, not a health spa, so "no consumptives" were allowed. Salisbury likely discovered the location, since Walker catered mostly to locals escaping the hot summers of the San Jacinto Valley.[31] She must have been excited to host the moving picture company, likely the first to film in the area.

The crew didn't have to venture far after a hearty breakfast in the lodge. Many views of the Keen Camp property, with its alpine meadows and rock outcroppings, match the film's terrain where Naturitch rescues Carston after he is struck by snow blindness. The snow scenes were demanding for the petite Red Wing. Not only did she have to brave the cold, but no stunt person hauled the massive Farnum out of the "poisonous cavern" onto the travois; it was Red Wing's task. The film shows her stumbling to get her bearings while she guides a horse through deep snow in her moccasins with the heavy load in tow.

A snapshot from DeMille's scrapbook shows Red Wing in costume standing next to DeMille in the snow. The area is hilly and dotted with fir trees, one of which they pose next to. DeMille, with hands on hips, looks directly into the camera. He wears a subtly rakish grin and is dapper in his stylish winter hat and fur-trimmed jacket. Red Wing, wearing the beaded headband and feather as usual, stands close to him. The hem of her fringed gown reaches the snow, and she is bundled in skin hides against the cold. Not much shorter than her director, she looks past him to something or someone beyond the picture taker. Her enthusiasm is evident in her radiant smile.[32]

Farnum wrote a friend about his experience at Camp Keen: "Last week, while going through a scene in which I am rescued from a hole, by Naturich, the squaw, the cow-pony which pulls me out developed stage fright, temperament or something and got to bucking. Well, I enjoyed ten minutes of royal rough riding. . . . All in all, acting before the camera is considerably more exciting than rehearsing on the stage. . . . It's a great life, full of thrills, requiring great patience and rewarding you with an exhilarating appreciation of the wonderful outdoors."[33]

Not long after, Blaisdell interviewed Farnum. Farnum agreed with Blaisdell that Red Wing "was splendid in her portrayal" of Naturitch, and then he shared two anecdotes about her. "Little Redwing came to me one day when we were getting near the end of the picture," he began, "and told me she had a beautiful pair of horns from a long-horned Texas steer which one of her relatives had mounted and of which she would like to make me a present." "Naturally surprised and perhaps pleased," he continued, "I tried to tell her how much I would appreciate the gift and how extremely generous she was, when I noticed her looking at me very fixedly. 'Just say yes or no,' she said shortly. In spite of education she got right down to cases."[34] Farnum probably misunderstood Red Wing's abrupt response. Calling attention to her gift was improper Ho-Chunk etiquette, and besides, he was probably a bit too effusive for her taste.

Farnum's second anecdote is more poignant and leaves unanswered questions about Red Wing and motherhood. "When we were rehearsing the scene where the baby is taken from Nat-u-Rich to be sent back to England, this pure-blooded Indian girl broke down and went into hysterics," Farnum told Blaisdell. "It was pitiful. It was twenty-five minutes before we could proceed with the picture. In all my years on the stage I never saw anything like it. It was absolutely the reverse of everything we have been taught about Indians."[35] Farnum construed Red Wing's reaction as uncharacteristic of an Indian, but there are certainly other ways to interpret her response. One film scholar suggests that her emotional outburst may have reflected the trauma of having been "ripped from the arms of her parents" to go to boarding school. But as we know, this doesn't exactly reflect her situation.

Certainly, Red Wing had a soft spot for the children she performed with, such as Violet Radcliffe. Maybe her emotion stemmed from realizing she would really miss her little costar, Carmen DeRue, as she perhaps missed Radcliffe. Or the scene brought up early memories of the loss of her own mother. After all, Naturitch's suicide leaves her son abandoned. On the other hand, what if Red Wing ached for children of her own? With her thirtieth birthday on the horizon, she approached the end of her reproductive years with no husband and no hope of a family. Finally, there is also nothing to discount whether Red Wing ever experienced pregnancy, miscarriage, or termination or gave up her own infant for adoption. Only Red Wing knew why the scene touched her so deeply.

The Lasky Company spent a week at Camp Keen and then, as the local newspaper reported, headed for San Diego to film the ship-burning scene. DeMille told Hemet's press he'd be back soon to film *Brewster's Millions*, but it's unclear whether he did. Red Wing and those not needed for the San Diego shoot returned to Hollywood.[36] A few days later, the cast and crew and their spouses dressed up to see the first showing of the film in the Hollywood barn. There were some problems with slippage because the perforations in the film weren't lined up accurately, but all in all, everyone was pleased. DeMille sent a telegraph to Samuel Goldfish in New York:

RAN "SQUAW MAN" COMPLETE FOR FIRST TIME. ALL WHO SAW IT VERY ENTHUSIASTIC. FARNUM WILL DELIVER TO YOU SUNDAY NIGHT. PROPER CUTTING TAKES GREAT DEAL OF TIME. RUNS JUST SIX THOUSAND FEET. . . . YOU MAY BE SATISFIED YOU HAVE A GOOD PICTURE.[37]

Farnum delivered the six-reel epic to the home office in New York, where Blaisdell interviewed him. "In nine weeks we have located grounds, engaged actors and built a studio, carpenter shop and scene dock," he recounted. "Just bear in mind we had twenty-one days of rain. I never saw such a conglomeration of weather in my life." Then he showed Blaisdell "a five-foot panoramic view of the coast studio with the players lined up in front"—now a well-known image of the first day of shooting at the barn. Red Wing in costume standing midphoto holds Carmen DeRue's hand. Farnum pointed out three men in the photograph, "a champion roper," "a champion rider," and "a six feet five inch tall Texan," who especially impressed him. Art Accord was certainly one of the three, as was, perhaps, Milt Brown. Farnum had found, to his delight, that all of the cowboys in the cast, though rough-and-tumble, had gentle souls. Yet, he added, he was most fascinated by "the Indians" and enjoyed studying their ways.[38]

When the conversation turned to the theme of *The Squaw Man*, "the inter-marriage of the white and the Indian," Farnum became thoughtful. "You know," he said, "the minute a man marries a squaw he is taboo." Still, he believed the "extenuating circumstances" shown by the film's dramatic portrayal "creates such a situation that no man with a heart in him can fail to forgive." These circumstances had everything to do with Red Wing's portrayal of the Indian maid saving the white man, a role she had honed over six years. The white man's transgression (getting her pregnant) can be forgiven, but, ironically, the Indian female's sexual availability and race (inextricably bound) can only be exonerated through her death. DeMille's film set this specifically American western narrative in stone with its trajectory that insures a happy ending for the white man—or at least America—but not ever for his Indian lover.[39]

On February 17 Lasky and Goldfish invited exhibitors and other trade people to a private showing at Broadway's Long Acre Theater on 48th Street in New York.[40] "The story is told in six parts and 264 scenes and is genuinely good," wrote an attendee.[41] The attendee felt the audience enjoyed Dustin Farnum's performance, as well as his supporting cast. He also complimented the cinematography, particularly the exterior shots. He concluded that the public would like the film as much as they had the play.

"D," the more erudite critic of the *New York Dramatic Mirror,* attended the preview and mused on his genuine surprise: "You [Lasky] jump into a game that many hard-working men have been studying for the past twenty years, and the very first time up to bat you pound out a home run." He found that the motion picture kept the audience's interest more than most, though he didn't think Singleton was suited for his role. Still, he found little else to criticize. He believed the film captured Farnum's "earnest acting . . . virile personality and powerful physique" just as well as the stage play had. Finally, he declared that the "personal touches" Red Wing brought to her part were "animated with the spark of life."[42]

The Lasky Company immediately hired the Lubin Manufacturing Company to fix the perforation issues and released the film to the public on February 23, Red Wing's thirtieth birthday.[43] The critical acclaim was fantastic. Lesley Mason of *Motion Picture News* announced the "First Lasky Production a Hit" and wrote that it lost nothing in the transformation from stage to film. Mason extolled Red Wing's snow scenes in particular: "The series of pictures delineating Jim's struggles across the snow-bound hills and Nat-U-Ritch's braving of 'The Evil Spirit' to save her hero from death, is in itself a masterpiece."[44]

The Squaw Man titles included a credit list reflecting the evolving film industry. Some publications such as the *New York Clipper* even printed a full list of the forty-seven cast members.[45] Red Wing, Farnum, and Elmer also appeared on the cover of *Moving Picture World* (March 28) posing in the saloon. Louis Reeves Harrison, one of the magazine's critics, gave the film a rave review: "One of the best visualizations of a stage play ever shown on the screen, 'The Squaw Man,' was a source of surprise and delight to me, and to the able critic at my side during the private exhibition, from beginning to end." Noting that Red Wing was a "remarkably fine actress," Harrison penned a romantic and incredibly lengthy panegyric highlighting her portrayal of the tragic Indian heroine. Harrison, an intellectual aesthete of his era, was absolutely smitten with Naturitch's tragic narrative thread, but he also gave credit where credit was due—to Red Wing herself: "It is not altogether a pleasing spectacle to see white women impersonating Indian squaws, and they are seldom, if ever, successful at it; on the other hand, Indian girls who can awaken and hold sympathy for their roles are few and far between, but Princess Redwing performs her part with exquisite fidelity and great depth of feeling. The play's highest merit is the opportunity it affords this accomplished actress."[46]

Jack C. Royle (Edwin Milton Royle's brother), journalist for Salt Lake City, Utah's *Goodwin's Weekly,* joined the chorus: "We saw the 'Squawman' pictures last Tuesday. They are tremendously effective and in places, truly beautiful. Farnum is charming in them and an Indian girl, Red Wing, was a revelation as 'Nat-U-Ritch.'"[47] The *Salt Lake Tribune* followed with more kudos for Red Wing: "The cast is wonderfully good. This is especially true of Princess Red Wing, the young Indian girl who plays the part of Nat-U-Ritch, the Indian wife and mother. After seeing the picture, one understands why Mr. Royle says she is a 'revelation' in the part. She has many splendid moments in the play, which she handles with exquisite feeling and consummate dramatic art."[48]

Red Wing's pride in her critically acclaimed performance is evident in the many times she mentioned the film during the rest of her life. Did she save the reviews? Did she congratulate herself on a job well done? Did she add another diamond ring to her finger? Finally, did she wonder how much better she would have fared in the film business had it not been for her loyalty to Young Deer? His last West Coast Studio production, *Against Heavy Odds*, was released in March. If she went to see the film, maybe she missed her husband and felt nostalgia for old times, but odds are she felt regret for putting his career before her own.

CHAPTER 14

In the Days of the Thundering Herd

Red Wing's leading men from West Coast Studio moved on. In March 1914 Joseph De Grasse signed on with the Universal Victor Company (where Fred Balshofer also found employment), and George Gebhardt signed on as a director for Ramo Film Company. Later in the year he left Ramo for Universal, where former Pathé West actor Douglas Gerrard also took a director's position. "Girls won't love him now," the *Los Angeles Times* teased, because Gebhardt was slated to play "heavies."[1] Red Wing moved from Edendale to an apartment on Sunset Boulevard. Tellingly, she listed her name in the Los Angeles city directory that year as "Lillian Redwing," not Lillian Youngdeer or Redwing Youngdeer, as she was usually known in the business.[2] She seemed to be turning a page in the book of her life. Even though the press still touted Princess Mona Darkfeather as "the famous Indian actress," and she had the wherewithal to play another "Red Wing" character in a film in April, Red Wing finally took the crown as western film's Indian *queen*.

Young Deer found employment with British and Colonial Kinematograph Company (B & C), a London firm known for its documentaries and crime dramas. In 1914 he directed the following B & C films: *The Black Cross Gang*, *The Water Rats of London*, *The World at War*, and *The Queen of the London Counterfeiters*. Interestingly, Lillian Wiggins starred in each film. Apparently, they developed a special relationship the exact nature of which is unknown.[3] On October 20 the year before, Wiggins left West

Coast Studio for Pathé American's new St. Augustine, Florida, plant to make animal pictures directed by Fred Wright.[4] When that production group broke up, Wiggins took a steamer to Europe, arriving in Paris on March 10, 1914. Wiggins claimed she began producing films for her own company but "tired of the responsibility" and "accepted an offer" with B & C. If Young Deer invited her to join B & C, she didn't say. Wiggins enjoyed her time in London, writing, "I have a dear little bungalow at Walton-on-Thames . . . directly on the river. . . . During my 'rest' between pictures I can fish just off my landing in front of my bungalow. Every morning I have my swim; it is really delightful."[5] Her flat, located in a London suburb near Ashbury Park, was probably not far from where Young Deer resided.

It's unknown what Young Deer was up to before he joined B & C. His Certificate of Registration of American Citizen states that he left the United States on December 8, 1913, and arrived in London on December 18 to reside at the Bedford Hotel.[6] He named his wife as "Lillian Red Wing" but lied that she resided in "New York City" and that she should be notified in case of emergency. The document also states that "picture producing" was his reason for coming to London. Presumably, he had contacts in the city.

On April 3 the *Los Angeles Times* printed a letter Young Deer had written to Judge Taft in early February. The reporter described him as "the Indian motion-picture man, who fled from this city after his arrest for misconduct with Miss Mason and Miss Wilkerson." He also said Young Deer's address was unknown. "Though I am many thousands of miles away from you . . . my promise is still fresh in my mind, and by the help of the Great Mystery and all that is good, I intend to keep it," Young Deer wrote. "I was told that the bond was laid aside for one year. I wanted to try and get some money, but everything was against me." He complained he lost $4,000 to $5,000 when the company he worked for rejected some of his pictures. If he meant Pathé Frères, he didn't say. Consequently, when he "got to New York," he "was worse off than ever." "Not a penny to my name, and since I came away, I have lost everything I had—horses, automobile that the lawyer took after I had paid him too." He further told the judge that he'd lost "his studio" and that it would take a long time to pay off his debts. He again claimed that he was innocent of the crimes against "Mason or that Wilkerson girl" and evoked God's mercy, pledging his honor on his "dead mother." "I was trying to make some money, but my heart was too sad. I can't work. I can't have anything, so I will keep my promise and come back though I haven't a penny." His letter was pathetic, but Taft still believed, "When an Indian pledges his word, he keeps it."[7]

If Red Wing hoped for his return, his letter did not mention her. It's likely Young Deer's sister Minnie Fossett sent the letter from New York. Young Deer may have been alerted that the last "white slavery ring" case had been resolved. In mid-January Frank Troxler pleaded guilty and was granted probation, and the rest of the cases had already been dropped.[8] Most of the accused, including Pat Hartigan, were none the worse for wear, which may have given Young Deer the confidence to write to Taft in February.

"P. C. Hartigan is back from New York with a trainload of scenery, leading women and star actors," the *Los Angeles Herald* reported in May, "and will establish a Pathe branch film factory here at once. He was gone several months and is glad to be back, betcherlife."[9] Former Bison Co. actor Howard Davies joined Hartigan's new venture, which was clarified by *Moving Picture World*.[10] "As the new directors for Pathe and the old directors working under new contracts, of course, want to engage their own people, it has been found unnecessary to keep the Pathe stock company other than those engaged in the 'Perils of Pauline.'"[11]

Red Wing and Young Deer's West Coast Studio was now dedicated to *The Perils of Pauline* series. The rest of the time it would serve "directors working under contract with Pathe." *Moving Picture World* likened Hartigan's company to "a book publishing house [that] handles the books written by its authors under contract." Instead of books, it would publish films. Instead of authors, it would contract film directors.[12]

Red Wing may have visited Nebraska in the early summer after discovering her sister Julia was seriously ill. Julia had been staying in Emerson with their sister Minnie, but by mid-June she had to be hospitalized in Sioux City.[13] At this time, Julia was in her midforties, and her son had just married. Fortunately, Julia recovered sometime later, but clearly life had not offered her nearly as many exciting opportunities as it had her youngest sister. Although both sisters were unlucky in love and Julia was as intelligent and gifted as her sister, Julia seemed to lack Red Wing's confidence, levelheadedness, charisma, and courage.

"After my own Co broke up," Red Wing wrote, "I played opposite Tom Mix in Selig's production 'The Thundering Herd.'" Selig Polyscope released the blockbuster *In the Days of the Thundering Herd* on November 30, 1914, nearly nine months after Red Wing's last film. It's unknown if she found any other work in between, but the November release would be her final prominent role in films. Red Wing as "Starlight" also played opposite Bessie Eyton, her former Pathé costar. Red Wing certainly had known Selig and Eyton for some time and likely knew the now famous cowboy actor Tom Mix because he worked next door to West Coast Studio. Selig had employed Mix since the year Red Wing came to Edendale after a representative from Selig's Chicago studio discovered him working for the Miller Brothers' 101 Ranch in Oklahoma.

Red Wing seems to have adored Mix. One 1960s newspaper report not only claimed she was one of his "most dedicated fans" but also erroneously declared, "She played in practically all of his pictures." The report also claimed that she "was with Tom when he bought his famous horse, Tony," and "loaned him some money to swing the deal." However, Mix stated that he bought the trick horse, Tony the Wonder Horse, "from his business partner, Pat Christman, for $600 in 1917," a year when Red Wing was probably not particularly flush.[14] Still, she may have been referring to one of his earlier horses.

Mix was born in Pennsylvania and had served during the Spanish-American War, but he slowly transformed his life story to match the public's perception of a western hero. He changed his birthplace to Oklahoma, gave his parents a western twang, and tacked on false claims here and there, such as that he had served as a U.S. marshal. By 1914 "Selig wanted to give Mix his own series," one biographer notes, "but before making the final decision Selig decided to test him in two special productions," *Chip of the Flying U* followed by *In the Days of the Thundering Herd*, both released in 1914. Mix's performances pleased Selig, and Selig

offered Mix "his own series," for which Mix "assembl[ed] his own production unit," including Red Wing's former employee, Hoot Gibson.[15]

In the Days of the Thundering Herd was an 1849 California gold rush
story written by Gilson Willetts. Selig Polyscope shot the film at Gordon
Lillie's Pawnee Ranch, which abutted the Pawnee Indian reservation in
Oklahoma.[16] The ranch was also home to one of the largest buffalo herds
in America, thanks in part to Lillie's wife, who became an expert buffalo
breeder. The film featured the buffalo herd and some seven hundred
Pawnee tribal members. As one review exclaimed, "You see [the buffalo]
sleeping, grazing, stampeding, hunted and killed by both rifle and bow
and arrow. There is a regular Indian village with its hundreds of redskins
in their original dress, and still maintaining their savage customs. They
fight the plainsmen and hunt the buffalo with their bows and arrows,
showing a skill with these instruments which has not been dulled by the
years of civilization."[17] The film also included "scores of prairie schooners"
for the white immigrant invaders.

Longtime Selig employee and Scotsman Colin Campbell served as
the film's director-producer. Wheeler Oakman, who was featured with
Eyton in the Selig silent classic *The Spoilers*, a film about Alaska's gold
rush, played Starlight's brother or father, Chief Swift Wing. Mix played his
almost namesake, Tom Mingle, while Eyton played Mingle's love interest,
Sally Madison. John Bowers acted as Dick Madison, Sally's strange and
hapless brother.

Selig Polyscope invited Lillie to see the film's preview in Chicago in
August, but it wasn't released to the general public until late November.[18]
Red Wing's Starlight, wearing the doeskin *Squaw Man* dress, would not get
her white man in the story, of course. "A series of the thrilling adventures
abound for Tom Mingle and Sally Madison," who are left the only survivors
of a group of immigrants who hazard a journey "across the plains to the
California gold fields where Sally's father is awaiting her." After Indians
wipe out their party, they take Tom and Sally prisoner. The couple is so
attractive that Swift Wing and Starlight "take a fancy to them." "After
many adventures they finally manage to escape," wrote *Moving Picture
World*'s critic, "and fall in with a band of buffalo hunters, who in turn are

almost wiped out by Indians. Help arrives in the nick of time and Sally and Tom at last reach their destination in safety."[19]

Help actually arrives in the character of Starlight, whose crush on the white hero is evident to the audience but not to him. "The poetic role of Starlight has been sustained most creditably by Red Wing, the full-blooded daughter of the Indian chief," stated *Moving Picture World*. "In a very subtle way, almost imperceptibly, she shows that she is in love with Tom Mingle and that her love is hopeless." The review further commended the film's closing scene, "in which Tom Mingle, Sally Madison and Starlight are shown as they set out for the land of promise. As we pathetically gaze at it, new vistas rise out of the saffron west, and we rub our eyes to find out whether or not we are dreaming."[20] Once again, Red Wing's character is doomed for eternity to love a white man and help his white beloved make him her own. The audience still loved to see Princess Red Wing play the third wheel in a mixed-race ménage à trois, particularly after her performance in *The Squaw Man*, but this would be their last chance to do so.

On September 23 Young Deer boarded the steamer *Cedric* at the port of Liverpool, the day after Wiggins left the country. The ship's manifest shows his birthplace as Dakota City, Nebraska, his home as Orange County, California, and his age several years younger than he was.[21] When the ocean liner embarked at the port of New York City on October 2, Young Deer may have sought out Wiggins, who lived in Brooklyn, or headed for Manhattan to see his widowed sister, Minnie, and his brother Harry Johnson, who worked as a waiter. If he saw Harry, it was for the last time. Harry suffered from a heart condition and died four months later, leaving his wife, Gertrude, and his daughter, Thelma, to live with Minnie.[22] Minnie still had no children and would marry native Virginian Alexander "Sandy" Moton, a chauffeur, the following year.

Just before he left Liverpool, Young Deer again wrote to Judge Taft. "I am returning to fulfill my promise to you. I almost regret making it for I am just about to do good here, but nevertheless my promise is to me more than anything else. It is bad enough for me to be accused of what I am, but I never hope to be accused of breaking a solemn promise or of betraying the confidence of my friends and bondsmen. I truly believe that I shall prove my innocence."[23]

On November 2 Young Deer surrendered to a Los Angeles constable and asked to be taken to Taft. "I promised him I would come back and stand trial," and "I want him to know I kept my word," Young Deer told a reporter. According to Young Deer, he suffered the conscience of a fugitive. "I would not live over the past year of my life for a million dollars. . . . The nervous strain of eluding officers for an entire year, is so great that I could no longer stand it. I am glad to get back, very glad. My wife is with me and we will get to work in the moving picture field again."[24]

Assuming his wife was still Red Wing, it's unknown how Young Deer returned to her good graces. She had made a real name for herself without him, but he told reporters that he had also earned some success. "In London I had many and varied experiences," but he "left the continent after the declaration of war because the moving picture business was all shot to pieces." He explained that he had directed "a moving picture producing company in London" and that "all we had to do was to take any kind of a drama, make the villain a German spy, the hero a British or French soldier, and worst the spy. With that your fortune was made."[25]

Carol Mason Burton's statutory rape case was set for a preliminary hearing in juvenile court in front of an unnamed judge for November 25. Marie Wilkerson's case was set for December 3, with Judge Taft presiding. Until then, Young Deer was "out on his own recognizance." However, his year of suffering was over. The court dropped both cases. Mason's witnesses could not be located in California, and Wilkerson "left the city and did not appear against him."[26]

In between the court dates on November 29, the *Los Angeles Times* ran a brief article describing Red Wing as "the clever Selig Indian actress." It erroneously claimed that she "rose to the playing of good parts" after being an extra "who played Indian types."[27] The next day, *In the Days of the Thundering Herd* was released. If Red Wing and Young Deer attended the premiere of the five-reel feature together, they would part ways very soon.

The next year, *Moving Picture World* published "Mecca of the Motion Picture," an informative and detailed account written by George Blaisdell of the current state of the Pacific coast film industry. Illustrated with the familiar photo, "Members of the Old-Time Bison Company," including Red Wing and Young Deer, Blaisdell's exposition offers an overview of the Los Angeles film studios of the day, showing the industry's progression since Red Wing stepped onto Alessandro Street five and a half years before. Blaisdell listed the companies that still believed in California's promise as a film mecca and so were expanding operations, such as New York Motion Picture Company, Keystone, Lasky, Essanay, Lubin, Metro-Rolfe, Famous Players, Universal, Balboa, and Kalem. He further described the newcomers, some of whom moved into old studios and some of whom built anew:

> David Horsely has just completed a large studio [in Hollywood]. . . . The Morosco-Bosworth is situated in a new structure of concrete and steel, built on advanced lines. . . . The Reliance Majestic studios at 4500 Sunset Boulevard are being constantly added to. The Albuquerque, now leasing from the Norbig company, has building plans under consideration. The Norbig, which has been doing commercial work, intends to begin production of western subjects. Quality Pictures is remodeling the old Nestor plant and installing an up-to-date laboratory, which will be operated under the name of F. B. Film Laboratories, of which the president as well as of the former corporation is Fred J. Balshofer. . . . The National Film Corporation has already produced four subjects in its studio that was formerly occupied by the Oz and then by the Famous Players, before removing to its new home.[28]

As far as is known, despite the growth of new studios Red Wing appeared in only two films released in 1915, *Fighting Bob* and *Carmen*. Her career slowed down drastically. She began to show her age and she had put on weight. She no longer looked the part of the little Indian maid, and ultimately the "perfect Indian type" she had single-handedly created was no longer in vogue.

Red Wing played Carmen, a matronly Spanish lady, in *Fighting Bob*, released by Metro Pictures on June 7.[29] B. A. Rolfe managed Metro, while John W. Noble, an ex–army officer, directed. *Moving Picture World* reported that the film was "based on the adventures of an American who joins the revolutionary army of a mythical republic" that was supposed to be located in Central America. Red Wing and her company traveled to a location south of the border in Juárez, Mexico, where "General Villa, who made his federal district just south of Juarez, granted the Rolfe concern carte blanche rights for staging the picture." Villa told a company representative that he was "willing to play a part" in the film, but his "service was declined with thanks."[30]

Metro staged the street-fighting scenes in the Plaza del Gobernador, "where the small low built adobe houses formed admirable backgrounds." The film starred Orrin Johnson as fighting Bob, while Broadway stage actress Olive Wyndham played Dulcina. The "big production" included 800 people and 250 horses. "The whole thing is chock full of boom, gallop, drive, charge, cannon roar, sizzle and war punch," *Moving Picture World*'s critic wrote, and came "at a most appropriate time, with war news in the paper on every side."[31] *Motion Picture News* reiterated that the film was "a most timely subject," because "President Wilson has just delivered his ultimatum to General Villa, Carranza, Zapata, and Jara and trouble is anticipated by Washington officials."[32]

None of the reviews mentioned Red Wing's performance. If Young Deer's exile blessed her career, Young Deer's return cursed it. They separated shortly after the film's release, if ever they had reunited in the first place. Without an anchor and with his already damaged reputation, Young Deer lost his bearings and ended up hospitalized after he tried to show his friends a new trick he'd learned. Cracking "a whisky glass with his teeth," he pretended to eat the broken glass, but when he tried hiding the glass in his palm instead, he cut his hand badly. "Then he fainted," according to the *Los Angeles Times*, "and was taken to the Receiving Hospital where the diagnosis was 'alcoholic hysteria.'" Perhaps the worst part was that the *Times* reporter identified him only as "Jim Youngdeer, Indian 'movie' actor who has figured in numerous escapades before the camera and elsewhere."[33]

Red Wing expanded her repertoire to again include cultural consultation for films. She also lent her beautiful *Squaw Man* dress to a young actress playing Naturitch onstage in Los Angeles. The dress, allegedly weighing thirty pounds, would become an integral part of Red Wing's future public appearances through the rest of her life.[34] In June she joined the cast of Lasky Company's *Carmen*. DeMille directed the film (released November 1), which was produced by Paramount Pictures. Prima donna Geraldine Farrar, who played Carmen for the popular Metropolitan Opera production, was cast as the lead. DeMille's brother, William C. DeMille, wrote the opera's screen adaptation. Broadway star Pedro De Cordoba and Wallace Reid, a popular film star, both played Carmen's leading men. Carmen, a "half-wild, fascinating creature—a gypsy by birth," was in many ways a liberated antiheroine who scratched, clawed, danced, and loved her way through life.[35]

Red Wing, probably thanks to DeMille, nabbed a bit part as Carmen's fellow worker in the cigar factory. Later she described her role as a "cigarette girl" to give it more glamour than it warranted. Still, she played the part with the same enthusiastic bravado she had given to all her leading roles. Her scenes, though few, are memorable because she expertly emotes and does not let the camera pass her by. When Carmen starts a catfight with one of the other factory girls, Red Wing, who appears much heavier than the year before, steps in to protect the girl and nearly steals the scene. It's obvious she refused to be pushed to the background, no matter how small her role.

After the filming was over Farrar threw a Hollywood party on August 15. If Red Wing attended the event, *Moving Picture World*'s coverage did not include her name.[36] Still, Red Wing counted the successful film as one of her career accomplishments. After *Carmen* Red Wing played a small part in *Tennessee's Pardner*, another film for the Lasky Company (released February 3, 1916). Directed by George Melford, the drama is based on Scott Marble's play *Tennessee's Partner*, which was in turn inspired by Bret Harte's famous tale. Well-known comedic stage actress Fannie Ward played the lead. The story was set at a California mission and was filmed north of Edendale at the San Fernando Mission.

Another forty-niner gold rush story, the dramatic western was a new genre for Ward: "Miss Ward will play the role of 'Tennessee,' a child whose parents are separated during the journey across the desert and who is left in care of her father's friend when her father is killed."[37] Red

Wing portrayed a mission Indian woman, but her name again appears in no reviews for the film. She appears prominently in three publicity stills, however, hair tied back, wearing a long calico dress and wool shawl, unlike her usual Indian attire. She stands in front of the San Fernando Mission with a man dressed as a padre and Fannie Ward dressed like Little Bo Peep. A stagecoach and a little girl also appear in the photos, while a few mission Indian characters, some apparently Native actors, stand in the background near the other padres.[38]

The film harked back to Red Wing's mission period. In the late summer of 1915, she visited the San Gabriel Mission to teach "chants and dances" to the Indians of the Mission Play company. One report claimed that she would star in the production, but she is not on the 1915 program, which lists scores of names.[39] Red Wing didn't go to San Gabriel alone. Accompanying her to help her instruct the Indian performers was an old friend, Luther Standing Bear.[40] The two were not at San Gabriel Mission just to teach the Mission Players the performance customs of their ancestors, however. Their presence served to promote their upcoming film, the most famous mission Indian story ever told.

CHAPTER 15

Ramona and Home Again

W. H. Clune's *Ramona* proved to be Red Wing's grand finale, although she may not have realized it at the time. Clune produced the twelve-reel epic, which was released on February 7, 1916, following his great financial success for D. W. Griffith's *Birth of a Nation*. The multitalented Donald Crisp, who later won an Academy Award for his performance in *How Green Was My Valley*, directed the film. California artist Alexander Harmer served as art director. Harmer certainly would have received an Oscar for his work on the film if such an award had existed. *Ramona* featured characters based on real Californios and spanned the state from Monterey to San Gabriel to San Jacinto to San Diego. Red Wing was too old to play the heroine, but who better to play Ramona's mother? Her part had a bit more substance than the character from Helen Hunt Jackson's novel. And unlike the novel, the film credits gave Red Wing's role a name, "Soft Wind." The image of Indian motherhood Soft Wind evokes is certainly more idealized than the one Jackson's nameless "squaw mother" elicits, and Red Wing may have inspired the name or come up with it herself.

Although *Ramona* was considered to be California's greatest romance, Jackson's conception of her heroine's real mother is far from romantic. Besides being nameless, she is a stereotypical Indian drudge, "notable for her many children and haggard body."[1] Her story line is woven into the narrative thread of wealthy ship owner and Scottish immigrant Angus Phail, who suffers because his love for a Californio maiden, Ramona Gonzaga, is unrequited. After Gonzaga breaks her vow to Phail and weds

Lieutenant Francis Ortegna, Phail wanders aimlessly for many years until he lands at the San Gabriel Mission, where a priest marries him to an "Indian squaw" who already has several children. She gives birth to their daughter, but Phail feels the baby is more his blood than hers. Consequently, he leaves his wife and takes their child.

When he hears that his first love, Ramona Ortegna, has remained childless for twenty-five years of marriage, he decides to rub salt in her wounds for rejecting him. He goes to her home near the Santa Barbara Mission and offers her his daughter. When the question arises as to the baby's mother, Phail replies, "That is nothing. She has other children, of her own blood. This is mine, my only one, my daughter. I wish her to be yours; otherwise, she will be taken by the Church." After he witnesses how lovingly Ramona accepts his child, his heart melts. She asks for the infant's name, and he replies, "The only woman's name that my lips ever spoke with love . . . was the name my daughter should bear."[2]

Knowing Red Wing, she made sure her portrayal left a better impression than Hunt intended. One precious photo exists of her as Soft Wind. She stands holding a pottery water jar in front of a real adobe brick house.[3] The house has a small corral and a weeping willow tree. An Indian man sits in the dirt at the corner of the house. Red Wing, hair tied back and barefoot, looks pensively into the distance. Although the exact story line for Soft Wind has been lost with the film (only one of the twelve reels of the film is extant), Clune put out a twenty-page lavish and artistically rendered program with illustrations and a story synopsis that suggests Red Wing's scenes:

> [Phail] drifted to the old San Gabriel Mission. He had reached the point where he was but the shell of a man and, falling ill one day before the hut of an Indian squaw, the Indian woman took him in and nursed him back to health. Later, Phail married the squaw and quietly settled down in the little Indian village, where a few years later, Ramona was born. This seemed to awaken in Phail a desire for the refinement of his earlier days. In comparing Ramona with the other children of the squaw and the careless manner in which they were raised, he conceived the idea of taking her to Ramona Ortegna, who still remained the ideal of his

dreams. Suffering great hardships on the way, he walked one hundred and twenty-two miles to Ramona Ortegna's home, and receiving the blessing and advice of Father Salvierderra, left his babe in her arms.

Now it happened that the Senora [*sic*] Ramona Ortegna had no children of her own, so all of her love was lavished on little Ramona Phail. The fact that her husband, greatly dissipated by constant drinking, was very brutal to her, only increased her love for the child, and Phail, realizing that his babe was in safe keeping, disappeared and was never heard from again.[4]

Soft Wind, whose name is also not given in the film's summary, is also "never heard from again." How Red Wing played her role is still the question. Did she portray Soft Wind as a neglectful mother with nurturing instincts only for Phail, or did Red Wing find an opening in the prejudicial story line to humanize Soft Wing's character? It's difficult to imagine Red Wing, with her love of children, portraying Soft Wing simply as Helen Hunt Jackson's Indian drudge. The name "Soft Wind" suggests she did not. The photo still from the film suggests she did not, but unless the film surfaces at a future date, we will never know.

Ramona's mother served the story as a degraded representative of her race. She is not portrayed at all in the 1928 version of *Ramona*, directed by Edwin Carewe (Chickasaw) and starring Dolores del Rio and Warren Baxter as Ramona and Alessandro. Nor does she appear in Darryl Zanuck's 1936 version, starring Loretta Young and Don Ameche.

How much internalized racism did Red Wing hold in her psyche? If we know her at all, she tried her best to uplift Phail's denigrated wife. Did her successful portrayal of Naturitch afford her some cachet to flesh out the role? It's hard to fathom Red Wing embodying a character that didn't show emotion when her "squaw man" leaves with her child. If the film included the moment when Phail takes Ramona from Soft Wing, surely her face conveyed loss—and not just her husband's abandonment. Perhaps the extant photograph represents this scene.

Soft Wind does not entirely vanish from the story, however. Her race marks a description of her daughter, Ramona, at nineteen (the inside quotation is from the novel): "Naturally a beautiful girl, her unassuming manner won the hearts of all who came in contact with her. 'She had just enough of olive tint in her complexion to underlie and enrich the skin and not make it swarthy. Indian mother's straight back, but her eyes were like her father's steel blue. Unless one came very near to Ramona, they were not sure that her eyes were not black, for her heavy black eye-brows and long black eye-lashes so shaded and shadowed them that they looked black.'"[5]

This description of Ramona is similar to late nineteenth-century fictional depictions of mulatto women. Ramona is not only beautiful but also exotic and erotic. She titillates as a "half-breed" because miscegenation is sinful and racial mixture fascinating. But like Hal in *The Squaw Man*, her inherited nature must be nurtured in civilization—even if it is a Californio Catholic version of it. Red Wing was familiar with the terrain not only in the moving pictures she acted but also in her own family history.

Adda Gleason played Ramona Phail, while Anna Lehr played her as a child. Monroe Salisbury played Ramona Phail's Indian lover and husband, Alessandro Assis. Jack London's niece and Red Wing's former costar Lurline Lyons played Señora Hermosa Gonzaga Moreno, whose character adopts Ramona as a child after Ramona Ortegna, Hermosa's sister, dies.[6] Victor Vallejo played Hermosa's biological son Felipe as a child, and N. de Builler played his father in the prologue, General Felipe Moreno, the "distinguished Mexican general." He also played the adult Felipe Moreno Jr., who carries a torch for his sister-cousin, Ramona, and ends up with her in the end when Alessandro dies. Others prominent in the cast were Mabel Van Buren as Ramona Gonzaga Ortegna, Arthur Tavares as Ramona's husband, Francis Ortegna, and Richard Sterling as Angus Phail. Hubert Whitehead portrayed Señor Gonzaga, Ramona's father and commander of the Santa Barbara Presidio; H. M. Best portrayed Father Salvierderra; and Alice Morton Otten portrayed Star Light, "Ramona Ortegna's Indian maid."[7] These are the characters that appear in the film's prologue, but many more are featured in act 1 and act 2, such as Luther Standing Bear, who plays Alessandro's father, chief of the Temecula Village Indians.

The story opens in 1847 with the marriage of Hermosa Gonzaga and Felipe Moreno at the Santa Barbara Mission. The wedding festivities include a barbecue, while Indian women make tortillas in the background. "As was the custom, the Indians took part in the peculiar dances of their kind," states Clune's program, "which were enjoyed by the Spanish Dons and ladies attending the wedding." It's likely that Red Wing and Standing Bear had a hand in the choreography, given their earlier engagement at the San Gabriel Mission. Red Wing probably also consulted on the film's third act, which opens in the home of a mission Indian, perhaps her own character, "engaged in basket-making, beadwork, and kindred occupations, while a group of Indians sing, play and dance."[8]

Journalist Grace Kingsley, who wrote about the making of the "California Epic," found Standing Bear of more interest than Red Wing: "Several hundred Indians are used in the picture, among whom the most interesting is Mato Najen (Chief Standing Bear,) a lithe, tall, erect and alert specimen of the Sioux brave at his best. . . . Chief Standing Bear is a graduate of Carlisle College, and one of the most interesting figures of his clan."[9] An illustration of Standing Bear accompanies the piece, along with a few other photos from the production. Standing Bear dons a Sioux headdress and a beaded loincloth that probably came from Red Wing's collection.

The film opened on February 6 at Clune's spectacular Los Angeles theater. One newspaper account mistook Red Wing and Standing Bear for the film's real "Indian Royalty." "Included in the hundred or more 'Mission Indians,' who take active part in 'Ramona,' are Princess Red Wing and Chief Standing Bear," the item stated, "two members of the ancient line who have ruled the Village of Temecula since time immemorial." The reporter also claimed that the producer had to get the padre's consent for their participation, "without which no Mission Indian will do anything for a white man." Driving home the point that Red Wing and Standing Bear were primitive Indians, the reporter contended that when "the Princess" and "the Chief" "were taken to Los Angeles they were visibly delighted when they recognized each other on screen."[10]

What probably delighted the "royals" was seeing each other in the same motion picture. As far as is known it was only film they made together. But what a significant film it was! Although many critics found *Ramona* at nearly three hours slow moving, "lugubrious," and a bit boring in places, almost everyone deemed it a masterpiece in filmmaking because the art direction and cinematography were simply stunning. Its "cinema-theatrical" presentation was particularly unique. Films were usually shown in stage theaters, and the art director took advantage of the stage in a way no film had done before. Certainly, the prologue, as described by *Moving Picture World*'s critic, was something Red Wing and filmgoers had never experienced: "Slowly the dark stage was changed from apparent night, to dawn, and the towering Santa Barbara mission was seen in dim and purple outline against the reddening sky. Natives emerged from the church and met others coming by. The scene was silent and impressive. Daylight came, and with it the songs of the happy people. Then the waning day and night, still and quietly thrilling." The set featured authentic mission bells, and each set onstage replicated the acts of the film. As *Moving Picture World*'s critic concluded, "The illusion was rather startling."[11]

Critics pointed out the film's innovative use of title cards and lauded its music production for its "effectiveness and beauty." Emil Bierman arranged the music, which had been selected by Clune's general manager, Lloyd Brown. Carlo Di Elinor, another Clune Theater mainstay, conducted the thirty-piece orchestra, while an additional twelve musicians played onstage. A vocal quartet also accompanied the musicians. As one critic wrote, the music combined "a strain of the Oriental, a touch of Spanish and a little Hawaiian."[12] The latter two ethnicities, in particular, reflected the heritage of the Southern California mission Indians. The audience understood the Spanish influence, but many did not realize the whaling industry brought Native Hawaiians to the California coast, and they intermarried with the local Indigenous population.

The film arrived at the Cort Theater in San Francisco on March 20 and then in Washington DC at the end of March. It then opened on April 5 on Broadway in New York City at the 44th Street Theater. A *New York Times* critic judged that the film should have been shortened to make it more entertaining, but he applauded the "sheep-shearing scenes" (done by Indians) and the "adorable performance" of the actress playing Ramona as a child. Gleason's and Salisbury's acting in particular showed how well they portrayed their "types."[13]

George Blaisdell was more enthusiastic, stating emphatically, "It is no exaggeration, it is expressing a plain fact, to say that 'Ramona' . . . marks a distinct advance in the motion picture industry." He found it faithful to Jackson's novel but, like other critics, felt it lacked enough drama to carry it through its long time span. Still, he explained, "It is a simple tale of life, from 1845 to 1881, staged in a picturesque country and treating of the love of Alessandro, a full-blooded Indian, and Ramona, the daughter of a Scotch father and an Indian mother." Although it was not a "spectacular story," he said, it was a "romance filled with heart interest" that highlighted the tragic plight of the mission Indians as Jackson had intended.[14]

Blaisdell also complimented Mexican-born Enrico Vallejo's stereo-scopic cinematography. "In distance, depth and composition it is unusual," he noted. He also, again, mentioned the fine stage settings, the first representing "the entrance to the Santa Barbara mission," the second, "the south veranda of the Moreno hacienda," and the third, "a remarkably picturesque canyon in towering San Jacinto." The last location suggests that Soboba Indians, as in *The Squaw Man,* may have appeared in the film.[15] Blaisdell further praised the performances of Gleason and Salisbury, as well as those of Sterling and Van Buren. He named Red Wing and Lurline Lyons among "the notable performances," but he made no mention of Standing Bear.

Even with *Ramona*'s great success Red Wing could not find work. That October 1916 she left her new apartment at 515 West 8th Street in Los Angeles and traveled to Klamath Falls, Oregon. The local newspaper reported that she was there on vacation but also had come to study the local Klamath Indians to research an upcoming film. The unnamed film never came to fruition. Red Wing also tested the waters for a new career venture, whether she knew it or not at the time.

German-born Anna K. Bath hosted Red Wing's visit.[16] How the two women connected is unknown. "Red Wing is no different from any other movie actress except that she is Indian," the local newspaper reported. "Her English is fluent and her education finished." The item listed several of Red Wing's films for which she was said to play "a leading role," including *Ramona, The Squaw Man, Red Wing's Gratitude, The Thundering Herd, Blue Wing and the Violinist, A Redskin's Appeal, A Cheyenne Brave, The Red Girl and the Child, Tennessee's Pardner*, and *Carmen*. She was further credited with writing scenarios for several of her films, as well as composing "poetry" for *The Red Girl and the Child*, though what poetry is a mystery. Red Wing apparently chose not to discuss with the reporter her years of collaboration with Young Deer. Instead, she highlighted her relationship with Standing Bear: "Red Wing comes from the Winnebago Indian reservation in Nebraska, and is the adopted niece of the Sioux chief Standing Bear, who is a brother-in-law of Hollow Horn Bear, the famous chief who died in Washington DC, a few years ago. Standing Bear gave her the name of Red Wing when he adopted her as his niece. This adoption is not a legal adoption as understood in the white man's law, but corresponds to what the white man would call becoming a godfather."[17]

Red Wing loaned her *Squaw Man* dress for display in the downtown hardware store. When *The Squaw Man* came to Klamath Fall's Star Theater in mid-November, she wore the dress to the screening and gave a lecture on the picture and, presumably, on Native culture.[18] Red Wing's visit to Klamath Falls reflects her early performances with Standing Bear, but it also presaged her future. With her film days mostly over, she needed to find another means of support. What else could she do with her talents and the skills she had acquired over the last seven years?

Red Wing had returned to Washington DC by the first of June 1917. In a way it must have been cathartic to revisit the place where she and Young Deer first met. Old memories didn't bring her back to the area, however; her sister did. Julia, "a well-educated Indian girl who has helped many of her red sisters and brothers in their efforts to secure justice from the Big White Father of this city," was still representing Winnebago people in heirship cases, as reported by an Omaha journalist stationed temporarily in the capital. The journalist couldn't help but find Julia's sister of interest, although he misnamed her "Vivian St. Cyr Johnston." "Nebraska has another moving picture heroine—one that rivals Pauline Bush Dwan for her screen title too," he wrote.[19] "She was here last week and to a World-Herald man who was permitted to glance nonchalantly at her pay check it was apparent that her starring qualities are well appreciated." He mentioned Red Wing's roles in *The Squaw Man* and *Ramona*, pronouncing:

"Movie artists from one end of the country to the other know her and speak very highly of her attainments in the silent drama."[20]

After Julia finished her duties, Red Wing returned with her to the reservation. At that time, brother Louis farmed his allotment, but brother David seems to have been unemployed. He'd become a convert to the new mescal religion—derogatorily called "the Peyote cult" but now known as the Native American Church. His former Hampton educators severely criticized his conversion, stating in an annual report that he was "no good to himself or others." Whether true or false, the prejudice held by Hampton educators ran deep against the new religion, which mixed "paganism" with Christianity.[21]

Red Wing reunited with her other sisters and their families. Annie's son Jason Owen had recently enlisted in the army infantry and was about to head out for training at Camp Cody, New Mexico. His sister Pauline, about thirteen, probably attended Genoa Indian Industrial School. Minnie Lowry had not remarried. Red Wing grew close to Minnie's daughters, particularly Alvina, a young woman full of promise. Red Wing's half brothers Levi and Abner were doing well. They had large families, and many of their children also attended Genoa. Abner worked as a teamster on the reservation, and Levi, who had previously found employment with the Indian Service in Kansas, was now back in Emerson farming. He continued singing in the Winnebago Quartet and was active in the Society of American Indians, the first national pan-Indian organization.[22]

By the summer of 1918, Red Wing had decided to seek employment. She may have hoped to escape publicity, but her appearance at the state employment agency in Sioux City resulted in a lengthy article headlined: "Indian Girl, Movie Actress, Is Doing Housework in Sioux City. It's a Far Call from Playing Opposite Dustin Farnum but Girl Is Happy." Although the reporter described her as an "Indian girl who bore the too undeniable traces of her race, the copper skin and the straight black hair," Red Wing's directness with Mrs. Larrimore, the employment agent, conveyed the attitude of a thoroughly modern Millie: "I am Lillian St. Cyr and my home is on the reservation of the Winnebago Indians. Have you any positions open for Indian girls?" Red Wing informed Larrimore that she "had done office work in Philadelphia." Two of her nieces accompanied her and easily found typing and stenographer jobs. However, Larrimore seems to have discouraged Red Wing in that line of work, opining that "the work of housemaid in a good home in Sioux City would not be distasteful to one who wanted to be near the home of her people." Consequently, a local housewife employed the former movie actress after hearing she'd worked as a housemaid for a Kansas senator. Pronouncing Red Wing "a housemaid a little better than the average," Larrimore concluded that she could serve as a role model for other "Indian girls who have good education, and who are willing to be employed."[23]

Meanwhile, Young Deer, who registered for the draft on September 12, 1918, claimed "Lilian Young Deer" as his wife on his registration form.[24] Tribal records also show him as her spouse that year, and, as mentioned, no records have been found documenting their final divorce decree. It's unknown if Red Wing ever returned to Los Angeles to be with him, and no documentation exists to show he traveled to Nebraska to be with her. Clearly, their marriage was over, but Young Deer refused to accept it.

The only other contact Red Wing had with the Los Angeles film industry was lending or selling Norma Talmadge her old beaded dress from Pine Ridge for Talmadge's starring role in *The Heart of Wetona* (released January 1919).[25] The public was more than happy to see Talmadge play an Indian maid while Red Wing took her proper place among the educated Indian housekeepers. How long Red Wing worked as a domestic is unknown, but in October 1919 she found brief employment with an Indian vaudeville entertainer known as Indian Joe Davis, aka White Eagle Jr.

Davis's Indian roots were as tenuous as Young Deer's. Allegedly born on a reservation in Nebraska, he promoted himself as the son of Pawnee chief White Eagle, though his birth occurred after the Pawnee left the state for Oklahoma, and tribal records for White Eagle Sr. don't support Davis's claim. Like Young Deer, he also falsely claimed he was a Carlisle graduate. In reality he'd performed for several Wild West shows before he created his act, including with Dick Elliott, Pawnee Bill, and Buffalo Bill Cody. It's likely Davis was a Mexican ranch hand and learned fancy rope training in Texas and Oklahoma, where he eventually married a Pawnee woman.

Besides performing at movie theaters, Davis took his act, funded by the YMCA, to schools, army camps, and hospitals. He advertised his show as "Instructive and Educational." During the war years he declared that Indians were as patriotic and willing to fight for their country as whites. He promoted his patriotism (and his act) by registering for the draft in Washington DC in September 1918, even though he was a bit too old to serve. Davis also espoused his views on Indians and the military with a letter published in *Wassaja*, a newsletter edited by Apache activist Dr. Carlos Montezuma:

> As I go through the country the people keep me busy explaining about the different tribes, for they do not seem to know much about them. My hair is very long and when I go to places people gaze at me as though I had just come out of the woods. Many of them think I am still wild like the Indians of a hundred years ago. I generally tell them that I may look wild, but I am not as wild as I look. If they ask me what I represent I generally tell them, personally of my race, and that I am here to explain about the Indians, and let them know that we Indians are not sleeping, but that we are really at work, so that we can take care of our ownselves and interests. We believe in justice, sticking together and living like brothers and sisters. Our blood is not going to pass out very soon. We have many of our boys in the service, and a few Indian girls are with the Red Cross in France. We are doing our bit. We are willing to fight in defense of the flag, which our forefathers never understood years ago—the Red, White and Blue.[26]

"All Indians are willing to fight in defense of the FLAG.—The Red, White and Blue," his ad for the Liberty Theater in Greenwood, South Carolina, likewise declared in July 1918. The same ad included a professional photo of Davis dressed in splendid Indian regalia as he holds an American colonial flag. His performance included a lecture on Indian lore and Thomas Ince's film *Custer's Last Fight*, as well as "native dances, war songs, fancy roping, and mysteries."[27]

Red Wing likely found Davis through a want ad, such as the one he placed in the June 1918 issue of *Billboard*: "Indian Joe Davis wants good Indian actress who can play the piano, sing or have some specialty."[28]

Not many apart from Red Wing could fill that bill. While Davis toured the Carolinas that fall he had paired up with Princess Blue Feather, also known as Wap-tuse-yose-yose. Billed as the "Sole Descendant of the Great Aztec King," she performed "Mexican Indian Dances," such as the "genuine War-Bell and Tom-tom," but left the act soon after.[29]

Red Wing certainly learned a few rope tricks from Indian Joe. On February 20, 1919, Davis took his act to Altoona, Pennsylvania, and was "assisted by Miss Red Wing of the Winnebago tribe."[30] Described as "thorough-bred Indians," the pair entertained over one thousand school children in all. Davis "executed many clever tricks with the lariat" that won him "deafening applause." He also performed standard magic tricks and lectured on Indian customs. Red Wing, returning to her old New York shtick, "sang a song in English" and accompanied herself on the piano. She followed her performance with a "native song." Afterward, she "explained the various musical instruments used at Indian festivities." She closed her part of the act with another old standby, "an Indian dance by the princess, accompanied on the tom-tom drum." Although Davis's stunning Indian regalia drew the children's attention, a newspaper noted that "Miss Redwing attired in buckskin and decorated in Indian beads was the centre of attraction of all eyes."[31] The report made no mention of Red Wing's film career.

The duo performed two days later at Red Wing's alma mater, Carlisle, although the Indian school had closed the year before due to the war and the lack of support for off-reservation education. The campus had been returned to the U.S. military. Davis and Red Wing gave one show at the General Army Hospital, housed on the school grounds, as well as two at the old Indian girls' dormitory. Carlisle's *Evening Herald* report didn't mention Davis's claim that he'd attended the Indian school, only that he had visited Carlisle several times. It did, however, confirm that Davis's assistant, "Lillian St. Cyr, also known as Red Wing," was a graduate of the school.[32]

By March, Davis had found work heading Chief Joe Davis's Indian Village with the Mighty Doris Exposition, a traveling circus featuring Wild West performers and acts like Haeman's Trained Wild Animal Arena and Howard's Congress of Fat Girls. At the end of March, the show performed in Richmond, Virginia, but if Red Wing was still with Davis, she wasn't making any press for it.[33]

Red Wing lost her best leading man in the spring of 1919, when George Gebhardt succumbed to heart failure at age thirty-nine. Gebhardt died in Los Angeles, leaving his widow, Madeline West.[34] If Red Wing had the financial means to attend his funeral, she also needed the emotional stamina to face Young Deer and the friends she'd left behind. Perhaps it was better to leave the past far behind her. By October, Julia St. Cyr had returned to Washington DC, supporting herself as a clerk for the Western Union while she represented heirship cases.[35] Red Wing may have joined her but probably returned to Emerson, because Minnie was seriously ill. On November 20, at only forty-nine, she died of an unnamed illness, leaving Alvina, Lillian, and Annie Lowry motherless. Although Ben Lowry had married other women "Indian custom" since he left the family, Minnie was still legally married to him upon her death. However, she had had the foresight to leave Ben one dollar in her will so that their daughters could inherit her allotment lands in full.[36] Alvina was still unmarried, but her sisters were married. Lillian married Nebraska Winnebago William Smith, and they had a daughter, Catherine Lucille, born in April. Just before she turned sixteen, Annie married Wisconsin Ho-Chunk and Carlisle alumnus Lester Young Thunder, and they had a son, William, born in June. Minnie experienced the joy of being a grandmother, if only briefly, before she passed on. Minnie's death dramatically changed the life course of at least two of her daughters. It would also assure Red Wing a future filled with family.

Fig. 25. "Selig Buffalo Picture," Red Wing and Tom Mix in *In the Days of the Thundering Herd. Moving Picture World*, November 14, 1914. Courtesy Media History Digital Library.

ℝED WING. Born in Nebraska, 1893. Her father was chief of the Sioux Indian Tribe. Was educated in Nebraska and started her picture experience with the forces of the New York Motion Picture Company under the direction of Chas. K. French, remaining there for one year. Her first picture was "The Cowboy's Narrow Escape." She then joined the Pathe Company, playing Indian leads and after remaining with them for three years joined the Laskey Features, her latest success being in "The Squaw Man."

Fig. 26. Red Wing in *Who's Who in the Film World*, 1914. Courtesy Media History Digital Library.

always studying them. Do I think Motion Pictures will ever outshine the stage? Well, so far as road shows are concerned, they already outshine the stage. But I dont think they'll *ever* outshine a Broadway production." and her voice sounded awfully home-sick. "Motion pictures will always cater to a larger audience, tho, and an audience that is much harder to please. I do not approve of the censorship of films. I consider it unnecessary, for so far as the Edison Company is concerned, I am sure Mr. Plimpton knows what is suitable and what to produce. Yes. I enjoy photoplays very much, and like them all—except Indians and Westerns."

The charming leading lady of the Jacksonville Edison Company was born in New York, but refuses to say where she was educated, for she says she does not think the public is interested enough in her to want to know that much about her. She does not believe in the fads of theosophy, mesmerism, and all that sort of thing, altho she considers Christian Science a wonderful thing. She loves swimming and is just learning. In fact, she likes all forms of exercise except walking, which she detests. She says she's a Democrat, altho she doesn't pretend to understand politics, and hasn't the slightest idea who the greatest living statesman is.

"How many hours a day, and how many days a week do you work?" was the next question, and Miss Trunnelle twisted her pretty face into a droll grimace.

"Well, that depends entirely upon the weather," she answered, "and if we stay in Florida long, we'll have to be retired on a pension." (In explanation, Florida, or at least this part of it, has been experiencing some of the worst weather known to even the "oldest inhabitant," and the three companies stationed here have been working Sundays to get out the necessary pictures.)

"It is impossible to say how many photo-plays I have worked in," she continued, "for I have been with Edison two years and with Majestic one year—the old Majestic, I mean, of course. I have worked in an average of one picture a week during the two years with Edison and two a week down at Majestic, so you can count it up for yourself."

She has never been in public print, and when in New York, lives in a hotel.

"There!" she said, as I rose to go. "That's the whole sad story of my life, and I certainly hope the public will be interested enough in me to read it."

And I am sure they will be!

PEARL GADDIS.

MONA DARKFEATHER, OF THE KALEM COMPANY

MONA DARKFEATHER is distinctly different. She is known all over the civilized world, and yet she has never worked outside of Los Angeles. She is recognized as one of the best Moving Picture Indians appearing on the screen, and yet she never set foot on the legiti-mate stage. She is a curiosity, has never had to travel to acquire a reputation, and yet she stands at the very head of her specialty. In-dian maidens, and altho the Moving Picture public associates her with Indian characters, she is really very versatile and will soon be as familiar in Western and society rôles as in Indian characterizations. She was the Indian maiden, however, when I met her at the Kalem studios at Glendale, and was ready to play her part in "The Invisible Vengeance," under the direction of Frank Montgomery. "Contrary to

Fig. 27. Mona Darkfeather, "Chats with the Players," *Motion Picture Story*, April 1914. Courtesy Media History Digital Library.

Fig. 28. Principals of W. H. Clune's *Ramona*. "Clune's Production of Ramona" program, 1915. Schmidt Litho. Co., Los Angeles.

Edendale Studios

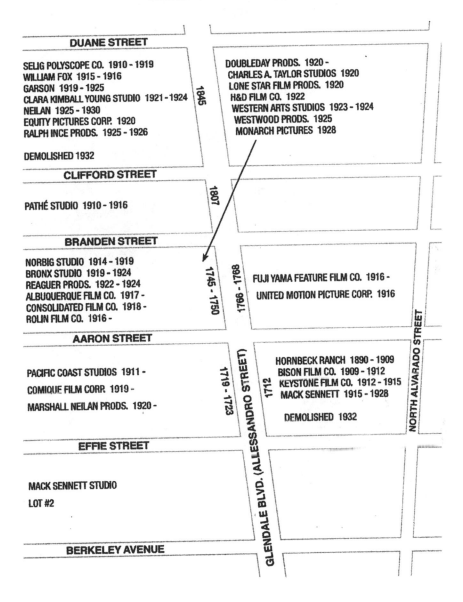

DUANE STREET

SELIG POLYSCOPE CO. 1910 - 1919
WILLIAM FOX 1915 - 1916
GARSON 1919 - 1925
CLARA KIMBALL YOUNG STUDIO 1921-1924
NEILAN 1925 - 1930
EQUITY PICTURES CORP. 1920
RALPH INCE PRODS. 1925 - 1926

DEMOLISHED 1932

DOUBLEDAY PRODS. 1920 -
CHARLES A. TAYLOR STUDIOS 1920
LONE STAR FILM PRODS. 1920
H&D FILM CO. 1922
WESTERN ARTS STUDIOS 1923 - 1924
WESTWOOD PRODS. 1925
MONARCH PICTURES 1928

1845

CLIFFORD STREET

PATHÉ STUDIO 1910 - 1916

1807

BRANDEN STREET

NORBIG STUDIO 1914 - 1919
BRONX STUDIO 1919 - 1924
REAGUER PRODS. 1922 - 1924
ALBUQUERQUE FILM CO. 1917 -
CONSOLIDATED FILM CO. 1918 -
ROLIN FILM CO. 1916 -

1745 - 1750

1766 - 1768

FUJI YAMA FEATURE FILM CO. 1916 -

UNITED MOTION PICTURE CORP. 1916

AARON STREET

PACIFIC COAST STUDIOS 1911 -

COMIQUE FILM CORP. 1919 -

MARSHALL NEILAN PRODS. 1920 -

1719 - 1723

GLENDALE BLVD. (ALLESSANDRO STREET)

1712

HORNBECK RANCH 1890 - 1909
BISON FILM CO. 1909 - 1912
KEYSTONE FILM CO. 1912 - 1915
MACK SENNETT 1915 - 1928

DEMOLISHED 1932

NORTH ALVARADO STREET

EFFIE STREET

MACK SENNETT STUDIO

LOT #2

BERKELEY AVENUE

Fig. 29. Map of Edendale Studios. Courtesy Marc Wanamaker, Bison Productions/Archives, Los Angeles.

Fig. 30. Bebe Daniels as a leading lady. *Moving Picture World*, June 12, 1920. Courtesy Media History Digital Library.

Fig. 31. Young Deer's "Watuska" cast. *Camera! The Digest of the Motion Picture Industry*, March 27, 1920 (back cover). Courtesy Media History Digital Library.

IN VAUDEVILLE

LILIA RED WING
Winnebago Indian Movie Actress will appear in person, giving a talk on movies; also give
songs in Indian and English.

NORMAN TYNDEL
Omaha Indian boy in native
songs and dances

Fig. 32. Left: Ad for Red Wing's tour of the Midwest. *Arkansas City Daily Traveler*, September 8, 1922.

Fig. 33. Right: Red Wing in Indian regalia sometime between 1920 and 1940. Courtesy Henry Payer, Ho-Chunk artist, Winnebago, Nebraska.

Fig. 34. The reunion of Red Wing and DeMille, Hollywood, California, 1951. Cecil B. DeMille Papers, L. Tom Perry Special Collections Library, Brigham Young University, Provo, Utah.

Fig. 35. Red Wing sewing a headdress. Meyer Berger interview, 1958. United Artists Collection (140949), Wisconsin Center for Film and Theater Research, Madison.

RED WING needs no introduction to the American public. She was the star of Cecil DeMille's first movie production "The Squaw Man" in which she played the part of Naturich opposite the late Dustin Farnum. She also appeared with the late Tom Mix. She played in the film version of "Ramona" and many other motion picture productions. Of recent years she has been engaged in educational work, giving instruction in Indian handcraft in the occupational therapy department of Bellevue Hospital.

Fig. 36. Red Wing wearing a headdress. Meyer Berger interview, 1958. United Artist Collection (140948), Wisconsin Center for Film and Theater Research.

Fig. 37. Henu Josephine Tarrant, 2018. Courtesy Henu Josephine Tarrant.

CHAPTER 16

Lilia Red Wing on Tour and the Visual Education Movement

After Minnie Lowry died, her daughter Lillian Lowry Smith and her husband moved to a large, modern rooming house in Omaha on Davenport Street, just west of the railroad tracks that bordered the Missouri River. Her husband worked for a meat-packing plant alongside one of the many stockyards in Omaha. Louis St. Cyr and his wife, Mabel Frenchman, also left their farm and relocated to Omaha, where Louis secured a job as a carpenter.[1] By January 1920 Red Wing had joined her family in Omaha, moving in with Louis and Mabel. The three shared a modest home on South 18th Street, a couple miles from the Smiths and not far from the bank of the Missouri River.

Omaha bustled in 1920. Fresh meat from the packing plants could be easily shipped because the city bordered the confluence of the Missouri and Platte Rivers. Red Wing's family moved to Omaha just after a terrible race riot culminated in the lynching of an African American man falsely accused of raping a white woman. Although white supremacists justified the murder, competition for jobs brought their hatred to a head. Stockyard and meat-packing employers found it financially expedient to recruit low-wage earners, particularly African Americans. What whites thought about Indians like Smith doing these jobs is unknown.

In days gone by, several tribes had made Omaha their home. Although the Omaha people were not one of these tribal groups, their government reservation sat between the city and the Winnebago reservation at the border of Iowa. When Omaha newspapers reported on local Native folks, news items usually involved illegal liquor sales to Indians (and by Indians), "immoral" Indian-custom marriages, the Winnebago's and Omaha's participation in the Peyote Religion, Indians in sports, or advertisements for local powwows. Other than that, most white city dwellers only knew American Indians through motion pictures. Westerns were still popular in Omaha's many theaters, but Native Americans in starring roles were rare. Theatergoers wanted to see the real thing up close and personal, some to learn about Native lifeways, but most to encounter the "wild Indian" before he or she supposedly vanished.

Red Wing understood these desires and more than most knew how to fulfill them.[2] Not long after she moved to Omaha, she took Joe Davis's lead and started to think about creating her own show. Elijah Tahamont and his wife, Margaret Camp, the Dark Clouds, also provided an example for her to follow, since they had lectured on "Indian life and customs" in theaters showing their Pathé films.[3] As one journalist declared, their presentation allowed audience members a chance to "witness . . . the last of this great and wonderful people which first inhabited this continent."[4]

Davis wasn't the only vaudeville Indian on the road in 1920. There were several other "chiefs," some with princess sidekicks, who appeared at movie theaters. Gowongo Mohawk was one of the more interesting performers. Born Caroline Mohawk in 1860 in Gowanda, New York, she toured in the summer of 1920 as Chief Wongo Nemah with "his squaw," Princess Floating Cloud. Previously, Mohawk was a rootin' tootin' lady Wild West rider for Buffalo Bill, but she also gained fame as the first Indian actress to have a stage career. Her chief and princess act included Indian dances and "a wonderful collection of Indian relics" on display in the lobby after a showing of Bison 101's blockbuster *Custer's Last Fight*.[5]

Chief Sheet Lightning, born Walter Battice (Sac and Fox), performed with Princess Little Eagle, a Stockbridge woman from Wisconsin.[6] Battice, also shown as Paw-me-waw-tha-skuk on tribal records, was a natural leader, serving as the secretary for the Sac and Fox Nation, which was removed from Iowa to Kansas in 1846 and then to Indian Territory (Oklahoma). Red Wing may have consulted Battice about his act, because her sister Julia attended Hampton Institute with him and considered him a good friend. But Red Wing probably knew him personally, since their paths crossed several times. As a young man, Battice taught at his reservation school, run by Quakers, but eventually joined the Miller Brothers' 101 Ranch as a performer. He took charge of the Indian Congress at the 1898 Omaha Exposition, and he managed the Indian performers at the 1907 Jamestown Exposition. In 1913 he played a role in San Gabriel's Mission Play as well.[7]

Battice and Little Eagle also performed that summer in tandem with *Custer's Last Fight*. Chief Hailstone, a self-described Cherokee, did the same.[8] The fact that all of these acts, including Indian Joe's, featured the 1912 Thomas Ince release was no coincidence. The performers most likely purchased rights to show the film.

Red Wing would do the same in 1920. "I bought the state rights for the Tom Mix pictures I played in," Red Wing later explained, "and traveled in many states with the pictures giving an educational program in conjunction with the pictures."[9] In another account she said she bought "states rights" to one Tom Mix picture, and, of course, technically she only made one film with him.[10] Advertisements for her act clear up the confusion. She actually performed with a 1919 release called *The Days of Daring*, a reedited version of *In the Days of the Thundering Herd*.[11] She didn't always perform with the Mix picture, but her appearance as Starlight in *The Days of Daring* lent her act more credibility and authenticity than any of the other vaudeville Indians touring at the time.

While Red Wing regrouped in Omaha, news surely came her way revealing how much her Native American roots boosted her husband's career. "James Youngdeer, motion picture producer, who has been in France for the past few years, directing pictures for Pathe, has returned to Los Angeles to begin production after the first of the year," *Moving Picture World* announced. "Miss Rita Nunn, new to pictures, will be the leading woman and several Indian girls belonging to the Creek tribe are members of the film company."[12]

The reference to his years in France fooled some, but most film industry locals knew Young Deer had struggled since his return to Los Angeles. "Jimmy Youngdeer is trying hard to get on top again, but this time, he says, he will not go to Paris," reported the *Herald*. "He has opened a one-reeler plant in the suburbs and works fourteen and sixteen hours a day."[13] In 1915 Young Deer leased the Norbig Studio, a block from his former studio. He directed a comedy for Hartigan's Pathé Exchange entitled *Just Tramps,* released the first week of May.[14] Press also stated he was busy producing a five-reel film entitled *The Savage* the same year. George Gebhardt and Bebe Daniels, who'd grown into a beautiful teenager, were supposed to star, and a big to-do was made about Young Deer's influence on Daniels's development as a child actress. However, the picture, if it was ever filmed, wasn't released. Subsequently, Gebhardt joined the Lasky Company and then went back to Universal Pictures in the fall. On the precipice of stardom the "dainty Bebe Daniels" became Rollin Film Company's leading lady under director Hal Roach, DeMille's five-dollar-a-day extra.[15]

By the fall, Young Deer had found a home at the Deer Film Company, headed by D. L. Burke. The company was probably named for him, but it was really Burke's baby. Deer Company produced pictures for the Associated Service (AS), a film distribution company also managed by Burke. Charles K. French, direct from Inceville, directed for AS's Navajo branch, while Frank Montgomery directed for its Monty division. Until the company's unexplained demise, Young Deer directed several films for Deer Company in 1915, at least two starring Lillian Wiggins.[16]

In 1916 Young Deer tried marketing comedies for Norbig Studios and writing scenarios, one of which became *The Great Secret,* starring Francis X. Bushman. By the summer of 1917, financial woes had forced him to return to acting. He appeared in a small role, "Lonesome Pete," for Metro-Yorke's *Under Handicap*. His old boss Fred Balshofer directed the film, which starred Harold Lockwood and Anna Little.[17] In 1919 Young Deer wrote scenarios for *Getting Acquainted* and *Neck and Noose*, Universal western shorts directed by George Holt. At some point he also worked and wrote scenarios with Alfred Santell, who later became a well-known Hollywood director. "I worked with Jimmie Youngdeer in the days when we doubled the cowboys as Indians and settlers and had them chasing themselves through two reels of thrilling westerns," Santell later recalled.[18] One of their shorts featured Australian actor Billy Bevan and Gebhardt's wife, Madeline West. After that work a company called

Circle C, headed by an unknown cowboy, supposedly hired Young Deer to direct pictures, but nothing came of it.[19]

In the late fall of 1919, Young Deer became director-general and treasurer of his own enterprise, Young Deer Productions, housed in the former Rollins Studio next to Norbig.[20] He wrote and directed the company's first film, *The Stranger*, exaggerated in the press as "five amazing reels." Young Deer utilized the new weekly Los Angeles trade magazine, *Camera! The Digest of the Motion Picture Industry,* to boost sales of the film with some advertising double-speak: "'A Photoplay Without a Known Star,' in a First National Exhibitor circuit house. This is an achievement that will be watched with eager interest by the general public."[21] But the magazine's editor, Elmer M. Robbins, published the name incorrectly as "Youngdeer Film Co." To set the record straight, Young Deer took out a full-page ad, stating, "I, James Youngdeer, who personally wrote and directed 'The Stranger,' wish to state that my publicity man advertised the production as a Youngdeer Film Co. picture. It has never been the property of Youngdeer Film Co. but was the property of the Youngdeer Production Co., which I formed for the purpose of producing said picture. Since that time, I have sold my interest in the Youngdeer Producing Co., and have since formed the Youngdeer Film Co., under which banner all of my future productions will appear."[22]

Young Deer intended to employ the same scheme as he had in *The Stranger*, promoting low-budget films with "no known stars" for his new venture, Young Deer Film Company. He placed a want ad in the *Los Angeles Herald* to recruit a cast for a future production he called "Watuska," though it's not mentioned in the ad: "WANTED—Young men of exceptionally good appearance; inexperienced: must honestly wish to make good in motion pictures. NOT A SCHOOL, but a high class producing company that offers an exceptional opportunity to exceptional people. Apply at once."[23] He also placed the same want ad to recruit young women.

Young Deer began casting for "Watuska," a "super seven reel production," in December 1919. His star, Miss Rita Nunn, mentioned previously, was actually Rita Harrison Nunn Gaisford, a former widow with two small children from Cape Girardeau, Missouri. Nunn married a second time to an auditor and lived with her toddlers and new husband in Los

Angeles.[24] Young Deer hid her motherhood and marital status and used her to promote his reputation as a director, as shown in a publicity piece for *Camera!*:

> Although Miss Nunn has never before appeared professionally, a great deal of her time has been devoted to dramatic study and training. She came to Los Angeles with the idea of taking up motion picture work and after careful observation she has placed herself under Mr. Youngdeer's direction, feeling confident that with practical application and experience he can develop her natural histrionic abilities. Miss Nunn has been familiar with the director's success in the past in drawing out and developing raw material into stardust. A few of Youngdeer's former protégés include Louis Glaum, Bessie Eyton, Jackie Saunders, Mary Miles Minter, Jewel Carmen [Evelyn Quick] and Douglas Gerard.[25]

The publicity piece also stated that Young Deer's stock company included eight unknown actors, among them "Chief Watuska, Wasona Silvermoon, and Princess Ane'-mone." It further claimed that "Wasona Silvermoon and Princess Ane'-Mone are both Indian girls, of the Creek tribe," Silvermoon a full blood and Ane'-Mone, the daughter of a chief and a French English woman. The ad didn't mention Chief Watuska's tribal affiliation. It also didn't disclose the film's narrative "theme," but, according to Young Deer's promotional ad in *Camera!*, "the general line-up promises some very high class productions."[26]

Young Deer's first choice for Princess Watuska didn't pan out. Either he couldn't develop Nunn's "histrionic" talents, or, more likely, serious financial conflicts came to a head. Young Deer's production company likely traded film acting training and a chance to become famous for pay. Nunn bowed out of the production, despite the director's promise to boost her to stardom. Nunn's career as a Hollywood actress ended as abruptly as it started.[27]

In February Young Deer placed another ad in the *Los Angeles Herald*: "I have made others; I can make you. I have directed Miss Glaum, Jackie Saunders, Bebe Daniels, Jules Carmen, and Bessie Eyton. I want 10 inexperienced men and women for my next picture. Just finished my second two-reel picture. (Good types and little talent required.) Call at once, as I expect to start a seven-reel superproduction in a few days."[28]

Young Deer took out several full-page ads in *Camera!* that appeared from December 1919 through April 1920. Nunn's photo appears in the first ad, but her image is replaced in the following ones by Princess Ane'-mone's. A photo of the "Creek princess" appears in a large circle in the center of the page surrounded by smaller circles. Over the course of the film's promotion, the circles contained question marks that eventually were replaced with the faces of the cast as they were hired or, rather, answered the want ad. The first of these shows Princess Ane'-mone smoking a cigarette and looking very Bohemian modern as "Princess Watuska in Reel Life." The final version of the ad series shows her in character, somber and thin in Indian costume, certainly a poor-man's version of Red Wing. *Camera!* reported that she was "the beautiful daughter of the Creek chief," whose name is conveniently omitted, and that the film was her first picture, "although she is well known throughout the east for her posing in vaudeville."[29] Under what name she played vaudeville is also omitted, but neither she nor Silvermoon, better known as Betty Cunard, were "Indian girls of the Creek tribe."

In the end, "Watuska" was not only "A Photoplay Without a Known Star," it was an Indian film without any Indians, except for one potential actor who may have been doing Young Deer a favor by lending his image to one of the cast circles. After Silverman's and Chief Watuska's photos disappeared from their respective orbits, Luther Standing Bear's image appeared in the chief's place as "Standing Bear."[30]

At the end of March, the popular *Film Daily* reported that "Youngdeer Productions" had been "formed on the coast." The name "Youngdeer's Film Co." just never caught on.[31] Editor Robbins had just died, and apparently his successor reversed the names again. *Camera!* also concurrently reported Young Deer's opinion about "the author" in filmmaking: "Jimmy Youngdeer says *the star* is the thing." He should have known. He couldn't afford to pay an accomplished actor, and apparently many of his amateurs weren't as desperate to claim the limelight as he'd hoped.[32] Accordingly, in May a judge in Los Angeles awarded $2,000 in salaries to two men "against Youngdeer Productions"—or was that the Young Deer Film Company?

"The complaint alleged that plaintiffs were taken on to learn the art of motion picture acting, and picked by Young Deer as his assistant directors." After nine weeks they were not paid.[33]

Young Deer did compensate his lead actor, however. On April 10, 1920, he married his star Princess, whose real name was Anomine Paige.[34] The same day *Camera!* reported, "James Youngdeer, director general of the Youngdeer Productions, will begin the filming of the plot proper of 'Watuska,' the prologue of which is not finished." Neither Youngdeer Productions nor Young Deer Film Company produced the film. Young Deer's dream of "developing raw material into stardust" turned into stardust itself. He changed his name to Edward R. Gordon and boarded another steamship for Liverpool. He moved to London and directed crime films for three years.[35] It's unknown what happened to his new bride.

Tribal and federal census records for 1920 marked Red Wing as officially "single" for the first time since her marriage. It was time to take her show on the road. On August 3 she gave her first performance at the Gem Theater in Clinton, Indiana, along with *Custer's Last Fight*. The fictionalized account of the Battle of the Little Big Horn starred Francis Ford and featured her old costar J. Barney Sherry. "A cast of 1,000 people supports Ford in this thrilling adventure picture, with its historical and exciting setting," an advertisement for her appearance announced. "It is a picture that will hold the interest of every spectator and based as it is on history, holds a deeper meaning than most pictures." To add "authenticity to the setting," "Princess Red Wing" would appear "in person" to "give a clear explanation of the picture." Her years of experience making westerns, including with Sherry, however, did not authenticate her. Her authenticity derived from the ad's false claim that she was "the daughter of one of the fighting Indian chiefs, who took part in the battle."[36] And thus Red Wing's Indian vaudeville tour began.

Following Indiana, Red Wing traveled to Ohio. By this time she had hired Charles H. Camp to manage her tour. Camp was a native Kansan who helped open the second movie theater in Abilene, Texas, about 1908. By 1911 he managed the Majestic Theater in Oklahoma City, Oklahoma. For the next six years, he managed the C. H. Camp Feature Film Company, the Strand Theater Company, and the Frankel Brothers and Camp Theatrical Agency.[37] However, it seems to have been his current position as the manager of the Educational Film Office, located in the Plaza Theater in Mount Vernon, Illinois, that led him to Red Wing or vice versa.

Camp's name first appears with Red Wing's in August 1920 in an ad for the Grand Theater in Hamilton, Ohio: "The Charles H. Camp Attractions Present Lilia Red Wing, The Noted Indian Princess and Actress in Person." The ad also noted that "Lillia Red Wing will be seen in the character of 'Star Light' in [*Days of Daring*] and with each showing of the picture will appear in person upon the stage and tell some of her interesting experiences as a motion picture star. . . . It is seldom that Hamilton is visited by a motion picture star so the visit of Miss Red Wing will be a real treat."[38]

Camp and Red Wing astutely realized that her film industry background deserved top billing, not some phony connection to Little Big Horn. In contrast, almost every Indian vaudeville act touring the country depended on promoting some connection to the Plains Indian wars, which she herself had exploited with the lie about her origins in Indiana. Now Red Wing's performances could confront the public's fantasy about wild Indians. Although Indian stereotypes appeared in the films accompanying her act, she planned to introduce a metanarrative of the *nonvanishing* Indian as *actor* in her own fate.

In November Camp placed ads in Coshocton and New Philadelphia, Ohio, that clearly announced Red Wing's past associations with prominent white actors such as Tom Mix, Dustin Farnum, and Geraldine Farrar. Ads also highlighted her prestigious graduation from Carlisle Indian Industrial School. Some even stated that she attended the school with Chief Bender and the Olympic star Jim Thorpe. Although Bender graduated from the school the same year she did, Thorpe enrolled two years later. No matter—her advertisements were more factual than most.

The following ad summed up Red Wing's solo act: "Miss Leilia Red Wing, of the Winnebago tribe in Nebraska, who is also a real movie actress will appear personally on the stage and lecture on the picture. She will also sing some genuine Indian songs in Indian and English, give an interesting talk on the movies and Indian life and do an Indian war dance."[39] Notably, her name received a significant update. She was no longer Lilian St. Cyr, Princess Red Wing, or Redwing Youngdeer. She appeared with the name her father penned on the letter just before he died, Lillia (or its various spellings Leilia, Lilia, or Lila). Her new moniker signified her rebirth as a single woman. The man she chose to honor was her father, not her husband.

Red Wing may have gone home to Omaha for the winter but was again in Ohio in the spring of 1921, appearing at Sandusky's Schade Theater in April, which was showing *The Last of the Mohicans*. DeMille's remake of *The Squaw Man* with Anna Little playing Naturitch also appeared in Sandusky at the time. For reasons unknown, Red Wing gave an interesting interview to a reporter from the *Sandusky Register* regarding her feelings on the segregation of Indians in society. Her opinions appeared in the first column of the front page of the newspaper and reflect her Indian boarding school education. More importantly, they reveal how she embraced her father's wishes for her education and how she bore the racism from which he sought to protect his children.

Red Wing conveyed Pratt's dictum that Indians be "permitted to mingle freely with the white people rather than be kept segregated upon the various reservations." But she tempered Pratt's fanaticism with Hampton's less strident view that assimilation cannot be forced; it takes time. The reporter noted that she was a cultured Carlisle graduate with "a passionate fondness for music" and that she "makes one pause in previous conceptions of what Indians are like." Red Wing responded, "You are not acquainted with the Indians. A chief's daughter could not feel otherwise. . . . The Indian has no chance such as even the poorest of the white race know. They are cribbed." She explained that most Carlisle graduates leave school inspired to help their race living on reservations, but they quickly "return to the blanket." "This is because upon the reservations they have no chance to do differently," she said, "and so, disappointed and to their thought outraged, they become more Indian than those who have never left the reservation." She said her father had received some education and "left strict instruction" that his children become educated to learn "the ways of the white race." "My mother, who was so good and kind, was uneducated," she added. The article reveals Red Wing as uncharacteristically outspoken in her expression of radical views for the time. The piece ended with a list of her film credits. As a minority in America, Red Wing experienced herself as irreconcilably different from how American society viewed her as an Indigenous woman. She left her white interviewer and his or her readers with something to think about beyond the Indian princess stereotype. She also revealed palpable symptoms of the historical trauma experienced by all Native people in the United States: "We have learned to expect betrayal. This is why, when we find a white person of truth and honesty toward us, we idolize them and are grateful beyond words to express."[40]

From Saturday, July 2, to Monday, July 4, Red Wing joined her nephew's half brother George Whitewing Jr. and Chief Deerfoot, an Italian American posing as a Cheyenne, in Algonac, Michigan. The trio met to perform in the centennial celebration for St. Clair County, Michigan.[41] The event was a typical American pageant to celebrate European American conquest. Like county histories written during the time, the celebration's narrative began with the primitive life of the local tribe and ended with the white settlers' victory over the Indians and the usurpation of their land. On Saturday Red Wing participated in the Indian Camp Meeting, where she, Whitewing, and Deerfoot assembled with a group of local Native people. The meeting included ceremonies and a meal to which other pageantgoers may have been invited. General events for the day also included boat races, field sports, a choral presentation, and church services. In addition, an unnamed Indian Band in Costume played for the three-day celebration.

The Indian Pageant began on Sunday morning. Red Wing was among the "full-blooded Indians" who depicted "early days when the Pioneers first invaded the Red Man's Territory." The Indian performers also put on snake dances, "some of which have never before been witnessed by the white man." The main attraction presented on July 4 was the "Night Spectacle." At 8:00 p.m. Native performers suddenly appeared "in war paint and costumes." After a thrilling war dance, perhaps choreographed by Red Wing, the Indians boarded canoes at Algonac's waterfront and rowed to nearby Russell's Island, where they pretended "to capture Fort Harsen and the pioneer village." Their feigned attempt resulted in a "great pyrotechnic display" that employed "aerial bombs, heavy artillery," and

"10,000 rounds of ammunition." From the mainland it looked like a forest fire was ravaging the island as white pioneer reenactors pretended to defend their log homes and the fort. The published program for the Algonac celebration concluded that the overall "effect" was "worthy of national appreciation," but no one recorded what the Native performers thought about their part in the reenactment.[42]

The Saint Clair centennial celebration included four other town pageants and resulted in an article titled "Behold! The Pioneers!" Although the title omits their presence, the body of the essay identifies the "Indian actors" and offers a different perspective of their role in the nationalistic narrative:

> This series of Historical Festivals and the Great Pageant reflected past history, present achievements and future desires and were built upon civic ideals. . . . The superb figure of Chief White Wing, advancing at the head of the Indian group to greet the Jesuit Fathers, La Salle and Hennepin, and make with them the solemn covenant of peace that blazed the way for the advance of the first planters into Michigan— this was a scene before which the descendants of those very planters bowed their heads. Chief White Wing is a Winnebago Indian from Nebraska who poses for statues in the Chicago Art Institute. Chief Deerfoot formerly of Buffalo Bill's Show; Lilia Red Wing, a Winnebago girl from Nebraska who has played opposite Dustin Farnum in The Squaw Man and many other pictures; and a large group of Algonquins now living on Walpole Island in the neighborhood of Algonac, comprised these Indian actors.[43]

Although the majority of modern European Americans thought the narrative of Native people's first contact with French Canadian colonizers (albeit religious ones) less worthy than their story of conquest, it was nonetheless vitally significant to many Native people in the old Northwest, including the Ho-Chunk. According to Ho-Chunk oral tradition, Jean Nicolet was the first European whom the Ho-Chunk encountered when they lived in present-day Green Bay at the Red Banks on Lake Michigan's southwestern shore. Red Wing and White Wing were certainly aware of the account as it passed down from generation to generation.

When the Ho-Chunk people espied Nicolet's ship in the bay in 1634, representatives cautiously edged to the Red Banks with their most sacred offerings, white deerskins and tobacco. Once the French Canadians saw these Indians, they saluted them with gunfire. Unfamiliar with such weapons, the Ho-Chunk representatives thought the strangers were thunderbirds and thus of the spirit world. On the other hand, Nicolet, seeking to reach China by an eastern route, was equally surprised when Indigenous people filled his hand with tobacco and poured tobacco on the heads of his crew. In turn, as tradition has it, one of Nicolet's men poured water on a Ho-chunk man because he was smoking.

Although the plot point is humorous, it reveals the Ho-Chunk's point of view. When the Frenchmen discovered the Indians had no metal tools, they showed the Indians how to chop down a tree with an axe. Consequently, an alliance was forged. The French brought new technology, while the Native people offered gifts of comfort and spirituality. From the Ho-Chunk's perspective, the axe and the guns appeared holy, but they eventually came to realize that the strangers were only human. Once they mastered the Frenchmen's technology, they began exchanging furs for guns and tools. Soon a party of French Canadian fur traders arrived from Montreal, including Joseph de Carries, Red Wing's great-great-great-grandfather.

The Ho-Chunk's story, at least as it was recorded in writing in the late nineteenth and early twentieth centuries, is similar to the contact narrative from "Behold! The Pioneers!" From the pageant program's perspective, Red Wing and her crew represented savage Indians who were simply the spoils of conquest. But from her oral tradition and "Behold! The Pioneers!" Ho-Chunk people began as equal agents in a trade alliance. The Native people desired the technological advances the French Canadians offered and chose to trade their furs. The strangers weren't interested in claiming the land so much as its resources. It was not until American settlers, squatters, and land speculators invaded French Canadian territory that they, in Red Wing's words, "learned to expect betrayal."

Red Wing returned to Nebraska to appear at the Colonial Theater in Lincoln the first week of November. According to the *Nebraska State Journal*, "Picturesque Red Wing, the famous Indian moving picture actress who has appeared here many a time in pictures, appears in person today with her entertaining offering consisting of songs, dances and stories."[44] From there she traveled to Missouri, performing with "four men and a little girl" at the Gayoso Theater in Kansas City. Since she had just left Nebraska, some of the five were probably family members. Two of the men also appeared with her at the Brooklyn Theater in the same city.[45]

Norman Tyndall, whose Indian name was recorded as Ge-ba-ha-gema (Come to Me, Go from Me), was likely one of these performers. He was a relative of the Omaha Indian family who went to school with the St. Cyrs in Philadelphia, and he became Red Wing's permanent partner during the rest of her tour. Usually described as an "Omaha boy" in ads, Tyndall was in his early twenties. In February 1922 the two performed in Maryville, Missouri, as "Princess Red Wing Indian Motion Picture Star and her Indian warrior."[46] Still managed by Camp, the duo performed in Moberly, along with another Tom Mix film titled *The Rough Diamond*, in March. In late April and early May they returned to Kansas City, first with a film starring the other popular cowboy of the day, William S. Hart (from Red Wing's West Coast Studio days), and then again with *Custer's Last Fight*.[47] In June they crossed the border into Kansas, performing in Osawatomie with the latter film, as well as Iola, where they did a special "Kiddies Show" along with *Days of Daring*.[48] "Miss Redwing does not pretend to be a vaudeville actress," one ad announced, "but will give a short talk on the movies and a few Indian songs and dances. There will also be an Indian boy in his native songs and dances."[49]

If Red Wing did "not pretend to be a vaudeville actress," it was not out of modesty. She was certainly more than confident in her performance abilities. The assertion reflects her unique approach to the Indian vaudeville circuit and her embrace of the new "visual education" movement. Distinguishing herself from other Indian vaudeville performers who played up a bogus connection to Plains Indian warriors, Red Wing embraced loftier aims—to teach the public and particularly children about real Native people as opposed to those portrayed on-screen.

Harley L. Clarke, "a utilities magnate," and Forest Ray Molton, a University of Chicago professor of anatomy, were instrumental in broadcasting the principles of the movement in which Red Wing invested her talents.

In 1919 they established the Society for Visual Education (SVE), a guild that endeavored to "produce films for use in school" and to incorporate existing motion pictures, as well as live performances, into school curricula.[50] The organization put out a journal "devoted to the cause of American education." Although Clarke sold the company in 1923, SVE continued through 1995. Not surprisingly, Thomas Edison supported visual education early on, claiming, "With the substitution of the motion picture for books in the elementary school we will make in twenty years an advance of ten centuries in civilization."[51]

Most educators were far less radical in their support of the cause, but many believed that introducing visual media in addition to standard textbooks could offer "great possibilities for advancement" and could "make study delightful." However, others thought visual education was only a passing fad. Time proved them wrong. Despite the fact that early proponents from the South found films like Griffith's *Birth of a Nation* fitting educational media, ethnically inclusive visual education remains an important component of school curricula.[52]

Red Wing's impressive career in film and live performance made a natural fit for the movement, but the question remains, how did she get involved in a national crusade to modernize education? It appears Camp was the conduit. As a 1922 newspaper interview explained, "With a boy of the Omaha tribe, she gives demonstrations of the tribal songs and dances. Their manager generally presents educational pictures, showing primitive Indian life and customs. In Chicago they were used as part of the new system of visual education for children."[53] It's unclear whether "they" refers to Red Wing and Tyndall or Red Wing and Camp; nonetheless, sometime between 1919 and 1922, Red Wing found her calling as an educator through performance.

Red Wing's cultural performances not only were visually educational but also included a musical component. Red Wing and Tyndall, dressed in all their Native finery, appeared on the January 1922 cover of the *Nebraska Teacher* with Thurlow Lieurance, who at that time taught at the University Conservatory of Music in Lincoln.[54] Lieurance was a noted composer and musicologist who collected "the music of primitive North American Indians." Lieurance made hundreds of recordings, adapting them into popular songs such as his most beloved, "By the Waters of the Minnetonka." From 1918 to 1927 Lieurance toured the country giving concerts inspired by his recordings. His non-Native wife, Edna Woolsey Lieurance, a mezzo-soprano, sang his songs dressed in Indian costume. By the time Red Wing sang for Lieurance, he'd spent two decades among at least thirty-one tribal groups in North America recording their music. "Hundreds of his records and notations are on file in the national and private museums of the country," according to a 1922 report, "and he has harmonized nearly 300 Indian melodies, all of which are in published form." "People usually think of Indian music as the monotonous humdrum they hear at Indian fairs and exhibitions. Nothing could be further from the truth," Lieurance told a journalist. "Whether it be a ceremonial dance, a flute call, a love song, or a lullaby, an underlying theme of pure melody will be found running thru all of them. There are working songs, play songs, hunting songs, society songs, and many of them are beautiful interpretations of legend."[55]

Red Wing and Tyndall made four records for Lieurance at his Lincoln studio. One of Red Wing's may have been titled "Winnebago Love Song." Tyndall probably contributed at least one ceremonial song from the Peyote Religion. Although Red Wing usually accompanied her songs with a hand drum, she may have also played an antique Winnebago flute for another recording.[56]

Red Wing and Tyndall visited Fort Scott, Kansas, in July 1922 and performed some of the composer's music. Alice G. McDermott, society column writer, covered the event, beginning, "Redwing, whose name in her language is Ru pa husa win and her English name, Lilian St. Cyr," is "well educated." After the introduction, which encompassed Red Wing's multiethnic modern Indian identity (and gave her Indian name in the Lakota language of Standing Bear), McDermott reported on Red Wing's musical performance. Red Wing sang either Lieurance's "By the Waters of Minnetonka" or "By the Weeping Waters." She also presented an ethnographic lecture that may or may not have been a mainstay of her regular act, but it was certainly representative of the visual education movement. McDermott, a second-grade teacher, and the rest of Red Wing's audience learned about Winnebago religious symbols and dances, feasts, and the practice of fasting and sweat baths to obtain mental, physical, and spiritual purification. In particular, she described Ho-Chunk Medicine Lodge religion and the kinds of visions practitioners might experience. She also explained that though the government forbid the Sun Dance to be performed, the Winnebago still held traditional medicine dances, as well as the "dance to the dead." She also explained traditional etiquette, such as the exchange of gifts between visiting tribes. In a discussion about "the origin of the Indian," Redwing expressed contemporary ethnic humor: "Some people believe that the Indians are the lost tribes of Israel, but it is not so for they can not make money like the Jews, and they like to spend it freely." Finally, she informed her audience about the esoteric significance of beadwork designs. As an example, she presumably wore her *Squaw Man* dress, which McDermott noted was "handsomely beaded" and valued at $300 to $400. Tyndall, dressed in "full regalia with eagle feather war bonnet," sang an Omaha brave song, danced a war dance, and explained a Peyote Religion legend.[57]

After the Fort Scott visit Indian Joe Davis joined Red Wing one last time, and with Tyndall they gave a performance in Chanute, Kansas, at the People's Theater. The theater showed a film starring Young Deer's old friend Lewis Stone. Davis contributed his "rope and spinning and magic."[58] Next, Red Wing and Tyndall appeared with a Pearl White film in Burlington, Kansas, and then in Cherryvale, where an ad characterized Red Wing's act as "a clean educational novelty." For at least the Cherryvale event, Tyndall exhibited his "large display of furs, eagle wings and other articles" in the theater lobby, while Red Wing loaned her beadwork, said to be worth $1,500, to a local clothing store to exhibit.[59]

A reporter noted that Red Wing and Tyndall toured "the country by automobile."[60] Who drove the vehicle wasn't mentioned. Near the end of July they motored to Independence, Kansas, performing with a Paramount comedy. Camp also added the Musical Bracken to the lineup. Billie Bracken, a red-haired country bumpkin comedian and musician, continued to tour on and off with Red Wing and Tyndall, adding some comic relief to their show. Bracken played twenty instruments, performed ventriloquism, imitated barnyard critters, and was advertised, as befit his co-performers, as "one of the cleanest and most entertaining act of vaudeville today."[61] In August the trio played in Coffeyville, Kansas, with a Charlie Chaplin film, among others. In early September Red Wing and Tyndall performed at a theater in Arkansas City, Kansas, along with another act that was not as squeaky clean: "Fatima, the most famous Turkish dancer in Vaudeville."[62]

Next, Red Wing and Tyndall drove to Winfield, Kansas, where they performed along with the newly released *The Mohican's Daughter*, a film based on Jack London's short story "The Story of Jees Uck." In Wellington their show accompanied *John Smith*, produced by Selznick Pictures Corporation, and, again, *Custer's Last Fight*. They performed in Vernon with a comedy, and for the first time along with Red Wing's Carlisle school credit the ad mentioned her attendance at Lincoln Institute. It also highlighted that she had been Senator Long's protégée, which makes sense, given he represented Kansas.[63] The duo ended their tour of Kansas in Greensburg, where an ad stated: "Bring the children to see the big Indian show, educational and instructive."[64]

Red Wing and her "Omaha boy" may have returned to Nebraska shortly after for a visit and a well-deserved rest. Although it would have been nice to spend Christmas with their families, the holiday season typically drew motion picture crowds, so the show was back on the road by mid-December. The last leg of their tour was the Lone Star State, where Camp's connections likely dictated the tour route.[65]

Red Wing and Tyndall spent six months in Texas, starting their tour near the border of Oklahoma at Vernon and Wichita Falls. Their next reported stop was Mexia, just south of the Fort Worth–Dallas area.[66] From there they went west to Abilene and Sweetwater. Their last performance ad for the Palace Theater in Sweetwater, dated May 11, 1923, represented their Texas tour:

> Hoot Gibson in 'The Lone Hand'
> Chas. H. Camp, Presents
> "The Musical Bracken's," 20 Musical Instruments, Ventriloquism and Imitating
> Also Lilia Red Wing Indian Movie Star in Person

She co-starred with Tom Mix in "Days of Daring." Also appeared with Dustin Farnum in "The Squaw Man." Miss Redwing was featured with the 101 Bison Films and also the Pathe Company. She will appear in person with Norman Tyndall, Omaha Indian Boy in a Genuine Indian Novelty Presenting—Talking, Singing and Dancing.[67]

By October 1923 Camp was still in Texas representing the Peerless Hawaiian Quartette, but Lilia Red Wing's vaudeville tour had come to a close. She celebrated her fortieth birthday on February 13, 1924, and except for a mysterious appearance that year "in original Indian costume" for a fabric exhibit at Philadelphia's Commercial Museum, "Indian princess Lilia Red Wing," disappeared from public record.[68]

Congress passed the Indian Citizenship Act in June 1924 under President Calvin Coolidge. The historic passage of this act, prompted by the military service provided by Native Americans to the country, seems to have fueled Red Wing's future political activism. However, first she went to New York and played a small part in the film *Soul Fire*. The role was far beneath her, but handsome and popular leading man Richard Barthelmess ensured the film's success. Barthelmess had recently worked out of Fort Lee, New Jersey, for Inspiration Pictures. The production company moved to the more modernized and convenient Tech-Art Studios on East 48th Street in Manhattan, where *Soul Fire* went into production. Cameras started rolling in February 1925. John S. Robertson directed the film. He gained his reputation for directing the popular 1920 version of *Dr. Jekyll and Mr. Hyde*, starring John Barrymore.

Shown in flashbacks, *Soul Fire*'s narrative is based on Martin Brown's melodramatic Broadway play *Great Music*. The play centered on the life of Barthelmess's character, a young musical genius, composer Eric Fane.[69] The action is set in Italy, Paris, and the Marquesas Islands, the latter the home of Teita, Fane's love interest. Bessie Love plays Teita, an English girl raised by the Indigenous people on her island. "The portion unfolding within the native hut of Teita is being filmed at the Tec-Art studios," reported a trade magazine, but "on March 1 Mr. Barthelmess and his company will go to Florida for the South Sea exteriors."[70] Red Wing acted her part outside Teita's hut, so she must have accompanied cast and crew to the Florida location.

Moving Picture World gave the motion picture a positive review and related that Fane eventually "finds peace and happiness and love" when "the natives," "playing their weird music," prepare for his and Teita's wedding feast.[71] But the natives not only played "weird music," they also danced to it. Red Wing, representing, as she later described it, "a South Seas maiden," danced with the other native character around a blazing fire that lights up the night sky.[72] Although she appears very briefly and is barely visible, Red Wing looks more matronly than maidenly in the film, but she is clearly—as always—leading the dance.

Apparently, Red Wing acquired the part after deciding to leave Nebraska for good and make New York her home. If she hoped to continue her film career on the East Coast, her appearance in the bit part failed to move her plan forward. *Soul Fire,* released on May 31, 1925, was her last feature film.

CHAPTER 17

The Metropolitan Group
of American Indians

Red Wing rented an apartment on the corner of West 113th Street and
Lenox Avenue at the southern end of Harlem just above Central Park in
New York City. No longer considered a viable movie actress in 1925, she
supported herself by making Indian costumes and regalia. According to
Meyer Berger, Red Wing purchased "her skins in the old swamp beside
the Brooklyn Bridge approach." Martin T. C. Waterman had a leather
goods store in the area, and he and Red Wing struck up a friendship
shortly after she moved to New York, indicating she did a lot of business
with him.[1] Her clients were white members of such organizations as the
Red Man's Order, theatrical producers, tribal members who wanted to
shine at the next powwow, and both real and faux Indian performers.
Joe Eaglefoot, whom Red Wing knew as a "show man," seems to have
belonged to the latter category. How long they had been acquainted is
unknown, but on July 2 Red Wing married Eaglefoot in a civil ceremony
in Manhattan. Waterman served as a witness.[2]

Red Wing with or without her new spouse traveled to Akron, Ohio,
for the city's centennial celebration shortly after her marriage. Her niece
Alvina "Vina" Lowry, a recent graduate of a business school in Philadel-
phia, came along too.[3] Both women appeared at a department store in
Akron on July 20 with Chief White Eagle. It's possible White Eagle was
Indian Joe Davis, but it could be that Deerfoot used the name. "Meet
Chief White Eagle," "Princess Red Wing," "and Morning Star" (Lowry),
the ad stated. "Lineal Descendants of the Indians Who Fished, Hunted

269

and Trapped for a Living in These Neighborhoods, In the Eighteenth Century. We extend an invitation to all children as well as to Centennial visitors and friends to meet these Indian descendants of a century ago."[4]

Other than that, most of Red Wing's activities for the remainder of the decade are unknown. In 1926 she appeared along with three other "theatrical stars" for "an old fashioned pageant" hosted by a Long Island society dame.[5] The next year she performed at a high school in New Jersey and then one in Yonkers, where she received a substantial review that was more a backhanded compliment than praise. "Her royal highness gave a one-woman variety show, providing much more noise than the usual vaudeville bill," according to the reviewer. "The renowned Princess Redwing" wore a "blue beaded dress . . . and sang, played on the piano, told stories and drew pictures on a blackboard." Her audience of students whooped and hollered, explained the reviewer, as she danced to "the monotonous 'tum-te-tum' of the tom tom," making "slightly contortionistic steps" that "didn't look as much like a dance as other things." The writer's sarcastic tone rang from the beginning to the end of the review. Asserting his or her preeminence as a theater connoisseur, the reviewer noted that "a small group of students applauded enthusiastically at the conclusion of the princess' performance, which was nothing if not very, very Indian."[6]

If Red Wing felt slighted by the review, it's unlikely her new spouse nursed her hurt feelings. It seems the relationship was not what she hoped for. Although the marriage certificate that Red Wing filled out states that her betrothed was of the "Red" race and born in New Mexico, it's highly unlikely.[7] Eaglefoot's identity remains a mystery. A photographer captured his image during a fair in Brockton, Massachusetts, in 1928. He appears as Joe Eagle Foot, Colorado, medicine man, with Chief Neptune and Joe Weeping Deer, two Passamaquoddy Indian performers. The three men wear Indian regalia, and Eaglefoot's accessories appear to be Red Wing's handiwork. Following the fair, someone stole Eaglefoot's beautiful Indian costume from his car, which would not have been the end of the world had he not already separated from his new wife.[8]

The couple divorced in March 1929, or the marriage was invalid to begin with, due to Red Wing's failure to complete her divorce from Young Deer. Three months later, Eaglefoot remarried. The new marriage record shows he was no longer a "Red show man" but a "white salesman." In 1930, still a white salesman, Eaglefoot had already divorced again.[9]

As the roaring twenties came to a close Red Wing found herself single once again. However, she had many friends and admirers in New York to keep her company. One of these was Anita De Frey, a soprano known as "the Modoc Sun Bird" (the Modoc tribe originated in northeastern California and central southern Oregon). De Frey adored Red Wing and admired her commitment to visual education. "Red Wing has always had a devotion to her people, not only the Winnebago Tribe, but all Indians of all of the tribes," De Frey later wrote, "and she has a profound knowledge of Indian history, customs and cultures." De Frey confirmed that Red Wing "always had a deep longing to have the Indian people truthfully presented to the world, and to correct so many erroneous impressions about them that have been foisted upon the public. She would especially like to have children taught the true facts about the history and civilization of the Red People of America."[10]

De Frey was not really a California Indian, but Red Wing appreciated De Frey's devotion to Native people. De Frey treasured the culture of Native Americans and avidly supported their civil rights. She created an Indian identity and modified her surname in part to promote her career but also to disguise her past. Born Anita Frey in San Francisco in 1892, De Frey's early childhood scarred her for life. Her parents, Margaret "Mattie" (née Dickey) and Gustave Frey, were white. Her father called himself a "speculator," but he was actually a crook and a murderer. When his marriage broke up he tried to reconcile with Mattie. She refused, so he threatened to kill Anita, their only child. Mattie pleaded with the San Francisco police to arrest him, but to no avail. When Anita was six years old, Frey shot and killed Mattie in the street in front of her residence and then turned the gun on himself. Mattie's brother and wife raised Anita to adulthood in a San Francisco suburb after the traumatic loss of her parents.[11] She attended Mills College in Oakland, California, and then received a bachelor of arts degree from New York City College.[12]

In 1956 Meyer Berger authored a brief sketch on De Frey in his About New York column titled "The New York metropolitan group of American Indians." His exposition provides insight as to why De Frey earned Red

Wing's trust and friendship. "Secretary, Tzika Subbas (Indian for the Sun Bird) is a California Modoc, a soft-voiced woman who sings professionally . . . and is probably the most earnest toiler in the New York group," he wrote. "She gets out all the group's correspondence there, works up Indian programs for schools, churches and for such places as Town Hall and Carnegie Hall." De Frey lived in a Greenwich Village flat that was "a museum of her people's handiwork—their weaving, painting, bead work, pottery and talismans," according to Berger. She also owned a "wardrobe of authentic Indian costumes." Berger wrote that her performances included "many of the songs of the Old Ones," as she called Native American elders, accompanied by "hand-drum obbligato." Her repertoire also included "forty Indian calls" or summons that she knew by heart. "She assembles her people for weddings, for funerals and for parties," said Berger, and "helps with suggestions for moves to try to stave off politicians' reservation-grabbing." "'Few white people know how poor and how unhappy some of our people are,'" De Frey told the journalist, but she only spoke for herself. She would not give Berger individual names of the New Yorker Indians because they "'might not welcome identification in print without their permission.'"[13]

Obviously, Red Wing and De Frey had much in common, particularly a deep respect for Native culture and a true desire to help American Indian people. De Frey was one among many posing Indian artists that Red Wing accepted into her world, but De Frey was especially kindhearted, considerate, and sensitive. As she told Berger in 1956, her "great fear was mostly for the Old ones," and Red Wing, an elder by that time, was certainly one of them.

Most of the Metropolitan Indians shared Red Wing's and De Frey's "deep longing" to educate the public about their people. In the late 1920s a group banded together to assert the importance of their heritage and to establish the Indian Unity Fraternal Organization, otherwise known as the Indian Unity Alliance. One of their objectives was to make Indian Day a national holiday. Fifteen other states had issued similar proclamations, but nothing had come of them. The Indian Unity Alliance also pushed for a holiday at the state level that would be similar to the holidays Illinois,

Colorado, and Washington had recently adopted. New York's governor would not agree to the exact date the Indian Unity Alliance requested, which was the fourth Friday in September.[14]

Still, on the fourth Friday in September 1929, Red Wing joined two hundred Native people and their friends in Brooklyn's Prospect Park for a show of unity "to preserve the identity of the Indian race" and to promote Indian Day. The *Brooklyn Daily Eagle* reported on the festivities, explaining: "Of the 250 Indians who reside in New York City, 200 make their homes in Brooklyn." The reporter explained that the men worked as "iron and steel workers, in the building industry, as actors, medicine showmen, some as professional men and many as sailors."[15]

According to the news coverage, Hurons, Abenaki, Caughnawaga (Kahnawake), Seneca, Onondaga, Tuscarora, Chickahominy, Yuma, Aztec, and San Blas (Kuna) participated in the gathering at the park. Many of the men came fully dressed in regalia, while most of the women simply added accessories like beaded headbands and Native jewelry to their everyday attire. It was a quiet gathering, except for the few who danced, sang, and played the tom-tom or flute. Some white attendees felt disappointed that the Indians in the park appeared more reticent than those in the motion pictures.

Walter Battice as Chief Sheet Lightning gave the opening address, and Father Francis Norman of St. Peter's Mission of Brooklyn followed him. Tom W. Shaw (Mohawk), also known as Tahowadeheto (Pulling the Boat), was the controversial political spokesperson for the day. Shaw lived in Brooklyn and served as the grand chief for the Indian Unity Alliance. He "reminded those present that the Indian race still totals half a million." He said that the fact that "the capitalist . . . absorbed Indian properties and robbed the Indian at large" warranted Indian unity. Shaw expressed radical views. He didn't believe Indians wanted to become citizens "or take part in any of the white man's forums." Rather, they wanted "to stand in the same light as Jefferson and Washington left them."[16]

Most if not all of the "honorary guests" who attended were performers. Chauncey Yellow Robe, a Rosebud Sioux leader, and Buffalo Child Long Lance, a writer and spokesperson for cultural preservation (whose undisclosed family roots matched Young Deer's) had just completed their acting roles in *The Silent Enemy*, an "anthropological documentary melodrama" about starvation among the Ojibwa.[17] Both men were also well-respected graduates of Carlisle Indian Industrial School. Red Wing and her sister Julia, identified as Henukaw White Wing, stood out among the honored women. Others included Princess Watawaso, a vocalist with the Redpath Chautauqua Circuit (Lucy Nicolar, Penobscot); "former Ziegfield girl" Princess White Deer (Esther G. Deer, Mohawk); the female lead in *The Silent Enemy*, Molly Spotted Elk (Penobscot); and her sister Darly Little Elk.[18]

Red Wing found support from and in turn supported these intelligent and talented men and women, who, like her, understood that their celebrity could shine a light on the plight of America's Indians. Gathered together in Prospect Park that autumn "Indian summer" day, Indian Unity Alliance members strived "to preserve the identity of the Indian race." They also challenged Pratt's dated directive, "Kill the Indian in him, and save the man." Nearly nine decades later, a national holiday honoring the American Indian has not come to pass.

The hopeful spirit of the roaring twenties came to an abrupt end exactly one month later when the stock market crashed. The devastating effect on the country's economy was immediate, and the Great Depression that resulted lasted until 1941. It was difficult for able-bodied white men to find employment, let alone a middle-aged Indian actress. As Louis Mofsie, Red Wing's great-nephew, related, the thirties and forties were hard times for his family. In the late 1920s his parents, Morris Mofsie, a Hopi artist, and Vina Lowry Mofsie moved to Manhattan, where their first child, Norton, was born.[19] Vina's sister Lillian Lowry Smith, divorced from her second husband, moved to the city about the same time with her two daughters, Lucille Smith and Delores Arroyo. Smith found work in a dressmaking factory. Shortly after her arrival to New York she wed Ernest Naquayouma, a Hopi silversmith who lived with the Mofsies. Red Wing's sister Julia also rented an apartment in Brooklyn by 1930.[20]

Red Wing later stated that when she returned to New York in 1925 "I worked in the famous Bellvue [*sic*] Hospital as an 'Occupational Therapist'" and "had a large class of boys and enjoyed my work with them."[21]

It's unknown if she acquired this job before or after the stock market crash. She may have found some work making costumes and regalia, but performance gigs were few and far between during the Great Depression.

Some Indian performers like Walter Battice still found employment at the beach resorts, but the stereotypical medicine show was his only recourse. The medicine show was far from prestigious employment, particularly for a respected tribal leader and political activist who had performed for the Miller Brothers, appeared onstage in Los Angeles, and lectured to the public about American Indian culture. Six months after Battice opened the proceedings at Prospect Park, he died at Coney Island of apoplexy at age fifty-five. Battice was not just respected; he was also beloved by Red Wing and her family. "I miss him more now than I did, when he first passed away," Julia St. Cyr wrote two years later to a former Hampton teacher.[22]

In the spring of 1931 Red Wing found a small job at the Wanamaker department store in Manhattan, which was doing a promotion for "Complete Camp Outfits." The event included Girl Scouts and a representative from *Redbook Magazine*'s education department. Red Wing brought Vina to appear with her. Her sister Julia and their niece Lillian (Lone Deer) probably joined them. "Come on . . . Let's go to Wanamaker's," an ad invited. "The Special Camp Display Opens Saturday, April 25th on the third floor, north building . . . Real Indian Princesses . . . Princess Red Wing and Princess Morning Star . . . in their real Indian Princess clothes . . . doing bead work and weaving baskets and making moccasins. . . . Come on . . . all you young campers. . . . [O]ur special guests will be here from ten o'clock in the morning till four-thirty in the afternoon. . . . [W]e'll expect you!"[23]

Howard W. Moore stopped by to watch Red Wing and her niece demonstrate their skills. He'd never met a "real Indian" before and was fascinated with how the women nimbly worked the beads. He decided to introduce himself and must have impressed Red Wing as much as she impressed him, because she introduced him to other family members.

Moore's natural curiosity and gentle nature made him an easy friend. His background was interesting as well. He was a conscientious objector who served in the army during World War I but would not take up arms. Eventually, he was court-martialed and sentenced to two years in military prison until officials released him on Thanksgiving Day in 1920. He moved back to his parents' Cherry Valley farm in upstate New York. He paid off the mortgage, reforested some of the land, and started a nursery business.[24] When a friend named Chinlund relayed to Moore that he planned to send his Chicago-born grandsons to camp in the Adirondacks, Moore invited the boys to spend the summer of 1931 in Cherry Valley instead. He had met an "Indian family" in New York, he told Chinlund, and they would care for the boys.

"Princess Red Wing was a talented Winnebago woman whom I had seen demonstrating bead and quill work. . . . She had an older sister and a niece Lone Deer who was married to a Hopi, Ernest Naquayouama [*sic*]. These four," he explained, "acted as counselors to the Chinlund boys and my two nephews." Red Wing's family and their charges camped in teepees near a spring-fed stream surrounded by a hemlock forest. Horses and ponies ready to ride grazed in a nearby pasture. When Moore visited the camp on weekends, he "found the boys having a wonderful time."[25] Red Wing undoubtedly enjoyed her time at the summer camp. Getting away from the city with her family, camping in the beautiful countryside, and pursuing one of her life goals—educating children about Indians— was not a bad gig.

Red Wing's experience in upstate New York seems to have inspired a performance idea she enacted when she returned to the city. On a sunny day, September 1, 1931, a camera filmed her "camping" atop the brand new Governor Clinton Hotel on Seventh Avenue and 31st Street. The forty-nine-second clip appears in a Universal Newspaper Newsreel.[26] The silent film star remained speechless, but the black-and-white newsreel featured "rapid-fire comment by Graham McNamee, talking reporter," as well as musical accompaniment by the Victor Concert Orchestra. Acclaimed for bringing "colorful scenes from many lands," Red Wing's four-subject newsreel also featured King George of England in "political strife," a national baby parade in Ashbury Park, New Jersey, visitors to the shrine of the Virgin of Guadalupe in Mexico City, and "Wolfgang

Von Gronau landing in Chicago after his epic flight from Germany to the Arctic regions."[27]

Red Wing's part in the black-and-white newsreel exhibits her sense of humor, as well as her Indian regalia. "New York, N.Y. Redskin lass dwells in skyscraper teepee!" reads the title page. "Princess Red Wing pitches native pent-house on heap big hotel." The first scene opens on the Clinton Hotel rooftop with a close-in shot of a tall teepee that Red Wing constructed with patterned Indian blankets. Next, a white-gloved butler arrives for "room service." He holds a silver tray of breakfast goodies and serves coffee from a silver pot to "Princess Redwing," who is sitting inside the teepee while she scoops out a bite of melon. Red Wing wears her *Squaw Man* dress and a beaded headband, and leather straps are wrapped around her two braids. She thanks the butler by nodding, and he departs.

The camera then pans up to the top of the teepee and farther up to the peak of the Empire State Building, which looms high in the background just to the right of the teepee. The next shot shows Red Wing outside the teepee on the rooftop wearing a Ho-Chunk bandolier bag over her dress. A beautiful Plains Indian bonnet crowns her head. She shades her eyes with her hand (Indian maiden style) and slowly turns her head to take in the impressive view that surrounds her. The film cuts to two construction workers on a skyscraper above her, while a third worker looks down at her and gives her a wave. Hand shading her eyes again, she peers into the distance as the film clip abruptly ends.

The tongue-in-cheek performance not only promoted her as an Indian actress—and a comic one at that—but also advertised her handiwork.[28] As a bonus, the Associated Press covered the filming, which led to even more publicity. Within the week, American newspapers treated citizens to an image of the Indian lass surrounded by skyscrapers.

Two different photos appeared with the various newspaper publications, one showing Red Wing with her arms outstretched to the sky and one in which she sips a cup of coffee on a balustrade at the edge of the hotel rooftop. In both she wears her Plains Indian bonnet. The AP story stated erroneously that Red Wing had just arrived in New York, further highlighting the newsreel's campy colonialist nostalgia. It introduced

Red Wing as a "dark-eyed cliff-dwelling" Indian maid from the Rocky Mountains in Colorado near Manitou Springs. "On her first real stay in New York she wishes to view the towering hand-made peaks reared by the 'pale face' since the development of his civilization which followed the purchase of Manhattan and the conquest of the continent."[29]

Her father was still Ho-Chunk, "Wank-shik-stohe-e-ga," or "gathers his people," but the writer took creative license with Red Wing's origins, not to mention the state of Minnesota's. Red Wing's grandfather, "a chieftain," gave his name to Red Wing, Minnesota, the publicity piece stated.[30] Red Wing "appeared as one of the ghosts of the city's earliest inhabitants as she walked noiselessly into her hotel" wearing red-and-white beaded moccasins. When she reached the hotel's rooftop, she "pitched her teepee." The piece explained why Red Wing declined the "downy bed in a softly-tinted, carefully appointed hotel room." She preferred familiar "wind-swept heights," and instead of the new-fangled radio, she favored the "faint 'tom-tom' of swift-moving motor traffic in the streets below" to "remind her of the music of the stirring mountain trees." When Red Wing had her say in the matter and in the piece, her words were more sophisticated than a primitive Indian maid's. "This is a marvelous, breath-taking city," she said as she looked over the skyscape. "But the red man would die, if he had to live in a one room kitchenette with electric refrigeration and steam heat."[31]

The day before Red Wing's "arrival," a *Brooklyn Daily Eagle* reporter surmised that the event was simply a ruse. "When Red Wing, that young Winnebago Indian lass, gets here," wrote the reporter, "she will park in a real Indian Tepee, on the Governor Clinton's roof." After "summering and wintering in the wide open spaces, where men are blanket weavers, and not press agents, she fears a hotel room will be too confining," the reporter continued. "What we really think she means is that a hotel room would be too confining on the imagination of the press agent. Anyway, it's an item."[32] He was wrong in part. After all, Red Wing had just returned from "summering" outdoors. Still, if "the red man" could not survive "a one room kitchenette," the thoroughly modern Indian gal who enjoyed the "marvelous, breath-taking city" padded back to her studio apartment on West 65th Street.[33]

In December the Brooklyn Writers' Group invited Red Wing to talk about her motion picture career, but it seems not much else came as a result of the publicity stunt atop the Clinton Hotel.[34] Still, her wholesome Indigenous approach to camp life inspired Moore to establish the Takaharawa American Indian Camp for Boys. He returned to New York to meet with Red Wing in the spring of 1932. She told him about New York's diverse Indian population and referred him to her Menominee friend, Isabella Erdlitz. Erdlitz was a singer known as Princess Valesta. According to Moore, she held a weekly tribal dance at her studio, which some forty-odd Metropolitan Indians attended. Since Red Wing had just gifted Moore "a beautiful Sioux costume," he joined their dance.[35]

Red Wing and her family members returned to Cherry Valley again that summer for the first season of Moore's official summer camp. *Redbook Magazine* gave the 1932 summer camp a great review, so Wanamaker's Astor Place store chose the camp for its 1933 camp exhibit. "The management cleared a whole floor, created an artificial lake bordered with living evergreens, put up tepees, and used my prospective counselors to bring the scene to me," recalled Moore. Moore gave a talk on Indian lore, while Red Wing and Wahnatahee, an Ojibwa woman, demonstrated beadwork and quillwork. Moore hoped to recruit more Indian counselors, so Red Wing introduced him to the event's Indian exhibitors, whom he had not met before. He met Nebabah (Penobscot), who "taught archery and fly-casting"; Red Eagle (Mohawk), a writer who told traditional stories; and White Cloud (Cheyenne), who "danced and played the tomtom." Max Big Man and Red Wing's niece Lillian as Lone Deer enacted an Indian marriage ceremony. "Additional publicity came," as Moore recalled, "when one of the major broadcasting stations arranged to have Charles Wakefield Cadman, composer of Indian songs, presented by our group with a Seneca cornhusk mask."

Red Wing shared Moore's goals for the 1933 summer camp, "freedom, self-reliance, responsibility, tolerance, and helpfulness." The fees Moore charged were just enough to "sustain the tribe," he said, and that would pose a problem. Enrollment was limited to twenty campers, but the ratio between Indian counselors and children was high. Moore created a progressive curriculum. Each night at the council fire the children decided the following day's activities, but Moore and the counselors set the pedagogical goal for each activity.[36] For example, if the children chose archery, it should not be practiced simply as a contest of skill but as the means "to cultivate alertness, observation coupled with quick action, and correct judgment, qualities required in the hunt." Similarly, hiking, though an excellent physical exercise, should lead to nature study. Children should learn about edible native plants, and if the children caught butterflies or other insects, counselors instructed them to closely examine and identify the species and "then let them go." Finally, all activities "led into dancing, for dancing, in the Indian mode, reflected individual experience," according to Moore. Thus, while the tom-tom accompanied their movements, the children might imitate a butterfly moving from flower to flower. It's easy to imagine who supervised this part of the program. Moore "was less interested in money than in the experiment itself," so his camp closed after the summer of 1933.

Red Wing continued to lend her name and performance skills to political events and powwows "to promote the general welfare of American Indians," as well as to push for a national Indian Day. De Frey noted that Red Wing was indeed "very active, attending all of the important Indian functions." Moreover, she declared, "Red Wing's "attendance . . . is always sought by the leaders of her people, and her presence on a platform attests both to its authenticity and to her belief in its sincerity of purpose."[37]

The Indian Unity Alliance held one such function in October 1934. Five hundred Native folks attended the event, held in Yonkers, New York. Yonkers resident William Spears, called Chief Sun Flower, headed the alliance. Members voted in as officers that day included Chief White Moon (Iroquois), Little Moose (Chippewa), Reindeer (Shoshone), White Elk (Osage), and "Princess Red Wing of the Winnebago Tribe, keeper of the wampum" (treasurer). "Assistant Chief Custalow of the Mattaponi Indians in Virginia" delivered a political address, evoking "the power of the great Virginia confederacy of 32 tribes under historic Powhattan." Custalow further declared that although his people "extended a hand of welcome to the visitors from across the water, the whites pushed them from their land, slew and scattered them and plowed up their burying grounds for corn fields."[38]

Red Wing performed and lectured with her niece's husband, Ernest Naquayouma, known today for his work on the Hopi language with prominent linguist Sapir Whorf. Even Julia St. Cyr sang a medicine song. The event's success compelled leaders of Yonkers's Museum of Science and Arts to sponsor an educational program in December to urge for a national Indian Day. Red Wing performed, but again the affair was too local to change enough minds about a national holiday.[39]

By 1934 performing prospects seemed to have been nearly nil. Red Wing did her Indian number in Yonkers for the Fellowcraft Club, but not much else appeared in the newspapers.[40] Her last filmed appearance atop the Clinton Hotel did little to kick-start her acting career. She performed for the Yonkers Masonic Lodge and a Yonkers department store, where she demonstrated the ever-popular Indian marriage ceremony with her Indian Unity Alliance colleague Little Moose. "Bring your husband" to "the Toy Floor!" the ad for the A & S men's store announced. "War dances! Tom toms! Sign Language Demonstration!"[41] Christmas was around the corner, so at least Red Wing had a chance to sell some of her exquisite handiwork.

Just after Christmas, news from Hollywood reignited Red Wing's star—if only briefly. Cecil DeMille decided to host the twenty-second reunion for *The Squaw Man*. DeMille was more than sentimental about his first picture. A savvy promoter, he realized that a widely publicized reunion would bring people to his concurrent film projects. His *Squaw Man* reunion was not the first. However, it launched him as Hollywood's first director, or at least the director of Hollywood's first *feature-length* film. David Horsley of the Nestor Motion Picture Company set up the first permanent studio in Hollywood two years before DeMille arrived on the scene. In fact, George Gebhardt starred in one of Horsley's first westerns.[42] However, Horsley produced one- or two-reelers, and they were not considered feature films. Moreover, D. W. Griffith first directed a four-reel film in Hollywood that rivaled *The Squaw Man* as the first feature.[43] Apparently, Griffith lacked DeMille's enterprising spirit, because he never overtly challenged him for the title.

On December 29, 1935, DeMille hosted a luncheon near the old barn where Red Wing first performed as Naturitch.[44] Fourteen of the original cast and crew attended. Several cast members whom Red Wing knew well were missing from the festivities. Art Accord and Milt Brown had passed away. Monroe Salisbury had died just that year. Dustin Farnum had died six years earlier in New York City.[45] Winifred Kingston (now Mrs. Carmen Runyon) couldn't be tracked down or didn't want to be. Red Wing was also conspicuously missing. "For several months, DeMille has been trying unsuccessfully to trace Red Wing, the little Indian girl, who played the squaw in 'The Squaw Man,'" one newspaper reported. "On other starting-date anniversaries she has communicated with him and he still has hopes."[46]

The press found Red Wing, but it was too late for her to come out to Hollywood. Her rediscovery became newsworthy, nonetheless. The AP broadcast the story across the United States. "Indian Movie Star Lectures. She Wears Native Costume When Going to Her Appointments," read one headline. The report recapped an interview with the former Indian movie star. Red Wing describes how she got the part in the film and how she informed DeMille that his leading man was lucky to work with a "100% American." She also related how her Indian name came from Standing Bear and that her last film was *Soul Fire*. "Today I lecture in the public schools on Indian lore, singing native songs and teaching sign language" and making "Indian things," she explained. She told the reporter she usually wasn't noticed, but "she always seems to collect a crowd of gapers" when she traveled to a "lecture appointment" dressed in her Indian garb.[47]

The New Year of 1936 brought few gapers because Red Wing gave few lectures, but the reunion publicity introduced her to the next generation as a primary Indian leading lady.[48] The press also honored her as a silent film pioneer. In fact, that summer DeMille told a reporter that he had looked "for another feminine Indian star as appealing as Red Wing." His new film, *The Plainsman*, described as "colossal, with Indians," inspired his declaration—whether it was true or not. The film featured nearly 2,500 Cheyenne to enact the battle at Little Big Horn. The incomparable western hero Gary Cooper played the lead, but DeMille claimed to the reporter that what really excited him was "the prospect of working with Indians once more." He also boasted again that he discovered Red Wing, which was a bit like saying that Columbus discovered America. He had no compunction in claiming title to Hollywood, so why not Red Wing, the girl he had "assigned the sympathetic role of the squaw" in his first film? "She was quite a sensation in her day," he told the reporter. "An appealing Indian girl would have great possibilities for the screen. . . . There has never been one of any prominence since Red Wing, but she was so successful that she made numerous pictures and a popular song bore her name."[49]

The remainder of 1930s held less heady praise for Red Wing. She occasionally donned her *Squaw Man* dress and beaded moccasins, silently plodding here and there to perform solo or with family members at various school and organization functions. She also got a job with the Works Progress Administration in 1939 that included making Christmas toys for children, and she continued her work with the Indian Unity Alliance. Due to the close-knit nature of the New York Native community, she had many friends who, like her, promoted the welfare of Indian people. Two of the most recent transplants came from Wisconsin. Ho-Chunk Sam Blowsnake (Big Winnebago) and his wife, Emma Sine, moved to Brooklyn for a time and worked making Indian crafts. Blowsnake also lectured about Indian culture for various organizations.[50]

Unfortunately, the late 1930s and 1940s brought Red Wing and her family many sorrows, the first the death of Norton Mofsie (Rolling Cloud) at seven years of age. Nottie, as the family called him, was already a Brooklyn celebrity. He had Red Wing's charisma and showed incredible promise as a traditional dancer and performer. Red Wing adored him as if he were her own. Tragically, Nottie's life was cut short when he was struck by an automobile and killed in front of his Brooklyn home on June 4, 1937.

The *Brooklyn Daily Eagle* reported that Nottie, born in Manhattan, "spent most of his earlier childhood touring the United States" when his parents performed.[51] The family was absolutely devastated, but Nottie's death also grieved the local Native community. In particular, his childhood friend, Gloria Miguel, still remembers the loss.[52] Their mothers were best friends and neighbors in Brooklyn's Little Caughnawaga neighborhood. The Mofsies and Miguels also shared performance as a calling. Sisters Muriel, Gloria, and Elizabeth Miguel founded the Spiderwoman Theater in 1976, the first Native American theater group established in New York.

Nottie left two siblings who were barely toddlers, Josephine and Louis Mofsie. They also became distinguished Native performers, seemingly touched with their brother's spirit. There's no telling how accomplished Nottie would have become.

In the summer of 1938, at age fifty, Louis St. Cyr also died. He had been working as a salesman in Nebraska but had a heart condition. He left a widow, Mabel Frenchman, sister of his first wife. The death of Red Wing's sister Annie St. Cyr Owen followed in 1939. She left a son and a husband (who would both die in 1942), as well as a married daughter. In 1940 Red Wing's eldest brother, David, succumbed to arteriosclerosis and diabetes. Her half brother Abner St. Cyr would pass on in 1944. How Red Wing coped with so many losses in so few years can only be imagined, but Nottie's death was like a blot on the sun. It made no sense, and it darkened every day.

In February 1940 the Indian Confederation of America, which seems to have merged with the Indian Unity Alliance, held a charity pageant at the Capital Hotel in Manhattan. Seven hundred people attended, including members from seventeen tribes. The program featured "Indian dances, songs and rituals," and proceeds went to "members of Brooklyn's colony of 800 Indians," which probably included Red Wing, though she lived in Manhattan. Performances featured the popular "squaw-hunters' dance," "tribal and dance songs," and "knife and hoop dances." To conclude the evening Sam Blowsnake led all the performers in a fabulous snake dance.[53]

The Museum of Modern Art in Manhattan put on an exhibit titled *Indian Art of the United States* also in February. To kick off the installation Columbia University professor of anthropology Dr. George Herzog gave a lecture on the music of American Indians in tandem with performances by Brooklyn Indians Blowsnake, White Bear (Henry White), his nephew, and Morris Mofsie, Vina's husband. Blowsnake sang several songs, some accompanied by his nephew. They included a medicine, Peyote, and doctoring song, as well as a love song, which he also played on the Winnebago flute. White Bear performed a double hoop dance. Mofsie's performance, described in the museum's press release, offers a significant summary of his talents and contributions to the local Indian community:

> Morris Mofsie, whose Indian name, Sekaqueftewa, means medicine cedar tree, is a Hopi living in Brooklyn. He is a craftsman and silversmith. He also paints, does beadwork and makes Kachina dolls. Mr. Mofsie will sing a Frog Dance song, accompanying himself with a notched-stick instrument called a rasping stick. He will also sing a corn grinding song, accompanying himself on the drum; a song of the ceremonial clowns, accompanying himself with a rattle; a buffalo dance song, accompanying himself on a drum; and a Kachina dance song, accompanying himself with a gourd rattle and a turtle shell rattle.[54]

Morris's performance demonstrates that Red Wing and Vina were not the only family members to teach the Mofsie children about Native culture. Their father in particular represented living proof that Indians had not vanished and that, in fact, many still passed on priceless esoteric cultural knowledge to the next generation.

However, tragedy struck again in May 1940, when Morris died at only thirty-five years of age.[55] Although Hopi, he was buried with his wife's Ho-Chunk family in the St. Augustine Cemetery, in Winnebago, Nebraska. How was Vina to cope with such great loss in so short a time? There was nothing to do but grieve and try to attend to the needs of her two small children. Red Wing worried that Vina was not up to it. She suggested to her niece that she take one of the children, probably Louis, and raise him herself. It was a shocking request, and Vina found it more than hurtful. She refused her aunt's offer, and Red Wing acquiesced.[56]

On September 29, 1940, a group of Indian hobbyist boys from the Salvation Army's Red Shield Club performed in Jamaica, New York, for Indian Day. Dressed in Indian regalia, they felt shy when they discovered that "some real Indians" had come to see them. However, they performed splendidly, and their performance so touched one audience member that she sent them a letter signed "Lilia Red Wing."

In behalf of the American Indian race, I tender my sincere thanks for the wonderful program you presented on Indian Day, September 29, 1940, at Chinquillas Indian Museum. The beauty, dignity and understanding with which it was presented will have a profound influence on the Youth of America and will promote a better understanding to all who are privileged to see it, of the culture and ideals of a race that has been sadly misunderstood. Again our sincere thanks and may the Great Spirit bless you and the great work you are doing.[57]

The club boys kept Red Wing's missive as "a precious framed trophy" for years. However, today we might scoff at Red Wing's unabashed support for non-Native people attempting to exhibit American Indian cultural practices. But we must put ourselves in her shoes to understand that she viewed these performances as promoting an appreciation for Indigenous people, who in the 1940s continued to endure viral racism and ethnocentric derision. Red Wing appears not to have had a racist bone in her body, and, of course, she also loved children. Her heartfelt letter suggests more than her open and supportive nature. It suggests that she grieved deeply for the little boy who had joined his "Great Spirit" in the eternal dance.

CHAPTER 18

Fare Thee Well and
Hollywood Reunion

From before the war years until the late 1950s, Red Wing lived in the Upper West Side in today's Lincoln Square neighborhood.[1] Her first apartment on West 65th Street bordered the often-violent San Juan Hill area, where the Charleston was born. Redevelopment has since flattened the hill, but during Red Wing's day more than five thousand African Americans, including jazz great Thelonious Monk, inhabited the neighborhood's low-rise tenements. The racial clash with the Irish of Hell's Kitchen to the south inspired *West Side Story*, whose opening scenes were filmed just before the hill was demolished in 1961. By 1945 Red Wing had moved a couple of blocks away to West 67th Street, and Vina and her two children moved into an apartment on the same street. Julia St. Cyr also found her own place nearby.[2] The family domain, nestled between Central Park on the east and the Hudson River on the west, was about as close to the great outdoors as one could get in Manhattan.

The area was a mecca of businesses and mom-and-pop stores. During the war years Red Wing could trade in her ration tickets without walking far, or she could ride on the city's first subway line if she needed to venture farther from home. Red Wing lived close to theaters, galleries, and museums, where she nurtured her creativity. According to Anita De Frey, however, Red Wing's "studio-domicile" was a museum in itself. In the following passage De Frey offers a close description of one of Red Wing's apartments.

It is in the heart of the business district, but is set back of a large courtyard, which her studio faces, and so she has quiet and privacy in the very center of the mad rat race that is today's New York. She is surrounded with practically a museum collection of Indian art treasures, among them pictures of her dear ones, those of the long ago, as well as . . . a fabulous collection of Indian art—bead work from the long ago that she inherited—and bead work of today she herself makes, holding strictly to the standards of artistic excellence learned from her people on the Reservation in the olden days. She makes authentic leather costumes and Indian feather ceremonial bonnets for the television and theatrical trades here in New York. The lovely white buckskin Indian dresses are all individual models, never two alike and they win unfailing praise wherever they are seen. Her feather bonnets and Chief's outfits are among the most striking seen at any of the ceremonies or pow wows, and the bead work with which she decorates them is exquisite. . . . A visit with her in her studio on the courtyard is an unforgettable experience—she is always happy to show her treasures to an interested visitor and to tell the wonderful stories of the long ago that are connected to each one of them.[3]

Young Deer's photo hung among "those of long ago," but Red Wing's relationship with her former partner and husband was complicated. Young Deer came back into her life in the 1940s, grieving and defeated, having exhausted all attempts to revive his career. In fact, film industry people considered him a has-been by the mid-1920s. After he returned from England, his career fell into a downward spiral. He moved to Pawhuska, Oklahoma, in the fall of 1924, where under the name J. Gordon Young Deer he planned to direct "special Indian subjects" for the newly incorporated Arrowhead Film Company, for which he was also general manager. Although *Moving Picture World* reported that a "charter naming the capital stock at $50,000, with $25,000 paid in cash, will be applied for at once," nothing came of the venture.[4]

In the throes of the Great Depression, Young Deer moved into a rooming house in the Mission District in San Francisco, where he claimed he was a theater instructor. He'd also changed his identity again to become an

Indian born in Oklahoma.[5] Young Deer applied for a government pension for his naval service in July 1930. He asked that the reply be sent to the address of his sister Minnie, who at that time lived in Harlem. Less than a week later and in his fifties, he married thirty-one-year-old Scottish immigrant Helen Gilchrist in Douglas, Arizona.[6] The couple had moved to Los Angeles by the fall, when Young Deer placed the following ad: "Motion picture director, 20 years experience, one of the pioneers of the motion picture industry, who has created many stars offers you the opportunity to participate and share in his future productions. Call, write or inquire. Mr. Youngdeer, Associated Studios. 3890 Mission Road."[7] Apparently, the ad had few if any takers.

It's more than likely that Young Deer struggled financially. At the end of 1930 he wrote the Navy Department seeking his discharge papers (which he said he'd lost) in order to complete his pension application. The monthly stipend, when he finally received it, helped ease his financial burdens somewhat.

In 1933 the Temple Theater in San Bernardino publicized a tryout for an upcoming production of *Neptune's Garden of Eden.* "James Gordon Youngdeer, director, will be present to give the screen tests," stated the ad. "He has discovered and directed such stars as Bebe Daniels, Hoot Gibson, Jules Carmon [*sic*] and others. He will give screen tests to all young men and women who fill out application blanks which may be secured at the Temple Theater." Again Young Deer sought out hopefuls who didn't expect much (or any) salary. Not surprisingly, his film, if made, was never released.[8]

The only other news about him concerned a house fire caused when his wife's curling iron touched her celluloid comb. "Mrs. Helen Young Deer, 35 years of age, wife of James Young Deer, Indian motion-picture director . . . was burned in the face and legs," the *Los Angeles Times* reported. Young Deer was also burned in the face and hands when he tried to put out the flames. The Youngdeers sued the owners of their apartment building for $95,000 in damages. Strangely, the item showed up in *Variety*, which reported, "The couple alleges that they were burned and disfigured when defective wiring started a fire in their apartment and their trained dog [was] lost."[9]

If the couple received a settlement, the money quickly disappeared into the abyss of their debts. It seemed life couldn't get much worse when Helen died of breast cancer on June 6, 1937. The service for the "beloved wife of J. Gordon Youngdeer" was held two days later, after which she was buried in the Inglewood Cemetery in Los Angeles. Today the only thing that marks her grave is a small stone that reads "2492."[10] The lack of tribute suggests Young Deer was flat broke.

An aging movie pioneer and widower with nothing left in his arsenal, Young Deer returned to New York to live on his pension.[11] He moved in with his widowed sister, Minnie, who worked as a dressmaking supervisor. If Red Wing was "glad to be rid of him," as Louis Mofsie thought, she was certainly not happy to learn he had moved practically next door on West 67th Street, where Minnie had resided for several years.[12] Still, Red Wing was patient and kind, so her heart may have gone out to the man she once loved.

Young Deer lived out his days incognito. Red Wing continued to stay relatively active and occasionally gave a public performance. She put on her usual show for a women's church group in Yonkers and later performed and lectured "on her people" to 130 attendees at the Hudson Museum Auxiliary. She donned her eagle headdress, but this time she wore sleigh bells on her ankles as she danced to the tom-tom. "She pictured the Red Men as a personally strong, self-contained people and not a race of 'worriers' like the white man," the newspaper reported. She informed her audience that "Indian babies . . . are bound on boards until they are three months old." Red Wing expressed her opinion that the custom "not only gives Indians straight backs throughout life but ingrains discipline and self-control in them." Red Wing grew bolder in pointing out the shortcomings of "the white man," who had in turn became more disposed to accepting criticism.[13]

She also joined Chief Rising Sun of the Cherokees, Chief Hill Canoe of the Navaho, and Peace Chief Lynx to provide entertainment for the Cub Pack of Flushing (Queens), as well as the Pelham Girl Scouts in Westchester County.[14] Morning Star (Vina) and her children, Green Rainbow (Louis) and Silver Cloud (Josephine), also performed in Indian-themed events around New York and elsewhere.[15]

Red Wing felt concern about Young Deer despite his many shortcomings. Louis Mofsie recalls his family "looking in on" him. Louis remembered that Young Deer was not what you'd call "a good person," but Red Wing was family, so the Mofsies put up with him. Young Deer had probably been in declining health for some time when he died in the Roosevelt Hospital of stomach cancer on April 6, 1946, just a few days after his seventieth birthday. Red Wing served as the informant for his death certificate, giving his name as James Y. Johnson. She also stated that she was his wife. Whether they mysteriously remarried after Helen's death or whether they were never divorced to begin with, Red Wing's marital status made her eligible to collect Young Deer's pension.

After Young Deer's death, Red Wing moved to 89 West End Avenue, closer to the waterfront and away from the hubbub of the busier streets. Julia moved a couple of blocks north on the same street, while Vina and the kids remained on West 67th Street, which bordered West End Avenue. Although Red Wing's and Julia's apartments were set back from the neighborhood bustle, Vina lived on a busy street. When the three women got together, the kids often went outside to play, but given the way her firstborn had died, Vina surely had one ear open at all times.

Weathermen predicted that the Great Snowstorm of 1947 would swallow up Manhattan over the holiday season, but on December 3 it only rained. On the world front, the Zionists and the Palestinians clashed, and the U.S. military began a propaganda campaign against Communism. While the *New York Times* advertised beaded evening bags as "better than mistletoe," the UN sent aid to war-torn children in Europe. Eleanor Roosevelt pressed for international civil rights, while Russian leaders demanded an investigation into "the Negro problem in the United States and conditions in colonial territories." The House Un-American Activities Committee sentenced pacifist screenwriter Dalton Trumbo for contempt and suspended his employment. "Urge Aid for Needy Navajos" also headlined the papers. As winter set in, President Truman proposed $2 million for the relief of the sixty-one thousand individuals who made up the Navajo Nation.

Julia St. Cyr, nearly eighty now, walked gingerly back from church that day, dodging puddles and trying to keep at least her head dry. She made it nearly to Vina's when a truck bolted out of nowhere and struck her down in front of the apartment building next door. If her life passed before her as she lay unconscious, she surely saw a vision of her only child, Leo White, now a married man living far away in Nebraska. Fortunately, he did not have to witness the accident or see her with her ribs and skull fractured, her brain lacerated, and one punctured lung filling up with blood. Someone rushed her to Roosevelt Hospital, but she died the next afternoon. Vina signed the death certificate, and if she heard the terrible collision, it surely shook her to her core.[16]

Julia's remains went to Winnebago, Nebraska, where she was buried on December 9. It's unknown whether Red Wing went to St. Augustine's, but certainly she felt some comfort burying her sister with their parents and siblings. Julia had watched over Red Wing all her life, and she had been so proud of her little sister's accomplishments. Julia's traumatic death must have been another tremendous life passage for Red Wing. Now she was the last surviving child of her dear mother and, except for her half brother Levi, the last of her father's children as well.

As the Christmas snowstorm transformed her world into a cold white landscape, grief over Julia's horrible death seems to have left Red Wing frozen as well. Newspapers failed to report her activities, but it's likely she suffered what all aging people do: the terrible and inevitable loss of loved ones, one by one.

Red Wing reemerged in 1948 to join the Long Island Indian Council, which established an annual powwow that year at "Springy Banks" in East Hampton. Due to the "scarcity" of local Indians, the group included "Narragansett, Cherokee, Choctaw, San Blas, Hopi, Schaghticoke, Nanticoke, Catawba, Peqot [sic] and Winnebago Tribes." The powwow featured a canoe race, a lacrosse game, Indian dancing, and ceremonies. Red Wing and other participants also displayed and sold their "Indian beadwork, basketry and silverware."[17]

In the fall she participated in Manhattan's first "county fair" at the Rockefeller Center. The fair was part of the Indians' exhibit at the Museum of Science and Industry. A photo shows Red Wing and Short Wing (Ho-Chunk) doing beadwork together while Louis Mofsie and others stand by. The fair wasn't a great success, and a reporter caught one of its moments: "A short flight below the main floor, only a group of Indians remained impassive over their souvenir collections of rings, belts, beads." The reporter approached Red Wing as she "quietly" played the tom-tom. She "fixed her feathers" and made it clear to him she was no princess and nobody's wife. "Red Wing—no miss or missus—just Red Wing," she told him.[18]

In January 1949 Red Wing attended a five-day powwow at the Rockefeller Indian Center, sponsored again by Radio City's Museum of Science and Industry. The powwow celebrated "President Truman's proclamation that all American Indians, whether on or off reservations, are full citizens with the privilege of voting" in the federal election. Representatives from several tribal groups came to the event, according to a newspaper report, including "Chief Crazy Bull of the Sioux tribe, the great grandson of Chief Sitting Bull of Custer Massacre fame," "Chief Young Deer of the Mohawks," his mother, "Princess Iona," and "Chief Little Moose of the Chippewa's." "Chief Short Wing, champion Indian chanter, war cry and sign language performer," and "Princess Red Wing, Indian lead in the 'Squaw Man' and 'Ramona,' of silent film days," represented the Winnebago.[19]

That winter, another Hollywood *Squaw Man* reunion passed her by, this one promoting "DeMille's latest Technicolor extravaganza," *Samson and Delilah*. The reunion also featured an exhibit with relics from the original film that included movie stills, a "rickety camera," Farnum's hat, and Red Wing's "Indian headgear."[20] Red Wing and her *Squaw Man* dress would have been a welcome addition.

The following spring Red Wing traveled to Otsego County, New York, to join an event for a group called American Restitution and Righting of Old Wrongs (ARROW). The new organization was established in 1949 to serve as the fund-raising arm of the National Congress of American Indians (NCAI) and allow it tax-exempt status.[21] ARROW was the brainchild of Will Rogers Jr., son of the western actor. Rogers served as president, but vice president Yeffe Kimball, recognized as a noted Osage artist, was ARROW's most visible New York presence.

In the spring the Richfield Springs Rotary Club launched a fundraising drive for ARROW that featured an authentic Native American dance program headed by Indian hobbyists Kenneth Laubin and his wife, Gladys. "Early hobbyists were galvanized by a deeply held belief that through their study of American Indian cultures, and especially through their dance performances," states scholar Clyde Ellis, "they hoped to save Native cultures from oblivion."[22] The Laubins further emphasized their relationship to living Indians. Sitting Bull's son Chief One Bull "adopted" Laubin when he "lived with the Indians," as an account stated. Furthermore, Laubin "received the highest honor the white man can receive from the Indian when the chief gave him his own name and that of his mother, Good Feather Woman, to Mrs. Laubin."[23]

The Laubins demonstrated sign language after Louis R. Bruce, a local Mohawk and early ARROW leader who later served as commissioner of Indians Affairs for President Richard Nixon, discussed "the plight of the Indian peoples," who he said lacked "educational facilities" and "adequate food." Moreover, he stressed that only half the Indian babies born each year would survive tuberculosis. He then presented "several Indian citizens," including Red Wing, who was there selling her "Indiancraft." Finally, he introduced Yeffe Kimball, "who outlined the plight of the Indians and explained what ARROW proposed to do about it."[24]

Kimball was a Bohemian fashion icon with a Frida Kahlo style. She is almost always pictured wearing two skinny dark braids that frame her delicately featured and angular face. She is usually smiling in photos and even hamming it up.[25] Red Wing and Kimball shared a friendship for the remainder of Red Wing's life, although they were polar opposites. Red Wing also became close to Kimball's husband, Harvey Slatin, an amiable Jewish intellectual and atomic physicist. Slatin "refused to work on weapons of war," but in 1942 he worked on the isolation of plutonium for the Manhattan Project at Los Alamos, New Mexico.[26] Slatin later described Kimball, whom he married in 1948, as "a powerhouse" who "easily won the affection of anyone who met her." "She had no hesitation to use anyone to accomplish her cause—to help the American Indian," as Harvey told his second wife, Anne Slatin. "She seemed to know everybody . . . senators, presidents, artists, musicians, you name it, came to our house." Harvey admitted to Anne, however, that they fought "like cats and dogs" because Kimball "was a very self-centered, ambitious, and jealous woman." He jokingly attributed their thirty-year marriage to the fact that "she was rarely home."[27]

Kimball moved to New York City in the 1930s and belonged to the Art Students League from 1935 to 1939. She began an affair with Herman B. Delman, an up-and-coming Jewish fashion shoe designer and manufacturer. When she met him, she was an aspiring though unremarkable European American painter, and he was making "crazy sketches" of shoes he would eventually design and manufacture, including a pair of moccasins.[28] They traveled to Europe together seeking the avant-garde. They went to Rome and Paris, where Kimball later claimed she studied cubism with Ferdinand Legér.[29] They married by 1940, and Delman's booming shoe business supported Kimball's artistic ambitions. When they divorced, Yeffe received "a fabulous divorce settlement," including "a triplex penthouse apartment in the Rockefeller Apartments on Park Avenue."[30]

Newly single Kimball enrolled at the New York School and moved to a Manhattan penthouse on 54th Street that afforded her a view of the sculpture gardens of the Museum of Modern Art. In 1946 she entered a small oil painting entitled *Sacred Buffalo* for "the First Exhibition of American Painting at the Philbrook Art Center in Tulsa, Oklahoma," according to art historian Bill Anthes. The primitivist work "depicted an iconic white buffalo, sacred to the Plains Indians, silhouetted against a dark and abstract night sky." However, to enter the competition Kimball described herself as an American Indian artist born "in a prairie dugout in Kiowa County, Oklahoma, to an Osage father and a white mother." Kimball's "Indian act" eventually paid off and "afforded her privileged access to the New York art world."[31] Henceforth she began subtracting years from her age and obscured the family tree that did not lend her the cachet she desired. Born Effie Violetta Goodman on March 30, 1906, not far from Kansas City in the small village of Rayville, Missouri, she was the fourth of at least nine children born to native Kansans Oather Alvis Goodman and Martha Clementine Smith. Kimball always claimed her real white mother as her own, but she created an American Indian father from her imagination, an Osage from Oklahoma whom she first called Good Man and later renamed Jesse W. Kimball.

"Yeffe's friends were captains of industry," Anne Slatin noted, and "just the sort of people who could afford to buy her paintings." Kimball also befriended many Harvard scientists, including Albert Einstein, who once hosted Harvey and her for dinner at his Princeton home. Kimball was indeed a ball of fire, and as Slatin recalled, her "social standing attracted a lot of interesting people who latched onto Harvey!" Kimball counted Red Wing as one of these "interesting friends," and Red Wing also latched onto Harvey, who unlike his wife was dependable and empathetic. "Yeffe was a rather mercurial individual," said Slatin, and Red Wing "was a very wise woman" who could "calm Yeffe down."[32]

Kimball was "a good friend" to the Indians, so Louis Mofsie believed her fake identity didn't really bother his great-aunt. It's important to note how both Kimball and De Frey differed from Indian hobbyists like the Laubins. The Laubins, like the Red Shield Club boys, attempted to sympathetically portray authentic Indians to the public but did not try to pass themselves off as Indians. Kimball and De Frey played Indian to enhance their careers and to divert attention from their origins—as Young Deer had done. If Red Wing felt the ends justified the means, she also understood the difference between her "authentic" self and the performance Indian persona she created.

With funerals behind her and new friends who would see her through the future, Red Wing looked at the world anew. She got a refreshing break from powwow circuits and the Cub Scouts when RKO Theaters invited her back on the road to promote *Broken Arrow*, a 1950 release starring Jimmy Stewart.[33] Publicity lauded the film, based on Tom Jeffards's experience in the Pony Express, as presenting *authentic* Indian culture. By today's standards that boast falls short, but *Broken Arrow* gave the most sympathetic portrayal of Indians in nearly two decades of popular westerns.[34]

Red Wing joined a troupe of four other American Indian performers who were "skilled in the song and dances of their people." They started a two-week tour on July 12, 1950, to RKO theaters in the metropolitan area. Their performances focused attention on the "authentic Indian folklore embodied in 20th Century–Fox Technicolored drama." Red Wing performed with Cherokee Tall Pine (Boyd Heath), a baritone who performed on Broadway; thirteen-year-old Green Rainbow (Louis Mofsie), skilled in hoop dancing; lovely Hote Mowee, "a Cherokee concert vocalist"; and fellow Ho-Chunk Short Wing, said to be "an authentic chieftain who is a recognized sign language expert and dancer."[35] The tour didn't exactly reignite Red Wing's film career, but she again gained recognition for her pioneering role in westerns.

After the tour Red Wing continued supporting ARROW under John C. Rainier (Taos Pueblo), the executive director of the National Congress for American Indians. ARROW sponsored a relief trip in 1951 to administer antibiotics, particularly for trachoma, to the Navajo of Arizona. The widow of Frederick de Groff Hyde, an archaeologist who "spent years among the Pueblos and Navajos," donated a Willys Jeep Station Wagon.[36] She intended to use the vehicle as a medical dispensary and drive it all the way to the Navajo reservation.

Red Wing and several others gave Hyde a publicity sendoff at the Park Lane Hotel on Central Park South. A photo shows the station wagon in the hotel lobby stuffed with people dressed in Indian garb rather than with medicine. Red Wing sits in the back, Yeffe and Harvey Slatin ham it up in the front, and Louis Mofsie and his sister lean on the vehicle's hood in a more dignified manner. Kimball stands out as the life of the party.[37]

That fall Red Wing treated herself to a special trip, one she had thought about for several years. By plane or train she traveled to Los Angeles to attend a celebration commemorating early Hollywood. As Cecil DeMille, Jesse Lasky, and Sam Goldwyn, now elderly men, stood on the corner of Vine Street and Selma Avenue on September 11, 1951, Red Wing surely watched in delight as an official attached a plaque marking "The Birthplace of Motion Pictures" to the exterior wall of the California Bank. The date of the ceremony coincided with the twenty-year anniversary of DeMille's 1931 rendition of *The Squaw Man*, but the plaque honored the first version of the film's production, when "Princess Redwing performed her part with exquisite fidelity and great depth of feeling."[38]

The next evening Red Wing attended a gala at the Ambassador Hotel at Cocoanut Grove honoring Lasky's thirty-eight years as a producer. Gloria Swanson presented him with the Screen Producers Guild Silver Wreath, the first award of its kind. The *Los Angeles Times* covered the extravagant fifteen-dollar-a-plate dinner, which featured six hundred "screen personalities," including many who worked with Lasky over the years.[39] George Jessel served as master of ceremonies, while DeMille, Goldwyn, and luminaries like Jack Benny, Mary Pickford, and Bob Hope delivered tributes to their old friend. Referring to the new and democratizing invention, the television, an ebullient DeMille exclaimed, "We are at the beginning of the dawn of what we set out to do—to have our pictures seen by EVERYONE!"[40]

Bob Hope cut up the crowd with several one-liners. "DeMille came out here originally as a used chariot dealer," he joked, referring to the director's blockbuster movie, *Samson and Delilah*. Lasky played "Stars and Stripes Forever" on his trumpet, which *Hollywood Variety* stated was the "happy highlight of a swell evening."[41] Virtually nothing was reported about *The Squaw Man*, however. The only mention quoted George Jessel, who announced to the audience that Mervyn LeRoy played "the Indian baby" in the film. Everyone's attention turned to the Academy Award–winning director, but Red Wing knew Jessel was lampooning LeRoy. "Therefore," Jessel quipped, "he has the honor of playing the first Jewish papoose in the United States."[42]

Red Wing spent a splendid evening hobnobbing with movie stars, who had become übercelebrities compared to her days in the industry. Mary Pickford attended the tribute, but it's unlikely Red Wing had a chance to speak with the popular actress and successful producer. The following day Red Wing went to the Paramount Studio wearing a simple belted floral dress and a prim little hat. She also donned some of her own beaded jewelry, though it didn't scream out "American Indian."

After DeMille supervised a publicity shoot with Bob Hope, star of his new comedy, *The Pale Face*, he posed with the former Indian actress he claimed to have discovered. The photos show that Red Wing's former director still held a special place in her heart.[43] One of the most endearing of the photos appeared in national newspapers. "Thirty-eight years after she was the slim heroine of Cecil B. DeMille's first movie, 'The Squaw Man,'" the caption read, "Miss Red Wing met DeMille while on her first visit to the studio in 30 years. He cancelled all appointments and screened his latest picture, 'The Greatest Show on Earth,' for his first leading lady."[44]

The happy reunion put Red Wing's career into its historical context. It also boosted her pride in her pioneering accomplishments. She always believed she was more than "she'll do," as Farnum told DeMille when he first saw her. If no one else realized it, she also knew that DeMille's phenomenal success began with *her*, the Indian actress who in her words "started him on his road to fame & fortune."[45] Now she was pronounced DeMille's "first leading lady" without the "Indian" qualifier. The retrospective established Red Wing's place as an *American* icon, 100 percent.

CHAPTER 19

The Moon Shines on Pretty Red Wing

> Now, the moon shines tonight on pretty Red Wing.
> The breeze is sighing, the night bird's crying.
>
> —KERRY MILLS, "Red Wing: An Intermezzo," lyrics by Thurland
> Chattaway (New York: F. A. Mills, 1907)

Except for John Ford's 1956 western, *The Searchers*, starring John Wayne and costarring Natalie Wood as the young Indian princess type, the western television series supplanted the western movie in the 1950s. If her Hollywood experience and its attending publicity boosted Red Wing's spirit, TV westerns also reminded her that no one had taken her place. No matter how carefully Red Wing watched the TV screen, she saw only white actresses playing Indians. It seems kismet engendered her historic place in the movie industry.

Red Wing passed the performance baton on to the Mofsie family but continued to attend functions as the first Indian movie star. Vina led the family of performers and became a respected elder and political leader in her community. Today Vina's children, grandchildren, and great-grandchildren continue to educate through performance while coalescing the diverse New York Native community. Vina's daughter Josephine married Samuel Tarrant in 1955. Their son Kevin married Murielle Borst, the talented daughter of the incomparable Muriel Miguel of the Spiderwoman Theater. Kevin and Murielle's marriage joined the two most prominent American Indian performing families in New York. Kevin founded and leads the Silvercloud Singers, an intertribal drumming and dance group that performs across the country. He also formerly served as the executive director of New York City's American Indian Community House. Murielle Borst-Tarrant earned a degree in theater and today is an award-winning playwright who has authored and performed in New York's cutting-edge Native theater.[1]

Louis Mofsie grew up to become a New York Indian community icon and traditional dancer. He helped found New York's first Native dance company in 1963, the Thunderbird American Indian Dancers. His dedication and talent resulted in a recent lifetime achievement award from the American Dance Guild for his invaluable contribution to preserving traditional dance.[2] He fondly recalls that Red Wing always encouraged him to pursue art and performance, and he still leads the intertribal dance at the American Indian Community Center, although he is in his golden years.[3]

Today actress Henu Josephine Tarrant, daughter of Kevin and Murielle, carries on the Mofsie-Miguel legacy. She has been performing traditional American Indian dances and songs since she was a small child. Now at nearly twenty-five, she performs, often in her mother's plays; dances and sings for American Indian functions; and has begun writing a cabaret-style musical play about her legendary great-great-great aunt Red Wing.[4] If anyone exhibits the unmistakable traits of the dynamic, effervescent, and multitalented Red Wing, it is she.

Newspapers reported on Red Wing's occasional appearances at high schools, Sunday schools, and other organizations for children, as well as annual powwows, such as Wyalusing Rocks (Prayer Rocks) in Pennsylvania, where she'd sometimes trill Kerry Mills's song "Red Wing: An Intermezzo" to an admiring audience. She also frequently appeared for the Quakers "wearing deerskin and an eagle feather bonnet." At age seventy a reporter caught her displaying her beautifully made handicrafts outside a meetinghouse during a Quaker fair. The reporter said she "chatted" with locals and reminisced about her "graduation from Carlisle College, and her Hollywood career." As usual, the children adored her. When asked why she was there, she answered emphatically, "Where you find the Quakers you will find me, because I love them."[5]

Meyer Berger wrote a column in 1956 titled "Redskin Colony of the Big City, Fifty Strong, Making Last Stand to Save Its Culture." The fifty belonged to the New York Metropolitan Group of American Indians, who, Berger said, held regular monthly meetings "to save their culture." The American Indian population had grown significantly since Red Wing first arrived in the city. Berger estimated that "600 to 800" American Indians lived around "Red Hook in Brooklyn." Most were Mohawk bridge and construction workers, but their population also included accountants, nurses, and a psychiatrist, as well as those who worked at the Wigwam, Tepee Town, and the Plume, Native handicraft stores that also served "as the Indian grapevine." Red Wing was one of the few who made doeskin dresses for ceremonials and powwows, which, Berger noted, "the old Winnebago movie star" regularly attended.[6]

Two years later Berger interviewed Red Wing at her West End Avenue studio, but that was the last year she lived there. Shortly after the interview, the Mayor's Committee on Slum Clearance leveled eighteen blocks of Red Wing's neighborhood. Red Wing was among the seven thousand poor families, mostly African American and Hispanic, displaced by the urban renewal project. Like the others, who were supposed to receive financial assistance from the city for their upheaval, redevelopment forced Red Wing to move to another low-income neighborhood without any recompense. She relocated to the Hell's Kitchen neighborhood, where she lived for nearly the rest of her life.[7]

In October 1959 *Life Magazine* published "De Mille's Epic Story of Film's First Epic," a story and photos that paid tribute to the prolific and successful director, who had died in January.[8] Red Wing appears in four large photos from *The Squaw Man* production, including one that shows her aiming a gun at Cash Hawkins. The next month *Life Magazine* printed a letter to the editor from *Film in Review* critic Jack Spears, who earlier had praised Red Wing for her "beautifully restrained performance" in *The Squaw Man*.[9] Spears contacted Red Wing and told *Life* readers what she was up to at the present time. A photo that accompanies his letter shows Red Wing and another woman, perhaps Anita De Frey, in Indian dress. The caption reads, "One of the few surviving members of the cast of Cecil B. DeMille's The Squaw Man."[10]

As one of the only surviving old-timers, Red Wing was invited as a guest of honor to the dedication of the new DeMille Theater in Times Square the first week in December 1959. The Loews Mayfair Theater was not actually new, but its name changed to honor the late legendary director. The theater planned to debut a new "AromaRama" version of *Behind the Great Wall*, complete with fragrances such as tangy orange and sandalwood to enhance the sight and sound of the Chinese travelogue.[11] *Motion Picture Daily* reported on the dedication, stating, "Redwing and Princess Juanita, stars of 'Squaw Man,' DeMille's first film, Jacqueline Logan, femme star of the classic 'King of Kings' and 'Fool's Paradise,' and Shannon Day, featured in 'Forbidden Fruit,' will be among the socialites, celebrities, civic officials and industry notables who will attend the debut of the film."[12] The event turned out to be a wonderful night for Red Wing and "Princess Juanita," who was not really a *Squaw Man* alum but Anita De Frey.

De Frey recorded her impressions of the evening that meant so much to her friend: "Red Wing was requested to appear there at the dedication ceremonies, which she most graciously consented to do, and she was acclaimed by a capacity audience, not only for the wonderful contribution her acting gave to the early days of the motion picture industry and to the success of this great producer, but for the dynamic and scintillating personality that is still hers, and that thrills the audience the moment she walks on stage." De Frey also averred that Red Wing and DeMille shared "a deep friendship" all his life.[13]

Red Wing celebrated her eightieth birthday with Long Island Indians and others in February 1964. The Indian League of America sponsored the event for her, and Vina, a leader of the organization, arranged a fabulous party in Manhattan for the grand dame of the New York Indians.[14] NBC news also interviewed her that day, but the broadcast has been lost. After a Nebraskan saw Red Wing on the news, the *Omaha Herald* reported on three other state residents who knew Red Wing. "Redwing has visited my grandmother's home many times," said one. "The last time I saw her was 30 years ago. I remember she was dressed in a long, white buckskin dress, hat and boots. Diamonds on three fingers of both hands. Quite fat but still beautiful." Still another said she'd received a letter from Red

Wing the previous summer. "I don't travel around as much as I used to," Red Wing wrote to her, "but New York is my headquarters and I made costumes (Indian) and headdresses or war bonnets for theatrical trade and television. . . . I haven't been to Nebraska since the Powwow at Winnebago about four years ago."[15]

As much as the 1950s were relatively happy years, the 1960s brought Red Wing the physical discomfort of an aging body, the social challenge of a generation gap, and the political effects of a revolutionary shift in consciousness. During her mideighties Red Wing began to suffer health problems, and in the late 1960s she was diagnosed with cancer. The disease remained in remission, fortunately, following surgery. Soon after, heart problems plagued her, so her doctor implanted a pacemaker, which at the time was a relatively new device.

Still, Red Wing fared better than most elderly American Indians across the United States. Vice President Hubert Humphrey headed the National Council of Indian Opportunity to "end moons of neglect" in 1968. The situation of "the nation's 600,000 Indians" was dire, reported the *New York Times*. Forty percent were unemployed, which was ten times the national average. High school dropouts were double the national average, and Indians lived "only about two-thirds as long as other Americans." Sympathizers rightly blamed government policies that supported "yesterday's bloody oppression and eviction to today's stultifying paternalism and neglect."[16]

The long-overdue reckoning inspired a celebration in Prospect Park in 1968. After forty years, Princess Morning Star (Vina) and Chief Running Horse, representing the Brooklyn Indians, received borough president Abe Stark's official proclamation that the fourth Saturday in September would be officially designated as Indian Day—at least in Brooklyn.[17]

The world dramatically changed by 1970. Many U.S. citizens held a patronizing view of America's Indigenous people that overshadowed Red Wing's desire and struggle to represent her people in a positive light. Although the idealistic and rebellious youth of the late 1960s embraced the communal and ecological values espoused by American Indians, their identification with Indigenous people expressed the generation gap more than political solidarity. Moreover, even with an awareness of cultural relativity, anthropologists and other academics ultimately defined Native culture for the masses, as Dakota intellectual Vine Deloria Jr. pointedly examined in his "Indian manifesto," *Custer Died for Your Sins*. The manifesto, published in 1969, accompanied the emergence of the American Indian Movement (AIM).

Deloria's words touched the heart and soul of Indian Country. AIM activists occupied Alcatraz Island in San Francisco Bay in 1968, while white upper-class and middle-class hippies came in droves to the City of Love looking for Utopia and seeking lost innocence. They appropriated braids, beads, and moccasins to signify their rejection of the social and political conservatism of their parents. As Spokane / Coeur d'Alene author Sherman Alexie humorously contends, "All the hippies were trying to be Indians."[18]

The fashionable and elite New York City folk upped the ante. They espoused the hippy ethos to become "radical chic," a term coined by New York journalist Tom Wolfe in 1970. Wolfe named and satirized the new movement in an article in *New York* magazine, "Radical Chic: That Party at Lenny's." With biting satire he chewed up and spit out the remains of a fashionable party given in January 1970 by composer Leonard Bernstein and his wife, Felicia Montealegre. The shindig was a fund-raiser for the Black Panther Party. Lenny and Felicia invited a few Black Panthers as guests of honor, but according to Wolfe, the soirée seemed like a cause célèbre to highlight the hosts' social standing and conspicuous consumption.

Lenny and Felicia lent their support to the radical cause of their black guests, but Wolfe's cultural critique reveals how the elite's desire to enhance their social status trumped political commitment and true empathy. "Lenny stands here in his own home radiating the charm and grace that make him an easy host for leaders of the oppressed," Wolfe ironically put it. Highlighting the difference between the manners and mien of the white elite and the Black Panther guests, Wolfe asserted that the latter elicited a kind of perverse desire in the former. "God, what a flood of taboo thoughts runs through one's head at these Radical Chic events," he wrote. "But it's delicious. It is as if one's nerve-endings were on red alert to the most intimate nuances of status. Deny it if you want to!

. . . It is like the delicious shudder you get when you try to force the prongs of two horseshoe magnets together . . . *them* and *us*." Wolfe's scathing reproach concluded that the radical chic couldn't support revolution as long as they embraced white privilege.[19]

The next summer Red Wing was invited to a similar party in Southampton, Long Island, but this time the hosts invited Indians as their oppressed minority. *New York Times* style writer Charlotte Curtis, whose column on Bernstein's party agitated Wolfe to write his essay, also covered Red Wing's gathering. "For a while there, it looked as if parties for minority underdogs of one sort or another would come to a screeching halt," she stated. "Mr. and Mrs. Leonard Bernstein were severely criticized for entertaining Black Panthers in their Park Avenue apartment. Mrs. Randolph Guggenheimer got it for her spaghetti dinner for the Puerto Rican Young Lords. And Andrew Stein was denounced for inviting Cesar Chavez's Mexican-American grape pickers to his family's palatial Southampton mansion. Mr. Stein, however, has refused to be intimidated. The young Assemblyman from Manhattan's Upper East Side was at it again last night—this time at a huge cocktail party in honor of the American Indian." Political activist LaDonna Harris (Comanche) and her husband, Democratic senator Fred R. Harris of Oklahoma, cohosted the event. Their daughter Laura handed out Americans for Indian Opportunity flyers for her mother. "Awareness is really the most important thing we'd like to project," LaDonna explained to Curtis, "No more of this, 'Lo, the poor Indian.' That's out. We want to be more positive." Red Wing shared Harris's new attitude, but she had done so all of her life.[20]

Several Indian representatives served double duty as party entertainment. Perry Horse (Kiowa) performed fancy dancing, and Floyd Westerman (Dakota) sang songs from his soon-to-be-released album, *Custer Died for Your Sins.* John Shopteese, a Potawatomi from the Department of Health, Education, and Welfare; William Seneca, governor of the Seneca Nation; and Long Island leaders Harry Williams (Shinnecock) and Junie Langhorn (Poospatuck) represented the Indians' governing body. José Torres, a Puerto Rican champion prizefighter, also accepted the invitation; however, Curtis reminded her readers that his nickname was "Everybody's Favorite Primitive."

The white elites, intellectual, political, and just plain wealthy, were well represented. The radical feminist icon Betty Friedan, author of *The Feminine Mystique* (1963), arrived with her housemate, Columbia University professor of sociology William J. Goode, known for *World Revolution and Family Patterns* (1963). New York senator Jacob K. Javits, an early opponent of the Vietnam War, stood in for liberal politicians. Eleanor Searle Whitney, former wife of Cornelius Vanderbilt Whitney and a philanthropist and evangelist singer; Ethel Redner, the wife of Robert Scull, Pop Art collector and Manhattan taxicab tycoon; and retired real estate mogul Joseph Weinstein represented the rich folk.

Curtis evidently planned to hone an ironic account of Andrew Stein's affair, since Wolfe had skewered her for her too-focused-on-style-and-not-on-substance take on Bernstein's party. Initially, Curtis set up Stein as her foil. Stein is known today for changing his political stripes, being convicted for a Ponzi scheme, and supporting his friend President Donald Trump through hell and high water. However, in the 1970s Stein still espoused liberal political views. "The American Indian got the biggest screwing in American history," Curtis quoted Stein. "This was their country and we took it away from them. We've ignored them for years. I think we should be doing what we can to correct this situation." Red Wing had some ideas on the matter, but apparently no one thought to ask her opinion.

Curtis let it be known that Stein didn't really intend to do much about "the biggest screwing in American history." Instead, he simply invited "scores of Indians and hundreds of frankly rich Southampton residents to his family's house," and they "predictably" accepted the invitation. Curtis further alluded to the irony in Stein's egalitarian employment of both "black and white maids" to serve the party's guests.

Curtis highlighted Eleanor Whitney's comments to further emphasize the disparity between the radical chic and their "pet primitives." "I've loved Indians all my life. . . . We must take action," Whitney told Horse and Shopteese, who "nodded politely, stared at her floppy red and white pajamas with the Navajo turquoise and silver jewelry, and indicated that they, too, had loved Indians all their lives." When Whitney walked away, Shopteese responded, "There are still lots of myths that have to be changed," including, he said, that Indians invented scalping.

Curtis wryly observed that Harris "crossed tribal lines" in her choice of attire, "a white pants suit printed with the Cherokee alphabet and a black, brown and white Cherokee alphabet scarf." Somehow Curtis missed the bigger picture when Harris explained to her, "It's the only Indian language that's written." Redner worried about the "motley crew" of guests, none of whom dressed like "real Indians." "Indians in coats and ties and paleface Southampton women in beads, feathers, fringed leather and all the other bits and pieces of what passes for Indian fashion" seemed to astonish her. Her assessment reveals why Red Wing had so much biracial business making Plains Indian regalia.

Friedan's housemate, Goode, said he was "staggered by the fashion" as well. "My God, the colors the [white] men allow themselves. It's one thing for the women, but the men!" Goode had a point. His attire, "fish net see-through shirt" with a metallic necklace and brown leather sandals, was neutrally toned. Betty Friedan merged fashion sense with gender politics, insisting, "I know people are going to criticize this thing . . . but I don't care. It's better to be radical chic than chic effete." Goode agreed. In response, Weinstein urged, "It was time for another Black Panther party."

Red Wing had the final say on the matter. Curtis cast her as the common man, the nonplussed Indian, and the aging silent film star: "Red Wing, an 87-year-old Winnebago princess said she'd never heard of the Panthers." "All I know," Red Wing remarked, "is Indians and how to make costumes for TV." Of course, she also reminded everyone, "I was in 'The Squaw Man' with Dustin Farnum. That was Cecil B. DeMille's first movie, you know."

As Farnum once noted, Red Wing "stuck to cases," but she also stuck out like a sore thumb amid the cultural revolution of the late 1960s and early 1970s. Most non-Native supporters, whether radical chic or just well-meaning, thought they really understood what had happened to the Indigenous people of their continent and what should be done about it. They were sorely misguided, as Deloria argued. What they thought they knew came from movies, from novels, and through the research of academics who utilized American Indians as objects of study. Most Americans were not versed in the situation of historic Native people—let alone contemporary ones.

The so-called crying Indian public service ad, released on Earth Day in 1971 and sponsored by the Keep America Beautiful campaign, signifies their misplaced identification. Iron Eyes Cody, dressed in buckskin, paddled a birch-bark canoe through littered waters as polluting factories smothered the landscape. When he shed a single tear, millions of liberals teared up in response. His stoic show of emotion heightened their alarm about the human degradation of Mother Earth. Everyone knew Indians only cried if things were truly dire. Moreover, Cody's portrayal of the crying Indian transformed the western movie actor into the ultimate representative of American Indians for a generation, even though he was an Italian American actor posing as a Sioux.

Red Wing knew Cody, but, as has been mentioned more than once, she was not one to harshly judge non-Native Indian performers. She further believed that the roles she played did not authenticate her as an American Indian. Her authenticity came from her origins. Today, when so many Native people are speaking out about what is culturally authentic, what qualifies as cultural appropriation, and what counts as respectful representation of Native Americans and their culture, Red Wing appears lacking. However, in her day, historical trauma was implicit, oppression was a given, inequality was a rule, disrespect was prevalent, and pity stood in for empathy. It took bold courage and splendid effervescence to shine her light through the barriers, barbs, and boundaries of a society that allowed for only the distorted and mostly negative view of American Indians.

In November 1971 Mary Pickford, who had left acting long before to run her own successful film production company, opened a letter sent to her Beverly Hills address from Jackson Heights, New York. It was not another fan letter but a request from Carol Delaine Bennett, who wanted to pay tribute to her friend Red Wing. Bennett was the widow of Harold Bennett, principal flutist for the Metropolitan Opera. She informed Pickford that she worked with "the American Indians." Her granddaughter confirms that she was involved in "the Native American civil rights movement" and also that she revered Native American culture. Bennett collected books on the subject, as well as "exquisite hand-carved totem poles" and other handcrafted items, some of which Red Wing probably made.

However, Red Wing's "fascinating career" and "remarkable personality" compelled Bennett to write to Pickford. After listing some of her film credits, including one Pickford shared, *The Mended Lute*, Bennett wrote, "Red Wing, despite her age and ill health . . . is reasonably active and is still a remarkably beautiful woman. Although she has worked with and associated with non-Indians most of her life, she has retained her Indian background, heritage, customs, and beliefs, and through her intelligence and personality wields considerable influence on the metropolitan Indian population as well as on her non-Indian friends."

Bennett told Pickford that Red Wing deserved "some definite recognition" and informed her that several of Red Wing's friends had urged her "to write her memoirs." Bennett noted that Red Wing at nearly ninety years old had a "fantastic memory" and "is still completely lucid." Bennett hoped to bring her tape recorder to Red Wing's apartment "and just let her talk." Red Wing had declined an offer for an interview with the woman's page editor at the *New York Times*. Bennett suspected Red Wing felt embarrassed to have the woman see her inelegant "surroundings." Yet like Meyer Berger and Anita De Frey, Bennett, as she told Pickford, found Red Wing's domicile "colorful and interesting" with its "enormous collection of the most exquisite Indian beadwork" and career memorabilia.

"We want very much to have Dick Cavett interview her on his TV Show," Bennett explained. Red Wing enjoyed *The Dick Cavett Show* and felt "a certain kinship" with her fellow Nebraskan. Although Bennett couldn't convince Red Wing to allow someone to write her memoirs, Red Wing had agreed to appear on TV. Bennett asked Pickford for the "prestige of your personal interest" and asked her if she would be "interested in being on the Cavett Show" with Red Wing.[21] She further pressed Pickford to use her influence and telephone or write to Red Wing "to encourage her to appear on the show and to consent to any interview worthy of her efforts." She also wondered if Pickford could locate any copies of Red Wing's movies that could be shown on TV and at a benefit Bennett was hosting to "bolster funds of the Red Wing St. Cyr Scholarship Fund for American Indian Students." "She is very proud to have appeared in films with you," Bennett wrote, and "hearing from you would be a very great thrill for her, as it would be for anyone."[22]

Pickford usually asked her assistant to answer her letters, but this one she answered personally. However, her response is unknown. Whatever her response, Red Wing never appeared on *The Dick Cavett Show*.

As her days grew fewer Red Wing left Hell's Kitchen and moved in with the Slatins. They lived in a brownstone walk-up in Greenwich Village at 11 Bank Street. Yeffe believed the house was haunted and had earlier invited Meyer Berger to attend a séance. He actually came. It's unknown if Red Wing was at the ritual or even if she believed in such things, but when she moved into the brownstone sometime between 1971 and 1974, the house was often full of spirited artists, intellectuals, scientists, and other Indians.

The social scene at Yeffe and Harvey's kept Red Wing in touch with important political events, like Watergate, as well as AIM's 1973 occupation of Wounded Knee. As Red Wing slowed down, the Red Power movement gained force. Red Wing celebrated her ninetieth birthday on February 13, 1974. Harvey more than Yeffe probably took care of Red Wing's daily needs. He just adored her, according to Anne Slatin, not to mention that her calming presence soothed his volatile wife. However, the love and care Red Wing received from the Slatins could not repair her failing heart. On March 12 her pacemaker stopped, and she was rushed to Roosevelt Hospital. At midnight on March 13, she died in Harvey's arms.[23]

Red Wing's remains went to New Jersey, where her body was cremated. Yeffe announced the funeral for the "Beloved Indian Leader" for March 15 in New York City. In lieu of flowers, Yeffe requested that contributions be sent to the Wounded Knee Defense Fund—a fitting tribute to the Indian actress and activist.

Eventually, the Mofsies returned Red Wing's remains to her first home. She was buried with her loved ones in the St. Augustine Cemetery on the reservation. Both "Lillian (Lily) St. Cyr" and "Red Wing of the Silent Film Era" are etched on her headstone, while her Indian name, Ah hoo such win gah (Wing Red Woman), is rendered there for eternity in the Ho-Chunk language rather than in the Lakota from which it came. Yeffe donated Red Wing's well-worn *Squaw Man* dress and some photographs to the Wisconsin Center for Film and Theater Research in Madison, where long ago Red Wing's ancestors celebrated the first Independence Day.

Red Wing outlived so many she had worked with, including nearly everyone, if not all, from the first *Squaw Man.* She also survived her former young partner, Norman Tyndall, who went on to train animals for Hollywood films and who died six weeks before her. Because she was one of the last surviving pre-Hollywood pioneers, scores of newspapers, including the *New York Times*, Omaha's *World-Herald*, the *Carlisle Sentinel*, and the *Los Angeles Times,* announced her passing.[24] After all, she was the *first* American Indian lady of the movies. Of all the eulogies she received, the Museum of the American Indian in New York perhaps characterized her best:

> We deeply regret the passing of a good friend of the Museum. Red Wing died on Tuesday, March 19th, after a long illness. She was ninety years old. She was well known as Nat-u-rich, the leading player in Cecil B. DeMille's 1914 film "Squaw Man," the first feature-length film to be made in Hollywood. To many of us, an even more memorable quality was her fine craftsmanship—she was an excellent beadwork artist. She was a student at Carlisle Indian School, and following graduation, she played for many years opposite Tom Mix and other stars of the silent screen era. She is the last of the true Old Timers, and the tune *Redwing* will always remind us of her vitality and beauty.[25]

APPENDIX A
Lilian Margaret St. Cyr Family

PARENTS: Mitchell St. Cyr Jr. (ca. 1835–89) and Julia Decora (ca. 1846–85)

FATHER'S PARENTS: Michel St. Cyr (adoptive) (ca. 1811–96) and Angelique Nausararesca (1824–ca. 1864)

MOTHER'S PARENTS: Tall "Baptiste" Decora (ca. 1820–83) and Younkaw (Queen Woman) (ca. 1819–1901)

FATHER'S FATHER'S PARENTS: Hyacinth St. Cyr (1784–1849) and Henokaw (unknown)

FATHER'S MOTHER'S PARENTS: unknown

MOTHER'S FATHER'S PARENTS: White War Eagle (son of Chougeka Decarrie (ca. 1750[?]–1836) and Carrimonie daughter (unknown)

MOTHER'S MOTHER'S PARENTS: unknown

LILIAN'S SIBLINGS:

1. David Rueben (1864–1940)

   •SPOUSE: Cora Frenchman (1866–1945)

   •several children

   •SPOUSE: Maggie Raymond Harden (ca. 1880–after 1940)

   •one child

2. Julia J. (1868–1947)

   •CHILD: Leo Cecil White (1891–1957); father: George Whitewing Sr. (ca. 1855–unknown)

   •SPOUSE: George A. Travis (1871–1926)

3. Annie (1869–1939)

- •SPOUSE: St. Pierre Owen (1871–1942)

- •CHILDREN: Devillo Jason Owen (1894–1942) and Pauline Addie Owen Gallup Lang (1905–87)

4. Minnie (ca. 1870–1919)

- •SPOUSE: Benjamin Lowry (1868–after 1940)

- •CHILDREN: *Alvina (1897–1986), Lillian Margaret (1901–67), and Annie St. Cyr Lowry (1903–82)

5. Louis Laurence St. Cyr (1877–1938)

- •SPOUSES: Mabel Frenchman (1887–1960) and Rosa Maria Frenchman (1882–1913) (sisters)

- •no children

6. Pauline (ca. 1878–before 1887)

7. Eugene (1881–before 1885)

LILIAN'S HALF BROTHERS: Abner (1869–1944) and Levi M. St. Cyr (1871–1953)

- •MOTHER: Ocseeahoononickaw (ca. 1830–before 1880)

- •SPOUSES: Elizabeth (ca. 1874–1947) and Annie Frenchman (1877–1930), respectively

- •CHILDREN: both brothers had several

*Alvina Lowry (1897–1986)

- •SPOUSE: Morris Mofsie (1906–41)

- •CHILDREN: Norton "Nottie" (1929–37), Josephine Mofsie Tarrant (1934–75), and Louis Mofsie (b. 1936)

APPENDIX B
James Young Johnson Family

PARENTS: George Durham Johnson (1844–78) and Emma Margaret Young (ca. 1844–90)

FATHER'S PARENTS: Major Clarke Johnson (1809–91) and Lydia Ann LeCount (1814–81)

MOTHER'S PARENTS: Morduit Young (ca. 1782–1844) and Anna (ca. 1812–78) (no surname; she and her children were born into slavery)

MOTHER'S SIBLINGS: James Rodney (ca. 1825–73), Maria A. "Minty" (ca. 1826–69), and William Pinckney (ca. 1830–94)

FATHER'S FATHER'S PARENTS: William Henry George Johnson (dates unknown) and Nancy Clark (dates unknown)

FATHER'S MOTHER'S PARENTS: James Le Count (1777–1860) and Elizabeth Munce (1783–1848)

MOTHER'S MOTHER'S PARENTS: unknown

MOTHER'S FATHER'S PARENTS: William Young Jr. (ca. 1745–before 1798) and Ruth Ann Jackson (ca. 1753–unknown)

JAMES'S SIBLINGS:

1. Marie Louise Johnson (ca. 1868–71)

2. George Durham Johnson Jr. (1871–after 1940)

   • SPOUSE: Lydia Annice Dickerson (ca. 1872–1931)

   • CHILD: Annice Kay Johnson (1898–1986)

3. Minnie Annie Johnson (ca. 1873–1948)

- •SPOUSES: William Henry Fossett (ca. 1874–after 1910) and Alexander "Sandy" Moton (1876–1936)

- •no children

4. Harry W. Johnson (1878–1915)

- •SPOUSE: Gertrude Alexander (ca. 1880–after 1920)

- •CHILD: Thelma Johnson (1908–after 1930)

JAMES'S COUSINS: James Le Count Jr. (1845–78) and his sister, Caroline Rebecca LeCount (1846–1923)

APPENDIX C
Red Wing's Filmography, 1908–1931

RELEASE DATE	TITLE	NOTATIONS FOR UNCONFIRMED FILMS
1908		
ca. May 8	*The White Squaw* (Kalem)	
1909		
May 3	*The Falling Arrow* (Lubin)	
June 25	*The Cowboy's Narrow Escape* (Bison Life Motion Pictures)	
July 2	*A True Indian's Heart* (Bison)	
August 5	*The Mended Lute* (Biograph)	
August 20	*Half Breed's Treachery* (Bison)	
August 23	*The Indian Runner's Romance* (Biograph)	
September 24	*A Squaw's Sacrifice* (Bison)	PROBABLY
October 8	*Dove Eye's Gratitude* (Bison)	
October 12	*Red Wing's Gratitude* (Vitagraph)	
October 22	*Iona, the White Squaw* (Bison)	POSSIBLY
November 5	*Young Deer's Bravery*	UNKNOWN
November 19	*An Indian's Bride* (Bison)	PROBABLY
December 3	*The Message of an Arrow* (Bison)	
December 17	*The Love of a Savage* (Bison)	PROBABLY

1910

January 7	*The Red Girl's Romance* (Bison)	
February 15	*Government Rations* (Bison)	
March 1	*The Cowboy & the Schoolmarm* (Bison)	
March 8	*The Indian & the Cowgirl* (Bison)	
April 1	*A Shot in Time* (Bison)	
April 8	*Red Wing's Loyalty* (Bison)	
April 15	*Red Wing's Constancy* (Bison)	
April 22	*The Adventures of a Cowpuncher* (Bison)	
May 6	*Love and Money* (Bison)	
May 27	*Perils of the Plains* (Bison)	
May 31	*The Tie That Binds* (Bison)	
July 15	*Red Fern and the Kid* (Bison)	PROBABLY
August 12	*The Red Girl and the Child* (Pathé Frères)	
August 24	*A Cheyenne Brave* (Pathé)	
September 10	*Appeal of the Prairie* (Pathé)	UNKNOWN
September 20	*For the Love of Red Wing* (Bison)	
October 4	*Young Deer's Return* (Bison)	
November 4	*Red Wing and the White Girl* (Bison)	
November 15	*The Flight of Red Wing* (Bison)	
December 31	*The Yaqui Girl* (Pathé)	

1911

January 4	*The Cowboy's Innocence* (Pathé)
February 11	*Silver Leaf's Heart* (Pathé)

February 18	*Lieutenant Scott's Narrow Escape* (Pathé)	
March 8	*Red Deer's Devotion* (Pathé)	UNKNOWN
March 25	*The Kid from Arizona* (Pathé)	
May 3	*Indian Justice* (Pathé)	UNKNOWN
August 3	*Blue Wing and the Violinist* (Pathé)	
August 19	*The Message of the Arrow* (Pathé)	PROBABLY
August 24	*The Cheyenne's Bride* (Pathé)	
August 31	*The Medicine Woman* (Pathé)	UNKNOWN
September 20	*An Up-to-Date Squaw* (Pathé)	UNKNOWN
September 21	*Starlight's Necklace* (Pathé)	
September 27	*Driven from the Tribe* (Pathé)	
October 5	*The Squaw's Mistaken Love* (Pathé)	UNKNOWN
October 12	*Romance of the Desert* (Pathé)	
November 2	*A Sioux Lover's Strategy* (Pathé)	UNKNOWN
November 16	*A Western Postmistress* (Pathé)	
November 29	*The Incendiary Indians* (Pathé)	UNKNOWN
December 2	*A Bear Hunt Romance* (Pathé)	PROBABLY
December 7	*Poisoned Arrows* (Pathé)	UNKNOWN
December 28	*His Daughter's Bracelet* (Pathé)	PROBABLY

1912

January 4	*The Rebuked Indian* (Pathé)	UNKNOWN
January 6	*The Cowboy's Sister* (Pathé)	UNKNOWN
January 17	*The Squaw Man's Revenge* (Pathé)	UNKNOWN
January 24	*The Sioux's Cave of Death* (Pathé)	UNKNOWN
January 27	*Swiftwind's Heroism* (Pathé)	

February 3	*Indian Blood* (Pathé)	PROBABLY
February 17	*Pawnee Love* (Pathé)	UNKNOWN
February 28	*The Squaw's Debt of Gratitude* (Pathé)	PROBABLY
March 6	*Cholera on the Plains* (Pathé)	UNKNOWN
March 16	*The Arrow of Defiance* (Pathé)	UNKNOWN
March 27	*A Victim of Firewater* (Pathé)	
April 25	*For the Papoose* (Pathé)	
May 1	*The Red Man's Honor* (Pathé)	UNKNOWN
May 2	*The Cowboy Girls*	
May 15	*Orphans of the Plains* (Pathé)	
May 16	*Justice of the Manitou* (Pathé)	UNKNOWN
May 26	*The Prospector's Sweetheart*	UNKNOWN
June 13	*A Redskin's Appeal* (Pathé)	
June 22	*An Indian Idyl* [sic] (Pathé)	PROBABLY
June 27	*The Deerslayer's Retribution* (Pathé)	
June 29	*The Squawman's Sweetheart* (Pathé)	
July 6	*The Wooing of White Fawn* (Pathé)	
July 12	*The Unwilling Bride* (Pathé)	
July 20	*The Half-Breed's Foster Sister* (Pathé)	UNKNOWN
July 24	*His Second Love* (Pathé)	UNKNOWN
August 14	*Silver Wing's Two Suitors* (Pathé)	
September 5	*The Penalty Paid* (Pathé)	
September 21	*Silver Moon's Rescue* (Pathé)	PROBABLY
October 10	*The Horse Thieves* (Pathé)	

November 13	*Red Eagle, the Lawyer* (Pathé)	PROBABLY
November 30	*The Winning of White Dove* (Pathé)	
December 28	*The Bear Trap* (Pathé)	

1913

January 2	*The Frame-Up* (Pathé)	
January 22	*The Unfulfilled Oath* (Pathé)	
February 6	*The Bear Hunter* (Pathé)	
February 27	*The Pioneer's Recompense* (Pathé)	
March 13	*The Love That Turned* (Pathé)	PROBABLY
April 23	*The Outlaw* (Pathé)	UNKNOWN
May 3	*General Scott's Protégé* (Pathé)	
May 14	*A Redskin's Mercy* (Pathé)	
May 31	*The Squaw Man's Awakening* (Pathé)	PROBABLY
August 13	*The Erring Brother* (Pathé)	UNKNOWN
August 14	*The House Divided* (Pathé)	PROBABLY
August 19	*The Mexican Gambler*	PROBABLY
September 6	*The Price of Jealousy* (Pathé)	UNKNOWN
September 24	*The Secret Treasure* (Pathé)	UNKNOWN
October 14	*A Yankee in Mexico* (Pathé)	UNKNOWN
October 17	*The Bullet's Mark* (Pathé)	UNKNOWN
November 27	*The Faithless Friend* (Pathé)	
December 3	*A Break for Freedom* (Pathé)	
December 5	*A Bear Escape* (Pathé)	UNKNOWN
December 23	*An Indian Don Juan* (Pathé)	
December 31	*By the Two Oak Trees* (Pathé)	

1914

February 15	*The Squaw Man* (Jesse Lasky)
November 30	*In the Days of the Thundering Herd* (Selig Polyscope)

1915

June 7	*Fighting Bob* (Metro-Rolfe)
November 1	*Carmen* (Jesse Lasky)

1916

February 6	*Tennessee's Pardner* (Jesse Lasky)
April 5	*Ramona* (Clune)

1925

May 16	*Soul Fire* (First National Pictures)

1931

January 1	*Red Lass on Skyscraper* (Universal Newspaper Newsreel)

* There are many more films listed in the book that Red Wing may have appeared in even when there was no "Indian girl" character.

NOTES

CDNC   California Digital Newspaper Collection, https://cdnc.ucr.edu
CO   City of Orange Public Library, http://history.cityoforange.org
FHC   Old Fulton New York Post Cards, fultonhistory.com
MHDL   Media History Digital Collection, mediahistoryproject.org
NARA   National Archives and Records Administration
NARA-CPR   NARA Central Plains Region, Kansas City, Missouri
NARA-DC   NARA Washington DC
NARA-SL   NARA St. Louis, Missouri
NPAC   NewspaperArchives, newspaperarchives.com
NPC   newspapers.com
RG   Record Group

INTRODUCTION

1. Meyer Berger, "Red Wing, Once a Film Star, Now Makes Indian Regalia on West End Ave.," About New York, *New York Times*, May 16, 1958.

1. LILIAN MARGARET ST. CYR OF THE WINNEBAGO

1. She signed her name "Lilian," though it often appears in print as "Lillian."
2. "1884–1885," Series 21: Reservation Censuses, 1867–1966, Textual, box 23 of 40, ARC 10: 6077651, RG75, NARA-CPR. My research on Ho Chunk families, particularly those with French Canadian ancestry, has been extensive. For the sake of brevity not all NARA tribal records are cited in the notes, please consult the bibliography.
3. Julia's parents had at least four more sons after her birth. Julia Decora also had two half brothers, one through her mother and one through her father.
4. Although her name has been interpreted as "Glory of the Morning" or "Coming of the Dawn," given its spelling and other similar names I've encountered, I think it may translate to something closer to "French Woman," "White Woman," or "Spirit Woman." The Ho-Chunk initially characterized the French Canadians who visited them with guns and domestic goodies as "spirits."
5. Smith, *Treaties and Agreements*, n.p.
6. Anthropologist Nancy Lurie explains the role of the civil chief, clarifying Lilian's lineage and her family's changing leadership role in the tribe: "In pre-contact and

early contact times . . . a dual chieftainship prevailed with the civil chief drawn from the Thunder Clan and a sort of police force with its chief drawn from the Bear Clan. As the Winnebago began to spread into western Wisconsin and northwestern Illinois . . . it appears that as greater band autonomy set in, each band tried to reproduce the system of dual chieftainship to order local affairs while recognizing the existence of a head or tribal chieftainship. However, the tribal chieftainship became more and more honorific rather than a politically significant office for both the Thunder and Bear chiefs who occupied it" ("A Check List," 50).

7. Decorah, "Narrative of Spoon Decorah," 448–49. "Zhuminaka" appears to be a Ho-Chunk term for "Fire Water." Sam Decora, Conokaw's grandson, rendered the name "Shu-me-na-gah" ("Estate of George Decora No. 1," 363–70, roll 86, M234, RG 75, NARA-CPR).

8. "De-ca-ri" (1825); "Hee-tshah-wau-sharp-skaw, kau, White War Eagle" (1829); and "Hee-tshah-wau-saip-skaw, skaw, White War Eagle, De-kaw-ray, sr. (1832)" (Smith, *Treaties and Agreements*, n.p.).

9. Diedrich, *Winnebago Oratory*, 44.

10. Kinzie, *Wau-bun*, 387.

11. Conokaw's baptismal name, recorded just before he died, was "John Schachip-kaka" (Hansen, "Records of St. John Nepomucene Catholic Church"; see also Mazzuchelli, *Memoirs*, for an account of Conokaw's baptism).

12. Diedrich, *Winnebago Oratory*, 66. He is referring to his baptism by a Catholic missionary, which probably occurred in the 1830s.

13. Conversation with David Lee Smith, tribal historian for the Winnebago Tribe of Nebraska, 2000.

14. Smith, *Treaties and Agreements*, 23, 33.

15. For the family relations between the St. Cyrs and the Ho-Chunk, see Waggoner, *"Neither White Men,"* 18, 36, 38–39, 118–19. The NARA tribal sources I've consulted are too numerous to cite. I've also consulted the tribal newspaper, *Winnebago Chieftain* (microfilm, Nebraska State Historical Society); Indian school newsletters, such as the *Peace Pipe* (microfilm, Ho-Chunk Historical Society); other Nebraska newspapers; the Papers of Alice Fletcher and Francis LaFlesche, MS 4558, Smithsonian National Anthropological Archives; and "Marriage Books," Thurston County Courthouse, Pender ne.

16. Schoolcraft passage quoted by Winnebago agent Jonathan C. Fletcher to confirm that Michel Sr. was a "Winnebago half-breed" and not a "Canadian half-breed" (*Wisconsin Historical Society Collections* 10:501).

17. "Michel St. Cyr, six years of age, the father being Hyacinth St. Cyr, Junior, the mother being a Winnebago woman named Josette" (Hansen, "Prairie du Chien Baptisms, 1817").

18. She has also been identified as Keenokou, the daughter of The Spaniard, who Michel St. Cyr, Sr. stated was "one of the first [principal] chiefs of the Winnebago

Nation" (Waggoner, *"Neither White Men,"* 39). George Catlin painted his portrait in 1828 (Catlin, *Letters and Notes,* 2:166). For the colored portrait, see Smithsonian American Art Museum, *Span-e-o-née-kaw, The Spaniard.*

19. No other American record of this man or someone with his surname comes up in an Ancestry.com search for the nineteenth century. Presumably he was white. However, a "Joseph-Marie Causic" appears in a French pension record index for this time (search at https://www.ancestry.com/).

20. Hansen, "Records of St. John Nepomucene Catholic Church." In 1860 St. Cyr's wife, as "Angelique Nansourerska," appears as a baptismal sponsor for Marie Therese Manigre [Manégre] ("Baptisms, 1856–1878, V. Sommereisen," New Ulm Historical Society, New Ulm MN). Angelique's sons, John and Hyacinthe St. Cyr, claimed she was "mixed blood," which usually signified mixed *Native* ancestry, while "half-breed" denoted European ancestry ("Alexander St. Cyr Heirship Case," roll 93, M234, RG 75, NARA-CPR). It has also been stated that she was related to the famous Ho-Chunk warrior Little Priest, but Michel St. Cyr's second (and plural) wife, Mink Woman, was his relation. A special note: The information about Joseph Causic as Mitchell's biological father was published in the *Sioux City (IA) Journal* in 2014 against my wishes. James Hansen of the Wisconsin Historical Society maintains the original source material and graciously shared it with me. I passed on the information about Causic to a relative of the St. Cyrs, who passed it on to the author of the newspaper article. Unfortunately, the St. Cyr family had not heard of Causic, which compels me to clarify the facts.

21. Today a bronze plaque on a granite boulder marks the site on Waconia Lane in Middleton, a suburb of Madison. It reads: "the Rowan-St Cyr fur-trade post 1832–1837" (Trading Post Oak, Lake Mendota). When St. Cyr bought the place it already had an impressive history. The year before Wallis constructed the trading post, military officials, headed by Wisconsin Territorial governor Henry Dodge, emphatically urged neutrality to some five thousand Ho-Chunk who were called there by runners during the Black Hawk War.

22. De La Ronde, "Personal Narrative," 360–61.

23. "Madison's Fur Traders." See also Draper, "Michel St. Cyr."

24. "Madison's Fur Traders."

25. In addition, the piece erroneously states, "Reportedly St. Cyr, a carpenter as well as trader and hosteler, helped to build the first post office in Madison, a log edifice located on the Capitol Square. He eventually moved on to Minnesota where he died in 1859" ("Madison's Fur Traders"). St. Cyr died in 1896.

26. Michael St. Cyr and Julia Angelique, Wisconsin Marriage Certificate, Iowa County, April 16, 1838. The year of his legal marriage to Angelique coincided with the disbursement of "mixed-blood" funds from the 1837 treaty. See Waggoner, *"Neither White Men."*

27. Hansen, "Records of St. John Nepomucene Catholic Church."

28. He was also paid fifteen dollars by the Winnebago agent for services rendered (roll 863, M234, RG 75, NARA-DC).

29. Their marriage was blessed on March 27, 1842 (Hansen, "The St. Cyr Family").

30. Paquette, "The Wisconsin Winnebagoes," 407.

31. Neill, *The History of Minnesota*, 483–87.

32. For example, Winnebago agent Jonathan E. Fletcher's 1853 report noted, "Michael St. Cyr has failed to give satisfaction as Farmer, not for lack of industry, but for want of energy and skill in the discharge of his duty; still in consideration of his connexion with the Indians his speaking their language, and his industry, I shall [see?] if the Department approves continue him in employ for the present, and pay him at the rate of $480.00 per annum, his contract with my provision[?] is $600 per annum" ("Report of the conduct"; see also Fletcher, "General Abstract").

33. The document reads: "We, Half-Breeds of the tribe are advised by the Indians to place our names to this. Alex Payeur, John B. Decarré, James Lequier, Simon Lequier, John Mayrand, Oliver Amelle, Alexis Lemier, Chas Chalefou, Wm Chalafou, John Pelky, Peter Perolt, Oliver Amell Jr, Michel St. Cyre, David Twiggs" (roll 932, M234, RG 75, NARA-DC). "John B[aptiste] Decarré" was apparently Tall Decora. In addition, the *St. Paul Pioneer Press* published a letter "bidding farewell" to one of the Catholic priests who headed the mission. Michel was also one of several cosigners of the letter published in *St. Paul Pioneer* Extracts, October 9, 1854, *Minnesota Genealogical Journal* 12. See also Hoffman, *The Church Founders*, 197–217.

34. "Julie St Seyre, Daughter of Michael St Cyre and of Angelique, his wife, was born the 28 of December, 1859" ("Baptisms, 1856–1878, V. Sommereisen," New Ulm Historical Society, New Ulm MN).

35. Donneley to Ramsey, "History," 2.

36. Galbraith to Thompson, No. 144, 266.

37. Anderson and Woolworth, *Through Dakota Eyes*, 1.

38. Carley, *The Dakota War*, 69. This number was reduced from 307.

39. Statement of Hyacinth St. Cyr (Alexander St. Cyr Heirship Case, roll 93, M234, RG 75, NARA-DC).

40. "Mitchell St. Cyr, 55 Half breed," wife and seven children received 80 acres in St. Clair, Minnesota (Irregularly Shaped Papers, 1849-1907, Item 103, Box 59, RG 75, Records of the Land Division, General Records, Bureau of Land Management, Springfield VA).

41. "Death of Mr. St. Cyr," *Mapleton Enterprise*, March 6, 1896, Blue Earth County Historical Society. His death record states he died February 27, 1896, of "senile debility" (Vital Records Office, Blue Earth County, Mankato MN).

42. "Winnebago Chiefs in New York City, 1866," Nebraska State Historical Society Photograph Collection. The photo may have been taken shortly after the delegation left Washington DC to visit New York, including the Brooklyn Naval

Yard ("The Army and the Navy," *Times-Picayune* [New Orleans LA], April 16, 1865, NPC). The individual chiefs were also photographed by a New York photographer at that time. See William Blackmore Collection.

43. The chiefs were Little Decora, Samuel King, Big Bear, Connohuttakaw, Good Thunder, One Horn, Little Thunder, Grey Wolf, Young Prophet, Young French, Old Laughter, Whirling Thunder, White Breast, and Young Rogue. See Sellers, "Diary," pt. 1:150.

44. Sellers, "Diary," pt. 1:159, 154. Paxson treated a wound for Mitchell's brother John St. Cyr, who served as captain of the Indian Police. An Indian woman had stabbed John in the knee, but Paxson gave no reason for the assault. Paxson also treated a "Mrs. St. Cyr" for an unknown condition. She may have been Mitchell's wife.

45. Sellers, "Diary," pt. 1:181–82.

46. Silas T. Learning of Decatur, Nebraska (who had also surveyed the Omaha reservation), surveyed the reservation. He is "Capt. Leamming" in Paxson's diary, apparently a mistranscription of the original diary. For an account of Learning, see Learning, "Personal Recollections," 77–83.

47. Sellers, "Diary," pt. 2:244–45.

48. Smith, *Ho-Chunk Tribal History*, 66.

49. These men were Bradford Porter, Big Head, No-so-ho-Kaw, Lieutenant Uptail, Charles English, Otter Smith, James Race [Rice], John Coo-Noo, Charles Mallory, Robert Lincoln, Henry M. Rice (Sellers, "Diary," pt. 2:273).

50. Good Red Bird Woman took care of her children after Sixth Daughter died sometime before 1880. Ocseeahoonoonickaw also had a daughter, born about 1859 in Minnesota, called Green Buffalo Woman.

51. "Enrollment of Winnebago Indians this Thursday & Friday December 9th & 10th 1880," Series 21: Reservation Censuses, 1867–1966, Textual, box 23 of 40, ARC ID: 6077561, RG 75, NARA-CPR.

52. "Still Pow-wowing," *Evening Critic* (Washington DC), August 24, 1881, Chronicling America: Historic American Newspapers, http://chroniclingamerica.loc.gov. The Omaha, on the other hand, complained that the Winnebago stole their horses, even though, "in 1864, as refugees, poor and naked, the Winnebago Indians came to the Omahas begging for a home." They asserted that the government's obligations to them, outlined in the 1865 treaty, in which they relinquished part of their reserve to the Winnebago, had not been fulfilled. Regarding the horses, one of the Ho-Chunk chiefs answered the charges: "The Winnebagoes have always been good friends to the Omahas—they smoked the pipe of peace with them." He also explained that the Winnebago stole horses in retaliation for the Omaha stealing their women (and implied that they valued horses more than women). One of the 1871 appointed Winnebago chiefs (who was initially a Métis interpreter) explained the situation but outlined a solution: "The great trouble was that the courts for the trial of theft

among them were very lax and the police system bad, and if they could have a court like the white people, petty crime would diminish. They have no proper jury system, and he suggested that a change in that direction should be made."

53. Harlan, *The Booker T. Washington Papers*, 88.

54. For this incident and Julia's relationship with Hampton Institute, see Waggoner, *Fire Light*, 53–55.

55. Mitchel St. Cyr to Isabel Eustis, February 17, 1882, Julia St. Cyr student file, Hampton University Archives, Hampton VA. The letter was penned for Mitchell by "Pre SND Martin, scribe."

56. See West, "Starvation Winter."

57. Fletcher, "A Phonetic Alphabet." The manuscript Fletcher used for her article shows it was signed while Fletcher was allotting land to the Nez Perce (series 26 and 27, Winnebago Field Notes to Winnebago Manuscript, box 31, Papers of Alice Fletcher and Francis LaFlesche, MS 4558, Smithsonian National Anthropological Archives).

58. Julia J. St. Cyr to Fletcher, June 28, 1885, series 1, Incoming Correspondence, 1884–85, Papers of Alice Fletcher and Francis LaFlesche, MS 4558, Smithsonian National Anthropological Archives.

59. St. Cyr to Fletcher, June 28, 1885. Julia J.'s brother David was working in Great Barrington, Massachusetts, when he wrote to Fletcher: "I just got a letter from Julia stating that Mother died on the 23 ult. and Father is getting worse with his eyes couldn't do any work and wishes me to come home which I could not do without your help so I will write you a letter I wish you would see the Commissioner as soon as you can and get him to get me a ticket from here to Chicago from there to Sioux City" (St. Cyr to Fletcher, July 7, 1885, series 1, Incoming Correspondence, 1884–85, Papers of Alice Fletcher and Francis LaFlesche, MS 4558, Smithsonian National Anthropological Archives).

60. St. Cyr to Fletcher, n.d., series 1, Incoming Correspondence, 1884–85, Papers of Alice Fletcher and Francis LaFlesche, MS 4558, Smithsonian National Anthropological Archives.

61. From "An Indian Graduate," *Southern Workman*, September 1886, Julia St. Cyr student file, Hampton University Archives, Hampton VA. Portraits taken of Mitchell during his 1881 visit to Washington DC indicate his eyes were infected. For example, see "Portrait of Winnebago man."

62. Julia again wrote Fletcher from the reservation: "I expected to go back to H[ampton] as Miss Richards wanted me to, also. There is not much going on here now. It is quite dull to me. I have gotten so used to the School. I was just completely lost when I came home" (series 1, Incoming Correspondence, July 20, 1885, Papers of Alice Fletcher and Francis LaFlesche, MS 4558, Smithsonian National Anthropological Archives).

63. Lindsey, *Indians at Hampton Institute*, 220. In October Julia wrote to the commissioner of Indian Affairs, according to Lindsey, detailing her complaints: "She had received lower wages than blacks," "Hampton refused to pay what it owed her," and "she had been made to scrub windows and cut wood, 'which is man's work.'"

64. "Winnebago Boarding School," 337.

65. Red Wing file, author's collection. Lilian kept the heirloom in a small manila envelope with the notation: "My father's letter to my sister Annie."

66. *The Executive Documents*, 407. Julia started work on July 1, 1888.

2. OCHSEGAHONEGAH AT THE LINCOLN INSTITUTE

1. "Indians Singing Pinafore," *Philadelphia Times*, March 3, 1889, NPC.

2. The reviewer actually said "a new line of usefulness and accomplishes for Lo" ("Indians Singing Pinafore," *Philadelphia Times*, March 3, 1889). The term "Poor Lo" derived from Alexander Pope's "An Essay on Man" (1732): "Lo, the poor Indian! Whose untutor'd mind / Sees God in clouds, or hears him in the wind." Although the term originally referred to the seventeenth century's romantic "noble Indian," by the nineteenth century, its meaning took on a darker ironic tone.

3. "Indians Singing Pinafore," *Philadelphia Times*, March 3, 1889, NPC. Sheridan denied he ever said, "The only good Indian is a dead Indian."

4. "Indians Singing Pinafore," *Philadelphia Times*, March 3, 1889, NPC.

5. "Indians Singing Pinafore," *Philadelphia Times*, March 3, 1889, NPC. Lilian often mentioned that she had graduated from Carlisle, but she left little account of her time in Philadelphia. Lincoln Institute school records have as yet not been found. The only reference I found in print regarding her attendance at Lincoln Institute besides the 1889 issue of the *Philadelphia Times* was forty years later in the "New Theatre Programme," *Harper (KS) Advocate*, October 26, 1922, NPC, and in only one of her scores of obituaries.

6. For a history of the Lincoln Institute, see "The Charity Case."

7. See Adams, *Education for Extinction*; and Ahern, "An Experiment Aborted."

8. "Educating Indian Boy," *Philadelphia Times*, February 8, 1889, NPC. It's likely that Julia St. Cyr contacted either the director of Hampton Institute or Alice Fletcher to request her siblings be taken to boarding school. The only list of Homes Indian students I discovered are from Church of the Ascension, Church of the Beloved, Church of the Epiphany, and Church of the Evangelist, Pennsylvania Church and Town Records, https://www.ancestry.com/. For a "census of children, between the ages of 5 and 18 years on the Winnebago Reservation" in 1893, see roll 312, M595, RG 75, NARA-DC. This list shows Lilian and Louis St. Cyr; Minnie and Annie were over eighteen at the time, so they are not listed.

9. "Lawyer Julia St. Cyr and Her Winnebago Folks," *Omaha Sunday World-Herald*, January 26, 1913, genealogybank.com; Meyer Berger, "About New York: Red Wing, Once a Film Star," *New York Times*, May 16, 1958.

10. See "The Home Probably to Close," *Philadelphia Times*, November 25, 1882, NPC.

11. See Eastman, *The Red Man's Moses*.

12. "A Creek Girl Writes of Our Trip to Philadelphia," *Indian Journal* (Muscogee OK), December 21, 1882, NPC. For another account of the parade and visit, see "The Indians," *Lancaster (PA) Daily Intelligencer*, October 27, 1882, NPAC.

13. Standing Bear, *My People the Sioux*, 148–49, 183.

14. "Lincoln Institution for Indian Girls," *Harrisburg (PA) Daily Independent*, November 24, 1882, NPC. See also "Lincoln Institution and Indian Girls," *National Republican* (Washington DC), December 12, 1882, NPC.

15. Eastman, *The Red Man's Moses*, 252.

16. For an overview of the validity of the fraud allegations, see Waggoner, *"Neither White Men,"* 1.

17. "The National Congress," *The Day* (New London CT), December 14, 1882, https://news.google.com. See also *Journal of the Senate*, December 11, 1882, 54. On November 30, 1883, the Educational Home under the general title of the Lincoln Institution also received $2,732.57 from Pennsylvania's State Treasury as a soldiers' orphan school (*Annual Report of the State Treasurer*, 43).

18. "School for Indian Children," *New York Times*, June 15, 1883.

19. "Indian Girls," *Lebanon (PA) Daily News*, September 20, 1883, NPC. See also "Ten Little Indian Girls," *Philadelphia Times*, September 19, 1883, NPC.

20. Iron Owl had more than one moniker, unless more than one great-niece of Sitting Bull attended the school. I'm assuming the names "Hattie Conkulu" and "Iron Owl" belong to the same girl. In addition, two accounts state that Bull on the Hill (or Tatanka-pabakan-najin, who signed the 1876 Treaty with the Sioux Nation) was the Sans Arc father of students Hattie Conkulu and Clara Richardson, who I'm assuming was Hattie's sister. To complicate matters, church records do not show these names. See "Sitting Bull at School," *Saint Paul (MN) Globe*, October 13, 1884; and "Homesick Indian Maidens," *Philadelphia Times*, August 3, 1886, NPC.

21. "100 Years Ago," *Gettysburg Times*, January 10, 1984, NPC. Regarding Pratt's students, see *Report of the Commissioner of Education*, 240. The number of girls adds up to forty-nine. The fiftieth student's name is unknown.

22. *Annual Report of the Board*, 15:36–37.

23. See Fear-Segal, "Nineteenth-Century Indian Education."

24. For Julia St. Cyr's experience at Hampton, see Waggoner, *Fire Light*, 51–53.

25. "Eighty-Four Indian Maids," *Philadelphia Times*, May 24, 1884, NPC.

26. *The Statutes at Large*, 1885, 92, 382.

27. For the Drexel family, see Sze, "St. Katharine Drexel." The Drexel Institute's most noted art instructor was Howard Pyle, the "father of American Illustration." One of his first and most gifted students was Ho-Chunk Angel De Cora (Lilian's cousin), who also attended Hampton Institute with Julia St. Cyr. Lincoln Institute also supplied models for some of De Cora's artwork ("Going to Teach Red Men," *Philadelphia Record*, March 2, 1899, https://news.google.com; see also Waggoner, *Fire Light*, for the life of Angel De Cora).
28. "Eighty-Four Indian Maids," *Philadelphia Times*, May 24, 1884, NPC.
29. Eva Johnson student file, Hampton University Archives, Hampton VA.
30. Cox quoted in "Philadelphia, September 7," *Railway News* 51:1156.
31. "Portrait of Winnebago man."
32. "Education and Training of American Indians," *Railway News* 51:1160–61.
33. Committee of the Social Science Section of the Civic Club, *Civic Club Digest*.
34. "Anna Bender," in Brudvig, "First Person Accounts."
35. "Eighty-Four Indian Maids," *Philadelphia Times*, May 24, 1884. For an account of her graduation that includes an illustration of Jane Eyre, see "Hundreds of Girl Graduates," *Philadelphia Times*, June 13, 1895; and "Indian Teachers Dined," *Philadelphia Times*, February 1, 1896, NPC. For her position as teacher, see *Annual Report of the Commissioner of Indian Affairs*, June 30, 1900, 728.
36. See Church of the Evangelist. Ancestry.com has indexed church records for students as "Roman Catholic," perhaps confusing this church with Philadelphia's St. John the Evangelist Catholic Church.
37. Whitaker confirmed Annie at the Church of the Epiphany with six other Lincoln Institute girls on April 7, 1889 (Church of the Epiphany).
38. When and if Annie St. Cyr was baptized are unknown, but she appears as a baptismal sponsor for two Winnebago girls, Margaret Beaver and Mary Yellowbank, at the chapel of the Educational Home in April 1893 (Church of the Evangelist). Today she lies in the Catholic cemetery in Winnebago with the rest of her family.
39. "Education and Training of American Indians," *Railway News* 51:1160–61.
40. "Education and Training of American Indians," *Railway News* 51:1160–61.
41. Welsh, *City and State*, 216–17.
42. Louis later played baseball in Nebraska and formed and captained a Winnebago football team partly composed of Carlisle alums ("City Eleven Now Forming," *Sioux City Journal*, December 5, 1911, NPC).
43. See "Chief Bender."
44. "Prev. Education: 2 yrs. Miss'n Educational Home, Phila. 3 mos. Govt. Genoa. Trade: Shoemaker. Wheelbarrow," Louis St. Cyr student file, Hampton University Archives, Hampton VA. Although this record said he attended the school for two years, Louis is shown at Philadelphia on the 1893 "census of children,

between the ages of 5 and 18 years on the Winnebago Reservation" (roll 312, M595, RG 75, NARA-DC).

45. *Annual Report*, vol. 23.

46. "School News and Notes," *Pipe of Peace* (Genoa NE), December 11, 1891, Ho-Chunk Historical Society.

3. ROLE MODELS AND VISITORS

1. For accounts of deaths at Carlisle, see "Excavating the Hidden History of Indian Children Who Died in Carlisle," *Inquirer Daily News* (Philadelphia), August 11, 2017, http://www.philly.com; and Fear-Segal and Rose, *Carlisle Industrial School*.

2. *Hiawatha* was also a typical production for Carlisle and Hampton Indian Schools.

3. Patterson, "The Spread Eagle Inn."

4. "Anna Bender," in Brudvig, "First Person Accounts."

5. "Sitting Bull at School," *Saint Paul (MN) Globe*, October 13, 1884, NPC. The article named Sitting Bull's great-niece "Hattie Conkuln" [*sic*], but as noted earlier, I believe she is the same person as Iron Owl.

6. "Sitting Bull at School," *Saint Paul (MN) Globe*, October 13, 1884, NPC.

7. "Indians at Play," *Philadelphia Times*, July 5, 1885, NPC.

8. "Philadelphia, Lincoln Institution," *Churchman*, May 2, 1885, 485, https://archive.org/details/TheMonthv51. The girls were left unnamed, and only one death record appears for only one girl at this time. Girls' deaths included Angie Jordan (September 30, 1884), Hattie Charko (March 14, 1886), Annie Afraid of Bear (March 11, 1887), Louisa Farnham (November 6, 1887), and Etta Springer (Omaha, April 23, 1890). Boys who died include Abraham Neck (February 14, 1885), John Robinson Long Neck (January 5, 1886), Frankie Bear (February 3, 1889), Samuel Porter (February 20, 1891), Charles A. Fisher (March 4, 1891), Charlie Hill (March 4, 1892), Edward Moore (June 20, 1892), and Joseph Norewas (April 5, 1893) (Philadelphia, Pennsylvania Death Certificates Index, 1803–1915). These children were all buried in the Woodlands Cemetery, located in the Woodlands National Historic Landmark District of Philadelphia. Later students who died were buried in the Fernwood Cemetery in Philadelphia.

9. Sue La Flesche to Rosalie La Flesche, October 24, 1886, La Flesche Family Papers, Green Library, Stanford University, Palo Alto CA.

10. "Homesick Indian Maidens," *Philadelphia Times*, August 3, 1886, NPC.

11. "Homesick Indian Maidens," *Philadelphia Times*, August 3, 1886, NPC. As earlier noted, two accounts identified Chief Bull on the Hill (Sans Arc) as the father of "Hattie Conkulu" (Iron Owl) and Clara Richardson (whose Indian name was said to be "Lucy").

12. Sue La Flesche to Rosalie La Flesche, October 24, 1886, La Flesche Family Papers, Green Library, Stanford University, Palo Alto CA.

13. For an insightful account about the development of pan-Indian identities in Indian boarding schools, see Lomawaima, *They Called It Prairie Light.*

14. See "Another Police Outrage," *Philadelphia Times,* February 19, 1892, and "Death after Disgrace," *Philadelphia Times,* February 21, 1892, NPC.

15. Philip C. Roubideaux and Nettie Hansell, 1893, Philadelphia Marriage Index, 1885–1951, https://www.ancestry.com/; Roland Mott (Matt?) Roubideaux baptism, May 14, 1894, Pennsylvania Church and Town Records, https://www.ancestry.com/; and Nettie Hansell Roubideaux, August 11, 1894, Pennsylvania, Philadelphia City Death Certificates, 1803–1915, https://www.familysearch.org/. Nettie and her son were buried in the Woodlands Cemetery in Philadelphia. A "Philip Roubideaux" received a reservation allotment on February 3, 1896 (Buffalo, South Dakota, U.S. General Land Office Records, 1776–2015, https://www.ancestry.com/).

16. "Great Chiefs in Town," *Philadelphia Times,* February 6, 1891, NPC.

17. "The Indian Chiefs Depart," *Philadelphia Times,* February 7, 1891, NPC. The Ghost Dance was the expression of a pan-Indian revival movement that predicted a flood would wipe out whites and bring back the Indians and the buffalo. The Paiute prophet Wovoka envisioned the Ghost Dance, and the movement spread to the Plains Indians. Ghost Dancers created "bulletproof" shirts and dresses that made the U.S. military nervous. Ghost Dancers also wore other items, as Lakota Plenty Eagles' letter to his sister reveals: "Now you must use every effort to come in possession of some Eagle's-down, and have them in readiness. From the time the grass starts you must be on the lookout and when a thunder storm comes you must attach them to your hair" (Gage, "Intertribal Communication").

18. McLaughlin told Herbert Welsh that this man was Bull Head. See "An Account of Sitting Bull's Death by James McLaughlin Indian Agent at Standing Rock Reservation (1891)," Archives of the West, PBS, http://www.pbs.org/weta/thewest/resources/archives/eight/sbarrest.htm.

19. "Great Chiefs in Town," *Philadelphia Times,* February 6, 1891, NPC.

20. "Great Chiefs in Town," *Philadelphia Times,* February 6, 1891, NPC.

21. "The Indian Chiefs Depart," *Philadelphia Times,* February 7, 1891, NPC.

22. "Great Chiefs in Town," *Philadelphia Times,* February 6, 1891, NPC.

23. Prucha, *Documents,* 175–76.

24. "Great Chiefs in Town," *Philadelphia Times,* February 6, 1891, NPC.

25. "Great Chiefs in Town," *Philadelphia Times,* February 6, 1891, NPC.

26. "Great Chiefs in Town," *Philadelphia Times,* February 6, 1891, NPC.

27. "Indians," *Philadelphia Times,* February 13, 1891, NPC.

28. "Braves from the West," *Philadelphia Times,* February 14, 1891, NPC. Those described as "very big injuns" were "Young-Man-Afraid-of-His-Horses, American Horse, Two Strikes, Little Wound, John Grass, Fast Thunder, Spotted Horse,

White Bird, Grass, High Pipe, High Frank, an Ogallala; Hollow Horn Bear, a Brule; Quick Bear, Spotted Elk, Big Mane, of Lower Brule; Medicine Bull, White Ghost, of Crow Creek Reservation; Wizi, Little-No-Heart, He Dog, Straight Head, Hump, Fire Lightning, One-to-Play-With, Big Road, Good Voice and Mad Bear, from Standing Rock."

29. "Braves from the West," *Philadelphia Times*, February 14, 1891, NPC. "Work was centered at Quaker Bridge ('Tunesassa'), NY where Friends established a boarding school in 1852 adjacent to the Allegany Reservation. Friends Indian School operated as a boarding school for Native Americans until 1938. The completion of the Kinzua Dam (Allegheny Reservoir) led to the flooding of much of the Allegany Reservation and the evacuation of Seneca families. Philadelphia Friends were active in helping the Seneca fight the construction of Kinzua" (Quaker and Special Collections).

30. "Braves from the West," *Philadelphia Times*, February 14, 1891, NPC.

31. "Braves from the West," *Philadelphia Times*, February 14, 1891, NPC.

32. "Braves from the West," *Philadelphia Times*, February 14, 1891, NPC. For Minnie, see also "Bright Young Indians, Graduates of the Lincoln Institutes Holding Honorable Positions," *Philadelphia Times*, January 22, 1892, NPC.

4. HOME AND AWAY AGAIN

1. The Autry Museum in Los Angeles holds Dixon's painting of Whitewing. See also Winther, "The Artist and His Model."

2. Julia St. Cyr to Samuel Armstrong, February 23, 1893, Julia St. Cyr student file, Hampton University Archives, Hampton VA.

3. See *Record of Indian Students Returned*.

4. *Record of Indian Students Returned*, 5.

5. See Cahill, *Federal Fathers and Mothers*.

6. Thurston County Nebraska marriages and Louis St. Cyr student file, Hampton University Archives, Hampton VA. Some scholars assert that Lilian lived with David St. Cyr during her childhood because they were not aware of her time in Philadelphia and because they probably misunderstood that Indian census rolls do not necessarily reflect where someone is living.

7. De Cora to Folsom, January 29, 1912, Angel De Cora student file, Hampton University Archives, Hampton VA.

8. Folder 7, Thomas Morgan Papers, Raynor Library, Special Collection and Archives, Marquette University, Milwaukee WI.

9. Conversation with Carma Foley, July 2014, St. Paul MN.

10. Lilian St. Cyr, Carlisle files, E1328, box 6, and E1329, box 1, RN 1327, Records of the Carlisle Indian Industrial School, RG 75.20.3, NARA-DC. The school register shows her date of enrollment as October 20. It also shows three Omaha children enrolling on that day: Mary Barada and Nettie and Henrietta Fremont

(Admitted—Register of Pupils, 1890–99, 53–54, series 1325, RG 75, NARA-DC, Carlisle Indian School Digital Resource Center, carlisleindian.dickenson.edu).

11. See map, "The Carlisle Indian Industrial School."

12. Landis, "About."

13. Pratt, *Battlefield and Classroom*, 192.

14. See Fear-Segal, "Nineteenth-Century Indian Education"; Landis, "About"; and Witmer, *The Indian Industrial School.*

15. Pratt, *Battlefield and Classroom*, 283. Pratt's infamous quote, "Kill the Indian in Him," comes from Richard H. Pratt, "The Advantages of Mingling Indians and Whites," in *Official Report of the Nineteenth Annual Conference of Charities and Correction* (1892), 46–59, reprinted in Prucha, *Americanizing the American Indians*, 260–71.

16. Eastman, *The Red Man's Moses*, 222.

17. Pratt did not join the growing ranks of the Social Darwinists like Armstrong who thought "progress" was limited by one's relative rung on the racial ladder. His views were born of the Enlightenment era, and he believed there were no essential rungs, only "the habit of civilization," which could, should, and would be taught to Indians if he had his way. See Fear-Segal, "Nineteenth-Century Indian Education."

18. Meyer Berger, "Red Wing, Once a Film Star, Now Makes Indian Regalia on West End Ave.," About New York, *New York Times*, May 16, 1958. The information on St. Cyr's outing families comes from 1900 federal census records and city directories at https://www.ancestry.com/.

19. Burlington County is also where the first Indian reservation in the nation was established for the Unami Indians; see "Friends School at Rancocas."

20. E1328*b*6, Records of the Carlisle Indian Industrial School, RG 75.20.3, NARA-DC.

21. E1328*b*6, Records of the Carlisle Indian Industrial School, RG 75.20.3, NARA-DC.

22. Comfort, *Just Among Friends*, 30.

23. Records of the Carlisle Indian Industrial School, E1328*b*6, RG 75.20.3, NARA-DC.

24. "Friends School at Rancocas."

25. Not everyone agreed with Lilian's assessment of Quakers. Gertrude Simmons Bonnin (Zitkála-Šá) wrote a scathing criticism of her time at a Quaker Indian school in Indiana. The article was published while she taught at Carlisle and while Lilian attended the school. Pratt raged over Bonnin's article because of her "ingratitude" for her Indian education. See Bonnin, "The School Days."

26. St. Cyr to Dr. Frissel, n.d., Julia St. Cyr student file, Hampton University Archives, Hampton VA.

27. *Southern Workman*, February 1899, David St. Cyr student file, Hampton University Archives, Hampton VA.

28. See Cahill, *Federal Fathers and Mothers.*

29. No title, *Indian Helper*, January 17, 1900, Cumberland County Historical Society.

30. Robert Blight from the Church of the Epiphany baptized Annie Frenchman and her sister, Rosa, along with a group of Lincoln Institute girls, including several from Winnebago, Nebraska, on August 10, 1890 (Church of the Epiphany). Annie, but not Rosa, Frenchman was also confirmed at the Chapel of the Educational Home on May 9, 1892 (Church of the Evangelist).

31. No title, *Indian Helper*, January 6, 1900, Cumberland County Historical Society.

32. Louis St. Cyr student file, http://carlisleindian.dickinson.edu/student_files/louis-st-cyr-student-file.

33. 1900 Massachusetts federal census, Essex County, Lynn Ward 4, District 0376, https://www.ancestry.com/.

34. These included the Nash children. For a complete list of Carlisle staff and students (and their tribal affiliations) for 1900, see 1900 Pennsylvania federal census, Cumberland County, North Middleton Township, Carlisle, ED 0167, https://www.ancestry.com/. Lilian appears as "Lillie St. Cyr."

35. He did so with the express invitation and ongoing support of the Indian agent, John Miles, who was a Quaker (Thiesen, "Every Beginning"). Samuel S. Haury was Elizabeth's brother-in-law. The mission burned down in 1882, taking the lives of four children, including one of Haury's.

36. At the same time, Haury and the Mennonites "extended their mission" to the vacated barracks at "the Cantonment on the North Fork of the Canadian [River]" (now Canton ok), where bands of Arapahoe and Southern Cheyenne made camp (Keeling, "My Experience").

37. The school was established in 1885 "in connection with the Mennonite Seminary at Halstead, Kansas." Ella and her brother may have been in the first group of fifteen Cheyenne students who were enrolled there. The school was moved to the Christian Krehbiel farm, one mile southeast of Halstead, two years later. "Here the school was conducted on a large family basis, the boys helping with the outside chores, the girls doing the housework" (Kaufman, "Mennonite Missions"). Ella's sister attended Haskell Indian School in Kansas while she and her brother were enrolled at Halstead.

38. "Ella Romero, Who Died at Newton, Kan.," *Fort Wayne (IN) Journal-Gazette*, February 5, 1903, NPC.

39. Ella Romero student information card, Carlisle Indian School Digital Resource Center, http://carlisleindian.dickinson.edu/student_files/ella-romero-student-information-card.

40. Romero, "Washita Battlefield." For various versions of Romero's story, see Berthrong, *The Cheyenne and Arapaho Ordeal*; Hardorff, *Washita Memories*; Harrison, *Yellow Swallow*; Philbrick, *The Last Stand*; Utley, *Custer*; Brennan, *An Autobiography*; and Cozzens, *Conquering the Southern Plains*.

41. The other interpreter was G. W. Fox. When the Cheyenne Agency dumped Romero from the payroll, Pratt hired him as a cook to retain his services as

interpreter. See Lookingbill, *War Dance at Fort Marion*, 44, 62, 80, and 87. A photo that became a stereoscopic was taken at Fort Marion by O. Pierre Havens. It was titled *Medicine Water and Wife, Mochi, with Romeo, the Cheyenne Interpreter in Native Costume Confined in Fort Marion, St. Augustine, Florida*, "Lawrence T. Jones, III, Texas Photographs," http://digitalcollections.smu .edu/cdm/ref/collection/jtx/id/1059.

42. Romero, "Washita Battlefield." This site does not mention the significance of Romero's name.

43. Hardorff, *Washita Memories*, 143n12. Hardorff claimed that Romero "served a vital role as an intermediary between Cheyennes and whites for more than thirty years."

44. Hardorff, *Washita Memories*, 231.

45. Cheyenne Kate Bighead gave an account to Little Big Horn historian Thomas Marquis in 1926. For information on Bighead's story and her picture, see Liberty, *A Northern Cheyenne Album*, 52.

46. Berthrong (*The Cheyenne and Arapaho Ordeal*) states that Ella's mother was also Mrs. Rufus Gilbert, but Indian census rolls (AC) show Gilbert's wife was Medicine Bear, the mother of Alice (also called Ella) Butts, who attended the missionary school in Halstead, Kansas, and lived until at least 1911. Medicine Bear, who lived until at least 1913, later married Walking Stone.

47. The similarities are that she was married at fifteen and had four children with three living. The children in the household are Minnie (born 1889) and McKinley (born 1898).

48. For example, in the early 1830s the Winnebago interpreter, Pierre Paquette, prostituted one of Conokaw Decora's daughters to a soldier at Fort Winnebago under the pretense it was a marriage. The soldier gave her a child and abandoned her (Kinzie, *Wau-bun*, 376–77). Alexander St. Cyr (son of Michel Sr.) also had similar "relationships" with desperate Dakota women at Crow Creek, apparently in trade for food and goods ("Alexander St. Cyr Heirship Case," roll 93, RG 75, M234, NARA-CPR).

49. "Girls of School Rooms 10 and 11 Have an Interesting Challenge Debate," *Red Man and Helper*, February 23, 1900, Cumberland County Historical Society.

50. "U.S. Returns from Regular Army Infantry Regiments, 1821–1916" (Hugh M. Lieder and Hugh Leider), and "U.S. Army, Register of Enlistments, 1798–1914," https://www.ancestry.com/.

51. No title, *Indian Helper*, March 9, 1900, Cumberland County Historical Society.

52. In May Ella also performed for the Academic Entertainment night, singing a duet with another student ("May Entertainment," *Red Man and Helper*, May 31, 1901, Cumberland County Historical Society).

53. "The Susan's Entertainment," *Red Man and Helper*, January 11, 1901, Cumberland County Historical Society.

54. Man-on-the-Bandstand's Corner, *Red Man and Helper*, July 26, 1901, Cumberland County Historical Society.

55. Conversation with Barbara Landis of the Cumberland County Historical Society, July 15, 1015.

56. M. Burgess, "Miss Ely Laid to Rest," *Carlisle Arrow*, September 4, 1914, Cumberland County Historical Society.

57. "General Items," *Red Man and Helper*, December 13, 1901, Cumberland County Historical Society.

58. David Lee Smith's old photograph collection. In fact, this photo was unidentified until I realized it was Lilian years after I had copied it.

59. Man-on-the-Bandstand's Corner, *Red Man and Helper*, August 15, 1902; and Man-on-the-Bandstand's Corner, *Red Man and Helper*, September 26, 1902, Cumberland County Historical Society.

60. Louis St. Cyr student file, Hampton University Archives, Hampton VA.

61. Lizzie was baptized in Philadelphia on January 18, 1890, with two other girls from Winnebago. Sponsors were Cox, Lucy Gordon, and Lucy Woods. She was confirmed on March 23, 1890 with several Lincoln Institute girls, including Ettie Tyndal (Church of the Epiphany, Pennsylvania Church and Town Records, images 314 and 358, https://www.ancestry.com/).

62. Man-on-the-Bandstand's Corner, *Red Man and Helper*, December 26 and January 2, 1903 (combined issue), Cumberland County Historical Society. Romero died at Calumet, Oklahoma, on July 2, 1902 (Hardorff, *Washita Memories*, 142–43n12).

63. "Ella Romero, Who Died at Newton, Kan," *Fort Wayne (in) Weekly Journal-Gazette*, February 5, 1903. In December of that year, Joel Welty also died "after a long illness" ("Joel Welty Dies after Long Illness," *Fort Wayne [IN] Sentinel*, December 21, 1903, NPC).

64. The article got the school wrong: "Lillian StCyr [*sic*], of Emerson Neb., spent Sunday night at the National, on her way to Medicine Lodge. Miss StCyr is a graduate from the Indian's school of north Omaha Neb., and she is going to Medicine Lodge to visit with Chester I. Long's this coming summer" ("Local News," *Barber County Index* [Medicine Lodge KS], May 6, 1903, NPC).

65. "The New Senator's Wife," *Kansas City (MO) Star*, January 25, 1903, NPAC.

66. Meyer Berger, "Red Wing, Once a Film Star, Now Makes Indian Regalia on West End Ave.," About New York, *New York Times*, May 16, 1958.

67. He married again, to Alice White, daughter of Geo White Bear and Buzz Woman, on March 3, 1903 (Thurston County Marriages Book, vol. 1, 617, Thurston County Courthouse, Pender NE).

68. Julia St. Cyr to Dr. Frissell, September 17, 1903, Julia's student file, Hampton University Archives, Hampton VA.

69. Over the top of Julia's letter, "refused" is written in someone else's handwriting.

70. "Lillian St. Cyr, class '05, is here for a short visit," "Miscellaneous Items," *Arrow*, October 6, 1905, Cumberland County Historical Society. She may have stopped at Carlisle before going to Washington DC.

71. "Washington Letter," *Scranton (PA) Republican*, February 12, 1905, NPC.

72. "Business Is Business," *Kansas City (KS) Daily Gazette*, November 24, 1906, NPC.

73. "Society," *Washington Post*, January 28, 1906, NPAC. Other invited guests were Mrs. W. A. Reeder, whose husband was a banker; Mrs. P. P. Campbell of Pittsburg, wife of Philip Pitt Campbell, author of the "Name on the Label" bill, which gave the public accurate information on manufactured goods; Mrs. Charles F. Scott of Iola, whose husband was a newspaper editor; and Mrs. Earl Ivan Brown, whose husband engineered large-scale river and harbor improvements and served in the Philippines (Guide to Earl Ivan Brown Papers).

74. Tyler, *Men of Mark*, 183–84.

5. JAMES YOUNG JOHNSON AND FAMILY SECRETS

1. For Leupp's views on art and his appointment of Angel De Cora to head Carlisle's new "Native Indian" art department, see Waggoner, *Fire Light*, 129–32.

2. "Lilian St. Cyr (Johnson) Saratoga Springs, NY Rel. to application for share of proceeds from sale of allottments of Tall Decora, Mrs. Tall Decora & Thomas Decora," Office of Indian Affairs, received August 21, 1906, Letters Received 1881–1907, 1906-72590 11E2 10/3/1, RG 75, NARA-DC.

3. "Indians to Graduate," *Harrisburg (pa) Telegraph*, March 17, 1906, NPC.

4. "Miscellaneous Items," *Arrow*, June 8, 1906, Cumberland County Historical Society; and "Washington, D.C. Marriage Licenses," *Evening Star* (Washington DC), April 10, 1906, NPC.

5. "J Younger Johnson and Margaret L St Cyr," April 9, 1906, District of Columbia Select Marriages, 1830–1921, https://www.ancestry.com/.

6. For George's family of origin, see Spruce Ward, Philadelphia, 1850 Pennsylvania federal census, and Ward 7, Philadelphia, 1860 Pennsylvania federal census, images 26 and 59, respectively, https://www.ancestry.com/. Joseph A. Romeo places the Johnson family within the so-called Moors of Delaware historical community ("Moors of Delaware"). See also "Free African Americans"; "Kent County's Moors"; "True Story of the Delaware Moors"; and "The Moors of Delaware."

7. George D. Johnson's voluntary enlistment states that he was dark skinned with hazel eyes (Compiled Military Service Records of Volunteer Union Soldiers Who Served the United States Colored Troops, Fold3, https://www.fold3.com /image/308783549; "George D. Johnson, 30 Sep 1869, Washington, District of Columbia, War Department, Freedman's Bureau," *Register of Officers and Agents, Civil, Military, and Naval in the Service of the United States, 1863–1959*,

1:218, https://www.ancestry.com/). For a description of the Freedman's Bureau of the District of Columbia at this time, see "A Descriptive Pamphlet," District of Columbia, Freedman's Bureau Field Office Records, 1863–72, https://www .familysearch.org/. For George's Washington DC residency and occupation, see *Washington, District of Columbia, City Directories*, 1867–75, https://www .ancestry.com/; and the 1870 federal census for Washington DC, Seventh Ward, image 221, https://www.ancestry.com/.

8. For George Johnson's work with the league, see "Another Convention," *Evening Telegraph* (Philadelphia), January 8, 1867, NPC; "The Colored School's Row," *Evening Star* (Washington DC), July 1, 1873, NPC; and "The New National Newspaper Suits," *Evening Star* (Washington DC), March 7, 1874, NPC. See also Taylor, "'To Make the Union.'"

9. "The Fifteenth Amendment," *Evening Star* (Washington DC), April 26, 1870, NPC. See also Students and Classes, 1870, District of Columbia, Howard University, 1870, U.S. School Catalogs, https://www.ancestry.com/.

10. LeCount is listed in the city directory, Washington DC, 1870, https://www .ancestry.com/. It's interesting to note that for three years, beginning in 1917, instead of "Johnson" or "Johnston" as before, tribal records list Lilian's husband as "LeClaire," which apparently has been erroneously transcribed from LeCount, as she did not remarry at that time. This indicated that Lilian knew something about her father-in-law's family by 1917. Lilian stated little or nothing about Johnson's true ancestry until well after his death, when she identified him as a Delaware Indian to Meyer Berger. Whether Delaware or, as some believe, Nanticoke describes her father-in-law's American Indian heritage is unknown.

11. James LeCount Jr. graduated from the Institute for Colored Youth along with four others in May 1863. His younger sister Caroline and he scored first and second, respectively, on the school's final examinations. Family legend says that when one of LeCount's young cousins "snuck into the coffin room during a game of hide-and-seek," he or she "found live people in the coffins; slaves James was helping escape" (Institute for Colored Youth).

12. His name is also recorded as Manduit, Mordrit, Mordret, and Mordecai (the latter may be his middle name).

13. William's siblings also owned land in the southeastern portion of the District of Columbia. Abraham Young inherited a farm on the northern portion of the Nock, while Elizabeth Young Wheeler inherited land that fronted the Anacostia River, where she and her husband ran a ferry. Today this area is Barney Circle. See "DC Genealogy," http://districtofcolumbiagenealogy.com/history/south _east_section.htm.

14. Vlach, "The Quest for a Capital."

15. See "Proposed Barney Circle Historic District."

16. Their names were "Wapping, Jack, David, Henry, Cinthia, Polly, Fanny, Jenny, Cyrus, Judeth, and Kate" (Rogers, *Freedom & Slavery Documents*, n.p.; and Index to Wills, William Young, Washington DC, Wills and Probate Records, https://www.ancestry.com/).

17. Ruth's father purchased three of her husband's slaves for her use, as shown by William Young Jr.'s probate record. The Proposed Barney Circle Historic District survey cites a book that states she had no slaves, but two are enumerated in the far right column of the 1800 census, which has been mislabeled "Georgetown" (1800 federal census for Washington DC, image 18, https://www.ancestry.com/). The 1810 census for the District of Columbia was destroyed.

18. Their farmhouse in today's Marshall Heights was still standing in 1917. For the history of the house and Morduit Young's time living there, see "The Rambler Visits Historic Eastern Branch Tract," *Evening Star* (Washington DC), March 11, 1917, NPC.

19. The property was described when it was sold after Morduit Young's death ("Valuable Land for Sale," *National Intelligencer* [Washington DC], August 27, 1844, NPAC).

20. Rogers, *Freedom & Slavery Documents*, 89.

21. 1820 federal census, south of Eastern Branch Potomac, Washington DC, image 1, https://www.ancestry.com/. The census shows that Morduit had four slaves: one male (fourteen to twenty-five), two boys (under fourteen), and a girl (under fourteen).

22. "Constable's Sale," *National Intelligencer* (Washington DC), August 6, 1825, NPAC.

23. Their twenty-six names did not include the four slaves she had earlier purchased from her son-in-law. To Ann, Morduit's eldest, "a woman called Catherine and her two children, Margaret and John"; to Amelia, "negro slave Flora and her two children, one called Mary and the other unnamed"; to Susana, "two negro boys, John and Lewis" (Ann Truman Beall Will, January 5, 1832, Wills, 1826–37, Washington DC Wills and Probate Records, https://www.ancestry.com/). She also willed one of his daughters "the money due me, from her father."

24. "Mordecai Young, Persons imprisoned for debt . . . secretary of state, Wednesday, December 14, 1836." In 1818 officials threatened to put several of his lots on the auction block for overdue taxes ("Sale of City Lots for Taxes," *National Intelligencer* [Washington DC], September 22, 1818, NPAC). A ferry and rowboat were seized to pay debts in 1825 ("Constable's Sale," *National Intelligencer* [Washington DC], August 6, 1825, NPAC).

25. Mandnit [*sic*] Young, July 15, 1839, Wills, 1837–47, Washington DC Wills and Probate Records, https://www.ancestry.com/.

26. "Deaths," *National Intelligencer*, July 24, 1844.

27. Davis, "Slavery and Emancipation."

28. Mandnit [*sic*] Young, July 15, 1839, Wills, 1837–47, Washington DC Wills and Probate Records, https://www.ancestry.com/.

29. Mandnit [*sic*] Young, July 15, 1839, Wills, 1837–47, Washington DC Wills and Probate Records, https://www.ancestry.com/.

30. "Public Sale," *Daily Intelligencer*, August 27, 1844, NPAC.

31. If the value of the seven adjoining lots and the personal property left to Ann is added to the evaluation of Morduit's slaves ($1,450), then the remainder of the estate willed to Elizabeth Young's daughters (and one only received money for a "morning suit") is far less than half what Ann and her children inherited. See Proposed Barney Circle Historic District.

32. The 1850 slave schedule census shows that Morduit's daughter Ann and her husband, Fielder Magruder, held seventeen slaves. His widowed daughter, Susana Sheriff, owned the same amount, while his daughter Amelia and her "planter" husband, James E. Hollyday, held forty-seven slaves.

33. His name is recorded as "Merrick" (but "Morduit" or a variation appears in directories that follow), *Washington, District of Columbia, City Directory*, 1863, 216, https://www.ancestry.com/.

34. See Brown, *Free Negroes*.

35. U.S. census mortality schedules, 1850–85, and 1870 District of Columbia federal census, Washington DC, https://www.ancestry.com/. The number of the household where she died corresponds to the household of Owen Fagan (a gardener) and family, two households away from her mother's.

36. The city directory for 1868 lists "Johnson, George D, clk [clerk], 179 F s," *Washington, District of Columbia, City Directory*, 1868, 292, https://www.ancestry.com/; "George D. Johnson, 30 Sep 1869, Washington, District of Columbia, War Department, Freedman's Bureau," *Register of Officers and Agents, Civil, Military, and Naval in the Service of the United States, 1863–1959*, 1:218, https://www.ancestry.com/. The census lists George D. Johnson's occupation as "clerk, F. bur." (short for Freedman's Bureau), 1870 federal census, Washington DC, Ward 7, https://www.ancestry.com/. The 1875 *Washington, District of Columbia, City Directory* also shows George D. Johnson, bookkeeper, living at 474 F Street SW (https://www.ancestry.com/).

37. "Johnson.—On the 23d instant at 7:30 a.m., Marie Louise, only daughter of George D. and Margaret E. Johnson. Funeral will take place at her father's residence, 474 F street south, Sunday, the 26th inst., at 2 pm" ("Died," *National Republican* [Washington DC], February 25, 1871, NPC). See also "Died," *Evening Star* (Washington DC), February 24, 1871, NPC.

38. See 1880 federal census, Washington City DC, 474 F Street SW, page 7, https://www.ancestry.com.

39. "Johnson, George D, bookkeeper, 474 F SW," *Washington, District of Columbia, City Directory*, 1873, 26, and *Washington, District of Columbia, City Directory*, 1875, 292, https://www.ancestry.com/. In 1874 his occupation is listed as "clk" (clerk). Both houses were later demolished for Interstate Highways 395 and 695.

40. "Young. On July 24, 1878, at 10:20 a. m. Mrs. Anna Young, after a long and painful illness. Funeral will take place from her late residence, No. 473 F street southwest, at 2 o'clock p.m. Friday, 26th. Friends and family are invited" ("Died," *Evening Star* [Washington DC], July 25, 1878, NPC).

41. District of Columbia Deaths, 1874–61, https://www.familysearch.org/; "Johnson, at 1:20 a.m., December 7th, 1878, George D. Johnson, aged thirty-four years. Funeral from the Fifteenth street Presbyterian Church, Tuesday afternoon, December 10th, at 2 o'clock" ("Died," *Evening Star* [Washington DC], December 9, 1878, NPC). See also "Died," *Philadelphia Inquirer*, December 9, 1878, NPC.

42. See "Caroline LeCount," Institute for Colored Graduates.

43. As one scholar has noted, Catto's "attendance signified . . . the newfound ability of hundreds of thousands of black men to portray themselves as saviors of the Union, rated as one of the most valuable political weapons in the black arsenal" (Taylor, "'To Make the Union,'" 335).

44. See "The Martyred Catto," *Cincinnati Times*, October 17, 1871, genealogybank.com.

45. "A Colored School Principal," *Philadelphia Inquirer*, August 25, 1891, NPC.

46. "Died," *Daily Critic* (Washington DC), August 11, 1890, NPC. The newspaper report says she was forty, but that is inaccurate. See also "Fifteenth Street Presbyterian Church"; Sluby, *Columbian Harmony Records*; and Columbian Harmony and Payne Cemetery Registers. The historic African American cemetery was eventually sold to investors, who reinterred remains in the National Harmony Memorial Park in Maryland.

47. "Estate of Emma Johnson; order of publication," "Probate Court," *Evening Star* (Washington DC), October 31, 1891, NPC; "Estate of Emma Johnson; letters of administration granted Elizabeth Savoy; bond, $2,600," "Probate Court," *Evening Star* (Washington DC), November 28, 1891, NPC; and "Estate of Emma Johnson; letters of administration granted Elizabeth E. Savoy, administratix, bonded and qualified," "Probate Court," *Evening Star* (Washington DC), December 7, 1891, NPC.

48. Savoy's mother, Lizzie Savoy, had been enslaved by U.S. Navy purser Timothy Winn and probably knew Ann Young. Savoy's formerly enslaved parents maintained strong ties to the civil rights movement in Washington DC. See Pippenger, *District of Columbia Probate Records*, 202–3. Savoy's father, a popular caterer in the city, was a congressional delegate for black suffrage in 1868. Her mother aided the Underground Railroad, raising money for Exodus Sufferers. Elizabeth and her mother taught in the segregated local public schools and were well respected by the city's African American community. Elizabeth never had children but helped her brother Edward Savoy with his brood after Edward's wife died. Edward was another accomplished African American role model. He "worked for 21 secretaries of state, through 14 presidencies from Ulysses S. Grant to Franklin Delano Roosevelt." Secretary of State Hamilton Fish hired fourteen-year-old Savoy to serve as his page in 1869. Savoy retired sixty-four years later, having attained the

position of chief messenger to the secretary of state, one of the highest government jobs available to an African American at that time ("Edward Augustine Savoy," Find a Grave Memorial #105942327, findagrave.com).

49. "On October 25, 1894, William Pinckney Young departed this life, at the age of sixty-one years. Funeral from his late residence, 474 F street southwest, Friday 3 p. m. Friends and relatives invited" ("Died," *Evening Star* [Washington DC], October 25, 1894, NPC).

50. Minnie's husband was the son of Jesse Fossett and the grandson of Joseph Jefferson Fossett, the nephew of President Thomas Jefferson's consort, Sally Hemings. Although Joseph gained his freedom, his wife and children were put on the auction block soon after Jefferson's death in 1826. However, Joseph managed to procure freedom for his wife and younger children, while his eldest son, Peter, did not gain his freedom for twenty-seven years. After having two more children, including Minnie's father-in-law, Joseph left Charlottesville, North Carolina, and migrated with his family to Cincinnati, located then in the free state of Ohio. See "Discovering More About the Fossett Family," Thomas Jefferson Foundation, https://www.monticello.org/site/plantation-and-slavery/discovering-more-about-fossett-family; "Joseph Fossett" (1780–1858), *Encyclopedia Virginia*, https://www.encyclopediavirginia.org/Fossett_Joseph_1780-1858; "Once the Slave of Thomas Jefferson," *Sunday World* (Cincinnati OH), January 29, 1898, reprinted in Frontline, https://www.pbs.org/wgbh/pages/frontline/shows/jefferson/slaves/memoir.html. See also "Jesse Fassett," 1850 federal census, Cincinnati Ward 6, Hamilton County OH, family no. 1150; "Jessee Fossitt," 1870 federal census, Cincinnati Ward 15, Hamilton County OH, Dwelling No. 2; "Jesoe Fossett," 1880 federal census, Cincinnati, Hamilton OH, House No. 181, Dwelling No. 55; and "William Fossett," 1900 federal census, Cincinnati Ward 16, Hamilton OH, House No. 761, Sheet No. 10, https://www.ancestry.com/.

51. Virginia Delayed Birth Records, 1854–1911, https://www.ancestry.com/.

52. The 1900 census lists them all as "black."

53. "Degrees Conferred in 1920, Bachelor of Arts," in *Calendar of Wellesley College, 1920–21*, 174, https://books.google.com; and the 1930 and 1940 federal censuses for Morristown, Morris County, New Jersey, https://www.ancestry.com/.

54. "Deeds in fee have been filed as follows . . . Emma Johnson to Elizabeth C. Savoy, pts. 16 and 14, sq. 172; $2,500" ("Transfers of Real Estate," *Evening Star* [Washington DC], June 23, 1890, NPC).

55. He also later rejected the Republican Party (beloved by African Americans at the time) because President McKinley "failed to raise his voice of the lynching of colored men in the south" ("F street southwest between 4 1-2 and 6th streets—Oliver C. Black et al., trustees to Minnie A. Fossett, George D. Johnson, James Y. and Harry W. Johnson, part original lot 20, square 496; $10," "Real Estate Transfers," *Evening Star* [Washington DC], March 15, 1901, NPC). For

Black's political activities, see "Commodore Wilson and the Dismissed Messenger, Black," *Evening Star* (Washington DC), March 19, 1883, NPC; "Shades of Color," *Daily Critic* (Washington DC), April 30, 1896, NPC; "The Color Line," *Washington Bee*, May 8, 1897; "Another Convert," *Washington Bee*, September 24, 1904, NPC; and "The Political Horoscope," *Colored American* (Washington DC), August 18, 1900, NPC.

56. See Taylor, "'To Make the Union.'"

57. The concept was introduced in the *Atlantic Monthly*. The quote is taken from *The Souls of Black Folk* by W. E. B. Du Bois.

58. Enlistments, 1898, USS *Vermont* at New York, Serial Number 3061 (or 3561), "Enlistment of Johnson James Young on the 8 October, 1898, as Mess Attendant," National Personnel Records Center. For a summary of his service, see Johnson, James Young, New York, Spanish-American War Military and Naval Service Records, https://www.ancestry.com/.

59. Johnson, James, 1900 federal census, Military and Naval Population, https://www.ancestry.com/; and USS *Celtic* (AF-2), 1891–1923.

60. James Young Johnson, Naval Record, National Personnel Records Center. One of the navy's means to keep order on the ship was to confiscate items left out by putting them in a storage locker called a "lucky bag." In order to get the articles back the loser had to undergo some form of punishment (to which both cases refer) or lose the item permanently when it went up for auction after a period of time.

61. James Young Johnson, Naval Record, National Personnel Records Center.

62. The "Report of Medical Survey" was addressed to the *Celtic* from the Navy's Department of Medicine and Surgery: "Sir in obedience to your order April 29, 1901, we have held a careful survey on Johnson, James Young Landsman, and beg leave to report as follows: 1. Present condition: Unfit for service 2. Disease or injury: *Epilepsy* [my emphasis] 3. Probable future duration: Permanent 4. Recommendation: That he be transferred to a Receiving Ship in the United States for discharge from the Naval Service. 5. Origin: not in line of duty—existed prior to enlistment, according to patient's accepted statement" (James Young Johnson, Naval Record, National Personnel Records Center).

63. James Young Johnson, Naval Record, National Personnel Records Center.

64. "Return of 'Globe Trotter,'" *Colored American* (Washington DC), February 22, 1902, NPC.

6. PRINCESS RED WING AND YOUNG DEER

1. Nothing else is known of his whereabouts until he married, except that he attended a picnic in Atlantic City hosted by the Keystone Beneficial Association in September 1902 ("Seaside Life in Gotham," *Colored American* [Washington DC], September 13, 1902, NPC). Pawnee Bill's Wild West Show maintained its headquarters in the seaside resort at this time, so perhaps this is when Johnson

entered show business ("Charter for Wild West Show Secretary of State's Office Incorporated Two Companies Today," *Trenton [NJ] Evening Time*, March 28, 1902, NPC).

2. 1905 New York state census, Manhattan, and 1910 New York federal census for Manhattan, https://www.ancestry.com/.

3. Bruchac, "Native Artisans."

4. "About three months ago I filed an application to draw my share of the proceeds from the sales of Tall Decora, Mrs. Tall Decora and Thomas Decora allottments," Lilian wrote Leupp, "at the time I was told that the deeds had been all signed and that we could receive our money in about a month" ("Lilian St. Cyr [Johnson], Saratoga Springs NY Rel. to application for share of proceeds from sale of allottments of Tall Decora, Mrs. Tall Decora & Thomas Decora," Office of Indian Affairs, received August 21, 1906, Letters Received 1881–1907, 1906-72590, 11E2, RG 75, NARA-DC).

5. *New York Hippodrome.*

6. Williams, "The Indian Colony."

7. "These names are exactly as furnished by the Presbyterian Minister at the Pine Ridge Agency" (*New York Hippodrome*, 15).

8. *New York Hippodrome*, 15.

9. Standing Bear, *My People the Sioux*, 278.

10. "Famous Indian Actress Visits Klamath Tribe," *Evening Herald* (Klamath Falls OR), October 26, 1916, NPC.

11. Red Wing's two autobiographical sketches, Red Wing file.

12. According to a Lakota language expert I spoke with in 2014, the name "is not exactly in the correct form for a woman's name." Lilian was the first of at least three nonbiological niece-uncle relationships Standing Bear nurtured during his life. Not until later did Lilian also claim that the song "Red Wing: An Intermezzo," patented in New York on March 22, 1907, was written for her. See "Musical Compositions," *Catalog of Copyright Entries*, pt. 3, vol. 2, January 1907, 575. No records contradict her claim, but neither does anything support it. Thurland Chattaway, the song's lyricist, would have had to have been a quick study to write "Red Wing" within a couple of months after *Pioneer Days* debuted, especially since it is doubtful she had yet acquired her name, Red Wing, by that time. It's also highly unlikely that Red Wing would have waited so long to announce her connection to the popular song.

13. See "Hippodrome Staff Seeks Summer Joys," *New York Times*, May 20, 1907.

14. Raheja, *Reservation Reelism*, 13. See also Moses, *Wild West Shows*; and Deloria, *Playing Indian.*

15. "Exonerated," *Indian News* (Genoa NE), October 1907, Ho-Chunk Historical Society. The headline in an Omaha paper was devastating: "Indian Woman Lawyer Indicted as Taking Excessive Pension Fee from a Blind Woman," *Evening*

World Herald, May 25, 1906, genealogybank.com. Worse, Julia was arrested on the reservation. Julia's brother-in-law St. Pierre Owen and a white merchant who ran Emerson's general store helped her to come up with the $500 bail. In October 1907 she was tried in Omaha. In securing a pension, attorneys were only allowed $10, and the charge levied at Julia was that she received over $300 from the widow of an Indian scout. Although the widow allowed her to take $391 from her pension check, Julia claimed it took her years to secure the pension, and it was not technically a fee. See *United States v. Julia St. Cyr*, United States District Court of Nebraska, no. 44-46; St. Cyr to Cora Folsom, Hampton, May 27, 1907, Julia St. Cyr student file, Hampton University Archives, Hampton VA; and "To Be Tried for Extortion," *Omaha Daily Bee*, October 9, 1907, and "Pension Case on File," *Omaha Daily Bee*, October 10, 1907, NPC.

16. *Moving Picture World*, May 6, 1911, 999, MHDL.
17. See "Hippodrome Staff Seeks Summer Joys," *New York Times*, May 20, 1907.
18. Wallis, *The Real Wild West*, 292–93.
19. Wallis, *The Real Wild West*, 292–93.
20. "One More Play in Town; Fun Galore at Beaches," *Brooklyn Daily Eagle*, August 4, 1907, NPC. It's unclear if Lilian and James actually worked directly for the Miller Brothers' 101 Ranch. See "Brighton Beach Music Hall," *Brooklyn Daily Eagle*, June 21, 1908, NPC. The Kemp Sisters' Hippodrome and Indian Congress, a lesser-known Wild West show, was booked at Brighton Beach during the summer of 1908. For a history of this Wild West show, run by the Kemp brothers of Gridley, Illinois, see "Kemp Genealogy."
21. See "Indian Guests at a Luncheon," *Brooklyn Daily Eagle*, August 11, 1908, NPC. The newspaper report claimed that Red Wing and Young Deer had worked for the show, but that they worked for it while "in the west." However, in a 1908 letter Red Wing penned for "Charging Hawk" that summer, she gave "101 Ranch, Brighton Beach" as his mailing address, suggesting they at least camped with the show
22. Originally from the Standing Rock Agency in South Dakota, Sherman's family relocated to the Rosebud reservation in 1882. He is listed with his parents on the U.S. Indian census for Rosebud, 1896, https://www.ancestry.com/. For his father's identity, see Wagner, *Participants*, 134. Artist Josef Scheuerle, whose friends included western stars Will Rogers and William S. Hart, painted Sherman Charging Hawk seated in profile in 1909.
23. Gracyk and Hoffman, *Popular American Recording Pioneers*, 187. The so-called dime museum had featured Sioux Indians before. In fact, a group from Pine Ridge appeared there in December 1890 to perform the Messiah Dance, also known as the Ghost Dance. It must have been an eerie and painful experience for the performers to learn about the massacre of Wounded Knee while performing the Ghost Dance for white New Yorkers ("Huber's Palace Museum," *New York Press*, January 16, 1891, FHC).

24. "A Holiday Grist of Plays," *New York Sun*, December 22, 1907, NPC.
25. "A Holiday Grist of Plays," *New York Sun*, December 22, 1907, NPC.
26. This view was given visual expression in the many before and after photographs of students Pratt commissioned.
27. Adams and Keene, *Women of the American Circus*, 7.
28. "There Were Some Bees at the Dime," *Philadelphia Inquirer*, January 7, 1908, NPC.
29. Luther Standing Bear's Carlisle file, 1321, box 60, 3019, RG 75, NARA-DC.
30. "Spanked a Paleface Boy," *New York Times*, February 17, 1908.
31. The lyrics of the former song (actually just titled "Navajo") were not only bawdy but also blatantly racist against African Americans, which is interesting, given Young Deer's family origins. Lyrics as performed by Harry MacDonough and recorded in 1904 (words by Harry Williams; music by Egbert Analstyne), History on the Net.
32. "Gotham Club Ghost Dance," *New York Times*, April 2, 1908.
33. "Gothamite's Occult Evening," *New York Sun*, April 2, 1908, NPC.
34. "Gotham Club Ghost Dance," *New York Times*, April 2, 1908.
35. Formerly Obermüller & Kern and then Obermüller & Son. A Google image search calls up several of his cabinet card photos.
36. About two years later, Obermüller, suffering from depression and business worries, crawled into his developing vat in his Cooper Square studio and drowned himself. His body was found three days later. See "Dead with Head in Tank," *New York Tribune*, November 17, 1910; and "Drowned in Own Tank," *Boston Globe*, November 17, 1910, NPC.
37. "'The White Squaw,'" *Concordia (KS) Blade-Empire*, February 3, 1909, NPC. Subtitled "Rescued from the Indians," it was also advertised as "A Thrilling and Exciting Story" and a "Very interesting picture of Indian life" ("Woodruff's," *Camden [NJ] Daily Courier*, June 3, 1908; and "The White Squaw," *Allentown [PA] Democrat*, September 18, 1908, NPC).
38. See "Kemp Genealogy."
39. "Big Shows at the Beaches and Elsewhere for Fourth of July Week," *Brooklyn Daily Eagle*, June 28, 1908, NPC.
40. "Seaside Amusements," *New York Herald*, July 5, 1908, NPC. See also "Big Shows at the Beaches and Elsewhere for Fourth of July," *Brooklyn Daily Eagle*, June 28, 1908, NPC.
41. For Boyington's involvement with the 101 Ranch, see Wallis, *The Real Wild West*, 290–91, 340. Boyington performed for the 1907 tour, but Wallis states that he rejoined the show in 1909, leaving one to infer that he was not working for the show in 1908. The Kemp Sisters seems to have been the only Wild West show in New York during the summer of 1908.
42. *Pearson's Magazine* 19 (January 1908): 164, googlebooks.com.

43. Indian Rights Association Papers, 1909, Green Library, Stanford University, Palo Alto CA. A postscript also stated: "Please notify the office at Washington or come & see then we can tell you all."

44. Indian Rights Association Papers, 1909, Green Library, Stanford University, Palo Alto CA.

45. "Varied Amusements by the Sea," *Brooklyn Daily Eagle*, July 19, 1908, NPC.

46. "Brighton Beach Music Hall," *Brooklyn Daily Eagle*, June 21, 1908, NPC.

47. "Indian Guests at a Luncheon," *Brooklyn Daily Eagle*, August 11, 1908, NPC. The caption shows that the men were Frank and Albert Gross and Harry C. B. Kederick. These men seem only to have been random fans of the trio.

48. A search of newspapers.com reveals that the term was first used in 1894. I'm told scholar Christine Bold has been researching Indian vaudeville, but she chose not to share a paper she gave on the subject for the Native American and Indigenous Studies Conference, Vancouver, British Columbia, 2017.

49. *Pantagraph* (Bloomington IL), June 28, 1909, NPC; and *Daily Times* (New Philadelphia OH), September 9, 1909, NPC.

50. Lydia died in 1931, and George remained there until 1940 and probably until his death. It's unknown when and if they ever reunited with Young Deer.

51. "Motion Pictures, 1894–1912," 19.

52. *Nickelodeon*, May 1909, 640, https://archive.org.

53. *Moving Picture World*, May 8, 1908, 594, MHDL. See also "Reviews of New Films," *New York Dramatic Mirror*, May 15, 1909, 15, FHC.

54. For Griffith and Biograph at Cuddebackville, see Griffith, *When the Movies Were Young*; and Neversink Valley Museum of History and Innovation, "Movies before Hollywood." Lester Predmore also speaks of Griffith in *Lester Predmore*. Griffith's first western, filmed in Little Falls, New Jersey, was entitled *The Redman and the Child*. As Griffith's wife, actress Linda Arvidson, recalled, "Charles Inslee was the big-hearted Indian chief in the story and little Johnny Tansy played the child" (*When the Movies Were Young*, 85–86).

55. Griffith, *When the Movies Were Young*, 117.

56. "The Singer Summit House."

57. Fleming, *Wallace Reid*, 41.

58. Griffith, *When the Movies Were Young*, 116. *The Mended Lute* survives today except for the last three minutes. See "Silent Hall of Fame."

59. Griffith, *When the Movies Were Young*, 118–19.

60. Henderson, *D. W. Griffith*, 77.

61. Fleming, *Wallace Reid*, 41.

62. Windeler, *Sweetheart*, 50. Lester Predmore, son of the innkeepers, mistakenly remembered Young Deer's name as "Dark Cloud" and said he showed the cast how to do Indian dances in the parlor. Dark Cloud was another Indian actor who later worked for Griffith (*Lester Predmore*).

63. Windeler, *Sweetheart*, 226.

64. *Moving Picture World*, August 14, 1909, 226, MHDL.

65. When Griffith was an actor at the turn of the century, he also picked hops in Ukiah, California, for income (Henderson, *D. W. Griffith*, 27). He certainly worked with local Pomo Indians, who often picked hops as a means of employment.

66. Ad for *The Indian Runner's Romance* in *Moving Picture World*, August 28, 1909, 294, MHDL.

67. *Moving Picture World*, August 7, 1909, 203, MHDL. Young Deer's expertise further shadowed his wife's when someone (probably Young Deer himself) bragged to a correspondent from the British publication *Kinematograph and Lantern Weekly*. In response, *Moving Picture World*'s critic rebutted, stating that the American correspondent "draws on his imagination when he says that the recent Biograph success, 'The Mended Lute,' was written and staged by James Young Deer, a full-blooded Indian. As a matter of fact, the play was staged by the Biograph Company's own producer and was not written by Young Deer. Both Young Deer and his wife have, however, appeared in Biograph productions" (*Moving Picture World*, October 9, 1909, 487, MHDL).

68. *Moving Picture World*, August 7, 1909, 203, MHDL.

69. Balshofer and Miller, *One Reel a Week*, 24.

70. Balshofer and Miller, *One Reel a Week*, 28.

71. Balshofer and Miller, *One Reel a Week*, 28. See Justice and Smith, *Who's Who in the Film World*, 229.

72. *Moving Picture World*, June 19, 1909, 840, and June 26, 1909, 871, MHDL. Balshofer recalled that *A True Indian's Heart* was the first film for which he hired the couple, but he does not mention *The Cowboy's Narrow Escape*. However, Lilian later stated that her first film for Bison was *The Cowboy's Narrow Escape*, which was released before *A True Indian's Heart*. See Balshofer and Miller, *One Reel a Week*, 28; and "Red Wing," in Justice and Smith, *Who's Who in the Film World*, 229. For *A Squaw's Revenge*, see *Moving Picture World*, June 5, 1909, 760, MHDL.

73. Katchmer, *A Biographical Dictionary*, 1.

74. *Moving Picture World*, June 26, 1909, 871, MHDL. The review stated that an Indian had "written the book," but I think the reviewer meant the film's narrative.

75. See Walker, *Max Sennett's Fun Factory* for Inslee's career.

76. Balshofer stated that he "could not measure up to the task" (Balshofer and Miller, *One Reel a Week*, 67).

77. *Moving Picture World*, July 3, 1909, 31, MHDL.

78. Meyers, "History of a Fort Lee Neighborhood."

79. Balshofer and Miller, *One Reel a Week*, 32, 33.

80. Balshofer and Miller, *One Reel a Week*, 33.

81. Balshofer and Miller, *One Reel a Week*, 34.

82. Balshofer and Miller, *One Reel a Week*, 36–37.

83. *Moving Picture World*, June 26, 1908, 890, MHDL.

84. Balshofer and Miller, *One Reel a Week*, 28, 40.

85. For prizes at the Indian dance, see *Winnebago Chieftain*, September 3, 1909, Ho-Chunk Historical Society. For Julia St. Cyr at the Omaha Exposition as part of the Indian Congress, see F. A. Rinehart's photo, "Mrs. Blackhawk and six others," American Indians 1898 Photo Album, "Trans Mississippi and International Exposition," http://trans-mississippi.unl.edu/photographs/view/TMI02043.html.

86. *Moving Picture World*, July 17, 1909, 81, MHDL.

87. Balshofer and Miller, *One Reel a Week*, 40.

88. Marubbio, *Killing the Indian Maiden*, 33–34. Andrew B. Smith noted that "Young Deer and Red Wing were central to Bison's early success. . . . In a period before the full emergence of the 'movie star' phenomenon, the actors became iconographic figures by which the movie going public identified Bison films" (*Shooting Cowboys and Indians*, 80).

89. Marubbio, *Killing the Indian Maiden*, 34–35.

90. *Moving Picture World*, September 25, 1909, 361, MHDL.

91. *Moving Picture World*, September 25, 1909, 429, MHDL; and Red Wing's autobiographical sketches, Red Wing file.

92. *Moving Picture World*, September 25, 1909, 429, MHDL.

93. *Moving Picture World*, October 9, 1909, 511, MHDL; and Red Wing's autobiographical sketches, Red Wing file.

94. *Variety*, October 1909, 12, MHDL.

95. Deloria, *Indians in Unexpected Places*, 88.

96. *Moving Picture World*, October 16, 1909, 545, MHDL; see also *Billboard*, October 16, 1909, 21, FIIC.

97. *Moving Picture World*, October 16, 1909, 545, MHDL.

98. *Moving Picture World*, November 6, 1909, 661, MHDL.

99. *Moving Picture World*, December 18, 1909, 882; ad, *Moving Picture World*, November 27, 1909, 787, MHDL.

100. *Moving Picture World*, December 11, 1909, 867, MHDL.

7. EDENDALE, CALIFORNIA

1. Balshofer and Miller, *One Reel a Week*, 54.

2. Colonel William N. Selig, a former vaudeville performer and photographer, started Chicago's Selig Polyscope Company in 1896. Frank Boggs established the company's Pacific coast branch, the first Los Angeles area film studio, in the spring of 1908 "at the corner of Seventh and South Olive streets, in Los Angeles." "James L. McGee, Thomas Santschi, James Crosby, Harry Todd, Gene Ward and Mrs. Boggs" accompanied Boggs. "It wasn't much of a place,"

according to one account, "a camera, a few lights and some painted scenery were about the entire equipment" (*Moving Picture World*, March 10, 1917, 1599–1603, MHDL).

3. For memorabilia of French's time with Bison Co., see the French Collection, folder 28.

4. Balshofer and Miller, *One Reel a Week*, 56.

5. Another report later erroneously claimed that Bison's first films were all westerns. It also stated that the Edendale studio was a block from Selig Polyscope, and it "consisted only of a horse corral and a stage" (*Moving Picture World*, March 10, 1915, 215–20, MHDL).

6. *Moving Picture World*, December 25, 1909, 907, MHDL; and *Story World and Photodramatist*, July 1923, http://archive.org/stream/storyworld.

7. See Smith (Bruzzel) Collection.

8. *Story World and Photodramatist*, July 1923, http://archive.org/stream/storyworld.

9. *Story World and Photodramatist*, July 1923, http://archive.org/stream/storyworld.

10. *Moving Picture World*, January 8, 1910, 33, MHDL.

11. See Jackson, *Ramona*. Jackson also wrote *A Century of Dishonor*, published in 1881. It is a nonfiction account of the nation's mistreatment of its Indians, including a chapter on the Winnebago.

12. For a contemporaneous account of this phenomenon, see James, *Through Ramona Country*. For a recent critical account, see Dorman, *Hell of a Vision*. For a critical reading of the annual Ramona Festival in Hemet, California, see Matson, "Performing Identity."

13. *Moving Picture World*, March 10, 1915, 215–20, MHDL. For an account of Biograph's first time in California, see Griffith, *When the Movies Were Young*, 134–72. See also California Mission Resource Center.

14. California's controversial saint, Father Junípero Serra, founded the mission. Many historians offer an account of this rebellion. See in particular Hackel, "Indian Testimony," 643–69.

15. Griffith, *When the Movies Were Young*, 169.

16. Balshofer and Miller, *One Reel a Week*, 74.

17. *Moving Picture World,* March 19, 1910, 429, MHDL.

18. *Moving Picture World*, January 8, 1910, 43, January 15, 1910, 70, and January 22, 1910, 92, 106, 108, MHDL.

19. *Moving Picture World*, February 12, 1910, 229, MHDL.

20. *New York Dramatic Mirror*, February 19, 1910, 19, FHC.

21. *Moving Picture World*, February 19, 1910, 276, and February 26, 1910, 300, MHDL.

22. "Quite a Colony," *Los Angeles Times*, February 1, 1910, NPC.

23. The article also ran in *Moving Picture World*, February 19, 1910, 256, MHDL. For whom the couple posed is a mystery. The term "perfect types of their race," however, was derived from the new discipline of anthropology. The

Smithsonian photograph of Red Wing's father (mentioned earlier) exemplifies this misperception, which usually entailed a front and side view of the subject in which cranium shape, jaw line, cheek bones, and, perhaps, nose (ironically, a Roman nose was "the perfect type" for Indian chiefs) were highlighted. As the Progressive Era progressed, it also came to be associated with a skewed kind of race pride that Red Wing may or may not have embraced.

24. Maison was born Carmen Edna K. Maisonave in 1886. For a brief biography of Maison, see "Edna Maison."

25. Daniels was born in Dallas, Texas, on January 14, 1901. She started as a child stage actor for the Belasco Stock Company ("Actresses—Comediennes," *Motion Picture Studio Directory*, 1919, 3150, https://www.ancestry.com/).

26. She played Blue Feather, daughter of a Cheyenne chief, in *Honor of the Tribe*, released January 16, 1912. New York's Museum of Modern Art has a viewing copy of this film, which also features J. Barney Sherry as Blue Feather's father.

27. For Peters's recollection of his early days with Bison Co., see "A Museum of Motion Picture History," GC 1026, box 1, unnumbered folder, Seaver Center, Los Angeles.

28. *Moving Picture World,* March 5, 1910, 353, MHDL.

29. *The Cowboy and the School-Marm*, Bison Life Pictures, 1910.

30. *Moving Picture World,* March 19, 1910, 426, 427, MHDL.

31. *Moving Picture World,* March 5, 1910, 302, MHDL; *Billboard*, March 5, 1910, 17, MHDL; and *New York Dramatic Mirror*, March 5, 1910, 8, FHC.

32. Red Wing is pictured in the ad for *A Shot in Time* (released on April 1), *Moving Picture World*, April 2, 1910, 495 (synopsis on 533), MHDL. For a review and photo, see *Moving Picture World*, April 16, 1910, 600, MHDL. The other film, *Romance of a Snake Charmer*, starred Evelyn Graham.

33. *Moving Picture World,* April 9, 1910, 539, MHDL.

34. *Moving Picture World,* April 16, 1910, 583, MHDL.

35. For story ad, synopsis, and review, respectively, see *Moving Picture World*, April 9, 1910, 539, April 16, 1910, 576, and April 26, 1910, 642, MHDL. I was able to further identify this film from unidentified stills in a scrapbook that belonged to Bison cameraman Maxwell Smith Bruzzel. See "Maxwell Smith Bruzzel Collection 1908–1912," Autry Museum, http://collections.theautry.org.

36. *Moving Picture World*, April 30, 1910, 690 (ad, April 9, 583; synopsis, April 16, 620), MHDL.

37. *Moving Picture World*, April 9, 1910, 583. See the French Collection, box 46, file 28, for another version of the scene, which shows Red Wing in the same pose with the same group behind her but no dead body. They are also pictured in front of a barn rather than on a grassy hillside.

38. *Moving Picture World*, April 16, 1910, 620, MHDL. I found the cowboys' names on a still from the French Collection, box 46, file 28.

39. "Tumbles from Buggy; Brain Slightly Hurt," and "Moving Pictures Show Accident to Actress," *Los Angeles Herald*, May 8 and 10, 1910, respectively, CDNC. Favar only suffered a concussion, but strangely, two weeks later her husband, a retired military officer, died from "a complication of diseases," which in fact was suicide. If Favar's life had been a movie, these events would have foreshadowed her murder on September 22, 1915, just before she reached the age of thirty. "Beside her was the body of J. C. Crowell of Greenwood, Miss., a millionaire. Their skulls had been crushed by some blunt instrument and an effort had been made to burn the bodies" ("Pay Tribute as Slain Actress Is Buried," *Los Angeles Herald*, March 23, 1916, CDNC). The police zoned in on a married man who had sent love letters to Favar, but his "trail led nowhere." Red Wing may have attended her funeral on March 23, 1916. If so, she was among those who, the *Herald* claimed, "forgot the shadow of the great tragedy and remembered [Favar] only as their friend . . . a beauty and a star." Favar was buried beside her mother, Alice, in the Hollywood Forever Cemetery. See also "Slain L.A. Actress to Be Buried Here" and "Heart Throb Missives to Actress," *Los Angeles Herald*, September 25 and 27, 1915, respectively, CDNC.

40. Smith (Bruzzel) Collection.

41. "Lawyer Julia St. Cyr and Her Winnebago Folks," *Omaha Sunday World-Herald*, January 26, 1913, genealogybank.com.

42. *Moving Picture World*, May 21, 1910, 834, MHDL.

8. NEW CAREERS WITH PATHÉ FRÈRES

1. Red Wing's autobiographies, Red Wing file.

2. Verhoeff, *The West in Early Cinema*, 162.

3. *Film Index*, July 23, 1910, 3, MHDL.

4. Pearl White's character, an Indian mother who saves her white husband from execution, is often mistaken for Red Wing. The two look nothing alike.

5. *Moving Picture World*, July 2, 1910, 24, MHDL.

6. My emphasis, *Nickelodeon*, June 15, 1910, 318, MHDL. Not all scholars are convinced that Young Deer directed this film, but Nickelodeon's description of its director points to none other. Indian men of prominence (or those purporting to be) were often called "chief" for no apparent reason.

7. *Technical World Magazine*, June 1910, 455, googlebooks.com.

8. Green Rainbow's father is unknown; his mother was called Logonoega. He had at least four wives and three daughters, two of whom he deserted. His only son lived less than a year. Green Rainbow died of pneumonia in 1926 ("Estate of Rosa Green Rainbow," roll 86, 417–19, and "Estate of Isaac Little Chief," roll 89, 399, RG 75, NARA-CPR; and "Deaths between 1925–1926," 1931 Winnebago census, https://www.ancestry.com/).

9. *Moving Picture World*, May 6, 1911, 999, MHDL.

10. *Moving Picture World* subsumed the publication in June 1911.

11. Larkin started playing vaudeville at sixteen and soon after began acting for the Edison Film Company. "His most spectacular fete" in motion pictures "was pretending to be shot and falling off a motorcycle going forty miles an hour." In 1914, when he worked for Universal Studios, he considered *A Cheyenne Brave* and *Under Both Flags* two of his most successful pictures (Justice and Smith, *Who's Who in the Film World*, 185).

12. *Film Index*, August 13, 1910, 16, 18, MHDL. Radcliffe was born in Niagara Falls, New York, in 1908. She debuted as an infant in *Quo Vadis* at eleven days old. *The Red Girl and the Child* appears to have been her first or second film (*Motion Picture Studio Directory*, 1919, 162, https://www.ancestry.com/). Radcliffe became a regular actor at West Coast Studio and then gained fame playing "tough boy parts."

13. *Film Index*, August 13, 1910, 3, MHDL. Later an article claimed that Red Wing "composed the poetry of 'The Red Girl and the Child.'" Perhaps it referred to the film's scenario, as there was no poem shown in the film.

14. *New York Dramatic Mirror*, August 20, 1910, 27, FHC. See also Horak, *Girls Will Be Boys*; and "1910—Movies, Reform, and New Women," in Keil and Singer, *American Cinema*, 31.

15. *Moving Picture World*, September 3, 1910, 518, MHDL.

16. *Film Index*, August 6, 1910, 3, MHDL; *Moving Picture World*, August 6, 1910, 518, MHDL.

17. *Moving Picture World*, August 20, 1910, 423, MHDL.

18. *Moving Picture World*, July 9, 1910, 125, and July 30, 1910, 245, MHDL. The ad has no picture, but Red Fern is described as "an Indian woman" in the story line summary.

19. "Winnebago Indians Are Registered at Nadeau," *Los Angeles Herald*, July 24, 1910, CDNC; and "Personal," *Los Angeles Times*, July 23, 1910, NPC.

20. *Film Index*, August 6, 1910, 3, MHDL.

21. See figure 29.

22. *Moving Picture World*, August 27, 1910, 471, MHDL.

23. Balshofer and Miller, *One Reel a Week*, 61.

24. Nestor released *The Plains Across* with a Red Wing character on July 19, 1911. See ad with photo of Red Wing character in *Moving Picture World*, July 22, 1911, 152, MHDL. Champion released *The Cowboy and the Squaw*, featuring Clara Hall as Red Wing, on July 27, 1911 (*Moving Picture World*, July 23, 1911, 217, MHDL).

25. "Deaths in Profession," *New York Clipper*, February 11, 1911, 1287, FHC.

26. See also "Actors, Characters . . . Charles K. French," *Motion Picture Studio Directory*, 77, https://www.ancestry.com/.

27. *New York Dramatic Mirror*, January 2, 1897, 2, FHC.

28. Balshofer and Miller, *One Reel a Week*, 63–64.

29. *Moving Picture World*, November 19, 1910, 1178, MHDL.

30. Balshofer stopped placing ads with images in July, and, apparently, because he was juggling so many things, he stopped placing ads altogether for several weeks. Consequently, *Moving Picture World* did not offer a scenario for *The Flight of Red Wing*. Unfortunately, I was unable to travel to London to view the British Film Institute's copy of the film.

31. See Spears, *Hollywood*, 394–95, for a sketch of Red Wing. Her name also appears in the book's acknowledgments section. However, Spears mistakenly credits Red Wing for *An Apache Father's Revenge*, although Bison 101 released the film in 1913. He also stated that one of her best-known Pathé films was *Back to the Prairie* rather than *Appeal of the Prairie*.

32. Smith (Bruzzel) Collection.

33. *Moving Picture World*, October 1, 1910, 7900.

34. *Moving Picture World*, September 16, 1910, 670, MHDL.

35. Smith (Bruzzel) Collection.

36. Another photo marked "The Flight of Red Wing" shows some of the same men in the same costumes attacking white men in front of a cabin while Young Deer places his knife on a white man's scalp. The photo reflects the story line of *For the Love of Red Wing* far better than it does *The Flight of Red Wing* (Smith [Bruzzel] Collection).

37. *Oakland (CA) Tribune*, October 30, 1910, 3, NPC. Balshofer's companion was Dr. C. L. Bennett of Oakland, California.

38. *Variety*, November 5, 1910, 14, MHDL.

39. I believe this was her first film ("Great Indian Western-Lyric," *Mount [PA] Carmel Item*, December 17, 1910, NPC; her name is listed as "Miss Nora Darkfeather"). For *A Child of the West,* see *Moving Picture World*, December 17, 1910, 1434, MHDL. "The part of the Indian girl in this picture is played by Miss Mona Darkfeather, a full-blooded Indian girl with strong and dramatic talent" ("Society and Personal," *Elwood [IN] Daily Record*, December 22, 1910, NPC).

40. For example, the finding aid for "American Indians in Silent Film" (Motion Picture & Television Reading Room, Library of Congress) lists the cast of *Little Dove's Romance* as "Red Wing, Charles Inslee, J. Barney Sherry, and Young Deer." I viewed the film, which shows Darkfeather, Charles Inslee, and Gebhardt in the leads. (J. Barney Sherry may have played Little Dove's father.) Neither Red Wing nor Young Deer appears in the film.

41. *Moving Picture World*, January 14, 1911, 90, MHDL. See also Richard Spencer column with photo of Chester, *Moving Picture World*, March 4, 1911, 466, and December 31, 1910, 1548, MHDL.

42. *Variety* (n.d., PDF 1343), FHC. See also *Billboard*, December 31, 1910, 26, MHDL.

43. The names, addresses, and occupations of the individuals in the company can be located by searching the 1910 and 1911 Los Angeles city directories, https://www.ancestry.com/; *Moving Picture World*, March 11, 1911, 520, MHDL.

44. "For Sale—or Exchange, 4-Cyl, 40 H.P. Thomas Detroit raceabout, 4-passenger, top glass front, speedometer, clock, magneto, etc., in good condition. Will trade for touring car. Let me know what you have. Address JAMES YOUNG DEER, West Coast Studio, Edendale" ("Classified Liners . . . Things on Wheels—All Sorts," *Los Angeles Times*, November 29, 1910, NPC).

45. These names have been confirmed and added to by merging the captions of two separate publications of the photo and the Los Angeles city directory.

46. See "Hoxie, Jack," in Katchmer, *A Biographical Dictionary*. Katchmer is incorrect about Hart's father, however. Hoxie's lengthy family story is included here because it represents an example, albeit extreme, of why so many western performers posed as Indian or part Indian. It also represents an example of how much research it takes to debunk an Indian poser. Hoxie's mother, Matilda, had taken the surname Quick by the time she was sixteen. Her mother had at least three husbands, one of them John Quick, but none of her known husbands seems to have been Matilda's father, unless it was John Dyer, a Michigan laborer born in England. At sixteen, Matilda, whose mother was of Pennsylvania Dutch ancestry, was married off to a nearly forty-year-old divorced Kansas farmer called Dr. Joseph M. Hoxie, with whom she had three children. Known locally as "an unsavory character," Hoxie was a farmer and stock raiser, but it's unclear whether he was a physician or a veterinarian. When Matilda parted ways with Hoxie at twenty-one years of age, she married nineteen-year-old Kansas native Calvin Scott Stone, apparently Hart Hoxie's real father.

A few years after Stone married Matilda, he was tried for rape but seems to have been let off the hook. He took the alias Doc Hoxie, after Matilda's ex-husband, and thus the confusion. About 1918 Stone was indicted for fraudulently claiming two homesteads and served some time in Oregon for the crime. Matilda left him before or after he went to prison and remarried.

Eventually, Scott Stone moved to Los Angeles probably to be near his two sons, Hart and Alton "Al" Jay Stone, who as Al Hoxie performed as Hart's stuntman. Scott Stone was eventually picked up for a "morals charge" involving an underage girl, for which he pleaded guilty. In 1925 he was sentenced to hang for the murder of two Los Angeles area sisters, age twelve and eight. A confession states that he lured the girls (and they weren't the first) into his apartment with the promise that they could meet his famous son, Hart. Apparently, when he tried to sexually assault the older girl, the younger girl protested, and he killed them both. Their bodies were discovered a year later in a sewage ditch. At the time, newspapers reported that the Hoxie brothers were related to Stone, but he was said to have been their stepfather. After some legal rigmarole, Stone's sentence was lessened to life in prison. He was paroled after fifteen years and released from San Quentin in 1941. Three years later, he died in Los Angeles. See "People v. Stone," https://casetext.com/case/people-v-stone-8; federal census records, https://www.ancestry.com/; "The Hoxie Brothers," http://www.b-westerns.com/hoxie1.htm; "Hart Hoxie," Find a Grave Memorial #71531019, findagrave.com; "A Disciple of Esculapius Ornamenting a Tree," *Atchison Daily Champion*, May 16, 1873, NPC; "All Around," *Lawrence Daily Journal*, May 20, 1873, NPC; "Joseph Hoxie vs. Maria C. Hoxie," *Belleville (KS) Telescope*, October 12, 1876; "Republic City News," *Belleville (KS) Telescope*, June 2, 1899, NPC; title illegible, *Belleville (KS) Republic County Press*, October 23, 1890, NPAC; Great-grandma Hoxie-Stone," http://alhoxietribute.blogspot.com/2007/11/great-grandma-hoxie-stone.html; and Catherine Quick marriages, http://berrien.migenweb.net/Biography_files/BrackettBios/Creitzer.html.

47. "Miss Bessie Eyton, formerly appearing in Pathe West Coast productions, has left the latter company and gone to the Selig Company, with whom he [she] has signed a contract" (*Moving Picture World*, May 20, 1911, 1125, MHDL). See also "Biography of Bessie (Harrison) (Eyton) (Coffey) Macdonald," http://mendoncafamily.com.s193431.gridserver.com/wp-content/uploads/2009/12/Biography-color-text.pdf.

48. *Motion Picture Story Magazine*, August 1912, 32, MHDL.

49. *Moving Picture World,* March 4, 1911, 466, MHDL. The 1900 federal census for San Francisco shows she was six years old (https://www.ancestry.com/). The Los Angeles federal census for 1910 shows her age as fifteen and that she was a musical comedy actress (https://www.ancestry.com/).

50. Lindvall, *Sanctuary Cinema*, 124. For Chester's role in Mena, see also *Moving Picture World*, December 1, 1917, 1311, MHDL; and "Virginia Chester," #91254155, findagrave.com.

51. *Moving Picture World*, January 30, 1911, 199, MHDL; and "Champion Rider Is Killed," *Urbana (IL) Daily Courier*, October 26, 1910, http://idnc.library.illinois.edu.

52. *Film Index*, January 7, 1911, 20, MHDL. Red Wing appears prominently in two stills for the film. The British Film Institute also holds a copy today, entitled *Celebrations on the Ranch*. I was not able to view the film, but the BFI's synopsis of the story mixes up the Indian girl character with a Mexican girl. See "Celebrations on the Ranch," http://collections-search.bfi.org.

53. *New York Dramatic Mirror*, September 1910–December 1911, FHC. See also *Moving Picture World*, January 7, 1911, 38–39, and January 14, 1911, 90, MHDL.

54. See *Moving Picture World*, January 14, 1911, 96, and January 28, 1911, 94, MHDL. For the new studio, see *Film Index*, February 11, 1911, 5, MHDL. It's often difficult to determine if a Pathé American film was made by Young Deer or by an East

Coast director unless the film has survived the ages. If so, the densely wooded East Coast scenery is easy to distinguish from Southern California's more arid landscapes. In addition, Red Wing's natural appearance and acting without fake Indian mannerisms make her films easier to identify when she is pictured.

55. *Nickelodeon*, January 28, 1911, 112, MHDL.

56. *Moving Picture World*, February 4, 1911, 243, MHDL. See also *Film Index*, January 21, 1911, 6, 16, MHDL; *Moving Picture World*, January 21, 1911, 151, and February 4, 1911, 243, MHDL.

57. *Moving Picture World*, February 18, 1910, 370, MHDL. Compare this review to the one in *Film Index*, an organ for Pathé: "Throughout this picture the action is sustained at a high pitch, so that there is not a dull moment in it. The photography is of good quality also" (*Film Index*, February 4, 1911, 4, MHDL).

58. *Moving Picture World*, January 21, 1911, 137, MHDL.

59. *Moving Picture World*, January 30, 1911, 199, MHDL.

60. *Moving Picture World*, February 11, 1911, 302, MHDL.

61. *Moving Picture World*, February 18, 1911, 360, MHDL. The accident was also reported in the French magazine *Cine-Journal*, March 4, 1911, 9, MHDL.

62. *Moving Picture World*, February 18, 1911, 360, MHDL.

63. Apparently, she did not bead the yoke, however, which has an interesting provenance. Ethnohistorian Clyde Ellis sent me a photograph of the same yoke worn by a little girl who was said to be Jesse Black Cat of the Rosebud Reservation. The photo was taken before 1912, when it appeared on the front cover of the *Indian Sentinel*, a missionary publication of the Catholic Church. See Jesse Black Cat Photo. In tracking down the identity of the little girl through Indian census rolls, the only candidate is Sallie Black Cat, who lived with her parents and siblings on the Pine Ridge reservation. She died from tuberculosis when she was twenty-five. I asked Fralin Museum (Charlottesville, Virginia) Curator of Indigenous Art Adrianna Greci Green in February 2017 if Red Wing's and Black Cat's yokes were the same, and she replied: "I agree it looks like the same beaded yoke, she [Red Wing] gussied it up with some fringe on the sleeve edges. I have never seen two dresses exactly the same as this seems to be, so although it is certainly possible that an artist might make similar or even perhaps the same design, I've never seen two to match." Since Julia St. Cyr collected Native clothing, it's possible she saved this piece for her sister. Or Red Wing bought the piece herself when Young Deer acquired the beaded vest from Pine Ridge.

64. *Film Index*, February 11, 1911, 5, MHDL.

65. *Moving Picture World*, February 18, 1911, 430. See also *Moving Picture World*, February 11, 1911, 320, MHDL; and *Nickelodeon*, February 11, 1911, 173, MHDL.

66. *Moving Picture World*, February 11, 1911, 302, MHDL.

67. *Film Index*, February 11, 1911, 5, MHDL. *Moving Picture World*, March 4, 1911, 482, MHDL.

68. *Nickelodeon*, March 11, 1911, 280, MHDL.

69. For *The Kid from Arizona*, see *Film Index*, March 25, 1911, 19–20; *Moving Picture World*, February 25, 1911, 416, and April 8, 1911, 782, MHDL. For *The Cattle Rustlers*, see *Moving Picture World*, April 8, 1911, 780, MHDL. Cinématèque Français, Paris, holds a copy of *The Sheriff's Daughter* (Verhoeff, *The West in Early Cinema*, 421).

70. See *Film Index*, March 11, 18, and 25, 1911, MHDL.

71. *Nickelodeon*, March 25, 1911, 336, MHDL.

72. *Moving Picture World*, March 25, 1910, 656, MHDL.

73. "Divorce Action Filed," *Los Angeles Herald*, March 5, 1911, CDNC; and "Divorce Suit Filed," *Los Angeles Times*, March 5, 1911, NPC. After a six-month search, following my visit to the Los Angeles County Courthouse, the Los Angeles County Courthouse Archives could not locate Red Wing's divorce filing.

74. *Moving Picture World*, March 4, 1911, 466, MHDL.

9. LEAVING YOUNG DEER

1. *Moving Picture World*, January 14, 1911, 93, and September 9, 1911, 718, MHDL. Coincidentally, Pat C. Hartigan from Bison Co., who played Red Wing's leading man, simultaneously left Edendale for New York for a career change. However, he returned by the summer to work for Kalem Company and directed Ruth Rolland as an Indian character in *A Chance Shot*.

2. "Under the Big Box," *Los Angeles Times*, March 12, 1911, CNDC.

3. "Under the Big Box," *Los Angeles Times*, March 12, 1911, CNDC.

4. "Under the Big Box," *Los Angeles Times*, March 12, 1911, CNDC.

5. *Moving Picture World*, March 25, 1911, 704, MHDL.

6. *Moving Picture World*, March 25, 1911, 644, and January 14, 1911, 93, MHDL.

7. *Moving Picture World*, April 22, 1911, 889, MHDL.

8. See "Benign Poker Davis Fleecing 'Em Again," "Finish of Tough Roadhouse," and "Woman's Name Let Out," *Los Angeles Times*, April 9, April 18, and June 13, 1911, respectively, NPC.

9. "Benign Poker Davis Fleecing 'Em Again," *Los Angeles Times*, April 9, 1911, NPC.

10. *Moving Picture World*, April 22, 1911, 889, MHDL.

11. *Moving Picture World*, April 29, 1911, 944, MHDL. Longpre died less than two months after Young Deer's visit.

12. "Coast News," *Madera (CA) Mercury*, July 6, 1912, CNDC.

13. *Moving Picture World*, April 29, 1911, 944, MHDL.

14. "Sioux Motion Picture Actor Goes on War Path," *Los Angeles Herald*, April 29, 1911, CNDC.

15. *Film Index*, April 29, 1911, 13, 22, MHDL. See also *Moving Picture World*, May 6, 1911, 1024, and May 20, 1140, MHDL.

16. "James Young Deer," *Moving Picture World*, May 6, 1911, 999, MHDL.

17. "James Young Deer," *Moving Picture World*, May 6, 1911, 999, MHDL.

18. *Moving Picture World*, May 20, 1911, 1116, MHDL.

19. *Moving Picture World*, May 27, 1911, 1186, MHDL.

20. "Indian Strikes Waiter; Crowd Chases on Street," *Los Angeles Herald*, May 25, 1911, CNDC. The article identified Morris as Choctaw. Apparently, he was David Morris, born in 1885. He appears on the Dawes Roll for the Choctaw for September 25, 1902, census card 515, Dawes Roll 1054, Native American Enrollment Cards for the Five Civilized Tribes, https://www.ancestry.com/.

21. *Indian Justice* was probably filmed in the Santa Monica Canyon location. Amsterdam's Filmmuseum (EYE) holds a copy of *The White Squaw* (titled *Indienne blanche*), which I have not seen. See Verhoeff, *The West in Early Cinema*, 419. Meanwhile, New Jersey's Pathé studio produced several westerns at this time, including *Old Indian Days*. Young Deer was mistakenly given credit in one newspaper for the film: "Manager director of a great Pacific coast studio, knows something about the real Indian as he was—No blood and thunder, but the free untrammeled life of the Red Man—He makes 'Old Indian Days'" ("Mr. James Young Deer," *Arkansas City [ks] Traveler*, July 22, 1911, NPC). It's not evident from the trade magazines if Pathé East Coast or West Coast made *The Passing of Dappled Fawn*. See *Film Index*, June 24, 1911, 4, 25, MHDL.

22. "Red Wing (who in private life is known as Mrs. James Young Deer), who plays Indian leads in Pathe Western stories, and who has been absent for several months visiting in New York City, is expected back this week" (*Moving Picture World*, May 20, 1911, 1125, MHDL).

23. *Moving Picture World*, June 10, 1911, 1302, MHDL.

24. *Moving Picture World*, June 17, 1911, 1382, MHDL.

25. *Moving Picture World*, June 10, 1911, 1302, and July 8, 1576, MHDL.

26. "Actor Loses Mind for over a Year," *San Francisco Chronicle*, March 26, 1913, NPC.

27. *Moving Picture World*, July 8, 1911, 1576, MHDL.

28. Red Wing stated she was in this film ("Famous Indian Actress Visits Klamath Tribe," *Evening Herald* [Klamath Falls OR], October 26, 1916, NPC). For the synopsis and review, see *Moving Picture World*, August 5, 1911, 306, and August 19, 1911, 463, MHDL.

29. "At the Bijou," *Wilmington (nc) Dispatch*, August 8, 1911, NPC.

30. From the *Spectator*, printed in the *New York Dramatic Mirror*, August 2, 1911, 21, FHC.

31. *Variety*, July 8, 1911, 1, MHDL; *Moving Picture World*, July 15, 1911, 22, and July 22, 1911, 114, MHDL.

32. Lillian St. Cyr Laverdue died in 2004. For her obituary, see "Lilian Laverdue," *Sioux City Journal*, August 19, 2004, https://siouxcityjournal.com.

33. The 1912 Indian census shows that Louis and Rosa were no longer married. Rosa died after giving birth to a son, Henry Bear ("Local Happenings," *Winnebago*

[*ne*] *Chieftain*, October 31, 1913, Ho-Chunk Historical Society). Her infant died shortly after. Keeping with family custom, Louis married Rosa's sister Mabel Frenchman sometime before 1918.

34. *Moving Picture World*, August 5, 1911, 228, MHDL.

35. Some of the following films identified as American Pathé's in trade magazines may have also been specifically West Coast Studio productions: *The Trapper's Fatal Shot* (released August 16), *The Message of the Arrow* (August 19), *The Ranch in Flames* (August 28), *For the Sake of the Tribe* (August 30), *The Medicine Woman* (August 31), *The Red Man's Dog* (September 7), *An Up-to-Date Squaw* (September 20), *The Squaw's Mistaken Love* (October 5), *The Ranch Girl's Terrible Mistake* (October 18), *The Renegade Brother* (October 19), *In Frontier Days* (October 26), *A Sioux Lover's Strategy* (November 2), *The Bandit's Bride* (November 10), *The Incendiary Indians* (November 29), and *Poisoned Arrows* (December 7).

36. *Moving Picture World*, September 9, 1911, 716, and August 19, 478, MHDL.

37. *Moving Picture World*, August 5, 1911, 276, MHDL.

38. *Moving Picture World*, August 19, 1911, 449, MHDL.

39. The film (which I have not seen) is held by the Cinématèque Français in Paris. See Nanna Verhoeff's excellent analysis of this film in *The West in Early Cinema*, 169.

40. "[A] most unexpected and attractive encounter," is written on the film's intertitle, as Verhoeff explains (*The West in Early Cinema*, 169).

41. *Moving Picture World*, October 7, 1911, 39, MHDL.

42. *Moving Picture World*, October 28, 1900, 290, MHDL.

43. *Moving Picture World*, September 30, 1911, 953, MHDL. "Anna Little, who was formerly with Ferris Hartman Musical Company, is one of the latest to join the motion pictures. She is now with the Bison company" (*Moving Picture News*, October 21, 1911, 27, MHDL). Regarding new talent, someone placed the following ad: "Wanted—Ladies and Gentlemen to interest themselves in moving picture acting, you may have talent for this art. Call and investigate, this school is directly connected with Pathe's West Coast Studio. Academy of Photoplay, 308 Broadway Central Bldg. office hours 10 to 4. WM Courtright, Manager" ("Wanted—Miscellaneous," *Los Angeles Times*, September 25, 1911, NPC). Gertrude Price's interview with DeGrasse states that he appeared in this film. See "This 'Bandit' of Movies Likes the Breezes and Balmy Weather," *Evansville (IN) Press*, June 9, 1913, 2, NPC.

44. *Motion Picture Story*, October 1911, "Gallery of Picture Players," MHDL.

10. KEEPING UP WITH THE COMPETITION

1. *Moving Picture News*, October 28, 1911, 26, MHDL.

2. Also known as the San Joaquin or Irvine Ranch, it's located about a mile from today's entrance to Irvine Park.

3. "At the Star," *Press and Sun-Bulletin* (Binghamton ny), January 25, 1911, 9, NPC.

4. "Moving Picture Concern Taking Cowboy Scenes on San Joaquin Ranch," *Santa Ana Register*, October 25, 1911, NPC.

5. Red Wing's autobiographies, Red Wing file.

6. Balshofer and Miller, *One Reel a Week*, 75–76.

7. *Moving Picture World*, June 8, 1912, 913, MHDL.

8. Balshofer and Miller, *One Reel a Week*, 75–76.

9. *Motography*, December 1911, 287, MHDL. *Nickelodeon* was *Motography*'s former name.

10. Balshofer and Miller, *One Reel a Week*, 80.

11. There is a lot of confusion about who leased what and when and whether Ince actually purchased 460 of these acres at the Sunset Boulevard / Pacific Coast Highway crossing. Some say the Miller Brothers owned some of the land and/or leased most of the land, but Michael Wallis (*The Real Wild West*) does not mention any land in the Santa Inez Canyon connected to the Miller Brothers at this time, only that the company was wintering and renting houses in Venice. In addition, Marc Wanamaker of Bison Company Productions/Archives in Los Angeles could not remember the exact details regarding ownership but thought that the Miller Brothers originally owned some of the Inceville land. Fred Balshofer (Balshofer and Miller, *One Reel a Week*) indicated that the land was the same as the Bison lease, though Ince may have leased and/or purchased additional land later.

12. Agnew, *The Old West*, 86.

13. Standing Bear, *My People the Sioux*, 283.

14. *New York Dramatic Mirror*, November 22, 1911, 28, FHC. Although the Internet Movie Database (IMDb) attributes the film to Pearl White and, thus, New Jersey Pathé, Red Wing played herself.

15. *Moving Picture World*, December 2, 1911, 724, MHDL.

16. *Moving Picture World*, November 19, 1911, 570, and December 9, 816, MHDL.

17. *Moving Picture News*, December 16, 1911, 29, MHDL.

18. Jim Sleeper (*Great Movies*) believes *Swiftwind's Heroism* was shot at the Orange County ranch, although this cannot be confirmed.

19. "Opera House Tonight," *Columbus (KS) Daily Advocate*, May 22, 1912, NPC.

20. "Indian Life and Customs," *Moving Picture World*, March 30, 1912, 1145, MHDL. These films included *The Sioux Cave of Death*, *The Chief's Talisman* (released April 22, 1911), *The Indian's Pride* (released July 6, 1911), and perhaps *For the Squaw* (released June 21, 1911). Andrew B. Smith mistakenly attributes *For the Squaw* to Young Deer (*Shooting Cowboys and Indians*, 96). However, Dark Cloud and Dove Eye appear in a film still with the caption "*For the Squaw* was produced at the Pathe eastern studio" (*Film Index,* June 17, 1911, 13, MHDL).

21. *Moving Picture World*, January 20, 1912, 238, MHDL.

22. See "Character Actors . . . Dark Cloud," *Motion Picture Studio Directory*, 76, MHDL. For genealogical data, see Elijah Tahamont, "Baptisms, Sorel, Protestant, 1863," AC. For the Camp and Tahamont families, see New York state census, Warren County, Caldwell, and 1880 and 1900 New York federal census, Warren County, Caldwell, https://www.ancestry.com/. For the Tahamonts' professional career, see "Remington's Model and Picture Show Hero Mourns for Woods," *Fort Worth Star-Telegram*, August 29, 1912, NPAC, as well as "An Indian Chief," *Houston Post*, June 23, 1912, NPAC.

23. Beulah Dark Cloud married famed Seneca anthropologist Arthur C. Parker, and their daughter, Bertha Parker, is known today as the first Native American woman anthropologist. She collected oral traditions of California Indians while working for the Southwest Museum in Los Angeles, California ("Biography: Bertha Cody"). Bertha Parker married western star (and non-Indian Indian) Iron Eyes Cody, famous for his 1970 ad about pollution (which will be discussed later).

24. Relatives Robert and Estella Tahamont attended Carlisle, however (http://carlisleindian.dickinson.edu).

25. "Remington's Model and Picture Show Hero Mourns for Woods," *Fort Worth Star-Telegram*, August 29, 1912, NPAC.

26. *Motography*, February 1912, 87, MHDL. See also "Pathe Motion Picture Company in the City," *El Paso Herald*, December 26, 1911, NPAC.

27. See London, *The Letters*, 296–97, 398–99.

28. Buck's family name is recorded a variety of ways, but he should not be confused with George V. Connor, who also managed for Buffalo Bill and the Miller Brothers' 101 Ranch. As usual, it's hard to distinguish fact from fiction when it comes to the families of early western actors. Although myth has it that Connors was born in San Saba, Texas, he was in fact born on November 22, 1880, in Streater, Illinois, to West Virginian William Connors and his wife, Leah Bowen, an Illinois native. After his mother died, the family moved to West Virginia. See George W. Connor, Social Security Life Claim; 1880 Illinois federal census, Streater (Bruce Township), La Salle County; and 1900 West Virginia federal census, Clay District, Marshall County, https://www.ancestry.com/. See also a biographical sketch of George Buck Connors at "The Old Corral," b-westerns.com. It notes that he didn't receive a Medal of Honor, but see the *Albuquerque Journal*, November 2, 1913, NPAC. Silva states that Connors retired in Quartzsite, Arizona, and died on a visit to Yuma on February 4, 1947.

29. *Variety*, January 30, 1909, 17, MHDL.

30. "Lassoes Girl in Secret Marriage," *Fort Worth Star-Telegram*, May 2, 1910, NPAC.

31. *Variety,* April 1, 1911, 11, MHDL.

32. "'Butch' Connors Has Gone to New Mexico," *Trenton (NJ) Evening Times*, December 10, 1911, 24, NPC. The newspaper reported that the independent film

company Powers Picture Plays Company employed him. The organization, from Bronx, New York, was run by Pat Powers. Either the reporter got the company name wrong or Young Deer quickly nabbed Connors from his competitor.

33. Lyons's stage career began as "a charter member of the Beta Sigma dramatic society of San Francisco." She played several leads for the group ("Society Girl to Join Nethersole," *San Francisco Call*, April 24, 1911, CDNC). Lyons was born in 1881 to an unknown Wisconsin-born mother and Julius Lyons, a Los Angeles attorney and the first court reporter appointed for the city. His father was a native of Maryland, but he was born in South America to a South American mother. After his wife died, he lived in Los Angeles with his mother and brother. Sometime before 1900, San Francisco merchant Willard L. Growall, who served as executor to Jack London's estate, and his wife, Emma, adopted Lyons (perhaps informally). Emma's family had also adopted Charmian Kitteredge, who became London's wife. Thus, Lyons was London's niece through marriage. For Lyons's marriages and children, see "Rubio Ranch House Rustic Retreat," *Star News Pasadena*, June 3, 1965, NPAC; "Marriages," *Los Angeles Times*, September 16, 1904, NPC; 1900 California federal census, San Francisco, District 121; 1900 California federal census, Los Angeles, District 5; Los Angeles city directory (1900); 1910 California federal census, Alameda, Berkeley, District 64; and 1930 California federal census, Los Angeles, District 721, https://www.ancestry.com/.

34. "Legal Documents," *Arizona Daily Star* (Tucson), February 27, 1912, NPC. Pathé West was not the only company filming in the area. Powers Picture Plays filmed at the San Augustin Ranch in the Organ Mountains, east of Alamogordo, New Mexico, while the Nestor Company filmed in Old Town in Albuquerque ("Mr. Horsley Takes Moving Pictures of the Town," *Albuquerque Journal*, February 21, 1912, NPAC). There's a lot of confusion about when and what Powers was filming. Some said *The Dude* was shot at the San Augustine Ranch in 1911, but an actual release date or synopsis of the film can't be found. However, the company released *Mexican Border Defenders* on April 6, 1912, which may be the Powers film described in a lengthy *Albuquerque Journal* article entitled "Fearful Battle with Rustlers in the Organs," February 28, 1912, NPAC. In addition, the Lubin Film Company filmed near the same time and place as Red Wing's crew, releasing *The Handicap* on March 7 and *The Mexican Courtship* on March 2. The latter similarly titled film beat West Coast Studio's release of *A Mexican Elopement* by nearly three weeks. See "Pictures of Ranch Life," *El Paso Herald*, February 15, 1912, 4, NPAC, for the filming locations.

35. See "American Has Close Call in Revolt," *Tucson Citizen*, August 28, 1911, genealogybank.com.

36. *Pawnee Love* (released February 17) and *Marriage or Death* (February 21) were probably East Coast Pathé films. In addition, the extant film held by EYE, *The Two Brothers* (released February 10), starring Octavia Handworth, a popular

East Coast Pathé stock player, is obviously by its landscape filmed in New Jersey. *Two Convict Brothers* was probably its sequel.

37. *Moving Picture World*, January 27, 1912, 324, MHDL. Lubin and Bison also produced films titled *Indian Blood* in 1911 and 1913, respectively.

38. *Moving Picture World*, February 24, 1912, 712, MHDL.

39. Although the title is off a bit, a fan magazine columnist stated, "Red Wing had the lead in 'A Slave [*sic*] to Firewater' (Pathé)," *Motion Picture Story*, July 1914, 165, MHDL. For *Cholera on the Plains,* see *Moving Picture World*, March 23, 1912, 1063, MHDL. For *The Arrow of Defiance,* see *Moving Picture World*, March 16, 1912, 996, and March 30, 1912, 1165, MHDL; for *The Price of Gratitude,* see *Moving Picture World*, March 16, 1912, 998, MHDL. In fact, none of these films has a scenario with a prominent Indian female.

40. *Moving Picture World*, March 23, 1912, 1096, MHDL.

41. *New York Dramatic Mirror*, May 8, 1912, 26, FHC. Glaum's character grows up with a white settler who adopts her after Indians killed her parents. An Indian, played by Inslee, also lived in the household, and their love story moves along nicely until an artist, played by Simmons, steals Glaum's heart and takes her back east to marry. The story ends with Inslee's forlorn noble Indian wandering the forest and carving the name of his love in the trees. See *Moving Picture World*, March 30, 1912, 1200, MHDL.

42. *Moving Picture World*, April 6, 1912, 66, MHDL. For Maison's role in the film, see "Edna Maison, at Home in the Rarefied Aria of Opera and Silver Screen," https://classicfilmaficionados.com.

43. *Moving Picture World* (March 25, 1912, 717, MHDL) published the following orchestra director's suggestion for the film's musical accompaniment. It offers a different view of the film synopsis normally presented in the magazine, reminding us that the public did not view silent films in silence:
   1. "Os-ka-loo-sa-loo" (Indian song) till change of scene.
   2. When he seizes girl short agitato till "That Same Night."
   3. Long, semi-mysterious agitato till Indian kills sleeping man.
   4. Hurry till "Next Morning."
   5. Indian music, sentimental order, till man throws cloth over Indian girl's head.
   6. Agitato till "Be Not Afraid, My Sister."
   7. Long, semi-mysterious till struggle.
   8. Hurry till man is seen dead.
   9. Sentimental Indian character (long) till end.

44. *Moving Picture World*, April 20, 1912, 262, and May 11, 527, MHDL. For an online view of the film (though the last part is damaged), see "For the Papoose," Library of Congress, https://www.loc.gov/item/90706439/.

45. *Moving Picture World*, May 18, 1912, 628, MHDL; also printed in *New York Clipper*, May 1, 1912, 6, MHDL. See also *Moving Picture World*, April 27, 1912, 360, MHDL. Also shown as *The Redmen's Honor*.

46. For *The Cowboy Girls*, see *Moving Picture World*, April 27, 1912, 360, MHDL. For *Orphans of the Plains*, see *Moving Picture World*, May 18, 1912, 658, MHDL. Cinématèque Français, Paris, holds a copy of the latter film, entitled *Les orphelins de la plaine* (Verhoeff, *The West in Early Cinema*, 420).

47. *Moving Picture World*, June 1, 1912, 830, MHDL. See also *Moving Picture World*, May 25, 1912, 760, MHDL. For *The Prospector's Sweetheart*, see *Moving Picture World*, June 8, 1912, 942, MHDL.

48. *Moving Picture World*, May 18, 1912, 658, and June 8, 942, MHDL.

49. *New York Dramatic Mirror*, May 1, 1912, 33, FHC. It's odd that Young Deer chose "Young Buffalo" for Gebhardt, given it was the white villain's name in *For the Papoose*.

50. *Motion Picture Story Magazine*, February 1912, 150, MHDL.

51. Gebhardt made a detour from Bison to Pathé, as shown in the following excerpt: "George Gebhart, formerly director of the Lux company at Hollywood, and later a leading man with the Nestor company, has gone over to Pathe Western company and will play all the Indian leads in the future. This is his forte and James Youngdeer, the Pathe director, is writing a series of Indian romantic dramas to feature Gebhart and Miss Winona [*sic*] Redwing, who is usually known in the pictures as 'Princess Redwing'" (*Moving Picture World*, June 8, 1912, 94, MHDL).

52. Young Deer's writing talents were also in competition with Bison, according to the following advertisement: "The Bison people say they are having difficulty getting photoplays and invite writers to submit scripts on the following subjects: Western Comedy, Military, Mining, Emigrant and Pioneer. Big Western stuff for two-reel productions is especially desired" (*Moving Picture World*, June 8, 1912, 913, MHDL).

53. "Over a Mile of Wonder Pageant," *Los Angeles Times*, May 11, 1912, NPC.

54. *Moving Picture World*, June 29, 1912, 1218–19, MHDL.

55. *Moving Picture World*, June 29, 1912, 1218–19, MHDL.

56. *Moving Picture World*, June 8, 1912, 914, MHDL.

57. His return was also reported in the Doings at Los Angeles column in *Moving Picture World*, June 8, 1912, 914, MHDL. See also *Moving Picture World*, June 8, 1912, 954, and June 29, 1912, 1226–27, MHDL. IMDb lists Buck Connors as the director of *A Redskin's Appeal*, but that was probably the writer's guess. On June 1 Pathé American released its "cowboy comedy" *A Whirlwind Courtship on Brandon's Ranch*. It's unknown if the film was a New Jersey or a California

production, but there seems to have been no Indian characters in the film (*Moving Picture World*, June 12, 1912, 760, MHDL).

58. *Moving Picture World*, June 8, 1912, 940, MHDL. "It was George Gebhardt, Jr., who played Strongheart in Pathe's 'A Redskin's Appeal'" (*Moving Picture World*, July 13, 1912, 39, MHDL). Strongheart was the namesake for a wildly popular 1905 play authored by Cecil B. DeMille's brother, William C. DeMille.

59. *Moving Picture World*, June 29, 1912, 1226–27, MHDL.

60. *Moving Picture World*, June 29, 1912, 1260, and July 13, 147, MHDL.

61. *Moving Picture World*, June 15, 1912, 1062, MHDL. "'Indian Idyll' was a Pathé Freres picture and taken at Los Angeles, Cal." (*Motion Picture Story Magazine*, March 1913, 140, MHDL).

62. A *Moving Picture World* columnist was under the impression that the company was headed for Lake Tahoe for the summer (*Moving Picture World*, June 8, 1912, 194, MHDL).

63. *Moving Picture World*, June 15, 1912, 1014, MHDL.

64. "Indians Will Run Wild in Canyon," *Santa Ana Register*, June 17, 1912, NPC.

65. Amusements, *Orange (CA) Daily News*, June 22, 1912, CO. See also the ad for the evening in the column Electric Theater, *Orange (CA) Daily News*, June 21, 1912, CO.

66. Over the years, Lavelle portrayed both Young Buffalo and Old Buffalo, to Cody's chagrin.

67. Amusements, *Orange (CA) Daily News*, June 22, 1912, CO.

68. Amusements, *Orange (CA) Daily News*, June 28, 1912, CO.

69. "Another Pathe Night" and Amusements, *Orange (CA) Daily News*, June 27 and 28, 1912, respectively, CO.

70. "Another Pathe Night," *Orange (CA) Daily News*, June 27, 1912, CO.

71. Amusements, *Orange (CA) Daily News*, June 28, 1912, CO.

72. See *Moving Picture World*, July 6, 1912, 35, MHDL.

73. Louis St. Cyr appears in a photo still of the film standing behind Gebhardt (see "Film Indentification, 101," https://nitrateville.com; "Living in California," 1912 Returned Students Evaluation, part of Louis St. Cyr student file, Hampton University Archives, Hampton VA).

74. *Moving Picture World* summarized the plot: "A squawman learns that his sweetheart back East is coming to visit him and he drives his squaw out. She, in retaliation, visits her tribe, tells her story, and after the Indians capture the white girl, the squawman is notified she will be killed. He succeeds in rescuing her, but is pursued by the Indians. After many thrilling adventures the pair finally escapes" (*Moving Picture World*, June 29, 1912, 1260, MHDL).

75. I have not seen the film, which is archived at Cinématèque Français, Paris. However, see Nanna Verhoeff's critique in *The West in Early Cinema* (167–68, and film archive list, 422). George Gebhardt and Joseph De Grasse also appear in the film.

76. *Moving Picture World*, July 13, 1912, 148, MHDL.

77. "Asks $5000 Poultice for Bite on Her Arm," *Los Angeles Herald*, July 27, 1912, CDNC. It's unclear if the case was ever filed, but it was indexed as Los Angeles County Court Case 93239, July 27, 1912: "Saunders, Jackie (plaintiff) Deer, James Young (defendant)," Los Angeles County Court Archives.

78. *Moving Picture World*, June 29, 1912, 1260, MHDL.

79. *Motion Picture Story Magazine,* March 1913, 134, MHDL. Joseph De Grasse played the husband.

80. *Moving Picture News*, July 13, 1912, 32, MHDL. Buster Emmons probably played the Indian lead.

81. *Moving Picture World*, July 13, 1912, 157; and *Moving Picture News*, July 13, 1912, 32, MHDL.

82. *Moving Picture World*, August 3, 1912, 476, MHDL. Joseph De Grasse and Edna Maison had the leads, though Red Wing may have appeared as De Grasse's Indian wife, who dies early in the story.

83. *Moving Picture World*, August 3, 1912, 476; *Moving Picture News*, July 20, 1912, 29; and *Motion Picture Story Magazine,* February 1913, 188, MHDL. Edna Maison and Joseph De Grasse played the leads.

84. *Moving Picture World*, August 3, 1912, 476, and August 10, 1912, 546; *Moving Picture News*, July 20, 1912, 30; *Motion Picture Story Magazine*, February 1913, 148, and August 1913, 142, MHDL. The leads in this film were Edna Maison and Joseph De Grasse.

85. For the former, see *Moving Picture World*, June 29, 1912, 1260; and *Motion Picture Story Magazine*, February 1913, 152, MHDL. For the latter, see *Moving Picture World*, July 13, 1912, 174, and August 3, 434, 445, MHDL; and "The Unwilling Bride," *Alton (IL) Evening Telegraph,* August 2, 1912, NPC.

86. IMDb lists Buck Connors as director and George Gebhardt and "his brother," Joseph, as the two brothers in the film. However, there was no Joseph Gebhardt. The error comes from a typo in *Motion Picture Story Magazine* (January 1913, 142, MHDL), which states, "Joseph Gebhardt was the leading man in the picture." *Motion Picture Story Magazine* often referred to George Gebhardt as "Joseph Gebhart."

87. *Moving Picture World*, June 29, 1912, 1260, MHDL.

88. "The Unwilling Bride," *Alton (IL) Evening Telegraph*, August 2, 1912, NPC.

89. *Moving Picture World*, August 3, 1912, 434, 445, and 476. See also *Moving Picture World*, July 13, 1912, 174, MHDL.

90. Electric Theater, *Orange (CA) Daily News*, July 12, 1912, CO.

91. *Moving Picture World*, August 17, 1912, 669, MHDL.

92. *Moving Picture World*, August 3, 1912, 476, MHDL.

93. *Moving Picture World*, August 31, 1912, 880, MHDL.

94. *Moving Picture World*, August 17, 1912, 690, September 7, 975; *Moving Picture News*, August 17, 1912, 29; and *Motion Picture Story Magazine*, February 1913, 158, MHDL.

95. *Moving Picture World*, August 17, 1912, 690; and *Motion Picture Story Magazine*, February 1913, 140, MHDL.

96. *Moving Picture World*, August 17, 1912, 690, and September 7, 976; *Moving Picture News*, July 20, 1912, 29, and August 17, 1912, 29–30; and *Motion Picture Story Magazine*, February 1913, 158, MHDL.

97. "Louise Glaum, one time leading woman with the Western Pathe Company, has been taking leads with two Nestor companies" (*Moving Picture World*, July 27, 1912, 33, MHDL). Young Deer also hired Fanchon Lewis that summer to act as leading lady for films made that summer at the ranch. Lewis, wife of local merchant M. S. Vandermast, was a Biograph transplant with equestrian skills (Amusements, *Orange [CA] Daily News*, February 11, 1913, CO).

98. *Moving Picture World*, August 10, 1912, 572, MHDL; and "The Orpheum," *Lexington (KY) Leader*, August 25, 1912, genealogybank.com.

99. *Moving Picture World,* August 31, 1912, 881, MHDL.

100. *Moving Picture World*, September 21, 1912, 1175, MHDL.

101. *Moving Picture World*, September 21, 1912, 1106, 1092, MHDL. See also *Rockford Republic*, October 24, 1912, genealogybank.com.

102. Stone later played Judge James Hardy in the *Andy Hardy* film series, starring Mickey Rooney.

103. "Closes Its Sessions," *Santa Ana Register*, August 19, NPC; and *Moving Picture World*, September 18, 1912, 1092, 1106, and October 5, 1912, 40, MHDL.

104. *Moving Picture World*, August 24, 1912, 760, MHDL.

105. It's unknown where the rest of the October releases were filmed. They included *Misleading Evidence* (October 19) with Gebhardt, De Grasse, and Edna Maison and *Little Raven's Sweetheart*, starring Radcliffe and probably Emmons.

106. *Moving Picture World*, September 14, 1912, 1067, MHDL.

107. *Moving Picture World*, September 14, 1912, 1067, and September 21, 1912, 1160, MHDL.

108. The African American man is pictured in a Bison Co. ad for the film (released February 25, 1910) (*Moving Picture World*, February 19, 1910, 282, MHDL).

109. See Dewitt Van Court's Column, *Los Angeles Times*, August 7, 1912, NPC.

110. Dewitt Van Court, "Rivers after Return Bout Finds Mandot Coy," *Los Angeles Times*, September 4, 1912, NPC.

111. Dewitt Van Court, "Tom Jones to Go East Today to Train Wolgast," *Los Angeles Times*, September 5, 1912, NPC.

112. *Moving Picture World*, September 28, 1912, 1266, MHDL. See also *New York Dramatic Mirror*, September 25, 1912, FHC.

113. "Rich Gold Ore Is Brought to Be Tested," *Arizona Daily Star* (Tucson), September 4, 1912, NPC.

114. "Killed Man He Thought to Be Wild Animal," *Arizona Daily Star* (Tucson), September 19, 1912, NPC. Smith's widow remarried the next year, and her brother Rea Hunt, also known as Ray Hunt, started his film career as an original Keystone Kop, ironically, working for the very company that fired Smith for stealing drawings of the inner workings of Balshofer's camera to give to patent detective Slim McCoy.

115. *Moving Picture World,* November 2, 1912, 461, 480–82, and November 23, 1912, 766, MHDL.

116. *Moving Picture World,* November 2, 1912, 482, MHDL.

117. *Moving Picture World,* November 30, 1912, 876; and *Motion Picture Story Magazine,* March 1913, 136, MHDL. The Cinématèque Français, Paris, may have a copy of *The Branded Arm* under the title *La marque reveleatrice* (The revealing brand) (Verhoeff, *The West in Early Cinema,* 419, listed as "c. 1912, Pathe: American Kinema, USA").

118. *Moving Picture World,* November 16, 1912, 696, MHDL.

119. *Fate's Decree* was released December 11 (*Moving Picture World,* December 28, 1912, 1291, MHDL). "Miss Mason was the mother in 'Fate's Decree'" (*Motion Picture Story Magazine,* April 1913, 164, MHDL). "Miss Maison was the girl in Her Faithful Yuma Servant (Pathe)" (*Motion Picture Story Magazine,* April 1913, 150). See *Moving Picture World,* January 11, 1913, 188, and February 1, 1913, 465, MHDL.

120. "Miss Maison was leading lady with the Pathe Western Company, for eighteen months" and "will replace Margarita Fischer in the Nestor company, under Director Ricketts" (*Moving Picture World,* November 30, 1912, 884, MHDL). For her return, see "Brevities of the Business," *Motography,* November 9, 1912, 377. For her change of mind, see *Motography,* December 7, 1912, 448, MHDL. Maison's home life seems to have been unstable. In 1913 she sued her husband, Tom Poste, a haberdasher (whom she married in Santa Ana in 1911 or 1912), for divorce. She provided her broken tooth to the court as evidence of his abuse (*San Francisco Dramatic Review,* June 24, 1913, 4, MHDL).

121. "Red Wing as White Dove," Bijou Theater, *Xenia (OH) Daily Gazette,* February 20, 1913, NPAC.

122. *Moving Picture World,* November 16, 1912, 694, MHDL. See also "Moving Pictures," *Milwaukee Journal,* November 19, 1912, NPC.

123. See "Jane Wolfe," IMDb.

124. *Motion Picture Story Magazine,* December 1912, 142, MHDL; and *New York Dramatic Mirror,* December 31, 1913, FHC.

125. Balshofer and Miller, *One Reel a Week,* 82–90. See "Mr. Thomas H. Ince: General Western Manager of the New York Motion Picture Company," *Motion Picture News,* October 26, 1912, 21, MHDL.

126. *Moving Picture World,* December 7, 1912, 969, MHDL.
127. *Motography,* December 7, 1912; and *Moving Picture World*, December 28, 1912, 1286, MHDL.
128. *Moving Picture World*, December 14, 1912, 1084, MHDL.
129. Slide, *The New Historical Dictionary*, 181.
130. "Uncanned," *Los Angeles Times*, December 26, 1912, NPC. See also "'Movies' Cowboys and Indians in Real Fight," *San Francisco Chronicle*, December 26, 1912, NPC.
131. "Uncanned," *Los Angeles Herald*, December 26, 1912, CDNC. The same issue of the *Herald* reported Young Deer's interest in another riot led by two Austrians who desecrated the American flag: "Mike Mott and George Zlomiclk, the alleged rioters, pleaded not guilty to charges of disturbing the peace. . . . Their trials were set for December 30 and bail fixed at $200 each. The regard in which the mass of citizens of Los Angeles hold the American flag is going to become impressed upon the minds of the world through the riot of Christmas day. . . . Young Deer, manager of the Pacific coast studio of Pathe brothers, today opened negotiations with Frank Schreiner, the policeman who put the rioters to flight, with a view to staging the whole affair for a moving picture."
132. Before his moving picture career, Pino (born about 1866) attended St. Catherine's Indian School in Santa Fe, then moved to Los Angeles and was employed as a janitor for the Indian Village in Eastlake Park not far from Edendale (1900 New Mexico census, Santa Fe, Santa Fe County; and 1910 California federal census, Los Angeles, Los Angeles County).

   Eagle Eye played at least two rolls as a Chinese character, one in 1916 and one in 1919. For the latter, newspapers reported: "William Eagle Eye, famous as a movie Indian character, has disclosed his real origin by converting his twin braids into the pigtail of his ancestors, who were Chinese, to play in Nazimova's 'The Red Lantern'" ("The Press Agents Say," *Bridgeport [CT] Evening Farmer*, June 4, 1919, genealogybank.com). Eagle Eye came to a tragic end in 1927 when he showed up drunk at the home of J. C. Spencer. After Eagle Eye allegedly picked a fight with Spencer, Spencer cracked Eagle Eye's skull on the sidewalk ("William Eagle Eye," Cavalry Cemetery, Los Angeles, findagrave.com).
133. "M. [George] Rizard then came to the Pathe West Coast studios where he remained two years photographing westerns under direction of James Youngdeer" (*American Cinematographer*, February 1, 1922, 17, MHDL).
134. *Moving Picture News*, January 11, 1913, 30; and *Motion Picture Story Magazine*, June 1913, 150, MHDL.
135. "Luna Theater," *Morning News* (Danville PA), March 3, 1913, NPC; and *Moving Picture World,* February 1, 1913, 495, and February 22, 1913, 780; *Moving Picture News*, February 1, 1913, 24; and *Motion Picture Story Magazine*, May 1913, 160, MHDL. A copy of the film, which I have not seen, is held by Cinématèque Français, Paris (Verhoeff, *The West in Early Cinema*, 416).

1. Curiously, *Mr.* Young Deer does not appear at this address: "Mrs Deer J Young: 1824 Allesandro," *Los Angeles City Directory*, 1913, https://www.ancestry.com/.

2. Gertrude M. Price, "Picturesque Indian Maid Is Fearless, Ambitious, Clever," *Tacoma (wa) Times*, February 4, 1913, NPC. Price's article is printed in several papers with the same headline, including the *Evansville (IN) Press*, April 23, 1913, NPC.

3. *Moving Picture World*, January 18, 1913, 251, MHDL; and "Earth's Garden," *Los Angeles Times*, January 2, 1913, NPC.

4. For photos of Keystone's entry, see "Looking for Mabel Normand."

5. *Moving Picture World*, January 18, 1913, 251, MHDL. See also "Earth's Garden," *Los Angeles Times*, January 2, 1913, NPC.

6. "Earth's Garden," *Los Angeles Times*, January 2, 1913, NPC.

7. *Moving Picture World*, January 18, 1913, 251, MHDL.

8. See *Motion Picture Story Magazine*, May 1913, 144, MHDL; *Moving Picture World*, January 4, 1913, 82, and January 25, 1913, 363, MHDL; and *Moving Picture World*, January 25, 1913, 388, and February 15, 1913, 679, MHDL. "George Gebhardt was the Indian chief in 'Saved by His Horse' (Pathe). There is only one Gebhardt with Pathe—George. He is such a good Indian that they always 'let George do it'" (*Motion Picture Story Magazine*, May 1913, 133, MHDL). Joseph De Grasse also starred with Peggy the horse in *An Equine Hero* (released March 6) (*Moving Picture World*, March 1, 1913, 922, and March 22, 1913, 1220, MHDL). See also *Motion Picture Story Magazine*, June 1913, 148, MHDL.

9. *Moving Picture World*, January 11, 1913, 188, and February 1, 1913, 465, MHDL. "Miss Maison was the girl in Her Faithful Yuma Servant (Pathe)" (*Motion Picture Story Magazine*, April 1913, 150, MHDL). For *The Halfbreed*, see *Moving Picture World*, January 18, 1913, 290, and February 8, 1913, 571, MHDL.

10. *Moving Picture World*, January 18, 1913, 264. See also *Moving Picture World*, December 28, 1912, 1326, MHDL.

11. *Moving Picture World*, January 18, 1913, 290, and February 8, 1913, 571. See also *Motion Picture Story Magazine*, May 1913, 134, and June 1913, 164, MHDL.

12. *Moving Picture World*, February 8, 1913, 571, MHDL.

13. *Moving Picture World*, January 4, 1913, 36, and February 8, 1913, 560, MHDL.

14. *Motography*, February 1913, MHDL. See also *Moving Picture World*, February 8, 1913, 560, MHDL.

15. "Photo Artists in Full Dress by Al G. Waddell," *Los Angeles Times*, February 15, 1913, NPC.

16. *Moving Picture World*, February 8, 1913, 560, MHDL.

17. "Photo Artists in Full Dress by Al G. Waddell," *Los Angeles Times*, February 15, 1913, NPC.

18. "Photo Artists in Full Dress by Al G. Waddell," *Los Angeles Times*, February 15, 1913, NPC.

19. *Moving Picture World*, January 25, 1913, 353, MHDL. IMDb lists only one film for an Olive Skinner, produced in 1925.

20. "From the Mason to the Majestic," *Los Angeles Times*, November 22, 1912, NPC. The show starred seductress Velasca Surrat. Wiggins played Lady Helen to positive and negative reviews but wowed the Los Angeles critic for her stand-in role as Mrs. Malaprop.

21. "Showgirl of Two Years Ago Today Is Star in the Movies," *Oregonian* (Portland), December 7, 1913, NPC.

22. "Showgirl of Two Years Ago Today Is Star in the Movies," *Oregonian* (Portland), December 7, 1913, NPC.

23. A Los Angeles reviewer of *The Kiss Waltz* also noted, "Lillian Wiggins . . . is considering an attractive offer to desert the stage in favor of the film studio out toward Edendale" ("From the Mason to the Majestic," *Los Angeles Times*, November 22, 1912, NPC).

24. *Motion Picture Story Magazine*, May 1913, 158, and July 1913, 66, MHDL. For a review, see "The Clutch of Conscience," *Sacramento Union*, March 1, 1913, NPC.

25. *Moving Picture World*, March 15, 1913, 1103, MHDL.

26. *Moving Picture World*, February 22, 1913, 766, MHDL. Anson Dudley Whittier, a relatively unknown sculptor who hailed from Canada, was the California artist.

27. *Moving Picture World*, March 8, 1913, 1020; and *Motion Picture Story Magazine*, July 1913, 133, MHDL.

28. *Moving Picture World*, April 12, 1913, 163; and *Motion Picture Story Magazine*, June 1913, 164, and March 1914, 133, MHDL.

29. *Variety*, April 1913, 15; and *Moving Picture World*, April 19, 1913, 288, MHDL.

30. *Moving Picture World*, April 26, 1913, 412, 704, MHDL. These films include *The Thwarted Plot* (released April 24) and *The Mexican's Defeat* (released April 30). *The Broken Idyll* (released April 5) probably starred Wiggins, but she definitely starred in *The Outlaw* ("'The Broken Idyll,' a Picture of the West by the Pathe Western Players," *Repository* [Canton OH], April 27, 1913, NPAC). See also *Moving Picture World*, April 19, 1913, 280, MHDL. The story summary has no Indians, but *Moving Picture News* (March 29, 1913, 27, MHDL) states that the film featured "a very pretty girl." For the latter film, see *Moving Picture World*, April 19, 1913, 304, and May 10, 1913, 595; and *Motion Picture Story Magazine*, December 1913, 154, MHDL.

31. Doings at Los Angeles, *Moving Picture World*, May 3, 1913, 268, MHDL.

32. *New York Dramatic Mirror*, May 7, 1913, 29, FHC.

33. Gertrude M. Price, "Picturesque Indian Maid Is Fearless, Ambitious, Clever," *Evansville (IN) Press*, April 23, 1913, NPC.

34. A photo shows French as a sheriff beginning to dance with Wiggins in a crowded saloon scene. Gebhardt on a stool eyes French suspiciously, while musicians, including a trombone player, play in the background (French Collection, box 46, file 5).

35. *New York Dramatic Mirror*, April 23, 1913, 27, FHC.

36. *Moving Picture World*, April 26, 1913, 412, and May 17, 1913, 703, MHDL.

37. *Moving Picture World*, April 26, 1913, 412; and *Moving Picture News*, April 26, 1913, MHDL.

38. "Fined for Inhumane Realism," Doings at Los Angeles, *Moving Picture World*, April 26, 1913, 367, MHDL.

39. For example, the following appeared in the local paper two years before: "Moving picture makers ran afoul the law yesterday when Charles Reel, who is aiding in the production of a 'wild west' film now under process of construction some 25 miles from here, was fined $50 in Justice Forbes' court on a charge of cruelty to animals. According to the evidence, Reel was using three half-starved and sore-backed animals in the aggregation of horse flesh necessary to represent his views of the 'wild west' days as they existed before the coming of the automobile" ("Moving Picture Maker Is Fined for Cruelty," *Los Angeles Herald*, May 17, 1911, CDNC).

40. "Fined for Inhumane Realism," *Moving Picture World*, April 26, 1913, 367, MHDL.

41. At the Sign of the Flaming Arcs, *Moving Picture World*, May 24, 1913, 820, MHDL. It's not clear how the horse scene fit into the film.

42. At the Sign of the Flaming Arcs, *Moving Picture World*, May 24, 1913, 820, MHDL.

43. *Moving Picture World*, June 14, 1913, MHDL.

44. "Moving Picture Outfit Camped in the Santiago," *Santa Ana Register*, April 29, 1913, NPC.

12. YOUNG DEER AND THE WHITE SLAVERY RING

1. For the subpoena-serving episode, see "In the Beginning Angrily Slaps Face She Says," *Los Angeles Times*, May 2, 1913, NPC; and "Serves Indian in Santiago," *Santa Ana Daily Register*, May 2, 1913, NPC.

2. George H. Bixby's relative Llewellyn Bixby had been co-owner of the "Irvine Ranch" ("Serves Indian in Santiago," *Santa Ana Daily Register*, May 2, 1913, NPC).

3. "White Slave Trials Postponed; Millionaire's Bum Nose Cause," *Modesto Evening News*, July 24, 1913, NPC.

4. "City News in Brief," "In the Beginning," and "Selling Souls for Hard Cash," *Los Angeles Times*, April 16, April 22, and May 2, 1913, respectively, NPC; *San Francisco Dramatic Review*, May 10, 1913, 12, MHDL; and *Variety*, May 9, 1913, 26, MHDL.

5. "Seek Many in High Places," *Los Angeles Times*, April 23, 1913, NPC.

6. "Girls Disgused [*sic*] as Boys Attend Prize Fight in Los Angeles," *Santa Ana Register*, May 21, 1913, NPC.

7. "At the Courthouse" and "August Trials," *Los Angeles Times*, June 5 and July 17, 1913, respectively, NPC. See also "Girl Victim of White Slavery Is Sent to Jail," *Santa Ana Register*, June 4, 1913, NPC.

8. "Information Given Police by Actress," *Oakland Tribune*, May 4, 1913, NPC.

9. In 1920 Young Deer claimed he had directed "Jules Carmen," who worked for him before she changed her name ("Motion Pictures," *Los Angeles Herald*, February 21, 1920, CDNC).

10. "La Casse Faces Girl Accuser," *Los Angeles Herald*, May 5, 1913, CDNC.

11. "Subpoena Server After Young Deer," *Los Angeles Herald*, May 1, 1913, CDNC.

12. *Moving Picture News*, May 10, 1913, 524, MHDL. See also *Moving Picture World*, May 10, 1913, 582, MHDL.

13. "Charges Piling Thick and Fast" and "Riverside," *Los Angeles Times*, April 27 and June 18, 1913, respectively, NPC.

14. "La Casse to Face Accusers," *Press Democrat* (Santa Rosa ca), July 10, 1913, CDNC.

15. "Engstrom Divorced in Fifteen Minutes," *Santa Ana Register*, July 16, 1913; and "August Trials," *Los Angeles Times*, July 17, 1913, NPC.

16. "Rivers in Condition," *Los Angeles Times*, February 18, 1913, NPC.

17. "August Trials," *Los Angeles Times*, July 17, 1913, NPC.

18. "15 New Arrests Asked in Jury Slave Probe," *Los Angeles Herald*, May 14, 1913, CDNC. Moreover, the *Herald* stated that the cases "revealed in Los Angeles a branch of the vicious cadet system which is in operation in some of the larger citits [*sic*] of the country."

19. "Young Deer has had Fagan on his Santa Ana ranch for the past six weeks and he has been gaining weight and doing some training and was never in better condition in his life," reported the *Los Angeles Times*. "Young Deer will back him to beat any middleweight in the country at 158 pounds" ("Deer Ambitious," *Los Angeles Times*, June 23, 1913, NPC). The *Times* sports columnist further reported: "Little Jimmy Youngdeer, the moving picture Indian, was threshing out, right and left, into the ribs of his neighboring spectators at the ring side and shrieking like a maniac" ("Leach Cross Battered Down Bud Anderson," *Los Angeles Times*, July 5, 1913, NPC).

20. Although *Moving Picture World*'s scenario summary only mentions two Indian warriors and a white heroine, the following shows that Red Wing was also featured: "Pathe—*A Redskin's Mercy*. A strong western drama, featuring George Gebhart and Princess Redwing" ("Luna Theater," *Morning News* [Dansville PA], August 4, 1913, NPC). See *Moving Picture World*, May 10, 1912, 624, and May 31, 1912, 920, MHDL.

21. For *Moving Picture World*'s coverage of these films, see May 24, 1913, 842; June 14, 1913, 1135, 1136, 1170; June 21, 1913, 1280; July 5, 1913, 48; July 12, 1913, 205,

232; July 19, 1913, 346; August 2, 1913, 536; August 16, 1913, 766; August 30, 1913, 960, 988; September 27, 1913, 1391, 1420; October 4, 1913, 47–48, 66; October 18, 1913, 263, 286; November 1, 1913, 496; November 15, 1913, 745; November 29, 1913, 1044; December 13, 1913, 1279; December 20, 1913, 1412, 1466, MHDL.

22. De Grasse's noble squaw man experiences an "awakening" after he rescues two white women against the wishes of his wife's tribe. Soon after, his Indian wife shoots him for his attraction to one of them (probably played by Virginia Chester). The story concludes when the squaw man sends his jealous wife and their "half breed" child back to her people and remains with the white women he loves. See *Moving Picture World*, May 24, 1913, 842, and June 14, 1913, 1136, MHDL; *News*, October 11, 1913, NPC; and "Filmographie Pathé," http://filmographie .fondation-jeromeseydoux-pathe.com/17016-appel-du-sang-l.

23. Not to be confused with the 1913 Bison 101 (Broncho Pictures) film *A House Divided* (released April 1, 1913).

24. By the reporter's account, the bear's health seemed less of a concern than it passing an illness to Youngdeer ("Bear Set Teeth in Actor's Face," *Orange [CA] Daily News*, July 7, 1913, CO).

25. "Disagreement; La Casse Jury," *Los Angeles Times*, July 26, 1913, NPC.

26. *The Erring Brother* was also released on August 13. See *Moving Picture World*, August 30, 1913, 960, MHDL.

27. *Moving Picture World*, August 16, 1913, 732, MHDL.

28. "Story of Gun Play among Motion Picture Actors," *Orange (CA) Daily News*, August 14, 1913, CO.

29. "Canned Drama Auto Pulled Off Scene without Camera," *Santa Ana Register*, August 30, 1913, NPC.

30. *Strand: An Illustrated Monthly*, January 1914, 102 (digitized by Princeton University, but source unknown).

31. "Rich Men Accused by Girl," *Oakland Tribune*, August 16, 1913, NPC.

32. "Wife Can't Testify; Burton Is Set Free," *Evansville (IL) Press*, August 26, 1913, NPC.

33. "Marriage Solves It," *Los Angeles Times*, August 23, 1913, NPC.

34. "End's Well—All's Well," *Los Angeles Times*, September 3, 1913. See also "Haskamp Up Today," *Los Angeles Times*, August 27, 1913; "To Release Haskamp," *Los Angeles Times*, September 2, 1913, NPC; and "Wife Can't Testify; Burton Is Set Free," *Los Angeles Herald*, August 26, 1913, CDNC.

35. "Paid Fines for Cruelty to Cow," *Santa Ana Register*, September 15, 1913, NPC. The men were listed as "Frank Berry, foreman, Leo Glines, R. J. Keith, George Sewards and Clarence Jones."

36. "Broadway Auto Crash Wounds Movie Actor," *Los Angeles Herald*, September 19, 1913, CDNC.

37. "Dismiss Case against Movie Manager," *Los Angeles Herald*, October 3, 1913, CDNC.

38. "Evelyn Nesbieth to Adopt Cloister Life," *Oakland Tribune*, November 2, 1913, NPC.

39. "Two Brought Up on Speeding Charge," *Orange (CA) Daily News*, October 10, 1913, CO; and "Preparing for Its Bantam Show," *Santa Ana Register*, October 22, 1913, NPC.

40. "Youngdeer Accused by Girl, Denies Her Acquaintance," *Los Angeles Herald*, November 24, 1913, CDNC.

41. Wilkerson's wedding in June 1916 was announced in "Society. Riverside," *Los Angeles Times*, June 18, 1916, NPC. She married Oliver Newhouse in Riverside, California. They are listed on the Riverside County 1930 and 1940 California federal censuses with their children. The latter census shows she only had one year of high school. Her death record states that Marie W. Newhouse was born in California on May 29, 1894, and died on November 9, 1988, in Riverside County ("California Death Index, 1940–1997," https://www.ancestry.com/).

42. The jail register shows he was arrested for a misdemeanor (James Youngdeer, 3120, Jail Register, 1913–1914: 82, Los Angeles County Records, Seaver Center, Los Angeles).

43. "And Arrested," *Los Angeles Times*, November 25, 1913, NPC.

44. "And Arrested," *Los Angeles Times*, November 25, 1913, NPC.

45. "Moving Picture Man Facing Accusation," *Orange (CA) Daily News*, November 25, 1913, CO. See also "Youngdeer, Accused by Girl, Denies Her Acquaintance," *Los Angeles Herald*, November 24, 1913, CDNC.

46. "Movie Stars Wait as Youngdeer Asks Delay of Hearing," *Los Angeles Herald*, November 28, 1913, CDNC.

47. *Moving Picture World*, November 15, 1913, 745, MHDL. Gebhardt's character is "abandoned on the desert by a false friend, whom he had just nursed back to health from smallpox. Indians find and take care of the sick hero and the villain marries the sweetheart, telling her that the other man is dead." Of course, pathos ensues, and "in his bitterness, the hero then joins the Indians and a few months later incites them to attack a caravan in which, it happens, are the faithless friend and the deceived sweetheart, now a wife." Red Wing's Indian helper character is not mentioned (*Moving Picture World*, December 13, 1913, 1279, MHDL).

48. "Youngdeer Is Held on Girl's Charges," *Los Angeles Herald*, November 29, 1913, CDNC. Papers across the country covered the story; for example, see "'Movie' Actor Held on Grave Charge," *Lincoln (NE) Star*, November 30, 1913, NPC.

49. "New Youngdeer Complaint," *Los Angeles Times*, December 2, 1913, NPC.

50. "Accuse Actor: Two Girls Involved," *Los Angeles Times*, November 30, 1913, 16, NPC.

51. "Youngdeer Is Held on Girl's Charges," *Los Angeles Herald*, November 29, 1913, CDNC; and "Youngdeer Gone, Officers Search," *Orange (CA) Daily News*, December 11, 1913, CO.

52. Jas Youngdeer, U.S., 53141, Consular Registration Certificates, 1907–18, https://www.ancestry.com/. The document states he left the United States on December 8, 1913, and arrived in London on December 18.

53. "Fear Youngdeer Has Fled," *Los Angeles Herald*, December 11, 1913, CDNC.

54. "Youngdeer Gone, Officers Search," *Orange (CA) Daily News*, December 11, 1913, CO.

55. "Youngdeer Gone, Officers Search," *Orange (CA) Daily News*, December 11, 1913, CO.

56. "Pleads Justice for the Indian," *Los Angeles Times*, December 27, 1913, NPC.

57. See "At the Courthouse" and "Pleads Justice for the Indian," *Los Angeles Times*, December 17 and 27, 1913, respectively, NPC; and "Court No Longer in Search of Youngdeer," *Los Angeles Herald*, December 26, 1913, CDNC.

58. *Moving Picture World*, December 30, 1913, 1466, MHDL.

59. *Moving Picture World* says her name was "Lillian Gibson," but I believe that's a typo (*Motion Picture News*, March 21, 1914, 14; *Moving Picture World*, March 7, 1914, 1296, and March 21, 1914, 1525, 1539, MHDL). *The Stolen Inheritance* was released on December 9. *Whom God Hath Joined* was released on January 6. Again, though I can't confirm it myself, IMDb shows that the film featured Gerrard, Lewis, Charles Stevenson, and Johnny Schiff (one of Young Deer's boxers). *Orphans of the Wild* was released on February 10. *Moving Picture World* (February 28, 1914, 1087, MHDL) states it features two children and a horse, and IMDb lists its cast as Tom Forman, Lillian Clark, Charles K. French, Eugene McConnell, and Violette Radcliffe. If French was in the film, it may have been made much earlier, however. *Where the Heart Calls* with Lillian Wiggins was released on February 19, but it was likely a Pathé American production and not from West Coast Studios. See *Moving Picture World*, March 7, 1914, 1237, MHDL.

60. Also written erroneously as *Down Low Gulp Way*.

61. *Moving Picture World*, December 27, 1913, 1582, MHDL.

62. "Portsmouth Theatre Programme," *Portsmouth (NH) Herald*, January 30, 1914, NPC.

63. *Moving Picture World*, January 31, 1914, 543, MHDL.

64. It's possible that Frank Montgomery and Mona Darkfeather acquired some of West Coast Studios' props and costumes: "Frank Montgomery, the Kalem director who specializes in Indian photoplays, has picked up the stock of two firms that went out of business here," *Moving Picture World* reported. "He secured a full equipment of costumes, war paraphernalia, head dress, and a number of other articles. He has a wonderful private collection of Indian relics. Mona Darkfeather received her share of the purchase, getting several new Indian dresses for her large wardrobe" (*Moving Picture World*, March 28, 1914, 1685, MHDL).

65. Gertrude M. Price, "Picturesque Indian Maid Is Fearless, Ambitious, Clever," *Seattle Star*, April 24, 1913, NPC.

13. CECIL B. DEMILLE AND *THE SQUAW MAN*

1. Jesse L. Lasky Feature Motion Picture Company elected the following officers: "Jesse L. Lasky, president; Cecil DeMille, general stage manager; Samuel Goldfish, treasurer and business manager, and Frank A. Tichenor, general sales manager." In addition, Goldfish was appointed in "charge of the commercial end of the

Lasky organization" (*Motion Picture News*, December 10, 1913, MHDL). See also *Moving Picture World*, December 20, 1913, 1419, MHDL.

2. *Motion Picture News*, December 10, 1913, 15, MHDL.
3. "A Man with the Bark On," *Moving Picture World*, March 7, 1914, 1243, MHDL.
4. Hayne, *The Autobiography of Cecil B. DeMille*, 78.
5. *Moving Picture World*, February 7, 1914, 689, MHDL.
6. "Dustin Farnum to Found Movie Camp," *Los Angeles Herald*, December 13, 1913, CDNC. DeMille's biographer Robert Birchard states that they arrived on December 20, but the *Herald* shows it was December 13 (*Cecil B. DeMille's Hollywood*, 5–7; see also Birchard, "The Squaw Man").
7. "Farnum Is Tired of Being a Hero," *Los Angeles Herald*, December 15, 1913, CDNC.
8. "Notes Re Barn via Stella Stray, March 19, 1956," DeMille Papers, MSS 1400, box 225, folder 8. For DeMille's "cast of characters" and script, see DeMille Papers, box 1227, folder 1. See also Guy Price, "Facts and Fables of the Foyer," *Los Angeles Herald*, December 24, 1913, CDNC.
9. Birchard, *Cecil B. DeMille's Hollywood*, 6.
10. Birchard, *Cecil B. DeMille's Hollywood*, 5–7.
11. "Indian Movie Star Lectures," *Ogden (UT) Standard*, December 29, 1935, NPC.
12. Hayne, *The Autobiography of Cecil B. DeMille*, 89. According to Birchard, Mona Darkfeather and Frank Montgomery were in the middle of producing their own film, to be released by Kalem (*Cecil B. DeMille's Hollywood*, 5–7).
13. Hayne, *The Autobiography of Cecil B. DeMille*, 81–82. DeMille kept the notebook in his safe. DeMille's notations for the first actress on the list, whose name is illegible, are "not pretty," "small fat," "okay," . . . "but no brains" (DeMille Papers, MSS 1400, box 237, folder 5: "Book of Notes of the First Squaw Man").
14. Later, Ford's younger brother John Ford directed Darwell in *The Grapes of Wrath*.
15. "Indian Movie Star Lectures," *Ogden (UT) Standard*, December 29, 1935, NPC.
16. *New York Clipper*, February 28, 1914, 15, MHDL. The Cahuilla reservation, near Anza, California, was established in 1875, and the reservation for the Soboba Band of Mission Indians in San Jacinto was established in 1913. A federal Indian census for the two groups was taken in 1904–7, and a special California census was taken in 1912–13, but I could not find these surnames listed (or on any other Indian census). The names listed were mostly of Hispanic origin. There were three men of the Soboba Training School Agency (1904) named Jack, but with different surnames (U.S. Indian Census Rolls, 1885–1940, https://www.ancestry.com/).
17. "'The Squaw Man' Has Private Showing," *Motography*, March 7, 1914, 69–70, MHDL.
18. For another view of killing off the tragic heroine, see Loraux, *Tragic Ways*.
19. "Star Indian Actress Shoots Self in Play," *Los Angeles Herald*, January 29, 1914, CDNC.
20. *Billboard*, February 7, 1914, 15, MHDL.
21. *Moving Picture World*, February 14, 1914, 824, MHDL.

22. A Hemet reporter later relayed Salisbury's description of the cliff-hanger scene: "The last time the stunt was pulled off [Salisbury] begged for 'more rope,' as the rope by which he had been suspended was hardly long enough to allow him to reach the ground" ("The 'Squaw Man' in Moving Picture Play," *Hemet News*, February 6, 1914, genealogybank.com).

23. Birchard, *Cecil B. DeMille's Hollywood*, 8–9. According to Stella Stray's account, DeMille began dictating the script to her on Friday, February 13, 1913, finishing on February 15, which was the film's release date (DeMille Papers, box 225, folder 8).

24. I believe DeMille confused *The Squaw Man* with his film *The Virginian*, filmed later in 1914. See "George Doane's Cabin"; and "Palomar History."

25. "Famous Melodrama to Be Pictured Here," *Hemet News*, February 13, 1914, genealogybank.com. The report noted that they had arrived on Monday.

26. The account of Muir's visit to Mount San Jacinto first appeared in Frederick, *Legends and History*.

27. "The 'Squaw Man' in Moving Picture Play," *Hemet News*, February 6, 1914, genealogybank.com. Today Mountain Center, a more recent census designation, is even closer than Idyllwild.

28. "Hemet Valley News," *Riverside (CA) Independent Enterprise*, February 4, 1914, 2, genealogybank.com. The newspaper erred in identifying the company, stating it was the "Alaskan Motion Picture Company" rather than the Lasky Company.

29. Her husband, Percy Walker, had drowned two years earlier, trying to save a swimmer in Lake Hemet, south of the resort.

30. "Keen Camp" (ad), Frederick Wagner, *Western Journal of Education*, October 1913, 5, https://archive.org.

31. Walker hosted deer hunters in the fall, as well as San Bernardino and Santa Ana locals who sought "the bracing mountain air" during August. The Garner Ranch next door was owned by the Garner family of Santa Ana.

32. For this photo and other film stills, see DeMille Papers, Cecil B. DeMille Photos, MSS P 146, box 25, folders 1–11, and box OS, 7, folders 1–3.

33. *Moving Picture World*, January 24, 1914, 421, MHDL. Farnum was born in Hampton Beach, Maine. His parents were in the theater, and he debuted in a stock company in 1897. His first theatrical success was *The Virginian*. His second was *The Littlest Rebel*, in which he acted with his brother, well-known screen actor William Farnum. He died of kidney failure in Queens, New York, in 1929 ("Dustin Farnum Dies after Long Illness," *New York Times*, July 5, 1929).

34. "A Man with the Bark On," *Moving Picture World*, March 7, 1914, 1243, MHDL.

35. "A Man with the Bark On," *Moving Picture World*, March 7, 1914, 1243, MHDL.

36. "The 'Squaw Man' in Moving Picture Play," *Hemet News*, February 6, 1914, genealogybank.com. Although, as previously mentioned, Robert Birchard states that the ship scenes were filmed in San Pedro, *Hemet News* reported, "In

the production of this play it will be necessary to make pictures of scenes from ocean to ocean. At San Diego the company will burn a ship to fill in a part of the drama." When the company left Keen Camp, a local reporter also noted that they were headed for San Diego with at least two actors who played the ship captain's wife and daughter: "Fifteen members of the Jesse Lasky Feature Play company, after a week's stay at Keen Camp, returned to Hollywood last week. They secured all the pictures necessary to complete the missing link in the 'Squaw Man' play, which is being made for the movies, and after a trip to San Diego the films will be ready for distribution to the various moving picture concerns throughout the country. . . . [T]he company will return in a few weeks to work on the new production, 'Brewster's Millions,' said Mr. de Mille" ("Famous Melodrama to Be Pictured Here," *Hemet News*, February 13, 1914, genealogybank.com).

37. Birchard, *Cecil B. DeMille's Hollywood*, 10.

38. *Moving Picture World*, March 7, 1914, MHDL.

39. *Moving Picture World*, March 7, 1914, MHDL. For example, *Broken Arrow*, the 1950 classic that revived the western genre and stars Jimmy Stewart, features an Indian princess who is shot and killed after she and Stewart's character share their wedding night. See also Marubbio, *Killing the Indian Maiden*.

40. Birchard, *Cecil B. DeMille's Hollywood*, 10–11.

41. *Motography*, March 7, 1914, 69–70, MHDL.

42. *New York Dramatic Mirror*, March or April 1914, FHC.

43. Birchard, *Cecil B. DeMille's Hollywood*, 10–11. For the actual release date, see DeMille Papers, box 1227, folder 1, and MSS P 146, box 220, folder 9.

44. *Motion Picture News*, February 28, 1914, 32, MHDL. "Besides having Dustin Farnum, who created the title role in the original play, to re-create it before the camera," he wrote, "every one of the big dramatic moments are incorporated in the film-play without the sacrifice of a single one of the features which gave the drama so wide and enduring a vogue in the heyday of its first popularity."

45. *New York Clipper*, February 28, 1914, 15, MHDL.

46. *Moving Picture World*, February 28, 1914, 1069, MHDL.

47. "The Rex," *Goodwin's Weekly* (Salt Lake City UT), March 7, 1914, NPC.

48. "Amusements," *Salt Lake Tribune*, March 10, 1914, NPC. One of the more unique reviews, which appeared in a North Carolina newspaper, stated that *The Squaw Man* featured a "variety of nationalities and denominations of any motion picture ever produced. Dustin Farnum is a true born American citizen; Princess Red Wing, the Indian actress, is a real American in every sense of the word; Dick La Reno, who plays 'Big Bill' in the piece, is a French-Canadian; Jack Ellis, who plays a prominent role, is a native of Sweden; Miss Kingston, 'Lady Elizabeth' of the picture, is a native of London, Eng., while Baby Derue [*sic*] is a native of Australia, and George Hawkins, the only colored man in the picture, comes

from Port-of-Spain, Trinidad, in the West Indian Islands. . . . Amongst the fifty cowboys used in the picture, are natives of Norway, Argentine, Brazil, Chili, Australia, New Zealand and Mexico. All in all, there are twenty-two national-ities and just by way of variety, one of the ordinary characters is played by J. F. Judkins, an out and out Mormon" ("We Beg to Announce," *Greensboro Daily News*, May 24, 1914, NPC).

14. *IN THE DAYS OF THE THUNDERING HERD*

1. For De Grasse, see Doings at Los Angeles, *Moving Picture World*, March 28, 1914, 1699, MHDL; for Gebhardt, see *Motion Picture Story Magazine*, July 1914, 165, MHDL; *Moving Picture World*, May 16, 1914, 942, MHDL; and "Girls Won't Love Him Now," *Los Angeles Times*, November 5, 1915, NPC.

2. "Lillian Redwing, actor h [head of house] 1807b Sunset blvd," *Los Angeles City Directory*, 1914, https://www.ancestry.com/.

3. For Wiggins and Young Deer's films together, see BFI (British Film Institute), http://www.bfi.org.uk/films-tv-people/4ce2b6f5cfda6, http://www.bfi.org.uk/films-tv-people/4ce2b6ba480a2, http://www.bfi.org.uk/films-tv-people/529540ec8c9c0, and http://www.bfi.org.uk/films-tv-people/4ce2b75e126b9.

4. "Pathe Establishes Florida Plant," *Motography*, November 1, 1913, 329, MHDL. See also *Motography*, November 15, 1913, 374; and *Moving Picture World*, October 25, 1913, 382, MHDL.

5. *Motion Picture Story Magazine*, March 1914, 128; *Motion Picture Magazine*, December 1914, 166–67; and *New York Clipper*, September 26, 1914, 14, MHDL.

6. Jas Youngdeer, U.S., 53141, Consular Registration Certificates, 1907-18, https://www.ancestry.com/.

7. "Fugitive Movie Man Promises to Return," *Los Angeles Times*, April 3, 1914, NPC.

8. "Pleads Guilty," *Los Angeles Times*, January 16, 1914, NPC. By July news was out that "Jimmie Youngdeer was in Londontown," indicating the lack of concern his absence elicited. After he wired his friend Jim Jeffries, former heavyweight champion, a sports columnist noted, "Youngdeer must have had a bet on Smith to whip Carpentier, as he says Smith was robbed. If Jimmy was coaching the defeat is not to be wondered at" ("Between You and Me," *Los Angeles Herald*, July 20, 1914, CDNC). *Variety* also stated, "James Youngdeer, former well known local theatrical and movie man, who mysteriously disappeared months ago, has been heard from. He's in London now. Jim Jeffries got a letter from him recently" (*Variety*, July 1914, 22, MHDL).

9. "Two New Stars for Pathe Films Arrive," *Los Angeles Herald*, May 23, 1914, CDNC. For Hartigan's activities with Pathé Exchange, see "Movie Co. Seeks Quarters at Beach" and "Evening Herald Sport Page," *Los Angeles Herald*, May 22 and June 3, 1914, respectively, CDNC; and Doings at Los Angeles, *Moving Picture World*, June 13, 1914, 1525, MHDL.

10. "Howard Davies, long associated with the Bison and Universal companies, has joined P. C. Hartigan, who is directing comedies for Pathe at the 'Zodiac' studios" (*Movie Pictorial*, June 27, 1914, 31, MHDL).

11. According to one report, Hartigan had some connection to the series: "P. C. Hartigan is leaving today for a short trip to Point Doom. He is going there to select a location for some more 'Perils of Pauline' pictures and will do considerable fishing before returning, if the fishies will bite" ("Between You and Me" and "Rare Species of Fish Caught at Point Dume," *Los Angeles Herald*, June 17 and June 19, 1914, respectively, CDNC). See also *Motography*, June 13, 1914, 440, MHDL.

12. *Moving Picture World*, July 25, 1914, 587, MHDL.

13. "Indian News," *Winnebago (NE) Chieftain*, June 12 and June 19, 1914, Nebraska State Historical Society.

14. Paul Seibel, "Fore and Aft," *Evening Times* (Sayre PA), July 13, 1964, NPC. For the Christman version, see Jensen, *The Amazing Tom Mix*, 36.

15. See Tom Mix Biography. The day before the film's release, the *Los Angeles Times* also reported: "In Tom Mix's company are five cowboys, chosen at first because of their riding and shooting accomplishments. These are Harry Lovern, Ed Jones (who is a wonderful shot,) and Pat Christman, Sid Jerdin and Dick Crawford" (Grace Kingsley, "Extra People in the Movies," *Los Angeles Times*, November 29, 1914, NPC).

16. For two photos with Red Wing, see "In the Days of the Thundering Herd," November 30, 1914, William N. Selig Collection, Special Collections, Academy of Motion Pictures Arts and Sciences Library, Margaret Herrick Library, Beverly Hills CA.

17. *Motion Picture News*, November 28, 1914, 68, MHDL. See also *Moving Picture World*, November 14, 1914, 949; *Motography*, November 28, 1914, 732, MHDL; and Kitty Kelly, "Flickerings from Film Land," *Chicago Tribune*, November 28, 1915, NPC.

18. "In the Days of '49," *Daily Review* (Decatur IL), August 5, 1914, 10, NPC.

19. *Motion Picture News*, November 28, 1914, 68, MHDL.

20. *Moving Picture World*, December 12, 1914, 1506, MHDL.

21. James Youngdeer, 115354 (departure date, September 23, 1914), UK, Outward Passenger Lists, 1890–1960, and James Youngdeer (arrival date, October 2, 1914), New York Passenger Lists, 1820–1957, https://www.ancestry.com/. For Wiggins's return to New York, see "Lillian Wiggins Said—but Read What Lillian Said," *Evening World* (New York), September 24, 1914, NPC.

22. *New York City Directory*, 1915, https://www.ancestry.com/. Gertrude lived at least until 1920, when she worked as a housekeeper to make ends meet. Thelma Johnson lived until at least 1930, when she worked as a maid in a dress shop. Federal census records show that Thelma's race defined her variously over three decades, first as mulatto (1910), then black (1920), and then Negro (1930) (https://www.ancestry.com/).

23. "Movie Manager Will Return to Face Trial," *Los Angeles Herald*, October 7, 1914, CDNC.

24. "Indian Surrenders," *Los Angeles Times*, November 3, 1914, NPC.

25. "Battles Conscience for Year, Then Surrenders," *Los Angeles Herald*, November 2, 1914, CDNC.

26. "Youngdeer Freed of Girl's Charges" and "Youngdeer Freed by Girl's Departure," *Los Angeles Herald*, November 25 and December 3, 1914, respectively, CDNC; and "Now She's Gone. And Youngdeer Freed," *Los Angeles Times*, December 4, 1914, NPC. As mentioned earlier in the notes, Wilkerson married in June 1916 in Riverside, California.

27. Grace Kingsley, "Extra People in the Movies," *Los Angeles Times*, November 29, 1914, NPC.

28. *Moving Picture World*, July 10, 1915, 215–20, MHDL.

29. She is listed as "Miss Redwing," *Variety*, June 1915, 18, MHDL.

30. See *Moving Picture World*, June 19, 1915, 1952, 2014, MHDL.

31. *Moving Picture World*, June 12, 1915, 1797, MHDL.

32. *Motion Picture News*, April 17, 1915, 55, MHDL.

33. "'Glass Eater' Has Trouble," *Los Angeles Times*, April 5, 1915, NPC. The following item also illustrates Young Deer's alcohol issues: "The theft of three cases of whisky, three cases of prepared cocktails, 16 quarts of vermouth and five dozen bottles of wine by burglars was reported to the police early today by J. Youngdeer of 1252 Lyman street. The burglars gained entrance to the Youngdeer cellar by use of a pass key" ("Cellar Robbed of Wines and Liquor," *Los Angeles Herald*, January 21, 1920, CDNC).

34. Grace Kingsley, "At the Stage Door," *Los Angeles Times*, February 22, 1915, 8, NPC.

35. See *Moving Picture World*, July 17, 1915, 473, 508; July 24, 1915, 660; August 7, 1915, cover; August 14, 1915, 1164; August 28, 1915, 1460, 1482; September 4, 1915, 1652; and November 6, 1915, 1208–10, MHDL.

36. *Moving Picture World*, August 28, 1915, 1483, MHDL.

37. *Motion Picture News*, January 22, 1916, 3627, MHDL. See also Grace Kingsley, "At the Stage Door," *Los Angeles Times*, November 22, 1915, NPC; and *Moving Picture World*, February 26, 1916, 1311, MHDL.

38. Paramount Collection Stills, *Tennessee's Pardner* (1916), Special Collections, Academy of Motion Pictures Arts and Sciences Library, Margaret Herrick Library, Beverly Hills CA.

39. The Mission Play program, San Gabriel, California, 1915.

40. *Moving Picture World*, September 18, 1915, 1985, MHDL. Another overexaggerated report stated that the two "made an exhaustive study of the chants and dances of the Mission Indians around Pala and Mesa Grande" ("Theater Notes," *Los Angeles Herald*, August 20, 1915, CDNC).

1. Marubbio, *Killing the Indian Maiden*, 12.
2. Jackson, *Ramona*, 28, 29.
3. The Bison Company Productions/Archives in Los Angeles holds a copy of the photo.
4. Clune's Production of *Ramona* Program.
5. Clune's Production of *Ramona* Program.
6. Lyons remained with Pathé Frères until 1914, when she helped to establish "a school of motion picture acting" in San Francisco and then returned to film acting (*Motion Picture News*, May 30, 1914, 29, MHDL).
7. After the film debuted, Mabel Van Buren joined the historic American Woman Film Company, run by writer May Whitney Emerson. Women made up most of the company with few exceptions, one of them Pat Hartigan. The company was located in San Rafael, California (Guy Price, "Confer on Border on Picture Plot," *Los Angeles Herald*, May 16, 1916, CDNC).
8. Grace Kingsley, "California Epic on Film," *Los Angeles Times*, January 30, 1916, 62, NPC.
9. Grace Kingsley, "California Epic on Film," *Los Angeles Times*, January 30, 1916, 62, NPC.
10. "Indian Royalty in 'Ramona,'" *Belvidere Daily Republican*, August 3, 1916, NPC.
11. *Moving Picture World*, February 26, 1916, 1284–85, MHDL. See also *Moving Picture World*, February 12, 1916, 959, and March 16, 1916, 1829, MHDL.
12. For an in-depth review about the intertitle cards, see *Moving Picture World*, June 17, 1916, 2034, MHDL.
13. "'Ramona' Shown upon the Screen," *New York Times,* April 6, 1916.
14. *Moving Picture World*, April 22, 1916, 640, MHDL.
15. *Moving Picture World*, April 22, 1916, 640, MHDL. See also Harvey S. Thew's review, *Motion Picture News*, April 22, 1916, 2380, MHDL; and *Moving Picture World*, May 13, 1916, 1150, MHDL. Fittingly, San Jacinto, from where *The Squaw Man*'s Soboba Indians hailed, began hosting the annual Ramona Pageant in 1923.
16. Anna's husband was Lewis H. Bath, born in Ohio. The Baths lived in Salinas, California, in 1910 (California federal census, https://www.ancestry.com/). Shortly after Red Wing's visit, Bath and her husband relocated to Butte, Montana ("Mrs. Bath Honored," *Evening Herald*, November 25, 1916, NPC).
17. "Famous Indian Actress Visits Klamath Tribe," *Evening Herald* (Klamath Falls OR), October 26, 1916, NPC.
18. "Famous Indian Actress Visits Klamath Tribe," *Evening Herald*, (Klamath Falls OR), October 26, 1916, NPC.
19. Known commonly as Pauline Bush, she was a Nebraska-born silent film actress and performer.

20. "Nebraska Affairs at Washington. Special to the World-Herald. Washington DC," *Omaha World-Herald*, June 27, 1917, genealogybank.com.

21. Louis St. Cyr and David St. Cyr student files, Hampton University Archives, Hampton VA.

22. "Deerfield, (Kan.) Echo," May 24, 1912, Local Happenings, May 2, 1913, Local Happenings, October 17, 1913, Local Happenings, March 6, 1914, and Correspondence, May 1, 1914, *Winnebago (NE) Chieftain*, Nebraska State Historical Society; title unknown, *Indian News* (Genoa NE), December 1915, 14; and "The Winnebago Quartette," *Indian News* (Genoa NE), February 1919, Ho-Chunk Historical Society.

23. "Indian Girl, Movie Actress, Is Doing Housework in Sioux City," *Waterloo (IA) Times Tribune*, August 11, 1918, NPAC; and "Indian Girl Was Once a Movie Actress," *Orlando (FL) Evening Star*, August 30, 1918, NPC. Both articles claimed that Red Wing returned home because two of her sisters had died, but none had. Red Wing may have believed her sister Minnie was terminally ill.

24. James Young Deer, Los Angeles, World War I draft registration cards, 1917–18, https://www.ancestry.com/.

25. See Talmadge in the dress (belted), in *Moving Picture World*, January 4, 1919, cover and 61. Red Wing later claimed, "I made the costume Norma Talmadge wore in the 'Heart of Wetonah'" ("Indian Movie Star Lectures," *Ogden [UT] Standard*, December 29, 1935, NPC).

26. Davis, "Democracy and Not Wardship for the Indians," *Wassaja* 3, no. 5 (August 1918).

27. "This Afternoon and To-Night Only at Liberty Theater," *Evening Index* (Greenwood SC), July 11, 1918, NPC.

28. *Billboard*, June 1918, 1, fhc.

29. "Grand Theater," *Alexandria (VA) Gazette*, September 20, 1918, NPC.

30. "Indian Joe Davis Here," *Altoona (PA) Tribune*, February 20, 1919, NPC.

31. "Indians Entertain at High School," *Altoona (PA) Tribune*, February 21, 1919, NPC.

32. "Indian Joe Davis to Entertain Tonight," *Carlisle (PA) Evening Herald*, February 24, 1919, 1, NPC.

33. See ad, "The Mighty Doris Exposition Shows Include," *Times Dispatch* (Richmond VA), March 30, 1919, NPC.

34. "George Gebhardt Passes Away," *Moving Picture World*, May 24, 1919, 1161.

35. Julia resided in Washington DC at the Vendome Hotel on Pennsylvania Avenue until April 1920 or 1921 ("In Washington most of the time—sometimes a lawyer—sometimes a clerk in the Western Union," notated Nebraska reservation visitor from Hampton, Julia St. Cyr student file, Hampton University Archives, Hampton VA).

36. "Winnebago agency probate, ca. 1910–1927," box 4, 36/8/9, 305–7, RG 75, NARA-CPR.

1. Louis St. Cyr, "'19 Working in Omaha," student file, Hampton University Archives, Hampton VA; 1920 Nebraska federal census, Douglas County, Omaha, https://www.ancestry.com/.
2. In February 1920 a newspaper reported that Red Wing performed the "clog dance" with an Irishman at a farmer's house in Marshall, Iowa. How and why the performance came about is a mystery, but clearly her dancing talents were not limited to the Indian war dance ("33 Years Ago," *Laurens [IA] Sun*, February 12, 1953, NPAC).
3. See "Indian Life and Customs," *Moving Picture World*, March 30, 1912, 1145, MHDL; and "An Indian Chief," *Houston Post*, June 23, 1912, "The Portal to Texas History," https://texashistory.unt.edu/.
4. "Remington's Model and Picture Show Hero Mourns for Woods," *Fort Worth Star-Telegram*, August 29, 1912, NPAC.
5. "Real Indians to Be Seen at the Grand Next Week," *Hamilton Evening Journal*, July 24, 1920, NPC. The combined name "Chief Wongo Nemah Gowongo Mohawk" appears in "At Grand Today—Last Day," *Tampa (FL) Times*, February 24, 1920, NPC. "Chief Wongo Nemah" was also performing in the South when Joe Davis was there in 1918 ("Liberty Theatre Tonight," *Evening Index* [Greenwood SC], June 20, 1918, 7, NPC). For the "Gowongo Effect," see Rebhorn, *Pioneer Performances*, 6–23. See also Hall, *Performing the Frontier*, 157–60. The following gives a rare biographical sketch of the performer: "Go-Won-Go Mohawk (1860–1924), also known as Caroline, was born on August 11, 1860 on the reservation in Gowanda, Cattaraugus County, New York, to chief and medicine man Dr. Alan Mohawk, and moved to Green, New York, at age one, living there until the death of her father in 1869. In 1870, Go-Won-Go moved with her mother, Lydia Hale Mohawk, to Painesville, Ohio, where she continued her education. Go-Won-Go was a self-proclaimed 'Indian Princess' with many talents. In addition to being a terrific athlete and sportswoman, Go-Won-Go was considered the first Indian actress to perform on the American stage. During the early 20th century, the two primary plays she starred in were 'The Indian Mail Carrier,' which she wrote and produced, and Lincoln Carter's 'The Flaming Arrow'" ("Go-Won-Go, Mohawk Indian Princess").
6. "Riley Theatre," *Daily Reporter* (Greenfield IN), June 7, 1920, NPC. See also "Bijou," *Times* (Munster IN), November 11, 1920, NPC. His name has also been translated as Struck Lightning or Lightning at a Distance.
7. St. Cyr to Folsom, March 5, 1932, Julia St. Cyr student file, Hampton University Archives, Hampton VA; "Obituary" for Battice, *Variety*, March 26, 1930, 76, MHDL; U.S. Indian census rolls, 1885–1940, https://www.ancestry.com/; and "Mission Play," *Los Angeles Times*, March 9, 1913, 29, NPC. See also Moses, *Wild West Shows*, 182–83.

8. "Cedar," *Philadelphia Inquirer*, August 15, 1920, NPC.
9. Red Wing autobiographies, Red Wing file.
10. Some film producers sold "states rights" for select films, allowing purchasers such as Red Wing to show the film in prespecified locales.
11. There is some confusion about the film, because Mix released another film with the same name in 1916, but the 1919 version was in fact adapted (edited) from *In the Days of the Thundering Herd*. See "The Palace," *Times Herald* (Orlean NY), June 23, 1919, NPC; and "Tom Mix at the Victor Today," *Akron (OH) Evening Times*, January 11, 1920, NPC. For the plot summary that matches *In the Days of the Thundering Herd*, see "Poseyville Theater," *Poseyville (IN) News*, July 23, 1919, NPAC.
12. *Moving Picture World*, January 17, 1920, 397, MHDL.
13. "Call Movies 'The Great Art Peril,'" *Los Angeles Herald*, May 22, 1915, CDNC.
14. "Pathé Exchange Inc. . . . Just Tramps, May 3–8.—A farce comedy produced by Youngdeer, and worthy of considerable praise. It has of course a great deal of the slapstick element, but this has, however, been worked into the picture in a more or less consistent manner. The two tramps discovered asleep in a freight car, follow a rude awakening with a tactful search for food" (*Moving Picture World*, May 8, 1915, 901, MHDL). For an account of Young Deer and the Norbig Studio, see "Call Movies 'The Great Art Peril,'" *Los Angeles Herald*, May 22, 1915, CDNC.
15. *Moving Picture World*, October 16, 1915, 448, MHDL. Even the *Los Angeles Times* reported, "Bebe Daniels, 14 years old, who plays the girl opposite George Gehard [*sic*] in James Youngdeer's latest five reeler, 'The Savage,' is the youngest of the screen's leading ladies. Five years ago when Mr. Youngdeer was sent from New York as special director for the New York Motion Picture Company, he wrote many child stories around little Bebe. Bebe was at that time playing Little Hal in 'The Squaw Man' with the Belasco company" ("Good for Bebe," *Los Angeles Times*, July 13, 1915, NPC). See also Epting, *Bebe Daniels*, 28. For other news about *The Savage*, see *Moving Picture World*, July 10, 1915, 294, October 9, 1915, 275, and October 16, 1915, 448, MHDL; *Billboard*, November 13, 1916, 53, MHDL; and *Movie Magazine*, August 1915, 24, googlebooks.com. For Gebhardt's career moves, see "Welcome Georgie!" and "Girls Won't Love Him Now," *Los Angeles Times*, May 13, 1915, and November 5, 1915, respectively, NPC.
16. Wiggins starred in the first Deer Co. film, *Her Atonement*, released September 29, 1915. She also appeared in *A Shattered Romance* (*Motion Picture News*, September 4, 1915, 100; September 11, 1915, 97; October 2, 1915, 81; and October 23, 1915, 592, MHDL). For a review of *Her Atonement*, see *Motion Picture News*, September 25, 1915, 122, MHDL. *Motion Picture News* also publicized the following Deer Co. films released in 1915 and January 1916: *Song of the Sea* and *The Bent Gun* (October 2, 1915, 41, 160, MHDL); *Love's Old Sweet Song*

(October 23, 1915, 554, MHDL); *The Courting of Misfortune* and *Rube's Delirium* (December 4, 1915, 1920, MHDL); *A Silk Stocking Romance* (December 11, 1915, 2100, MHDL); *Taking Chances* (December 18, 1915, 2271, MHDL); *Billy Comes Home* (December 25, 1915, 32, MHDL); *A Peaceful Agitator* (January 1, 1916, 117, MHDL); and *False Rumors* (January 8, 1916, 18, MHDL), the last film released, on January 3, 1916. See also *Motion Picture News*, June 12, 1915, 46; July 17, 1915, 261; and October 16, 1915, 278, MHDL.

17. *Billboard*, November 13, 1916, 53, MHDL; Daisy Dean, "News Notes from Movie Land," *Janesville Daily Gazette*, February 7, 1917, NPC; and *Moving Picture World*, June 30, 1917, 2106, MHDL. Young Deer is pictured in a still from the film in Fred J. Balshofer's Scrapbook #1, 1916–17, Academy of Motion Pictures Arts and Sciences Library, Margaret Herrick Library, Beverly Hills CA. See several of Young Deer's scenarios (none of which are very good) in Youngdeer, James, Scenario, folder 982, 1–9, Mack Sennett Collection, Academy of Motion Pictures Arts and Sciences Library, Margaret Herrick Library, Beverly Hills CA.

18. "He Likes 'Em Wild," *Photoplay Magazine*, July 1920, 94, MHDL.

19. *Variety*, June 1919, 29, MHDL; *Camera! The Digest of the Motion Picture Industry*, June 15, 1919, 3, MHDL; *Moving Picture World*, June 14, 1919, 1674, MHDL; *Motion Picture News*, November 8, 1919, 3427, MHDL; and "*Neck and Noose* copyrighted; story by Jim Youngdeer, scenario by Anthony Coldeway, directed by George Holt. 2 reels. C, July 21, 1919, Universal film mfg. co., Inc. New York" (*Catalog of Copyright Entries*, pt. 1, vol. 16:2, 838, googlebooks.com).

20. The following shows the members and capital stock of the company: "Incorporations . . . Fictitious Firm Names . . . Youngdeer Production Co., 1745 Allesandro St. [address of Norbig] Motion pictures. Members: Hugh B. Evans, Jr. . . . Robert G. Boyd . . . and Jas. Deer, 4041 Munroe St" (*Southwest Builder and Contractor*, vol. 54:29, googlebooks.com); "Incorporations . . . Youngdeer Productions, Los Angeles, Capital stock, $50,000; subscribed $500. Directors: J. Perrin Willis of San Francisco, and Emily B. Down and James Youngdeer of Los Angeles. Attorney: J. Perrin Willis, 303 Hearst Bldg. San Francisco" (*Southwest Builder and Contractor*, vol. 55:34, googlebooks.com).

21. *Camera! The Digest of the Motion Picture Industry*, January 17, 1920, 3, 16, MHDL; and *Film Daily*, March 30, 1920, 629, MHDL.

22. *Camera! The Digest of the Motion Picture Industry*, January 24, 1920, 2, MHDL.

23. "Youngdeer Film Co.," *Los Angeles Herald*, January 24, 1920, CDNC. The address given was "SUNSET STUDIOS, 123 Henne bldg., 3rd and Spring sts." The following men were said to be part of the company: Harry Keaton, not only to star but also as casting director; Ralph Staub as cameraman; and Bob Renzia as assistant director (*Camera! The Digest of the Motion Picture Industry*, January 24, 1920, 11, MHDL). Later *Camera!* (March 27, 1920, 3, MHDL) reported that S. F. Rogers, a pudgy older comedian, would direct the film. Cecil De Freitas replaced

Ralph Staub and took out his own ads as the film's photographer-cameraman (*Camera! The Digest of the Motion Picture Industry*, March 27, 1920, 3, MHDL). Additionally, "James Youngdeer has engaged the services of Captain Earl T. Martin to play the lover in 'Watuska.' John Wallace will do Chief Ironside in the same production" (*Camera! The Digest of the Motion Picture Industry*, March 27, 1920, 20, MHDL).

24. "Rita Nunn" is described as the widow of Joel T. Nunn in "Cakes.—The Arcade" (*Sikeston [MO] Standard*, January 27, 1920, NPC).

25. *Camera! The Digest of the Motion Picture Industry*, December 20, 1919, 3, MHDL.

26. *Camera! The Digest of the Motion Picture Industry*, December 20, 1919, 3, MHDL.

27. 2017 correspondence with Marie Gaisford, who remembered her aunt as a beautiful, loving woman. According to Gaisford, Nunn left the movie business and led a very long and happy life.

28. "Motion Pictures," *Los Angeles Herald*, February 21, 1920, CDNC.

29. *Camera! The Digest of the Motion Picture Industry*, December 20, 1919, 14, MHDL.

30. *Camera! The Digest of the Motion Picture Industry*, February 28, 1920, 3; March 6, 1920, 3; March 27, 1920, 3, 20, MHDL; and *Atlanta Constitution*, February 29, 1920, NPC.

31. "Youngdeer Prod. is the name of a newly formed company. The officers are J. P. Willis, president; Mrs. Emily Dow, vice-president and James Youngdeer director-general and treasurer" (*Film Daily*, March 30, 1920, 629, MHDL).

32. *Camera! The Digest of the Motion Picture Industry*, March 13, 1920, 4, MHDL. Robbins's death was announced in *Film Daily*, March 23, 1920, n.p., MHDL.

33. "Film Employees Win in $2000 Wage Suit," *Los Angeles Herald*, May 13, 1920, CDNC.

34. *Camera! The Digest of the Motion Picture Industry*, April 10, 1920, 15, MHDL. The marriage may have been illegal, since, as previously mentioned, he and Red Wing may have never divorced. Young Deer's marriage record to Anomine shows she was twenty-two and that Young Deer reduced his age five years. His parents are listed as James and Emma Deer. Anomine's father is listed as William Paige, but her mother's name is "unknown" (Los Angeles County marriages, GS film number: 2074260, digital folder number: 004280710, image number: 00017, https://www.familysearch.org/). A records search on https://www.ancestry.com/ shows several females named "Anonyme Page" born in Canada, beginning in the 1600s.

35. The following items refer to Young Deer's time in London: "'The Haigh Serial' being produced by Frederick White under the direction of Edward R. Gordon, is working on schedule. It stars Ernest Haigh" (*Camera! The Digest of the Motion Picture Industry*, August 20, 1921, 3, MHDL). "The directors are George K. Arthur, Flora le Breton, Edward R. Gordon and an up to now anonymous renter, said to be American. Their first effort will be a five-reel drama" (*Variety*, April 22, 1922,

39, MHDL). "Edward R. Gordon (Young Deer) is producing the new George Arthur film. 'Rounded Corners.' The principal parts are played by George K. Arthur and Flora le Breton" ("London Film Notes," *Variety*, May 19, 1922, 43, MHDL). "'B. and Z.' a new British producing firm boast they have let all territory in their first picture 'Repentance' by individual effort and without having to go to one of the established renting firms as is generally the case. Peggy Hathaway is the leading lady and the producer is the American James Gordon sometimes known as 'Young Deer'" (*Variety*, July 23, 1922, 31, MHDL). "Repentance. London, Sept. 15. This, the first picture made by Geoffrey Benstead, with the 'B. & Z.' brand, is good dramatic entertainment. The story is an original one, written by *Lilian* [my emphasis] and Edward R. Gordon, the latter having directed the production" (*Variety*, September 29, 1922, MHDL). "London, July 27 . . . Among the few producing concerns which are working are . . . George K. Arthur Productions are on 'The Night Errant' which is being directed by Edward R. Gordon ('Young Deer')" (*Variety*, August 11, 1922, MHDL). "Star Productions, a new concern, has just completed a five-reeler under the direction of Ed R. Gordon ('Youngdeer') and Wm. S. Charlton. The cast includes Flora le Breton, Doris Lloyd, Marie Gerald, George K. Arthur, George Turner, William Lugg, Bertie Wright and Sir Simeon Stuart. If the story and production are equal to the cast the picture should be a winner" (*Variety*, April 19, 1923, 34). The reference above to Gordon's wife "Lilian" is perplexing. Should this have said "Anomine," or did this refer to Red Wing (who was on tour in the States) or even Lillian Wiggins?

Edward R. Gordon was also the name of an actor performing in Hollywood at this time. Not surprisingly, the two are often confused. The following filmography for Edward R. Gordon *as director* belongs to Young Deer, although the British Film Institute (BFI) web site gives the birth and death dates for the actor Edward R. Gordon: 1921: *The Prodigal Son*; *Mother's Darling*; *Lost, Stolen or Strayed*; *The Case of a Packing Case*; *The Notorious Mrs. Fagan*; *The Stolen Jewels*; *The Lady in Black*; *The Girl Who Came Back*; and *Fight in a Thieves Kitchen*; 1922: *His Wife's Sweetheart* (producer/script); *Love's Influence*; *Repentance* (director and script writer); 1923: (none recorded); 1924: *Lieutenant Daring RN and the Water Rats*; and date unknown: *Something in the City* (BFI, http://www.bfi .org.uk/films-tv-people/4ce2b9fb4e44d). Young Deer was also involved with *Rounded Corners* (as noted above); *Leaves from My Life* with Edward Haigh, released in 1921; and *Belle of the Gambling Den* (Goble, *The Complete Index*, 202; and Gifford, *British Film Catalogue*).

36. "Gem," *Daily Clintonian* (Clinton IN), August 2, 3, 1920, NPC.
37. Charles H. Camp was born on December 10, 1880 (World War I draft registration, 1917–18, Jefferson County, New York, September 5, 1918, A 955, https:// www.ancestry.com/). "Mr. Camp and Ray Stinnett opened the second picture

show in Abilene some fifteen years ago. Mr. Camp now operates a string of picture shows in southern Illinois and conducts road shows as well" ("Vaudeville Acts at Queen Pronounced as Splendid," *Abilene [TX] Daily Reporter*, May 8, 1923, NPAC). See also "U.S. City Directories, Oklahoma City, Oklahoma," 1911, 196, 1912, 186, and 1917, 129, https://www.ancestry.com/; "Oklahoma Charter Grants," *Wichita (KS) Beacon*, June 4, 1917, NPC. Also see "Daugherty After Theater Manager," *Daily Oklahoman* (Oklahoma City), February 7, 1912, NPC, regarding Camp's violation of the child labor law.

38. "Tom Mix and Lillia Red Wing at the Grand in 'The Days of Danger,'" *Hamilton (OH) Daily News*, August 20, 1920, NPC.

39. "Heart Interest Film of American Frontier Life and Hardships at the Mystic Theater," *Coshocton (OH) Tribune*, November 22, 1920, NPC; and "Star Theater," *Daily Times* (New Philadelphia OH), November 8, 1920, NPC.

40. "Indian Actress Here Says Segration Here People Great Mistake," *Sandusky (OH) Register*, May 1, 1921, NPC. Headline is shown as it appeared, with misspellings.

41. Deerfoot, who admitted his real name was Will. S. Beecher, claimed his mother was Cheyenne and his father was a Scotsman born in New York. In 1923 he also admitted he had two brothers, Robert and John Beecher, who lived in Philadelphia. All three boys are listed with their father, born in Italy, and mother, from South Carolina, on the 1900 federal census for Philadelphia (Ward 39, District 1009, 6B). He is also listed as "white" for the 1920 census for St. Johnsville, Montgomery County, New York, https://www.ancestry.com/. See "Lucky Oil Strike," *Fort Plain (NY) Standard*, April 26, 1923, Chronicling America: Historic American Newspapers, http://chroniclingamerica.loc.gov.

42. "Indian Pageant," 23, souvenir program, Saint Clair County.

43. Armes, "Behold! The Pioneers!," 171, 181.

44. Another issue gave the standard list of her latest film roles, but it's unknown with what moving picture she appeared ("Indian Moving Picture Actress Will Appear in Person at the Colonial," *Nebraska State Journal* [Lincoln], November 6, 1921, NPC).

45. *Billboard*, December 10, 1921, 156, FHC. "Miss Redwood [*sic*], the Indian Movie Actress will appear in person in a 20 minute vaudeville act. Also two Indian dances by fullblood Indians at 9 o'clock" ("Brooklyn. Big Show Tonight," *Kansas City [MO] Star*, December 13, 1921, NPAC).

46. "Empire Theatre," *Democrat Forum* (Maryville mo), February 3, 1922, NPC.

47. "Bonadventure Shows" and "Alamo 34th and Main," *Kansas City (MO) Star*, April 25 and May 5, 1922, respectively, NPAC.

48. "Indian Actress Coming," *Osawatomie (KS) Graphic*, June 22, 1922, NPC; and "Grand Tonight," *Iola (KS) Daily Register*, July 8, 1922, NPC.

49. "4th Street Theater," *Moberly (MO) Democrat*, March 2, 1922, NPC.

50. "Clarke sold the company to Marie Witham who continued the business on a smaller scale. In 1923 she introduced the Picturol range. Maintains largest slide film library" ("Society for Visual Education"). In 1922 the society debuted its journal, the *Educational Screen: The Independent Magazine Devoted to the New Influence in National Education.*

51. "Committee of Teachers, Investigating Visual Education, Seeks Equipment," *Lincoln (NE) Star*, October 23, 1921, NPC.

52. See "Motion Pictures as a Factor in Public School Education," *Atlanta Constitution*, September 18, 1921, NPC.

53. "Society News," *Fort Scott (KS) Daily Tribune-Monitor*, July 7, 1922, NPC.

54. *Nebraska Teacher*, January 1922, 187–88, googlebooks.com (the cover showing Red Wing and Tyndall is on page 168). For the composer's views on Native Americans and their music, see Lieurance, "The Musical Soul."

55. "Events in Society, Lieurance Recital," *Colorado Springs (CO) Gazette*, June 18, 1922, NPC.

56. "Redwing made records for insurance for two prominent manufacturers. She secured from an old chief Four Legs an antique Indian flute. They would not permit anyone else to have it. In singing, Redwing accompanies herself on an Indian drum" (Alice McDermott, "Society News," *Fort Scott [KS] Daily Tribune-Monitor*, July 7, 1922, NPC). Four Legs was living in Portage, Wisconsin, in 1832. See also the finding aid for the Thurlow Lieurance Collection, Special Collections and University Archives, Wichita State University, Wichita, Kansas.

57. Alice McDermott, "Society News," *Fort Scott (KS) Daily Tribune-Monitor*, July 7, 1922, NPC.

58. "People's Theater (Chanute's Brightest Spot)," *Chanute (KS) Daily Tribune*, July 8, 10, 1922, NPC.

59. "Lilia Redwing Here," *Daily Republican* (Cherryvale KS), July 26, 1922, NPC.

60. "Lilia Redwing Here," *Daily Republican* (Cherryvale KS), July 26, 1922, NPC.

61. Bracken was also described as a "Clean, Classy, Clever, Comical Cuss" ("Picture Shows Tonight," *Independence [KS] Daily Reporter*, July 31, 1922, 1, NPC).

62. "Tackett's Theatre," *Coffeyville (KS) Daily Journal*, August 4, 1922, NPC; "In Vaudeville" and "Rex Today (last time)," *Arkansas City Daily Traveler*, September 8, 9, 1922, NPC; and "Vaudville [*sic*] Acts at Queen Pronounced Splendid," *Abilene (TX) Daily Reporter*, May 8, 1923, NPAC.

63. "New Theatre Programme," *Harper (KS) Advocate*, October 26, 1922, NPC.

64. "Special Added," *Kiowa County Signal* (Greensburg KS), November 2, 1922, NPC; "Wed. and Thursday Noted Movie Actor 'Lilia Redwing,'" *Winfield (KS) Daily Free Press*, September 12, 1922, NPC; "Wellington to Have a Real Movie Actress," *Wellington (KS) Daily News*, September 23, 1922, NPC.

65. Red Wing's Texas tour followed the path of Camp's former business interests and family. A native Kansan, Camp had lived in Dallas and Abilene with his

wife and kids. Camp's wife lived in Fort Worth with his two daughters by 1920 but was listed as a widow on census records (1900 Texas federal census, Dallas County, Dallas, and 1920 Texas federal census, Tarrant County, Fort Worth, https://www.ancestry.com/).

66. "Special Attraction Is Secured for Majestic," *Wichita Daily Times*, December 24, 1922, NPAC; "Wednesday and Thursday 3 Acts," *Vernon (TX) Record*, December 12, 1922, NPC; and "The Opera House," *Mexia (TX) Daily News*, April 27, 1923, NPAC.

67. "Hoot Gibson in the 'Lone Hand,'" *Sweetwater (TX) Daily Reporter*, May 11, 1923, NPAC. As previously mentioned, Red Wing only appeared in Bison Life Films, as far as is known.

68. *Commercial America* 21, Philadelphia Commercial Museum, 1924 (only partial view), 179, googlebooks.com.

69. Hischak, *Broadway Plays*, 178.

70. *Exhibitors Herald*, March 7, 1925, 49, MHDL. Regarding the move of Inspiration Pictures from Fort Lee to Manhattan, see Koszarski, *Hollywood on the Hudson*, 88. See also *Exhibitors Herald*, January 3, 1925, 82, MHDL.

71. *Moving Picture World*, May 15, 1925, 316, and May 23, 1925, 475, MHDL.

72. "Indian Movie Star Lectures," *Ogden (UT) Standard*, December 29, 1935, NPC.

17. METROPOLITAN GROUP OF AMERICAN INDIANS

1. For Waterman, see 1920 New York federal census, Brooklyn Assembly District 18, Kings County, and 1925 New York state census, Brooklyn Assembly District 18, Kings County, https://www.ancestry.com/.

2. State of New York Certificate of Marriage, No. 22709, July 2, 1925.

3. Josephine Tarrant said Alvina's family believes she went to school in Philadelphia.

4. "Akron's Quality Store," *Akron (OH) Beacon Journal*, July 20, 1925, NPC. John Freeman Craig also performed as "White Eagle" during this time. He was born about 1866 in Wisconsin to Ezekiel Lawton Craig (Scotch Welsh) and an alleged "Indian mother," Alvina Dunn (Wisconsin Marriage Index, 1820–1907, Sheboygan, vol. 1:34, https://www.ancestry.com/). However, Alvina's parents, Orrin Hammond and Rachel Stone, were both New Yorkers. See 1880 Wisconsin federal census, LaGrange, Monroe County, https://www.ancestry.com/; and Washington Deaths, 1883–1960, https://www.ancestry.com/. See also Craig, *Chief White Eagle*.

5. "'Olde Fashioned Pageant' at Home of Mrs. Ferdinand J. Kuhn to Attract Fashionable Attendance," *New York Evening Post*, June 23, 1926, FHC; and "Pageant at Bernardsville on Saturday," *Plainfield Courier-News* (Bridgewater NJ), June 24, 1926, NPC.

6. "Plainfield High School Notes," *Plainfield Courier-News* (Bridgewater NJ), March 24, 1927, NPC; and "Royalty at Gorton High," *Yonkers (NY) Statesman*, April 15, 1927, FHC.

7. No. 22709, State of New York Certificate of Marriage. Eaglefoot's parents are listed as "Byol" and "Ana Janer [or Jauer]." A search for them proved fruitless. Not surprisingly, given the era, Red Wing shaved ten years off her age, while Eaglefoot's age reads "32," though he was probably in his late twenties.
8. See "Big Brockton Fair Attracts Thousands on Opening Day" and "Three Bold Braves," *Boston Herald*, October 2, 1928, and October 21, 1962, respectively, genealogybank.com; and "50 Years Ago," *Pittsburgh Press*, February 19, 1978, NPC.
9. Eaglefoot married Louise Mantino, a housekeeper (No. 22203, Application for Marriage License, County of Lebanon, Pennsylvania). The 1930 Illinois federal census, Chicago, Cook County, lists him as "divorced." His name disappears from records after 1930.
10. Anita De Frey, "Red Wing (a Biographical Sketch)," Red Wing file.
11. Anita's mother was the daughter of an Irish mother and a Pennsylvanian farmer who was a native Missourian and son of German immigrants. See "Double Tragedy at San Francisco," *San Francisco Call*, November 30, 1897, CDNC. De Frey sought her birth certificate in 1954, but there was no record of it in San Francisco. See California Biographical Collection: Responses to Vital Record Inquiries, 1822–1964, Anita Veronica Frey, images 2121–22, https://www.ancestry.com/; "Deaths . . . Cook," *San Francisco Chronicle*, May 26, 1930, genealogybank.com; Margaret Frey, Union Cemetery, Redwood City ca, findagrave.com; Frey, Gustave, 1890 and 1892 California voter registrations; *San Francisco City Directory*, 1891; 1910 California federal census, Redwood City, San Mateo County (Joseph Dickey family), https://www.ancestry.com/.
12. Meyer Berger, "New York Metropolitan Group of American Indians," *New York Times*, March 18, 1956.
13. Meyer Berger, "New York Metropolitan Group of American Indians," *New York Times*, March 18, 1956.
14. "Redmen, Reduced 80 Percent; but Remainder Is Playing Important Role in Nation," *Brooklyn Daily Eagle*, May 8, 1927, NPC. The report also stated that Michigan, "the first state to grant the Indians full rights as citizens," agreed to set aside the New Yorkers' chosen date "to be observed hereafter" as Indian Day.
15. "Unification to Preserve Identity of Indian Race Urged at Park Conclave," *Brooklyn Daily Eagle*, September 30, 1929, NPC.
16. "Unification to Preserve Identity of Indian Race Urged at Park Conclave," *Brooklyn Daily Eagle*, September 30, 1929, NPC.
17. Buffalo Child Long Lance (born Sylvester Clark Long), like Young Deer deemed "mulatto," hid his African American identity and claimed to be half Cherokee when he enrolled at Carlisle. Although he did have some Native ancestry, he later wrote an autobiography in which he falsely claimed to be the son of a Blackfoot chief. He was an activist for Indian causes and had a brief film career until he committed suicide in 1932 because his African American

identity was about to be exposed. One of the people who allegedly sought this exposure was his costar Chauncey Yellow Robe. See Smith, *Chief Buffalo Child Long Lance*.

18. Molly Spotted Elk or Mary Alice Nelson was born on Indian Island, Maine, in 1906. Her family called her Molliedell. Her sister Darly (short for Darling) was born Mildred Nelson and was one of Molly's seven siblings. For a fascinating comparison to Red Wing's career, see McBriee, *Molly Spotted Elk*.

19. Morris Mofsie attended the Phoenix Indian school, where he played in the band ("Roster of Band," *Arizona Republic* [Phoenix], November 5, 1924).

20. Alvina Mofsie recorded the 1922 date on Julia's death certificate, and the 1930 tribal census shows her living in Brooklyn.

21. Red Wing file.

22. St. Cyr to Folsom, March 5, 1932, Julia St. Cyr student file, Hampton University Archives, Hampton VA; and obituary for Battice, *Variety*, March 26, 1930, 76, MHDL. His obituary stated he had two daughters, Cora Ellis and Red Wing (who traveled in Australia at the time of his death). Cora Ellis was in fact his married daughter, as tribal records show (U.S. Indian Census Schedules, 1885, 1940, https://www.ancestry.com/), but this particular Red Wing was a probably a young performing partner, not a daughter. While Lilia Red Wing toured the Midwest, Battice and "Miss Red Wing," said to be a "Cherokee maid," performed a mock wedding in New York in 1923. Supposedly, the mock wedding turned out to be real, according to the report. See "Promoter of 'Mock' Wedding Loses Cherokee Maiden's Hand," *Baltimore Sun*, May 19, 1923, NPC. For more on Cora Battice Ellis, see Cora Battice student file, Carlisle Indian School Digital Resource Center, http://carlisleindian.dickinson.edu.

23. "Oh Gee! I Want to Go to Camp!," *New York Evening Post*, April 23, 1931, FHC.

24. Howard W. Moore Papers, 1915–93, SC20795, Finding Aids, Manuscripts and Special Collections, New York State Library, http://webcache.googleusercontent .com/search?q=cacheiu9tzaz6liAKgJ:www.nysl.nysed.gov/msscfa/sc20795 .htm&num=1&hl=en&gl=us&strip=1&vwsrc=0.

25. Moore, *Plowing My Own Furrow*, 166–70.

26. See "Actress Lillian St. Cyr wearing a native costume eats in a tepee on penthouse patio of a hotel in New York, United States," Critical Past, http://www .criticalpast.com.

27. "Redskin Princess Is Shown in Reel," *Philadelphia Inquirer*, September 8, 1931, NPC. See also "Great Britain Strife Shown in 'Times' Reel," *Los Angeles Times*, September 9, 1931, NPC. These clips can be viewed at Critical Past, http://www .criticalpast.com/video.

28. The production serves as a testament to Michelle H. Raheja's postmodern concept of "visual sovereignty." "Laughing at the camera confronts the spectator with the often-absurd assumptions that circulate around visual representations of Native

Americans," she explains. Not only was Red Wing "flagging" her "involvement and complicity in these often disempowering structures of cinematic dominance and stereotype," in Raheja's words, but she was also reappropriating these structures to promote herself as a performer and likely as a skilled craftsperson of regalia. See Raheja, *Reservation Reelism*, 193. Other works relevant to Indians playing Indians or "redfacing" include Moses, *Wild West Shows*; Deloria, *Playing Indian*; Trachtenberg, *Shades of Hiawatha*; Wilmer, *Native American Performance*; and Vizenor, *Manifest Manners*.

29. "Indian Maid's Camp Site High Skyscraper Roof," *Spokane (WA) Daily Chronicle*, September 2, 1931, https://news.google.com.

30. The city was named after Red Wing, but that Red Wing was a leader of the Dakota people.

31. "Indian Maiden, Modern Cliff Dweller, Pitches Her Tepee atop New York Skyscraper," *Miami (OK) New Record*, September 6, 1931; also published in the *Republic* (Columbus IN), September 1, 1931, NPC.

32. "Yawn Department," *Brooklyn Daily Eagle*, September 1, 1931, NPC. The next year two Indians copied Red Wing's publicity stunt: "Here are Chief Little Bear and Chief Crazy Horse of the Sioux tribe, shown with their tepee which they pitched on the roof of a hotel in New York. They refused to sleep in the rooms. They are there to attend the tenth annual meeting of the Izaak Walton League and enter their pleas for federal permission to fish in the famed Winnesniek [*sic*] refuge near Genoa, Wis." ("Camp on Skyscraper Roof," *Ottawa Citizen*, April 28, 1932, NPC).

33. Although Red Wing's apartment at 170 West 65th Street was demolished, she would be happy to find that today the address sits between the Film Society of Lincoln Center and the Lincoln Center Theater.

34. "Indian Princess Tells Experiences in Films at Writer's Assembly," *Brooklyn Daily Eagle*, December 9, 1931, NPC. The next December she was also invited to sing Indian songs and lead carols for the American Woman's Association to help needy children ("300 Children in Yule Fete," *New York Times*, December 22, 1932).

35. Erdlitz lived at 171 West 97th Street. She and Red Wing gave similar performances. Born Isabella F. Erdlitz in 1889 in Marinette, Wisconsin, her parents were Joseph and Elizabeth Erdlitz. Her father was a Bohemian immigrant and her mother was a Wisconsin Menominee. Erdlitz trained as a nurse and joined the Red Cross in Chicago, serving overseas during the war. In 1944 she recruited nurses for the war effort. She died four years later in Manhattan (*Independent Record*, August 12, 1944, NPC). See also "The Honor Roll."

36. Moore, *Plowing My Own Furrow*, 166–70. Katherine Cloud, who claimed to be the niece of artist and ornithologist Louis Agassiz Fuertes, was one of Moore's new counselors. Agassiz's father was Puerto Rican, and Cloud's Indian heritage is doubtful.

37. De Frey, biographical sketch of Red Wing, Red Wing file.
38. "Alliance of Indians to Gather for Pow-Wow at Nodine Field," *Herald Statesman* (Yonkers NY), October 24, 1933, FHC; and "5,000 See Paleface Mayor Made Chief Great River at Pow-Wow," *Herald Statesman* (Yonkers NY), October 30, 1933, FHC.
39. "National Day to Honor Indians Urged by Speaker at Museum," *Herald Statesman* (Yonkers NY), December 12, 1933, FHC.
40. "23 Prizes Awarded at Bridge Party of Fern Brook Unit," *Herald Statesman* (Yonkers NY), May 1, 1934, FHC.
41. "Thistle Lodge," *Herald Statesman* (Yonkers NY), September 30, 1935, FHC; and "Abraham & Straus Dept. Store," *Brooklyn Daily Eagle*, December 11, 1935, NPC.
42. "Nestor Studio."
43. For example, Hollywood journalist Bob Thomas wrote: "I don't want to seem disrespectful of public monuments, but I believe I detected an error in one the other day. While walking down Vine street, I noticed a bronze tablet on the corner of a bank. It proclaimed that on that spot was produced 'the first feature-length picture made in America.' The picture was said to be 'The Squaw Man,' produced by Cecil B. Demille, Jesse Lasky and Samuel Goldwyn in December, 1913. The record books indicate otherwise. The best authorities declare D. W. Griffith, who originated most movie advances, made the first length picture in the U.S. It was 'Judith and Bethulia,' a four-reeler made earlier in 1913" ("Lana Turner Plans Heavy Work to Forget Troubles," *Alton Evening Telegraph*, October 29, 1951, 12, NPC).
44. "Film Group Has Reunion," *Los Angeles Times*, December 29, 1935, NPC. See also *Motion Picture Herald*, January 4, 1936, 52, MHDL; and "Original Cast of the Squaw Man Enjoys Reunion," *San Bernardino (CA) County Sun*, January 5, 1936, NPC.
45. "Dustin Farnum Dies after Long Illness," *New York Times*, July 5, 1929.
46. "Reunion in Hollywood," *Trenton (NJ) Evening Times*, December 29, 1935, NPC.
47. "Indian Movie Star Lectures," *Ogden (UT) Standard*, December 29, 1935, NPC.
48. It was reported that she appeared with Morris Mofsie (Sharp Shooter) at the YMCA ("Collector Gives Club Expert Advice about Pictures in the Home," *Long Island Daily Press* [Jamaica NY], October 15, 1936, FHC).
49. "Redskins Whoop It Up in Hollywood," *Richmond (VA) Times Dispatch*, August 4, 1936, NPC.
50. Blowsnake, also known as Sam Carley, and his brother, Jasper Blowsnake, became well-known subjects of ethnologist Paul Radin's *The Autobiography of a Winnebago Indian* and *Crashing Thunder*. Besides Radin's work, Blowsnake is known for his performances at the Standing Rock Ceremonial in the Dells, Wisconsin. For Brooklyn performances, see "Mohawk Indians Dance, Sing for Old Brooklynites Society" and "Representative of 17 Tribes Hold Indian

Charity Pageant," *Brooklyn Daily Eagle*, February 2 and February 10, 1940, respectively, NPC. See also the 1940 New York federal census, Kings County, Brooklyn.

51. "Boro Pals Mourn Indian Boy," *Brooklyn Daily Eagle*, July 2, 1937, NPC. The article is accompanied by a photo of darling Norton posing in a Plains Indian bonnet. See also "Indian Rites Mark Birthday of Auto Victim," *Brooklyn Daily Eagle*, November 15, 1937, NPC.

52. Conversations with Henu Josephine Tarrant, 2018. See "Spider Woman Theater."

53. "Representative of 17 Tribes Hold Indian Charity Pageant," *Brooklyn Daily Eagle*, February 10, 1940, NPC.

54. "The Museum of Modern Art."

55. Morris was the son of Jack Mofsie and Mina Jasenvensie ("New York, New York City Municipal Deaths, 1795–1949," Brooklyn, May 3, 1941, https://www .familysearch.org/; and 1940 New York federal census, Brooklyn, Kings County, https://www.ancestry.com/). For a photograph of Alvina Mofsie at this time, see "Alvina L. Mofsie (Alvina Lowery), Winnebago [Nebraska], 1897–1986," February 22, 1943, http://collections.si.edu/search/results.htm?view=&dsort =&date.slider=&q=alvina.

56. Conversation with Henu Josephine Tarrant, 2018.

57. "Indian Summer," *Baltimore Sun*, August 31, 1947, NPC.

18. FARE THEE WELL AND HOLLYWOOD REUNION

1. By 1937, according to three Social Security number applications, she lived on West 65th Street, West 67th, and finally, her favorite residence, on West End Avenue. She applied for Social Security under different first names: Adrienne St. Cyr, June 14, 1937, 170 West 65th Street; Lily St. Cyr, March 2, 1945, 202 West 67th Street; and Lilian St. Cyr, February 10, 1950, 189 West End Avenue, Applications for Social Security Account Number, Social Security Administration. Why she used the name "Adrienne" is unknown.

2. They lived in the vicinity of Amsterdam Avenue to West End Avenue between West 66th and West 67th Streets (Julia St. Cyr, September 22, 1943, 251 West 66th Street, Application for Social Security Account Number, Social Security Administration). By 1947 Alvina had moved from 34 Douglas Street in Brooklyn (1930 New York federal census) to 214 West 67th Street (Julia St. Cyr's death certificate, source below).

3. De Frey, biographical sketch of Red Wing, Red Wing file. De Frey was called the "Modoc Sun Bird" but was also known as Juanita or Nita De Frey. Kerry Mills (composer of "Red Wing") also wrote a song called "Sun Bird," which may have inspired De Frey's Indian name. In the 1920s De Frey, a soprano, performed at movie theaters, and in the 1930s she sang for radio. In the 1950s she performed with Louis Mofsie. See "Here to Please You Warburton Theatre,"

Yonkers (NY) Statesman, May 13, 1921, FHC; "Radio Programmes," *Standard Union*, January 27, 1932, FHC; and Meyer Berger, "About New York," *New York Times*, July 27, 1956.

4. *Moving Picture World*, March 14, 1925, 138, MHDL. See also *Variety*, November 19, 1924, 21, MHDL; *Film Daily*, November 26, 1924, 5, MHDL; "In Filmland," *Tipton (IN) Daily Tribune*, December 29, 1924, NPAC; "Trip to Hell Is Described in 'Inferno,'" *World-Herald,* January 25, 1925, genealogybank.com; and *Variety*, March 11, 1925, 36, MHDL.

5. 1930 California federal census, San Francisco County, San Francisco, https://www.ancestry.com/.

6. Jas Youngdeer and Helen Gilchrist, Cochise County, Arizona, marriage certificate, July 18, 1930, https://www.ancestry.com/; and "Tombstone Ore Outlook Good," *Arizona Daily Star* (Tucson), July 27, 1930, NPC.

7. "Business Opportunities of Many Kinds," *Los Angeles Times* (classified ads), November 27, 30, 1930, and December 1, 3, 5, 15, 19, 20, 1930, NPC.

8. "Temple to Hold Screen Contest," *Sun* (San Bernardino CA), March 26, 1933, NPC.

9. *Variety*, July 25, 1933, 58, MHDL. See also "Director's Wife Burned by Comb," *Los Angeles Times*, July 18, 1932, NPC.

10. A photo of the stone can be viewed at Helen Gilchrist Young Deer, Inglewood Cemetery, Los Angeles, California, Find a Grave Memorial #110287022, findagrave.com; "Helen Gilchrist Youngdeer," died June 6, 1937, Maywood, Los Angeles, "J. Gordon Youngdeer" (husband and death informant, lived at 1149 Las Palmas), Standard Certificate of Death, State of California, Department of Public Health, Vital Statistics, https://www.ancestry.com/. Gilchrist, born in Whitemich, Scotland, arrived in Detroit on March 1, 1926 (Detroit Border Crossings and Passenger and Crew Lists, 1905–57, https://www.ancestry.com/). See her funeral notice, "Youngdeer," *Los Angeles Times*, June 7, 8, 1937, NPC.

11. 1940 New York federal census, Manhattan Borough, New York County, https://www.ancestry.com/.

12. Application for Social Security Account Number, Lily St. Cyr, March 2, 1945. Minnie Moton lived at 231 West 67th Street (1940 federal census, New York, https://www.ancestry.com/). When she died on August 13, 1948, Minnie lived at 250 West 67th Street, New York (New York City Municipal Deaths, 1795–1949, https://www.familysearch.org/).

13. "Hudson Museum Auxiliary Holds Its Annual Luncheon," *Herald Statesman* (Yonkers NY), June 15, 1943, FHC.

14. "Methodists See Indian War Dances" and "Hudson Museum Auxiliary Holds Its Annual Luncheon," *Herald Statesman* (Yonkers NY), April 2 and June 15, 1943, respectively, FHC; "Indian Chiefs Visit Flushing Cub Pack," *Long Island Star-Journal* (Brooklyn NY), November 9, 1943, NPC; and "Indian Program Will Be Given for Girl Scouts," *Pelham (NY) Sun*, April 27, 1944, FHC.

15. "Whisky Interest Too Big for Show," *New York Sun*, April 13, 1944, FHC; *New York Star* (East Hampton NY), September 13, 1945, FHC; and "Indians to Be Present at County Hobby Show," *Herald Statesman* (Yonkers NY), May 27, 1947, FHC.

16. "Julia St. Cyr Travis," 165 West End Avenue, died December 4, 1947, certificate of death, 26160, New York Department of Health, Borough of Manhattan (Alvina Mofsie, informant).

17. "Indian Pow Wow Next Week-End," *New York Star* (East Hampton), June 17, 1948, FHC.

18. "New York Holds Its First County Fair," *New York Times*, September 14, 1948. Short Wing Winneshiek was a well-known Ho-Chunk chief in the mid- to late nineteenth century. Presumably, this Short Wing's last name was Winneshiek, but I have not been able to figure out exactly who he was. He is pictured in Indian regalia in "Ancient Color Returns as Redskins Dance on Springy Banks," *County Review* (Riverhead NY), July 7, 1949, nyshistoricnewspapers.org.

19. "Fred P. Shaw Becomes Chief at Rockefeller Center," *Bath (ME) Independent*, January 13, 1949, NPAC.

20. *Lubbock (TX) Avalanche Journal*, December 11, 1949, NPC.

21. Cowger, *The National Congress*, 9–71.

22. "Hobbyist groups proliferated in the 1950s and 1960s at an astonishing rate, and by 1963 there were a dozen groups in Texas alone and more than thirty nationwide with thousands of members," Clyde Ellis told me in April 2016. Ellis also explained, "The Indian hobbyist movement was drawn largely from Boy Scouting's Indian lore–themed program, the Order of the Arrow."

23. "Indian Dances Superb Arrow Drive Launched," *Richfield Springs (NY) Mercury*, April 20, 1950, FHC; "'Arrow' Drive for Indians Is Commenced," *Otsego Farmer* (Cooperstown NY), April 21, 1950, nyshistoricnewspapers.org. For the establishment of ARROW, see Cowger, *The National Congress*, 70–71.

24. "Indian Dances Superb Arrow Drive Launched," *Richfield (NY) Springs Mercury*, April 20, 1950, FHC.

25. A photo with Secretary of the Interior Stewart Udall and his wife with Maria Martinez shows Kimball jutting her face into Martinez's personal space, apparently trying to get the great Pueblo potter to crack a smile. Photo by U.S. Department of the Interior, Collection of Harvey Slatin.

26. Harvey L. Slatin obituary, *Daily Star*, February 2013, http://obituaries.thedailystar.com/obituary/harvey-slatin-1915-2013-733206662.

27. Correspondence with Anne Pratt Slatin, March 28, 2014; and Anthes, *Native Moderns*, 121.

28. "Collection of Historic Shoes," *Miniota (MB) Herald*, November 7, 1933, NPAC. Delman owned five hundred pairs of historic shoes, including the boots Amelia Earhart wore during her flight to Paris.

29. Ship manifests show Kimball as sometimes single and sometimes married, probably because Delman had a wife and son. Her birthplace is given as Mountain Park, Oklahoma, the city where her real parents were married. See New York, Passenger Lists, 1820–1957 (for Effie Delman, Series T715, 1897–1957, roll 5312; for Yeffe V. Kimball, Series T715, roll 5542 and roll 5371; for Yeffe Violette Kimball, Series T715, roll 6381) and 1940 New York federal census, New York, https://www.ancestry.com/.

30. Correspondence with Anne Pratt Slatin, April 14, 2014.

31. Anthes, *Native Moderns*, 117, 121.

32. Correspondence with Anne Pratt Slatin, April 14, March 27, 2014.

33. For example, Omaha's *World-Herald* reported that she appeared at the Shinnecock Powwow in Southampton, New York, in September and that she and the Mofsie children gave a performance for the East Rockaway Cub Scouts in October ("Nebraskan to Pow Wow in New York State," *World-Herald*, September 3, 1950, genealogybank.com).

34. White actors like blonde Jeff Chandler played the principal Indian roles, which included a stereotypical Indian princess, played by a red-faced Natalie Wood, who is fittingly killed right after she marries Jeffards.

35. "Indians Tour RKO Theaters," *Brooklyn Daily Eagle*, July 7, 1950, NPC; and "Indians to Boost New Roxy Movie," *Daily News* (New York), July 9, 1950, NPC. I was not able to find anything else about Hote Mowee.

36. "Indian Drums Beat in Hotel Here to Start Health Wagon to Navajos," *New York Times*, April 24, 1951.

37. "Indian Drums Beat in Hotel Here to Start Health Wagon to Navajos," *New York Times*, April 24, 1951.

38. Scrapbook vol. 30, *Hollywoodian*, MS 1400, DeMille Papers.

39. "Producers Fete Lasky as Pioneer Film Maker," *Los Angeles Times*, September 13, 1951, NPC.

40. Scrapbook vol. 30, *Hollywood Reporter*, September 14, 1951, MS 1400, DeMille Papers.

41. Scrapbook vol. 30, *Hollywood Variety*, September 14, 1951, MS 1400, DeMille Papers.

42. Scrapbook vol. 30, *Variety*, September 13, 1951 [first page?], MS 1400, DeMille Papers.

43. There are three photos. In one, Stella Stray, both Red Wing's and DeMille's former stenographer, is pictured with Red Wing and DeMille. See the Business Yearbook, 1951, box 187, folder 2, "Cecil B. DeMille and Red Wing," and "Stella Stray, Cecil B. DeMille, and Red Wing," "13 September 1951, reunion, *The Squaw Man*, 1931," 34-6-9785-86 and 34-6-9787; and Scrapbook vol. 30, *Los Angeles Herald*, September 19, 1951, MS 1400, DeMille Papers.

44. Helen Bower, "Star Gazing," *Detroit Free Press*, November 11, 1951, NPC. See also "Historic Film Spot Marked by Plaque," *Los Angeles Times*, September 12, 1951, NPC; and Scrapbook vol. 30, *Hollywoodian*, MS 1400, DeMille Papers.

45. Red Wing autobiography, Red Wing file.

19. THE MOON SHINES ON PRETTY RED WING

1. Conversation with Henu Josephine Tarrant, daughter of Kevin and Muriel, 2018. I was delighted to see Henu Josephine Tarrant perform in her mother's play, *"Don't Feed the Indians!": A Divine Comedy Pageant*, at the La Mama Theater in New York City in 2014. I also saw her perform a solo fancy shawl dance at New York City's Indian Community House the next night. Louis Mofsie led the intertribal dance and also, like his great-aunt before him, sold Indian crafts before and after performing.

2. See Thunderbird American Indian Dancers.

3. Conversation with Louis Mofsie, 2014.

4. Conversation with Henu Josephine Tarrant, 2018.

5. "Queen Is Belle of County Fair," *Daily Register*, September 14, 1964, http://209.212.22.88/data/rbr/1960-1969/1964/1964.09.14.pdf.

6. Meyer Berger, "Redskin Colony of the Big City, Fifty Strong, Making Last Stand to Save Its Culture," About New York, *New York Times*, March 18, 1956.

7. "How Lincoln Center Was Built (It Wasn't Pretty)," *New York Times*, December 21, 1917. Red Wing lived at 458 West 35th Street (1959 Manhattan phone book and documents in Red Wing file). At some point late in life Red Wing had a male companion. Louis Mofsie remembered he was a Japanese actor who appeared either on the stage or the screen in *Anna and the King*. Although Mofsie doesn't recall his name, he said the actor was much younger than Red Wing and had admired her from her silent film days. When the relationship began and how long it lasted he couldn't say.

8. "De Mille's Epic Story of Film's First Epic," *Life Magazine*, October 19, 1959, 154–68.

9. Spears, *The Golden Age of Hollywood*, 394.

10. Letters to the Editor, *Life Magazine*, November 9, 1959, 10.

11. *Motion Picture Daily*, December 10, 1959, cover, MHDL.

12. *Motion Picture Daily*, December 3, 1959, 2, MHDL.

13. De Frey, biographical sketch, Red Wing file.

14. "Indians to Hail at Birthday Fete," *Long Island Star-Journal*, February 14, 1964, FHC.

15. "Pretty Red Wing," *Omaha World-Herald*, March 1, 1965, genealogybank.com.

16. "Ending Moons of Neglect," *New York Times*, March 9, 1968.

17. "Annual Indian Day," *Brooklyn Daily Eagle*, September 27, 1968, NPC.

18. Alexie, *The Lone Ranger*, 24.

19. Tom Wolfe, "Radical Chic: That Party at Lenny's," *New York*, June 8, 1970, http://nymag.com/news/features/46170/.

20. Charlotte Curtis, "Comanche, Kiowa, Potawatomi and Social Tribes Attend," *New York Times*, July 13, 1970.

21. Carol Bennett to Mary Pickford, November 1, 1971, 265/f-2474, Mary Pickford Collection, Academy of Motion Pictures Arts and Sciences Library, Margaret Herrick Library, Beverly Hills CA.

22. Note on envelope, postmarked November 5, 1971, says, "Esther I answered this."

23. "Lillian Red Wing St. Cyr," 11 Bank Street, "widowed," actress, died March 13, 1974, death certificate, 156-74-104816 (Yeffe Slatin, death informant), the City of New York Vital Records Certificate. Both Louis Mofsie and Anne Pratt Slatin informed me about the circumstances of Red Wing's death.

24. "Red Wing, 90, Star in 1913 'Squaw Man'" (with her picture from the film), *New York Times*, March 14, 1974; "Red Wing Dies, Retired Actress," *World-Herald* (Omaha NE), March 14, 1974, genealogybank.com; "Lillian St. Cyr," *Carlisle (PA) Sentinel*, March 26, 1974, NPC; "Lillian St. Cyr, Early Star Dies," *Los Angeles Times*, March 15, 1974, NPC.

25. Berkman, "Lillian Red Wing St. Cyr," Obituaries, in Berkman, ed., *Indian Notes*.

BIBLIOGRAPHY

Adams, David Wallace. *Education for Extinction: American Indians and the Boarding School Experience 1875–1928*. Lawrence: University Press of Kansas, 1995.

Adams, Katherine H., and Michael L. Keene. *Women of the American Circus, 1880–1940*. Jefferson NC: McFarland and Company, 2012.

Agnew, Jeremy. *The Old West in Fact and Film: History versus Hollywood*. Jefferson NC: McFarland and Company, 2012.

Ahern, Wilbert H. "An Experiment Aborted: Returned Indian Students in the Indian School Service, 1881–1908." *Ethnohistory* 44, no. 2 (1997): 263–304.

Aleiss, Angela. *Making the White Man's Indian: Native Americans and Hollywood Movies*. Westport CT: Praeger, 2005.

Alexie, Sherman. *The Lone Ranger and Tonto Fistfight in Heaven*. New York: Harper Perennial, 1994.

Almeida, Diedre Ann. "The Role of Western Massachusetts in the Development of American Education Reform Through the Hampton Institute's Summer Outing Program (1878–1912)." EdD diss., University of Massachusetts, 1992.

Anderson, Gary Clayton, and Alan R. Woolworth, eds. *Through Dakota Eyes: Narrative Accounts of the Minnesota Indian War of 1862*. St. Paul: Minnesota Historical Society Press, 1988.

Annual Report of the Board of Commissioners of Public Charities. Vol. 15. Pennsylvania Board of Public Charities. https://books.google.com.

Annual Report of the Board of Commissioners of Public Charities. Vol. 23. Pennsylvania Board of Public Charities. https://books.google.com.

Annual Report of the Commissioner of Indian Affairs, June 30, 1900. Part 1. United States Office of Indian Affairs. https://books.google.com.

Annual Report of the State Treasurer of the Commonwealth of Pennsylvania for the Fiscal Year Ending November 30, 1884. Harrisburg: Lane S. Hart, State Printer, 1885.

Anthes, Bill. *Native Moderns: American Indian Painting, 1940–1960*. Durham NC: Duke University Press, 2006.

Armes, Ethel. "Behold! The Pioneers! The Historical Pageants of Michigan." *Playground* 16, no. 4 (1922): 171. https://books.google.com.

Ashley, James R. *The Rise and Fall of the Silent Film Era: Vol. III: The Movie Studios and Directors.* Kindle ed. Copyright 2015 James R. Ashley.

Balshofer, Fred J., and Arthur C. Miller. *One Reel a Week.* Berkeley: University of California Press, 1967.

Bataille, Gretchen M., and Kathleen Mullen Sands. *American Indian Women: Telling Their Lives.* Lincoln: University of Nebraska Press, 1984.

Behrens, Jo Lea Wetherilt. "Defense of 'Poor Lo': National Indian Defense Association and Council Fire's Advocacy for Sioux Land Rights." South Dakota Historical Society, 1994.

Beider, Robert E. *Native American Communities in Wisconsin 1600–1960: A Study of Tradition and Change.* Madison: University of Wisconsin Press, 1995.

——— . "Scientific Attitudes toward Indian Mixed-Bloods in Early Nineteenth Century America." *Journal of Ethnic Studies* 8 (Summer 1980): 17–30.

Bell, Genevieve. "Telling Stories out of School: Remembering the Carlisle Indian Industrial School, 1879–1918." PhD diss., Stanford University, 1998.

Berger, Meyer. *Meyer Berger's New York: A Great Reporter's Love Affair with a City.* New York: Fordham University Press, 2004.

Berkhofer, Robert F., Jr. *The White Man's Indian: Images of the American Indian from Columbus to the Present.* New York: Vintage Books, 1979.

Berkman, Kathy, ed. *Indian Notes: Museum of the American Indian Quarterly* 10, no. 2 (Spring 1974). http://archive.org/stream/indiannotes1021974muse/indiannotes1021974muse_djvu.tx.

Bernardi, Daniel, ed. *The Birth of Whiteness: Race and the Emergence of U.S. Cinema.* New Brunswick NJ: Rutgers University Press, 1996.

Berthrong, Donald J. *The Cheyenne and Arapaho Ordeal: Reservation and Agency Life in the Indian Territory, 1875–1907.* Norman: University of Oklahoma Press, 1976.

Bible, Karie, Marc Wanamaker, and Harry Medved. *Location Filming in America.* Charleston SC: Arcadia Publishing, 2010.

"Biography: Bertha Cody, Native American Archaeology." http://www.theheroinecollective.com/bertha-cody/.

Biography of Bessie (Harrison) (Eyton) (Coffey) Macdonald. http://mendoncafamily.com.s193431.gridserver.com/wp-content/uploads/2009/12/ Biography-color-text.pdf.

Birchard, Robert S. *Cecil B. DeMille's Hollywood.* Lexington: University Press of Kentucky, 2004.

——— . "The Squaw Man." http://americanfilm.afi.com/issue/2014/2/archives#.WYTPlIqQym0.

Blair, Emma H., ed. *The Indian Tribes of the Upper Mississippi Valley and Region of the Great Lakes, as Described by Nicolas Perrot, French Commandant in the Northwest; Bacqueville de la Potherie, French Royal Commissioner to Canada;*

Morrell Marston, American Army Officer; and Thomas Forsyth, United States Agent at Fort Armstrong. Cleveland: Arthur H. Clark, 1911.

Bold, Christine. *The Frontier Club: Popular Westerns and Cultural Power, 1880–1924*. New York: Oxford University Press, 2013.

Bonnin, Gertrude Simmons (Zitkála-Šá). "Impressions of Indian Childhood." *Atlantic Monthly*, January 1900.

———. "An Indian Teacher among Indians." *Atlantic Monthly*, March 1900.

———. "The School Days of an Indian Girl." *Atlantic Monthly*, February 1900, 185.

Brennan, Stephen, ed. *An Autobiography of General Custer*. New York: Skyhorse Publishing, 2012.

Brown, Jennifer S. H. *Strangers in Blood: Fur Trade Company Families in Indian Country*. Vancouver: University of British Columbia Press, 1980.

Brown, Letitia Woods. *Free Negroes in the District of Columbia, 1790–1846*. New York: Oxford University Press, 1972.

Brownlow, Kevin. *The War, the West, and the Wilderness*. New York: Knopf, 1978.

Bruchac, Margaret. "Native Artisans and Trade in the Saratoga Region." Saratoga Native American Festival Program, 27–28. https://repository.upenn.edu/anthro _papers/157.

Brudvig, Jon L., ed. and comp. "First Person Accounts as Written by American Indian Students at Hampton Institute, 1878–1923." http://www.twofrog.com /hamptonstories1.html.

Brumble, H. David, III. *American Indian Autobiography*. Berkeley: University of California Press, 1988.

Buscombe, Edward. *"Injuns!": Native Americans in the Movies*. London: Reaktion Books Ltd., 2006.

Buscombe, Edward, and Roberta E. Pearson. *Back in the Saddle Again: New Essays on the Western*. London: British Film Institute, 1998.

Cahill, Cathleen D. *Federal Fathers and Mothers: A Social History of the United States Indian Service, 1869–1933*. Chapel Hill: University of North Carolina Press, 2011.

California Mission Resource Center. http://www.missionscalifornia.com/stories /movies-missions.html.

Carley, Kenneth. *The Dakota War of 1862: Minnesota's Other Civil War*. 2nd ed. St. Paul: Minnesota Historical Society Press, 1976.

"The Carlisle Indian Industrial School: Assimilation with Education after the Indian Wars." Teaching with Historic Planes, National Park Service, 12. https://www .nps.gov/subjects/teachingwithhistoricplaces/upload/Twhp-Lessons_Carlisle -School2016.pdf.

Carlisle Indian School Digital Resource Center. carlisleindian.dickinson.edu.

Catalog of Copyright Entries. https://books.google.com.

Catlin, George. *Letters and Notes on the American Indians, Two Volumes in One*. Reprint. North Dighton MA: JG Press, 1995.

"The Charity Case, Hidden City." http://hiddencityphila.org/2012/08/the-charity-case.

The Cheyenne's Bride. Pathé Frères (West Coast), 1911. EYE (Eye Film Museum, Amsterdam, the Netherlands), https://www.eyefilm.nl/en.

"Chief Bender." Society for American Baseball Research. https://sabr.org/bioproj /person/03e80f4d.

Child, Brenda J. *Boarding School Seasons: American Indian Families, 1900–1940.* Lincoln: University of Nebraska Press, 2000.

Church of the Epiphany. Pennsylvania Church and Town Records. Image 357. https:// www.ancestry.com/.

Church of the Evangelist. Pennsylvania Church and Town Records, October 1889. Image 186. https://www.ancestry.com/.

Clifton, James A., ed. *Being and Becoming Indian: Biographical Studies of North American Frontiers.* Chicago: Dorsey Press, 1989.

Clune's Production of *Ramona* Program. clunesproductionooclunrich.pdf.

Columbian Harmony and Payne Cemetery Registers. http://www.dclibrary.org /node/44933.

Comfort, William Wistar. *Just among Friends: The Quaker Way of Life.* New York: Macmillan Co., 1941. archive.org.

Commercial America. Vol. 21. Philadelphia Commercial Museum, 1924 (partial view). https://books.google.com.

Committee of the Social Science Section of the Civic Club, comp. *Civic Club Digest of the Institutions and Societies in Philadelphia.* Philadelphia: University of Pennsylvania, 1895.

Connelly, Robert B. *The Motion Picture Guide: Silent Film, 1910–1936.* Chicago: Cinebooks, 1986.

The Cowboy and the School-Marm. Bison Life Pictures, 1910. EYE (Eye Film Museum, Amsterdam, the Netherlands), https://www.eyefilm.nl/en.

Cowger, Thomas. *The National Congress of American Indians: The Founding Years.* Lincoln: University of Nebraska Press, 1999.

Cozzens, Peter. *Conquering the Southern Plains.* Volume 3 of *Eyewitness to the Indian Wars, 1865–1890.* Mechanicsburg PA: Stackpole Books, 2003.

Craig, John Freeman. *Chief White Eagle: Fifty Years on the Warpath.* Washington DC: Independent Publishing Company, 1929 (Kessinger Legacy Reprints).

Crary, Margaret. *Susette La Flesche: Voice of the Omaha Indians.* New York: Hawthorne Books, 1973.

D'Agostino, Annette, comp. *Filmmakers in the Moving Picture World: An Index of Articles, 1907–1927.* Jefferson NC: McFarland and Company, 1997.

Davis, Damani. "Slavery and Emancipation in the Nation's Capital: Using Federal Records to Explore the Lives of African American Ancestors." *Prologue Magazine* 42 (Spring 2010): 1.

Decorah, Spoon. "Narrative of Spoon Decorah." In *Wisconsin Historical Collections* 13, edited and annotated by Rueben Gold Thwaites, 448–62. Madison: State Historical Society of Wisconsin, 1895.

Degrees Conferred in 1920, Bachelor of Arts. *Calendar of Wellesley College, 1920–21.* https://books.google.com.

De La Ronde, John T. "Personal Narrative." In *Wisconsin Historical Collections* 7, edited by Lyman Copeland Draper, 345–65. Madison: State Historical Society of Wisconsin, 1876.

Deloria, Philip J. *Indians in Unexpected Places.* Lawrence: University Press of Kansas, 2004.

——. *Playing Indian.* New Haven CT: Yale University Press, 1998.

Deloria, Vine, Jr. *Custer Died for Your Sins: An Indian Manifesto.* Norman: University of Oklahoma Press, 1988.

DeMille, Cecil B., Papers. L. Tom Perry Special Collections Library, Brigham Young University, Provo UT.

Diedrich, Mark, ed. *Ho-Chunk Chiefs: Winnebago Leadership in the Era of Crisis.* Rochester MN: Coyote Books, 2001.

——. *Winnebago Oratory: Great Moments in the Recorded Speech of the Hochungra, 1742–1887.* Rochester MN: Coyote Books, 1991.

Dippie, Brian W. *The Vanishing American: White Attitudes and U.S. Indian Policy.* Lawrence: University Press of Kansas, 1982.

Donneley, Lieutenant Governor Ignatious, to Governor Alexander Ramsey. "History of the Indian War." No. 2. August 29, 1862. In *Annual Report of the Commissioner of Indian Affairs for the Year 1862.* Washington DC: Government Printing Office, 1862.

Dorman, Robert L. *Hell of a Vision: Regionalism and the Modern American West.* Tucson: University of Arizona Press, 2012.

Draper, Lyman Copeland. "Michel St. Cyr, an Early Dane County Pioneer." *Wisconsin Historical Collections* 6. Madison. State Historical Society, 1872.

Du Bois, W. E. B. *The Souls of Black Folk.* 1903. Kindle edition.

Eastman, Elaine Goodale. *The Red Man's Moses.* Norman: University of Oklahoma Press, 1935.

Edmonds, I. G. *Big U: Universal in the Silent Days.* South Brunswick NJ: A. S. Barnes and Company, 1977.

Edmunds, R. David, ed. "'Unacquainted with the Laws of the Civilized World': American Attitudes toward the Métis Communities in the Old Northwest." In *The New Peoples: Being and Becoming Métis in North America*, edited by Jacqueline Peterson and Jennifer S. H. Brown. Lincoln: University of Nebraska Press, 1985.

"Edna Maison, at Home in the Rarefied Aria of Opera and Silver Screen." https://classicfilmaficionados.com/2015/03/20/edna-maison-at-home-in-the-rarefied-aria-of-opera-and-silver-screen.

Elting, Mary. *The Hopi Way*. Illustrated by Louis Mofsie. New York: M. Evans and Company, 1969.

Epting, Charles L. *Bebe Daniels: Hollywood's Good Little Bad Girl*. Jefferson NC: McFarland and Company, 2016.

The Executive Documents of the House of Representatives for the First Session of the Fifty-First Congress, 1889–1890. United States Congressional serial set, issue 2725. Washington DC: Government Printing Office, 1890.

Fear-Segal, Jacqueline. "Nineteenth-Century Indian Education: Universalism versus Evolutionism." *Journal of American Studies* 33, no. 2 (1999): 323–41.

Fear-Segal, Jacqueline, and Susan B. Rose, eds. *Carlisle Industrial School: Indigenous Histories, Memories, and Reclamations*. Lincoln: University of Nebraska Press, 2016.

"Fifteenth Street Presbyterian Church, African American Heritage Trial." https://www.culturaltourismdc.org/portal/fifteenth-street-presbyterian-church-african-american-heritage-trail.

Fleming, E. J. *Wallace Reid: The Life and Death of a Hollywood Idol*. Jefferson NC: McFarland and Company, 2007.

Fletcher, Alice. "A Phonetic Alphabet Used by the Winnebago Tribe of Indians." *Journal of American Folklore* 3, no. 11 (October–December 1890).

Fletcher, Jonathan E. "General Abstract of Disbursements Made by J. E. Fletcher, Indian Agent, within the Winnebago Agency for the Year Ending June 30, 1855." Ho-Chunk Historical Society.

——— . "Report of the Conduct of Employees at the Winnebago Agency during the Quarter Ending September 3rd 1853." Ho-Chunk Historical Society.

For the Papoose. Pathé Frères (West Coast), 1912. Library of Congress. https://www.loc.gov/item/90706439.

Frederick, K. P. *Legends and History of the San Jacinto Mountains*. Long Beach CA: Self-published, 1926.

"Free African Americans of Virginia, North Carolina, South Carolina, Maryland and Delaware." http://www.freeafricanamericans.com.

"Friends School at Rancocas." http://www.rancocasfriendsschool.org/SchoolHistory/FriendsHistory.html.

French, Charles K., Collection. Series 2.8, P-26, Motion Picture Collection. Seaver Center, Los Angeles.

Gage, J. R. "Intertribal Communication, Literacy, and the Spread of the Ghost Dance." scholarworks.uark.edu/cgi/viewcontent.cgi?article=2417&context=etd:.

Galbraith to Clark W. Thompson. No. 144. *Report of the Commissioner of Indian Affairs for the Year 1863*. Washington DC: Government Printing Office, 1863.

Gallop, Alan. *Buffalo Bill's British Wild West*. Phoenix: Sutton Publishing, 2001.

"George Doane's Cabin in 1914 Movie." https://palomarmountainnews.wordpress.com.

Gifford, Denis, ed. *British Film Catalogue, Vol. 1: The Fiction Film, 1895–1994*. London: Routledge, 2016.

Gilman, Rhoda R. "The Fur Trade in the Upper Mississippi Valley, 1630–1850." *Wisconsin Magazine of History* 58 (Autumn 1974–75).

Goble, Alan, ed. *The Complete Index to Literary Sources in Film.* London: Bowker Saur, 1999. https://books.google.com.

"Go-Won-Go, Mohawk Indian Princess." https://www.liveauctioneers.com/item /11718641_293-go-won-go-mohawk-indian-princess-and-wild-west-show.

Gracyk, Tim, and Frank Hoffman. *Popular American Recording Pioneers: 1895–1925.* London: Routledge, 2008. https://books.google.com.

Great-Grandma Hoxie-Stone. http://alhoxietribute.blogspot.com/2007/11/great -grandma-hoxie-stone.html.

Griffith, Mrs. D. W. (Linda Arvidson). *When the Movies Were Young.* New York: E. P. Dutton & Co., 1925.

Guide to Earl Ivan Brown Papers, 1900–1936. http://library.duke.edu/rubenstein /findingaids/brownearlivan/.

Hackel, Steven W. "Indian Testimony and the Mission San Gabriel Uprising of 1785." *Ethnohistory* 50, no. 4 (Fall 2003).

Hall, Roger A. *Performing the Frontier.* Cambridge: Cambridge University Press, 2001.

Hansen, James L. "'Half-Breed' Rolls and Fur Trade Families in the Great Lakes Region—an Introduction and Bibliography." In *The Fur Trade Revisited: Selected Papers of the Sixth North American Fur Trade Conference,* edited by Jennifer S. H. Brown, W. J. Eccles, and Donald P. Heldman. Mackinac Island: Michigan State University Press, 1994.

———. "Prairie du Chien Baptisms, 1817." Transcribed by James Hansen. *Minnesota Genealogical Journal* 4.

———. "Records of St. John Nepomucene Catholic Church, Little Chute, Wisconsin, 1836–1851." Unpublished.

———. "The St. Cyr Family of Prairie du Chien." Unpublished.

Hardorff, Richard G. *Washita Memories: Eyewitness Views of Custer's Attack on Black Kettle's Village.* Norman: University of Oklahoma Press, 2006.

Harlan, Louis R., ed. *The Booker T. Washington Papers, Volume 2: 1860–89.* Urbana: University of Illinois Press, 1972.

Harrison, Peter. *Yellow Swallow: Custer's Lost Son.* Edited by Gary Leonard. Southampton, UK: Chetwynd Press, 2014.

Hayne, Donald, ed. *The Autobiography of Cecil B. DeMille.* Englewood Cliffs NJ: Prentice-Hall, 1959.

Hearne, Joanna. *Native Recognition: Indigenous Cinema and the Western.* Albany: SUNY Press, 2012.

Henderson, Robert M. *D. W. Griffith: The Years at Biograph.* New York: Farrar, Straus and Giroux, 1970.

Hill, Edward E. "Winnebago Agency, 1826–76." In *Historical Sketches for Jurisdictional and Subject Headings Used for the Letters Received by the Office of*

Indian Affairs, 1824–80. Washington DC: National Archives and Records Service, 1967.

Hischak, Thomas S. *Broadway Plays and Musicals: Descriptions and Essential Facts of More Than 14,000 Shows through 2007.* Jefferson NC: McFarland and Company, 2009.

History on the Net. http://www.authentichistory.com/diversity/native/ns2-princess/19040000_Navajo-Harry_MacDonough-lyrics.html.

Hoffman, M. M. *The Church Founders of the Northwest.* Milwaukee: Bruce Publishing Company, 1937.

Honor of the Tribe. Bison Life Pictures, 1912. Celeste Bartos International Film Study Center, Museum of Modern Art, New York.

"The Honor Roll of Menominee County, Michigan in the World War 1917–1918–1919." https://archive.org/stream/4763157.0001.001.umich.edu/4763157.0001.001.umich.edu_djvu.txt.

Horak, Laura. *Girls Will Be Boys: Cross-Dressed Women, Lesbians, and American Cinema, 1908–1934.* New Brunswick NJ: Rutgers University Press, 2016.

Horan, James D. *The McKenny-Hall Portrait Gallery of American Indians.* New York: Bramhall House, 1986.

Horsman, Reginald. *Race and Manifest Destiny: The Origins of American Racial Anglo-Saxonism.* Cambridge MA: Harvard University Press, 1981.

The Hoxie Brothers. http://www.b-westerns.com/hoxie1.htm.

Hoxie, Frederick E., ed. *Talking Back to Civilization: Indian Voices in from the Progressive Era.* Boston: Bedford / St. Martin's, 2001.

Hughes, Thomas. *History of Blue Earth County.* Chicago: Middle West Publishing Company, 1901.

——— . *Indian Chiefs of Southern Minnesota: Containing Sketches of the Prominent Chieftains of the Dakota and Winnebago Tribes from 1825 to 1865.* Minneapolis: Ross & Haines, 1969.

Hultgren, Mary Lou, and Paulette Fairbanks Molin. *To Lead and to Serve: American Indian Education at Hampton Institute 1878–1923.* Virginia Foundation for the Humanities, 1989.

Hutchinson, Elizabeth West. "Progressive Primitivism: Race, Gender and Turn-of-the-Century American Art." PhD diss., Stanford University, 1998.

Ingersoll, Thomas N. *To Intermix with Our White Brothers: Indian Mixed Bloods in the United States from Earliest Times to the Indian Removals.* Albuquerque: University of New Mexico Press, 2005.

Institute for Colored Graduates. http://exhibits.library.villanova.edu/institute-colored-youth/graduates/.

Institute for Colored Youth in the Civil War Era, Classes of 1856–1864. https://exhibits.library.villanova.edu/institute-colored-youth/graduates/.

Jacobs, Margaret D. *White Mothers to a Dark Race: Settler Colonialism, Maternalism, and the Removal of Indigenous Children in the American West and Australia, 1880–1940*. Lincoln: University of Nebraska Press, 2009.

Jackson, Helen Hunt. *A Century of Dishonor: A Sketch of the United States Government's Dealings with Some of the Indian Tribes*. 1885. Reprint, Norman: University of Oklahoma Press, 1995.

———. *Ramona*. New York: Penguin Books (Signet Classic), 1988.

James, George Wharton. *Through Ramona Country*. Boston: Little, Brown and Company, 1909.

Jensen, Richard D. *The Amazing Tom Mix: The Most Famous Cowboy of the Movies*. New York: iUniverse, 2005. https://books.google.com.

Jensen, Richard E. *The Indian Interviews of Eli S. Ricker, 1903–1919*. Lincoln: University of Nebraska Press, 2005.

Jesse Black Cat Photo. http://digitalmarquette.cdmhost.com/cdm/ref/collection/p128701coll3/id/1904.

Jones, John Alan. *Winnebago Ethnology*. New York: Garland Publishing, 1974.

Jones, Tom, et al. *People of the Big Voice: Photographs of Ho-Chunk Families by Charles Van Schaick, 1879–1942*. Madison: Wisconsin Historical Society Press, 2011.

Journal of the Senate, December 11, 1882, 54. *Congressional Series*, vol. 2,072.

Justice, Fred C., and Tom R. Smith. *Who's Who in the Film World: Being Biographies with Photographic Reproductions of Prominent Men and Women Who Through Their Genius and Untiring Energy Have Contributed So Greatly toward the Upbuilding of the Moving Picture Industry*. Los Angeles: Film World Publishing Co., 1914.

Katchmer, George A. *A Biographical Dictionary of Silent Film Western Actors and Actresses*. 2002. Reprint, Jefferson NC: McFarland and Company, 2009. https://books.google.com.

Kaufman, Edmund G. "Mennonite Missions among the Oklahoma Indians." http://digital.library.okstate.edu/Chronicles/v040/v040p041.pdf.

Keeling, Henry C. "My Experience with the Cheyenne Indians." *Chronicles of Oklahoma* 3, no. 1 (1925): 79–53.

Keil, Charlie, and Ben Singer, eds. *American Cinema of the 1910s: Themes and Variations*. New Brunswick NJ: Rutgers University Press, 2009.

Kellogg, Louise Phelps. *The French Régime in Wisconsin and the Northwest*. Edited by Joseph Scharfer. New York: Cooper Square Publishers, 1968.

———. "Glory of the Morning and the Decorah Family." *Madison Democrat*, February 21, 1912. Wisconsin Local History and Biography Articles, Wisconsin Historical Society. http://www.wisconsinhistory.org.

———. "The Removal of the Winnebago." *Transactions of the Wisconsin Academy of Sciences, Arts and Letters* 21 (1924): 23–29.

"Kent County's Moors." http://nativeamericansofdelawarestate.com/MoorsOfDelaware/moor4.html.

Kilpatrick, Jacquelyn. *Celluloid Indians: Native Americans and Film*. Lincoln: University of Nebraska Press, 1999.

Kinzie, Juliette M. *Wau-bun: The "Early Day" in the North West, 1856*. National Society of the Colonial Dames of America, 1948. Reprint, Menasha WI: George Banta Publishing Company, 1989.

Koszarski, Richard. *Fort Lee: The Film Town*. Rome: John Libbey Publishing, 2004.

———. *Hollywood on the Hudson: Film and Television in New York from Griffith to Sarnoff*. New Brunswick NJ: Rutgers University Press, 2010.

Krupat, Arnold. *Ethno-criticism: Ethnography, History, Literature*. Berkeley: University of California Press, 1992.

———. *For Those Who Come After: A Study of Native American Autobiography*. Berkeley: University of California Press, 1985.

Landis, Barbara. "About the Carlisle Indian Industrial School." http://home.epix.net/~landis/histry.html.

Lass, William E. "The Removal from Minnesota of the Sioux and Winnebago Indians." *Minnesota History* 38, no. 8 (1963): 353–64.

Learning, Capt. S. T. "Personal Recollections of Early Days in Decatur." *Proceedings and Collections of the Nebraska State Historical Society*, vol. 15. Lincoln: Jacob North and Co., Printers, 1907.

Lester Predmore about D. W. Griffith at Cuddebackville 1971. youtube.com.

Liberty, Margot, ed. *A Northern Cheyenne Album: Photographs by Thomas B. Marquis*. Norman: University of Oklahoma Press, 2006.

Lieurance, Thurlow. "The Musical Soul of the American Indian." *The Etude*, October 1920, 655–56. https://books.google.com.

Little Dove's Romance. Bison Life Pictures, 1911. Green Library, Stanford University, Palo Alto CA.

Little Hill. "The Uprooted Winnebago." In *Native American Testimony*, edited by Peter Nabakov. Rev. ed. New York: Penguin Books, 1999.

Lindsey, Donal F. *Indians at Hampton Institute 1877–1923*. Urbana: University of Illinois Press, 1995.

Lindvall, Terry. *Sanctuary Cinema: Origins of the Christian Film Industry*. New York: New York University Press, 2007.

Lomawaima, K. Tsianina. *They Called It Prairie Light: The Story of Chilocco Indian School*. Lincoln: University of Nebraska Press, 1994.

London, Jack. *The Letters of Jack London: 1913–1916*. Edited by Earl Labor, Robert C. Leitz III, and I. Milo Shephard. Vol. 3. Stanford CA: Stanford University Press, 1988.

Lookingbill, Brad D. *War Dance at Fort Marion: Plains Indian War Prisoners*. Norman: University of Oklahoma Press, 2006.

"Looking for Mabel Normand (Marilyn Slater)." http://looking-for-mabel.webs.com.

Loraux, Nicole. *Tragic Ways of Killing a Woman.* Translated by Anthony Forster. Cambridge MA: Harvard University Press, 1987.

Lubman, Hyman. "A History of the Nebraska Winnebago Indians with Special Emphasis on Education." MA thesis, University of Omaha, Nebraska, 1962.

Ludlow, Helen. "Indian Education at Hampton and Carlisle." *Harper's Monthly Magazine,* April 1881, 659–75.

Lund, Karen C., comp. American Indians in Silent Film Finding Aid. Motion Picture and Television Reading Room. https://www.loc.gov/rr/mopic/findaid /indian1.html.

Lurie, Nancy Oestreich. "A Check List of Treaty Signers by Clan Affiliation." *Journal of the Wisconsin Indians Research Institute* 2 (June 1966): 50–73.

————. "Cultural Change among the Wisconsin Winnebago." *Wisconsin Archeologist* 25, no. 4 (1944): 119–25.

————, ed. *Mountain Wolf Woman: The Autobiography of a Winnebago Indian.* Ann Arbor: University of Michigan Press, 1961.

————. "Winnebago." In *Northeast,* edited by Bruce G. Trigger, 690–707. Vol. 15 of *Handbook of North American Indians,* general editor, William C. Sturtevant. Washington DC: Smithsonian Institution Press, 1978.

————. *Wisconsin Indians.* Madison: State Historical Society of Wisconsin, 1987.

MacCann, Richard Dyer. *The First Film Makers.* Metuchen NJ: Scarecrow, 1989.

"Madison's Fur Traders: The First White Men in Wisconsin." wisconsinhistory.org.

Mark, Joan. *A Stranger in Her Native Land: Alice Fletcher and the American Indians.* Lincoln: University of Nebraska Press, 1988.

Marks, Paula Mitchell. *In a Barren Land: American Indian Dispossession and Survival.* New York: Quill, 1998.

Marubbio, M. Elise. *Killing the Indian Maiden: Images of Native American Women in Film.* Lexington: University Press of Kentucky, 2009.

Matson, Barb Ann. "Performing Identity, Staging Injustice: California's Ramona Festival as Ritual." PhD diss., University of Colorado, 2006.

Mazzuchelli, Samuel Charles. *Memoirs, historical and edifying, of a missionary apostolic of the order of Saint Dominic among various Indian tribes and among the Catholics and Protestants in the United States of America.* Pioneering the Upper Midwest: Books from Michigan, Minnesota, and Wisconsin, ca. 1820–1910. Library of Congress, General Collections and Rare Book and Special Collections Division. American Memory. http://memory.loc.gov/cgi-bin.

McBriee, Bunny. *Molly Spotted Elk.* Norman: University of Oklahoma Press, 1995.

McKenny, Thomas L. *Sketches of a Tour to the Lakes.* 1827. Reprint, Minneapolis: Ross and Haines, 1959.

Merrell, Henry. "Pioneer Life in Wisconsin." In *Wisconsin Historical Collections* 9, edited by Lyman C. Draper, 366–404. Madison: State Historical Society of Wisconsin, 1882.

Meyers, Tom. "History of a Fort Lee Neighborhood." http://patch.com/newjersey /fortlee/history-of-a-fort-lee-neighborhood-coytesville.

Michelson, Truman. "Some Notes on Winnebago Social and Political Organizations." *American Anthropologist* 37 (July–September 1935).

Minnesota Genealogical Journal. 38 vols. Roseville MN: Park Genealogical Books, 1984–2006.

The Mission Play Program, San Gabriel, California, 1915.

Moore, Howard W. *Plowing My Own Furrow.* Syracuse NY: Syracuse University Press, 1993.

"The Moors of Delaware." http://nativeamericansofdelawarestate.com/MoorsOf Delaware/trirace3.html.

Moses, L. G. *Wild West Shows and the Images of American Indians, 1883–1933.* Albuquerque: University of New Mexico Press, 1996.

"Motion Pictures, 1894–1912." Library of Congress, April 8, 1909. http://archive.org /stream/motionpict18941912librrich/motionpict18941912librrich_djvu.txt.

Murphy, Lucy Eldersveld. *A Gathering of Rivers: Indians, Métis, and Mining in the Western Great Lakes, 1737–1832.* Lincoln: University of Nebraska Press, 2000.

"The Museum of Modern Art: For Immediate Release." http://www.moma.org /docs/press_archives/672/releases/MOMA_1941_0011_1941-02-14_41214-10 .pdf?2010.

Musical Compositions, Library of Congress. In *Catalog of Copyright Entries.* Vol. 2. Washington DC: Government Printing Office, 1907.

The Nebraska Teacher. Vols. 24–25, January 1922. https://books.google.com.

Neill, Edward Duffield. *The History of Minnesota.* Philadelphia: J. B. Lippincott & Co., 1858.

Nestor Studio. http://hollywoodlostandfound.net/locations/nestorstudio.html.

Neversink Valley Museum of History and Innovation. "Movies before Hollywood: A Legacy of Film Making in the Tri-State Area." http://neversinkmuseum.org /our-resources/movies-before-hollywood-a-legacy-of-film-making-in-the-tri -state-area/.

New York Hippodrome. New York: Comstock Programme Company, 1907.

Nott, J. C. "The Mulatto a Hybrid—Probable Extermination of Two Races If the Whites and Blacks Are Allowed to Intermarry." In *American Journal of the Medical Sciences* 6, edited by Isaac Hays. Philadelphia: Lea & Blanchard, 1843.

"The Old Corral." http://www.b-westerns.com.

"Palomar History." http://www.peterbrueggeman.com/palomarhistory/.

Paquette, Moses. "The Wisconsin Winnebagoes." In *Wisconsin Historical Collections* 12, edited by Reuben Gold Thwaites, 399–433. Madison: State Historical Society of Wisconsin, 1892.

Patterson, Emma C. "The Spread Eagle Inn." Radnor Historical Society. June 2, 1950. http://radnorhistory.org/archive/articles/ytmt/?p=58.

Peterson, Jacqueline. "Many Roads to Red River: Métis Genesis in the Great Lakes Region, 1680–1815." In *The New Peoples: Being and Becoming Métis in North America*, edited by Jacqueline Peterson and Jennifer S. H. Brown, 35–71. Lincoln: University of Nebraska Press, 1985.

——. "The People in Between: Indian-White Marriage and the Genesis of a Métis Society and Culture in the Great Lakes Region, 1680–1830." PhD diss., University of Illinois at Chicago Circle, 1981.

Peterson, Jacqueline, and Jennifer S. H. Brown, eds. *The New Peoples: Being and Becoming Métis in North America*. Lincoln: University of Nebraska Press, 1985.

Philadelphia, Pennsylvania, Death Certificates Index, 1803–1915. https://www.ancestry.com/.

Philbrick, Nathaniel. *The Last Stand: Custer, Sitting Bull, and the Battle of the Little Bighorn*. New York: Viking (Penguin Group), 2010.

Pippenger, Wesley E. *District of Columbia Interments (Index to Deaths): January 1, 1855 to July 31, 1874*. Westminster MD: Willow Bend Books, 1999.

——. *District of Columbia Probate Records: Will Books 1 through 6, 1801–1852 and Estate Files, 1801–1852*. Westminster MD: Family Line, 1996.

"Portrait of Winnebago man, Michel St Cyr before 1884." Negative 3760A. National Anthropological Archives. http://collections.si.edu.

Pratt, Richard Henry. *Battlefield and Classroom: Four Decades with the American Indians, 1867–1904*. Edited by Robert M. Utley. Norman: University of Oklahoma Press, 2003.

"Proposed Barney Circle Historic District." https://planning.dc.gov/publication/proposed-barney-circle-historic-district.

Prucha, Francis Paul. *American Indian Policy in Crisis: Christian Reformers and the Indian, 1865–1900*. Norman: University of Oklahoma Press, 1976.

——. *American Indian Treaties: The History of a Political Anomaly*. Berkeley: University of California Press, 1994.

——, ed. *Americanizing the American Indians: Writings by the "Friends of the Indian," 1880–1900*. Cambridge MA: Harvard University Press, 1973.

——. *Documents of United States Indian Policy*. 2nd ed. Lincoln: University of Nebraska Press, 1990.

Quaker and Special Collections. https://www.haverford.edu/library/special/aids/pymic/.

Radin, Paul. *The Autobiography of a Winnebago Indian*. 1920. Reprint, New York: Dover Publications, 1963.

——. *Crashing Thunder: The Autobiography of an American Indian*. New York: Appleton and Company, 1926.

——. "The Influence of Whites on Winnebago Culture." In *Proceedings of the State Historical Society of Wisconsin for 1913–14*. Paul Radin Papers, Marquette University Archives, Milwaukie WI.

————. *The Winnebago Tribe*. Lincoln: University of Nebraska Press, 1990.

Ragan, David. *Who's Who in Hollywood*. New Rochelle NY: Arlington House Publishers, 1976.

Raheja, Michelle H. *Reservation Reelism: Redfacing, Visual Sovereignty, and Representations of Native Americans in Film*. Lincoln: University of Nebraska Press, 2010.

Railway News and Joint-Stock Journal. June 22, 1889. London: Office of the Railway News, 1889. https://books.google.com.

Rebhorn, Matthew. *Pioneer Performances: Staging the Frontier*. London: Oxford University Press, 2012.

Record of Indian Students Returned from Hampton Institute, 1892. 52nd Cong., 1st sess., Senate Ex. Doc. No. 31.

Red Girl and the Child. Pathé Frères (West Coast), 1910. Celeste Bartos International Film Study Center, Museum of Modern Art, New York.

Reentmeesters, Les, and Jeanne Reentmeesters. *The Wisconsin Creoles*. Melbourne FL: Self-published, 1987.

————. *The Wisconsin Fur-Trade People*. Melbourne FL: Self-published, 1991.

Report of the Commissioner of Education for the Year 1883–'84. Washington DC: Government Printing Office, 1885.

Rogers, Helen Hoban, comp. *Freedom & Slavery Documents in the District of Columbia, Volume 3, 1816–1822*. Baltimore MD: Otter Bay Books, 2009.

Rollins, Peter C., and John E. O'Connor, eds. *Hollywood's Indian: The Portrayal of the Native American in Film*. Lexington: University Press of Kentucky, 1999.

Romeo, Joseph A. "Moors of Delaware: Genealogical Records of the Descendants of a Colonial Delaware Isolate Community." http://www.moors-delaware.com /gendat/moors.aspx.

Romero, Raphael. "Washita Battlefield, National Historic Site, Oklahoma." https:// www.nps.gov/waba/learn/historyculture/raphael-romero-ca-1843-1902.htm.

Rydell, Robert. *All the World's a Fair: Visions of Empire at American Expositions, 1876–1916*. Chicago: University of Chicago Press, 1984.

Scanlan, Peter L. *Prairie du Chien: French, British, American*. Prairie du Chien WI: Prairie du Chien Historical Society, 1998.

Scarangella McNenly, Linda. *Native Performers in Wild West Shows: From Buffalo Bill to Euro Disney*. Norman: University of Oklahoma Press, 2012.

Schraeder, Julie Hiller. *The Heritage of Blue Earth County*. Dallas: Curtis Media, 1990.

Schultz, Duane. *Over the Earth I Come: The Great Sioux Uprising of 1862*. New York: St. Martin's Press, 1992.

Sellers, James L. "Diary of Dr. Joseph Paxson, Physician to the Winnebago Indians, 1869–1870." *Nebraska History* 27, no. 3 (July–September 1946): 143–204, and 27, no. 4 (October–December 1946): 244–75.

Shoemaker, Nancy, ed. *Negotiators of Change: Historical Perspectives on Native American Women*. New York: Routledge, 1995.

"Silent Hall of Fame." http://silent-hall-of-fame.org/index.php/1905–1909/143-the
-mended-lute-1909-with-film.

"The Singer Summit House." http://singersummithouse.com/ssh.htm.

Sleeper, Jim. *Great Movies Shot in Orange County*. Trabuco Canyon: California Classics, 1980.

Sleeper, Susan. *Indian Women and French Men: Rethinking Cultural Encounter in the Western Great Lakes*. Amherst: University of Massachusetts Press, 2001.

Slide, Anthony. *The New Historical Dictionary of the American Film History*. Lanham MD: Scarecrow Press, 1998.

Sluby, Paul E. *Columbian Harmony Cemetary Records, District of Columbia, 1831–1899*. Washington DC: The Columbian Harmony Society, ca. 1993.

Smith, Andrew Brodie. *Shooting Cowboys and Indians: Silent Western Films, American Culture, and the Birth of Hollywood*. Boulder: University Press of Colorado, 2003.

Smith, David Lee. *Folklore of the Winnebago Tribe*. Norman: University of Oklahoma Press, 1997.

——— . *Ho-Chunk Tribal History: The History of the Ho-Chunk People from the Mound Building Era to the Present Day*. Self-published, 1996.

——— . *People of the Parent Speech*. Winnebago NE: Ho-Chunk Historical Society, 1996.

——— , comp. *Treaties and Agreements with the Winnebago Tribe, 1816–1928*. 1998. Self-published.

Smith, Donald B. *Chief Buffalo Child Long Lance: The Glorious Imposter*. Red Deer AB: Red Deer Press, 1999.

Smith, Huron H. "Among the Winnebago." In *Yearbook of the Public Museum of the City of Milwaukee 1928*, edited by S. A. Barret. Milwaukee, 1929.

Smith, Paige. *America Enters the World: A People's History of the Progressive Era and World War I*. New York: Penguin Books, 1985.

Smith (Bruzzel), Maxwell, Collection, 1908–12. Autry Manuscript Collections, Institute for the Study of the American West, Autry National Center, Southwest Museum, Los Angeles, http://collections.theautry.org.

"Society for Visual Education: 1919–1995." http://collection.sciencemuseum.org
.uk/people/cp117319/society-for-visual-education-inc.

Soul Fire. Directed by John S. Robertson. First National Picture, 1925.

Southwest Builder and Contractor. Vols. 54 and 55. https://books.google.com.

Souvenir Program, Saint Clair County, Centennial and Home-Coming Celebration, July 1921. https://archive.org/stream/3117212.0001.001.umich.edu#page/n0/mode/2up.

Spears, Jack. *Hollywood: The Golden Era*. New York: Castle Books, 1971.

Spehr, Paul C., and Gunnar Lundquist. *American Film Personnel and Company Credits, 1908–1920*. Jefferson NC: McFarland and Company, 1996.

"Spider Woman Theater." https://www.spiderwomantheater.org/blank-mpvle.

The Squaw Man. Directed by Oscar Apfel and Cecil B. DeMille. Jesse L. Lasky Feature Motion Picture Company, 1914.

Standing Bear, Luther. *My People the Sioux.* Lincoln: University of Nebraska Press, 1975.

The Statutes at Large of the United States of America, from December 1883 to March 1885 and Recent Treaties, Postal Conventions, and Executive Proclamations. Vol. 23. Washington DC: Government Printing Office, 1885.

Stephanson, Anders. *Manifest Destiny: American Expansion and the Empire of Right.* New York: Hill and Wang, 1995.

Stephens, E. J., and Marc Wanamaker. *Early Poverty Row Studios.* Images of America Series. Charleston SC: Arcadia Publishing, 2014.

Szasz, Margaret Connell. *Between Indian and White Worlds: The Cultural Broker.* Norman: University of Oklahoma Press, 1994.

Sze, Corinne P. "St. Katharine Drexel." http://newmexicohistory.org/people /katharine-drexel.

Takaki, Ronald. *Iron Cages: Race and Culture in 19th-Century America.* Rev. ed. New York: Oxford University Press, 2000.

Talbot, Edith Armstrong. *Samuel Chapman Armstrong: A Biographical Study.* New York: Doubleday, Page and Co., 1904.

Tanner, Helen Hornbeck, Adele Hast, Jacqueline Peterson, and Robert J. Surtees, eds. *Atlas of Great Lakes Indian History.* Norman: University of Oklahoma Press, 1987.

Taylor, Brian M. "'To Make the Union What It Ought to Be': African Americans, Civil War Military Service and Citizenship." PhD diss., Georgetown University, 2015. https://repository.library.georgetown.edu/bitstream/handle/10822 /760870/Taylor_georgetown_0076D_12985.pdf?sequence=1]https://repository .library.georgetown.edu/bitstream/handle/10822/760870/Taylor_georgetown _0076d_12985.pdf?sequence=1.

Technical World Magazine 13 (June 1910): 455. https://books.google.com.

Thiesen, Barbara A. "Every Beginning Is Hard." *Mennonite Life* 15, no. 2 (June 2006).

Thunderbird American Indian Dancers. https://thunderbirdamericanindiandancers .wordpress.com.

Thwaites, Reuben Gold. *Wisconsin: The Americanization of a French Settlement.* Boston: Houghton Mifflin Co., 1908.

Tom Mix Biography. American National Biography. http://www.anb.org/articles /18/18–00851.html.

Trachtenberg, Alan. *Shades of Hiawatha: Staging Indians, Making Americans, 1880– 1930.* New York: Hill and Wang, 2004.

Trading Post Oak, Lake Mendota. http://dnr.wi.gov/topic/ForestManagement /EveryRootAnAnchor/documents/013-tradingPostOak.pdf.

Trennert, Robert A. "Educating Indian Girls at Non-reservation Boarding Schools, 1878–1920." In *The American Indian: Past and Present*, 3rd ed., edited by Roger L. Nichols, 218–31. New York: McGraw Hill, 1986.

"True Story of the Delaware Moors." http://nativeamericansofdelawarestate.com /MoorsOfDelaware/moor2.html.

Turner, Andrew Jackson. *The Family Tree of Columbia County*. Portage: Press of the Wisconsin State Register, 1904.

Turner, Frederick Jackson. *The Character and Influence of the Indian Trade in Wisconsin: A Study of the Trading Post as an Institution*. Edited by David Harry Miller and William W. Savage Jr. Norman: University of Oklahoma Press, 1977.

Tyler, Lyon Gardiner. *Men of Mark in Virginia: Ideals of American Life*. Vol. 2. Washington DC: Men of Mark Publishing Co., 1907.

United States v. Julia St. Cyr. United States District Court of Nebraska, no. 44-46. Filed October 9, 1907.

USS *Celtic* (AF-2), 1891–1923. Fleet Provisions Store Ship. http://freepages.military .rootsweb.ancestry.com/~cacunithistories/USS_Celtic.html.

Utley, Robert M. Utley. *Custer: Cavalier in Buckskin*. Norman: University of Oklahoma Press, 2001.

Van Kirk, Sylvia. *"Many Tender Ties": Women in Fur Trade Society, 1670–1870*. Norman: University of Oklahoma Press, 1983.

Verhoeff, Nanna. *The West in Early Cinema: After the Beginning*. Amsterdam: Amsterdam University Press, 2006.

Vizenor, Gerald. *Manifest Manners: Narratives on Postindian Survivance*. Lincoln: University of Nebraska Press, 1999.

Vlach, John Michael. "The Quest for a Capital." http://freepages.genealogy.rootsweb .ancestry.com/~hurdelswebpage/beallindex.html.

Waggoner, Linda M. *Fire Light: The Life of Angel de Cora, Winnebago Artist*. Norman: University of Oklahoma Press, 2008.

——, ed. *"Neither White Men nor Indians": Affidavits from the Winnebago Mixed-Blood Claim Commissions, Prairie du Chien, Wisconsin, 1838–1839*. Roseville MN: Park Genealogical Books, 2002.

———. "Sibley's Winnebago Prisoners: Deconstructing Race and Recovering Kinship in the Dakota War of 1862." *Great Plains Quarterly*, Winter 2013.

Wagner, Frederick C., III. *Participants in the Battle of Little Big Horn: A Biographical Dictionary of Sioux, Cheyenne and United States Military Personnel*. 2nd ed. Jefferson NC: McFarland and Company, 2016. https://books.google.com.

Walker, Brent E. *Max Sennet's Fun Factory: A History and Filmography of His Studio and His Keystone and Mack Sennett Comedies, with Biographies of Players and Personnel*. Jefferson NC: McFarland and Company, 2010.

Wallis, Michael. *The Real Wild West: The 101 Ranch and the Creation of the American West*. New York: St. Martin's Griffin, 1999.

Wassaja 3, no. 5 (August 1918). https://repository.asu.edu/attachments/179934/content/WHS_Wassaja_V3_No5OCR.txt.

Welsh, Herbert, ed. *City and State* 6, no. 13 (March 13, 1899): 216–17.

West, Helen B. "Starvation Winter of the Blackfeet." *Montana: The Magazine of Modern History* 9, no. 1 (January 1959).

White, Richard. *The Middle Ground: Indians, Empires, and Republics in the Great Lakes Region, 1650–1815.* 5th ed. Cambridge: Cambridge University Press, 1995.

William Blackmore Collection. www.britishmuseum.org.

Williams, Allen S. "The Indian Colony in New York City." *Phrenological Journal* 120 (March 1907).

Wilmer, S. E., ed. *Native American Performance and Representation*. Tucson: University of Arizona Press, 2009.

Windeler, Robert. *Sweetheart: The Story of Mary Pickford*. New York: Praeger Publishing, 1974.

"Winnebago Boarding School, Employees in Indian Schools, Omaha and Winnebago Agency, Nebraska Agency." In *Annual Report of the Commissioner of Indian Affairs to the Secretary of the Interior for the Year 1887*. Washington DC: Government Printing Office, 1887.

Winnebago Tribe. *Laws and Regulations Adopted by the Winnebago Tribe of Indians: In Council Held at the Winnebago Agency, Nebraska, July 21st, A.D. 1868*. Miami, n.d. Reprint from Omaha Daily Herald Book and Job Printing Establishment, 1868.

Winther, Barbara. "The Artist and His Model: The Crossing Paths of Maynard Dixon and George Whitewing." *Western Historical Quarterly* 49, no. 3 (2018): 335–42.

Wisconsin Historical Society Collections. 31 vols. Madison: Wisconsin Historical Society, 1855–1931.

Witmer, Linda. *The Indian Industrial School: Carlisle, Pennsylvania 1879–1918*. Carlisle PA: Cumberland County Historical Society, 2002.

Wolf, Tom. "Radical Chic: That Party at Lenny's." *New York Magazine,* June 1970.

Yarsinske, Amy Waters. *Jamestown Exposition: American Imperialism on Parade*. Vol. 1. Images of America Series. Charleston SC: Arcadia Publishing, 1999.

Young, Robert. *Colonial Desire: Hybridity, Race and Theories of Culture*. London: Routledge, 1995.

INDEX